SEARCH
FOR
HUMAN UNDERSTANDING

SEARCH
FOR
HUMAN UNDERSTANDING
A Reader in Psychology

Second Edition

Edited by
Michael Merbaum
University of Haifa

and

George Stricker
*Institute of Advanced Psychological Studies,
Adelphi University*

Holt, Rinehart and Winston, Inc.
New York   Chicago   San Francisco   Atlanta
Dallas   Montreal   Toronto   London   Sydney

The cover photograph is reproduced by courtesy of Joseph Neumayer and Authenticated News International. All other photographs are reproduced by courtesy of Fred Weiss.

Library of Congress Cataloging in Publication Data

Merbaum, Michael, comp.
    Search for human understanding.

    Includes bibliographies.
    1. Psychology.   I. Stricker, George, joint comp.
II. Title.   [DNLM: 1. Psychology—Collected works.
BF121 M552s]
BF121.M48   1975   150'.8   74–22248
ISBN: 0–03–089229–5

Preface

The readings in this supplementary textbook are designed to acquaint the introductory psychology student with a compelling and informative record of the activities of psychologists and of the findings of psychological inquiry. The usual approach to the construction of an introductory readings text—the culling of professional literature on research—was rejected for an obvious reason: professional literature is almost always beyond the grasp of the beginning student. And although we wish to inform the student of some of these areas of investigation, we prefer to do so in a manner consistent with the individual's current level of experience and interest.

The vehicle we have chosen to accomplish this purpose is the popular press. Quality newspapers and magazines often carry articles discussing the results of psychological investigation. These articles, frequently written by or in collaboration with professional psychologists, are aimed at an audience of intelligent but untrained laymen who are unfamiliar with technical jargon. This target group, the intelligent lay reader, more closely resembles the introductory psychology student than does the target group for professional journal articles. Thus, as an educational technique, the presentation of good, solid research and theoretical material in this form should generate greater student enthusiasm and motivation to read the assigned material.

In selecting these articles, we used two basic criteria. First, the article had to contain psychologically sound and accurate information. Second, the article had to be interesting and readable. In almost every case, these two criteria were satisfied by material drawn from popular sources. In those few cases in which articles were taken from journals, the journal material was selected to meet the above conditions.

Our readings were chosen and organized to emphasize the main features of introductory psychology courses. There are sections dealing with basic psychological processes and with the developing human organism. There are also specialized sections on such subjects as the identification and treatment of abnormal behavior, and the impact and relevance of psychology in our time. A wide variety of groups—beginning psychology students in high schools, community colleges, junior colleges, and traditional four-year colleges—should find this collection appealing. In addition, introductory social science and education courses could make significant use of these supplementary readings.

To aid the student in making effective use of this book we have included a number of study aids. These include (1) a prefatory essay, which introduces each chapter by describing the content and its importance within the science of psychology. Also included are (2) suggested readings, which follow each chapter, made up a list of pertinent books from the professional literature, along with a brief description of the content of each book. Following the annotated readings there are (3) discussion questions which either can be used by students individually to stimulate thought about issues raised by the selections, or can be used by classes as a basis for discussion. (As an aid for the instructor, a booklet containing multiple-choice questions for each article is available.)

This volume is the second edition, and follows in both style and approach the orientation of the first edition. It represents, however, a thorough revision in content, as nearly three-quarters of the selections are new. This modification was necessary in order to keep up with the rapid growth of knowledge and interest within psychology.

A number of individuals have generously contributed their time and effort in the preparation of this volume. We are pleased to acknowledge our debt and appreciation to Barbara Cohen and Lee Geisen, graduate students in the Institute of Advanced Psychological Studies, who contributed a great deal to every stage of compiling this book.

At this point an explanation about authorship is in order. Each editor participated equally in all phases of the preparation of this book. The sequence of authorship, therefore, rested entirely on the outcome of a game of chance and skill. It should be noted in passing that the first author claims the latter, while the second author is quite convinced of the former.

And finally to our wives, Marta Merbaum, and Joan Stricker, who gave continuing moral support to the project, we express our gratitude.

M. M.
G. S.

Garden City, New York
July 1974

Contents

Chapter 1
The Great Psychologists

Man's intense curiosity about himself is an ancient preoccupation. Since the dawn of time, brilliant thinkers have reflected upon man and passionately searched for the key to greater human understanding. Psychology, the scientific study of behavior, is an evolutionary product of this ancestral heritage.

The true beginnings of modern psychology, however, did not emerge until the latter part of the nineteenth century, with the opening of the first experimental psychological laboratory by the German philosopher-psychologist Wilhelm Wundt. Until that time, psychology was the handmaiden of philosophy, physiology, biology, and medicine. From these roots psychological thought grew and eventually established itself as a separate scientific discipline. Perhaps in many ways this was inevitable, for man's relation to his body and to his social and physical environment is so complex that a comprehensive understanding necessarily requires creative efforts from many different perspectives. This is both the challenge and beauty of contemporary psychology.

Our significant intellectual advances are the result of a delicate balance between the genius of men and the social forces that provided the framework for their achievements. Yet in the final analysis it is the men that we remember. The great names in the history of thought have left a legacy in the content of their intellectual endeavors as well as in the stimulation they provided countless others in refining and broadening these lines of inquiry. In this spirit, it is appropriate to introduce some significant contributors in psychology, both past and contemporary, and survey their impact on this ever-widening area of science.

The first paper in this chapter by David C. McClelland highlights the similarities and contrasts in the personality and professional accomplishments of two eminent psychologists, Sigmund Freud and Clark L. Hull. In the history of psychology both men occupy positions of extreme importance. Freud is most widely known as the father of psychoanalysis. His scientific work centered on the understanding and treatment of mental disorders, although his theories have reached far beyond this problem. The insights derived from psychoanalysis have been applied in the study of art, literature, anthropology, sociology, biology, and almost every conceivable human enterprise. To a large extent Freud never entered the

mainstream of experimental psychology. However, his thinking has dominated clinical psychology and strongly influenced developmental and
child psychology. This is quite reasonable, given the subject matter
studied by psychoanalysis and the therapeutic techniques which evolved
out of direct clinical contact with patients. The major dependence on
clinical observation to the exclusion of rigorously controlled experimentation has been severely criticized by many behaviorally oriented psychologists. Nonetheless, the impact of psychoanalysis has been considerable,
particularly in personality research.

The only theory as ambitious and complex as Freud's in the experimental psychology of learning was developed by the American psychologist Clark L. Hull. Hull was dedicated to the idea that psychology is an
objective, quantitative science; thus he closely followed in the Pavlovian
tradition. However, where Pavlov used dogs as his primary subjects, Hull
experimented with the white rat.

Hull's psychological system is a complicated stimulus–response
theory. The environmental events which affect the organism are the
stimuli, and the behaviors of the organism in reaction to these stimuli are
the responses. In order to make his system complete, Hull sought to
define the changes occurring within the organism by inferring certain symbolic constructs such as drive, motivation, and inhibition. By observing
the effects of stimuli and adding to the equation the influence of the various internal processes, Hull hoped to be able to predict behavioral responses in precise mathematical terms. How two scientists, so widely
separated by social background and scientific tradition, could create systems of thought so similar and yet so dissimilar in overall design is deftly
presented in McClelland's paper.

The behaviorist tradition in American psychology has had its share
of brilliant and energetic champions. One of the most significant is
Burrhus Frederic Skinner, who is intimately portrayed in an article found
in *Time* magazine. But before we talk about Skinner it is important to go
back a few years and briefly mention a predecessor of Skinner who still
exerts a powerful influence in the area of learning and conditioning.

In psychology the name of Pavlov is immediately associated with the
experimental procedure called conditioning. It is interesting to discover,
however, that Ivan Pavlov, the great Russian psychologist, regarded himself not as a psychologist but as a physiologist, and that his Nobel Prize
was awarded for his original work on digestion. In fact, Pavlov viewed the
term "psychology" as prescientific and nonobjective and censured its mention in his laboratories. Despite this dissatisfaction for the psychology of
that early period his emphasis on the biological basis of behavior was soon
to be part of behaviorism, a new wave in psychology. In America the new
psychology found its way through the influence of John B. Watson, a
young psychologist from the University of Chicago. In 1913, Watson proclaimed in bold terms that "psychology as the behaviorist views it is a

purely objective branch of natural science. Its theoretical goal is the prediction and control of behavior." The term "conditioning" became the rallying point for those psychologists committed to an experimental psychology based upon objective stimulus–response relationships. American psychology, therefore, readily adopted Pavlov's experimental methods but concentrated mainly on learning in a psychological sense, generally to the exclusion of more physiological considerations. Thus it is important to note that Pavlov and Skinner are products of a similar objective scientific tradition, although their studies reflect some relevant differences. Pavlov hoped eventually to localize the process of conditioning in various biological systems, while Skinner over the years has devoted himself to the identification and the control of the environmental conditions that predictably influence behavior. B. F. Skinner is best known for his systematic development and refinement of operant conditioning, a variant and perhaps extension of Pavlov's classical conditioning procedures.

In classical conditioning, the typical procedure is to present the organism (for example, a dog) with an unconditioned stimulus (meat powder), which then elicits the unconditioned response (salivation). When a conditioned stimulus (a tone) is paired simultaneously with the unconditioned stimulus (meat powder), it acquires, after a number of these simultaneous presentations, the capacity to elicit a conditioned response (salivation) similar to the unconditioned response (salivation). When the conditioned stimulus alone predictably elicits the conditioned response, conditioning has occurred. In classical conditioning the organism is usually a passive participant. He is presented the meat powder and he salivates. There is little he can do to alter the procedure or the consequences. In operant conditioning, however, the organism acts or instrumentally operates on the environment to obtain certain consequences or reinforcements. The behavior is emitted rather than elicited by specific stimuli, and the frequency of the behavior depends upon its effect on the environment and the environment's effect on the individual organism. Thus, for Skinner, behavior is controlled by environmental reinforcement. Because of his rigorous commitment to an objective theoretical system, Skinner will admit no references to hypothetical causes of behavior. For example, he would not say that a dog eats because he is hungry but, rather, that specific conditions are present which reliably accompany the behavior (eating). The task of the scientist is to define objectively these environmental events. If one understands what variables affect behavior then control is possible, and that is the ultimate goal of science. Skinner's uncompromising views have attracted many followers, and operant conditioning principles are now regularly applied in education, advertising, psychopharmacology, and treatment of the mentally ill, to name just a few areas.

The article presented in this chapter describes Skinner's theoretical views and offers an intimate portrait of Skinner the person. He is still a controversial figure in American psychology, and the publication of his recent book *Beyond Freedom and Dignity* has reinforced this image. Independence of thought is not new to Skinner—some years before, he wrote a provocative novel, *Walden Two,* about a plan for a utopian community. A part of this article describes a real-life Walden Two community, Twin Oaks. This community was designed according to the principles of operant conditioning and is the kind of social experiment Skinner had in mind when he wrote his novel. While it is apparent that Twin Oaks has not yet achieved complete utopian perfection, as a social psychological experiment it stands out as an important contribution. This article shows how direct psychological principles can be translated into codes or rules for community living.

The most renowned figure in developmental child psychology is the Swiss psychologist Jean Piaget. The article by David Elkind is both an affectionate and scholarly portrait of this remarkable man.

Piaget has devoted over thirty years of study to the experimental and theoretical analysis of the structure of intelligence and general cognitive processes such as moral judgment and reasoning. To him, intelligence is the culmination of an interaction between the organism and his environment. To amplify this point, Piaget postulates various stages of sensory-motor development, beginning with the appearance of hereditary reflex functions at birth and progressing to advanced mental operations such as invention and ingenuity in the final stages. The alive and vital development sequence from infancy through childhood is highly complex, as evidenced by the truly phenomenal output of books, monographs, and research papers by Piaget and his co-workers. The paper by Elkind is an overview of Piaget's creative contributions.

Psychoanalyses, as represented in the works of Freud, and behaviorism, as seen in both Hull and Skinner, have been the most powerful sources of influence on modern psychology. Recently a third force, humanistic psychology, has attracted a great number of adherents, and developments in this area are described in the contribution of Severin. This article is unlike the others in the chapter in that it does not focus on a single great psychologist, but rather on a body of thought embracing the creative contributions of many psychologists. The humanistic approach is an orientation to human behavior which focuses on growth, consciousness, and self-determination, arising in opposition to the deterministic orientations of behaviorism and psychoanalysis. Proponents of humanism have been accused of being simplistic and anti-intellectual, and in return have labeled much of contemporary psychology mechanical and sterile. It is the task of the student to discard the name-calling and find what there is of value in each of the approaches.

"Here are two men who differed radically in personality, in cultural background, in scientific approach, in the kind of behavior they cared about, yet both are major figures in contemporary psychology."

Freud and Hull were born in extremely dissimilar social and intellectual environments. Freud grew up in an urban, traditionally Jewish culture which emphasized learning and scholarship. In contrast, Hull was raised in a rural, Protestant environment. Interestingly enough, both became famous psychological theorists whose theories shared many important similarities.

To a group of psychologists at least, an attempt to discuss these two men at the same time would be somewhat surprising—Sigmund Freud, the cultured European, expert on dreamlife, founder of psychoanalysis; Clark L. Hull, backwoods American, expert on learning, founder of a kind of latter-day Newtonian system of behavioral psychology. Yet both claimed to be scientists, both contributed in a major way to psychological theory, and both are key figures in contemporary psychology. Certainly no Ph.D. candidate in psychology today can safely ignore either of them and even most undergraduate students of psychology must study rather carefully both psychoanalysis and Hull's system of behavior theory.

So we have an apparent paradox: here are two men who differed radically in personality, in cultural background, in scientific approach, in the kind of behavior they cared about, yet both are major figures in contemporary psychology. Why is this? To try and find an answer, let us look at some of these differences a little more closely. Fortunately we have at least an eminently sane and thorough biography of Freud by Ernest Jones (3) which gives a great many details about Freud's early scientific career which have subsequently been lost sight of in the furious controversies over psychoanalysis. As for Hull, he is too recently dead for anyone to have attempted a systematic evaluation of his career, but we do have his own autobiographical statement (2) and in his case I can draw on my own personal knowledge since I studied under him at Yale University in the late 30's. Freud (1856–1939) lived most of his life in Vienna, and was in many ways a vintage product of a rich center of European culture. His family was not very well off and he was always short of money in his student days, but he was nevertheless encouraged in his early intellectual and cultural interests by the traditional Jewish respect for knowledge and learning. He grew up to be a true scholar in the old sense, knowing some eight different languages, and being well-versed in the classics of all cultures. He is one psychological scientist who has sometimes been more accepted in literary circles than in scientific ones. He started his professional career as a physiologist and neuro-anatomist but was forced, in the end, to go into the practice of medicine to earn a living.

Hull (1884–1952) by way of contrast, was almost the stereotype of an American pioneer. He was brought up in a log cabin in Michigan and spent his early years attending a one-room school and clearing stumps from the land to prepare it for farming. His formal education was as poor as Freud's was rich, although he seems to have read a good deal on his own, and mentions in particular Spinoza's *Ethics*. His father was practically illiterate and did not finish learning to read until his wife taught him after they were married. The family had been strongly Protestant, but his parents were "free thinkers," just as Freud's parents were with respect to their strong Jewish tradition. Hull originally planned to enter some practical profession like mining engineering but on a summer job he contracted poliomyelitis (at the age of 24) which permanently crippled one leg and forced him to change his occupation to that of school teaching—fortunately for science. What could be a more extreme difference in background than this—Freud, the cultured, well-educated European; Hull, the practical pioneer American! How they both ended up in psychology is a fascinating problem in itself, but we cannot take time to dwell on it here. It will have to do to say that Hull apparently decided quite on his own during his prolonged convalescence from poliomyelitis that psychology was the field for him and got his mother to read him James' *Principles of Psychology* since his own eyes were too weak at the time. Freud on the other hand, seems to have been drawn into psychology gradually from the experience he had in his clinical practice with "nervous" cases.

As psychologists they differed greatly. Freud began his professional life by studies in neuro-anatomy and then moved on to the aphasias as being somewhere between physical and mental disease and finally ended up in the functional neuroses with studies of dream-life, hypnosis, sexual instincts, and the like. In his work we run across concepts like libido, repression, defense mechanisms, the censor, the unconscious, the Super-ego, etc. In Hull we find a totally different line of development. He began working with serial verbal learning, then turned to aptitude testing, and finally spent the major portion of his career dealing with data derived from studies of learning functions in the white rat at Yale University. At only one point did their empirical interest overlap. They both studied hypnosis—neither, it may be noted in passing, with much success. Freud gave it up because it was an undependable therapeutic instrument, and Hull gave it up partly because he thought that he had demonstrated that it was merely a form of suggestibility similar in kind, if not in extent, to waking suggestibility, and partly because of the opposition of medical authorities in New Haven. Hull dealt in concepts like habit strength, excitatory potential, reactive inhibition, drive and the like. His mature and most developed work is represented by a page of definitions, axioms, deductions, and equations, whereas Freud's is represented by a page of closely reasoned analysis of inner mental life. It is small wonder that people have doubted whether they were in the same field.

In fact, throughout the last twenty or thirty years there hasn't been much tendency to treat them as part of the same discipline. Psychoanalysis grew up quite independently of academic psychology and American behaviorists were not slow in following their European colleagues in branding Freud both unscientific and absurd. Unfortunately we do not have recorded what these two men thought of each other. In fact, we could not really expect that Freud would have taken time out in his late seventies to read Hull's aggressively behavioristic papers which began to appear around 1930, fully 35 years after Freud's major work had begun. The best that we could expect from psychoanalysts on Hull is a terse "no comment," meaning perhaps that most of Hull's system is irrelevant to human psychology. On the other hand, Hull certainly knew about Freud's work through the influence of men like Professor John Dollard whom he knew at Yale, but it does not seem to have influenced his thinking much. Perhaps his comment on one of his early teachers at Wisconsin, the clinical psychologist Jastrow, will serve to represent somewhat his attitude toward men like Freud; "His mind could scintillate in a brilliant fashion, but his approach to psychology was largely qualitative and literary . . . He would sometimes lecture for five minutes at a time in perfectly good sentences, yet hardly say a thing" (2, p. 147).

Yet this is clearly not the whole story. Two facts stand out as contributing strongly to the impression that Freud and Hull basically had something very important in common. First, some of the most extreme systematic behaviorists of the Hull school have had a great personal interest and respect for psychoanalysis. Perhaps it was because Hull's system had little to say about their inner experiences and their own personal problems. So they turned to psychoanalysis as a personal, originally non-professional interest, perhaps, one might almost say, as providing a philosophy of life. A number of these behaviorists were psychoanalyzed. Secondly, Professors Dollard, Miller, and others at Yale attempted formally to state some of the psychoanalytic concepts in terms of the Hullian principles of behavior. Oddly enough, this did not prove a very difficult task, at least in its initial stage, a fact which strongly suggests that there must have been some basic similarities in approach between the two men. Some of their values at least should have been similar.

Let us look for a moment for these similarities. On the personal level, despite their enormous difference in background, they were alike in several important respects. Both were prodigiously hard workers. Freud, when he was writing "The Interpretation of Dreams," often saw patients eight to ten hours a day and then worked past midnight writing his books. Hull's working habits were the opposite although they were equally intense. He used to wake early in the morning around 5:00 A.M. and think in bed several hours before rising and going to his office at Yale. He kept "a permanent notebook of original ideas, concerning all sorts of psychological subjects as they came to me" (2, p. 147).

At his death he had some twenty-eight such volumes in which his ideas had been persistently and continually worked through to their ultimate implications. Freud published more, partly because his active psychoanalytic period lasted for fully 40 years while Hull's mature work was all done in about 18 years between 1930 and 1948. But behind every page of Hull's work there was a vast amount of intricate reasoning and calculation, much of which could be condensed to a single equation taking up one line.

Both men were also tremendously courageous and honest. They both believed the truth must be pursued at all personal cost. The attacks that Freud had to suffer because he was a Jew and because he persisted in attributing sexuality to infants are too well known to need review here. Hull never was as violently and personally attacked, but it is certain that he came in for his share of ridicule over the tedious and elaborate proofs of his theorems and propositions. Such challenges seem to have led both of them to redouble their efforts to do what they thought the science of psychology needed most.

Thirdly, they were both what might be called "close thinkers." Although Freud's thinking did not result in carefully worked out geometrical or algebraic proofs, no one who has read his works can deny that he wrestled with a problem as closely and thoroughly as did Hull, particularly in his early years when he was still formulating some of his basic ideas. Finally, both men had a grand vision of the great new science of psychology which spurred them on to tremendous efforts. Someone has said that to make a great contribution to any field of knowledge, one must have an image of one's own greatness. It can be said that both Freud and Hull had an image of greatness. Both were modest about it, but the idea that a real science of psychology was possible gripped both of them and they both felt that it was their sacred duty to show how this could be done. And both had confidence in their ultimate success: "We shall win through in the end" (Freud). "It would be nice to know how these and similar scientific problems turn out" (Hull). Neither of them had the slightest doubt that ultimately the problems of understanding human behavior scientifically would be solved.

What was the science of psychology to be like? Again we find they had much in common. Both were extremely anti-religious and deterministic. Both openly disbelieved in God, and Freud nearly caused a family crisis by refusing at first to go through the "superstitious nonsense" of a Jewish wedding ceremony. Hull reacted violently against his narrow sectarian upbringing and felt that "religious considerations interfere with the evolution of science" (2, p. 162). Their determinism was thoroughgoing and can perhaps best be illustrated by the way both of them treated the problem of "free will" or "spontaneity." Freud recognized characteristically that the subjective feeling of free will was an important psychological fact to be explained. His explanation consisted of demonstrating that so-called chance acts or trivial "choices" really have an unconscious motive behind them which a skillful analyst can always discover Thus, no act is uncaused and the *illusion* of free will simply comes from the fact that some of our motives are unconscious (3, p. 365). Hull, on the other hand, in his presidential address before the American Psychological Association in 1936 spends a good deal of time getting rid of such notions as "consciousness" or "spontaneity" as being thoroughly unnecessary in a scientific system. His explanation is, in principle, the same as Freud's. Two acts, A and B, may have different strengths, so that A appears rather than B. But if A is unsuccessful in satisfying a need (motive) its strength will gradually diminish according to known laws of the extinction process, and finally B will "spontaneously" appear because its strength is now relatively greater than A's. No "free choice" is involved. In his own words, "This theorem is noteworthy because it represents the classical case of a form of spontaneity widely assumed, as far back as the Middle Ages, to be inconceivable without presupposing consciousness" (1, p. 12). Both men believed firmly in natural law and took much delight in explaining traditional moral and religious concepts as perfectly natural phenomena.

Their psychologies were also to be quantitative. This comes as no surprise in the case of Hull who spent the last years of his life trying to set up scales and units for measuring his basic concepts like habit strength, but it is perhaps unusual to claim that Freud, who appeared so qualitative in his writing, was also really quantitatively oriented. Yet Ernest Jones, who has analyzed Freud's earliest "general theory" which was never published, leaves no doubt about Freud's ultimate way of thinking about mental phenomena. Jones describes the work thus:

> The aim of the "project" is to furnish a psychology which shall be a natural science. This Freud defines as one representing psychical processes as quantitatively determinate states of material elements which can be specified. It contains two main ideas: (1) to conceive in terms of Quantity which is subject to the general laws of motion, whatever distinguishes activity from rest; (2) to regard the neurones as the material elements in question" (3, p. 385).

In another place Freud speaks of a goal which plagues him, "To see how the theory of mental functions would shape itself if one introduced quantitative considerations, a sort of economics of nervous energy" (3, p. 347). It is quite clear from his subsequent work which deals with the libido, or drive concept, and its various ways of being checked and diverted that he had fundamentally in mind a quantitative concept of neural or electrical energy which was seeking to be discharged.

Both men also felt that psychology ultimately rests first on physiology and ultimately on physics. This is clear from the statement quoted above about Freud's first "general theory" and it is well known that Hull always hoped to find some confirmation of his theory at the physiological level. Both men ultimately were disappointed in not being helped more by nerve physiology and had to go on without it, but they believed that ultimately the laws of physiology and psychology would be found to be similar or at least consistent with one another.

Finally, in both of their systems the organism is conceived as being guided in its functioning by the satisfaction of needs or the "discharge of tension." It is difficult here to use words that will apply equally well to both systems of thinking, but clearly they both have very much the same idea in mind. It runs something like this: The organism seeks to preserve a state of equilibrium; anything which disturbs it will call out adjustive responses which will continue until the equilibrium is restored. Freud had in mind apparently a simple reflex model in which a stimulus sets up an excitation which "sets out" through the nervous system until it can discharge itself in a response. Generalizing this idea, he spoke of states of "unpleasure," or, as it has been more recently translated, tension, which keep the organism upset and active until they are discharged either directly or indirectly. The direct discharge, or primary process, as it was called, may simply involve the hallucination of the desired state of affairs as in a dream. The indirect, or secondary process, involves an instrumental adaptive response in real life which produces the desired event in fact rather than in fancy. Hull did not concern himself at all with the primary process since, as a behaviorist, he did not concern himself with dreams and the like, but the secondary process describes almost exactly the way he thought the organism functioned. Certain biological needs like hunger, thirst, and sex (here a bow to the Freudians, although he never worked with sex as a drive) made the organism active until it successfully discovered a response which reduced the need. Then in the proposition which is basic to his whole system, Hull postulated that the reduction in need automatically strengthens the connection between the stimulus and response preceding it, a statement of the well-known "law of effect," which is usually thought to have been formulated first by Thorndike in this country. It is interesting to observe, however, that Freud, thinking along very similar lines, had come to an identical conclusion in the 1890's: "When this [the process of satisfying a desire] occurs, associations are forged . . . with the perceptual image of the satisfying object on the one hand, and on the other hand, the information derived from the motor activity that brought that object within reach" (3, p. 392). In Hull's terms, he is saying that need reduction forges a connection between the "stimulus" and the response-produced stimulus, a conception quite similar to Hull's in most respects. It is probably because the basic "model" of how the organism functioned is so similar for the two men that it was so easy to incorporate certain Freudian notions into Hull's system. Both men were essentially natural scientists, who had been strongly influenced by the theory of evolution, and who tended, therefore, to think of the organism as responding and adapting to changes in the environment so that it could survive or maintain its equilibrium.

Having covered some of the superficial differences between the two men and some of their basic similarities, we are in a better position to summarize how they differed in their approach to the scientific study of psychology. In the first place, they differed markedly in their attitude toward experimentation. Freud was no experimenter, as Jones makes very clear. His early success in the laboratory was with the microscope where he spent hours and hours dissecting, inventing new methods of staining, and analyzing different kinds of nervous tissue. He tried experimentation three times, all unsuccessfully according to Jones (3, p. 54). His last attempt was to measure the effects of cocaine on muscular strength as measured by a dynamometer, a problem which, except for the nature of the drug used, was quite similar to many similar studies performed by academic psychologists like Hull and others. Freud had a marked preference for "seeing" over "doing." He spoke of experimentation in terms of "mutilating animals or tormenting human beings" (3, p. 53). One of his objections to hypnosis was that it was a "coarsely interfering method." Instead, he preferred to listen carefully and analyze. Hull was much more the practical American "doer." He thought that much valuable time was wasted in controversy that could better be settled by the resort to experiment. In his autobiography he quotes with favor Thorndike's comment "that the time spent in replying to an attack could better be employed in doing a relevant experiment" (3, p. 154). It is true, however, that most of his own experiments, particularly in his later years, were done not with human beings, but with rats. So one might argue that the logical superiority which experimentation should have given him over Freud was dissipated to a considerable extent because he did not employ it in the areas where it might have revealed the most useful facts for understanding human nature.

Another really basic difference between the two men was in the kind of behavior in which they were interested. Hull, true to the American tradition, was concerned almost wholly with the psychology of learning, with discovering how the organism adapts to new situations. He wanted to know what shape the learning curve took, what its major determinants were, what happened when practice ceased, etc. In all of this he was satisfied to use white rats because they seem to learn pretty much the same way as human beings do, at least so far as the simple kinds of associative learning are concerned in which Hull was interested. Freud, on the other hand, was interested in dreaming rather than in learning. Dreaming provides of necessity a kind of psychological data which belongs exlusively to the human sphere and which leads readily into studies not only of abnormal psychology but of art and literature. It involved Freud in problems of memory for content and of perception, problems which Hull failed to deal with satisfactorily in his system. To the extent that Hull neglected dream life, Freud neglected the psychology of learning. If one may presume to stand in judgment, we might conclude that to the extent that both of them tried hard to build general systems of psychology, each began from too narrow a base. But this has always been true in the history of science. If each man pushes his insights to the limit, perhaps some future genius can see how they fit together, as Einstein could for certain physical phenomena.

Finally and most important of all, they differed enormously in the relative emphasis they placed on induction and education. Hull was fascinated by deductive systems from his earliest youth. While in his teens he "tried to use the geometrical method to deduce some negative propositions regarding theology" (2, p. 144). Later in college he constructed a "logic machine" which would satisfactorily "deduce" all the implications of a set of propositions plugged into it. But then let him put it in his own words. "The study of geometry proved to be the most important event of my intellectual life; it opened to me an entirely new world—the fact that thought itself could generate and really prove new relationships from previously possessed elements" (3, p. 144). It is probably fair to say that all of his serious intellectual work was patterned after the geometrical model. He worked out a number of miniature systems complete with axioms, definitions, and derivations of theorems which he would then put to the "observational check." He believed that all secondary laws of human behavior could be derived from certain primary laws and so he dedicated his life to discovering the primary laws "together with the scientifically true and unmistakable definitions of all critical terms involved. These laws should take the form of quantitative equations readily yielding unambiguous deductions of major behavioral phenomena, both individual and social" (3, p. 162). It was his particular bête noire to read theorists whose propositions and principles were so unclear, confusing and ambiguous that it was impossible to test any of them experimentally.

Freud, on the other hand, took quite a different tack. He feared the deductive method and consciously set himself against using it for fear that it would lead him into empty philosophical speculation. Here we must invoke the difference in the historical periods in which the two men grew up. In Freud's time it was revolutionary to be empirical, to turn one's attention to actual observation of human behavior. To be excessively theoretical was to be identified with philosophers whom one was revolting against. By Hull's time, however, there had already been a considerable mass of data collected by experimentation and observation, and Hull felt that the real problem was now to bring some order into it. He had nothing but contempt for the man who came into his office on Monday morning and looked around the laboratory asking, "Now what shall I do next?" He felt that this "dry as dust" empiricism was getting nowhere, that it did not lead to an accumulation of knowledge in a systematic form.

Even though the difference between the two men can readily be explained in historical terms such as these, it remains a fact that Freud, as a person, was always much more impressed by the singular observed fact than Hull was. Freud stayed much closer to his data. After all, his theories had their basis in the consulting room and he had to check them constantly against the symptoms of his patients. In the early days when he was attempting to check his hypothesis that hysteria, as a neurosis, always had a sexual etiology, he had to test it against case after case as they came to him for consultation. He felt that he had to explain every little fact, no matter how small and how apparently insignificant. (See, for example, his "Psychopathology of Everyday Life".) Hull, on the other hand, was much more willing to attribute things to "chance" and in this sense was not so thorough-going a determinist, at least in practice. When a particular rat did not behave the way he was supposed to according to Hull's theory, it did not concern him unduly because, by this time, statistical considerations could be invoked and it was possible to attribute the deviation to some chance factor and still argue that the general results of the experiment were in agreement with the hypothesis. Freud retained throughout his long life the basic conviction that "theory is all very well, but it does not prevent [the facts] from existing" (3, p. 208). The same could not be said of Hull in practice, though I am sure that he would have subscribed to this sentiment in theory. When facts turned up which seemed actually to be inconsistent with his theory his common reaction was: "Give me time. It is not possible to make all deductions at once; the system must be built up gradually." This is certainly a justifiable attitude, but in the end his loyalty was primarily to the system (as indeed it might well be, considering the amount of energy and time he had put into it) rather than to curious, apparently inexplicable, facts in themselves.

As a result of this last difference in particular, both men had their characteristic weakness as scientists. In Freud's case, he kept so close to his observations over the years as an inductive scientist that his theoretical system was constantly in a state of flux. The concepts used did not relate to each other in any clear systematic way because they were constantly growing, changing and developing as new observations were made. One may argue that a scientist must keep his theorizing flexible, but one also has a right to expect that it is not so flexible as to make it impossible to test systematically. Freud, himself, was temperamentally disinclined to follow up on the detailed checking of his insights, as Jones points out, and this shows in the end in his system. He could have used some of Hull's rigor.

As for Hull, his weakness ultimately lay in the fact that he whittled away at the inductive process until observation became merely a means of checking his previous theoretical assumptions. This has the disadvantage which has characterized all such elaborate deductive systems in the past. It leads its exponents to look at only those phenomena which are covered by the system. Other phenomena tend to be neglected, though they may be equally important, simply because they do not "fit" in the system anywhere and to make them fit may cause a radical, not to say painful, revision in the enormous superstructure of propositions and derivations which the system involves. Hull speaks rather fondly in his autobiography of a machine which he built over a number of years which would calculate coefficients of correlation automatically. He relates that many of his friends joked with him about it, claiming that it would never work. "But," he concludes, somewhat proudly, "it really worked, exactly according to plan" (2, p. 15). What he failed to add was that although it did work, no one ever used it, partly because other more efficient ways of calculating coefficients of correlation had developed in the meantime, and partly because psychologists became more interested in statistical measures which had to be calculated with other types of machines. Some psychologists have the same thing to say in effect about his mathematico-deductive systems. They work all right, and they stand perhaps as a model of what can be done, but it is doubtful if they will be used, partly because there will be more efficient ways of accounting for the same facts, and partly because there are important facts which will have to be accounted for by other theoretical models.

But what is our final evaluation of the contribution of these two men to the scientific study of psychology? To begin with, we must not underestimate the fact that they both inspired in a number of younger men the firm conviction that a science of psychology was possible. Such a belief has not been widely held, and, as we have seen, they both fought valiantly againt doubts on this score wherever they arose, but particularly in religious circles. Then if we were to summarize Freud's lasting contribution in one word, it would have to be "ideas." He left behind him probably more important ideas about the nature of human psychology than any other man since Aristotle. Many of these ideas have not been checked by what most of us would regard today as adequate scientific methods, but they are a rich legacy which psychologists will draw on for years to come.

To summarize Hull's lasting contribution in one word, we would have to choose "system." By this we need not refer to his own elaborately worked out mathematico-deductive models. It is more the attitude which his models imply than the particular models themselves. No one, and here I speak from personal experience, could be long associated with Hull without catching some of his enthusiasm for exactitude, clarity, and system in stating propositions and ideas. The following comment is typical:

Too often what pass as systems in psychology are merely informal points of view containing occasional propositions. . . . Some authors are prone to the illusion that such propositions could be deduced with rigor in a few moments if they cared to take the trouble. Others assert that the logic has all been worked by them "in their heads," but that they did not bother to write it out; the reader is expected to accept this on faith. Fortunately, in science, it is customary to base conclusions on faith (1, p. 30).

It would be difficult to make much of a case for Hull as an original thinker or for Freud as a systematic one, but certainly we may agree that the "system" of the one and the creativity of the other are both absolutely essential for a successful scientific approach to psychology.

References

1. Hull, C. L. Mind, mechanism and adoptive behavior, *Psychol. Rev., 44*, 1–32, 1937.
2. Hull, C. L. Autobiography, in *A History of Psychology in Autobiography*, Vol. IV. Worcester, Mass.: Clark Univ. Press, 1952.
3. Jones, E. *The Life and Work of Sigmund Freud*, Vol I. New York: Basic Books, 1953.

"Skinner's reasoning is that freedom and free will are no more than illusions: Like it or not, man is already controlled by external influences."

Skinner's greatest contribution to psychology is in helping to clarify the role of reinforcement in the learning process. In his early works Skinner designed a box, aptly called a Skinner box, containing a lever and a mechanism delivering a pellet of food to the animal once the lever is depressed. In a classic cartoon two rats discuss their situation. The caption reads, "Boy, have I got this guy conditioned! Every time I press the bar down, he drops in a piece of food."

> I've had only one idea in my life—a true *idée fixe*. To put it as bluntly as possible—the idea of having my own way. "Control" expresses it. The control of human behavior. In my early experimental days it was a frenzied, selfish desire to dominate. I remember the rage I used to feel when a prediction went awry. I could have shouted at the subjects of my experiments, "Behave, damn you! Behave as you ought!"
>
> B. F. Skinner's *Walden Two*. 1948

The speaker is T. E. Frazier, a character in *Walden Two* and the fictional founder of the utopian community described in that novel. He is also an alter ego of the author, Burrhus Frederic Skinner, who is both a psychology professor and an institution at Harvard.

Skinner is the most influential of living American psychologists, and the most controversial contemporary figure in the science of human behavior, adored as a messiah and abhorred as a menace. As leader of the "behavioristic" psychologists, who liken man to a machine, Skinner is vigorously opposed both by humanists and by Freudian psychoanalysts. Next week that opposition is bound to flare anew with the publication of Skinner's latest book, *Beyond Freedom and Dignity* (Knopf: $6.95). Its message is one that is familiar to followers of Skinner, but startling to the uninitiated: we can no longer afford freedom, and so it must be replaced with control over man, his conduct and his culture. This

Reprinted by permission from *Time*, The Weekly Newsmagazine, September 1971, pp. 47–53. Copyright Time Inc.

thesis, proposed not by a writer of science fiction but by a man of science, raises the specter of a 1984 Orwellian society that might really come to pass. It accounts, also, for the alarm and anger that Skinner's current popularity arouses in his opponents.

Like the utopians who preceded him, Skinner hopes for a society in which men of good will can work, love and live in security and in harmony. For mankind he wants enough to eat, a clean environment and safety from nuclear cataclysm. He longs for a worldwide culture based on the principles of his famous didactic novel, *Walden Two*. Those principles include: communal ownership of land and buildings, egalitarian relationships between men and women, devotion to art, music and literature, liberal rewards for constructive behavior, freedom from jealousy, gossip, and—astonishingly—from the ideal of freedom. *Beyond Freedom and Dignity,* in fact, is really a nonfiction version of *Walden Two*.

Disastrous Results

Skinner acknowledges that the concept of freedom played a vital role in man's successful efforts to overthrow the tyrants who oppressed him, bolstering his courage and spurring him to nearly superhuman effort. But the same ideal, Skinner maintains, now threatens 20th century man's continued existence. "My book," says Skinner, "is an effort to demonstrate how things go bad when you make a fetish out of individual freedom and dignity. If you insist that individual rights are the *summum bonum,* then the whole structure of society falls down." In fact, Skinner believes that Western culture may die and be replaced, perhaps, with the more disciplined culture of the Soviet Union or of China. If that happens, Western man will have lost the only form of immortality he can hope for—the survival of his way of life.

Skinner's reasoning is that freedom and free will are no more than illusions; like it or not, man is already controlled by external influences. Some are haphazard; some are arranged by careless or evil men whose goals are selfish instead of humanitarian. The problem, then, is to design a culture that can, theoretically, survive; to decide how men must behave to ensure its survival in reality; and to plan environmental influences that will guarantee the desired behavior. Thus, in the Skinnerian world, man will refrain from polluting, from overpopulating, from rioting, and from making war, not because he knows that the results will be disastrous, but because he has been conditioned to want what serves group interests.

Is such a world really possible? Skinner believes that it is; he is certain that human behavior can be predicted and shaped exactly as if it were a chemical reaction. The way to do it, he thinks, is through "behavioral technology," a developing science of control that aims to change the environment rather than people, that seeks to alter actions rather than feelings, and that shifts the customary psychological emphasis on the world inside men to the world outside them. Central to Skinner's approach is a method of conditioning that has been used with uniform success on laboratory animals: giving rewards to mold the subject to the experimenter's will. According to Skinner and his followers, the same technique can be made to work equally well with human beings.

Underlying the method is the Skinnerian conviction that behavior is determined not from within but from without. "Unable to understand how or why the person we see behaves as he does, we attribute his behavior to a person inside," Skinner explains. Mistakenly, we believe that man "initiates, originates and creates, and in doing so he remains, as he was for the Greeks, divine. We say that he is autonomous." But Skinner insists that autonomy is a myth, and that belief in an "inner man" is a superstition that originated, like belief in God, in man's inability to understand his world. With the rise of behavioral science, understanding has grown, and man no longer needs such fictions as "something going on inside the individual, states of mind, feelings, purposes, expectancies and all of that." The fact is, Skinner insists, that actions are determined by the environment: behavior "is shaped and maintained by its consequences."

Avoiding Punishment

To Skinner, this means that there is nothing wrong, emotionally or morally, with people who behave badly. For example, youths who drop out of school or refuse to get jobs behave as they do not because they are neurotic or because they feel alienated, but "because of defective social environments in homes, schools, factories and elsewhere." As Skinner sees it, environments are defective when they fail to make desirable behavior pay off and when they resort to punishment as a means of stopping undesirable behavior.

In short, it is punishment or reward that determines whether a particular kind of behavior becomes habitual. But Skinner believes that punishment is generally an ineffective means of control. "A person who has been punished," he writes in his new book,

> is not less inclined to behave in a given way; at best, he learns how to avoid punishment. Our task is not to encourage moral struggle or to build or demonstrate inner virtues. It is to make life less punishing, and in doing so to release for more reinforcing activities the time and energy consumed in the avoidance of punishment.

The way to release that time and energy is "to build a world in which people are naturally good," in which they are rewarded for wanting what is good for their culture.

But arranging effective rewards, complicated enough in the laboratory, is even more complex in the real world. Why not solve society's problems by using the much simpler physical and biological technologies we already have? Because, Skinner says, that will not work.

> Better contraceptives will control population only if people use them. A nuclear holocaust can be prevented only if the conditions under which nations make war can be changed. The environment will continue to deteriorate until pollution practices are abandoned. We need to make vast changes in human behavior.

Soap Mouthwash

A matter that might interest President Nixon is Skinner's belief that new ways must be found to persuade people that work is worthwhile. "Behavior used to be reinforced by great deprivation; if people weren't hungry, they wouldn't work. Now we are committed to feeding people whether they work or not. Nor is money as great a reinforcer as it once was. People no longer work for punitive reasons, yet our culture offers no new satisfactions." Moreover, "we can't control inflation if everything we might do is a threat to somebody's freedom. Yet in the long run, we are all going to suffer much more than if we were slightly restricted."

Skinner came rather slowly to his conviction that such changes can be made; his early interests, in fact, were far from psychology. Born in Susquehanna, Pa., in 1904, he was the elder son of Grace Burrhus, an amateur musician who sang at weddings and funerals, and William Skinner, a lawyer who was "a sucker for book salesmen." In his "Sketch for an Autobiography," Skinner describes his early life as "warm and stable." He lived in the same house until he went to college. He was never physically punished by his father and only once by his mother—when she washed out his mouth with soap for using a "bad word." Nevertheless, young Skinner was "taught to fear God, the police and what people will think," and his Grandmother Skinner "made sure that I understood the concept of hell by showing me the glowing bed of coals in the parlor stove." To deter him from a life of crime, Skinner's father conducted him through the county jail and on a summer vacation took him to a lecture with colored slides that depicted life in Sing Sing.

From his childhood years, Skinner was mechanically inclined. He built roller-skate scooters, steerable wagons, rafts, water pistols from lengths of bamboo, and "from a discarded water boiler a steam cannon with which I could shoot plugs of potato and carrot over the houses of our neighbors." He also devised a flotation system to separate green from ripe elderberries, which he used to sell from door to door. Although his attempts to build a glider and a perpetual motion machine ended in failure, his innovative tinkering was to pay off handsomely in the laboratory in later years.

In high school, Skinner earned money by lettering advertising show cards, played in a jazz band, and with three other boys organized an orchestra that performed two nights a week in a local movie theater. A good student, he demonstrated a flair for writing, and when he got to Hamilton College (Clinton, N.Y.) in 1922, decided to major in English.

In college, by his own admission, young Fred never fitted into student life, but became a rebel whose lack of self-understanding now amazes him. He wrote an editorial attacking Phi Beta Kappa, helped cover the walls at Class Day exercises with "bitter caricatures of the faculty," and made such a shambles of commencement ceremonies that he was warned by the college president that he would not get his degree unless he quieted down.

But at the same time he had what classmates recall as a brilliant mind, and he made full use of it. For one thing, he wrote short stories, and in his senior year sent three of them to Robert Frost, who praised them warmly.

That encouragement convinced Fred Skinner that he should become a writer. The decision, he says, was "disastrous." Recalling those "dark years," living first at home with his family and then in New York's Greenwich Village, he admits that he frittered away his time, read aimlessly, wrote very little—"and thought about seeing a psychiatrist." In his own words, he "failed as a writer" because he "had nothing important to say."

But that failure allowed Skinner to swing his attention back to one of the pet interests of his youth: animal behavior. As a boy, he had had toads and chipmunks. He also had a vivid memory of watching a troupe of trained pigeons at a county fair play at putting out a fire. Besides, he had read and been excited by some Bertrand Russell articles in the old *Dial* magazine about Johns Hopkins Psychologist John B. Watson, father of behaviorism. It was with Watson, in 1913, that psychology really emerged from its origins in philosophy to become a full-fledged scientific discipline.

Early Christian thinkers pondering the mystery of man believed that it was the "soul" that set human beings apart from animals. To them, the essence of man was his God-given spirit, immaterial, impalpable, otherworldly, something quite outside the natural world. But with the decline of religion and the rise of materialism, 17th and 18th century philosophers like Thomas Hobbes and Julien de La Mettrie increasingly viewed the soul as an aspect of the body, man as an animal, both men and animals as machines.

It was this kind of thinking that influenced Watson. Drawing, too, on the work of Pavlov, he repudiated the subjective concepts of mind and emotion and described human behavior as a succession of physical reflex responses to stimuli coming from the environment. It was the environment alone, he felt, that determined what a man is: "Give me a dozen healthy infants," he wrote in 1925, "and I'll guarantee to take any one at random and train him to become any type of specialist I might select—doctor, lawyer, even beggarman and thief, regardless of his talents, penchants, tendencies, abilities." The goal of this Watsonian behaviorism was the prediction and control of behavior—which suited Skinner to perfection.

Bach Fugues

And so, in 1928, Skinner entered Harvard with a new goal: a doctorate in psychology. His regime was spartan: "I saw no movies or plays, had scarcely any dates, and read nothing but psychology and physiology. The second year I bought a piano; but there was discipline even so; I played Bach fugues or nothing."

In these years—and subsequently—Skinner disciplined not just himself but also rats. The rats, and later pigeons, became the center of laboratory experiments in which he controlled behavior by setting up "contingencies of reinforcement"—circumstances under which a particular bit of desired behavior is "reinforced" or rewarded to make sure it will be repeated. The behavior Skinner demanded of his pigeons was bizarre—for pigeons. He made them walk figure eights, for example, by reinforcing them with food at crucial moments. The process as explained by Skinner:

> I watch a hungry pigeon carefully. When he makes a slight clockwise turn, he's instantly rewarded for it. After he eats, he immediately tries it again. Then I wait for more of a turn and reinforce again. Within two or three minutes, I can get any pigeon to make a full circle. Next I reinforce only when he moves in the other direction. Then I wait until he does both, and reinforce him again and again until it becomes a kind of drill. Within ten to 15 minutes, the pigeon will be doing a perfect figure eight.

By a similar process, Skinner has taught pigeons to dance with each other, and even to play Ping Pong. During World War II, he conceived the idea of using pigeons in guided-missile control; three birds were conditioned to peck continuously for four or five minutes at the image of a target on a screen. Then they were placed in harness in the nose of a missile, facing a screen on which the target would appear when the missile was in flight. By pecking at the image moving on the screen, the pigeons would send corrective signals that moved the missile's fins and kept it on target. The missile, called the Pelican, was never used in warfare; the pigeon-aided equipment was so complex and bulky that the missile could carry little high explosive. Furthermore, Skinner mourns, "our problem was no one could take us seriously."

All of these conditioning feats were accomplished with the now-famous Skinner box. It is a soundproof enclosure with a food dispenser that a rat can operate by pressing a lever, and a pigeon by pecking a key. The dispenser does not work unless the animal has first performed according to a specially designed "schedule of reinforcement."

Explains Skinner:

> One of the most powerful schedules, the variable-ratio schedule, is characteristic of all gambling systems. The gambler cannot be sure the next play will win, but a certain mean ratio of plays to wins is maintained. This is the way a dishonest gambler hooks his victim. At first the victim is permitted to win fairly often. Eventually he continues to play when he is not winning at all. With this technique it is possible to create a pathological gambler out of a simple bird like a pigeon.

Venture in Self-Therapy

For a while, that beguiling possibility and others suggested by Skinner left the academic world pretty cold, as did his first book, *The Behavior of Organisms,* published in 1938. "People didn't reinforce me, but my rats did," Skinner says regretfully, remembering how rewarded he felt every time his command to "Behave, damn you!" was obeyed.

He was rewarded in a different way—his first general public recognition— when in 1945 the *Ladies' Home Journal* printed a piece about another kind of Skinner box, the so-called air crib. . . . By the time the *Journal* was printed, Skinner had finished writing his second book, though he did not find a publisher for it until 1948. The work was *Walden Two,* completed in seven weeks of impassioned creativity. Writing it, says Skinner, was "pretty obviously a venture in self-therapy in which I was struggling to reconcile two aspects of my own behavior, represented by Burris and Frazier." Even today, both characters represent Skinner himself. Burris is a professor with traditional ideas, acquired in childhood, about freedom, dignity and democracy. Frazier is the antidemocratic creator of a controlled society whose views about human behavior correspond to Skinner's laboratory findings.

Visiting Frazier's planned community, Burris is both attracted and repelled —attracted by the seeming contentment of its inhabitants, repelled by their voluntary submission to the maneuverings, however well-intentioned, of its Planners and Managers. In the end, his skepticism overcome, he decides to join the community and with "euphoric abandon" wires his college head: "My dear President Mittelbach, you may take your stupid university . . ."

Pigeons Aren't People

Unlike Burris, the numerous and articulate anti-Skinnerians remain skeptical, if not downright hostile toward him and his followers. Yet they feel that his long, patient campaign against freedom must be studied and understood. Their criticism is directed not at Skinner the scientific technician (the soundness of his laboratory work is seldom questioned) but at Skinner the philosopher and political thinker; his proposal for a controlled society, they say, is both unworkable and evil.

Giving as an example the failure of the North Koreans to brainwash many of their G.I. war prisoners, Stanford Psychologist Albert Bandura asserts that control of human behavior on the scale advocated by Skinner is impossible. Psychologist Ernest Hilgard, also of Stanford, thinks control of mass behavior is theoretically possible but realistically improbable, because there are too many bright people who would never go along.

Skinner himself admits that "pigeons aren't people," but points out that his ideas have already been put to practical use in schools, mental hospitals, penal institutions and business firms. Skinner-inspired teaching machines have begun to produce what amounts to an educational revolution. It was after a visit to his daughter's fourth-grade arithmetic class that he invented the first device for programmed instruction in 1954. Having seen "minds being destroyed," he concluded that youngsters should learn math, spelling and other subjects in the same way that pigeons learn Ping Pong. Accordingly, machines now in use in scores of cities across the country present pupils with a succession of easy learning steps. At each one, a correct answer to a question brings instant reinforcement, not with the grain of corn that rewarded the pigeon, but with a printed statement—supposedly just as satisfying—that the answer is right.

Juvenile Offenders

Some critics, loyal Skinnerians among them, argue that this teaching process bores all but the dullest students, and that there is little solid evidence as to how well programmed instruction sticks. But Skinner insists that his devices teach faster than other methods and free teachers to give personal attention to students who are trying to master complex subjects.

In some mental hospitals, reinforcement therapy inspired by Skinner is helping apathetic or rebellious patients to behave more like healthy human beings. The staffers of one institution, for instance, were troubled by patients who insisted on trailing into the dining room long after the dinner bell sounded. Attendants tried closing the doors 20 minutes after the bell rang, refusing admittance to those who showed up any later. Gradually, the interval between bell and door closing was shortened to only five minutes, and most patients were arriving promptly. "You shift from one kind of reinforcement—annoying the guards and getting attention—to another, eating when you're hungry," says Skinner. To charges that this kind of conditioning is sadism, he replies that "the patients are going in quickly because they want to." That is strange logic;

he seems to ignore the fact that the patients are compelled to "want to" unless they care to go hungry.

In yet another practical example of Skinnerism in operation, a point system for good behavior was set up for juvenile offenders—armed robbers, rapists and murderers—in the Robert F. Kennedy Youth Center in West Virginia. Though no requirements were imposed on the delinquents, they earned points if they voluntarily picked up books, or went to lectures and managed to learn something from them. With the points they could then buy such rewards as better food, a private room, or time in front of the TV set.

"All their lives," says Skinner, "these boys had been told that they couldn't learn and that they were useless. But under conditions that reinforced them every time they progressed, their morale improved enormously. Moreover, the return rate to the school dropped from 85% to 25% after the method was instituted."

The same kind of positive reinforcement was tried a few years ago by Emery Air Freight of Wilton, Conn. To reduce the breakage that resulted when goods were packed in the wrong boxes for shipping, supervisors began complimenting packers when the correct boxes were chosen. Taking new pride in their work, the employees made virtually no mistakes, breakage ceased, and the company saved $600,000 in a year.

Mothers who practice Skinnerism—knowingly or by instinct—have an easier time with their youngsters when they reward good behavior instead of punishing bad. Explains Skinner: "If a mother goes to her baby only when he yells, she reinforces fussing. But when she goes to him while he's happy and perhaps saying 'Mama' softly, the baby will always speak to her that way."

Uncompromising View

Though such apparent successes persuade Skinnerians that reinforcement is eminently practical, critics find the technique philosophically distasteful and morally wrong.

Many of their objections center around the ancient, crucial argument over free will v. determinism; is man in charge of himself and his destiny, or is he not? Skinner argues that belief in free will comes only from man's need to be given credit for his "good" behavior and achievements. "Consider a woman who has a baby. It cost her a lot of pain and trouble to have it. But she didn't design that baby; it was all settled at the moment of conception what the baby was going to be like. The same thing is true when a man writes books, invents things, manages a business. He didn't initiate anything. It's all the effect of past history on him. That's the truth, and we have to get used to it." Theologians, humanists and conventional psychologists, including Freudians, cannot accept this uncompromising view. "The chief source of man's destiny," Reinhold Niebuhr wrote, "is man's essential freedom and capacity for self-determination." Carl Rogers has asserted that "over and above the circumstances which control all of us, there exists an inner experience of choice which is very important. This is the kind of thing Skinner has never been willing to recognize."

Skinner's detractors attack the whole concept of behaviorism, which Novelist Arthur Koestler, who has high amateur standing in psychology and other sciences, maintains is nothing but pseudoscience, " a monumental triviality that has sent psychology into a modern version of the Dark Ages." In ignoring consciousness, mind, imagination and purpose, Koestler says, Behaviorist Skinner and his admirers have abandoned what is most important. Similarly, Historian Peter Gay speaks of "the innate naiveté, intellectual bankruptcy and half-deliberate cruelty of behaviorism."

The gravest menace from Skinner is his authoritarianism in the view of his critics. They reject the notion that man can no longer afford freedom and believe in fact that he cannot afford the opposite. Says Harvard Social Psychologist Herbert C. Kelman: "For those of us who hold the enhancement of man's freedom of choice as a fundamental value, any manipulation of the behavior of others constitutes a violation of that essential humanity, regardless of the 'goodness' of the cause that this manipulation is designed to serve." To Kelman, the "ethical ambiguity" of behavioral manipulation is the same whether the limitation on choice comes "through punishment or reward or even through so perfect an arrangement of society that people do not care to choose."

Existential Psychoanalyst Rollo May believes that Skinner is a totalitarian without fully knowing it. "I have never found any place in Skinner's system for the rebel," he says. "Yet the capacity to rebel is of the essence in a constructive society." Richard Rubenstein, professor of religion at Florida State University, wonders what might happen to would-be rebels in a Skinnerian society: "Suppose some future controller told dissenting groups to 'behave, damn you!' What would prevent the controller from employing his own final solution?"

Skinner is skeptical about democracy. Observing that society is already using such ineffective means of behavioral control as persuasion and conventional education, he insists that men of good will must adopt more effective techniques, using them for "good" purposes to keep despots from using them for "bad" ones. In his planned society, he says, control would be balanced by countercontrol, probably by "making the controller a member of the group he controls." This would help to ensure that punishment would never be inflicted, Skinner maintains, adding that it was the use of "aversive control" (punishment) that doomed Hitler: "The Nazi system had its own destruction built right into it. When you control that way, people are out to get you."

The ultimate logical dilemma in Skinner's thinking is this: What are the sources of the standards of good and evil in his ideal society? Indeed, who decides even what constitutes pleasure or pain, reward or punishment, when man and his environment can be limitlessly manipulated? Skinner himself believes in Judeo-Christian ethics combined with the scientific tradition. But he fails to answer how it is possible to accept those ethics without also accepting something like the "inner person" with an autonomous conscience.

Skinner has never responded fully to any of his critics, despite their number and stature. Often he has failed to understand them. Sometimes he has even branded them as neurotic or even psychotic. Occasionally he has seemed to imply that he himself is beyond criticism. "When I met him, he was convinced he was a genius," Yvonne Skinner remembers. And in *Walden Two*, Skinner's alter ego, Frazier, assuming the posture of Christ on the cross, says that there is "a curious similarity" between himself and God—adding, however, that "perhaps I must yield to God in point of seniority."

In another *Walden Two* passage, Skinner sketches a more realistic self-portrait. With some bitterness, his alter ego Frazier addresses Burris: "You think I'm conceited, aggressive, tactless, selfish. You're convinced that I'm completely insensitive to my effect upon others, except when the effect is calculated. You can't see in me any personal warmth. You're sure that I'm one who couldn't possibly be a genuine member of any community . . . Shall we say that as a person I'm a complete failure and have done with it?"

This awareness that he is unfit for communal life may be one reason that Skinner has never tried to start a real Walden Two, never sent a Dear-President-Mittelbach telegram to the president of Harvard. In addition, he likes his own kind of life too well to give it up even for an ideal in which he believes so intensely, and even if he felt otherwise, his wife is opposed to the idea.

Says Yvonne Skinner, a former University of Chicago English major who studied with Thornton Wilder and is herself a gifted writer: "We had tremendous arguments about *Walden Two*. I wouldn't like it: I just like change and privacy."

Refusing Invitations

Fred and Yvonne Skinner live in an attractive, modern Cambridge house complete with swimming pool, a stereo system, a grand piano, a clavichord and, in the basement study, a small organ. In a sense Skinner's own life-style is highly controlled and conditioned. His study contains a special clock that "runs when I'm really thinking. I keep a cumulative record of serious time at my desk. The clock starts when I turn on the desk light, and whenever it passes twelve hours, I plot a point on a curve. I can see what my average rate of writing has been at any period. When other activities take up my time, the slope falls off. That helps me to refuse invitations."

Skinner rises at 5 a.m., writes for three hours, then walks to his Harvard office, sometimes memorizing poetry (Shakespeare or Baudelaire) on the way. There he charts the sales of *Walden Two* on a graph over his desk; the total should reach the million mark sometime in 1972. In the course of the day, he gives an occasional lecture and records his ideas in notebooks that he has always at hand. "He thinks of himself as an event in the history of man, and he wants to be damned sure the record is straight," a colleague observes.

Skinner nonetheless allows himself some relaxation. He drinks vodka and tonic in the late afternoon, sees an occasional movie, reads Georges Simenon detective novels once in a while, and enjoys the company of friends, his two children and his grandchildren. It sounds fulfilling, but a poignant passage from a personal journal several years ago suggests an underlying sadness: "Sun streams into our living room. My hi-fi is midway through the first act of *Tristan and Isolde*. A very pleasant environment. A man would be a fool not to enjoy himself in it. In a moment I will work on a manuscript which may help mankind. So my life is not only pleasant, it is earned or deserved. Yet, yet, I am unhappy."

That sort of unhappiness wells from deep personal sources. Yet it is also related to his more universal concerns. Skinner worries about the fact that, as *Walden Two*'s Frazier put it, "our civilization is running away like a frightened horse. As she runs, her speed and her panic increase together. As for your politicians, your professors, your writers—let them wave their arms and shout as wildly as they will."

That may be an accurate description of society's dilemma, but Skinner's solution seems equally frightening. To Theologian Rubenstein, *Beyond Freedom and Dignity* is an important but "terrifying" book. Skinner's "utopian projection," he says, "is less likely to be a blueprint for the Golden Age than for the theory and practice of hell."

Twin Oaks: On to Walden Two

At first glance, it looks like a movie set for *Walden Two*. There is a shop building called Harmony, a farmhouse called Llano, and a dormitory called Oneida. Bulletin boards list upcoming cultural events, and young people lounge on hammocks, reading and engaging in serious discussions. The smell of farm-fresh cooking is everywhere. The resemblance to Walden Two is more than superficial. Twin Oaks, a 123-acre farm commune nestled in the foothills of Virginia's Piedmont, is a remarkable attempt to create a utopian community governed by Skinner's laws of social engineering.

Work is allocated by an intricate system of labor credits so that none of the 35 members have unequal burdens. Titles and honorifics have been done away with so that, in the words of the community's code, "all are entitled to the same privileges, advantages and respect." Private property is forbidden, except for such things as books and clothing, and even with that loophole, most members draw their clothing, right down to their underwear, from a massive community closet. No one is allowed to boast of individual accomplishments, to gossip ("negative speech") or to be intolerant of another's beliefs.

Behavioral engineering goes on every minute of the day. A member who gets angry, who makes demands or who gives ultimatums is simply not "reinforced," to use the behavioral term. He is ignored. What is considered appropriate behavior—cooperating, showing affection, turning the other cheek and working diligently—is, on the other hand, applauded, or "reinforced," by the group. Members are singled out for compliments if they do a job well; signs are put up telling who cleaned a room, for example. Smokers who wanted to break the cigarette habit formed a group to help one another. Cigarettes were put in progressively more inconvenient spots, and each member of the group received congratulations for every day he spent without tobacco.

The use of tobacco and alcohol is, in fact, discouraged at Twin Oaks, and all drugs, including marijuana, are banned. So is television, which is considered a cultural poison. "We decided that we just weren't strong enough to stand up to television," says Kat Griebe, one of Twin Oaks' charter founders and, at 40, one of the oldest members. "Its powerful message is that of middle-class American values, which we reject—a high level of consumption, streamlined cosmetic standards of beauty, male dominance, the use of violence as a problem solver, and the underlying assumption that life should be a constant state of titillation and excitement. Life just isn't like that."

Especially life at Twin Oaks. The favorite sports are "cooperation volleyball" and skinny-dipping in the South Anna River—false modesty is another of the sins that are not reinforced—and there is plenty of folk singing and dancing. In a departure from Skinner's rather puritanical Walden Two, sex is considered, as one member put it, a "pleasant pastime, like anything else." Adds Kat: "We don't have a very high opinion of marriage—it often becomes possessive. We do have a high regard for what Skinner calls 'abiding affection.' "

As yet there are no children at Twin Oaks. There is not enough "surplus labor" to care for infants, and there is no space for a separate Skinnerian nursery. Besides that, the reasoning goes, it is better not to bring children into the equation until all the adults have developed "appropriate" behavior; otherwise, bad habits would simply be reproduced in the young.

All of the utopian ventures of the early and mid-19th century—from Indiana's New Harmony on the Wabash River to Massachusetts' famed Brook Farm—eventually foundered, and Twin Oaks, too, has its problems. The major one appears to be financial. "Skinner never wrote about a poor community," laments Gabe Sinclair. "He wrote about a rich one." After starting with only $35,000, Twin Oaks, four years later, still finds survival a struggle. The farm brings more emotional than monetary rewards; members would find it cheaper to work at other jobs and buy their food at the market. The community's chief source of income is the sale of hammocks stitched together in Harmony, but it is not enough to make ends meet: several members are forced to take outside jobs in Richmond and Charlottesville—a direct contradiction to Walden Two's basic premise that all time should be spent in a totally controlled environment.

Beyond economics, there are serious psychological problems at Twin Oaks and few members have stayed very long. Turnover last year was close to 70%. The ones who leave first, in fact, are often the most competent members, who still expect special recognition for their talents. "Competent people are hard to get along with," says Richard Stutsman, one of Twin Oaks' trained psychologists. "They tend to make demands, not requests. We cannot afford to reinforce ultimatum behavior, although we recognize our need for their competence. So often we have given in to them on little things, and then when a big demand arises we have to deny them." When they leave, the community not only loses their skills but also sacrifices a potential rise in its standard of living.

While it is considerably poorer than Walden Two, Twin Oaks has gone farther toward the goal of behavioral control than might have seemed reasonably possible. It is too soon, however, to call the commune much more than a fascinating experiment.

In 1945, when Deborah Skinner was eleven months old, she had a rather dubious distinction; she was the most talked-about infant in America—the famous "baby in a box." The box, or "air crib" as her father called it, was his own invention, a glassed-in, insulated, air-controlled crib that he thought would revolutionize child rearing and, in line with his behavioral theories, produce happier, healthier children.

One of the major practical problems in raising a young baby, Skinner reasoned, is the simple one of keeping it warm. The infant is usually covered by half a dozen layers of cloth—shirt, nightdress, sheet and blankets—that not only constrict movement and cause rashes, but sometimes even pose the danger of strangulation. Then there is the mother's labor in dressing and undressing the child, plus the considerable expense of buying and laundering all those clothes and blankets.

To eliminate those troubles, Skinner designed Deborah's crib with temperature and humidity controls so that she could be warm and naked at the same time. Besides the hoped-for results—Deborah never suffered from a rash, for instance—the crib provided an unexpected fringe benefit: the Skinners discovered that the baby was so sensitive to even the slightest change in temperature that she could be made happy simply by moving the thermostat a notch or two. "We wonder how a comfortable temperature is ever reached with clothing and blankets," Skinner wrote in a 1945 issue of *Ladies' Home Journal.* "During the past six months, Deborah has not cried at all except for a moment or two when injured or sharply distressed—for example, when inoculated."

The air in the box was passed through filters, keeping Deborah free from germs and so clean that it was necessary to give her only one bath a week. There was the usual diaper change, but little other laundering; a single, 10-yd.-long sheet was stored on a spool at one end of the compartment and rolled through into a hamper on the other end as it was soiled, it had to be laundered just once a week. The box was partially soundproofed, and a shade could be drawn over the plate-glass windows.

Skinner was sensitive to criticism that Deborah was isolated. In his articles and lectures, he took pains to stress that she could watch everything that was taking place in the room about her, and that she was frequently taken out for cuddling and play. To many people, however, the air box sounded and looked like an atrocious human goldfish bowl.

The continuing controversy about the box may have partially offset the good effects Skinner hoped for when he designed it. Says Deborah, who is now an art student in London: "It was spread around that because of the box I had become psychotic, had to be institutionalized, and had even attempted suicide. My father was very concerned about these rumors as was I. He thinks they may have affected me. After college, I had a typical half-year of depression, the sort of identity crisis that everybody I've ever known has gone through. At this point my father brought up the idea that I don't have enough faith in myself, and that the rumors may have had something to do with this."

In fact, Deborah, a slightly shy and earnest but nonpsychotic young woman of 27, seems to have survived the rumors rather well. Her 2½ years in the box, she thinks, did her only good. "It wasn't really a psychological experiment," she says, "but what you might call a happiness-through-health experiment. I think I was a very happy baby. Most of the criticisms of the box are by people who don't understand what it was."

Though something like 1,000 of the air cribs are in use today, Skinner's idea has not caught on with very many parents and has yet to revolutionize child rearing.

"Piaget argues that much of our knowledge about reality comes to us not from without like the wail of a siren but rather from within by the force of our own logic."

Jean Piaget, now 79 years old, is a major figure in contemporary psychology. During one period of research investigation he carefully studied the mental growth of his own children and three significant books resulted from these observations. Piaget's discoveries in children's language and thought are currently exerting considerable influence in education and child psychology.

In February, 1967, Jean Piaget, the Swiss psychologist, arrived at Clark University in Worcester, Mass., to deliver the Heinz Werner Memorial Lectures. The lectures were to be given in the evening, and before the first one a small dinner party was arranged in honor of Piaget and was attended by colleagues, former students and friends. I was invited because of my long advocacy of Piaget's work and because I had spent a year (1964–65) at his Institute for Educational Science in Geneva. Piaget had changed very little since I had last seen him, but he did appear tired and mildly apprehensive.

Although Piaget has lectured all over the world, this particular occasion had special significance. Almost 60 years before, in 1909, another famous European, Sigmund Freud, also lectured at Clark University. Piaget was certainly aware of the historical parallel. He was, moreover, going to speak to a huge American audience in French and, despite the offices of his remarkable translator, Eleanor Duckworth, he must have had some reservations about how it would go.

Piaget's apprehension was apparent during the dinner. For one who is usually a lively and charming dinner companion, he was surprisingly quiet and unresponsive. About half way through the meal there was a small disturbance. The room in which the dinner was held was at a garden level and two boys suddenly appeared at the windows and began tapping at them. The inclination of most of us, I think, was to shoo them away. Before we had a chance to do that, however, Piaget had turned to face the children. He smiled up at the lads, hunched his shoulders and gave them a slight wave with his hand. They hunched their shoulders and smiled in return, gave a slight wave and disappeared. After a moment, Piaget turned back to the table and began telling stories and entering into animated conversation.

Although I am sure his lecture would have been a success in any case and that the standing ovation he received would have occurred without the little incident, I nonetheless like to think that the encounter with the boys did much to restore his vigor and good humor.

It is Piaget's genius for empathy with children together with true intellectual genius, that has made him the outstanding child psychologist in the world today and one destined to stand beside Freud with respect to his contributions to psychology, education and related disciplines. Just as Freud's discoveries of unconscious motivation, infantile sexuality and the stages of psychosexual growth changed our ways of thinking about human personality, so Piaget's discoveries of children's implicit philosophies, the construction of reality by the infant and the stages of mental development have altered our ways of thinking about human intelligence.

The man behind these discoveries is an arresting figure. He is tall and somewhat portly, and his stooped walk, bulky suits and crown of long white hair give him the appearance of a thrice-magnified Einstein. (When he was at the Institute for Advanced Study at Princeton in 1953, a friend of his wife rushed to a window one day and exclaimed, "Look, Einstein!" Madame Piaget looked and replied, "No, just my Piaget.") Piaget's personal trademarks are his meerschaum pipes (now burned deep amber), his navy blue beret and his bicycle.

Meeting Piaget is a memorable experience. Although Piaget has an abundance of Old-World charm and graciousness, he seems to emanate an aura of intellectual presence not unlike the aura of personality presence conveyed by a great actor. While as a psychologist I am unable to explain how this sense of presence is communicated, I am nevertheless convinced that everyone who meets Piaget experiences it. While talking to me, for example, he was able to divine in my remarks and questions a significance and depth of which I was entirely unaware and certainly hadn't intended. Evidently one characteristic of genius is to search for relevance in the apparently commonplace and frivolous.

Piaget's is a superbly disciplined life. He arises early each morning, sometimes as early as 4 A.M., and writes four or more publishable pages on square sheets of white paper in an even, small hand. Later in the morning he may teach classes and attend meetings. His afternoons include long walks during which he thinks about the problems he is currently confronting. He says, "I always like to think on a problem before reading about it." In the evenings, he reads and retires early. Even on his international trips, Piaget keeps on this schedule.

Each summer, as soon as classes are over, Piaget gathers up the research findings that have been collected by his assistants during the year and departs for the Alps, where he takes up solitary residence in a room in an abandoned farmhouse. The whereabouts of this retreat is as closely guarded as the means of depositors in numbered Swiss bank accounts; only Piaget's family, his long-time colleague Bärbel Inhelder and a trusted secretary know where he is. During the summer Piaget takes walks, meditates, writes *and* writes. Then, when the leaves begin to turn, he descends from the mountains with the several books and articles he has written on his "vacation."

Although Piaget, now in his 72d year, has been carrying his works down from the mountains for almost 50 summers (he has published more than 30 books and hundreds of articles), it is only within the past decade that his writings have come to be fully appreciated in America. This was due, in part, to the fact that until fairly recently only a few of his books had been translated into English. In addition, American psychology and education were simply not ready for Piaget until the fifties. Now the ideas that Piaget had been advocating for more than 30 years are regarded as exceedingly innovative and even as avant-garde.

His work falls into three more or less distinct periods within each of which he covered an enormous amount of psychological territory and developed a multitude of insights. (Like most creative men, Piaget is hard put to it to say when a particular idea came to him. If he ever came suddenly upon an idea which sent him shouting through the halls, he has never admitted to it.)

During the first period (roughly 1922–29), Piaget explored the extent and depth of children's spontaneous ideas about the physical world and about their own mental processes. He happened upon this line of inquiry while working in Alfred Binet's laboratory school in Paris where he arrived, still seeking a direction for his talents, a year after receiving his doctorate in biological science at the University of Lausanne. It was in the course of some routine intelligence testing that Piaget became interested in what lay behind children's correct, and particularly their incorrect, answers. To clarify the origins of these answers he began to interview the children in the open-ended manner he had learned while serving a brief interneship at Bleuler's psychiatric clinic in Zurich. This semi-clinical interview procedure, aimed at revealing the processes by which a child arrives at a particular reply to a test question, has become a trademark of Piagetian research investigation.

What Piaget found with this method of inquiry was that children not only reasoned differently from adults but also that they had quite different worldviews, literally different philosophies. This led Piaget to attend to those childish remarks and questions which most adults find amusing or nonsensical. Just as Freud used seemingly accidental slips of the tongue and pen as evidence for unconscious motivations, so Piaget has employed the "cute" sayings of children to demonstrate the existence of ideas quite foreign to the adult mind.

Piaget had read in the recollections of a deaf mute (recorded by William James) that as a child he had regarded the sun and moon as gods and believed they followed him about. Piaget sought to verify this recollection by interviewing children on the subject, and he found that many youngsters do believe that the sun and moon follow them when they are out for a walk. Similar remarks Piaget either overheard or was told about led to a large number of investigations which revealed, among many similar findings, that young children believe that anything which moves is alive, that the names of objects reside in the objects themselves and that dreams come in through the window at night.

Such beliefs, Piaget pointed out in an early article entitled "Children's Philosophies," are not unrelated to but rather derive from an implicit animism and artificialism with many parallels to primitive and Greek philosophies. In the child's view, objects like stones and clouds are imbued with motives, intentions and feelings, while mental events such as dreams and thoughts are endowed with corporality and force. Children also believe that everything has a purpose and that everything in the world is made by and for man. (My 5-year-old son asked me why we have snow and answered his own question by saying, "It is for children to play in.")

The child's animism and artificialism help to explain his famous and often unanswerable "why" questions. It is because children believe that everything has a purpose that they ask, "Why is grass green?" and "Why do the stars shine?" The parent who attempts to answer such questions with a physical explanation has missed the point.

In addition to disclosing the existence of children's philosophies during this first period, Piaget also found the clue to the egocentrism of childhood. In observing young children at play at the *Maison des Petits,* the modified Montessori school associated with the Institute of Educational Science in Geneva, Piaget noted a peculiar lack of social orientation which was also present in their conversation and in their approaches to certain intellectual tasks. A child would make up a new word ("stocks" for socks and stockings) and just assume that everyone knew what he was talking about as if this were the conventional name for the objects he had in mind. Likewise, Piaget noted that when two nursery school children were at play they often spoke *at* rather than *to* one another and were frequently chattering on about two quite different and unrelated topics. Piaget observed, moreover, that when he stood a child of 5 years opposite him, the child who could tell his own right and left nevertheless insisted that Piaget's right and left hands were directly opposite his own.

In Piaget's view, all of these behaviors can be explained by the young child's inability to put himself in another person's position and to take that person's point of view. Unlike the egocentric adult, who can take another person's point of view but does not, the egocentric child does not take another person's viewpoint because he cannot. This conception of childish egocentrism has produced a fundamental alteration in our evaluation of the preschool child's behavior. We now appreciate that it is intellectual immaturity and not moral perversity which makes, for example, a young child continue to pester his mother after she has told him she has a headache and wishes to be left alone. The preschool child is simply unable to put himself in his mother's position and see things from her point of view.

The second period of Piaget's investigations began when, in 1929, he sought to trace the origins of the child's spontaneous mental growth to the behavior of infants; in this case, his own three children, Jaqueline, Lucienne and Laurent. Piaget kept very detailed records of their behavior and of their performance on a series of ingenious tasks which he invented and presented to them. The books resulting from these investigations, "The Origins of Intelligence in Children," "Play, Dreams and Imitation in Children" and "The Construction of Reality in the Child" are now generally regarded as classics in the field and have been one of the major forces behind the scurry of research activity in the area of infant behavior now current both in America and abroad. The publication of these books in the middle and late nineteen-thirties marked the end of the second phase of Piaget's work.

Some of the most telling observations Piaget made during this period had to do with what he called the *conservation of the object* (using the word conservation to convey the idea of permanence). To the older child and to the adult, the existence of objects and persons who are not immediately present is taken as self-evident. The child at school knows that while he is working at his desk his mother is simultaneously at home and his father is at work. This is not the case for the young infant playing in his crib, for whom out of sight is literally out of mind. Piaget observed that when an infant 4 or 5 months old is playing with a toy which subsequently rolls out of sight (behind another toy) but is still within reach, the infant ceases to look for it. The infant behaves as if the toy had not only disappeared but as if it had gone entirely out of existence.

This helps to explain the pleasure infants take in the game of peek-a-boo. If the infant believed that the object existed when it was not seen, he would not be surprised and delighted at its re-emergence and there would be no point to the game. It is only during the second year of life, when children begin to represent objects mentally, that they seek after toys that have disappeared from view. Only then do they attribute an independent existence to objects which are not present to their senses.

The third and major phase of Piaget's endeavors began about 1940 and continues until the present day. During this period Piaget has studied the development in children and adolescents of, those mental abilities which gradually enable the child to construct a world-view which is in conformance with reality as seen by adults. He has, at the same time, been concerned with how children acquire the adult versions of various concepts such as number, quantity and speed. Piaget and his colleague have amassed, in the last 28 years, an astounding amount of information about the thinking of children and adolescents which is only now beginning to be used by psychologists and educators.

Two discoveries made during this last period are of particular importance both because they were so unexpected and because of their relevance for education. It is perhaps fair to say that education tends to focus upon the static aspects of reality rather than upon its dynamic transformations. The child is taught how and what things are but not the conditions under which they change or remain the same. And yet the child is constantly confronted with change and alteration. This view of the world alters as he grows in height and perceptual acuity. And the world changes. Seasons come and go, trees gain and lose their foliage, snow falls and melts. People change, too. They may change over brief time periods in mood and over long periods in weight and hair coloration or fullness. The child receives a static education while living amidst a world in transition.

Piaget's investigations since 1940 have focused upon how the child copes with change, how he comes to distinguish between the permanent and the transient and between appearance and reality. An incident that probably played a part in initiating this line of investigation occurred during Piaget's short-lived flirtation with the automobile. (When his children were young, Piaget learned to drive and bought a car, but he gave it up for his beloved bicycle after a couple of years.) He took his son for a drive and Laurent asked the name of the mountain they were passing. The mountain was the Salève, the crocodile-shaped mass that dominates the city of Geneva. Laurent was in fact familiar with the mountain and its name because he could see it from his garden, although from a different perspective. Laurent's question brought home to Piaget the fact that a child has difficulty in dealing with the results of transformations whether they are brought about by an alteration in the object itself or by the child's movement with respect to the object.

The methods Piaget used to study how the child comes to deal with transformations are ingenuously simple and can be used by any interested parent or teacher. These methods all have to do with testing the child's abilities to discover that a quantity remains the same across a change in its appearance. In other words, that the quantity is conserved.

To give just one illustration from among hundreds, a child is shown two identical drinking glasses filled equally full with orangeade and he is asked to say whether there is the "same to drink" in the two glasses. After the child says that this is the case, the orangeade from one glass is poured into another which is taller and thinner so that the orangeade now reaches a higher level. Then the child is asked to say whether there is the same amount to drink in the two differently shaped glasses. Before the age of 6 or 7, most children say that the tall, narrow glass has more orangeade. The young child cannot deal with the transformation and bases his judgment on the static features of the orangeade, namely the levels.

How does the older child arrive at the notion that the amounts of orangeade in the two differently shaped glasses is the same? The answer, according to Piaget, is that he discovers the equality with the aid of reason. If the child judges only on the basis of appearances he cannot solve the problem. When he compares the two glasses with respect to width he must conclude that the wide glass has more while if he compares them with respect to the level of the orangeade he must conclude that the tall glass has more. There is then no way, on the basis of appearance, that he can solve the problem. If, on the other hand, the child reasons that there was the same in the two glasses before and that nothing was added or taken away during the pouring, he concludes that both glasses still have the same drink although this does not appear to be true.

On the basis of this and many similar findings, Piaget argues that much of our knowledge about reality comes to us not from without like the wail of a siren but rather from within by the force of our own logic.

It is hard to overemphasize the importance of this fact, because it is so often forgotten, particularly in education. For those who are not philosophically inclined, it appears that our knowledge of things comes about rather directly as if our mind simply copied the forms, colors and textures of things. From this point of view the mind acts as a sort of mirror which is limited to reflecting the reality which is presented to it. As Piaget's research has demonstrated, however, the mind operates not as a passive mirror but rather as an active artist.

The portrait painter does not merely copy what he sees, he interprets his subject. Before even commencing the portrait, the artist learns a great deal about the individual subject and does not limit himself to studying the face alone. Into the portrait goes not only what the artist sees but also what he knows about his subject. A good portrait is larger than life because it carries much more information than could ever be conveyed by a mirror image.

In forming his spontaneous conception of the world, therefore, the child does more than reflect what is presented to his senses. His image of reality is in fact a portrait or reconstruction of the world and not a simple copy of it. It is only by reasoning about the information which the child receives from the external world that he is able to overcome the transient nature of sense experience and arrive at that awareness of permanence within apparent change that is the mark of adult thought. The importance of reason in the child's spontaneous construction of his world is thus one of the major discoveries of Piaget's third period.

The second major discovery of this time has to do with the nature of the elementary school child's reasoning ability. Long before there was anything like a discipline of child psychology, the age of 6 to 7 was recognized as the *age of reason*. It was also assumed, however, that once the child attained the age of reason, there were no longer any substantial differences between his reasoning abilities and those of adolescents and adults. What Piaget discovered is that this is in fact not the case. While the elementary school child is indeed able to reason, his reasoning ability is limited in a very important respect—he can reason about things but not about verbal propositions.

If a child of 8 to 9 is shown a series of three blocks, ABC, which differ in size, then he can tell by looking at them, and without comparing them directly, that if A is greater than B and B is greater than C, then A is greater than C. When the same child is given this problem, "Helen is taller than Mary and Mary is taller than Jane, who is the tallest of the three?" the result is quite different. He cannot solve it despite the fact that it repeats in words the problem with the blocks. Adolescents and adults, however, encounter no difficulty with this problem because they can reason about verbal propositions as well as about things.

This discovery that children think differently from adults even after attaining the age of reason has educational implications which are only now beginning to be applied. Robert Karplus, the physicist who heads the Science Curriculum Improvement Study at Berkeley has pointed out that most teachers use verbal propositions in teaching elementary school children. At least some of their instruction is thus destined to go over the heads of their pupils. Kurplus and his co-workers are now attempting to train teachers to instruct children at a verbal level which is appropriate to their level of mental ability.

An example of the effects of the failure to take into account the difference between the reasoning abilities of children and adults comes from the New Math experiment. In building materials for the New Math, it was hoped that the construction of a new language would facilitate instruction of set concepts. This new language has been less than successful and the originators of the New Math are currently attempting to devise a physical model to convey the New Math concepts. It is likely that the new language created to teach the set concepts failed because it was geared to the logic of adults rather than to the reasoning of children. Attention to the research on children's thinking carried out during Piaget's third period might have helped to avoid some of the difficulties of the "New Math" program.

In the course of these many years of research into children's thinking, Piaget has elaborated a general theory of intellectual development which, in its scope and comprehensiveness, rivals Freud's theory of personality development. Piaget proposes that intelligence—adaptive thinking and action—develops in a sequence of stages that is related to age. Each stage sees the elaboration of new mental abilities which set the limits and determine the character of what can be learned during that period (Piaget finds incomprehensible Harvard psychologist Jerome Bruner's famous hypothesis to the effect that "any subject can be taught effectively in some intellectually honest form to any child at any stage of development.") Although Piaget believes that the order in which the stages appear holds true for all children, he also believes that the ages at which the stages evolve will depend upon the native endowment of the child and upon the quality of the physical and social environment in which he is reared. In a very real sense, then, Piaget's is both a nature *and* a nurture theory.

The first stage in the development of intelligence (usually 0–2 years) Piaget calls the sensory-motor period and it is concerned with the evolution of those abilities necessary to construct and reconstruct objects. To illustrate, Piaget observed that when he held a cigarette case in front of his daughter Jaqueline (who was 8 months old at the time) and then dropped it, she did not follow the trajectory of the case but continued looking at his hand. Even at 8 months (Lucienne and Laurent succeeded in following the object at about 5 months but had been exposed to more experiments than Jaqueline) she was not able to reconstruct the path of the object which she had seen dropped in front of her.

Toward the end of this period, however, Jaqueline was even able to reconstruct the position of objects which had undergone hidden displacement. When she was 19 months old, Piaget placed a coin in his hand and then placed his hand under a coverlet where he dropped the coin before removing his hand. Jaqueline first looked in his hand and then immediately lifted the coverlet and found the coin. This reconstruction was accomplished with the aid of an elementary form of reasoning. The coin was in the hand, the hand was under the coverlet. Such reasoning, it must be said, is accomplished without the aid of language and by means of mental images.

The second stage (usually 2–7 years), which Piaget calls the preoperational stage, bears witness to the elaboration of the symbolic function, those abilities which have to do with representing things. The presence of these new abilities is shown by the gradual acquisition of language, the first indications of dreams and night terrors, the advent of symbolic play (two sticks at right angles are an airplane) and the first attempts at drawing and graphic representation.

At the beginning of this stage the child tends to identify words and symbols with the objects they are intended to represent. He is upset if someone tramps on a stone which he has designated as a turtle. And he believes that names are as much a part of objects as their color and form. (The child at this point is like the old gentleman who, when asked why noodles are called noodles, replied that, "they are white like noodles, soft like noodles and taste like noodles so we call them noodles.")

By the end of this period the child can clearly distinguish between words and symbols and what they represent. He now recognizes that names are arbitrary designations. The child's discovery of the arbitrariness of names is often manifested in the "name calling" so prevalent during the early school years.

At the next stage (usually 7–11 years) the child acquires what Piaget calls concrete operations, internalized actions that permit the child to do "in his head" what before he would have had to accomplish through real actions. Concrete operations enable the child to think about things. To illustrate, in one study Piaget presented 5-, 6- and 7-year old children with six sticks in a row and asked them to take the same number of sticks from a pile on the table. The young children solved the problem by placing their sticks beneath the sample and matching the sticks one by one. The older children merely picked up the six sticks and held them in their hands. The older children had counted the sticks mentally and hence felt no need to actually match them with the sticks in the row. It should be said that even the youngest children were able to count to six, so that this was not a factor in their performance.

Concrete operations also enable children to deal with the relations among classes of things. In another study Piaget presented 5-, 6- and 7-year-old children with a box containing 20 white and seven brown wooden beads. Each child was first asked if there were more white or more brown beads and all were able to say that there were more white than brown beads. Then Piaget asked, "Are there more white or more wooden beads?" The young children could not fathom the question and replied that "there are more white than brown beads." For such children classes are not regarded as abstractions but are thought of as concrete places. (I once asked a pre-operational child if he could be a Protestant and an American at the same time, to which he replied, "No," and then as an afterthought, "only if you move.")

When a child thought of a bead in the white "place" he could not think of it as being in the wooden "place" since objects cannot be in two places at once. He could only compare the white with the brown "places." The older children, who had attained concrete operations, encountered no difficulty with the task and readily replied that "there are more wooden than white beads because all of the beads are wooden and only some are white." By the end of the concrete operational period, children are remarkably adept at doing thought problems and at combining and dividing class concepts.

During the last stage (usually 12–15 years) there gradually emerge what Piaget calls formal operations and which, in effect, permit adolescents to think about their thoughts, to construct ideals and to reason realistically about the future. Formal operations also enable young peope to reason about contrary-to-fact propositions. If, for example, a child is asked to assume that coal is white he is likely to reply, "But coal is black," whereas the adolescent can accept the contrary-to-fact assumption and reason from it.

Formal operational thought also makes possible the understanding of metaphor. It is for this reason that political and other satirical cartoons are not understood until adolescence. The child's inability to understand metaphor helps to explain why books such as "Alice in Wonderland" and "Gulliver's Travels" are enjoyed at different levels during childhood than in adolescence and adulthood, when their social significance can be understood.

No new mental systems emerge after the formal operations, which are the common coin of adult thought. After adolescence, mental growth takes the form—it is hoped—of a gradual increase in wisdom.

This capsule summary of Piaget's theory of intellectual development would not be complete without some words about Piaget's position with respect to language and thought. Piaget regards thought and language as different but closely related systems. Language, to a much greater extent than thought, is determined by particular forms of environmental stimulation. Inner-city Negro children, who tend to be retarded in language development, are much less retarded with respect to the ages at which they attain concrete operations. Indeed, not only inner-city children but children in bush Africa, Hong Kong and Appalachia all attain concrete operations at about the same age as middle-class children in Geneva and Boston.

Likewise, attempts to teach children concrete operations have been almost uniformly unsuccessful. This does not mean that these operations are independent of the environment but only that their development takes time and can be nourished by a much wider variety of environmental nutriments than is true for the growth of language, which is dependent upon much more specific forms of stimulation.

Language is, then, deceptive with respect to thought. Teachers of middle-class children are often misled, by the verbal facility of these youngsters, into believing that they understand more than they actually comprehend. (My 5-year-old asked me what my true identity was and as I tried to recover my composure he explained that Clark Kent was Superman's true identity.) At the other end, the teachers of inner-city children are often fooled by the language handicaps of these children into thinking that they have much lower mental ability than they actually possess. It is appropriate, therefore, that pre-school programs for the disadvantaged should focus upon training these children in language and perception rather than upon trying to teach them concrete operations.

The impact which the foregoing Piagetian discoveries and conceptions is having upon education and child psychology has come as something of a shock to a good many educators and psychological research in America, which relies heavily upon statistics, electronics and computers. Piaget's studies of children's thinking seem hardly a step beyond the pre-scientific baby biographies kept by such men as Charles Darwin and Bronson Alcott. Indeed, in many of Piaget's research papers he supports his conclusions simply with illustrative examples of how children at different age levels respond to his tasks.

Many of Piaget's critics have focused upon his apparently casual methodology and have argued that while Piaget has arrived at some original ideas about children's thinking, his research lacks scientific rigor. It is likely that few, if any, of Piaget's research reports would have been accepted for publication in American psychological journals.

Other critics have taken somewhat the opposite tack. Jerome Bruner, who had done so much to bring Piaget to the attention of American social scientists, acknowledges the fruitfulness of Piaget's methods, modifications of which he has employed in his own investigations. But he argues against Piaget's theoretical interpretations. Bruner believes that Piaget has "missed the heart" of the problem of change and permanence or conservation in children's thinking. In the case of the orangeade poured into a different-sized container, Bruner argues that it is not reason, or mental operations, but some "internalized verbal formula that shields him [the child] from the overpowering appearance of the visual displays." Bruner seems to believe that the syntactical rules of language rather than logic can account for the child's discovery that a quantity remains unchanged despite alterations in its appearance.

Piaget is willing to answer his critics but only when he feels that the criticism is responsible and informed. With respect to his methods, their casualness is only apparent. Before they set out collecting data, his students are given a year of training in the art of interviewing children. They learn to ask questions without suggesting the answers and to test, by counter-suggestion, the strength of the child's conviction. Many of Piaget's studies have now been repeated with more rigorous procedures by other investigators all over the world and the results have been remarkably consistent with Piaget's findings. Attempts are currently under way to build a new intelligence scale on the basis of the Piaget tests, many of which are already in widespread use as evaluative procedures in education.

When it comes to criticisms of his theoretical views, Piaget is remarkably open and does not claim to be infallible. He frequently invites scholars who are in genuine disagreement with him to come to Geneva for a year so that the differences can be discussed and studied in depth. He has no desire to form a cult and says, in fact, "To the extent that there are Piagetians, to that extent have I failed." Piaget's lack of dogmatism is illustrated in his response to Bruner:

> Bruner does say that I "missed the heart" of the conservation problem, a problem I have been working on for the last 30 years. He is right, of course, but that does not mean that he himself has understood it in a much shorter time . . . Adults, just like children, need time to reach the right ideas . . . This is the great mystery of development, which is irreducible to an accumulation of isolated learning acquisitions. Even psychology cannot be constructed in a short time.

(Despite his disclaimer, Piaget has offered a comprehensive theory of how the child arrives at conservation and this theory has received much research support.)

Piaget would probably agree with those who are critical about premature applications of his work to education. He finds particularly disturbing the efforts by·some American educators to accelerate children intellectually. When he was giving his other 1967 lectures, in New York, he remarked:

> If we accept the fact that there are stages of development, another question arises which I call "the American question," and I am asked it every time I come here. If there are stages that children reach at given norms of ages can we accelerate the stages? Do we have to go through each one of these stages, or can't we speed it up a bit? Well, surely, the answer is yes . . . but how far can we speed them up? . . . I have a hypothesis which I am so far incapable of proving: probably the organization of operations has an optimal time . . . For example, we know that it takes 9 to 12 months before babies develop the notion that an object is still there even when a screen is placed in front of it. Now kittens go through the same sub-stages but they do it in three months—so they're six months ahead of the babies. Is this an advantage or isn't it?
>
> We can certainly see our answer in one sense. The kitten is not going to go much further. The child has taken longer, but he is capable of going further so it seems to me that the nine months were not for nothing . . . It is probably possible to accelerate, but maximal acceleration is not desirable. There seems to be an optimal time. What this optimal time is will surely depend upon each individual and on the subject matter. We still need a great deal of research to know what the optimal time would be.

Piaget's stance against using his findings as a justification for accelerating children intellectually recalls a remark made by Freud when he was asked whatever became of those bright, aggressive shoeshine boys one encounters in city streets. Freud's reply was "They become cobblers." In Piaget's terms they get to a certain point earlier but they don't go as far. And the New York educator Eliot Shapiro has pointed out that one of the Negro child's problems is that he is forced to grow up and take responsibility too soon and doesn't have time to be a child.

Despite some premature and erroneous applications of his thinking to education, Piaget has had an overall effect much more positive than negative. His findings about children's understanding of scientific and mathematical concepts are being used as guidelines for new curricula in these subjects. And his tests are being more and more widely used to evaluate educational outcomes. Perhaps the most significant and widespread positive effect that Piaget has had upon education is in the changed attitudes on the part of teachers who have been exposed to his thinking. After becoming acquainted with Piaget's work, teachers can never again see children in quite the same way as they had before. Once teachers begin to look at children from the Piagetian perspective they can also appreciate his views with regard to the aims of education.

"The principal goal of education," he once said,

> is to create men who are capable of doing new things, not simply of repeating what other generations have done—men who are creative, inventive and discoverers. The second goal of education is to form minds which can be critical, can verify, and not accept everything they are offered. The great danger today is of slogans, collective opinions, ready-made trends of thought. We have to be able to resist individually, to criticize, to distinguish between what is proven and what is not. So we need pupils who are active, who learn early to find out themselves, partly by their own spontaneous activity and partly through materials we set up for them; who learn early to tell what is verifiable and what is simply the first idea to come to them.

At the beginning of his eighth decade, Jean Piaget is as busy as ever. A new book of his on memory will be published soon and another on the mental functions in the preschool child is in preparation. The International Center for Genetic Epistemology, which Piaget founded in 1955 with a grant from the Rockefeller Foundation, continues to draw scholars from around the world who wish to explore with Piaget the origin of scientific concepts. As Professor of Experimental Psychology at the University of Geneva, Piaget also continues to teach courses and conduct seminars.

And his students still continue to collect the data which at the end of the school year Piaget will take with him up to the mountains. The methods employed by his students today are not markedly different from those which were used by their predecessors decades ago. While there are occasional statistics, there are still no electronics or computers. In an age of moon shots and automation, the remarkable discoveries of Jean Piaget are evidence that in the realm of scientific achievement, technological sophistication is still no substitute for creative genius.

4 Third Force Psychology: A Humanistic Orientation to the Study of Man
Frank T. Severin

"No science, least of all psychology, can be value free."

The humanistic orientation to psychology is based upon the idea that psychology must be relevant to the human condition. Man lives in a world of values, and to ignore the importance of values in determining consciousness, volition, and life style in general is to deny the dynamic quality of man's existence. Severin presents some of the individuals who have been most influential in establishing this third-force psychology.

One of the most relevant questions anyone can ask is, "Who am I?" The reason is that an understanding of basic nature as well as one's own individual characteristics is a key factor in personality integration. Just as a traveller can never reach his destination until he knows where he wishes to go, no one can become a fully-functioning person unless he understands what it means to be truly human.

Psychology, too, struggles in its own way with the question, "What is man?" Each answer that is given is almost necessarily culture-bound, and reflects a particular phase in the development of psychological science. In order to have some systematic framework for the study of man, the earliest psychologists envisioned their discipline as a kind of mental chemistry. Their task, as they saw it, was to explain complex inner experiences in terms of simple conscious elements, such as images, feelings, and muscular tension. Sigmund Freud was concerned with a different problem. His clinical work with neurotic patients led him to picture the human individual as the battleground where three conflicting inner tendencies, the id, the ego, and the superego, are locked in a never-ending struggle. By contrast, John B. Watson, the spokesman for behaviorism, was interested only in externally observable behavior—that is, in the subject studied from the outside as a stimulus-response organism while ignoring or even denying what went on inside the individual's head.

Such models or analogies are legitimate guides for certain areas of research as long as they are not considered to be an adequate description of human beings. Unfortunately, they have a way of becoming elevated into dogmas about what people are really like, especially by consumers of psychological research. Partly as a result of this, more and more psychologists have become aware of several grave deficiencies in the theories of behaviorism and psychoanalysis, the two leading forces, or influences, in American psychology. Humanistic psychology came into existence to call attention to these deficiencies and to work toward eliminating them. How may we characterize this movement?

One aim of humanistic psychology is to present a more accurate picture of mankind—one that does not conflict with the way we experience ourselves and others. The image currently projected by psychology is at variance in certain respects with what we ourselves have learned about mankind by being human. If psychology makes the claim of being a relevant science, one of its first concerns should be to propose a model for living that is credible and authentic.

Unity of the Person

The ongoing processes of the human organism—what transpires within us at any given moment—are incredibly complex. Unlike the working of a machine whose individual operations are related to each other in a fixed, mechanical way, human psychophysical processes interact in a manner that defies description. Even as simple an action as pointing to a bird and following its path in flight requires a feedback mechanism in the nervous system so complex that only now are we beginning to understand it. Greeting a friend on the street occurs too routinely to be given a second thought, yet much more than the vocal apparatus is involved in this bit of commonplace behavior. We have to see the person, recognize him, scan our memories to determine whether we are on speaking terms, decide what words to use, and then say them.

And then there are the all-pervading effects of emotional reactions. If a man with ulcers catches a glimpse of his favorite enemy, he may be indisposed for the rest of the day. It would be relatively simple to show from changes in blood pressure, galvanic skin response, and respiration that his entire bodily functioning has been affected. If our man meets his fiancée instead, the type of organic reaction he experiences may differ, but again the whole person will get into the act.

A psychologist who wants to understand the person-as-a-whole rather than one routine action encounters much greater difficulty than he did in monitoring a single response. He can accurately observe only one or at most a few distinct processes at a time. If he has a sense of humor he may begin to feel some vague empathy with the weak-eyed Mr. Magoo, who, while concentrating on the single feature of a situation that he can see, often misinterprets the whole state of affairs.

Psychologists have traditionally used procedures borrowed from the natural sciences, which inevitably fractionate the total human individual into a multitude of small, isolated processes such as learning, perception, and motivation. Doing so permits them to study each process in depth, but it exacts a heavy price. The overall coordination and mutual interaction of ongoing activities, which characterize them as human, escape through the meshes of the scientific net, and what remains frequently has little relevance to real-life problems.

Analysis, or the breaking down of complex objects into simpler elements, is a powerful tool of science, but it is not the only one. Besides taking things apart to see how they work, we must also be able to piece together wholes from parts. This procedure is called *synthesis*. Sometimes parts can be understood only in terms of what they contribute to the total operation. A small, strangely shaped metal component that falls out of a desk calculator would be a homely example. How to study the human individual in larger chunks—or better yet, the whole man in real-life circumstances as the insight clinician must —is a problem that intrigues humanistic psychologists. Some tentative new directions will be sketched in a later section. Here we continue with our description of the humanistic image of man.

Autonomy

Suppose that you were asked to explain what you understand by *wholesome personality*. How would you answer? You might say that the fully integrated individual is spontaneously alive. Unlike a machine that sits quietly at rest until set into operation by someone pressing a button, the human individual is an active instigator of behavior rather than a passive reactor to stimuli: the motive to be up and doing comes mainly from within on one's own initiative. You might also say that personality is not, like physical growth, something that just happens to the self. To a large extent it is a do-it-yourself product, fashioned out of the raw material of hereditary endowment under the influence of practical experience in living—including the significant choices one makes.

Such an outlook presupposes that the human individual is free to choose one course of action rather than another. His behavior is not always predetermined by forces over which he has no control. He cannot, of course, jump 15 feet high or speak a language he has never heard. But in situations that permit reasoned choice he can usually decide what to do and then do it. Even though conscious motions or unconscious impulses may sway him more in one direction than another, such persuasive influences need not imply complete control unless the person is so overwhelmed that normal functioning is inhibited. Neither the victim of a hard-sell huckster nor the girl who realizes only vaguely that she is marrying to escape an unhappy home life have necessarily lost all freedom to make an opposite choice.

It may come as a surprise to the student that many psychologists begin with the assumption that man is not a free agent. The reason often given is reminiscent of the student who first looks up the answer to a textbook problem and then works backward to make the solution fit. A true science, some psychologists say, cannot deal with freedom. In order to have a psychology worthy of the name, they argue, every human act must follow natural laws as inexorable as the conditions under which hydrogen and oxygen combine to form water. If the individual could make choices on his own initiative, we could never establish invariable principles of behavior. The argument stops here, but the implication is that since psychologists are determined to have a *natural* science of man, come what may, the human individual *must* be passively determined by fully predictable forces, just as any other object in nature.

But it is imperative that we begin with man as we find him, not as we might wish him to be. Most research methods used in psychology are modeled on those of nineteenth-century physics. The scientists who originated these and similar methods were not concerned about conscious experience or self-determination, because they were dealing with inanimate nature. Later we will maintain that a truly human science implies more than applying such procedures to the study of man. Methods which are suitable for investigating those characteristics which are uniquely human must also be devised.

How would the assumptions of determinism affect human living? This question is discussed in considerable detail in other publications such as Allport (1955); May (1969b); and Severin (1973). Perhaps the following questions will be helpful in thinking through the matter. Why is it that persons who deny human freedom continue to examine evidence and make choices in everyday life? Are they consciously indulging an illusion? If a scientist's actions are fully determined by factors he cannot control, how can he perform a meaningful experiment? Not only must he know what measures to take, he must also be free to carry them out as planned without interference from other sources.

No one can be held responsible for doing something that he cannot avoid doing. Unless human beings are autonomous, how can any one be held legally or ethically responsible for his behavior? If a careless driver is no more free than his automobile which runs down a pedestrian, it would make more sense to arrest the car rather than its operator. The reader might be interested in thinking through for himself what effect determinism would have on society and on his ability to become the kind of person he wishes to be.

It should be noted that a scientist's decision about freedom or determinism is made long before he enters the laboratory. It is not based on experimental data; the only empirical evidence either for or against freedom is one's own experience of self determination. The problem of determinism falls more naturally under the heading of philosophy, although no psychologist can long avoid taking a stand on the issue. Part of the confusion arises from the use of such terms as "will" and "freedom" whose meaning has been blurred by past debates. Many psychologists who are repelled by these terms might not object to the underlying notions if they were called by other names. But regardless of the words used, the matter should be clear. If the human individual can exert an influence on *some* of his activities *by his decision to do so,* to that extent he is capable of self-determination.

Human Goals and Values

Still another facet of humanistic psychology's image of man is his ceaseless striving toward goals he sets for himself. Bühler (1959), Frankl (1966), Maslow (1970, Ch. 3), May (1969a), Rogers (1961), and others have shown, at least by implication, the fallacy of explaining all human motivation in terms of homeostasis. The theories of psychoanalysis and behaviorism notwithstanding, man's goal is not to achieve a quiescent state of reduced tension. Quite the contrary: When psychological stress is at a minimum, a person becomes bored and is likely to set out in search of excitement. Sensory deprivation studies have shown the debilitating effect of too little stimulation. Frankl has vividly described a type of neurosis characterized chiefly by apathy, boredom, and mild depression. He attributes these symptoms to what he calls an "existential vacuum," or lack of meaning in life. To regain his former zest for living the sufferer must discover some purpose for his existence, something worthwhile on which to spend himself. Rather than reduce psychological tension, he must increase it to an optimal level and employ it in the quest of some significant value.

Other theories of self-actualization also stress the apparent universal need of well-integrated persons to develop their potentialities. Rogers, among others, views the good life, not as a fixed state of being, but as a continuous process of becoming. The individual who progressively opens himself up to the full range of human experience becomes more creative and trustful of himself. As defenses drop one by one, he feels himself at long last coming to life as a fully-functioning person. Maslow (1970) labels as a *higher* need the insistent urge many people feel to become the best possible "I." It remains latent until lower basic needs for love, status, and security have been satisfied. Both types of needs are considered inborn. Bühler (1959, 1968) has devoted many years to investigating the life goals to which people commit themselves. Frankl (1967) insists that everyone is endowed with a wealth of potentialities, but not all are of equal value. Many are not worth the time and effort required to develop them and would not gratify the individual at the deepest level. Given a limited life span and the circumstances of one's existence, each individual must choose in a responsible way which latent capacities to actualize. Such choices should not be made in terms of shortsighted satisfaction, but in terms of life's meaning and values. In this sense self-transcendent aims become a basic feature of human motivation.

Research into the problem of values has long been delayed by a mistaken assumption that science has nothing to do with value judgments. Now that this notion is rapidly being dispelled by new insights into the theory of science, more exploratory studies in this important area can be expected. Without a knowledge of values, goals, and purposes, human behavior will forever remain a mystery. Frequently it is less revealing to know *what* a person does than *why* he does it. Suppose that a student walks out of the classroom during a lecture and slams the door. Was it because he felt that his basic value system was being attacked? Or did he just remember an important engagement? Or was he feeling faint? Much overt behavior is quite ambiguous when isolated from what goes on in a person's mind.

The Uniqueness of Man

Another misgiving about the typical textbook description of mankind is that it is based preponderantly upon animal experimentation. If an investigator begins his research with the assumption that man differs in no essential way from lower animals instead of looking intently for just such differences, it should not be surprising if his conclusions reflect this assumption. Any genuine dissimilarities that do exist are likely to be ruled out of the experiment as irrelevant or to be classified as "error variance." Something like this seems to have happened in psychology: Learning and motivation are usually defined in such a way as to apply almost identically to both animals and man. Experiments in which lower animals learn to respond differentially to perceptual stimuli such as variously shaped triangles or patterns with unequal numbers of items are often interpreted in terms of human experience, and treated as evidence of concept formation or counting. A simpler, and more plausible, explanation is that animals can tell such stimuli apart on a concrete sensory basis because they look different—not because the animals understand the abstract significance of symbols. The fact that a rat can learn that the correct turn in a maze is the one marked with a triangle does not necessarily mean that it grasps *conceptually* what a triangle is: Rather one concrete perceptual shape becomes associated with the presence of some reinforcer such as food while other perceptual forms do not. Neither does an animal's correct motor response to a stimulus card showing a given number of dots imply that the animal assigns numbers to items the way we count (Severin, 1973, Ch. 7). It is enough that patterns look different.

In spite of this many psychologists are reluctant to accept mankind as a unique species. There are at least two reasons for this reluctance. The first stems from one version of the theory of evolution. It is generally agreed that the progressive anatomical changes from one species to the next consist of slight modifications of previously existing species. Many theorists take this to imply continuity not only in structure but in every ability as well. If they are right, then the difference between lower animals and man is merely a matter of degree.

Teilhard de Chardin (1965) disagrees with this view. First, he shows that evolution can be explained more satisfactorily in terms of a progressive *sharpening of awareness* rather than mere change in anatomy. Secondly, he explains that at certain critical points in evolution a qualitative difference between species occurred. In other words, the new organism that appeared could not be totally accounted for in terms of the more primitive forms that preceded it: Something new had been added. One example of such a profound inner change is the passage from nonlife to life. Even though plants are composed of chemicals, growth and reproduction cannot be understood in terms of chemical activities but only in terms of the new organization of matter. The laws of chemical combination are still retained but a higher level of organization has been introduced (Polanyi, 1962).

The classic experiment of Gardner and Gardner (1969) in teaching sign language to a chimpanzee has aroused great interest and not a little controversy. The Gardners do not claim that this type of communication is human language, even though the animal used a large number of signs spontaneously and appropriately for whole classes of objects and frequently combined two or more signs. This question, they state, is foreign to the spirit of their research.

Premack (1970a, 1970b) and his associates have taught their chimpanzee, Sarah, to use 120 different plastic cut-outs which are placed on a magnetic "language board" as concrete signs for objects and their manipulation. Thus when Sarah places the pieces in the arrangement, "Mary give Sarah banana," she expects to receive this kind of fruit. Premack believes that Sarah has acquired a conceptual language. He contends that a psychological theory of language should emphasize function rather than structure, so he began by "relieving" language of its exclusive human form. For example, one plastic form was designated "same" and another "different." He then taught Sarah to place the former between pairs of objects which were identical and the latter between nonidentical pairs. The conclusion Premack drew was that the animal was answering the question he had in mind, "What is the relation between these two objects—are they the same or different?" Next, he complicated the problem still further by introducing a plastic cut-out which he called a question mark and others with such labels as "if–then" which he felt confident were demonstrating the animal's ability to understand abstract relationships of the kind involved in human language.

Since I have dealt with the issue of animal communication at greater length elsewhere (Severin, 1973, Ch. 7), only a brief outline will be given here. English and English (1958, p. 106) define the term *concrete attitude* as the "tendency to react to the immediately given object or situation without considering its relationships or classification." By contrast, an *abstract attitude* implies that ". . . the person reacts not so much to the sensory impressions of a given situation as to its abstract qualities." In other words, abstract knowledge consists in the understanding of what makes a thing, such as a home, what it is without reference to the individual characteristics of any actually existing home. The idea applies in exactly the same way to any and every structure that can be considered a human dwelling.

The concrete way of knowing is based on the specific sensory qualities belonging to individual objects. It relies upon perception, imagination, and the reorganization of images (remembered sensations) into new patterns—this particular person or thing, or the combination of parts of past sensations in an original way which need not correspond to any actually existing thing. Köhler's chimpanzee can be understood to have solved the stick–banana problem by such a spontaneous reorganization of imagery. When Sultan accidentally pushed the end of one stick into the joint of the other, he was then able to picture the stick and the banana in a new relationship on a *concrete* basis without the *aha* experience of Archimedes and other human beings who would recognize the principle involved.

Concrete relationships are certainly involved in perception—a series of dots may be arranged to form a star; the correct turn in a maze may be to the subject's right or left—yet it is not the relationship *as a relationship* that is understood. Instead, certain specific *sensory* qualities are associated with other *sensory* qualities or with specific features of the external environment. A chimpanzee can be taught to find food hidden in one of several boxes—the one painted red. There is no need to postulate that it makes the abstract intellectual generalization, "I will always find food in the red box," which would be necessary to communicate in a human fashion. All that is required is for the animal to associate the color of the box with food. In other words, it is operating on a concrete, perceptual level rather than at the abstract, conceptual level.

Cassirer (1944, pp. 31–35) deals with the same topic from a slightly different point of view. He discriminates clearly between signs or signals on the one hand and symbols on the other. A signal is part of the physical world, such as Pavlov's bell in conditioning a dog to salivate or the rattling of a food dish which achieved the same result. Premack's plastic cut-outs, which he calls "words," also belong to the physical world. They are specific, concrete objects which can be associated with specific behaviors using a conditioning technique where there is only one particular unknown at a time to learn. There is indeed great flexibility in animal behavior because imagery deals with perceptual or sensory qualities which can be recombined in different ways to solve practical problems.

A symbol belongs to the world of meaning. The idea of *dog* is an example. First of all, the notion has been stripped of all sensory characteristics. It is not a St. Bernard nor a Chihuahua, it is not young or old, brown, black, or white. No perceptual elements remain; only the abstract understanding of what makes a dog and nothing else. We might say then, to quote Cassirer, "... the animal possesses a practical imagination and intelligence, whereas man alone has developed a new form: a *symbolic imagination and intelligence.*"

Cassirer goes on to illustrate how Helen Keller, a girl born blind and deaf, at first responded to words spelled into her hand through a manual alphabet as though they were signals applying to only one particular object, such as the pump she was touching at the time. Once she had made the breakthrough from words as signals to words as symbols—so that she now realized that common names apply in exactly the same way to every member of a class—it was like living in a different world and her education advanced rapidly.

What has been said about the experiments by Premack and the Gardners applies equally to more recent research in teaching a chimpanzee to communicate by pressing buttons on a computer panel (Rumbaugh and von Glaserfield, 1973). By progressively complicating the stimulus situation to which a chimpanzee must react, psychologists can test the limits of its ability to associate sensory signals with definite behaviors, but even if it were capable of stringing together human words, more would be required to have a language. Bronowski and Bellugi (1970) have analyzed the general features of language to determine how closely chimpanzee sign communication approximates human language. They concluded that chimpanzees share some of these elements in a rudimentary fashion but lack the human logical capacity to understand their environment and to deal with it correspondingly. A true language requires the user to analyze his experience into meaningful parts which can be manipulated as objects and regrouped in an unlimited number of ways. More impressive still is the failure of chimpanzees to develop a language in their natural habitat. If these animals possess the highly developed capacity for conceptual language that some psychologists attribute to them, it seems strange indeed that over many millions of years they should have been unable to evolve a primitive language and some beginnings of a culture.

Current attempts to teach language to animals revive all the excitement and drama created by the amazing feats of intelligence of the horse, Clever Hans, that enlivened the closing years of the last century. The animal, a trotter owned and lovingly trained by a German schoolmaster named von Osten, to all appearances understood and used language. Not only did it respond to spoken commands, but could count by tapping with its hoof, work problems in arithmetic, correct its errors, select a ribbon of the color requested, recognize persons from their photographs, tell time, and shake its head to indicate misplayed notes in music. The exciting story of how psychologists proved that the trainer, not the horse, unwittingly did the thinking is related by Pfungst (1965). Unconscious cues from the trainer, such as minimal nods of the head or relaxation of facial tension, directed the animal in its tasks.

The shortcomings of current research consists not so much in defective laboratory procedures as in the interpretation of data. The observed behaviors can be explained in terms of perception, imagery, and learning on a concrete level, that is, as responses to signals. Abstract symbols which form the basis of conceptual language are the product of a set of abilities that are unique to man.

Reductionism

A favorite method of investigation in the natural sciences is *reductionism.* According to this point of view a complex object or process can be analyzed into elemental parts which fully explain the operation of the whole. Many psychologists who rely chiefly upon natural-science methods favor the supposition that man is not unique, because such an assumption fits nicely into the theory of reductionism. Classical behaviorism, for instance, explained all psychological functioning in terms of conditioned responses. By making the further assumption that conditioned responses are almost identical in all species, it was thought that the basic features of human behavior could be discovered by studying the simpler responses of animals. For this reason the white rat became the favorite surrogate for learning about man.

Another example of reductionism is the attempt to explain all human and animal motivation as drive reduction. The theory might be applied to a newborn baby as follows: Since the infant acts mainly to relieve bodily needs, it is readily seen how its mother gains in importance by keeping it well-fed, dry, and comfortable. This physiologically based love of the child for the mother is then used by her as a lever in shaping the child into an image of the prevailing culture. In this connection she can be thought of as a secondary reinforcer. Her response in giving or withholding approval, which now has become associated with need satisfaction, serves as a powerful reinforcement in socialization and ethical training. Some reductionists have considered these beginnings to be the first links in an incredibly long chain of higher-order conditioned responses that extend throughout one's entire life span. Theoretically, even as adults, all motives, however noble or altruistic could allegedly be traced backward along this chain to the original primary motive of ridding one's self of physical discomfort. Such an explanation does not require a qualitative difference between any human and animal motives.

While reductionistic studies serve a useful purpose in many areas of research, it is a mistake to press this method too far. Perhaps the chief contribution of gestalt psychology consists in showing that wholes contain certain properties not found in the sum of the parts. When four matchsticks are arranged in the form of a square, something new emerges. By the same token, all our reductionistic studies taken together can never add up to a viable human being, for processes studied in isolation from what else is going on within the individual are less than human. An effort must be made to deal with behavior in larger chunks, preferably the individual-as-a-whole.

In summary, we have seen that the majority of humanistic psychologists consider mankind to be a unique species capable of making meaningful choices that imply personal responsibility. The human individual is more accurately pictured as a profoundly integrated self than as a loose federation of discrete psychological processes. Normally, a person works purposefully toward goals, including the actualization of potential abilities and even self-transcendence.

For a discussion of still other characteristics of humanistic psychology's image of man, the reader is referred to "A Fresh Look at the Human Design," by Hadley Cantril (1967).

The Need for a Human Science

A psychologist's belief about the nature of science will determine to a great extent how he thinks about man. Since the time of John B. Watson, the American psychological tradition has been largely behavioristic. Repelled by the excessive dependence upon introspection by Titchener and others, Watson determined to make psychology a purely natural science modeled on physics. The theory of science current at that time has long since been abandoned by physicists and philosophers of science, but only recently have psychologists begun to examine how these changed concepts affect the way we should study man.

Nineteenth-century physics conceived of science as being completely objective. It was commonly believed that no assumptions were made or conclusions drawn except those demanded by the data in hand. The investigator thought of himself as standing outside the framework of his experiment, so that his manipulations did not influence the results. By implication, experimental observations were considered self-interpreting as well as self-correcting when contradicted by the results of later experiments.

In contrast, the present trend in the theory of science is to recognize that the so-called subjective and objective methods—one taking note of what the individual experiences here and now, the other attempting to study him impersonally from the outside—are but the two extremes of a continuum. Even the physicist makes many subjective judgments in setting up and performing an experiment, and frequently influences the results by his intervention. Furthermore, the data that he gathers is not very meaningful until its implications have been spelled out in detail, and two scientists with different perspectives may draw opposite conclusions from the same set of observations.

Actually the chief difference between science and nonscientific disciplines lies in the way that the original observations are validated. The whole machinery of scientific methodology has but one purpose: to guarantee the accuracy of the raw data in so far as this is humanly possible (Rogers, 1955). From this point onward the scientist must rely upon logical methods to explicate the meaning of his raw data, to elaborate theories, and to devise further hypotheses. Although he usually makes use of mathematical procedures when this is possible, this part of scientific research does not essentially differ from the way that nonscientific disciplines solve their problems.

Thomas Kuhn (1970) has shown from a historical perspective that science does not progress merely by accumulating facts but more dramatically by occasional shifts in what he calls paradigms. This is a name for the conglomeration of assumptions, rules, and attitudes for the practice of science. Although they are unwritten, yet they are known by every competent scientist in a given field. A piece of research is evaluated as brilliant or defective in terms of the paradigm; an article is accepted for publication or rejected by editors on the same basis. Each paradigm is based on our limited knowledge of the subject matter and accordingly contains many arbitrary elements which may not be recognized at the time. When we look backward, for example, to the pre-Copernican conception of the universe, we can more easily identify these arbitrary elements. Polanyi (1962) goes still farther in showing that all knowledge contains implicit components which can not be specified, so that, even in theory, completely objective knowledge is an impossible goal.

Public and Private Events

Due to the influence of behaviorism which insisted on studying man from the outside as any other object in nature, most psychologists shy away from investigating human experience firsthand. Somehow data gathered with the aid of sophisticated instruments seem more properly scientific even when the conclusions they father turn out to be trivial and have little bearing on the important problems that people worry about. What gives rise to this dilemma is an exaggerated distinction between public and private events. A *public event* is a response that is at least potentially discernible to an outside observer. The turn a rat makes in running a maze, or the change in the electrical resistance of a human subject's skin, is a public event that can be recorded objectively. Checking the reliability of such data is greatly simplified by the fact that the entire process is open to repetition by any number of observers. By contrast, *private events* are those—such as thought, feeling, and other conscious processes—that can be verified directly only by the person experiencing them. Such processes can, however, be made public in a number of ways. Subjects' descriptions of their perceptual experience in psychophysical studies were accepted as respectable data even by classical behaviorists who renamed them *verbal reports* because they could be written down and processed as any other data. Gestures or questions are often useful as when one person says to another, "Look at that object in the sky" or an experimenter asks his subject, "What do you see on the screen?" If the experience of both agree, the former private event is now a public one.

Using similar methods of intersubjective verification it is possible to infer with reasonable certainty what another person perceives in a given situation. Conclusions by way of inference are very common in the natural sciences. Most of what we know about atomic physics has been inferred from such sources as tracks on photographic film and X-ray diffraction. The theory of evolution is also based on inference.

Some Limitations of Objective Methodology

There is no denying the tremendous advantage of direct observation over inference, especially inferences about human experience, but at the same time we should not overlook the limitations of natural science methodology when applied to the study of man. First of all, since these procedures were devised to study inanimate nature, no provision was made for investigating conscious processes. Great emphasis was placed on experimental procedures and measurement, not because this is the most effective approach in every situation, but because measurement is especially appropriate for this type of subject matter

(Giorgi, 1966, 1970). If what a person thinks, feels, and intends is considered important, other methods of investigation must also be included within the framework of psychology.

Several limitations of the natural science approach to the study of man were mentioned earlier. First of all, attention is focused on individual processes to the exclusion of all the interactions taking place within the integral organism. The picture one gets, to use Maslow's analogy, is like a single frame of a movie film. As a result, the conclusions that are drawn tend to be trivial and they are essentially abstract generalizations or constructs which describe the individual, not as he actually is, but as he appears from a single point of view external to him. The kind of data an experimenter gets peering into the subject from the outside is different than the subject gets on the inside looking out. Both kinds of data are valid and both are needed for a psychology that wishes to study *man-as-a-person* rather than *man-as-an-object*.

Some of the abstractions that are most commonly used in psychology are exceedingly difficult to define. Kagan (1967) comments that what psychologists call *reinforcement* can be a shock to an animal's paw, a scolding, a smile, a food pellet, a sign indicating relaxation, or watching a killer get caught in a Hitchcock movie—in fact, anything which helps learning. All that these items have in common is the name *reinforcement*. Likewise, the strength of a stimulus or of reinforcement depends upon the state of the subject's organism as well as fluctuations in attention. What is a stimulus at one moment may not be at the next. Frequently something directly in front of the eyes is ignored in favor of an object across the room. It is a mistake to consider either the stimulus or reinforcement mechanically as a fixed quantity. Jessor (1961) adds that stimulus–response or S–R psychology might be reconciled with a more subjective approach if *stimulus* and *response* were defined in psychological and meaningful terms rather than in terms of physical quantities.

All the problems that plague psychological experimentation and measurement cannot be mentioned here, but one should be noted. It is presumed that a subject entering the experimental situation will not only cooperate willingly but also function as normally as he would in a neutral setting. This presumption can be frequently challenged. In addition, the typical subjects who are college freshmen and sophomores constitute a select sample which is not a representative cross-section of the total population. Ordinarily they "volunteer" because of the moral pressure brought to bear upon them by an investigator in need of subjects. It is not unlikely that many such subjects have negative attitudes toward participating in research or are suspicious of being deceived about the nature of the study. Others may misinterpret the experimental task. Few experimenters take the trouble to determine whether all their presumptions about their subjects are correct.

The Need for Additional Methods

Objective methodology is necessary in psychology, but it is not enough. Much more has been written about its virtues than about its limitations. It is hoped that by presenting the negative side of the picture here, the need for other approaches will become evident. The development of alternative approaches and techniques lies largely in the future. As long as the natural science approach was considered the only legitimate one, very little effort was made to discover new directions. More recently some beginnings have been made in the form of phenomenological methods, projective techniques, Q-sort, semantic differential, achievement motivation, and ways of assessing a client's improvement in psychotherapy. Giorgi (1970, p. 214) points out that scientists, including behaviorists, actually do make use of a method of thinking through the implications of their data which is more subjective than objective. They critically examine the writings of other scientists, summarize the points they make, and repeatedly ponder their meanings until all the implications have been worked out in great detail. This procedure does not differ radically from the way a paleontologist traces the evolutionary development of animals from clues provided by fossils, or historians determine the causes of World War I. The formal recognition of this method as being largely experiential would be a step in the right direction.

The Aims of Humanistic Psychology

Having discussed several dimensions of humanistic psychology, we must now bring its primary concerns into focus. Before summarizing them it should be emphasized that this new movement is not a school of thought as structuralism, behaviorism, or psychoanalysis are schools of thought. Rather, it is an *orientation* to psychology—a way of thinking about man and the whole scientific enterprise that modifies our image of human beings and frees psychology from several artificial restrictions placed upon it by theories that now appear outmoded. Its proponents are active in every phase of psychology, particularly in applied areas. There is no basic philosophy common to all, but humanistic psychologists are generally sympathetic toward a number of positions held by gestalt, Adlerian, neo-Freudian, Jungian, phenomenological, existential, and ego psychologists. Although not every humanistic psychologist would subscribe to all the statements listed below, there is substantial agreement about them.

1. The image of man that emerges from an exclusive stimulus–response approach to psychology does not do justice to the human individual. We experience ourselves and others, not as passively responding organisms who are fully determined by forces we cannot control, but as spontaneous, self-determining persons striving creatively toward self-fulfillment and other goals. Moreover, man is a unique species that can not be fully explained in terms of lower animals.

2. While it is useful to study isolated human processes such as learning and emotion, much more attention should be devoted to investigating the mutual interaction of *all* the *ongoing activities* within the integral human individual. Emphasis on the concept of *self* might effectively counteract the tendency to fractionate, or reduce, the person to a number of separate processes.

3. Consciousness is the most basic human process, and every operation of science is wholly dependent upon it. Immediate experience is the fundamental reality, not laws and generalizations which are systematically derived from it. For this reason every objective study must begin with experience, and scientific conclusions must in turn be applicable to experience if they are to be useful. Similarly, private and public events should

be considered as the two terminals of a continuum rather than radically different sources of data.

4. The traditional concept of psychological research is based upon several postulates of classical physics which are now outdated. Newer insights into the nature of science have broken down the sharp dichotomy between subjective and objective methodology (Kuhn, 1970; Polanyi, 1962, 1968). The door should now be open for the development of a truly human science.

5. For several decades psychology has been method-centered rather than problem-centered. Too frequently the criterion for choosing research topics has not been their relevance to the individual and society but rather methodological considerations—"Does this problem lend itself to the use of automatically recording instruments and a 'tight' experimental design?"

6. No science, least of all psychology, can be value free. Instead of avoiding questions of choice and preference, special treatment ought to be given to such topics as self-actualization, commitment, responsibility, and life goals.

7. Psychologists should be more deeply concerned about important human issues, for example, the crises in society, one's own growth as a person, and a humanistic approach to education. Professional responsibility requires us to use our expertise to help resolve these thorny problems.

8. Research on topics that currently seem far-out should not be discouraged. At one time the Copernican world view and the notion of diseases being caused by microscopic germs seemed even more improbable than parapsychology and similar topics do today.

9. In keeping with its other objectives, humanistic psychology repudiates the traditional goal of prediction and control as its primary end. Rather it seeks to *understand* behavior with a view of expanding the individual's autonomy.

In a word, the thrust of humanistic psychology is toward broadening our perspectives on what constitutes a human science. It proposes that we take a fresh look at the so-called "organism" that is man. With a revolution well under way in the theory of natural science, the time has come for psychology to develop methods of its own that are more in keeping with its unique subject matter.

In addition to the books already mentioned, the student who wishes to know more about humanistic psychology may wish to consult such publications as Ansbacher (1971), Bugental (1963, 1967) Bühler and Allen (1972), Chein (1962), Goble (1970), Hammes (1971), Jourard (1968), Maslow (1968, 1970), Matson (1973), May (1967), and Rogers (1969, 1970).

References
Allport, G. W. *Becoming: Basic considerations for a psychology of personality.* New Haven: Yale University Press, 1955.

Ansbacher, H. L. Alfred Adler and humanistic psychology. *Journal of Humanistic Psychology,* 1971, *11,* 53–63.

Bronowski, J. and Bellugi, U. Language, name and concept. *Science,* 1970, *168,* 669–673.

Bugental, J. F. T. Humanistic psychology: A new breakthrough. *American Psychologist*, 1963, *18*, 563–567.

Bugental, J. F. T. *The challenges of humanistic psychology.* New York: McGraw-Hill, 1967.

Bühler, C. Theoretical observations about life's basic tendencies. *American Journal of Psychotherapy*, 1959, *13*, 561–581.

Bühler, C. and Massarik, F. (Eds.) *The course of human life.* New York: Springer, 1968.

Bühler, C. and Allen, M. *Introduction to humanistic psychology.* Monterey, Calif.: Brooks/Cole, 1972.

Cantril, H. A fresh look at the human design. In J. F. T. Bugental (Ed.), *The challenges of humanistic psychology,* New York: McGraw-Hill, 1967.

Cassirer, E. *An essay on man.* New Haven: Yale University Press, 1944, pp. 31–39.

Chein, I. The image of man. *Journal of Social Issues,* 1962, *13,* 1–35.

Frankl, V. E. *Man's search for meaning: An introduction to logotherapy.* Boston: Beacon Press, 1966.

Frankl, V. E. *Psychotherapy and existentialism: Selected papers on logotherapy.* New York: Washington Square Press, 1967, Ch. 3.

Gardner, R. S. and Gardner, B. T. Teaching sign language to a chimpanzee. *Science,* 1969, *165,* 664–672.

Giorgi, A. Phenomenology and experimental psychology. *Review of Existential Psychology and Psychiatry,* Winter 1966, *6,* 37–50.

Giorgi, A. *Psychology as a human science: A phenomenologically based approach.* New York: Harper & Row, 1970.

Goble, F. *The third force: The psychology of Abraham Maslow.* New York: Grossman, 1970.

Hammes, J. A. *Humanistic psychology: A Christian interpretation.* New York: Grune & Stratton, 1971.

Jourard, S. A. *Disclosing man to himself.* New York: Van Nostrand, 1968.

Kagan, J. On the need for relativism in psychology. *American Psychologist,* 1967, *22,* 131–142.

Kuhn, T. S. *The structure of scientific revolution* (Rev. ed.) Chicago: University of Chicago Press, 1970.

Maslow, A. H. A philosophy of psychology: The need for a mature science of human nature. *Main Currents in Modern Thought,* 1957, *13,* 27–32.

Maslow, A. H. *Motivation and personality* (Rev. ed.) New York: Harper & Row, 1970.

Matson, F. W. *Without/within: Behaviorism and humanism.* Monterey, Calif.: Brooks/Cole, 1973.

May, R. *Psychology and the human dilemma.* Princeton, N.J.: Van Nostrand, 1967.

May, R. (Ed.) *Existential psychology* (Rev. ed.) New York: Random House, 1969a.

May, R. *Love and will.* New York: Norton, 1969b.

Pfungst, O. *Clever Hans: The horse of Mr. von Osten.* R. Rosenthal (Ed.), New York: Holt, Rinehart and Winston, 1965.

Polanyi, M. *Personal Knowledge* (Rev. ed.) Chicago: University of Chicago Press, 1962. (Also published as a paperback by Harper & Row)

Polanyi, M. Logic and psychology. *American Psychologist,* 1968, *23,* 27–42.

Premack, D. A functional analysis of language. *Journal of the Experimental Analysis of Behavior,* 1970a, *14,* 107–125.

Premack, D. The education of Sarah: A chimp learns the language. *Psychology Today,* 1970b, *4*(4), 54–58.

Rogers, C. R. Persons or science? A philosophical question. *American Psychologist,* 1955, *10,* 267–279.

Rogers, C. R. *On becoming a person.* Boston: Houghton & Mifflin, 1961.

Rogers, C. R. *Freedom to learn.* Columbus, Ohio: Merrill, 1969.

Rogers, C. R. *Carl Rogers on encounter groups.* New York: Harper & Row, 1970.

Rumbaugh, M. D. and von Glaserfield, E..C. Reading and sentence completion by a chimpanzee (Pan). *Science,* 1973, *182,* 731–733.

Severin, F. T. *Discovering man in psychology: A humanistic approach.* New York: McGraw-Hill, 1973.

Teilhard de Chardin, P. *The phenomenon of man.* New York: Harper & Row, 1965.

Suggested Readings for
Chapter 1

Boring, E. G. *A History of experimental psychology.* (2nd ed.) New York: Appleton-Century-Crofts, 1957. A classical history of psychology with a scholarly and thorough analysis of the factors involved in the growth of psychology as an experimental science.

Krawiec, T. S. *The psychologists.* New York: Oxford University Press. Vol. I, 1972; Vol. II, 1974. This is a two-volume work consisting of autobiographical essays describing the life and work of a number of outstanding contemporary psychologists. It is both readable and instructive.

Postman, L. (Ed.) *Psychology in the making.* New York: Alfred A. Knopf, 1962. The presentation, in historical context, of eleven research areas that have significant implications for psychology as a science.

Skinner, B. F. *Beyond freedom and dignity.* New York: Alfred A. Knopf, 1971. An exciting and controversial study of man by a prominent psychologist.

Watson, R .I. *The great psychologists.* (2nd ed.) Philadelphia: J. B. Lippincott Company, 1967. An excellent survey of psychological thought from early times to the recent past. Watson ties together the philosophical, biological, and social foundations of psychology as a science.

Discussion Questions

1. What are the different conceptions of man implied by the men discussed in this chapter?

2. Skinner's Utopia is described in one article. What would Utopia be like for the other psychologists? For you?

3. The "third force" is a reaction to the first two forces—psychoanalysis and behaviorism. What aspects of these two forces is it reacting to, and what does it offer as alternatives?

4. If psychology can reach the point where it can predict and control human behavior, would this represent a gain or loss for society?

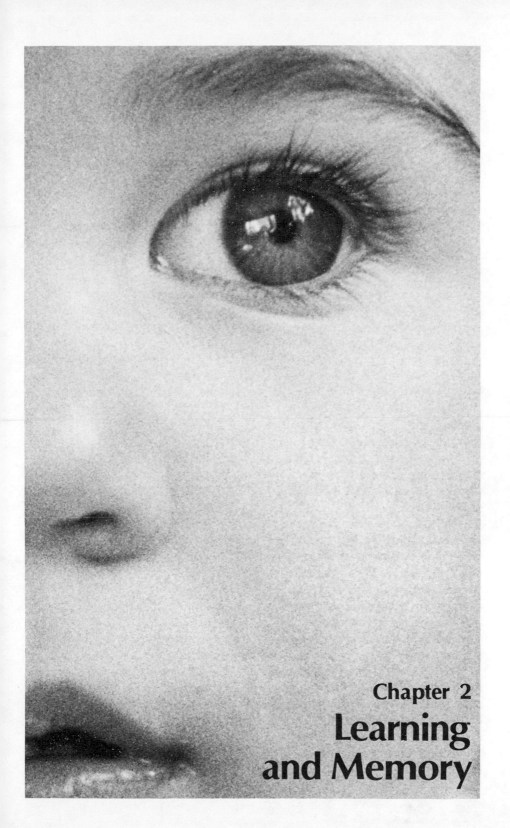

Chapter 2

Learning and Memory

The study of learning is perhaps the most significant and popular area of psychological investigation. It is common knowledge that all people do learn, but the critical scientific issues involve how learning develops, the various kinds of learning, and the conditions necessary for learning to take place. To this end, psychologists have created elaborate theoretical systems and have carried out extensive research to refine the concept and properties of learning.

Learning is closely tied to the past experience of the individual. Maturation, on the other hand, is a consequence of natural biological growth. Both concepts involve behavior change, and in this sense they are closely related. However, the label "learning" is used specifically to identify the acquisition or occurrence of behavior that is not a direct function of automatic biological development. For example, each child eventually acquires the physiological capacity for speech, which is associated with his maturation or growth. But his construction of words, phrases, intonations, and other social language qualities are outgrowths of learning.

At this point a distinction should be made between learning and performance. Learning in a strict theoretical sense is never directly observed. What one sees is performance. Learning is a construct that is inferred from observable behavior, that is, performance. By the same token, performance does not necessarily indicate that a person has, in fact, learned. Changes in behavior can also result from heightened motivation, changes in environmental conditions, physiological insults, or accelerated physical growth. While there are many conditions which result in behavior change, learning is the most durable and stable of these.

In Chapter 1, two of our most prominent contemporary learning theorists are represented—Hull and Skinner. Both are intimately associated with the theoretical explanation and experimental techniques of conditioning. In the course of his work, each was known for a specific kind of research environment specially designed to test his particular theoretical ideas. In his research Hull often used mazes that provided the environment for white rats to scurry about seeking the location of food. Skinner devised boxes with levers and pecking bars for his rats and pigeons in order to measure their response rates under different schedules of reinforcement. Pavlov, who is also mentioned in the introduction to Chapter 1, harnessed his dogs and applied unconditioned and conditioned stimuli to increase common functions such as salivation and other physiological processes. A fascinating description of learning theory is found in a science-fiction tale by James McConnell about a psychologist captured by visiting aliens from another planet. This story speculates on what would happen if a psychologist were suddenly to find himself in a research situation in which he were the subject. How would he react to mazes, Skinner boxes, and other ingenious psychological devices set up to study learning? This story provides an entertaining and informative excursion into the rigors of experimental psychology as seen through the eyes of an unwilling subject.

The application of principles of learning to the treatment of behavior problems is now quite widespread. Behavior therapy methods of treatment often take a relatively short time to produce positive behavioral changes and are therefore a new and exciting alternative to more traditional forms of treatment. The paper by Marvin Goldfried and Michael Merbaum is an overview of a treatment procedure called self-control. This paper shows how self-control can be learned by training an individual to be his own therapist. In these training methods the person learns to identify the stimuli, both internal and external, which control and maintain his behavior. Once these relevant variables are identified the next step is to arrange conditions to control their influence on behavior. Through the proper use of the principles of self-control, problems such as obesity, smoking, alcoholism, anxiety, and depressive states can potentially be modified.

An extremely important educational problem frequently found in relatively young children is called dyslexia. Dyslexia involves distortions in perception and learning and is therefore a complicated process to understand and treat. The article by Michele Maquard provides a general review of the symptoms characteristic of this disorder. Difficulties in learning to read and write and in the perception of visual material are typical of children who are labeled dyslexic. While there are many theories about dyslexia, there is unfortunately a lack of clarity about the causes of this disorder. Often the impaired learning and perception are variously attributed to hereditary deficiencies, physiological disturbances, or even poor reinforcement histories in childhood. This article, in clear language, attempts to explain the many faces of this disorder and presents some of the experiments and remedial procedures which are being developed to help children struggling with this crippling educational problem.

Perception is a much researched area which concerns the reception and organization of sensations from the outside world, and we have already associated the process of learning with the acquisition of skill, knowledge, and the ability to solve problems. However, the retention of these behaviors so that they can be reproduced in the future involves memory. It is, of course, a little difficult to disentangle memory, learning, and perception since both perception and learning are obviously dependent in part on memory. When we learn, we are not simply tackling each situation independently; rather we are using the related skills and knowledge accumulated over past experiences and applying them to the current situation. This is where memory comes into action. Furthermore, it is not essential that we be consciously aware of the relevant memories in order for them to be useful. This is not to say that personal awareness is not helpful, but in many cases it can interfere with the smooth execution of behavior. For example, if one has gone through the process of learning a musical instrument this point is clearly illustrated. At the beginning the notes are learned consciously and deliberately. The finger movements are then coordinated with the conscious set to execute this movement or to achieve a particular sound. After endless practice the result is, hopefully, an effortlessness and smooth presentation of what has been learned. To go back now and consciously repeat the earlier self-instructions, such as moving the hand in a particular way, would completely disrupt the integration of the learned sequence of behavior. The memory of the correct hand movement has become automatically involved in the entire performance.

Memory as a cognitive process takes many forms and is a general heading which includes related phenomena such as forgetting, remembering, retention, and recognition. Furthermore, different principles seem to be involved in short- and long-term memory. As a general rule it can be said that the percentage of forgetting is greatest immediately after something has been learned and then levels off at a slowly decreasing rate. In addition, the more meaningful the material to be learned, the more easily it is retained.

Memory, as a mental ability, shows a fairly set pattern of development. There are, of course, individual variations in this capacity related to innate intelligence or to an environment that emphasizes intellectual achievement. But by the time the child has reached the age of two, memory begins to shape itself from primitive sense impressions to include the faculties of language and speech. How this developmental sequence unfolds is the topic of the article by Flora R. Schreiber entitled "Watching Johnny's Memory Grow."

5　Learning Theory
James V. McConnell

"Yes, there I was walking through the woods minding my own business...when the transition took place."

Imagine yourself an unwilling captive in an alien spaceship trying to survive under extraordinarily perplexing circumstances. Add to this fantasy the discovery that alien psychologists are using *you* as an experimental subject for their studies. How our earth psychologist hero outfoxes his alien counterparts is delightfully recorded in McConnell's tale.

It's better to be wanted for murder than not to be wanted at all."—Marty Winch (via Don Lewis)

I am writing this because I presume He wants me to. Otherwise He would not have left paper and pencil handy for me to use. And I put the word "He" in capitals because it seems the only thing to do. If I am dead and in hell, then this is only proper. However, if I am merely a captive somewhere, then surely a little flattery won't hurt matters.

As I sit here in this small room and think about it, I am impressed most of all by the suddenness of the whole thing. At one moment I was out walking in the woods near my suburban home. The next thing I knew, here I was in a small, featureless room, naked as a jaybird, with only my powers of rationalization to stand between me and insanity. When the "change" was made (whatever the change was), I was not conscious of so much as a momentary flicker between walking in the woods and being here in this room. Whoever is responsible for all of this is to be complimented—either He has developed an instantaneous anesthetic or He has solved the problem of instantaneous transportation of matter. I would prefer to think it the former, for the latter leads to too much anxiety.

Yes, there I was walking through the woods, minding my own business, studiously pretending to enjoy the outing so that I wouldn't mind the exercise too much, when the transition took place. As I recall, I was immersed in the problem of how to teach my class in Beginning Psychology some of the more abstruse points of Learning Theory when the transition came. How far away and distant life at the University seems at the moment! I must be forgiven if now I am much more concerned about where I am and how to get out of here than about how freshmen can be cajoled into understanding Hull or Tolman.

Problem One. Where am I? For an answer, I can only describe this room. It is about twenty feet square, some twelve feet high, with no windows, but with what might be a door in the middle of one of the walls. Everything is of a uniform gray color, and the walls and ceiling emit a fairly pleasant achromatic light. The walls themselves are of some hard material which might be metal since it feels slightly cool to the touch. The floor is of a softer, rubbery material that yields a little when I walk on it. Also, it has a rather "tingly" feel to it, suggesting that it may be in constant vibration. It is somewhat warmer than the walls, which is all to the good since it appears I must sleep on the floor.

The only furniture in the room consists of what might be a table and what passes for a chair. They are not quite that, but they can be made to serve this purpose. On the table I found the paper and the pencil. No, let me correct myself. What I call paper is a good deal rougher and thicker than I am used to, and what I call a pencil is nothing more than a thin round stick of graphite which I have sharpened by rubbing one end of it on the table.

And that is the sum extent of my surroundings. I wish I knew what He has done with my clothes. The suit was an old one, but I am worried about the walking boots. I was very fond of those boots—not because of any sentimental attachment nor because they had done me much good service, but rather because they were quite expensive and I would hate to lose them.

The problem still remains to be answered, however, as to just where in the hell I am—if not in hell itself!

Problem Two is a knottier one—why am I here? Were I subject to paranoid tendencies, I would doubtless come to the conclusion that my enemies had kidnapped me. Or perhaps that the Russians had taken such an interest in my research that they had spirited me away to some Siberian hideout and would soon appear to demand either cooperation or death. Sadly enough, I am too reality oriented. My research was highly interesting to me, and perhaps to a few other psychologists who like to dabble in esoteric problems of animal learning, but it was scarcely startling enough to warrant such attention as kidnapping.

So I am left as baffled as before. Where am I, and why?

And who is He?

2

I have decided to forego all attempts at keeping this diary according to "days" or "hours." Such units of time have no meaning in any present circumstances, for the light remains constant all the time I am awake. The human organism is not possessed of as neat an internal clock as some of the lower species. Far too many studies have shown that a human being who is isolated from all external stimulation soon loses his sense of time. So I will merely indicate breaks in the narrative and hope that He will understand that if He wasn't bright enough to leave me with my wristwatch, He couldn't expect me to keep an accurate record.

Nothing much has happened since I began this narrative, except that I have slept, been fed and watered, and have emptied my bladder and bowels. The food was waiting on the table when I awoke last time. I must say that He had little of the gourmet in Him. Protein balls are not my idea of a feast royal. However, they will serve to keep body and soul together (presuming, of course, that they *are* together at the moment). But I must object to my source of liquid refreshment. The meal made me very thirsty and I was in the process of cursing Him and everybody else when I noticed a small nipple which had appeared in the wall while I was asleep. At first I thought that perhaps Freud was right after all, and that my libido had taken over control of my imagery. Experimentation convinced me, however, that the thing was real, and that it is my present source of water. If one sucks on the thing, it delivers a slightly cool and somewhat sweetish flow of liquid. But really, it's a most undignified procedure. It's bad enough to have to sit around all day in my birthday suit. But for a full professor to have to stand on his tiptoes and suck on an artificial nipple in order to obtain water is asking a little too much. I'd complain to the Management if only I knew to whom to complain!

Following eating and drinking, the call to nature became a little too strong to ignore. Now, I was adequately toilet-trained with indoors plumbing, and the absence of same is most annoying. However, there was nothing much to do but choose a corner of the room and make the best of a none too pleasant situation. (As a side-thought, I wonder if the choosing of a corner was in any way instinctive?). However, the upshot of the whole thing was my learning what is probably the purpose of the vibration of the floor. For the excreted material disappeared through the floor not too many minutes later. The process was a gradual one. Now I will be faced with all kinds of uncomfortable thoughts concerning what might possibly happen to me if I slept too long!

Perhaps this is to be expected, but I find myself becoming a little paranoid after all. In attempting to solve my *Problem Two*, why I am here, I have begun to wonder if perhaps some of my colleagues at the University are not using me as the subject in some kind of experiment. It would be just like them to dream up some fantastic kind of "human-in-isolation" experiment and use me as a pilot observer. You would think that they'd have asked my permission first. However, perhaps it's important that the subject not know what's happening to him. If so, I have one happy thought to console me. If any of them are responsible for this, they'll have to take over the teaching of my classes for the time being. And how they hate teaching Learning Theory to freshmen!

You know, this place seems dreadfully quiet to me.

3

Suddenly I have solved two of my problems. I know both where I am and who He is. And I bless the day I got interested in the perception of motion.

I should say to begin with that the air in this room seems to have more than the usual concentration of dust particles. This didn't seem particularly noteworthy until I noticed that most of them seemed to pile up along the floor against one wall in particular. For a while I was sure that this was due to the ventilation system—perhaps there was an out-going air duct there where this particular wall was joined to the floor. However, when I went over and put my hand to the floor there, I could feel no breeze whatsoever. Yet even as I held my hand along the dividing line between the wall and the floor, dust motes covered my hand with a thin coating. I tried this same experiment everywhere else in the room to no avail. This was the only spot where the phenomenon occurred, and it occurred along the entire length of this one wall.

But if ventilation was not responsible for the phenomenon, what was? All at once there popped into my mind some calculations I had made back when the rocket boys had first proposed a manned satellite station. Engineers are notoriously naive when it comes to the performance of a human being in most situations, and I remembered that the problem of the perception of the satellite's rotation seemingly had been ignored by the slip-stick crowd. They had planned to rotate the doughnut-shaped satellite in order to substitute centrifugal force for the force of gravity. Thus the outer shell of the doughnut would appear to be "down" to anyone inside the thing. Apparently they had not realized that man is at least as sensitive to angular rotation as he is to variations in the pull of gravity. As I figured the problem then, if a man aboard the doughnut moved his head as much as three or four feet outwards from the center of the doughnut, he would have become fairly dizzy! Rather annoying it would have been, too, to have been hit by a wave of nausea every time one sat down in a chair. Also, as I pondered the problem, it became apparent that dust particles and the like would probably show a tendency to move in a direction opposite to the direction of the rotation, and hence pile up against any wall or such that impeded their flight.

Using the behavior of the dust particles as a clue, I then climbed atop the table and leapt off. Sure enough, my head felt like a mule had kicked it by the time I landed on the floor. My hypothesis was confirmed.

So I am aboard a spaceship!

The thought is incredible, but in a strange way comforting. At least now I can postpone worrying about heaven and hell—and somehow I find the idea of being in a spaceship much more to the liking of a confirmed agnostic. I suppose I owe my colleagues an apology—I should have known they would never have put themselves in a position where they might have to teach freshmen all about learning!

And, of course, I now know who "He" is. Or rather, I know who He *isn't*, which is something else again. Surely, though, I can no longer think of Him as being human. Whether I should be consoled at this or not, I have no way of telling.

I still have no notion of *why* I am here, however, nor why this alien chose to pick me of all people to pay a visit to His spaceship. What possible use could I be? Surely if He were interested in making contact with the human race, He would have spirited away a politician. After all, that's what politicians are for! Since there has been no effort made to communicate with me, however, I must reluctantly give up any cherished hopes that His purpose is that of making contact with *genus homo*.

Or perhaps He's a galactic scientist of some kind, a biologist of sorts out gathering specimens. Now, that's a particularly nasty thought. What if He turned out to be a psychologist, interested in cutting me open eventually to see what makes me tick? Will my innards be smeared over a glass slide for scores of youthful Hims to peer at under a microscope? Brrrr! I don't mind giving my life to Science, but I'd rather do it a little at a time.

If you don't mind, I think I'll go do a little repressing for a while.

4

Good God! I should have known it! Destiny will play her little tricks, and all jokes have their cosmic angles. He is a *psychologist!* Had I given it due consideration, I would have realized that whenever you come across a new species, you worry about behavior first, physiology second. So I have received the ultimate insult—or the ultimate compliment. I don't know which. I have become a specimen for an alien psychologist!

This thought first occurred to me when I awoke after my latest sleep (which was filled, I must admit, with most frightening dreams). It was immediately obvious that something about the room had changed. Almost at once I noticed that one of the walls now had a lever of some kind protruding from it, and to one side of the lever, a small hole in the wall with a container beneath the hole. I wandered over to the lever, inspected it for a few moments, then accidently depressed the thing. At once there came a loud clicking noise, and a protein ball popped out of the hole and fell into the container.

For just a moment a frown crossed my brow. This seemed somehow so strangely familiar. Then, all at once, I burst into wild laughter. The room had been changed into a gigantic Skinner Box! For years I had been studying animal learning by putting white rats in a Skinner Box and following the changes in the rats' behavior. The rats had to learn to press the lever in order to get a pellet of food, which was delivered to them through just such an apparatus as is now affixed to the wall of my cell. And now, after all of these years, and after all of the learning studies I had done, to find myself trapped like a rat in a Skinner Box! Perhaps this was hell after all, I told myself, and the Lord High Executioner's admonition to "let the punishment fit the crime" was being followed.

Frankly, this sudden turn of events has left me more than a little shaken.

5

I seem to be performing according to theory. It didn't take me long to discover that pressing the lever would give me food some of the time, while at other times all I got was the click and no protein ball. It appears that approximately every twelve hours the thing delivers me a random number of protein balls—the number has varied from five to fifteen so far. I never know ahead of time how many pellets—I mean protein balls—the apparatus will deliver, and it spews them out intermittently. Sometimes I have to press the lever a dozen times or so before it will give me anything, while at other times it gives me one ball for each press. Since I don't have a watch on me, I am never quite sure when the twelve hours have passed, so I stomp over to the lever and press it every few minutes when I think it's getting close to time to be fed. Just like my rats always did. And since the pellets are small and I never get enough of them, occasionally I find myself banging away on the lever with all the compulsion of a stupid animal. But I missed the feeding time once and almost starved to death (so it seemed) before the lever delivered food the next time. About the only consolation to my wounded pride is that at this rate of starvation, I'll lose my bay window in short order.

At least He doesn't seem to be fattening me up for the kill. Or maybe he just likes lean meat.

6

I have been promoted. Apparently He in His infinite alien wisdom has decided that I'm intelligent enough to handle the Skinner-type apparatus, so I've been promoted to solving a maze. Can you picture the irony of the situation? All of the classic Learning Theory methodology is practically being thrown in my face in mockery. If only I could communicate with Him! I don't mind being subjected to tests nearly as much as I mind being underestimated. Why, I can solve puzzles hundreds of times more complex than what He's throwing at me. But how can I tell Him?

7

As it turns out, the maze is much like our standard T-mazes, and is not too difficult to learn. It's a rather long one, true, with some 23 choice points along the way. I spent the better part of half an hour wandering through the thing the first time I found myself in it. Surprisingly enough, I didn't realize the first time out what I was in, so I made no conscious attempt to memorize the correct turns. It wasn't until I reached the final turn and found food waiting for me that I recognized what I was expected to do. The next time through the maze my performance was a good deal better, and I was able to turn in a perfect performance in not too long a time. However, it does not do my ego any good to realize that my own white rats could have learned the maze a little sooner than I did.

My "home cage," so to speak, still has the Skinner apparatus in it, but the lever delivers food only occasionally now. I still give it a whirl now and again, but since I'm getting a fairly good supply of food at the end of the maze each time, I don't pay the lever much attention.

Now that I am very sure of what is happening to me, quite naturally my thoughts have turned to how I can get out of this situation. Mazes I can solve without too much difficulty, but how to escape is apparently beyond my intellectual capacity. But then, come to think of it, there was precious little chance for my own experimental animals to get out of my clutches. And assuming that I am unable to escape, what then? After He has finished putting me through as many paces as He wishes, where do we go from there? Will he treat me as I treated most of my non-human subjects—that is, will I get tossed into a jar containing chloroform? "Following the experiment, the animals are sacrificed," as we so euphemistically report in the scientific literature. This doesn't appeal to me much, as you can imagine. Or maybe if I seem particularly bright to Him, He may use me for breeding purposes, to establish a colony of His own. Now, that might have possibilities . . .

Oh, damn Freud anyhow!

8

And damn Him, too! I had just gotten the maze well learned when He upped and changed things on me. I stumbled about like a bat in the sunlight for quite some time before I finally got to the goal box. I'm afraid my performance was pretty poor.

9

Well, it wasn't so bad after all. What He did was just to reverse the whole maze so that it was a mirror image of what it used to be. Took me only two trials to discover the solution. Let Him figure that one out if He's so smart!

10

My performance on the maze reversal must have pleased Him, because now He's added a new complication. And again I suppose I could have predicted the next step if I had been thinking along the right direction. I woke up a few hours ago to find myself in a totally different room. There was nothing whatsoever in the room, but opposite me were two doors in the wall—one door a pure white, the other jet black. Between me and the doors was a deep pit, filled with water. I didn't like the looks of the situation, for it occurred to me right away that He had devised a kind of jumping-stand for me. I had to choose which of the doors was open and led to the food. The other door would be locked. If I jumped at the wrong door, and found it locked, I'd fall in the water. I needed a bath, that was for sure, but I didn't relish getting it in this fashion.

While I stood there watching, I got the shock of my life. I mean it quite literally. The bastard had thought of everything. When I used to run rats on jumping stands, to overcome their reluctance to jump, I used to shock them. He's following exactly the same pattern. The floor in this room is wired but good. I howled and jumped about and showed all the usual anxiety behavior. It took me less than two seconds to come to my senses and make a flying leap at the white door, however.

You know something? That water is ice-cold!

11

I have now, by my own calculations, solved no fewer than 87 different problems on the jumping stand, and I'm getting sick and tired of it. One time I got angry and just pointed at the correct door—and got shocked for not going ahead and jumping. I shouted bloody murder, cursing Him at the top of my voice, telling Him if He didn't like my performance, He could damn well lump it. All He did, of course, was to increase the shock.

Frankly, I don't know how much longer I can put up with this. It's not that the work is difficult. But rather that it seems so senseless, so useless. If He were giving me half a chance to show my capabilities, I wouldn't mind it. I suppose I've contemplated a thousand different ways of escaping, but none of them is worth mentioning. But if I don't get out of here soon, I shall go stark raving mad!

12

For almost an hour after it happened, I sat in this room and just wept. I realize that it is not the style of our culture for a grown man to weep, but there are times when cultural taboos must be forgotten. Again, had I thought much about the sort of experiments He must have had in mind, I most probably could have predicted the next step. Even so, I most likely would have repressed the knowledge.

One of the standard problems which any learning psychologist is interested in is this one—will an animal learn something if you fail to reward him for his performance? There are many theorists, such as Hull and Spence, who believe that reward (or "reinforcement," as they call it) is absolutely necessary for learning to occur. This is mere stuff and nonsense, as anyone with a grain of sense knows, but nonetheless the "reinforcement" theory has been dominant in the field for years now. We fought a hard battle with Spence and Hull, and actually had them with their backs to the wall at one point, when suddenly they came up with the concept of "secondary reinforcement." That is, anything associated with a reward takes on the ability to act as a reward itself. For example, the mere sight of food would become a reward in and of itself—almost as much as a reward, in fact, as is the eating of the food. The sight of food, indeed! But nonetheless, it saved their theories for the moment.

For the past five years now, I have been trying to design an experiment that would show beyond a shadow of a doubt that the sight of a reward was not sufficient for learning to take place. And now look at what has happened to me!

I'm sure that He must lean towards Hull and Spence in his theorizing, for earlier today, when I found myself in the jumping stand room, instead of being rewarded with my usual protein balls when I made the correct jump, I discovered . . .

I'm sorry, but it is difficult to write about even now. For when I made the correct jump and the door opened and I started toward the food trough, I found it had been replaced with a photograph. A calendar photograph. You know the one. Her name, I think, is Monroe.

I sat on the floor for almost an hour weeping afterwards. For five whole years I have been attacking the validity of the secondary reinforcement theory, and now I find myself giving Him evidence that the theory is correct! For I cannot help "learning" which of the doors is the correct one to jump through. I refuse to stand on the apparatus and have the life shocked out of me, and I refuse to pick the wrong door all the time and get an icy bath time after time. It just isn't fair! For He will doubtless put it all down to the fact that the mere sight of the photograph is functioning as a reward, and that I am learning the problems merely to be able to see Miss What's-her-name in her bare skin!

Oh, I can just see Him now, sitting somewhere else in this spaceship, gathering in all the data I am giving Him, plotting all kinds of learning curves, chortling to Himself because I am confirming all of His pet theories, I just wish . . .

13

Almost an hour has gone by since I wrote the above section. It seems longer than that, but surely it's been only an hour. And I have spent the time in deep thought. For I have discovered a way out of this place, I think. The question is, dare I do it?

I was in the midst of writing that paragraph about His sitting and chortling and confirming his theories, when it suddenly struck me that theories are born of the equipment that one uses. This has probably been true throughout the history of all science, but perhaps most true of all in psychology. If Skinner had never invented his blasted box, if the maze and the jumping stand had not been developed, we probably would have entirely different theories of learning today than we now have. For if nothing else, the type of equipment that one uses drastically reduces the type of behavior that one's subjects can show, and one's theories have to account only for the type of behavior that appears in the laboratories.

It follows from this also that any two cultures that devise the same sort of experimental procedures will come up with almost identical theories.

Keeping all of this in mind, it's not hard for me to believe that He is an iron-clad reinforcement theorist, for He uses all of the various paraphernalia that they use, and uses it in exactly the same way.

My means of escape is therefore obvious. He expects from me confirmation of all His pet theories. Well, He won't get it any more! I know all of His theories backwards and forwards, and this means I know how to give Him results that will tear his theories right smack in half!

I can almost predict the results. What does any learning theorist do with an animal that won't behave properly, that refuses to give the results that are predicted? One gets rid of the beast, quite naturally. For one wishes to use only healthy, normal animals in one's work, and any animal that gives "unusual" results is removed from the study but quickly. After all, if it doesn't perform as expected, it must be sick, abnormal, or aberrant in one way or another . . .

There is no guarantee, of course, what method He will employ to dispose of my now annoying presence. Will He "sacrifice" me? Or will He just return me to the "permanent colony?" I cannot say. I know only that I will be free from what is now an intolerable situation. The chance must be taken.

Just wait until He looks at His results from now on!

II

From: Experimenter-in-Chief, Interstellar Labship PSYCH-145
To: Director, Bureau of Science

Thlan, my friend, this will be an informal missive. I will send the official report along later, but I wanted to give you my subjective impressions first.

The work with the newly discovered species is, for the moment, at a standstill. Things went exceedingly well at first. We picked what seemed to be a normal, healthy animal and smattered it into our standard test apparatus. I may have told you that this new species seemed quite identical to our usual laboratory animals, so we included a couple of the "toys" that our home animals seem to be fond of—thin pieces of material made from woodpulp and a tiny stick of graphite. Imagine our surprise, and our pleasure, when this new specimen made exactly the same use of the materials as have all of our home colony specimens. Could it be that there are certain innate behavior patterns to be found throughout the universe in the lower species?

Well, I merely pose the question. The answer is of little importance to a Learning Theorist. Your friend Verpk keeps insisting that the use of these "toys" may have some deeper meaning to it, and that perhaps we should investigate further. At his insistence, then, I include with this informal missive the materials used by our first subject. In my opinion, Verpk is guilty of gross anthropomorphism, and I wish to have nothing further to do with the question. However, this behavior did give us hope that our newly discovered colony would yield subjects whose performance would be exactly in accordance with standard theory.

And, in truth, this is exactly what seemed to be the case. The animal solved the Bfian Box problem in short order, yielding as beautiful data as I have ever seen. We then shifted it to maze, maze-reversal and jumping stand problems, and the results could not have confirmed our theories better had we rigged the data. However, when we switched the animal to secondary reinforcement problems, it seemed to undergo a strange sort of change. No longer was its performance up to par. In fact, at times it seemed to go quite berserk. For part of the experiment, it would perform superbly. But then, just as it seemed to be solving whatever problem we set it to, its behavior would subtly change into patterns that obviously could not come from a normal specimen. It got worse and worse, until its behavior departed radically from that which our theories predicted. Naturally, we knew then that something had happened to the animal, for our theories are based upon thousands of experiments with similar subjects, and hence our theories must be right. But our theories hold only for normal subjects, and for normal species, so it soon became apparent to us that we had stumbled upon some abnormal type of animal.

Upon due consideration, we returned the subject to its home colony. However, we also voted almost unanimously to request from you permission to take steps to destroy the complete colony. It is obviously of little scientific use to us, and stands as a potential danger that we must take adequate steps against. Since all colonies are under your protection, we therefore request permission to destroy it in toto.

I must report, by the way, that Verpk's vote was the only one which was cast against this procedure. He has some silly notion that one should study behavior as one finds it. Frankly, I cannot understand why you have seen fit to saddle me with him on this expedition, but perhaps you have your reasons.

Verpk's vote notwithstanding, however, the rest of us are of the considered opinion that this whole new colony must be destroyed, and quickly. For it is obviously diseased or some such—as reference to our theories has proven. And should it by some chance come in contact with our other colonies, and infect our other animals with whatever disease or aberration it has, we would never be able to predict their behavior again. I need not carry the argument further, I think.

May we have your permission to destroy the colony as soon as possible, then, so that we may search out yet other colonies and test our theories against other healthy animals? For it is only in this fashion that science progresses.

Respectfully yours,
Iowyy

"The potential for external control has become more frightening in recent years."

What control does the individual have over his own fate? Is he really helpless to change his conditions of life? This article is quite optimistic. It emphasizes the active possibilities for change that each person can learn to recognize in order to better control his own directions.

What role does man play in determining his own life, his future, his fate? Is each person the product, the prisoner or the creative collaborator with his environment? In reality, how actively can each one of us participate in shaping the world we so intimately represent? The study of self-control has attempted to grapple directly with these issues.

Although man's ability to control his own world is clearly not a concern of only recent origin, the nature of our current society is such that questions of man's personal autonomy have achieved more widespread and serious consideration. The size and complexity of our contemporary civilization makes it more difficult for any one individual to exert an influence on his environment. To complicate matters even further, we are living at a time when social change is most rapid, providing ever-shifting requirements and values which guide and limit our behavior.

Definition of Self-Control

In *Behavior Change through Self-Control*, we offer the following definition of self-control: "*Self-control represents a personal decision arrived at through conscious deliberation for the purpose of instigating action which is designed to achieve certain desired outcomes or goals as determined by the individual himself.*"

Essential to the exercise of self-control is the use of one's higher mental processes. It is also important to recognize that attempts at self-regulation do not occur when all is going well, but rather when the individual has experienced some difficulty in coping with his environment. In some instances, the individual himself is capable of standing back and taking stock of his inability to function. In other instances, perhaps because the problem behaviors may not be all that apparent to the individual, some prod from external sources may be necessary.

Specially prepared for this volume.

An important example of this involves the Surgeon General's report which pointed out the adverse effects of cigarette smoking. Whether it is done on one's own, or with the assistance of external sources, the crucial point is that the person himself recognizes that certain things he is doing or not doing are ultimately resulting in negative consequences.

A comprehensive definition of self-control, then, includes the following points:

1. It is the individual himself who determines the goal or direction of the change. Although it is clear that his decision will be susceptible to external advice and influence, the ultimate decision remains his own.
2. In addition to specifying the goal, the person must be aware of the specific steps which must be taken to achieve this goal. This means that he must be willing to deliberately and consciously arrange his life, or his environment, so that each of these steps may be pursued.
3. Self-control is best defined according to the outcome. Thus, one would view self-control in terms of the success of one's actions, rather than solely the actions themselves.
4. Self-control does not refer to some global characteristic of the individual, but a set of abilities. A person can have good self-control in some aspects of his life, and poor self-control in others.
5. Finally, and most important of all, self-control does not result from any innate growth process, but is acquired through learning. The implications of this final point are indeed far-reaching, suggesting that almost any individual, given the proper learning experiences, is capable of gaining some control over his problematic behaviors.

Self-Relaxation

One of the most disturbing difficulties which plagues modern man is the problem of anxiety. A most effective way in which behavior therapists teach individuals to deal with anxiety is through *relaxation training*. Based on the procedure described by Jacobson in 1938, the individual goes through a series of exercises which eventually allows him to achieve a deep state of relaxation. The relaxation exercises themselves begin with practice sessions where the person, sitting in a comfortable chair or lying on a bed, alternately tenses and then relaxes various groups of muscles throughout his entire body. After a period of several practice sessions, one then utilizes an abbreviated set of exercises. Instead of deliberately tensing one's muscles before relaxing, the person instead "tunes in" on whatever tenseness may already exist and relaxes away this tension. Although trained professionals are typically required in order to implement the relaxation training, learning to relax is frequently enhanced by at-home practice sessions—using tape-recorded or self-instructions.

Once the individual has learned to relax himself, he is then ready to gradually become exposed (in imagination or in real life) to anxiety provoking situations or objects. Clinical reports and research evidence have all indicated that this procedure has proved to be a highly effective means for reducing fears and phobias. In addition, more recent attention has been paid to the possibility of utilizing this approach for providing the individual with a more generalized coping skill. Thus, by training the person to become sensitive to his bodily signs of tension, and then have these feelings serve as a signal for him to relax away the tension, it is possible for a person to achieve a relatively general state of calm in a wide variety of situations which might previously have been upsetting.

Rational Reevaluation

Still another method for the self-control of anxiety which appears to have great potential is based on the *rational-emotive* approach of Albert Ellis. In a number of instances, an individual becomes upset not because of the objective nature of the situation, but rather by the way in which he *interprets* the situation. On the basis of early learning experiences, individuals frequently develop misconceptions about certain situations and how they must perform in them. One frequently held irrational expectation is that it is essential to be perfect in everything one does. When confronted with an objectively minor failure, such an individual is apt to respond with disproportionate upset—which may be anxiety, depression, anger, or feelings of inadequacy. The upset in this case is not so much the result of the situation, but rather what the person tells himself about it. Consequently, an individual may learn to control his negative emotional reactions by having this upset serve as a signal that he should reevaluate more rationally what he is telling himself about the situation which is so disturbing. With repeated practice, it is possible for the person to eventually correct many of his misconceptions, and approach the situation in a more realistic and comfortable fashion.

Self-Administered Aversion Therapy

There are certain problems in our lives which exist because we find ourselves tempted by situations and objects which are potentially harmful—either physically or psychologically. Take, for example, the case of an obese person who is trying to control his temptation for certain appealing, but high-caloric foods. The sight, smell, and indeed even the thought of food has such a strong attraction that the person may be unable to resist the urge to eat. In such cases, the general strategy is to neutralize this positive attraction by associating certain foods with unpleasant feelings. Within the context of self-control, this can be accomplished as follows: The person can imagine himself in his kitchen, looking up at the chocolate cake on top of the refrigerator. He becomes more and more aware of the powerful temptation to walk over, take the cake down, and help himself to a large slice. As he starts approaching the refrigerator, he imagines himself getting more and more sick to his stomach. The closer he gets to partaking of the forbidden food, the more and more nauseous he imagines himself, until he does, in fact, vomit. This entire sequence is rehearsed again and again in imagination, and an actual attempt to conjure up such negative associations is made when the person is actually tempted to eat in the real life situation.

The procedure of self-administered aversive therapy has been successfully applied to a number of other problems where the long-term consequences are negative, but where the more immediate impact is pleasurable—such as drinking, smoking, and various deviant sexual activities.

Stimulus Control

Another way in which a person can gain control over problem behaviors is by directly altering those environmental cues which lead to these behaviors. In the self-control of cigarette smoking, for example, one stimulus-control procedure involves a buzzer which signals the availability of a cigarette for smoking. The buzzer may be directly built into a cigarette case, or may consist of a small parking meter timer worn on a key chain. By lengthening the interval between buzzes, individuals can voluntarily increase the time between signals and thus cut down the number of cigarettes smoked. Still another procedure is to make a firm commitment to smoke solely in an area designated as "the smoking place." It should be arranged, however, so that no other activity, such as reading, watching TV, or holding a conversation is carried out in this "smoking place." The theory behind this is that if smoking can be detached from all the stimuli which appear to increase its reinforcement value (e.g., the social context), then a considerable amount of smoking could be curtailed.

There are a number of other problem areas which can be dealt with by directly manipulating one's environment. The likelihood of eating chocolate cake is reduced by not having such food around the house. The tendency to become involved in other things when one should be working can be handled by doing one's work in a location relatively free from distractions. And the tendency to shut off one's alarm and go back to sleep in the morning can be minimized by placing the clock at the far end of the room.

Self-Instructions

In a sense, the use of self-instructions as a means of gaining control over one's behavior is involved in all attempts at self-control. In making a deliberate decision to use a self-control technique, the person must "tell himself" to relax, to reevaluate a situation rationally, to imagine himself becoming nauseous, or to modify his environment in a particular way. Above and beyond the use of self-instructions in conjunction with other self-control techniques, behavior therapists have found that people can learn to "talk to themselves" in certain ways which can have profound effects on their behavior. For example, impulsive children have been found to moderate their activity by continually instructing themselves to "slow down." When placed in a situation where good performance on a task would increase their chances of getting a prize, grade-school boys were able to resist temptations to cheat by continually reminding themselves of the task instructions.

Training in self-verbalization has also been applied in more complex instances such as in deciding on the most effective course of action when confronted with a problematic situation. For example, D'Zurilla and Goldfried have outlined a number of steps which one can follow in coping with difficult life situations, such as defining the exact nature of the situation and the issues to be handled, creatively generating a number of potential alternatives, and deciding on what is likely to be the most effective course of action. Such use of self-instructions is particularly useful as a means of independence training—that is, "thinking things out" on one's own.

Self-Reinforcement

Much of what we do in our daily lives is maintained by its consequences. For the most part, we tend to do things that somehow "pay off," and avoid that which does not. Within the context of self-control, the important point here is that positive consequences—or reinforcement—can be just as effective when administered by the individual himself as when it comes from some external source. The self-reinforcement may consist of some material reward, a pleasurable activity, or perhaps even self-praise. Take, for example, the student who has difficulty in sitting down to study, where the temptation instead is to read a magazine, watch TV, or do something else more enjoyable. In addition to arranging his environment to minimize associations with other activities (e.g., studying at a desk which is used *only* for that purpose), the self-reinforcement may very well consist of those very activities which are likely to interfere with the studying. Thus, rather than watching TV or going to the movies instead of, or even before studying, one would do so only *after* the studying has been completed.

Prospects for the Future

The increased interest in the importance of self-control appears to have paralleled the fear that man is becoming more and more controlled by agencies external to himself. The potential for external control has become more frightening in recent years, partly because we have become more aware of its existence, but also because our control by others has, in fact, become more pervasive and effective. Perry London has beautifully described the moral and ethical questions associated with being controlled. As a way of dealing with this danger, he notes the following:

> In order to defend individual freedom, it is necessary to enhance the power of individuals. If behavior technology endangers freedom by giving refined power to controllers, then the antidote which promotes freedom is to give more refined power over their own behavior to those who are endangered. Since everyone is endangered, this means facilitating self-control in everyone.

Because of the importance of this issue, one of the significant contributions that the behavioral sciences can offer to our society is to help translate the promise of self-control into a reality. Our group and personal integrity is likely to depend on this.

References

D'Zurilla, T. J. and Goldfried, M. R. Problem solving and behavior modification. *Journal of Abnormal Psychology*, 1971, *78*, 107–126.

Goldfried, M. R. Systematic desensitization as training in self-control. *Journal of Consulting and Clinical Psychology*, 1971, *37*, 228–234.

Goldfried, M. R. Reduction of generalized anxiety through a variant of systematic desensitization. In M. R. Goldfried and M. Merbaum (Eds.), *Behavior change through self-control*. New York: Holt, Rinehart and Winston, 1973.

Goldfried, M. R., Decenteceo, E. T., and Weinberg, L. Systematic rational reconstructuring as a self-control technique, *Behavior Therapy*, 1974, *5*, 247–254.

Goldfried, M. R. and Merbaum, M. (Eds.) *Behavior change through self-control*. New York: Holt, Rinehart and Winston, 1973.

Jacobson, E. *Progressive relaxation*. Chicago: University of Chicago Press, 1938.

Meichenbaum, D. and Goodman, J. Training impulsive children to talk to themselves: A means of developing self-control. *Journal of Abnormal Psychology*, 1971, *77*, 115–126.

O'Leary, K. D. The effects of self-instruction on immoral behavior. *Journal of Experimental Child Psychology*, 1968, *6*, 297–301.

"Dyslexia may be accompanied by a variety of symptoms: language disorders, orientation difficulties in space and time, or emotional disturbances."

Dyslexia is a poorly understood syndrome which involves a variety of symptoms. Usually, dyslexia refers to difficulty in learning to read and write—a condition which plagues a huge number of children in our public schools. This article attempts to give a perspective on this puzzling disorder and points out some of the treatment possibilities that are currently available.

Difficulty in learning to read and write is a specific obstacle to success at school, and fairly recently acquired disease status when it came to be known as "dyslexia." But is it a medical problem? It has been likened to the alexia seen in adults, a loss of understanding of the written word that is not associated with loss of vision. James Kerr was the first, in 1896, to report cases of children with symptoms of "pure word blindness," a kind of "visual agnosia," or inability to recognize known objects in spite of unimpaired vision. Ombredane a little later reported similar cases, and since then many investigations have tried to clarify the problem.

Following the advent of school health services, more and more children have been examined, and many of them treated for dyslexia; these children became the raw material for studying the "disease." Opinions differ as to whether it is a generalized disorganization or a specific disorder of language or of perception. Certainly the many definitions that exist do not simplify matters.

Generally speaking, three categories of dyslexia are recognized: difficulty in learning to read or write among children of normal intellectual ability; persistent difficulty in reading or spelling after two, three or four years of schooling; and generalized difficulty in learning due to slow development.

Many theories have been put forward about dyslexia—that it is a hereditary constitutional disorder, for example. Other suggested causes are a lack of maturity or lesions of the central nervous system, or disturbances of hemispheric

From *World Health*, the magazine of the World Health Organization, August–September 1972.

dominance: the brain is divided into two hemispheres, and one of the hemispheres is more concerned than the other in the control of a given function; for example, the left-hand hemisphere is usually dominant for speech.

Dyslexia may be accompanied by a variety of symptoms: language disorders, orientation difficulties in space and time, or emotional disturbances. Not one of these symptoms, however, is associated with every type of reading difficulty. What is more, any of them may occur in disorders other than those associated with reading. It is not possible to describe the characteristics of all dyslectic children, just as it would be impossible to find a control group of children with similar characteristics but who had learned to read.

Poorly Understood

Specialized services come across children taken to them for other reasons—who are backward, deficient in notions of space or time, or who have difficulty with language—but who nevertheless have learned to read and write. Other children have had a difficult early childhood, but their ability to learn to read and write remains unaffected. Even among children with poor spatial organization or laterality (dominance of one side of the body), a striking proportion have no difficulty in learning to read and write.

It is thus evident that dyslexia is as yet poorly understood, and it is hardly surprising that vague and often erroneous ideas about it are fairly widespread. The press and television, teachers and parents, and the children themselves discuss the problem with varying degrees of knowledge and insight. According to Mucchili, dyslexia has become "the disease of the century." Certainly, since it was recognized as an obstacle to school learning, a good many children have been freed from the accusation of being lazy or stupid, and the demand for remedial teaching is constantly increasing.

Although such teaching is both useful and necessary for a number of children, it cannot guarantee their future scholastic success. The results, indeed, vary considerably: the child may catch up completely, or show a total lack of interest in the written language. The outcome depends not only on the child's specific disability at reading and writing, but also on his intellectual potential and capacity for emotional adjustment, as well as on the socio-cultural level of the family, to say nothing of the remedial means applied.

Dyslexia is often confused with dysgraphia. In fact, each relates to a different aspect of written language—decoding (reading) and encoding (writing). Follow-up studies of children with dyslexia and dysgraphia show that, whether or not they receive special training, they progressively compensate for their difficulties in reading. Indeed, at a certain stage in their school career they achieve satisfactory marks for reading. On the other hand, more than half of them remain considerably backward in writing, even after remedial teaching. Spelling is apparently a much more serious difficulty to the schoolchild than reading.

This leads to the following important question: are reading and writing difficult only for children said to be suffering from dyslexia and dysgraphia, or are they difficult for other children also? Clearly this "disease," which manifests itself in the context of school learning, would not exist at all if children did not have to learn to read and write. Is dyslexia thus an educational problem? School learning is the result of the child's activity when confronted with a skill that he is expected to acquire, under conditions established by the school. The relationships between these three .entities—the child, the skill and the school—must account for success or failure in learning to read and write.

Scholastic Difficulties

The modern tendency in investigating the problem is to gather general information about children and the conditions under which they are expected to learn. Studies of this kind tend to show that failure in learning to read, the first skill taught at school, is directly related to scholastic difficulties in general. According to Chiland, "no child who fails completely in reading or writing, or whose performance is inadequate or only fair, will complete his primary schooling without having to repeat at least one class. Marks for reading and writing have the greatest value for general scholastic achievement." In 1965, Haramein, in Geneva, noted that those pupils who "completed the full course of compulsory schooling were usually those who managed the first three years easily."

The following statistics are of interest. In 1965, in Geneva, 46 per cent of pupils aged 15 had not reached the class corresponding to their age. In 1971, in France, 10 per cent of pupils were ahead for their age by the end of their compulsory schooling, 40 per cent finished on time, and 50 per cent were behind for their age, 17 per cent being behind by two years or more.

In France, the proportion of failures in reading, which is taught during the first vital years of school, is between 31 and 33 per cent when based on the criterion of repeating a year, and 41 per cent when based on the level of accomplishment in reading and writing. Similar proportions are found in some other countries.

Average marks for writing are invariably lower than average marks for other subjects. The conclusion is, therefore, that approximately one child in two is a poor pupil when judged by the criteria of the institution responsible for teaching him to read and write.

The problem is thus a very general one and not just a matter of some more or less specific pathological condition affecting a comparatively small number of children. There are good grounds for asking whether it is not rather a social problem. Analysis of the failures indicates that the children who have the most difficulties come mainly from the socio-culturally underprivileged sections of society. At primary school, the proportion of children who have to repeat a year is one in three among children from working-class families, but only one in seventeen among the more comfortably off. This is true of various countries in which the problem has been studied, even though social conditions may be different and language may not have the same cultural overtones.

There is a universal tendency to overemphasize the cultural importance of both the spoken and the written word. To write well is everywhere considered the key to speaking well, hence the saying "to speak like a book." Nevertheless, surveys show that 60 per cent of parents keep no books in the house and never read, or at most read a sports newspaper. A child's development depends in part on his identification with other people, those he takes for a model; this suggests at least one reason why his performance varies according to whether he comes from an economically favored or a disadvantaged home environment.

Language is one of the major differences between these two types of environment. At the one extreme, both the spoken and the written language are much used, sometimes simply for the pleasure of talking, even if one has nothing to say. Ideas are given elaborate expression. At the other, language is perhaps mainly used to talk about one's emotions and needs, and to transmit factual information. Children from such a background are slower to adapt to the type of verbal activity common in schools—for example, answering questions that are not really questions, since the child knows quite well that the teacher knows the answer, and that there is only one correct answer; or analyzing language simply as an exercise, which means detaching oneself from its emotional content. Even the form of the language used is different, so that the child may find himself practically in a bi-lingual situation with regard to the vocabulary and syntax used at home and used at school by the teacher and in the textbooks. As many as 50 per cent of common words used by children from working-class families at the age of six do not form part of the school vocabulary. These children, therefore, are in a very different situation from that of their class-mates, trained in the use of language at an earlier age and already convinced that the written message is of interest.

The reaction of parents to failure is greatly influenced by what they expect of their child. Accepting or refusing failure affects the parents' attitude to the child and determines whether they take steps to overcome his difficulties, in particular through seeking remedial teaching.

A school expects all children of the same age to satisfy its requirements. When they fail to do so, an unbridgeable gulf separates the privileged who succeed from those who do not, who become "education cripples," though it is well known that children progress at different speeds and that consequently children of the same age are not necessarily at the same stage of educational readiness.

The Best Age

The question of which is the best age for starting to learn to read—that is, the age at which failure is least likely to occur—is crucial. The best age seems to be six or seven, though the conclusions of psychologists on the subject rarely coincide with what happens in schools or with the wishes of parents, who usually want their children to be taught earlier. Were the age to be raised, the method of teaching would probably prove to be of minor importance, and learning time would be much reduced.

A child's ability to learn to read arises in the course of his development. If the preconditions for learning the art of reading are fulfilled, then the actual method of teaching cannot matter much. Nevertheless educationalists' discussions all too often reduce the question to a search for superior methods. Yet precise and impartial experimental studies show that the success rate at the end of the learning period is practically the same, whatever method is used. Such differences as do occur are found during the different stages of teaching by the various methods.

Malmquist, a world expert on reading problems, considers that the best guarantee of success is a well-trained teacher with at least ten years' experience. Thus it is not the method itself that can cause failure, but the way it is applied by the teacher coupled with the child's own situation at the moment of teaching. Dyslexia, therefore, does not result from the use of any particular method.

In any discussion of teaching methods, the importance of the content of what is taught cannot be underestimated. Better teaching depends on a better comprehension of what is to be taught. This applies less to reading, for which numerous techniques of proven value are available, than to spelling. Dictation, for example, is sacrosanct in the syllabus yet far from satisfactory to teachers, since although it can be used for testing the pupil's command of spelling, it does not help him to acquire it.

Investigations and experiments aiming to provide more insight into the written language and to modify the conditions under which it is taught are still few in number and give rise to much controversy. Yet psycholinguistic research on the acquisition of language by the child may provide the beginning of an answer to the problem, while studies of the special way in which written language works as compared to spoken language could well lead to the development of new ways of teaching.

These various considerations place the problem of failure to learn to read and write in a new perspective. The child's potential at the time he first enters school is determined by numerous factors relating both to the child himself and to his environment. The extent to which he succeeds in learning to read and write, or the difficulties he encounters, depend on his teachers, the programme of study, and the school's criteria for success.

In any event, learning takes time and must involve trial and error. Children who are poor learners are characteristically slow, and make repeated and frequent mistakes. However, their mistakes in reading and spelling are the same as those made in the initial stages by children who learn well. What distinguishes the good learners is the fact that they are gradually able to eliminate their mistakes. Their less fortunate companions, on the other hand, are constantly grappling with a skill they fail to master but are expected to use to an increasing extent. Thus the gap between the two groups widens. What might have been only a temporary setback threatens to become a permanent disability, as a result of which the child will be poorly equipped to acquire new knowledge.

Disturbances manifest themselves in different ways, according to which of the many causative factors predominate. Each failure, therefore, must be considered individually if it is to be properly understood and a suitable remedy found. Dyslexia-dysgraphia, and its treatment through remedial teaching, is only one aspect of a more general problem.

It is to be hoped that for future generations reading and writing will carry less weight as criteria for scholastic success, and that every child will easily acquire within the time allocated the fundamentals of the written language upon which our culture is based. The means to this end remain to be found.

"Most children...remember what they see longer than what they hear."

Most parents would certainly agree that watching a child's memory development is an exciting game. Flora R. Schreiber's description of how this sequence unfolds is entertaining as well as informative. Of special interest are the various roles that maturation and learning play in this process.

One Sunday morning an astute mother listened as her 19-month-old son hung a first picture on memory's wall. The week before he had stood outside the guest room, murmuring "Cora's sleeping." Now, even though Cora was in her own home, he again stood before what had been her door, repeating "Cora's sleeping." It was his way of recalling a week-old event.

"No," the mother carefully explained, "Cora is not here. That was last Sunday—a week ago."

"Week," the child echoed as he made his first primitive connections between that word and his new sense of time.

Such moments, when rightly interpreted as milestones along memory's path, can be the means of deepening relationships between parents and children and an important gauge for child care. Yet, although we've charted Johnny's speech development, fretted about why he can't read, and, of course, worried about how he behaves, we've largely overlooked memory—which deeply affects each of these.

Dramatic are the changes that convert your infant, lying in his crib, kicking his feet, crying, experiencing sense impressions in their pure and primitive form into the two-year-old, whose memory is beginning to be similar to your own; or into the five-year-old, who can remember four digits, sentences consisting of eight and in some cases 13 to 35 syllables and who not only recognizes people, places, and things, but who even displays those more complicated abilities of memory—the capacity to remember concepts and the ability to recall.

Beginning with no past on which to draw, without, as Arthur T. Jersild puts it in his *Child Psychology*, "special meanings that come to be associated, as time passes, with the happenings of everyday life," Johnny does commence to show signs of memory by the time he is three months old.

From *Today's Health*, October 1966. Published by The American Medical Association. Reprinted by permission.

These first memories are responses to direct appeals to the senses and to strong emotional experiences, chiefly painful ones. These memories are also a form of adaptation to the immediate environment, and, as tests of immediate memory reveal, are only for what just occurred. Three-month-old Johnny in the test situation searches for and is disturbed by the disappearance of the tester's face after it has appeared and been withdrawn. Five-month-old Johnny shows memory by looking "searchingly" in the direction in which a toy that was given him has been deliberately removed.

A test for the 10-month-old gives him the opportunity to show memory when in short succession he is presented with two hollow balls to which he is expected to react. The first contains a chicken which he releases while playing with the ball. The second, although it looks exactly like the first, does not contain a chicken. Since his attention was diverted while the first ball was removed, he naturally thinks there is only one ball. He therefore shows memory in the way he reacts when he squeezes the ball and finds no chicken. He may, for instance, look questioningly at the tester's face or put his finger in the hole through which the chicken failed to appear.

At 10 months this memory for the lost chicken is about one minute. (Five months later it will be eight minutes, and 11 months later 17 minutes.)

Watching Johnny's memory grow can be a fascinating game, a family adventure. Suddenly he seems to remember what his rattle, his bottle, and his blanket are like, what they can do to him and he to them. When you approach his crib and he stops crying, he does so because he remembers that previous approaches meant coddling and being cared for.

When Johnny coos not only at your approach, but at his father's or his big brother's, but bawls when his grandfather from a distant city visits for the first time, he displays memory by differentiating between the familiar and the unfamiliar. When, like a child studied from earliest infancy until his third birthday, he recognizes photographs and mirror images of people he knows, but not of himself, he again shows this discrimination. After all, the others were familiar; he himself a stranger, at least visually.

Before the end of Johnny's first year, an important development begins to take place: Along with the swift, transient memory that you have been watching is something that can be described as *permanent memory*. This permanent memory is evident in the first glimmers of an ability to retain and to act in terms of past impressions even when an outside, memory-provoking stimulus is absent.

Johnny, for instance, gets hold of a spoon covered with a napkin or keeps his eyes fixed on the door through which you have disappeared. The spoon is not visible, but he remembers it. Mother is not present, but she lingers in memory.

As Johnny enters his second year, he embarks on a period of important memory changes. Even though permanent memory will come chiefly in glimmers until the fourth year, Johnny's second-year transient memories are becoming increasingly reliable. He can now be expected to respond to simple commands and to understand when you tell him something is "all gone." Previously he has responded only to outside stimuli, but now he is capable of evoking simple memories from within. By the second half of the year, for instance, he not only looks searchingly at a door through which you have disappeared as he did his first year, but in your absence also talks of "my Mommy."

A sense of time, the expression of a growing memory, is another second-year characteristic. "Cora's sleeping" is one example. Johnny also learns to distinguish between Sundays and weekdays by the fact that Daddy is home on Sundays. Past and future, however, are still hazy. Only a few two-year-olds use the past tense correctly.

In the second half of the second year belongs the important capacity for storing up memories which become the bedrock of later learning. Passages from Sophocles read to a baby (who had no other contact with Greek) from the time he was 15 until he was 18 months, for instance, made it possible for him at eight and a half years to memorize these passages after 317 repetitions while he required 435 repetitions to memorize passages that had not been read to him when he was a baby!

In his second year you can give Johnny some small sense of responsibility and can expect him to carry out a few simple commands. Now, too, you can begin to stimulate him to artistic appreciation through books and other intellectual materials, as the incident of the Greek passages from Sophocles shows, that are patently beyond him at that time.

Johnny in his third year copes with time more effectively than in his second year. Gradually, for instance, he acquires some notion of what is meant by a minute or a day. While at two years he typically uses the word "today," which reveals his sense of the present, he shows a sense of the future at two and a half when he uses "tomorrow" and of the past at age three when "yesterday" enters his vocabulary. A three-year-old girl, making deals through the use of "tomorrow" told her mother "If I go to sleep, let me wear my skirt with buttons *tomorrow.*" By now Johnny can describe in detail events that took place a month or two, and in some cases, even a year before.

Johnny also shows a new deftness in manipulation. A study of two- to four-year-olds revealed, for instance, that while two-year-olds, without fumbling or redirection, could remember the correct technique for opening boxes for three to eight days, four-year-olds could do so for seven to 20 days. This capacity, more than doubled at four, was steadily growing during the third year.

Other new aptitudes include a memory for colors and an increased memory span.

Mothers can take clues for child care from these changes. You can take advantage of the growing sense of present, past, and future in teaching Johnny to tell time. It is important, too, to be precise with him when you talk, especially about time. By using loose phrases like" Just a minute," which might mean many minutes, you only confuse him. Since he is likely to be entranced about hearing about his own unremembered past and to beg you to tell him about "When I was a baby," use the occasion to fill in memories for him and to give him a sense of their chronological order.

You can make his new deftness of manipulation the opportunity for teaching him simple household tasks. Because of his memory for color, you can ask him to pass the "red" pitcher or hand Daddy the "blue" tie or to know one traffic light from another. You can even begin encouraging him to paint or look at paintings. While his memory span is still very limited, nevertheless he is becoming more capable of paying attention to an idea or task and for the first time has staying power.

The fourth year, a time of imaginative expansiveness, ushers in a Johnny who is coming of age vocally and linguistically spurts forth the charged overflow of rapidly developing memory. His sense of time has improved sufficiently for him to tell you whether it is morning or afternoon and how old he is. He can count in sequence up to 10, usually beginning with a number higher than one. His rattling off in sequence of numbers, for instance, from three to 10, is in most cases a mere matter of rote memory, however. He does not really know the meaning of the numbers. If you show him several objects, he can count only three of them. He can, in all likelihood, remember four digits and the future tense has entered his vocabulary (if only as a means of referring to later today).

Now, because of the expansiveness that characterizes all aspects of his behavior, Johnny's memories pour out in stories, in endless, unrelenting narratives. If you and he look at two pictures and you ask him to point to one of them, he will point to both. He will not only point but will also hold forth. "This one is bigger. This one is smaller. This one is nice. This one is funny. This frame is dirty," he will say, rambling on and on. One four-year-old Johnny in every four will actually attempt to tell you what the picture means.

One thing leads to another and Johnny talks and talks. He makes many, many free associations as his memory runs rampant. His memory has developed to the point where any tiny detail is enough to set him off on a tangent of reminiscing.

More and more, since the end of his third year, Johnny has shown facility in understanding what is not present. Even so, he cannot yet easily imagine himself in a situation beyond his experience. If you ask him what he would do if he were separated from you in a crowded store, he is likely to be unable to answer. His capacity for generalizing, a process of drawing inductions from memories, is steadily growing, however. When asked what he must do when hungry, he replies not "I eat" as he did before, but simply "eat." He thus shows that he knows not only that he eats, but that everyone else does.

This fourth year is noteworthy, too, for the true onset of permanent memory. What permanent memories he has had before, as in the case of the 15-month-old who absorbed Greek passages, were chiefly unconscious ones.

These permanent memories, which first appear when an impression is made in the brain of sufficient depth to be retained through life and which are almost always precipitated by strong emotions, are the ones that will linger into old age when, as Galsworthy puts it, "Birth calls to Death." Among the first enduring memories that have been described to investigators: moving into a new house, meeting a playmate, having a picture taken, writing letters to Santa Claus on a frosted window pane, and of Indians coming to a village.

Parents during this fourth year need a world of imagination and patience to deal with Johnny's expansiveness and to protect him, too, against those not infrequent moments when he reveals chinks in the armor of his vaunting self-esteem.

Johnny's major fifth-year gain is an ability to remember *concepts*. If you were to have told four-year-old Johnny that one man is considered as good as the other, he might ingenuously have asked which man was the "one" and which the "other." At five, however, he understands that in speaking of "one man" and the "other" you are using general ideas and do not mean individual persons.

Now the child understands not only what is, but also what could be. Ask him what he must do before he crosses the street and he will tell you. "Wait for the light to change," or "Wait till the policeman signals," or something similar. Ask him what he would do if he lost his mother in a crowded store and he will answer, "Look for her," or "Get somebody to help me find her."

This recalls the story of how, when Jacqueline Kennedy was this age and became separated from her nurse in Central Park, she calmly went up to a policeman and gave him her home phone number. When a call had brought her mother to the scene, she announced that not she but her nurse had been lost.

This new ability to understand what could be and to remember as he looks ahead can make you feel more secure about your child's safety. You can now let him be more independent, more self-reliant. You can expect him to remember most instructions.

He should of course not be taxed beyond his capacities. Since he can still remember only four digits—the address for example of Aunt Ethel who lives at 2042 Main Street—he should not be scolded for not remembering a telephone number: 666-2264. Since he can remember sentences consisting of some eight syllables (or if he is very advanced from 13 to 35 syllables), he should not be expected to memorize a poem of some 60 syllables.

Johnny at five still recognizes more than he recalls (he will all his life; so do you and I). Presented with 10 pictures he has seen before, he is likely to recognize at least five of them. To recall these same five pictures, however, without the stimulation provided by seeing them again is very difficult. Yet Johnny has much less difficulty in recalling than he had two years earlier. He now remembers what is read to him. Without any prompting from you or any other external stimulation, he will say, "Pooh did so and so," or "Robin Hood said so and so." Books, radio, television, and records therefore can now have a greater influence on Johnny than they ever had. In what he remembers and recalls from the books read him are direct influences on his thinking, his behavior, and his conduct.

Johnny enters the first grade with a memory span for about five numerals. He can call back correctly a string of five numbers immediately after hearing them once. At this time he has the beginnings of organized, continuous memories rather than the piecemeal, episodic ones of the pre-school years. In later life he will therefore have much less difficulty in remembering his school years than his pre-school ones.

The impression Johnny makes at school will be strongly influenced by his memory, for children with memory deficiencies are poor readers, poor spellers, and poor speakers. Speaking badly, reading badly, spelling badly, they are mistaken for stupid children, irrespective of how intelligent they may be.

Do not, therefore, jump to grim conclusions about your child's intelligence merely on the basis of what seems to be memory slowness. Four-year-old Harriet just could not remember and retain words, just as some children with a stomach disorder cannot hold food. Although she understood what people said and could occasionally repeat one or two sounds accurately immediately after she heard them, never could she repeat more than two sounds.

Other children, able to repeat several sounds immediately after hearing them, are unable to do so again a few seconds later. Naturally, these children, using only one- and two-syllable words—no matter how high their IQ's—will have stunted vocabularies and appear stupid. It may be that their memory deficiencies can be improved through speech therapy.

Some children with low IQ's on the other hand, have outstanding memories linked with special ability in a particular field. One Japanese boy with a low IQ is a genius in painting.

In general, the more intelligent the child, the earlier will his memory develop and the more vivid and enduring will it become. While most children show the true onset of permanent memory in the fourth year, it has been recorded for some as early as 18 months and as late at the eighth year. Although the average child generally will not be able to retain and to act upon a past impression until his fourth year, a gifted boy of a year and a half was able to note that a canary he had seen in a room six weeks earlier was not there when he visited the room a second time.

Even a year-old gifted girl held and acted upon an impression after two months. Finding a cookie under her grandmother's sofa at 10 and a half months, she looked for it again when she returned two months later.

Though most five-year-olds are doing extremely well by remembering 35 syllables, Thomas Edison, before he was five, could remember in full the work songs of the lumbermen and canal men whom he met.

In studying the immediate memory of children of normal and subnormal intelligence, Beate Hermelin and N. O'Connor of Medical Research Council, Social Psychiatry Unit, Institute of Psychiatry, Maudsley Hospital, London, found that memory fades faster for the subnormal than for the normal child. The initial impression made on the child with a low IQ, these investigators also noted, is weaker than on the normal child. The low IQ children could not even recognize pictures which had previously been presented to them. Nor could they distinguish between words they had just heard and new words.

When Johnny fails to remember, you are perhaps all too likely to consider him either stupid or stubborn. Just because he doesn't remember instructions, he may seem a disciplinary problem. Poor behavior, however, may be due only to his not being ready to remember instruction. How "good" or how "bad" he is and how well he concentrates are markedly influenced by the stage of memory he has achieved.

You may perhaps feel that your child lacks stick-to-itiveness and doesn't "try." Not "trying," however, might be interpreted as not being ready to try. The average duration of sustained attention, for instance, of children presented with a jack-in-the-box and asked to watch it until it was opened was eight seconds at three and four years, about 17 seconds at five, and about 28 seconds at six.

Binet, the famous intelligence tester, moreover, has evaluated the memory span for digits as the means of measuring not only digits, but even more importantly as a gauge of the child's capacity for effort. You can judge how limited this capacity is in the pre-school years from the fact that Johnny doesn't remember even as many as four digits until somewhere between his fourth and fifth years. How can he be reasonably expected to put forth any sustained effort before then? As, however, his memory span for digits increases to five digits between the sixth and eighth years, six digits between ages nine and 12, and seven digits beyond 12, more and more concentration can be expected of him.

Speech also is a gauge of Johnny's developing memory. Until his memory is ready, he does not begin to speak. His first words come only after he has made appropriate connections between the objects, events, and people he sees and hears and the words that represent them. Each time you prepare to take Johnny out, you may say "Go bye-bye." Before he can name that for himself, he must learn to understand the meaning of the concept of being taken out of the house. He must make a generalization from his memories of a number of particular experiences in which he was taken out of doors. It actually takes some two to seven months of remembering from the toddler's first hearing of a word or phrase—"go bye-bye" or any other—until his first meaningful utterance of it.

During this time when appropriate connections are made and memory leads to speech, the child can learn a second language as easily as a first. Doing so now, he will master the second language without an accent and will be able to think in it. If, however, as Dr. Wilder Penfield of McGill University in Montreal has shown, he doesn't acquire the second language until five or six, likely he will have an accent and will find it difficult to think in the language, even though he will still grasp it more readily than would an older person.

Some children are late speakers because their memories are not sufficiently developed for them to recognize, identify, or remember the connections between a sound and what the sound means. Four-year-old Anne, for instance, failed to see any connection between the ringing of the doorbell and the fact that her grandfather was calling to take her for a walk, a daily ritual. She could hear, but, when the bell rang, she acted as though she were deaf. Such a child is said to have no memory for audible symbols.

Children like three-year-old Joseph talk late because of a poor memory for sounds. Words and the sounds of which they are composed just passed him by, making no impression. He was not deaf, but acted as though he were. He did not learn to speak until his memory for sounds was improved through speech therapy.

Parents can do much. Since Johnny's memory can be no better than the memory "input," to use the word currently in vogue in memory research, parents should fill his world with the stimulation of ideas, music, books, radio, television, and animated conversation. Given stimulation, even Hermelin's and O'Connor's subnormal children improved. These children, for instance, remembered nouns that were accompanied by pictures better than words without visual aids. Pictures following a presentation of corresponding words, however, were recognized better than the words themselves.

Most children—average and gifted as well as slow—remember what they see longer than what they hear and therefore respond well to having words reinforced by pictures. This depends, however, on whether the child is primarily eye-minded or ear-minded.

Simple tests given either at private psychological laboratories or at those connected with colleges or universities will determine the type. The Knox Cube test measures transient visual memory; the Digit Span, transient auditory memory. Testing can take place even before the child knows how to read, for the printed word can always be replaced by pictures.

As the well-known memory expert Bruno Furst points out, "Testing for type is especially important for children who are below average in reading.

writing, or spelling. The help these children need depends largely on the type to which they belong."

If Johnny is eye-minded, you can help him with his reading by printing certain words in exaggeratedly large size. If he is ear-minded, you can teach him words by appealing to his sense of rhyme and rhythm. The strongest approach to his memory, however, consists of the triple impact of eye, ear, and speech. When what is seen and heard is put into speech, the memory becomes more lasting than when it remains simply an appeal to the eye or to the ear.

Hardly any two children remember the same objects with equal ease. One shows an outstanding memory for numbers, another for maps or architecture, while a third amazes everybody by quoting long passages of prose or poetry by heart. What Johnny remembers best gives you a clue to his interests, his inclinations, and his abilities. Careful attention to each of these may help you to steer him toward his future career. (Were our educational system more memory-conscious, such observations of memory would play a crucial role in vocational guidance.)

Retention is important, since it is upon retention that school success is largely based. Recitation is an excellent aid to retention, for the more opportunities you give Johnny to rehearse aloud what he reads, the more certain will he become of his knowledge, the fewer blunders and erroneous recalls will he make, and the greater will be his ability to organize his material in usable form. Poems are learned more effectively when they are read from beginning to end than when verses are learned separately and later connected. Retention is improved, too, particularly for ear-minded children, when words, names, and dates to be learned are cast into verse form. The strongest spur to retention, however, is the deliberate intent to memorize.

More intelligent children naturally memorize more easily than less intelligent ones. But for all children, bright as well as slow, memorizing is impeded by boredom, worry, a scolding, or daydreaming. For all, too, memorizing has marked limits, for, as Dr. Arthur I. Gates of Columbia University's Teachers' College discovered by subjecting beginning school children for three months to long practice with numbers, memorizing did not even permanently strengthen their memories for numbers. Nor, of course, did this memorizing in one field lead to improved memory in any other.

James V. McConnell, professor of psychology at the University of Michigan and the chief experimenter on the RNA molecule and memory transfer, suggests that the child of the future may be endowed with memory and knowledge that is transmitted to him by extracting RNA from the brains of his parents and other adults of a preceding generation. For the present, however, the ancients who named Memoria "the mother of the muses" and said "we know as much as we hold in memory," still have the answer. Since Johnny knows as much as he "holds in memory," his memory becomes an accessible tool for understanding and molding him.

**Suggested Readings for
Chapter 2**

Bandura, A. & Walters, R. H. *Social learning and personality development.* New York: Holt, Rinehart and Winston, 1963. An examination of socialization and personality development through the process of imitation and other learning theory principles.

Goldfried, Marvin R. & Merbaum, Michael (Eds.) *Behavior change through self-control.* New York: Holt, Rinehart and Winston, 1972. This volume presents classic articles in the area of self-control, emphasizing theory and therapeutic applications.

Hilgard, E. R. & Bower, G. H. *Theories of learning.* (3d ed.) New York: Appleton-Century-Crofts, 1966. A broad and scholarly survey of contemporary theories of learning. New advances in neurophysiology and mathematical learning theories are also examined.

Skinner, B. F. *Walden two.* New York: The Macmillan Company, 1948. An interesting and controversial novel about a utopia designed on the basis of operant conditioning principles.

Voeks, V. *On becoming an educated person.* (2d ed.) Philadelphia: Saunders, 1964. A practical application of learning theory to personal problems in developing good study skills and exam-taking attitudes.

Discussion Questions

1. Control is often considered to be the opposite of freedom. How is self-control related to personal freedom?

2. Learning traditionally has been an area of central concern to psychologists. Why is it of such importance that we understand principles of learning?

3. In what ways does our system of education employ principles of learning? In what ways does it seem to ignore these principles?

4. How can an understanding of learning and memory help you to be a better parent?

Chapter 3

Intelligence

Over the years, a number of different theories about the nature of intelligence have been formulated. Each has received some support, although not enough to determine which is the most adequate in explaining intelligence. One theory suggests that there is a general amount of intelligence, called the "g factor"; the more this "g factor" that people possess, the smarter they are. This "g factor" was originally conceived in the first decade of this century by a psychologist named Charles Spearman. Spearman developed his theory through the use of a sophisticated correlational technique called factor analysis. By intercorrelating many different intellectual abilities, Spearman discovered that a "g factor" seemed to underlie most of these abilities. Simply stated, this general theory of intelligence postulates that there is one major factor (g) which characterizes human intelligence. Furthermore, he found that the kinds of tests which characterize this factor were those that involved reasoning and judgment. Many years later another scientist by the name of Lewis Thurstone developed statistical procedures which were more sophisticated than Spearman's. Thurstone further reinforced Spearman's ideas about intelligence and added about a dozen primary abilities (verbal comprehension, word fluency, number space, reasoning, etc.) which had been subsumed under the general heading of this "g factor."

This one-factor theory is at odds with another approach which holds that there are a number of primary abilities, such as mathematical ability, verbal ability, and so on which cannot be put under one general heading of intelligence. A person can be quite well endowed with one of these primary abilities without necessarily being as competent in areas which require other primary abilities. In many ways these two theories are not as radically different as they might seem at first glance, since both accept the fact that there are general and specific types of intelligence. They do differ, however, in terms of the relative importance of each. Recent theories have subdivided primary abilities to such an extent that over a hundred such components of intelligence have been identified. Some recent original and interesting work has attempted to identify two major types of intelligence. One type, called fluid intelligence, refers to a general, untrained kind of intelligence; it is due largely to physiological, probably inherited processes and seems to resemble the g factor very closely. The other major type of intelligence is called crystallized intelligence; it is more dependent on the environment and on specific learning experiences. A frequent question which has considerable social significance is whether intelligence is inherited or acquired. Recent evidence appears to indicate that fluid intelligence is predominately inherited and that crystallized intelligence is predominately acquired. This, in fact, is consistent with the general resolution of most heredity–environment controversies. Both factors play a role in determining most behavior, and it is nearly impossible to separate the relative contributions of each.

While it has been proven extremely difficult to define intelligence, to understand its basic structure, and to separate it from related traits like creativity, psychologists have not been deterred from constructing innumerable tests of intelligence. Some of these are carefully assembled, well standardized tests which present a clear picture of the subject's full range of intellectual abilities. Others are tests hastily thrown together which represent the author's conception of intelligence and relate to intelligence only in some incidental way. Even among the many established and reputable tests of intelligence, form and content differ widely from test to test. A few tests require individual administration while a larger number, in order to economize on time, are constructed for group administration. The tester can be much more sensitive to some of the idiosyncratic factors that influence test scores in the individual administration situation, but as a general rule the scores should be comparable. However, where tests are administered for other than routine purposes—to a distractable child, an underachiever, or a child from a culturally different background—idiosyncratic features are more likely to be present. In these cases the flexibility of the individual intelligence test makes it a far better choice. Some tests are constructed to emphasize verbal skills and abilities, whereas others place more weight on nonverbal skills, such as spatial relations, puzzle solving, and ability with numbers. Since these skills are unevenly distributed among people, an individual's IQ score will depend, at least partially, on the nature of the particular test he has taken. While it is common in an educational setting to hear teachers, parents, or students ask about a particular student's IQ, it is rare to hear any questions raised about the particular test that was used. This slight sign of sophistication would be of much help in interpreting the score, if it were accompanied by a knowledge of the properties of the various tests.

The article by David C. McClelland deals with many serious issues which underlie the intelligence test movement. As McClelland perceptively points out, intelligence testing has become extraordinarily widespread and furthermore has gained enormous power in determining the educational fate of many students. In this article McClelland questions many of the almost sacred notions which the advocates of intelligence testing have assumed to be valid. He presents alternative interpretations of research evidence and in general is not enthusiastically supportive of the use of intelligence tests in making crucial educational decisions.

The article by Mary Jo Bane and Christopher Jencks is an extension and an elaboration of McClelland's point of view. Bane and Jencks highlight five myths about IQ and offer some hard observations about the looseness of thinking that goes into the interpretation of intelligence test material. One of the major myths they attempt to discredit is that the IQ is overwhelmingly a function of heredity or genetic endowment. This is a controversy that has existed in psychology for many years but was more recently brought to the forefront by the controversial claim of Arthur Jensen that genes account for an overwhelmingly significant percentage of variation in children's intelligence test performance. This very complicated statistical, theoretical, and empirical question is assessed by Bane and Jencks, who feel that Jensen overestimates the importance of genetic endowment in intelligence test performance. This paper is a refreshing antidote to some of the more pompous claims of professional psychologists who are wedded to IQ testing without sufficient awareness of recent experimental evidence questioning their uncritical use.

Perhaps the most widely used and well established of the individual intelligence tests is the series developed by David Wechsler. He has constructed separate forms for the preschool child (4–6 years of age), the school-age child (5–15 years of age), and the adult (16 and older). All these tests yield separate verbal and performance IQs as well as a full-scale IQ. For this reason, they provide a great deal more information about a person's intellectual functioning than a raw summary number. In his article, Wechsler discusses a number of issues about the development and interpretation of the IQ test, and he relates this to recent developments concerning the use of such tests with people from varying cultural groups. It is important to recognize that the IQ does not purport to measure innate potential. Although it will be relatively stable if the person remains in stable circumstances, it is quite responsive to actual changes in the person's functioning. If an individual does poorly on a test because his cultural background has not prepared him for such an examination, it is not unlikely that he is also poorly prepared to function in school, which requires similar skills. If he can become better prepared, through any number of training experiences, his school work will improve dramatically and so should his IQ. Perhaps an appreciation of this would make the IQ of more value to the teacher whose misinterpretations of it can harm the students by placing them in inappropriate groupings.

The major contributions to our culture have not come, as a general rule, from displays of raw intellectual power alone, but rather from the creative use of the talents of the contributor. Because of this, there has recently been a great deal of interest in the area of creativity. Some psychologists feel that creativity and intelligence are separate and independent. Others insist they are not and maintain that the creative person is always intelligent. Wallach and Kogan describe a study in which they successfully developed separate measures of intelligence and creativity. They discuss the characteristics of children with varying combinations of the two factors, and they conclude by suggesting that children who score high in intelligence and low in creativity, or vice versa, suffer from motivational difficulties that would be responsive to proper teaching. If this is true, and if proper teaching could make these children score high in both qualities, which has not yet been demonstrated, then one must wonder about the extent to which these qualities are truly independent.

"In this sense the test becomes an instrument for those in power to screen out those who do not know the right words and who are therefore 'unqualified' to be lawyers in the minds of those who control such things."

This article by David C. McClelland studies some of the potential mis-uses of testing. Tests are being used all over the world as predictors of academic success and vocational excellence although the claims for the value of testing are sometimes outrageous. McClelland questions many of the assumptions which underlie the testing movement and, being a very reputable and gifted psychologist, his words are thoughtful and provocative.

Psychology has one great practical success to its credit in the twentieth century—namely the intelligence testing movement. Many tests have been devised which predict success in school with remarkable regularity. Literally tens of thousands of validity coefficients have been calculated, demonstrating that those who score higher on aptitude or intelligence tests usually do better in their school work. Selecting, at random, a finding which is quite typical for the United States, I recently observed in a longitudinal study to be reported by Costa that Kuhlman-Anderson I.Q. scores obtained in the sixth grade correlated 0.59 with twelfth-grade rank in class. In other words knowing how a child scores on an intelligence test when he is eleven or twelve years old enables you to predict fairly accurately how well he will be doing in school some six or seven years later. Rank in class at graduation from secondary school in turn predicts whether he can go on to the university and how good a university he will get into. As a consequence, knowing a person's intelligence-test score or scholastic-aptitude-test score has become a matter of great importance in the United States, not only to admissions officers who use it to pick people for college but also to businesses and civil service commissions who use it to decide who is "bright enough" to be a policeman, a social worker or a fireman.

Testing has therefore become big business. The Educational Testing Service which gives the Scholastic Aptitude Test used by most of the better-known colleges and universities in the United States employs around two thousand people and has a large plant spread over hundreds of acres in Princeton, New Jersey. Thousands of young people pay to take its tests annually to see if they are qualified to get into the college of their choice. The testing technology has been so sold to the American public that only in a few of the more "backward" parts of the society is it not used in the schools or businesses or civil service. And of course it is spreading fast to the rest of the world, which is beginning to discover the utility of tests for picking those who will do well in school.

To be sure, the testers themselves loudly insist that there are other important human qualities besides the ability to take scholastic aptitude tests, but as Wing and Wallach have shown, admissions officers may believe they take these other qualities into account but in fact their selection decisions can be almost perfectly predicted by aptitude-test scores alone. The desire to select more "intelligent" people for schooling or for almost any occupation proves overpowering. It quickly reduces other qualifications to insignificance.

While the intelligence-testing movement in the United States has been moving on from one triumph to the next, some questions have been raised about its theoretical underpinnings, both by scholars and by policy makers who wonder if its growing power over people's lives is justified. One difficulty with tests has long been known but little commented on perhaps because its seriousness has not been fully appreciated. It is very simply that if academic achievement tests are taken seriously as measures of real competence, then the *quality* of education does not seem to contribute to improving competence. Back in the 1930's in the United States, a number of private schools tried to improve the quality of their education as part of what was then known as the "progressive education movement." Standardized scholastic achievement tests were used to evaluate the effects of this supposedly improved education as compared with more traditional teaching.

By and large no effects of the supposedly higher-quality education could be discovered in the test scores. The educators felt they were doing a better job but the test scores did not indicate that they were. The same findings has turned up again and again since that time. Certain colleges in the United States are widely acknowledged to be better than other colleges—in the sense that they have better faculties, more books in the library, higher endowments, better laboratory facilities, and so forth. Yet repeated studies as summarized by Jacob have failed to show any test-score differences attributable to the better education supposedly obtained in the elite colleges. If the graduates of those colleges perform better on achievement tests, it is because they scored higher on them at entrance to college, not because they received a better education subsequently.

Most recently in a very important social document on equality of educational opportunity, Coleman again showed that the *quality* of education (here in secondary school) seemed to have very little effect on the academic achievement test scores of children. In other words the children who went to poor schools with poorly trained teachers, dilapidated buildings, and crowded classrooms did no worse on the tests than children who went to excellent, well-equipped schools with low teacher-pupil ratios, once one had corrected for the initial differences in intelligence and social background of the pupils attending the two types of schools. In other words what the test results seem to have shown over and over again is that quality of education makes no difference in improving competence.

What does make a difference are the attributes of the people getting the education—their intelligence, their social characteristics and so forth. Why then should citizens spend so much money trying to improve education? Why should educational psychologists be trying to find better ways of educating pupils? Why is money wasted on conferences to try to find ways of improving education —if in fact the data clearly show that educational variations have very little effect on academic achievement, which in turn is considered the main measure of competence for life's tasks?

One reason is that we keep suspecting that the educators may be right in continuing to think that the quality of education does make a difference. It may be the psychological testers who are wrong: their tests may simply not be adequate measures of the competence which better education produces. In fact there may even be a built-in theoretical reason why most existing tests are inadequate measures of variations in the quality of education. Most testers have worked hard to create tests which are reliable—that is, which will give the same score when the same individual is tested again. An instrument which is designed to be very reliable may not be very sensitive to changes that have actually taken place in the person through education.

But this theoretical problem has never shaken the self-confidence of the testing movement. It has continued to roll on like a juggernaut overwhelming all such doubts.

When many psychologists began to examine really seriously for the first time the assumptions on which the intelligence testing movement had been built, it took them no time at all to discover that many intelligence tests had a built-in middle-class bias. The vocabulary used in the tests was so-called "standard English," not the dialect spoken in many ghetto communities. So the children from these communities often did not even understand the instructions for the tests, let alone the words they were supposed to identify which were not part of the vocabulary in common use in their community. Correct answers to questions also often assume a standard midddle-class way of life. For example a child is asked on an intelligence test, "What would you do if you were sent to the store by your mother to buy something and you found the store didn't have it?" The "intelligent" or correct answer is supposed to be that you would go to another store to see if they had it. However this is certainly not an intelligent answer for a ghetto child who is under strict orders from his mother to come straight home from the store because she is afraid he might be robbed or beaten if he strayed too far from familiar territory. Yet if he says he would go home he is judged by the testers to be less intelligent. It is also easy to see from these examples why there is a correlation between test performance and later performance in school because the teacher, as a representative of standard middle-class culture, will expect the same language and types of behavior as the person who made up the so-called intelligence test. The teacher will either not understand the dialect that is used in class or will give the child a lower mark for using "bad" language and the ghetto child will before long go through life stigmatized as being less intelligent and a poor student.

Looking at the problem this way forced psychologists to consider seriously another possible explanation for many of the existing correlations between intelligence test scores, doing well in school, and holding down higher-status jobs later in life. Those who control not only economic and social opportunities but also what language and values are the standards by which others will be judged, may in fact be able to use test scores to maintain their power. All one needs to assume is that more powerful families are in a much better position to help their children get higher-status jobs: they know the right people; they can send their children to the right schools; they can use their influence to get them jobs directly. So it turns out that people in higher-status jobs score higher on so-called intelligence tests.

But where is the direct evidence that the higher score on the test in fact indicated that the person was better able to do the higher-status job? As every psychologist knows, correlation does not mean causation. It doesn't follow that because professionals score higher than laborers on certain tests that it is the ability to perform those particular tests which enabled them to be professionals rather than laborers. The reason why people have assumed that causation was involved is that the test scores were supposed to indicate how intelligent the person was, and it seems reasonable to assume that being a professional requires more of something called intelligence than being a laborer does. However it is by no means as self-evident as it once was that these test scores measure the kind of intelligence implied by the logic of this argument. They may simply indicate that the person has the *credentials* that the power elite insists that he must have in order to hold a higher-status job. The connection between test performance and job performance may well be extrinsic rather than intrinsic. That is, being able to use the right words may have nothing to do intrinsically with whether a person is a cleverer lawyer, but those in power in a society simply decree that a person cannot be a lawyer unless he uses the correct vocabulary. In this sense the test becomes an instrument for those in power to screen out those who do not know the right words and who are therefore "unqualified" to be lawyers in the minds of those who control such things. Now such a selection procedure may be justifiable in one way or another but it does serve to make clear that the central issue is who is in power and controlling resources, not who is genetically inferior in intelligence.

American psychologists have long accepted without question Professor Terman's conclusion that his gifted children (those with higher intelligence test scores) grew up to be more successful occupationally, maritally, and socially than those of average intelligence and that they showed fewer "morally deviant" forms of psychopathology such as alcoholism or homosexuality. Yet the power analysis just carried out suggests that neither Professor Terman nor anyone else has as yet brought forward conclusive evidence that it is giftedness per se as he measured it that is responsible for these happier life outcomes. For his gifted children were also drawn very disproportionately from the ranks of the educated, the wealthy, and the powerful. This means that they had not only a better chance to acquire the characteristics measured in the test but also to be happier (since they had more money) and also to have access to higher occupations and better social standing. Maybe test scores measuring "giftedness" are simply another symptom of their generally more favorable social status.

"Parents' and teachers' anxieties have been further intensified as a result of claims that IQ scores are largely determined by heredity."

The public at large has many stereotypes about the IQ. Some of the more prominent of these myths are discussed in this article by Bane and Jencks and their validity carefully examined. As you will see, many of these myths are quite controversial and have raised commotions not only in the public's mind but also in professional quarters. The authors use research evidence to clarify some of the issues in this interesting and complicated area.

Standard IQ tests purport to measure "intelligence," which is widely viewed as the key to adult success. As a result, children with low IQ scores* are the subject of anxious solicitude from their parents, while groups that test badly, notably blacks, are constantly on the defensive. This is doubly true when, as usually happens, those who do poorly on IQ tests also do poorly on school achievement tests that measure things like reading comprehension and arithmetic skills.

Parents' and teachers' anxieties have been further intensified as a result of claims that IQ scores are largely determined by heredity. If an individual's genes determine his IQ, and if IQ then determines his chances of adult success, it is a short step to the conclusion that there is nothing he can do to improve his prospects. Moreover, if life chances are determined at birth, many recent efforts at social reform have obviously been doomed from the start.

The controversy over IQ and achievement tests has become so bitter that it is almost impossible to discuss the subject rationally. Neither social scientists nor laymen seem to have much interest in the actual facts, which are extremely complex. The best currently available evidence suggests that:

* An intelligence quotient is computed by ascertaining a person's mental age on the basis of a standardized intelligence test, and multiplying the result by 100. That result is then divided by the person's chronological age, to yield the IQ. Thus, the average IQ of the population is (and arithmetically must be) 100. About one person in six has an IQ under 85, and about one in six has an IQ over 115. About one in forty is under 70, and about one in forty is over 130.

▶ IQ tests measure only one rather limited variety of intelligence, namely the kind that schools (and psychologists) value. Scores on the tests show remarkably little relationship to performance in most adult roles. People with high scores do a little better in most jobs than people with low scores, and they earn somewhat more money, but the differences are suprisingly small.

▶ The poor are seldom poor because they have low IQ scores, low reading scores, low arithmetic scores, or bad genes. They are poor because they either cannot work, cannot find adequately paying jobs, or cannot keep such jobs. This has very little to do with their test scores.

▶ Claims that "IQ scores are 80 percent hereditary" appear to be greatly exaggerated. Test results depend almost as much on variations in children's environments as on variations in their genes.

▶ While differences in the environments that children grow up in explain much of the variation in their test scores, differences in their school experiences appear to play a relatively minor role. But even socioeconomic background has a quite modest impact on test scores. Many factors that influence the scores seem to be unrelated to either school quality or parental status. At present, nobody has a clear idea what these factors are, how they work, or what we can do about them.

▶ If school quality has a modest effect on adult test scores, and if test scores then have a modest effect on economic success, school reforms aimed at teaching basic cognitive skills are likely to have minuscule effects on students' future earning power.

Each of these conclusions contradicts a commonly accepted myth about IQ.

Myth 1: IQ Tests Are the Best Measure of Human Intelligence

When asked whether IQ tests really measure "intelligence," psychologists are fond of saying that this is a meaningless question. They simply define intelligence as "whatever IQ tests measure." This is rather like Humpty-Dumpty, for whom words meant whatever he wanted them to mean, and it was just a question of who was to be master. The trouble is that the psychologists are not the masters of language, and they cannot assign arbitrary meanings to words without causing all kinds of confusion. In the real world, people cannot use a term like intelligence without assuming that it means many different things at once—all very important. Those who claim that "intelligence is what intelligence tests measure" ought logically to assume, for example, that "intelligence is of no more consequence in human affairs than whatever intelligence tests measure." But people do not think this way. Having said that "intelligence is what IQ tests measure," psychologists always end up assuming that what IQ tests measure must be important, because "intelligence" is important. This road leads through the looking glass.

What, then, does the trem "intelligence" really mean? For most people, it includes all the mental abilities required to solve whatever theoretical or practical problems they happen to think important. At one moment intelligence is the ability to unravel French syntax. At another it is the intuition required to understand what ails a neurotic friend. At still another it is the capacity to anticipate future demands for hog bristles. We know from experience that these skills are only loosely related to one another. People who are "intelligent" in one context often are remarkably "stupid" in another. Thus, in weighing the value of IQ tests, one must ask exactly what *kinds* of intelligence they really measure and what kinds they do not measure.

The evidence we have reviewed suggests that IQ tests are quite good at measuring the kinds of intelligence needed to do school work. Students who do well on IQ tests are quite likely to get good grades in school. They are also likely to stay in school longer than average. But the evidence also suggests that IQ tests are *not* very good at measuring the skills required to succeed in most kinds of adult work.

Myth 2: The Poor Are Poor Because They Have Low IQs.
Those with High IQs End up in Well-Paid Jobs

The fact is that people who do well on IQ and achievement tests do not perform much better than average in most jobs. Nor do they earn much more than the average. There have been more than a hundred studies of the relationship between IQ and people's performance on different jobs, using a wide variety of techniques for rating performance. In general, differences in IQ account for less than 10 percent of the variation in actual job performance. In many situations, there is no relationship at all between a man's IQ and how competent he is at his job. IQ also plays a modest role in determining income, explaining only about 12 percent of the variation. Thus, 88 percent of the variation in income is unrelated to IQ.

Nor do IQ differences account for much of the economic gap between blacks and whites. Phillips Cutright of the University of Indiana has conducted an extensive investigation of blacks who were examined by the Selective Service System in 1952. These men all took the Armed Forces Qualification Test, which measures much the same thing as an IQ test. In 1962, the average black in this sample earned 43 percent less than the average white. Blacks with AFQT scores as high as the average white's earned 32 percent less than the average white. Equalizing black and white test scores therefore reduced the income gap by about a quarter. Three quarters of the gap had nothing to do with test scores. This same pattern holds for whites born into working-class and middle-class families. Whites with middle-class parents earn more than whites with working-class parents, but only 25–35 percent of the gap is traceable to test-score differences between the two groups.

None of this means that a child with a high IQ has no economic advantage over a child with a low IQ, nor that a child with high reading and math scores has no economic advantage over a child with low scores. It just means that the economic effect is likely to be much smaller than anxious parents or educational reformers expect. Among white males, those who score in the top fifth on standardized tests appear to earn about a third more than the national average. Those who score in the bottom fifth earn about two-thirds of the national average. These differences are by no means trivial. But they do not look very impressive when we recall that the best paid fifth of all workers earns six or seven times as much as the worst paid fifth. Most of that gap has nothing to do with test scores, and cannot be eliminated by equalizing test scores.

How can this be? We know that test scores play a significant role in determining school grades, in determining how long students stay in school, and in determining what kinds of credentials they eventually earn. We also know that credentials play a significant role in determining what occupations men enter. Occupations, in turn, have a significant effect on earnings. But at each stage in this process there are many exceptions, and the cumulative result is that exceptions are almost commonplace. A significant number of students with relatively low test scores earn college degrees, for example. In addition, a significant number of individuals without college degrees enter well-paid occupations, especially in business. Finally, people in relatively low-status occupations (such as plumbers and electricians) often earn more than professionals (think of teachers and clergymen). Overall, then, there are a lot of people with rather low test scores who nonetheless make above-average incomes, and a lot of people with high IQs but below-average incomes.

The limited importance of test scores is also clear if we look at the really poor—those who have to get by on less than half the national average. Nearly half of all poor families have no earner at all, either because they are too old, because they are headed by a woman with young children, or because the father is sick, alcoholic, mentally ill, or otherwise incapacitated. These problems are a bit more common among people with low IQs, but that is not the primary explanation for any of them.

This does not mean that financial success depends primarily on the socioeconomic background, as many liberals and radicals seem to believe. Socioeconomic background has about the same influence as IQ on how much schooling a person gets, on the kind of occupation he enters, and on how much money he makes. Thus we can say that *neither* socioeconomic background *nor* IQ explains much of the variation in adult occupational status or income. Most of the economic inequality among adults is due to other factors.

Unfortunately, we do not know enough to identify with much precision the other factors leading to economic success. All we can do is suggest their complexity. First, there is a wide variety of skills that have little or no connection with IQ but have a strong relationship to success in some specialized field. The ability to hit a ball thrown at high speed is extremely valuable, if you happen to be a professional baseball player. The ability to walk along a narrow steel beam 600 feet above the ground without losing your nerve is also very valuable, if you happen to be a construction worker. In addition, many personality traits have substantial cash value in certain contexts. A man who is good at figuring out what his boss wants, or good at getting his subordinates to understand and do what he wants, is at a great premium in almost any large hierarchical organization. While these talents are doubtless related to IQ, the connection is obviously very loose. Similarly, a person who inspires confidence is likely to do well regardless of whether he is a doctor, a clergyman, a small businessman, or a Mafioso, and inspiring confidence depends as much on manner as on mental abilities.

Finally, there is the matter of luck. America is full of gamblers, some of whom strike it rich while others lose hard-earned assets. One man's farm has oil on it, while another man's cattle get hoof-and-mouth disease. One man backs a "mad inventor" and ends up owning a big piece of Polaroid, while another backs a mad inventor and ends up owning a piece of worthless paper. We cannot say much about the relative importance of these factors, but when it comes to making a dollar, IQ is clearly only a small part of a big, complicated picture.

Myth 3: Your IQ Is Overwhelmingly Determined by Your Genetic Endowment

Over the past decade, an enormous number of school reform programs have attempted to raise the scores of those who do poorly on standardized tests. These programs have involved preschool education, curriculum development, teacher training, compensatory education, administrative reorganization, and many other innovations. None appears to have produced the promised results on a permanent basis. This has led many people to the conclusion that variations in IQ scores must reflect innate genetic differences between individuals and groups. This is a logical non sequitur. But more important, the theory that IQ scores are determined at the moment of conception is not supported by the evidence. Genes clearly have a significant influence on IQ and school achievement scores, but so does environment. The reason reform programs have failed to improve test scores is not that the environment is irrelevant but that the reforms have not altered the most important features of the environment.

Much of the continuing furor over IQ scores derives from Arthur Jensen's controversial claim that genes "explain" something like 80 percent of the variation in children's performance on IQ tests. We have reviewed the same evidence as Jensen, and while it certainly shows that genes have *some* effect on IQ, we believe that his 80 percent estimate is much too high. The details of the argument are extremely complicated, but the basic reasons that Jensen overestimated the role of heredity and underestimated the role of environment are fairly easy to understand.

First, Jensen estimated the influence of genes on IQ scores largely by using data from studies of twins. Some of these studies dealt with identical twins who had been separated early in life and brought up by different parents. Identical twins have exactly the same genes. When they are brought up in different environments, all differences between them can be attributed to the effects of their environments.

Other studies compared identical twins who had been reared together with fraternal twins who had been reared together. Fraternal twins have only about half their genes in common; identical twins have all their genes in common. Thus if identical twins were no more alike on IQ tests than fraternal twins, we would have to conclude that genetic resemblance did not affect the children's test scores. But identical twins are in fact considerably more alike than fraternal twins, so it seems reasonable to suppose that genes have a significant effect on test scores. (Identical twins may also be treated somewhat more alike than fraternal twins, but the effect of this appears to be small.)

It is perfectly legitimate to use twin studies to estimate the relative influence of heredity and environment on test scores. But we can also estimate the effects of environment by measuring the degree of resemblance between adopted children reared in the same home. When we do this, environment appears to have somewhat more effect than it does in twin studies, while genes appear to have somewhat less effect. No one has ever offered a good explanation for this discrepancy, but that does not justify ignoring it. The most reasonable assumption is that the true effect of heredity is somewhat less than that suggested by twin studies but somewhat more than that suggested by studies of unrelated children in the same home.

A second difficulty with Jensen's estimate is that it is based on twin studies in England as well as in the United States. When we separate the American and

English studies, we find that genetic factors appear to be more important in England than in America. This suggests that children's environments are more varied in the United States than they are in England. Other evidence, as well as common-sense observation of the two cultures, supports this interpretation. Consequently, when Jensen pools English and American data to arrive at his estimate of the effects of genes on IQ scores, he overestimates the relative importance of genes in America and underestimates their importance in England.

A third problem: Jensen assumes that the effects of genes and those of environment are completely independent of one another. In fact, since parents with favorable genes tend to have above-average cognitive skills, they tend to provide their children with unusually rich home environments. Our calculations suggest that this double advantage accounts for about a fifth of the variation in IQ scores.

After correcting all these biases, our best estimate is that genes explain 45 rather than 80 percent of the variation in IQ scores in contemporary America. This 45 percent estimate could easily be off by 10 percent either way, and it might conceivably be off by as much as 20 percent either way. The estimate would change if the range of environments were to increase or decrease for any reason. Genes are relatively more important in small homogeneous communities, where children's environments are relatively similar, than in America as a whole. By the same token, genes are relatively less important among groups whose environments are unusually diverse. If, for example, there were a sharp increase in the number of children suffering from acute malnutrition, or if large numbers of children were excluded from schools, environmental inequality would increase, and the relative importance of genes in determining IQ scores would decrease.

While genes probably account for something like 45 percent of the variation in IQ scores, it does not follow that genetic differences in actual learning capacity account for anything like this much variation. Genes influence test scores in two quite different ways. First, they influence what an individual learns from a given environment. Placed in front of the same TV program, one child may remember more of what he sees than another. Confronted with subtraction, one child may "catch on" faster than another. These differences derive partly from genetically based differences in learning capacity. In addition, however, genes can influence the environments to which people are exposed. Imagine a nation that refuses to send children with red hair to school. Under these circumstances having genes that cause red hair will lower your reading scores. This does not tell us that children with red hair cannot learn to read. It tells us only that in this particular situation there is a socially imposed relationship between genes and opportunities to learn. In America, the genes that affect skin color have an indirect influence on an individual's opportunities and incentives to learn many skills. So too hereditary appearance and athletic ability influence a youngster's chance of getting into many colleges, and thus affect his or her later test scores.

Beyond all that, a person's genes may influence his actual learning capacity, which may then affect his opportunities and incentives to learn. If an individual has low test scores for genetic reasons, he may be assigned to a "slow" class where he learns less. Or he may be excluded from college. Such practices tend to widen the initial test score gap between the genetically advantaged and the genetically disadvantaged. The resulting inequality is thus due *both* to genes *and* to environment. Yet conventional methods of estimating heritability impute the entire difference to genes.

When we say that genes "explain" 45 percent of the variation in test scores, we are talking about their overall effect, including their effect both on the capacity to learn and on opportunities and incentives to learn. No one has yet devised a method for separating these two effects. But if opportunities and incentives to learn were absolutely equal, genetically determined differences in learning capacity would account for considerably less than 45 percent of the variation in IQ scores.

Myth 4: The Main Reason Black Children and Poor White Children Have Low IQ Scores Is That They Have "Bad" Genes

Children from poor families tend to get lower scores on both IQ and school achievement tests than children from middle-class families. This difference is apparent when children enter school, and it does not seem to change much as children get older. Many liberals argue that the reason poor children do badly on these tests is that the tests are biased. Most of the tests contain items that are culturally loaded, in the sense that they presume familiarity with certain objects or assume the correctness of certain attitudes. The bias in these items always appears to favor children from middle-class backgrounds. Yet when psychologists have examined children's answers to these "loaded" items, they have not found that poor children did particularly badly on them. Nor have they found that eliminating such items from tests reduced the disparity in overall performance between poor and middle-class children. Middle-class children outscore poor children by as much on "culture free" tests as on "culturally loaded" tests. This suggests that what poor children lack is not specific information but more basic skills that are relevant to many different kinds of tests.

These findings seem to support the theory that test-score differences between rich and poor derive from genetic differences between rich and poor children. Like the "cultural bias" explanation, this "genetic" explanation has considerable logical appeal. Everyone who has studied the matter agrees that genes have *some* influence on test scores, that test scores have *some* influence on education attainment, and that education has *some* influence on adult success. It follows that there must be *some* genetic difference, however small, between economically successful and unsuccessful adults. If this is true, there must also be some genetic difference between children with successful and unsuccessful parents.

The evidence suggests, however, that genetic differences between successful and unsuccessful families plays a very minor role in determining children's IQs. Studies of adopted children indicate that genes may account for as much as half the observed correlation between parental status and children's test scores. Indirect evidence, derived from the relationship between test scores and parental success, suggests that the relationship is even weaker. Overall, our best guess is that genetic differences between social classes explain no more than 6 percent of the variation in IQ scores, while cultural differences between social classes explain another 6–9 percent.

This conclusion means that the average middle-class child may have a small genetic advantage over the average working-class child. But it also means that there are more working-class children than middle-class children with high genetic potential. This is because there are more working-class children to begin with. While their average score is a little lower than that of middle-class children, the difference is very small, and nearly half of all working-class children are above the middle-class average.

Furthermore, while differences between rich and poor whites are probably partly genetic, this tells us nothing about the origins of differences between whites and blacks. Blacks have lower IQ and achievement scores than whites, even when their parents have similar economic positions. But blacks also grow up in very different social and cultural environments from whites, even when their parents have the same occupations and incomes. We have no way of measuring the effects of these cultural differences. Our personal feeling is that black-white cultural differences could easily explain the observed IQ difference, which is only about 15 points. Differences of this magnitude are often found between white subcultures. Both black and white scores on military tests rose about 10 points between World War I and World War II, for example. Whites in eastern Tennessee improved by almost this much between 1930 and 1940, apparently as a result of the introduction of schools, roads, radios, etc.

The key point is that *it doesn't much matter whether IQ differences between blacks and whites are hereditary or environmental.* IQ accounts for only a quarter of the income gap between blacks and whites. Therefore, even if genes accounted for *all* the IQ gap between blacks and whites, which is hardly likely, they would account for only a quarter of the economic gap. In all probability their role is far smaller. The widespread obsession with possible genetic differences between races is thus a diversion from the real problem. We ought to worry about eliminating the discrimination that still accounts for most of the observed economic difference between blacks and whites. If this could be done, the average black would be earning almost as much as the average white, and the pointless debate about possible genetic differences would no longer seem important to most sensible people.

**Myth 5: Improving the Quality of the Schools Will Go a Long Way
toward Wiping Out Differences in IQ and School Achievement
and Therefore in Children's Life Chances**

Whether we like it or not, the quality of a child's school has even less effect than his social class on his test scores. The best evidence on this still comes from the 1965 Equality of Educational Opportunity Survey, whose first and most famous product was the Coleman Report. This survey did not give individual IQ tests to children, but it did give "verbal ability" tests that are very similar. It also gave reading and math tests. The results of this survey have aroused all sorts of controversy, but they have been confirmed by several other large surveys, notably the national study of high schools conducted by Project Talent throughout the 1960s. These surveys show that the differences among students in the same school are far greater than the difference between the average student in one school and the average student in another.

The surveys also show that test score differences between the alumni of different schools are largely due to differences between the entering students. Those from high-status families who enter school with high test scores tend to end up with high scores no matter what school they attend. Conversely, students from low-status families with low initial scores tend to end up with low scores even in what most people define as "good" schools. It follows that even if all schools had exactly the same effects on students' scores, the variation in students' IQ and achievement scores would decline very little. Qualitative differences among elementary schools seem to account for less than 6 percent of the variation in IQ test scores. Qualitative differences among high schools account for less than 2 percent.

In theory, of course, we could give students with low initial scores *better* schooling than students with high initial scores. This would allow us to reduce initial differences by more than 6 percent. The difficulty is that nobody knows how to do this. There is no consistent relationship between the amount of money we spend on a school and the rate at which children's test scores improve after they enter. Indeed, while school expenditures nearly doubled during the 1960s, a recent Project Talent survey shows that eleventh graders' school achievement scores hardly changed at all during that decade. Nor is there a consistent relationship between any specific school resource and the rate at which students' test scores rise. Neither small classes, well-paid teachers, experienced teachers, teachers with advanced degrees, new textbooks, nor adequate facilities have a consistent effect on students' scores.

Compensatory educational programs aimed at boosting the test scores of disadvantaged students have also produced discouraging results. Some studies report big gains, but others show that students who were not in the program gained more than those who were. Taken as a group, these studies suggest that students' scores do not improve any faster in compensatory programs than elsewhere. Thus, while there are good theoretical reasons for assuming that we can improve the test scores of those who enter school at a disadvantage, there is also strong evidence that educators simply do not know how to do this at the present time. (Neither, we should add, do educational critics, including ourselves.)

Racial and economic segregation may have slightly more effect than school expenditures on IQ test scores. The evidence, however, is by no means conclusive. Blacks who attend what we might call "naturally" desegregated schools, that is, schools in racially mixed neighborhoods, generally have higher test scores than blacks who attend segregated schools. These differences are apparent when students enter first grade, but they increase over time. This suggests that attending a racially mixed school boosts test scores somewhat faster than attending an all-black school. But the cumulative difference over six years of elementary school is small enough so that the effect in any one year is likely to be almost undetectable.

When we turn from "naturally" desegregated schools to schools that have been desegregated by busing, the evidence is more ambiguous. Some busing studies report that blacks showed appreciable gains. Very few report losses. Most show no statistically reliable difference. Since most of the studies involve small samples and short periods of time, this is not surprising. Taken together, the studies suggest that *on the average* busing probably increases black students' test scores, but that there are plenty of exceptions. Our best guess, based on evidence from both studies of busing and studies of naturally desegregated schools, is that desegregated schools would eventually reduce the test score gap between blacks and whites by about 20 percent. This is, however, only an educated guess. The evidence on this question remains inconclusive, despite some recent extravagant claims to the contrary.

Nor is there any obvious reason to suppose that either decentralization or community control will improve students' test scores. Among whites, relatively small districts score at about the same level as large ones, once other factors are taken into account. Neither decentralization nor community control has been tried on a large enough scale in black communities to prove very much. But predominantly black suburban school districts like Ravenswood and Compton in California, do not appear to have produced particularly impressive results. Neither have they done particularly badly.

None of this means that we should spend less on schools, stop trying to desegregate them, or reject decentralization or community control. Quite the contrary. If additional expenditures make schools better places for children, then they are justified regardless of their effects on reading comprehension, or IQ scores. If school desegregation reduces racial antagonism over the long run, then we should desegregate even though the students' test scores remain unaffected. And if community control gives parents the feeling that the schools belong to "us" rather than "them," this too is worthwhile for its own sake. Given the slim connection between test scores and adult success, it would be myopic to judge any sort of school reform primarily in terms of its effect on either IQ or school achievement.

Because a student's mastery of the skills taught in school provides a very poor measure of how well he will do once he graduates, reforms aimed at teaching these skills more effectively are not likely to take us very far toward economic prosperity or equality among adults. We have noted that only 12 percent of the variation in men's earnings is explained by their test scores. We have also seen that reducing inequality in test scores is very difficult. Under these circumstances it makes little sense for economic egalitarians to concentrate on equalizing IQ and achievement scores. Instead, they should concentrate on eliminating the other sources of income inequality, which cause 88 percent of the problem.

To be sure, this is more easily said than done. Those who do well in the present economic system inevitably resist reforms that would reduce their privileges. Those who do poorly in the present system are for the most part too demoralized to protest in any effective way. So long as this persists, there will be little chance of reducing economic inequality.

The complacency of the rich and the demoralization of the poor are reinforced by theories that attribute economic success to genetic superiority and economic failure to genetic deficiency. These theories are nonsense. In 1968, the income difference between the best and worst paid fifth of all workers was about $14,000. Of this, perhaps $500 or $1,000 was attributable to genetically determined differences in IQ scores. The idea that genetic inequality explains economic inequality is thus a myth. Like the divine right of kings, such myths help legitimize the status quo. But they should not be taken seriously by those who really want to understand the modern world, much less those who want to change it.

"...More,
rather than less, testing
is needed."

Intelligence has often been defined as whatever an intelligence test measures. The most popular intelligence tests are the creations of Dr. David Wechsler, who has done more to develop intelligence testing, and thereby to define intelligence, than any other psychologist.

It is now two years since the New York City school system eliminated the I.Q. from pupil's records. Banned under the pressure of groups that claimed the I.Q. was unfair to the culturally deprived, it has been replaced by achievement tests. Meanwhile, a great deal of effort is being put into developing new, non-verbal scales to measure schoolchildren's abilities while eliminating the troublesome factor of language.

Neither of these substitutes is an adequate replacement for the I.Q. In my opinion, the ban was misdirected in the first place and we should restore the I.Q. to its former position as a diagnostic tool as soon as possible. The substitutes simply do not test enough of the abilities that go to make up individual intelligence.

To understand what I.Q. tests do, and why they are valuable, we must first be clear about what intelligence is. This is a surprisingly thorny issue. Too much depends upon how one defines intelligence. In this respect psychologists are in no better agreement than the lay public. Divergency of view stems largely from differences in emphasis on the particular abilities thought to be central to the definition one envisages. Thus, an educator may define intelligence primarily as the ability to learn, a biologist in terms of ability to adapt, a psychologist as the ability to reason abstractly and the practical layman as just common sense.

One difficulty is similar to what a physicist encounters when asked to state what he means by energy, or a biologist what he means by life. The fact is that energy and life are not tangible entities; you cannot touch them or see them under a microscope even though you are able to describe them. We know them by their effects or properties.

The same is true of general intelligence. For example, we must assume that there is something common to learning to count, avoiding danger and playing chess which makes it possible for us to say that they are evidence of intelligent behavior, as against learning to walk, being accident prone and playing bingo, which seemingly have little if anything to do with it.

Intelligence, operationally defined, is the aggregate capacity of the individual to act purposefully, to think rationally and to deal effectively with his environment. Although it is not a mere sum of intellectual abilities, the only way we can evaluate it quantitatively is by the measurement of various aspects of these abilities.

Any test is primarily a device for eliciting and evaluating a fragment of behavior. An intelligence test is one by which an examiner seeks to appraise this bit of behavior insofar as it may be called intelligent. Various abilities can be used for this purpose because manifestations of ability are the means by which a subject can communicate and demonstrate his competences. To this end it is not so much the particular ability that is tested which is important, as the degree to which it correlates with posited criteria. A test is considered a good measure of intelligence if it correlates, for example, with learning ability, ability to comprehend, evidence of capacity to adjust and so on. If it does so to a satisfactory degree it is said to be valid. But, even when a test has been established as valid, there still remains a question: For what class of subjects is it valid? The answer will depend in a large measure upon the population on which the test was standardized—for example, middle-class white children, Southern Negro children or recently arrived Puerto Ricans.

Thus I.Q. tests are attacked on the ground that they are over weighted with items depending on verbal ability and academic information. Individuals with limited educational backgrounds are obviously penalized, and non-English-speaking subjects are admittedly incapable of taking the tests at all. This is an important stricture and test makers, contrary to some opinion, are fully aware of it. One way of "solving" the problem would be to provide separate normal or average scores for different populations, but apart from the practical difficulty of obtaining such norms, there is always the stricture that they bypass rather than meet the central issue. A compromise approach is practiced in some school systems, where intelligence tests continue to be used—under the more acceptable name of "aptitude tests."

Almost from the start, psychologists have sought to cope with the problem of literacy and language disability by devising nonverbal tests of intelligence. Thus, soon after the Binet tests were introduced more than a half-century ago, two American psychologists, Pintner and Paterson, developed the Non-Language Individual Performance Scale for non-English-speaking subjects. Similarly, when the Army Alpha (the main verbal test of World War I) was devised for the military services, a companion nonverbal test (the Army Beta) was prepared along with it.

The Pintner-Paterson scale required the subject to give evidence of his capacities by filling in appropriate missing parts on familiar pictures, putting together form boards, learning to associate signs with symbols, etc. The Army Beta consisted of such tasks as following mazes, reproducing picture designs, counting cubes, etc.—with directions presented to the subject by gesture or mime.

Many similar tests—the so-called "culture-free" or "culture-fair" tests—have followed. The most recent one reported is the Johns Hopkins Perceptual

Test devised by Dr. Leon Rosenberg and associates at the Johns Hopkins School of Medicine. This test was initially developed for children who did not speak or who were handicapped by certain functional or organic disorders; it has also been recommended as a more effective intelligence test for the very young and for culturally deprived children.

The Johns Hopkins Perceptual Test consists of a series of designs from which a child is asked to choose appropriate patterns to match others shown to him. Its primary merit is that it eliminates the factor of language. It is also claimed to be less dependent than verbal tests upon acquired skill, which, of course, depend to some extent upon a child's environmental experience. But this test, like other performance tests, does not measure a sufficient number of the abilities that go to make up the total picture of intelligent behavior.

Contrary to claims, the results of performance tests have been generally disappointing. The findings indicate that while they may be useful in certain situations, and for certain diagnostic groups, they prove quite unsatisfactory as alternates for verbal scales. They correlate poorly with verbal aptitudes and are poor prognosticators of over-all learning ability as well as school achievement. Above all, they have turned out to be neither culture-free nor culture-fair.

Culture-free tests fail to attain their end because, in the first place, the items usually employed are themselves subject to particular environmental experiences. A circle in one place may be associated with the sun, in another with a copper coin, in still another with a wheel. In some places a dog is a pet, in others a detested animal. Pictures, in the long run, are just symbols and these may be as difficult to understand and recognize as words; they have to be interpreted, as anyone who has attempted to learn sign language knows. Putting together blocks may be a challenge or a threat, working fast a sign of carelessness or an incentive to competition. Nonverbal, even more than verbal tests, need to be related to particular environments and, from a practical point of view, are both limited in range and difficult to contrive.

Finally many performance items when increased in difficulty tend to become measures of special abilities rather than having any significant correlation with over-all measures of intelligence. Thus, while tests of visual motor coordination may be useful items on intelligence tests for young children they are no longer effective at later ages. Copying a diamond is a good test at the 7-year level, but whether a child of 12 can produce a complicated design has little to do with his general intelligence and represents at most a special ability.

The effect of culture on test performance is a subject that demands serious concern, but here one deals with the problem of what one understands by the word "culture." In the United States there is a strong trend among contemporary writers to identify the term with socio-economic levels. This is in contrast to the historic and broader meaning of the term, which covers all human as well as environmental influences that serve to characterize the intellectual and moral status of a civilization.

Not all the poor are culturally deprived. Although standards may differ widely, "culturally different" does not mean "culturally deprived." The Jews and Italians who lived on the Lower East Side had their culture, and so have the Negroes in the slums of Harlem. They differ widely in respect to almost any variable one might employ, and culture is no exception. What this implies is that "culture" no more than color of skin should be a basis for assessing individuals.

The comments relating to the question of cultural impact apply with equal force to the problem of racial and national differences. One may start with the hypothesis that such differences exist and not necessarily be overwhelmed by their importance. This, in the writer's opinion, is a reasonable position.

This opinion is based on studies done in the field and, in particular, on data from World War I and World War II United States Armed Forces testing programs. The data from World War I included not only tables for the over-all draft population but for a great many subgroupings. Among these were separate test-score summaries according to national origin of the draftees, and a particularly detailed one comparing Negroes and whites. As might have been expected, differences between groups compared were found, and as might also have been expected invidious comparisons were immediately made and exploited. Particularly emphasized were the lower scores made by Negroes as compared with those made by white soldiers. Neglected, on the other hand, were the differences found between occupational levels and the more general ones between urban and rural populations.

It was not too difficult to correct the erroneous inferences made by the racists. But, in disposing of the racial claims, some authors went much beyond what the data warranted. Eventually, statements were made that other test findings revealed no significant differences between any national or racial groups —a fact which is equally questionable, and in any event still needs to be demonstrated. In the author's opinion, national and racial differences do exist—probably of both genetic and environmental origins, in varying degree. But the fact is that these differences are not large or relevant in the individual case.

We now come to the biggest bugaboo of intelligence testing—the I.Q. itself. The scientific literature on it is as large as its assailants are numerous. It has been attacked by educators, parents, writers of popular articles and politicians. During the Korean War it was investigated by Congress. Now that we are once more having trouble with draft quotas, the I.Q. will most likely be investigated again. It is doubtful whether the I.Q. can be brought into good grace at this time, but perhaps much of the fire sparked by the I.Q. can be quenched by an objective explanation of what it really is.

An I.Q. is just a measure of relative brightness. It merely asserts that, compared with persons of his own age group, an individual has attained a certain rank on a particular intelligence test. For example, a 10-year-old takes the Stanford-Binet test and attains a certain score, which happens to be that for the statistically average 8-year-old. We then divide the child's mental age (8) by his chronological age (10) and obtain a quotient, which we multiply by 100 simply to remove the inconvenience of decimal points. The result is called the Intelligence Quotient (or I.Q.)—in this case, 80. This particular figure tells us that, as compared with others in his age group, the child has performed below normal (which would be 100).

When this procedure of comparative grading is applied to a geography or bookkeeping test—when a teacher apportions class grades on a bell curve or a sliding scale—nobody gets excited. But when it is used with a mental test the reaction is quite different.

Opposition is generally focused not on the way that I.Q.'s are computed, but, more pointedly, on the way they are interpreted and utilized. One interpretation that has caused understandable concern is the notion that a person is "born with" an I.Q. which remains immutable. This is an allegation proclaimed by those who are opposed to the I.Q. rather than a view maintained by psychologists. What is asserted by psychologists, and supported by test-retest findings, is that I.Q.'s once accurately established are not likely to vary to any considerable degree. This does not mean that an I.Q. never changes, or that the conditions under which it was obtained may not have affected its validity.

The so-called constancy of the I.Q. is relative, but compared with other commonly used indexes, it is surprisingly stable. It is much more stable, for instance, than an individual's electrocardiogram or his basal metabolism level, which are accepted without question.

There are always exceptional cases which cannot be overlooked or bypassed. But one does not throw out the baby with the bath water. When for any reason a subject's I.Q. is suspect, the sensible thing to do is to have him retested. I.Q.'s, unlike the laws of the Medes and the Persians, are not irrevocable, but they should be respected.

While retest studies show that I.Q.'s are relatively stable, they also reveal that in individual cases large changes may occur—as much as 20 points or more. Thus, conceivably, an individual could move from the "dull normal" group to "average," or vice versa.

Much depends upon the age at which the original test was administered and the interval between testings. In general, I.Q.'s obtained before the age of 4 or 5 are more likely to show discrepancies between test and retest; those in the middle years least. Discrepancies are also likely to be larger as the intervals between retests increase. All this evidence points to reasons for not making a definite intelligence classification on the basis of a single test, and more especially on one administered at an early age. This precaution is necessary not because the tests are unreliable but because rates of mental maturity are often factors that have to be taken into account. Such variations tend not only to penalize slow developers but also to overrate early bloomers.

Various skills are required for effective test performance at different age levels. The fact that they are not present at a particular age level does not indicate that a child who lacks them is necessarily stunted. It may only be that these skills have not as yet emerged. Early training has a bearing on test readiness, but it is not true that if a child has not had this training at one age, he will not develop the skills required at a later age. On the other hand, deliberately teaching a child skills in order to have him "pass" an intelligence test, as now seems to be the vogue, is not the answer to acquiring a high I.Q.

An important conclusion to be drawn from the above is that more, rather than less, testing is needed. Unfortunately, when this is suggested, one encounters the objection that extended testing programs in public schools would be too costly. The expensiveness of school testing has been greatly exaggerated, especially when considered in relation to the over-all cost of keeping a child in school (an average of $600 to $700 per child per year in most parts of the country).

Particularly neglected is the individual intelligence examination, which at present is administered in most public schools only to "problem cases." In the author's opinion, an individual intelligence examination ought to be given to all children as they enter school. Most private schools require such an examination, and there is good reason why the public schools should also provide it.

Allowing $50 per examination administered once over a four-year period, the cost would be a minuscule addition to the school's budget. In return, a systematic individual examination could serve as a means of evaluating a child's assets and liabilities before he was subjected to the hazards of arbitrary placement. Finally, it must be borne in mind that intelligence tests are intended as a means not merely for detecting the intellectually retarded, but also for discovering the intellectually gifted.

In discussions of the merits and limitations of intelligence tests, one important aspect, frequently overlooked, is their basic aim. This objective is most effectively summed up in the late Professor Irving Lorge's definition of what intelligence tests aim to measure—namely, "the ability to learn and to solve the task's required by a particular environment."

This definition implies a multiple approach to the concept of intelligence and intelligence testing. In the latter process, one is of necessity engaged in evaluating an individual's particular abilities. Of course, in doing so, one obtains information regarding a subject's liabilities and handicaps. This information is both useful and important, but is really only an incidental aspect of what one wishes to discover from an intelligence test.

When it is asserted that intelligence tests are unfair to the disadvantaged and minorities, one must be mindful of the fact that they are simply recording the unfairness of life. They show also, for example, that our mental abilities, whoever we may be, decline with advancing age—(Of course, this decline is in many cases counterbalanced by increased experience.)

Intelligence tests were not devised for the handicapped alone but for everybody. What then can be the reason for believing they may not be suitable for the major segments of our population—or for prohibiting their administration to the majority of children in a school system? The current New York City I.Q. ban is a case in point, and especially discouraging when one sees what is being used instead.

The tests that have been substituted are a series of achievement tests—in particular, reading tests. Of all the possible choices, one can hardly imagine a worse alternative. For of all areas in which the disadvantaged child is handicapped, reading heads the list. The main difference between an intelligence (or aptitude) test and an achievement test is that the former is less tied to curriculum content. If it is true that a low score on an intelligence test presents a misleading picture of a pupil's learning capacity, how much more unfair would be an even lower score on an achievement test. It is possible that the I.Q. was banned in New York because those who supported the ban wished primarily to combat what they believed to be a widespread view that the I.Q. is "somehow a fixed, static and genetic measure of learning ability." One may wonder, however, whether political pressures may not have played some role in the decision —and one may hope that the ban will soon be retracted.

The I.Q. has had a long life and will probably withstand the latest assaults on it. The most discouraging thing about them is not that they are without merit, but that they are directed against the wrong target. It is true that the results of intelligence tests, and of others, too, are unfair to the disadvantaged, deprived and various minority groups but it is not the I.Q. that has made them so. The culprits are poor housing, broken homes, a lack of basic opportunities, etc., etc. If the various pressure groups succeed in eliminating these problems, the I.Q.'s of the disadvantaged will take care of themselves.

"...Creativity is a different type of cognitive excellence than general intelligence."

Are all intelligent children creative? Are all creative children intelligent? Wallach and Kogan would answer both questions with "No." How can we help all children, regardless of their intelligence, to develop their creativity? This is one of the major problems facing education today, as the following article reveals.

While there has been a great deal of discussion in recent years concerning the importance of fostering "creativity" in our children, there is little solid evidence to support the claim that creativity can be distinguished from the more familiar concept of intelligence. To be sure, the word "creativity" has caught the fancy of the culture—frequent reference is made to creativity in contexts as diverse as education, industry, and advertising. Time and time again, however, the "proof" offered to support the existence of a type of cognitive excellence different from general intelligence has proven to be a will-o'-the-wisp.

The logical requirements for such a proof can be put as follows. The psychological concept of *intelligence* defines a network of strongly related abilities concerning the retention, transformation, and utilization of verbal and numerical symbols: at issue are a person's memory storage capacities, his skill in solving problems, his dexterity in manipulating and dealing with concepts. The person high in one of these skills will tend to be high in all; the individual who is low in one will tend to be low in all. But what of the psychological concept of *creativity*? If the behavior judged to be indicative of creativity turns up in the same persons who behave in the ways we call "intelligent," then there is no justification for claiming the existence of any kind of cognitive capacity apart from general intelligence. We would have to assert that the notion of greater or lesser degrees of *creativity* in people simply boils down, upon empirical inspection, to the notion of greater or lesser degrees of general *intelligence*. On the other hand, in order to demonstrate that there are grounds for considering creativity to be a kind of cognitive talent that exists in its own right, another kind of proof would be required. It would be necessary to demonstrate that whatever methods of evaluation are utilized to define variations in creativity from person to person result in classifications that are different from those obtained when the same individuals are categorized as to intelligence.

When we reviewed the quantitative research on creativity, we were forced to conclude that these logical requirements were not met. Despite frequent use of the term "creativity" to define a form of talent that was independent of intelligence, examination of the evidence indicated that the purported measures of creativity tended to have little more in common with each other than they had in common with measures of general intelligence. If one could do about the same thing with an I.Q. measure as one could with the creativity measures (regarding who should be considered more creative and who should be considered less creative), it was difficult to defend the practice of invoking a new and glamorous term such as "creativity" for describing the kind of talent under study.

While varying conceptions of the meaning of creativity had been embodied in the measures used, they all shared one thing in common: they had been administered to the persons under study as *tests*. From the viewpoint of the person undergoing assessment, the creativity procedures, no less than an intelligence test, carried the aura of school examinations. They were carried out with explicit or implicit time limits in classroom settings where many students underwent the assessment procedures at the same time. Indeed, we even found that the creativity procedures had been described to the students as "tests" by the psychologists who gave them.

We were suspicious that such a test-like context was inimical to the whole-hearted display of cognitive characteristics which could be correctly referred to as being involved in creativity. Hence we believed that creativity had not yet been given a fair chance to reveal itself as a different form of excellence than intelligence. These suspicions were reinforced when we considered what creative artists and scientists have said concerning creative moments in their own work.

Their Creative Elders

In their introspections one finds an emphasis upon the production of a free flow of ideas—the bubbling forth of varieties of associations concerning the matter at hand. Einstein, for example, refers to the need for "combinatory play" and "associative play" in putting ideas together. Dryden describes the process of writing as involving "a confus'd mass of thoughts, tumbling over one another in the dark." Poincaré talks about ideas as having "rose in crowds" immediately prior to his obtaining a significant mathematical insight. These associations, moreover, range with high frequency into the consideration of unique, unusual possibilities, but ones which are nevertheless relevant to the issue rather than just bizarre. When we look into the conditions under which an abundant flow of unique ideational possibilities has been available, the artists and scientists indicate that the most conducive attitude is one of playful contemplation—if you will, of permissiveness. Creative awareness tends to occur when the individual—in a playful manner—entertains a range of possibilities without worry concerning his own personal success or failure and how his self-image will fare in the eyes of others.

With this in mind we formulated a research program that involved the extensive study of 151 fifth-grade children. They were of middle-class socio-economic status, and boys and girls were about equally represented in our sample. The work, which was supported in part by the Cooperative Research Program of the United States Office of Education, has been described in detail in our book, *Modes of Thinking in Young Children: A Study of the Creativity-Intelligence Distinction* (Holt, Rinehart and Winston, 1965).

From the introspections of scientists and artists arose some ground rules concerning what creativity might rightfully signify if in fact it constitutes a type of excellence different from intelligence. These ground rules might be put in terms of the following two injunctions:

First, study the flow of ideas—consider how unique and how abundant are the kinds of ideas that a child can provide when contemplating various sorts of tasks. One is talking here, of course, about relevant ideas, not about ideas that might earn the status of being unique only because they are so bizarre as to have no relevance at all to the task.

Second, provide an atmosphere that convinces the child that he is not under test—that the situation is one of play rather than one where his intellectual worthiness is under evaluation by others. This second injunction may be a particularly difficult one to fulfill on the American educational scene, where testing and the feeling of undergoing personal evaluation are ubiquitous. Yet if our considerations were correct, it obviously was essential to fulfill it if creativity was to receive a fighting chance to display itself.

Accordingly, we mustered every device possible to place the assessment procedures in a context of play rather than in the typical context of testing with which the children were all too familiar. There were no time limits on the procedures. They were administered to one child at a time rather than to groups of children seated at their classroom desks. The adults who worked with the children, moreover, had already established relationships in the context of play activities. We even took pains to avoid the customary vocabulary of tests and testing in connection with the research enterprise as a whole—in our talk with the children we described the work as oriented to the study of children's games for purposes of developing new games children would like.

The procedures involved such matters as requesting the child to suggest possible uses for each of several objects, or to describe possible ways in which each of several pairs of objects are similar to each other. For example, in one procedure the child was to suggest all the different ways in which we could use such objects as a newspaper, a cork, a shoe, a chair. "Rip it up if angry" was a unique response for "newspaper," while "make paper hats" was not unique. In another, he was to indicate similarities between, for example, a potato and a carrot, a cat and a mouse, milk and meat. "They are government-inspected" was a unique response for "milk and meat," while "they come from animals" was not unique. In yet another, he was to indicate all the things that each of a number of abstract drawings might be. For a triangle with three circles around it, "three mice eating a piece of cheese" was a unique response, while "three people sitting around a table" was not unique. For two half-circles over a line, "two haystacks on a flying carpet" was a unique response, while "two igloos" was not unique.

Our interests were in the number of ideas that a child would suggest, and the uniqueness of the suggested ideas—the extent to which a given idea in response to a given task belonged to one child alone rather than being an idea that was suggested by other children as well. In addition, we used a variety of traditional techniques for assessing general intelligence with the same children.

When the results of the creativity assessment procedures were compared with results of the intelligence measures, a definite divergence was obtained—the kind that had not been found in earlier studies. They had already shown, and so did our study, that a child who scores at the high intelligence end of one intelligence test will tend to score that way in other intelligence tests as well. In addition, however, our research revealed two further facts which tended to be different from earlier studies:

The various measures of creativity that we utilized had a great deal in common with one another: a child who scored at the high creativity end of one of our creativity measures tended to score at the high creativity end of all the rest of these measures.

Of particular importance, the indices of creativity and the indices of intelligence tended to be independent of each other. That is to say, a child who was creative by our measures would just as likely be of low intelligence as of high intelligence. Likewise, a child who was relatively low in creativity by our measures would as likely be of high intelligence as of low intelligence.

In short, the obtained facts *did* support the view that in school children creativity is a different type of cognitive excellence than general intelligence. Such an outcome was especially striking in light of the fact that our procedures for assessing creativity of necessity called upon the child's verbal ability in some degree—and verbal ability is known to contribute substantially to performance on I.Q. tests. Despite this possible source of commonality, the chances that a child of high intelligence would also display high creativity by our measures were no more than about 50-50.

What are some of the characteristics, then, of children in our four categories: intelligent and creative; neither intelligent nor creative; intelligent but low in creativity; and creative but low in regard to intelligence? The composite pictures that emerged from the experiments and observations that we carried out are composites in the sense that some portions of the evidence upon which they are based were more clear for the boys, while other parts of the evidence were more clear for the girls. However, the general pictures that emerged for the two sexes tended to suggest the same underlying characteristics.

High Creativity–High Intelligence

In many respects these children earn the most superlatives of any of the four groups. For example, when they are observed in the classroom they tend to be particularly high in degree of attention span and concentration upon academic work. At the same time, their academic bent does not put them at a social disadvantage. Quite to the contrary, they are observed to be the most socially "healthy" of the four groups: they have the strongest inclination to be friends with others, and others also have the strongest inclination to be friends with them. (These observations were made during play periods as well as during class sessions.)

These children, in addition, are the least likely of all four groups to behave in ways that suggest disapproval or doubt concerning oneself, one's actions, and one's work. However, this isn't merely a question of behaving in a manner most in harmony with the society's expectations, for these children also demonstrate a strong inclination to engage in various sorts of disruptive activities in the classroom. It's as if they are bursting through the typical behavioral molds that the society has constructed.

What are some of the underpinnings of the general behaviors just described for this group? For one thing, they are likely to see possible connections between events that do not have too much in common. The members of this group, in other words, are more willing to posit relationships between events that are in many respects dissimilar. For another thing, these children are particularly good at reading the subtle affective or expressive connotations that can be carried by what goes on in the environment. These two matters are not entirely separate— a sensitive, aesthetic "tuning" to the possible expressive meanings conveyed by human gesture or by abstract design forms involves seeing possible linkages between quite different kinds of objects and events. The children high in both creativity and intelligence seemed to be most capable of all the groups regarding this kind of aesthetic sensitivity.

To illustrate how we studied the child's ability to read subtle expressive connotations, consider the following example. We confronted the child with a picture of a straight line and asked him to imagine that he was looking down from above at a path that someone had made. The child was to tell us what sort of person made this trail. Our interest was in determining whether the child's response conveyed information about the kinds of emotional experience that might characterize the person in question, or on the other hand conveyed information only about the superficial character of what the person did. An example of a response showing sensitivity to possible expressive meanings was: "Someone very tense; because if he were relaxed he might wander all over; somebody mad." On the other hand, here is an example of a response that did not show expressive sensitivity: "Man was traveling on a highway; he met people in a huge car; it had a lot of people and it was crowded; they traveled together and got food in restaurants; when they got where they were going, they had a nice vacation."

Turning finally to the way these children describe their own feeling states, we find a tendency for them to admit to experiencing some anxiety, some disturbance—neither a great deal nor very little. It may be that experiencing some anxiety serves an energizing function for them: it is not so much anxiety as to cripple them, and not so little anxiety as to leave them dormant. Also, their total mode of adaptation does not minimize the experience of anxiety for them.

Low Creativity–High Intelligence

In what respects are the children who are high with regard to general intelligence but low in creativity different from those who are high in both? Let us return first to behavior observed in classroom and play settings. While the high intelligence-low creativity children resembled the high creativity-high intelligence children in possessing strong capacities for concentration on academic work and a long attention span, in other respects they were quite different. Those of high intelligence but low creativity were least likely of all four groups to engage in disruptive activities in the classroom and tended to hesitate about expressing opinions. In short, these children seemed rather unwilling to take chances.

Parallel behavior was observed in their social relations with other children; while others had a strong inclination to be friends with them, they in turn tended to hold themselves aloof from interaction with other children. The high intelligence-low creativity children, therefore, seemed to be characterized by a coolness or reserve in relations with their peers. Others would seek out the high intelligence-low creativity children for companionship, possibly because of this group's high academic standing. The children in question, however, tended not to seek out others in return. Perhaps this group felt themselves to be on top of the social mountain, as it were—in a position where they could receive homage from others without any need for requital.

The observations regarding a tendency toward caution and reserve on the part of the high intelligence-low creativity children receive further corroboration in other areas of their functioning. For example, when asked to make arrangements and groupings of pictures of everyday objects in whatever ways they considered most suitable, they preferred to make groupings that were more conventional in nature. They tended to avoid making free-wheeling, unconventional arrangements in which there would be greater free play for evolving unique combinations of objects. For instance, a more conventional grouping would be assembling pictures of a lamppost, a door, and a hammer, and calling them "hard objects." A more unconventional grouping, on the other hand, would be putting together pictures of a comb, a lipstick, a watch, a pocketbook, and a door, and describing them as items that concern "getting ready to go out." It is as if a greater fear of error characterizes these children, so that when left to their own devices, they tend to gravitate toward ways of construing the world that are less open to criticism by others.

We also found out that if you *request* these children to try to behave in a manner that involves establishing more free-wheeling linkages among objects, they are capable of doing so. It is not that they lack the ability to look at the world in this manner, but the inclination. When an adult in their environment comes along and makes it clear that they are expected to consider unusual and possibly bizarre ways in which objects can be linked, they are able to conform to this task demand with skill. But most of the time, their environment tells them that the more unconventional ways of proceeding are more likely to lead them into error and be criticized as wrong. Since the possibility of error seems particularly painful to these children, their typical behavior is to proceed in a manner that is less likely, on the average, to bring them criticism.

Another example of the same sort of process is provided when we consider how the high intelligence-low creativity group reads the possible affective meanings that can be possessed by the behavior of others. As in the case of arranging objects into groups, one can contrast more conventional, expected ways and more unconventional, unusual ways of construing what the behavior of others may signify. For example, an angry figure can be described as "angry" with little risk of error. It requires acceptance of unconventional possibilities, on the other hand, for the child to admit the idea that this figure might be "peaceful" or might be "searching." It turns out that the group in question is least likely to entertain the possibility of the more unconventional, unusual kinds of meanings. They seem locked, therefore, in more conventional ways of interpreting their social world as well as their physical world. Again, fear of possible error seems to be at work.

Since the high intelligence-low creativity children seem to behave in a manner that should maximize correctness and minimize error, we can expect them to be in particularly good standing in their classroom environment. Given their apparent tendency to conform to expectations, their mode of functioning should be maximally rewarding and minimally punishing for them. In short, there should be a high degree of fit between customary environmental expectations and their way of conducting themselves. We find, in fact, that this group admits to little anxiety or disturbance when asked to describe their own feeling states. Their self-descriptions indicate the lowest levels of anxiety reported by any of the four creativity-intelligence groups. Since this group behaves in a manner that should minimize worry or concern for them, their minimal level of reported anxiety probably represents an accurate description of how they feel. But at a cost, as we have noted, of functioning in a constricted manner.

High Creativity–Low Intelligence

Turning to the group characterized by high creativity but relatively low intelligence, we find, first of all, that they tend to exhibit disruptive behavior in the classroom. This is about the only respect, however, in which their observable conduct in the usual school and play settings resembles that of the group high in both creativity and intelligence. Of all four groups, the high creativity-low intelligence children are the least able to concentrate and maintain attention in class, the lowest in self-confidence, and the most likely to express the conviction that they are no good. It is as if they are convinced that their case is a hopeless one. Furthermore, they are relatively isolated socially; not only do they avoid contact with other children, but in addition their peers shun them more than any other group. Perhaps, in their social withdrawal, these children are indulging fantasy activities. At any rate, they are relatively alone in the school setting, and in many respects can be characterized as worse off than the group low in both creativity and intelligence.

It should be borne in mind that the high creativity-low intelligence children nevertheless give evidence of the same kind of creative thinking capacities as are found in the high creativity-high intelligence group. Again, for example, we find a greater likelihood of seeing possible connections between events that do not share much in common. The high creativity children, whether high or low regarding intelligence, are more willing to postulate relationships between somewhat dissimilar events.

Apparently, the kinds of evaluational pressures present in the case of intelligence and achievement testing as well as in the typical classroom environment serve to disrupt cognitive powers which can come to the fore when pressure is reduced. An interesting complementarity seems to exist with regard to the psychological situations found for the high creativity-low intelligence group and the low creativity-high intelligence group; while members of the former seem to perform more effectively when evaluational pressures are absent, members of the latter seem to work more adequately when evaluational pressures are present. It is as if the former children tend to go to pieces if questions of personal competence and achievement enter the picture, while the latter children have difficulty if they are denied a framework of standards within which they can evaluate what is required of them if they are to seem competent in the eyes of adults.

Low Creativity–Low Intelligence

While the children in this group show the greatest cognitive deprivation of the four groups under study, they seem to make up for it at least to some degree in the social sphere. From observations of their behavior in school and at play they are found to be more extroverted socially, less hesitant, and more self-confident and self-assured than the children of low intelligence but high creativity. The members of the low-low group are particularly poor regarding the kinds of aesthetic sensitivity that were mentioned earlier—for example, they show the weakest tendencies to respond to the possible expressive meanings that abstract line forms may convey. Despite such deficiencies, however, this group does not seem to be the maximally disadvantaged group in the classroom. Rather, the low-low children seem to have worked out a modus vivendi that puts them at greater social ease in the school situation than is the case for their high creativity-low intelligence peers.

The Motivational Hurdle

Now that we have characterized the four groups of children, let us finally consider the implications of the relative roles played by ability and by motivational factors in a child's thinking. The only group that looks like it is in difficulty with regard to ability—and even in their case we cannot be sure—is the group low in both intelligence and creativity. In the cases of the two groups that are low regarding one cognitive skill and high regarding the other—the low intelligence-high creativity group and the high intelligence-low creativity group—our evidence suggests that, rather than an ability deficiency, the children in question are handicapped by particular motivational dispositions receiving strong environmental support. For the low intelligence-high creativity children, the difficulty seems to concern excessive fear of being evaluated; hence they perform poorly when evaluational standards are a prominent part of the setting. For the high intelligence-low creativity children, on the other hand, the difficulty seems to concern a fear of not knowing whether one is thought well of by significant others. The possibility of making mistakes, therefore, is particularly avoided. Further, if evaluational standards are not a clear part of the setting, so that the child does not know a right way of behaving in order to fulfill the expectations of others, performance will deteriorate because the problem of avoiding error becomes of prime importance.

In theory, at least, these kinds of motivational hindrances could be rectified by appropriate training procedures. If one could induce the low intelligence-high creativity children to be less concerned when evaluational standards are present, and the high intelligence-low creativity children to be less concerned when evaluational standards are absent, their thinking behavior might come to display high levels of both intelligence and creativity.

Suggested Readings for
Chapter 3

Hunt, J. McV. *Intelligence and experience.* New York: Ronald, 1961. A discussion of the nature and development of intelligence, with particular emphasis on the role of heredity and environment.

Matarazzo, J. D. *Wechsler's measurement and appraisal of adult intelligence.* (5th ed.) New York: Williams and Wilkins, 1972. This is an updating and revision of Wechsler's classic book defining intelligence and describing his approach to its measurement. It contains a great deal of data as well as a good literature review and thorough description of the test.

Piaget, Jean. *The origins of intelligence in children.* New York: W. W. Norton & Co., 1963. In this volume Jean Piaget, the world-famous Swiss developmental psychologist, describes his theories concerning the stages through which children go as they develop the ability to use intelligence in their functioning.

Terman, L. M. & Oden, M. H. *The gifted group at mid-life.* Stanford University Press, 1959. The most recent follow-up of a group of gifted children identified at an early age and studied systematically since then.

Wallach, M. A. & Kogan, N. *Modes of thinking in young children.* New York: Holt, Rinehart and Winston, Inc., 1965. An examination of the distinction between intelligence and creativity which expands upon the material in the selection in this chapter.

Discussion Questions

1. What is intelligence?

2. How does intelligence differ from creativity?

3. What are the relative contributions of heredity and environment to the development of intelligence?

4. Do IQ tests measure intelligence?

Chapter 4
The Human Body

The scientific study of human behavior is so vast an undertaking that almost all scientific disciplines have contributed to its evolution. This fact is a testimony to the interrelatedness of science as well as a tribute to the complexity of the human organism. Over the past few decades a great store of information has been acquired concerning the physiological and biological processes that underlie behavior. Scientific studies have revealed much about the function of bodily systems in their various structural, electrical, chemical, and molecular attributes, and research has begun to tell us what the body does, how it works, its relationship to human actions, and possible consequences if the system is impaired. Through the cross-fertilization of psychology with other sciences, man is becoming more knowledgeable about the physiological aspects of his behavior and the ways it can be predicted and controlled.

The body is a unitary system acting in concert with its parts. In this sense, most bodily organs are necessary for life, although some are more central than others. In psychology, the structures that command most attention are located in the central nervous system, composed of the brain and the spinal cord. These systems harbor the responsible agents for consciousness, thought, intelligence, reception and organization of sensations from the external environment and other higher order faculties. In addition, the central nervous system is the prime control center for the integration of the biological system with its environment. The one possession that distinguishes man from lower animals is his highly developed brain. This is a great convoluted mass, composed of millions of nerve cells that channel information in the form of neural impulses to and from all parts of the body. In the course of its development the brain has become differentiated into subdivisions that appear to have both general and specific functions. For example, the cerebral cortex (our most recent acquisition in evolutionary development) concerns itself with voluntary movement such as thinking, consciousness, speech, and sense perception. The cortex is divided into halves called the right and left cerebral hemispheres, each hemisphere containing four parts: frontal, parietal, occipital, and temporal lobes. In a gross way these sections of the brain have either sensory or motor capabilities established at birth. In the first paper in this chapter Beach outlines the anatomical organization and the many varied physiological systems that make up the nervous system.

The article by José M. R. Delgado, entitled "Psychocivilized Direction of Behavior," reviews some of the author's work in the technology and theory of brain control. Delgado is a researcher who has pioneered the exploration of the brain through the use of very sophisticated electrostimulation techniques. Through the implantation of microelectrodes into various parts of living brains, Delgado has been able to investigate experimentally both animal and human learning, thinking, and behaving. Delgado assures us that these procedures are safe, painless, and have apparently not interfered with the normal activities of patients who received such electrical stimulation implants. As a medical procedure, electrical implantations have been used with patients suffering from epilepsy, intractable pain, involuntary movements, and illnesses which have been resistant to other forms of therapy. But the crux of Delgado's paper is not simply a description of a unique medical technology but a serious attempt to state the philosophical implications which underlie the use of these techniques. For many, the idea of brain manipulation evokes images of 1984, and reinforces fears that our technology is suffocating more intimately human concerns such as freedom, dignity, and so on. Delgado, for his part, is very sympathetic with the work of B. F. Skinner and is notably impressed by his recent book *Beyond Freedom and Dignity*.

More and more scientists are examining the correlations between biological functioning and overt behavioral action. A specific area of investigation carrying enormous implications for society are the ways in which brain functioning tends to shape and/or initiate violent behavior. The origins of aggression have been the object of heated theoretical debate. One theoretical position presented forcefully by Konrad Lorenz and other ethologists is that aggression is basically a biological predisposition which can be successfully redirected but not necessarily eliminated through environmental interventions. On the other hand, learning theorists such as John Paul Scott stress an alternative view that environmental training is the principal variable in the development of violent behavior and that biological instincts play only a minor role in determining human behavior. At this point, the evidence seems to be that neither view can be successfully defended. As Gene Bylinsky points out in his article, "New Clues to the Causes of Violence," the biological and environmental causes of violence must be carefully examined and the effects of each identified. There appears to be little question that a social environment which reinforces violent behavior will increase the probability of future violent behavior. Furthermore, it seems likely that early patterns of environmental action are imprinted upon the young brain and produce patterns of brain functioning which could eventually be identified through a careful study of the chemical and electrical functioning of the brain itself. There is also well-documented evidence that injuries, lesions, or tumors in various parts of the brain such as the hypothalamus or the amygdala can turn a nonviolent person into a violent one. Evidence is also cited suggesting that males have more brain cells that are involved with aggression than females. Consequently, boys may inherit more aggressive tendencies than girls, and this may account for what is characterized as masculine behavior. Evidence is also accumulating that males who are born with an extra Y chromosome (in an XYY chromosomal pattern), seem to have a greater probability of acting in a violent manner than males who are born with the conventional XY chromosomal pattern. This problem is complicated by the suggestion that the XYY male will be more or less aggressive depending upon whether he inherited his Y chromosome from a peaceable or violent father. These later results are mainly the outcome of experiments with rats, and thus their clear applicability to humans is at this juncture somewhat questionable. From the psychological side, important studies by Albert Bandura have shown that subjects who are exposed to influential models are apt to adopt the behavioral characteristics of these models and act similarly. For example, after observing a film of aggressive adults, children who were given the opportunity to play out these roles in real life showed more aggression towards each other than they had before being exposed to these aggressive models. The basic theme of this paper is that both biological and learning factors are involved in aggression. Which one plays the most important role is yet to be determined. However, it is clear that both sets of variables can affect each other. To understand the causes of aggression and the means to prevent excessive violence is a matter of basic survival. Our destructive technology is so awesome in its size and power that even a little bit of violence and aggression in the wrong hands could put an end to a lot of potentially peaceable citizens.

We live in a stressful society. Competition, social mobility, and the tremendous urge to better oneself economically and materially produce emotional stresses which seem to have unpleasant physical consequences. Recent research cited by Walter McQuade in his article, "What Stress Can Do to You," suggests that middle-aged men are particularly prone to a variety of serious diseases that may be caused by stress. One excellent example of the presence of stress, as well as the frantic attempts people use to avoid stress, can be illustrated by the increasing market for medications, tranquilizers, and other "soothing" drugs. These drugs not only include the most conventionally acceptable mood modifiers such as barbiturates to soothe one down and amphetamines to boost one up, but also equally destructive drugs such as alcohol and cigarettes. One of the most insightful researchers in the area of stress has been a scientist by the name of Hans Selye. Selye's theory suggests that there are certain individuals who are prone to experience severe physical reactions to stress resulting in extreme physiological disability. Selye's work, focusing on cardiovascular disease, is extraordinarily important because heart disease is still the principal cause of death among people of all ages in our society. Once identifying the problem, the real issue is how to solve it, or at least to minimize the risks that are realistically involved in living within a stressful world.

Our body is our most important possession. We look at it, we feel it, we sense it, we experience it, and sometimes we either love it or we hate it. The body, as Seymour Fisher points out in his article, "Experiencing Your Body: You Are What You Feel," is our unique base of personal identity. Fisher has carried out a substantial body of research to study how people relate to their body image. In these studies he used the Rorschach inkblot test as a method for obtaining personal information about how people felt about their body. The Rorschach is a psychological test composed of ten relatively ambiguous inkblots. Fisher discovered that people will express different associative symbols on the Rorschach depending upon how they feel about their body. For example, he found that individuals who feel secure about their body boundaries have a tendency to produce images that have sheltering qualities such as caves with rocky walls, turtles with hard shells, and so on. Other fascinating findings are reported in this article.

" The computer is the brain, and it has subparts that receive and integrate information from the various sense organs."

There is no organ more crucial to man's humanness than his brain. It is the seat of consciousness and the main instigator of behavior. This paper by Dr. Beach studies brain processes and the research which has revolutionized our understanding of the human brain as a living, growing, and changing organ.

In the discussion of sensation and perception, we visualized the human being as a roving information gatherer that had specialized sensing devices mounted on it. These sensing devices relayed messages to a central computer, which in turn interpreted and interrelated the messages in order to derive a coherent, unified evaluation of the things that were being sensed. The discussion that followed focused on the sensing devices and on the resulting evaluations, but not much was said about the intermediate steps of transmission of the information to the computer or about the computer itself. This appendix supplements that earlier discussion by describing how the transmission occurs and how the computer works. Unfortunately, many important questions about the operation of the computer are still unanswered; but the basic picture is becoming clear, and while this description will, by necessity, be abbreviated, you can get at least a general idea of what that picture looks like.

Some Basic Concepts

For the time being let us continue to rely on our analogy between the human being and the hypothetical information gatherer. The gatherer's basic components would be (1) the *sensing devices* that receive and code incoming information, (2) *transmission cables* for the coded incoming information, (3a) the *computer*, (3b) subsections of the computer that receive and interpret *incoming information* from specific sensing devices, (3c) an *integration system* that interrelates subsections of the computer and regulates the flow of incoming information and outgoing messages, (3d) subsections that initiate *outgoing messages* in reply to the incoming information, (4) *transmission cables* for the outgoing messages that cause some parts of the system to act upon either the sensed objects in the environment or upon the sensing devices themselves (for example, to turn them off or to change their focus of attention). This sort of design would permit our hypothetical device to gather information, interpret and integrate it, and initiate actions in light of it.

Let us look at the physiological counterparts of this system in human beings. The sensory devices are your sense organs, which, as you know, react to patterns of light, sound, pressure, temperature, chemistry, gases, gravity, and so on, and they code what they sense into patterns of electrical activity. The transmission cables are your nerves. They react to the sense organs' patterns of electrical activity by themselves becoming electrically active and thereby carrying the coded information to the brain. The computer is the brain, and it has subparts that receive and integrate information from the various sense organs. Roughly speaking, there is a central clearinghouse in the center of the brain which receives the information first; from this clearinghouse visual information goes to the back of the brain, auditory information goes to the sides, touch and muscle information goes to the top, and information about the body's vital functions and about posture and muscle movement goes to the bottom of the brain. In each case, the incoming information is also integrated with other incoming information (you *hear* a man speak and *see* his lips move at the same time) and with information from past experience that already is stored in the brain's memory (you *understand* what the man says because you already have learned the language).

After the incoming information is received and interpreted, it is checked to see if a reply is necessary. If so, an outgoing message is transmitted through the outgoing cables to the appropriate muscles or organs. For example, an outgoing message to your eye muscles may change the direction in which you are looking in order to see some object better. Or if your body temperature were too high or too low, an outgoing message would call for sweating or shivering in an attempt to solve the problem.

This is all very complex—indeed, the brain is more complex than any computer we can imagine. As a result, our analogy only begins to give the flavor of what is actually going on.

Transmission Cables:
Nerves and Neurons

Most of the transmission cables are bundles of lines a bit like a telephone cable. These bundles are called *nerves* and the component lines are called *neurons*. Usually a neuron is fairly short and does not extend the full length of the nerve. Rather, neurons pass their electrical activity (called *impulses*) from one to another in a chain, and this chain extends from the sense organ to the brain.

Neurons look generally like the diagram in Figure A2.1. The *cell body*, as with all cells, supplies the nutrients that keep the cell alive and functioning at its best. The *dendrites* are short arms that extend from the edges of the cell body, and the *axon* is a long tail that has brushlike arms at its end, called *end brushes*.

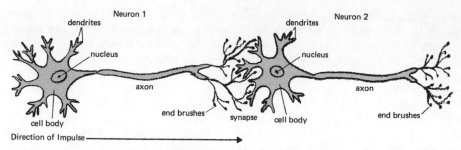

FIG. A2.1   Typical neurons. Stimulation of the dendrites of neuron 1 causes an electrical impulse to travel down the axon of the neuron to the end brushes. After reaching the end brushes, this electrical impulse initiates chemical changes in the synapse which, in turn, result in the stimulation of the dendrites of neuron 2.

Electrical transmission of impulses within a neuron always begins at the dendrites and moves down the axon toward the end brushes. Electrical transmission between neurons occurs when the end brushes of the axon of one neuron stimulate the dendrites of the next neuron. The end brushes and dendrites do not actually touch each other; transmission occurs because of chemical activity occurring at the *synapse* (the gap between the end brushes of one neuron and dendrites of another neuron). This chemical activity is initiated by the electrical impulse reaching the end brushes; the chemical activity causes an electrical impulse to be initiated in the second neuron. This impulse travels down the axon of the second neuron to its end brushes where again chemical activity at the synapse causes stimulation of the dendrites of the third neuron, and so on.

Some Limitations on Transmission

The transmission of impulses from one neuron to another is, of course, not as simple as this description might imply. First, a specific amount of chemical activity is required at the dendrites of a neuron in order for its electrical impulse to be triggered. This specific amount is called the neuron's *threshold*, and sometimes more than one neuron acting on the dendrites are needed to exceed this threshold. When the threshold is exceeded, the electrical activity always occurs at full strength (called the *"all-or-none"* principle because electrical activity either occurs or it does not).

Second, after having transmitted its impulse, there is a very short period during which the neuron is fairly insensitive to stimulation of its dendrites. That is, the threshold is high immediately after the neuron has been active. As the neuron recovers its sensitivity, the threshold level decreases to normal. But until full recovery occurs, only strong activity on its dendrites will induce another spasm of activity.

Third, transmission of the impulse from neuron to neuron can be influenced at the synapse by other neurons which meet at the same synapse. Depending upon the circumstances, this influence can result in decreased or increased activity, phenomena known as *inhibition* and *facilitation*, respectively.

These three limitations on a neuron's activity (threshold, recovery times, and inhibition and facilitation) are thought to interact so that a bundle of neurons, a nerve, ends up transmitting complex codes from the sense organs to the brain. All three limitations influence impulse transmission and, therefore, information which eventually reaches the brain can be coded in a variety of ways—in terms of the pace, duration, and patterning of impulses.

The Spinal Cord

Nerves from throughout the trunk and limbs of the body go to the spinal column where they enter between the bones and form a large cable called the *spinal cord* (Fig. A.2.2). Some of the nerves in the spinal cord relay incoming information to the brain and some relay outgoing information back to the body. The nerves relaying information about the senses in the head (eyes, ears, taste, smell, scalp, face, and so on) all connect directly to the brain and are not part of the spinal cord.

The Somatic and Autonomic Systems

The nervous system has two components. The first, the *somatic system*, relays messages to and from the muscles and sense organs, permitting movement and sensory functioning. The second, the *autonomic system*, carries messages to and from internal organs such as the heart, lungs, stomach, and so forth. The autonomic system can either arouse the body to action by increasing heart rate, blood pressure, the adrenalin in the blood, sweating, and overall alertness or relax it by decreasing heart rate, blood pressure, and so on. Thus, the autonomic system can arouse you to fight or escape from danger, or it can relax you so you can peacefully digest a meal or doze pleasantly in the sun.

The Computer:
The Brain and Its Parts

It is customary to discuss the structure and function of the brain as though it were composed of many rather independent subparts, but this is done only in order to simplify discussion. From the beginning you should understand that this is only a fiction; the brain is a highly integrated system. Some parts of the brain appear to be more or less specialized, but every job executed by the brain involves many different parts. Moreover, in many cases there are back-up systems, so that if one part of the brain is damaged through disease or accident, other parts eventually take over at least some of the function of the damaged part.

General Structure

Figure A2.3 shows a diagram of the general shape and structure of the human brain. It is slightly bigger than a man's two clenched fists held side by side. It is divided into two halves, left and right, that are connected to one another in the middle by a large cable of neurons called the *corpus callosum*. Were it not for this connection, the two halves would operate essentially as two separate brains. Strangely enough, the two halves control the opposite sides of the body; the left side of the brain controls the right side of the body, and the right side of the brain controls the left side of the body. Thus, if a person has a stroke or accident that damages the left side of his brain, his right arm and leg

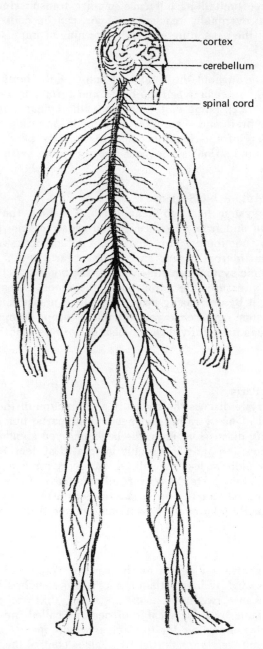

cortex

cerebellum

spinal cord

FIG. A2.2 Nerves carrying information to and from the trunk and limbs of the body connect to the brain via the spinal cord.

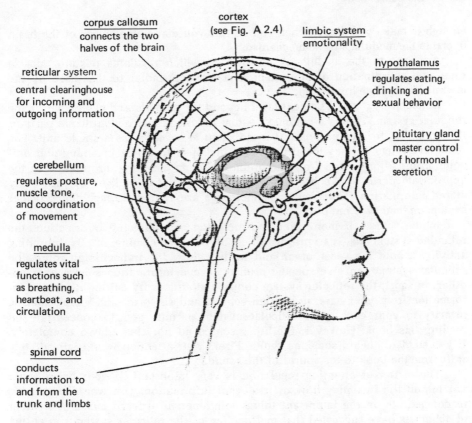

corpus callosum
connects the two
halves of the brain

cortex
(see Fig. **A** 2.4)

limbic system
emotionality

hypothalamus
regulates eating,
drinking and
sexual behavior

reticular system
central clearinghouse
for incoming and
outgoing information

pituitary gland
master control
of hormonal
secretion

cerebellum
regulates posture,
muscle tone,
and coordination
of movement

medulla
regulates vital
functions such
as breathing,
heartbeat, and
circulation

spinal cord
conducts
information to
and from the
trunk and limbs

FIG. A2.3   The inside of the brain.

are likely to be paralyzed. In most animals the two halves of the brain are pretty much equal partners, but for human beings one side is *dominant*. For most of us, the left half is dominant, which may account for the fact that most of us are right handed.

Parts of the Brain

Medulla and Cerebellum   Let us begin our discussion of the various parts of the brain with the parts that lie near the bottom. These parts are located in the area where the spinal cord connects with the brain; they play an important role in routing information in and out of larger parts of the brain and in regulating various body processes and emotional activities. At the top of the spinal cord is the medulla, which regulates such vital functions as breathing, heartbeat, circulation, and the like. For example, it receives information through spinal nerves about the carbon dioxide content of the blood and the muscle tension in the muscles that move the chest cavity and expand the lungs. Using this information, the medulla can *excite* the muscles so that you inhale when you need to and then *inhibit* this excitement so that you can exhale when necessary. Of course, it is not simply a mechanical activity because you can inhale or exhale voluntarily. Or you can hold your breath until the carbon dioxide level gets high enough to make you dizzy; when you do this you make other parts of the brain override the medulla's basic mechanism.

Adjacent to the medulla is *cerebellum,* which regulates posture, muscle tone, and coordination of movement in a manner similar to that used by the medulla to regulate breathing.

Reticular System   The next level beyond the medulla and cerebellum is the *reticular system.* This is a complex system involving many identifiable parts of the brain, but for our purposes it is sufficient to regard it as a single unit. The reticular system acts as the central clearinghouse for most incoming and outgoing information to and from the brain. It directs incoming information to the appropriate parts of the brain where it is interpreted in light of previously stored information. Then, outgoing messages are routed through the reticular system on their way out of the body.

In the course of monitoring the incoming and outgoing information, the reticular system also assigns priorities to what is coming in. By inhibiting activity at both the sense organ and further along the transmission route, the reticular system can give specific priority to one information source over another; in short, the reticular system controls attention. By cutting down the information from your ears, nose, skin senses, and so forth, and giving specific priority to your eyes, your reticular system permits you to concentrate on reading this book. However, the other senses do not close down completely. If you suddenly heard someone shout "Fire!" your attention would immediately shift from the book to the source of the sound.

The matter of attention regulation is very important. If your brain could not inhibit the incoming flow of irrelevant information, you would be unable to concentrate on the important things long enough to learn much. A number of scientists have suggested that malfunction of the reticular system's attention mechanism may be one underlying reason that some mentally retarded people can't learn quickly. Some retarded people can learn some tasks as quickly as normal people once they focus on the important components of the task—it merely takes them longer to focus. The suspicion is that their reticular systems are not permitting them to exclude the irrelevant; their attention is diverted so easily that they are unable to concentrate on the task long enough to learn it. While this hypothesis is still unproved, it may turn out to be a key to understanding and eventually helping some mentally retarded people.

Another function of the reticular system's control of attention is that it can close down virtually all senses and let you sleep. Indeed, unless there is information to process, the reticular system will not keep you awake. So, when you want to sleep you lie down in a quiet, dark room so that your senses transmit very little information. Most animals sleep whenever the information isn't very interesting, day or night. Human beings are one of the few animals that try to stay awake for long stretches at a time in spite of how dull it may be. We also apparently are the only animals who suffer from insomnia (the inability to go to sleep). This is probably because only human beings have to turn off a flood of complex information from memory, imagination, contemplation, and so forth in order to go to sleep.

Hypothalamus   Working closely with the reticular system is an important regulatory system called the *hypothalamus.* The hypothalamus regulates eating, drinking, and sexual behavior. Apparently, we would continue to eat or drink until we overflowed if it were not for inhibitory control by the hypothalamus. The hypothalamus receives information about the blood-sugar level, the fullness of the stomach, the muscle action of chewing and swallowing, and so forth, and uses it to determine when to inhibit eating. It uses signals concerning the concentration of chemicals in the blood and the blood volume to determine thirst. It can even stop thirst before these adverse signals disappear; it takes a little while for the water to go from the stomach into the blood so that the hypothalamus can detect a change, but the hypothalamus apparently can compensate for this delay and inhibit drinking before too much water has been taken in. It is not clear how sexual behavior is regulated in human beings. In most other animals, sexual behavior is controlled by hormonal changes in the female, regulated in part by the hypothalamus, which controls the *pituitary gland* (the master control of hormonal secretion). The sight and smell of a sexually ready female arouses a male animal (apparently this is also dependent upon hormonal regulation by the hypothalamus).

The hypothalamus is of particular interest to psychologists because it seems to play a role in the reactions of animals to reward and punishment. That is by means of an electrode that is like a long needle (the brain has no pain receptors, so it doesn't hurt), weak electrical stimulation of specific parts of the hypothalamus and surrounding areas will act as reward or punishment and thus promote learning by rats, monkeys, cats, and other animals. Stimulation of some of these areas apparently is pleasurable; rats, for instance, can be taught to press a switch which will deliver a short burst of electricity to a particular area. Indeed, they will sit and work the switch several thousand times an hour until they drop from exhaustion. Electrical stimulation in other parts of the brain apparently is unpleasant; animals will quickly learn to switch off such stimulation or even to press a switch to prevent it when a warning light is turned on.

No one is quite sure whether the feeling arising from this kind of artificial brain stimulation is similar to the pleasantness we feel when we are elated, sexually aroused, or happy or to the unpleasantness we feel when we are depressed, rejected, unhappy, and so on. However, it seems plausible that the stimulation is mimicking the neural activity that takes place when we feel such emotions. This seems even more reasonable when we consider that the hypothalamus is closely linked to the system which will be discussed next, a system that primarily is involved with emotionality.

Limbic System   The limbic system surrounds the reticular system and feeds information into it through the hypothalamus and other centers. Moreover, it sends and receives information to and from the senses as well as to and from other parts of the brain. Research thus far is quite incomplete, but the limbic system clearly plays a role in emotionality. A wild animal that has had damage done to a specific part of his limbic system becomes docile and friendly; a wildcat that couldn't be approached before, for example, can be safely petted. Damage to other parts of the system can do just the opposite; a normally gentle white rat will turn into a vicious, ill-tempered beast who will attack anything and anybody. Damage in yet other areas of the system produces an animal that has difficulty in learning to anticipate and avoid painful experiences. In a normal animal, the fear emotion produced by a dangerous situation is sufficient to motivate it to learn to get out of the situation. While it is not really

Box A2.1
ESB: Electrical Stimulation of the Brain

Because the nervous system is an electrochemical device, it is not surprising to find that it can be influenced by electrical stimulation. This was first demonstrated in 1791 when an Italian physiologist, L. Galvani, noted that if an electrical current was applied to an amputated frog leg, it would cause the leg to kick. While interest in this phenomenon prompted quite a lot of physiological research, it was not until the rather recent development of sophisticated surgical and electronic techniques that its psychological implications could be examined. Among these was the development of electrodes, thin needlelike wires that can be inserted painlessly into the living brain. After insertion it is possible to use the electrodes either to record the brain's own electrical activity or to send very small impulses into the brain, a process known as *electrical stimulation of the brain* (ESB), which, by the way, also is painless.

Through precise placement of the microelectrodes, ESB can be used to trigger behavior. The triggered behavior often is fairly stereotyped and predictable in lower animals, in part, perhaps, because these animals' ordinary behavior is heavily based on reflexes and instincts. In human beings, however, ESB-triggered behavior appears to be less predictable. This may be because our ordinary behavior is more heavily based on our past experiences rather than upon innate programing. But it also may be that research has failed to find much stereotyped behavior because ESB is done on human beings only as part of medical treatment and, as a result, there understandably is less experimentation and less is known about its effects on human beings than on animals.

Predictable or not, ESB-induced behavior in both animals and human beings is not wholly rigid but usually takes the situation at hand into account. For example, Dr. José Delgado, a physiologist at Yale University and one of the best-known investigators of ESB found that when some of the monkeys in a rhesus monkey colony were made aggressive through ESB, they never attacked a monkey who was higher than they were in the monkey colony's social hierarchy.* Even human beings when made aggressive through ESB express their aggressiveness in socially acceptable ways (for example, tearing up a piece of paper rather than hitting someone). Clearly, ESB does not produce totally mechanical behavior like something out of a science fiction fantasy; it apparently can initiate or inhibit existing behavior, but the actual expression (or inhibition) of the behavior is also dependent upon past experiences and the usual social and moral constraints that normally influence the things we do. In short, ESB cannot make us into robots.

Dr. Delgado has performed some extraordinary experiments using ESB to inhibit behavior. It is possible to connect the electrodes to "stimo-

* J. M. R. Delgado, *Physical Control of the Mind: Toward a Psychocivilized Society.* New York: Harper & Row, 1969.

ceivers" (so called because they can both *stimulate* the brain and *receive* electrical information from the brain) that are fastened to the heads of animals and of human beings. This permits ESB to be done via radio transmission, eliminating the need for wires and allowing the animal or human being to move freely. Using this technique, Dr. Delgado has been able to stop a charging bull in its tracks, which is most impressive. He also has shown that when ESB is used to inhibit the aggressiveness of the "boss" monkey in a colony, the monkey soon loses his dominant status. The monkey's aggressiveness and status come back after ESB is discontinued, but if his stimoceiver is controlled by a lever in the cage, other monkeys in the colony soon learn to press the lever to give him a calming dose of ESB whenever he starts to get too aggressive. In yet another experiment, Dr. Delgado demonstrated that ESB could make a monkey stop eating a banana and even spit out the part that remained in his mouth.

The fact that ESB can initiate and, more important, inhibit some kinds of behaviors provides promise for the treatment of certain kinds of medical and psychological problems. For example, treatment of chronically depressed persons with ESB has been successfully demonstrated. In the future, a person who suffers from bouts of extreme depression may elect to have electrodes and a stimoceiver implanted in his brain; when depression sets in, he merely will have to administer ESB to himself and his mood will change. Current research using ESB to treat epilepsy has also been quite successful. The day may come when an epileptic can have a stimoceiver implanted in his brain in order to monitor his brain's activity. The information would be relayed to a computer, which would analyze it for signs of the beginning of an epileptic seizure. When such signs appeared, the computer would instruct the stimoceiver to administer ESB to stop the seizure before it began. Experiments have been carried out using ESB to treat intractable pain, tremors, schizophrenia, aggressiveness, anxiety, fear, and obsessive and compulsive behaviors.

Most of the ESB research is still in the experimental stages where it is proving valuable in investigating the functions of various parts of the brain. Once these functions are better understood, ESB may well be the key to treating a variety of medical and psychological problems (such as those mentioned above) that currently are difficult to treat. Of course, like any experimental technique, ESB may have its dangers if not used with restraint and with respect for personal rights. Doubtless, few of us would want to see it used as a method of crime control or political pacification. But this is somewhat unlikely, since use of ESB requires a great deal of knowledge and skill in medicine, electronics, and so on. Also, it should be remembered that ESB cannot introduce new behaviors. All it can do is initiate or inhibit behaviors that already exist in the behavior repertory of the animal or human being. Since its potential for good is so great, abandonment of ESB for fear of its misuse might be rash.

clear-cut, the research suggests that some kinds of limbic damage prevent the fear emotion and thus interfere with learning to avoid danger. At any rate, these observations demonstrate the involvement of the limbic system with emotion.

Reception, Integration, and Response-Formulation Centers   Thus far, we have followed incoming information from the senses through the spinal cord, through or by the medulla and cerebellum to the recticular system from which it goes to the hypothalamus, limbic systems, and to the *cortex*. The cortex consists of the large puffy parts of the brain in Figure A2.3. It is made up of literally millions of neurons that are complexly interconnected. Some parts of the cortex receive information from specific senses while other parts play a role in formulating outgoing messages in response to this information. All of this involves use of information from past experience that is stored in memory, but no one knows how it all works. The best that scientists have been able to do is to discover the parts of the cortex that appear to be specifically involved with information from specific senses and with formulation of response messages to specific parts of the body.

Frontal-Parietal Cortex As you can see in Figure A2.4, there are four general divisions of the cortex that seem to be assigned to specific senses. The *frontal-parietal cortex* is primarily for the body senses. Figure A2.5 shows how it is schematically arranged. Sensory information from the various parts of the body is received in this area. Movement of the corresponding body parts is controlled by the adjacent areas. Of course, the interpretation of the information and the particular movements that are made in response involve many other parts of the brain.

Occipital Cortex The *occipital cortex* is involved in vision. Figure A2.6 shows how the optic nerves come out of the back of the eyeballs, divide, and end in the occipital cortex. The result is that information on the right half of the retina of each eye goes to the right half of the occipital cortex and that on the left half of the retina of each eye goes to the left half of the occipital cortex.

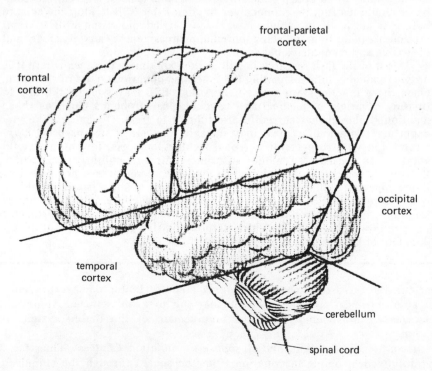

FIG. A2.4 The outside of the brain.

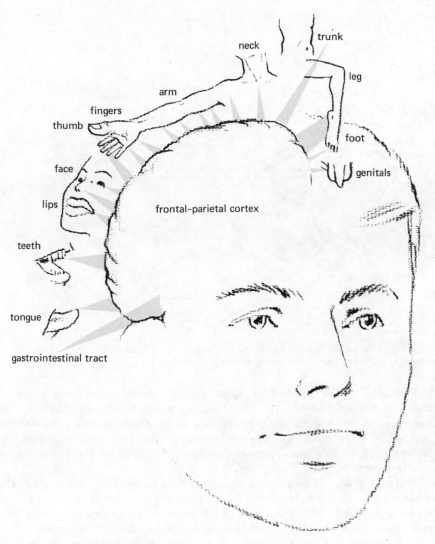

neck

trunk

leg

arm

fingers

thumb

foot

face

genitals

lips

frontal-parietal cortex

teeth

tongue

gastrointestinal tract

FIG. A2.5 A schematic arrangement of the specific areas in the frontal-parietal cortex where sensory information from various parts of the body is received.

If one of the halves of the occipital cortex is damaged (say in an accident or through disease), the person loses the ability to see one half of his visual field.

The occipital cortex is only beginning to be understood. The neural elements in the retina are interrelated in complex ways so that they are sensitive to particular colors, shapes, and directions of movement of light patterns. This information is relayed to the occipital cortex where different areas of the cortex specialize in specific kinds of information from specific parts of the retina. Then, together with information from the other senses and from memory, this information is interpreted and the appropriate response is formulated. Again, no one knows how the integration or response formulation takes place.

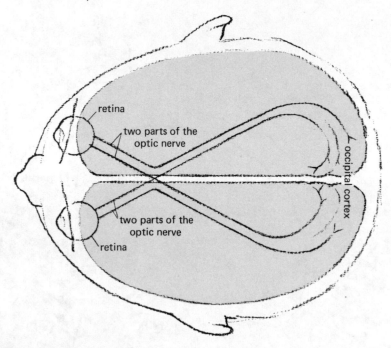

FIG. A2.6   The neural pathways from the eyes to the occipital cortex. This view is as though you were above the brain, looking downward.

Temporal Cortex   The third major sensory areas is the *temporal cortex* which receives auditory information. It is organized in a fairly simple manner; different parts are specifically for different sounds. Again this information is combined in some unknown way with information from past experience and from other senses to yield meaningful auditory perceptions and prompt appropriate responses to them.

Frontal Cortex   If you'll look at Figure A2.3 again, you will see that there are large parts of the cortex that haven't been discussed. Aside from a part of the temporal area in the left half of the brain which is pretty specific to the comprehension and production of speech, the remainder of the cortex is somewhat of a mystery. Parts of the cortex near the areas that have just been discussed are in some way related to aiding those areas in doing their job, but just how isn't clear. In fact, for medical reasons it is sometimes necessary to surgically damage or remove parts of these auxiliary areas, and strangely enough, there frequently is little or no obvious effect on the patient's behavior. What effect there is seems related to the amount of cortex that is damaged rather than to the specific locality of the damage.

The *frontal cortex* was at one time thought to be where thinking took place. This idea seemed reasonable because this area of the brain is larger for human beings than for other animals and, therefore, might be expected to reflect the uniquely human characteristics of prolonged and abstract thought. But again, removal or damage of this part of the cortex produces problems only when large areas are affected. Such results have dashed hopes that this area might be the primary storage location of past experience, that is, of memory. Indeed, memories are probably stored all over the brain (for example, the electrical stimulation of some temporal areas will cause the patient to remember things he probably could not voluntarily recall).

A Final Note

It is impossible to appreciate fully how little is actually known about how the brain works unless you ponder the stunning complexity of its organization and the overwhelming amount of information it so skillfully integrates. For example, imagine yourself at a very bad symphonic concert. As you sit there squirming in your seat, twisting your program, listening to the orchestra butcher your favorite overture, and watching the various musicians, you become aware of the fact that you are sleepy, even though you also are rather angry about the performance. Adding to your discomfort, the salt on the food you had for dinner has made you very thirsty.

Now, consider some of the major things that are going on in your brain. Your frontal-parietal cortex is receiving information about the hardness of the seat and at the same time is causing you to squirm to relieve the numbness. It also is regulating your fingers' nervous play with the program. Your temporal cortex is receiving information about the music, which is then compared to your information from past experience about how this music *ought* to sound. Your eyes dart about from one part of the orchestra to another, receiving a bewilderingly complicated sequence of visual impressions that are relayed to the occipital cortex where they are somehow interpreted as violinists, drummers, clarinetists, and so forth. Your limbic system is involved with your disgust about the poor performance. Your hypothalamus is reacting to the effect of the salt on your blood and is screaming for water. Finally, your reticular system is fighting a losing battle to keep you awake and to keep your attention on the music. When you view all of this activity as happening simultaneously and when you realize that this brief description is really giving you only the grossest picture of what is actually going on, maybe you can get a feeling for how truly amazing and complicated the nervous system and brain actually are.

Summary

1. *Neurons* and bundles of neurons, *nerves,* are transmission cables that run from the senses to the brain. They also are the stuff of which the brain is made. Impulses are initiated at the neuron's *dendrites* and proceed along the *axon* to the *end brushes* where chemical activity at the *synapse* transmits the impulse to the dendrites of the next neuron.
2. The nervous system has two components, the *somatic system* for muscles and the sense organs and the *autonomic system* for internal organs.
3. The brain receives, integrates, and formulates responses to the information received through the nervous system. It is composed of a number of highly integrated parts, primary among which are the *medulla* and the *cerebellum,* which regulate the body's vital functions; the *reticular system,* which is the clearinghouse for incoming and outgoing information; the *hypothalamus,* which controls eating, drinking, and sexual

behavior (in animals, at any rate); the *limbic system,* which plays a role in emotionality; and the *cortex,* which receives and integrates information and initiates responses.

Further Reading

Asimov, I. *The Human Brain: Its Capacities and Functions.* New York: New American Library, 1965 (c. 1963), 357 pages (paperback). Well known as an excellent writer of science fiction, Asimov is also known for the clarity of his writing on almost any detailed scientific topic. In this particular book, he describes how the brain organizes and controls the total functioning of the individual through its control over the nervous system, the senses, the glands, and the hormones.

Crichton, M. *The Terminal Man.* New York: Alfred A. Knopf, 1972, 247 pages. A novel about an attempt to control a violent man by connecting his brain to a computer. Although this book is fiction, it is based on actual research. It also touches on the social implications and moral issues of electrical stimulation of the brain (ESB). Entertaining as well as informative.

Delgado, J. M. R. *Physical Control of the Mind.* New York: Harper & Row, 1971 (c. 1969), 288 pages (paperback). A fascinating book about control of behavior through electrical stimulation of the brain (ESB). ESB experiments done with cats, bulls, monkeys, chimpanzees, and human beings are described and possible future uses of ESB are discussed.

Stevens, C. F. *Neurophysiology: A Primer.* New York: Wiley, 1966, 182 pages. A well-written description of the structure and properties of neurons and of how neurons interact with each other in the nervous system. The author also discusses how information gets in and out of the nervous system and the various methods for determining the functions of groups of cells. Although this book is fairly detailed, its clarity and its use of many simple diagrams make it easy to understand.

Tart, C. T. *Altered States of Consciousness.* New York: Wiley, 1969, 575 pages. Although technical at times, this is a fascinating book of readings about the physiological behavior and thought processes that occur during altered states of consciousness. Covers the topics of sleep and dreams, meditation, hypnosis, and drugs. Some articles are strongly research oriented while others are speculative and thought provoking.

"There are several medical reasons for implanting electrodes in man."

The pioneering research work by Delgado using electrical stimulation techniques in the brain is an exciting and controversial area of research. By stimulating various specific regions in the brain, Delgado has been able to evoke emotions and to induce various types of behavior in both animal and man. This article describes not only the research but also the implications which may follow from these investigations.

Insiders and Outsiders: Reaching for the Mind in the Depth of the Brain

In their attempts to understand man, philosophers and scientists usually function as spectators in the theater of nature, as outsiders who perceive the world through sensory inputs; they do not understand those mechanisms of the mind where all information is evaluated for the initiation of feelings, thoughts, and actions. Until recently, mental functions eluded scientific experimentation because cerebral activity could not be detected, measured, or modified by any known physical or chemical means. Behavior was investigated by simple observations: Human beings looked at other human beings, provided them with specific information or education, and attempted to estimate the influence of these sensory inputs on behavioral outputs. Even the process of introspection consisted of analyzing the effects of information received from the environment.

The essential link between sensory inputs and behavioral outputs lies within cerebral structures and involves neurological mechanisms, chemical reactions, and electrical phenomena that are absolutely prerequisite for every mental manifestation. Perhaps because these processes were unknown or unreachable, they were often considered irrelevant to understanding the mind, and even in psychology the brain was referred to as a "black box" outside the realm of investigation. This situation would be comparable to our being denied entrance to an automobile factory and, from the outside, being able to observe the delivery of steel, rubber, glass and other raw materials, and the exit of smoke, refuse, and finished cars. As outsiders it would be difficult for us to assess the organization of the factory, the processes involved, and the machinery

This article first appeared in The Humanist March/April 1972, and is reprinted by permission.

used. It would be even more difficult to understand the policies of the company, to predict future models, or to influence the decisions of the board of directors. If, however, we could place inside the factory a net of agents equipped with cameras, microphones, tape recorders, and other sensors to transmit information to the outside, our understanding of the internal organization and our prediction of present and future activities would be greatly facilitated. If, beyond that, our agents had the skill and power to influence behavior and decisions of the workers and directors, we on the outside could modify internal activities and influence the products manufactured.

Modern techniques for brain exploration give us precisely these alternatives. In many laboratories throughout the world, mechanical, thermal, electrical, and chemical sensors and stimulators are being placed inside the working brain. With these instruments it is possible to detect the synchronous pulsing of neuronal pools or even the electrical discharges of single nerve cells. We can correlate physical phenomena of specific areas of the brain with determined sensory stimulation of sounds or shapes, and we can identify certain electrical wave patterns as indicators of ongoing behavioral responses such as learning or problem solving. Miscroscopic amounts of chemicals—such as catecholamines or amino acids—have been introduced into a small cerebral area, and, depending on the selected substance and neuronal region, the intervention has been found to increase or decrease sleep, sex, appetite, or a variety of other functions. We are learning about the cerebral basis of behavior, and how and where human experiences are stored in the brain. Memory, for example, is somehow related to the stereochemical synthesis of proteins; richness or poverty of early sensory experience is manifested in the thickness of the cerebral cortex, in the submicroscopic structure of neuronal connections, and in the enzymatic composition of the brain.

Investigation and manipulation of the physiological mechanisms of mental and behavioral activities should provide a better understanding of man's biological, intellectual, and emotional capabilities and limitations, and also should help us clarify fundamental questions about personal identity, consciousness, education, freedom, and the very purpose of life.

Technology and Possibilities of Brain Control

The reception of a sensory input is accompanied by electrical and chemical phenomena that are detectable in the depth of specific areas of the brain. These phenomena are considered normal because they are activated by the organism's physiological portals of entry, that is, by the sensory receptors. Although the concept of normality is disputable, it is convenient to differentiate the effects of these inputs from those responses evoked by agents that modify the brain without sensory intervention. The latter may be classified in three groups: psychoactive drugs, psychosurgery, and direct chemical or electrical stimulation of the brain. In this article we shall briefly consider the last method.

The brain is like an ocean through which, by relying on instrumental guidance, we can navigate without visibility and reach a specific destination. Using suitable cerebral maps, oriented according to stereotaxic coordinates, we can blindly but quite accurately place electrodes within any desired brain structure. Guided by micromanipulators, assemblies of very fine wires are introduced through a small opening in the skull. The terminal contacts remain outside the skin and are used for electrical stimulations or recordings. Surgery is performed under anesthesia. As the electrodes may remain implanted for months or years, studies can be carried out with completely awake subjects who are engaged in normal activities. We can therefore experimentally investigate human and animal neuronal mechanisms related to learning, thinking, and behaving.

Experience has shown that this procedure is safe and painless. Patients wired for months have not expressed concern or discomfort; they have enjoyed normal activities and returned to the hospital only for periodic examination. There are several medical reasons for implanting electrodes in man. In some cases of drug-resistant epilepsy, it is necessary to explore the depth of cerebral structures involved in order to locate areas with abnormal discharges and to orient subsequent surgery. Patients with intractable pain, anxiety neurosis, involuntary movements, and other illnesses have also benefited from cerebral explorations without the stress and confinement of the operating room. Actually, the use of electrodes represents a more conservative approach than destruction of portions of the brain performed by neurosurgeons in the treatment of neurological disturbances. In some cases, programmed stimulation may be able to replace lesions as therapy, thereby avoiding the permanent destruction of cerebral tissue. In addition to these therapeutic values, implanted electrodes are important tools for the investigation of neurophysiological processes of animals such as monkeys and chimpanzees.

The presence of leads connecting the experimental subject to the recording instruments has represented an obstacle for free behavioral expression and for long-term stimulation. This problem has been solved by means of miniaturization and tele-control. The instrument called stimoceiver, developed in our laboratory at Yale, permits both transmission and reception of several channels of electrical messages to and from the brain, using frequency-modulated radio links. A more advanced instrumentation, also developed by our group, is the multichannel transdermal stimulator, consisting of integrated circuits enclosed in biologically inert silicon. This instrument is implanted subcutaneously. It has no batteries; energy and signals are transferred through the intact skin by radio induction. The subject, animal or human, may thus be instrumented for life.

In animals, electrical stimulation of the brain's motor areas results in well-organized movements that are indistinguishable from voluntary activities. Some of the effects are simple responses: flexing a leg, closing an eye, opening the mouth. Stimulation of other areas may evoke sequential acts of varying complexity. Excitation of the red nucleus in monkeys, for example, produced a change in facial expression followed by head-turning, standing on two feet, circling, walking on two feet, climbing, low-toned vocalization, threats, and approaches to other animals. This complex and ordered sequence was repeated as often as the red nucleus was stimulated. The effects produced were reliable if the situation remained constant, but could adapt to environmental changes. For example, waving the catching net in front of the monkey induced a precipitous escape, inhibiting most of the motor effects evoked by cerebral simulation, unless the applied electrical intensity was rather strong. The conclusion reached after considerable experimentation was that behavior is organized as motor fragments that have anatomical and functional representation within the brain. These fragments may be combined in different ways, like the notes of a melody, resulting in a succession of motor acts such as walking or eating. The formulas of motor activity may be activated in a similar way by the spontaneous "will" of the subject or by artificial electrical stimulation, which provides an excellent opportunity for analysis of the cerebral mechanisms of behavioral performance.

Even more interesting have been the results obtained by stimulating areas of the brain that play a role in emotional responses. In these cases, the evoked effect is not a stereotyped movement, but a change in general reactivity toward environmental inputs. For example, in restrained monkeys, stimulating the tegmentum, central gray, midline thalamus, and several other cerebral structures evoked a typical offensive reaction with showing of teeth, low-toned vocalization, flattening of ears, staring, restlessness, and a generally threatening attitude. When the same areas were stimulated by radio while the monkey was completely free and formed part of a colony, the results depended on the hierarchical status and the social situation. Thus when radio stimulation was applied to the boss, his aggression was directed against a particular monkey, an unfriendly male, and never against his favorite female. It should be emphasized that the increased aggressiveness depended on the electrical stimulation of the brain; the motor details of aggressive performance and the direction of hostility were determined by the previous experience of the animal and by the location and reactions of his enemies. This fact proved that the emotional state of anger could be differentiated experimentally from the actual aggressive performance and suggested that they were related to different cerebral mechanisms that could be influenced independently of each other.

The results obtained by cerebral stimulation of some of our patients agreed with these findings. For example, in a boy with temporal lobe epilepsy, electrical excitation of the second temporal convolution elicited an eight-fold increase in friendly manifestations and in verbal output. The effect was highly specific because it did not appear when other areas of the brain were stimulated. While the increase in communication and in affectivity depended on the artificially applied electricity, the facial expression, words chosen, phrases used, and ideological content of the conversation were in agreement with the patient's education and mental capacity. His basic personality had not been modified; only his affective tone and expressive aspect.

These results introduce many important questions about cerebrobehavioral correlations. Could friendliness be related to functional activation of determined areas of the brain? May this activation be induced in a similar way by specific psychic messages and by unspecific electrical signals? Can we interpret emotional tone as a cerebral bias that will modulate sensory input from the environment? Obtaining answers to these and many other questions will require more experiment and intellectual elaboration. The results already obtained in animals and humans, however, show that we have the tools necessary to investigate the neuronal basis of emotional and behavioral reactions and also that we can influence psychic functions by direct stimulation of the brain. These facts indicate that the brain and its functional counterpart, mental activities, are within experimental reach. What is necessary now is a great effort to investigate the basic cerebral mechanisms related to the essence of man, and to direct our intellect toward the understanding and control of our emotional and behavioral activities.

Limits of Brain Manipulation

The main (and fortunate) limitation of brain interventions, whether by surgery or the application of electricity or chemicals, is that they can only trigger or modify what is already in the brain: They do not provide information or skills. Electrical stimulation may activiate physiological mechanisms, but it does not create them. We cannot force a subject to fly unless it already knows how and possesses wings; we cannot teach mathematics by sending a few volts to certain neurons, we cannot implant ideas electronically; we cannot transform an organism into a radio-controlled robot.

We must realize that even during activation of the normal mechanisms of physiological performance, the nerve impulse merely initiates preestablished processes. For example, the voluntary flexion of a limb is triggered by neural messages from the brain, but it depends on a sequence of genetically determined events, including very complex chemical reactions of sugars and proteins, all of which result in the mechanical shortening of muscle fiber. Electrically evoked behavior is like a chain reaction in which the final result depends more on the structure and organization of the components than on the trigger. In a similar way, we could ask whether the finger of the officer pushing a button to launch a man into orbit is responsible for the performance of the assembled, complicated machinery. Obviously his finger, like the electrical stimulus, is only the trigger of a well-programmed series of interdependent processes; consequently, the officer should not take much credit for the feat of orbiting astronauts around the earth.

In addition, behavioral responses are determined by a constellation of factors among which brain stimulation is only one. A play of forces may result if the natural and artificial orders are contradictory. In one of our experiments, radio stimulation of the central gray in a monkey induced aggressive behavior manifested as vocalization, threatening, chasing, and biting other animals. But when exactly the same stimulation of the same animal was repeated in a different social setting, in the presence of a new monkey who dominated the stimulated one, it did not produce hostility; to the contrary, the monkey displayed submissive behavior such as grimacing.

These experimental facts illustrate the limitations of electronic control of the brain and should mitigate fears of its misuse. As discussed more extensively in my recent book *Physical Control of the Mind: Toward a Psychocivilized Society,* by stimulating the brain we cannot substitute one personality for another. It is true that we can influence emotional reactivity and perhaps make a patient more aggressive or amorous, but in each case the details of behavioral expression are related to the individual's past experience, which cannot be created by electricity. The classical methods of punishment and reward through normal sensory inputs are more effective than direct brain stimulation in inducing purposeful changes in behavioral activity. Ideologies, prejudices, beliefs, and customs are a part of the cultural setting inculcated during early childhood through normal sensory inputs, and they cannot be transmitted by direct excitation of the brain.

We must conclude that messages with complex meaning, the building blocks of personal identity, must reach the brain through the senses, and that the power of brain stimulation is far more modest. The great potential interest of cerebral explorations is that they will provide the clues for understanding normal and abnormal behavior, paving the way for a more intelligent direction of education, and clarifying the biological possibilities and limits of the human mind.

Shaping the Mind by Operant
Conditioning and Brain Manipulation

As demonstrated by B. F. Skinner and his school, operant conditioning, teaching machines, and programmed learning are powerful tools for shaping animal and human behavior. These procedures have been useful for educating normal and mentally deficient students and also as therapy for different types of deviant behavior, from homosexuality to phobias. Professor Skinner's recent book, *Beyond Freedom and Dignity*, represents a significant contribution to science and philosophy. I admire and agree with a good part of Skinner's ideas, including the necessity to design cultures and establish intelligent purpose in the behavioral shaping of the individual.

While recognizing the theoretical and practical importance of operant conditioning, I would like to point out that it is an "outsider" approach to the study of behavior: The scientist or educator offers a reward or punishment for performance of a determined response without necessarily being concerned with the intracerebral mechanisms involved. In Skinner's words, "Many physiologists regard themselves as looking for the physiological correlates of mental events. They regard physiological research as simply a more scientific version of introspection. But physiological techniques are not, of course, designed to detect or measure personalities, feelings, or thoughts." Although it is true that present methodology does not supply "very adequate information about what is going on inside a man as he behaves," I do not think that physiologists are merely interested in correlates of mental activity. With the new telemetric methods for radio communication with the brain, we have the tools to investigate not only behavioral correlates, but basic mechanisms. When movement is induced, affectivity changed, friendliness increased, or hostility manipulated in animals and humans by direct stimulation of specific cerebral structures, we are in touch with the neuronal circuits and functions responsible for these manifestations, and we can analyze their intimate activities. When we collect perfusates from the amygdala or the thalamus in awake primates, in order to follow the *in vivo* synthesis of catecholamines or amino acids during different behavioral responses, we may gain a deeper knowledge of the regional chemistry of emotions. When in response to a determined pattern of shapes or movements, unitary responses can be detected in occipital neurons, we are examining the essential events of visual perception.

It would be naive to look only to biochemical concepts and electrical fields for an explanation of the thinking process, just as it would be misleading to describe a painting only in chromatic terms. In the study of mental activity we must distinguish between the *material carriers* of coded information, which can be expressed as physical and chemical events of the neurons, and the *symbolic meaning*, which is molded by individual experience. The same symbol (for example, a red triangle) should activate the optic receptors similarly in different subjects, but, depending on a person's previous associations with this image, it may represent punishment or reward or may be neutral. The meaning is not in the material carrier, but in temporal associations among different carriers. We therefore need to correlate physical and psychological concepts that will supplement each other. Intracerebral studies can provide essential data for the understanding of how sensory input (education) is related to motor output (behavior). Ideally, then, when investigating the processes of human behavior, we should be both "outsiders" and "insiders."

Freedom

Behavioral freedom may be expressed as the conscious choice of one pattern of response from among several available alternatives, involving a rational evaluation of determinants and consequences. Biological, psychological, social, and economic factors form part of the situation to be evaluated. Accordingly, if we do not have money or proper clothing, we may be barred from access to a fancy restaurant; or from a smorgasbord table full of appetizing dishes, we may select varying amounts of several kinds of food, according to their aspect and our taste, hunger, mood, company, and other factors.

Automatism, on the other hand, is the antithesis of freedom: It is a response determined by the rigidity of the mechanisms involved; it requires a minimum of awareness, choice, or rationality. For example, the pupil constricts when exposed to light and dilates in darkness.

Freedom of action is relative, because it is determined and limited by the functional characteristics of supporting neurological mechanisms. Individual responses are a reaction to sensory stimulation, and are patterned according to the frame of reference constructed within each individual by his past learning and experiences. Freedom is certainly a choice, but the number of choices is limited; the reasons for the choice are within the limits of rationality, and the performance is in agreement with biological laws and acquired skills. For example, I do not have the freedom to talk a language that I do not know, nor can I see if I am blind.

Freedom is also related to multiplicity of available choices and to technology. Primitive man was bound to a small territory and always had to search for food, while today we can travel to distant lands, taste exotic foods and live in sophisticated homes, enjoy the music of many cultures, and communicate instantaneously with any corner of the world. In addition, we enjoy the freedom of a greater awareness, the luxury of thinking, studying, exploring, comparing, and deciding. This is perhaps the highest quality of man and the most important function of the human brain: the rational evaluation of multifactorial situations in order to plan a strategy and to follow paths of action oriented toward preestablished aims, directing the forces and resources of nature, and educating the functions and development of our own neurons. Freedom is not a spontaneous and natural result of brain physiology, but the sophisticated product of civilization, education, and the humanization of man. It is increased by education. The neuronal mechanisms of rationality, the elements of knowledge, the evaluation of received information, the flexibility of responses, and other aspects of freedom are greatly influenced by the educational molding of the brain.

Choice involves mental effort. A rational evaluation of possibilities and consequences is time-consuming, requires responsibility, and may cause anxiety. Too many choices are tiresome. In order to perform efficiently, the brain stores symbols and sequences of responses that later will be used automatically. For example, most motor acts are performed according to ideokinetic formulas. These do not exist in the newborn brain, but are learned slowly by trial and error and then stored in memory. Thus, learning to walk is a tedious process, begun with clumsy movements and precarious equilibrium, and it occupies many months of a baby's life. After the formulas for performance are learned, however, they are used without awareness. Behavioral freedom requires a balance between this kind of automatic performance and conscious choice. To learn to walk we do not need to know about muscle spindles, the cerebellum, or cardiovascular adaptation. But for a scientifically sound program of children's education or rehabilitation, or for the diagnosis and therapy of walking disturbances, we need to know as much as possible about the biological mechanisms involved.

Liberal societies are based on the principle of self-determination. They assume that each person is born free and has the right and ability to develop his own mind, shape his own behavior, construct his own ideology, and express his personality without external pressures or indoctrination. The role of education is to help natural development without trying to change the individual. Privacy has a high priority, including its intellectual, emotional, material, and territorial aspects. Personal freedom is limited only when there is interference with the rights of others.

This nonrestrictive orientation has great appeal, especially for those educated in liberal societies, but unfortunately its assumptions are not supported by neurophysiological or psychological studies of intracerebral mechanisms. While an infant may have the theoretical right to "be free," he has neither the option nor the biological mechanisms for free behavior. For his brain lacks the stored information, neuronal circuitry, and functional keyboards that are prerequisites for the formulation of choices. The brain per se with all its genetic determination is not sufficient for the development of a mind. Mental structure depends on external information that will be stored as symbolic codes with material traces carved in the proteic flesh of the neurons; to evaluate sensory messages and determine a course of action, one must correlate present information with past experience. This fact is rather important, because without a frame of reference, evaluation of reality is not possible, and a frame of reference is not provided by the genes. The empty brain of the newborn lacks the necessary information and neuronal mechanisms to process the almost infinite number of inputs from the environment. Since only a limited number are used to structure each individual, their initial selection depends on chance and on such variables as the presence and behavior of parents and teachers. During the early years of childhood, the individual is unable to search independently for alternatives. Until our capacity for intelligent choice, or even resistance, has emerged, our personality is structured in a rather automatic way.

Personal freedom, then, is not a biological gift, but a mental attribute that must be acquired and cultivated. To be free is not to satisfy sexual instincts, to grow long hair, or to kill someone who annoys us. It requires the recognition of biological drives, the understanding of their underlying mechanisms, and the intelligent direction of behavior. Our task is not to discover a "true" personality, because the search for absolute values is fantasy. Rather, we must investigate the origin, reception, intracerebral circulation, and behavioral manifestations of the sets of values that form the relative frame of reference of each individual. With this approach, immutability of values and fatalistic determination of destiny are rejected. Instead of accepting natural fate, we gain greater freedom by using intelligence; we consider that ideological systems and behavioral reactivity are only relative human creations that can be improved and modified by the feedback of reason.

Who Is To Decide?

Our understanding of intracerebral mechanisms is growing at an impressive rate. Our power to influence the physical and functional properties of the brain is also increasing rapidly, and very soon we may be able to enhance or diminish specific behavioral qualities. Who, then, is going to decide the mental shape of future man, and what will be the basis for his decisions? Should we encourage individuality or conformism, rebellion or submissiveness, emotion or intellect? What are the risks of misusing this as yet incalculable power? What ethical principles should be established?

Rejecting the myth that each individual is born with a mental homunculus, and accepting the fact that we are merely a product of genes plus sensory inputs provided by the surroundings, we approach a conclusion similar to that formulated so lucidily by Skinner: Cultures must be designed with a human purpose. Just as we have developed city planning, we should propose mental planning as a new and important discipline to formulate theories and practical means for directing the evolution of future man. We should not consider ourselves the end product of evolution; rather, we should try to imagine that thousands of years from now the inhabitants of the earth could differ more from present man than we differ from gorillas and chimpanzees. The key factor for our future development is human intelligence, which could play a decisive role in evolution.

In confronting the question "Who is to decide the qualities of future men?" we should remember that when a machine or an ideology has enough appeal and applicability, it will spread and it will be used. Our present task is to investigate the biological and mental capabilities of man and to evaluate the choices for future development. Then these choices should be made available to society and to the individual.

On one fundamental point I differ with Skinner: In cultural design, individual freedom should not be played down, but up. We should explain to the mature individual that a collection of frames of reference, including cultural prejudices, factual knowledge, conditioned reactions, and emotional settings, have been inculcated in him during his childhood; that this was done hopefully for a good purpose, but without his permission, because his brain could not develop in a vacuum of sensory inputs, and he did not have the appropriate mentality to make his own choices. Then he should be trained and encouraged to use the given building blocks of his personality in some original way, according to that unique combination of circumstances which constitutes his personal identity. It should also be made clear that we do not really own, nor have we invented, our frames of reference. They are simply borrowed from culture, although we may modify them by a process of intelligent feedback.

A Proposal

The present crisis in ideology, ethics, and human relations is in part determined by the internal contradictions of evolving civilization, including the lack of balance between rapid technological or material evolution and the slow pace of mental evolution. This imbalance is partly due to methodological problems. Study of the essential and continuous dependence of the mind on sensory reception will favor man's social integration, because it demonstrates that we cannot live alone, and that our mental survival depends upon a constant stream of information from the environment. At the same time, exploration of the genetic, environmental, and intracerebral elements that determine mental structure will favor the intelligent selection of these elements, and thus increase the basis for individual differentiation and personal freedom.

What I propose is the adoption of a strategy for mental planning. The project of conquering the human mind could be a central theme for international cooperation and understanding, because its aim is to know the mechanisms of the brain that make all men behave and misbehave, give us pleasure and suffering, and promote love and hate. The differences in genetic potential among men are magnified grotesquely, like shadows on a wall, by their educational environment. Even if political ideas, cultural values, and behavioral reactivity vary, the basic physical, intellectual, and emotional needs of men are the same, and they must have similar neurophysiological mechanisms. Hate and destruction are not functional properties of the brain, but elements introduced through sensory inputs; they originate not within the person, but in the environment.

"Other researchers have recently traced three generations of human parents who batter and abuse their children."

Expressions of violence have reached epic proportions in the United States. In some parts of the country, especially in urban areas, citizens express great fear about being free to walk wherever they want or talk with whomever they want. The causes of violence are many and complex and Bylinsky attempts to clarify some of the current research taking place in many psychological and medical laboratories around the country.

Assassinations, vicious muggings, and the high and rising U.S. murder rate have pushed the subject of violence to the forefront among American concerns. At times, the nation appears to be oddly fascinated by the phenomenon. Consider, for example, the recent proliferation of grisly movies, some of which seem to glorify violence as a cult. We have been hearing an abundance of theories about the causes of violence, which variously attribute it to the war in Vietnam, to permissiveness, to drug addiction, to racial frustrations, and even to the legacy of the wild frontier.

Now science is venturing into this area of speculation and dispute. A broad interdisciplinary effort is getting under way to explore the biological nature and origins of violence. Biologists, biochemists, neurophysiologists, geneticists, and other natural scientists are probing with increasingly precise tools and techniques in a field where supposition and speculation have long prevailed. Their work is beginning to provide new clues to the complex ways in which the brain shapes violent behavior. It is also shedding new light on how environmental influences, by affecting the brain, can trigger violence. In time, these insights and discoveries could lead to practical action that may inhibit violent acts—perhaps, for example, a change in the way children are brought up, or treatment with "anti-violence" drugs. Such preventive steps might in the long run be more effective in controlling violent crime than either "law and order" or social reform.

By tradition, students of aggression and violence have been divided into

Reprinted from the January 1973 issue of *Fortune* Magazine by special permission; ©
1973 Time Inc. Research associate: Bro Uttal.

two separate camps that hardly ever communicated with each other. On one side stood the ethologists, students of animal behavior in the wild, many of whom held that man is biologically fated to violence. At the other extreme were social scientists, who knew, or cared, little about biology. They argued that violent crime is strictly a social phenomenon, best dealt with by eliminating slums, urban crowding, and racial discrimination, and by alleviating poverty and improving the prison system.

An Imprint on the Brain

The most recent research suggests that the biological and environmental causes of violence are so closely intertwined as to require a less fragmented search for remedies. The research is showing, among other things that the environment itself can leave a physical imprint on a developing brain. The wrong kind of upbringing can make a young animal, and probably a child too, more inclined to violent behavior as an adolescent or an adult. The hopeful augury of this research is that such behavior can be prevented if steps are taken to assure that young brains develop properly.

Until a few years ago, scientists knew comparatively little about the intricate inner mechanisms of the brain that initiate and control violence. These mechanisms lie deep in an inaccessible area called the limbic system, wrapped around the brain stem, as shown in the drawing. In the limbic system, the hypothalamus stands out as the single most important control center. Regulating many of man's primitive drives, its networks of nerve cells, or neurons, direct not only aggressive and violent behavior but also the states of sleep and wakefulness, as well as sexual and feeding behavior. The front part of the hypothalamus contains networks of nerve cells that promote calmness and tranquility. The back part regulates aggression and rage.

Restraining the Hypothalamus

Nearby lies the almond-shaped amygdala, which restrains the impulses from the hypothalamus. Another close-by structure, the septum, seems to inhibit messages from both the hypothalamus and the amygdala. The cerebellum, the large structure at the back of the brain, filters sensory impulses. The hippocampus, a short-term memory bank in front of the cerebellum, is importantly involved in ways that brain researchers do not yet adequately understand.

All these structures are functionally as well as anatomically interrelated. Electrical signals, arising in response to sensory or internal cues (e.g., sight or thought), speed along nerve pathways to activate or block the function of other nerve cells. Chemicals such as noradrenaline and dopamine, which are normally present in the brain and are known as neurotransmitters, apparently ferry these electrical signals across the tiny gaps between nerve cells, called synapses, to such control centers as the hypothalamus. At the same time, the neurons are constantly bathed in waves of background electrical activity. In still unknown ways, this background "music" apparently conveys information, too.

So complex are the organization and function of the human brain that some of its estimated 10 billion nerve cells may have as many as 100,000 con-

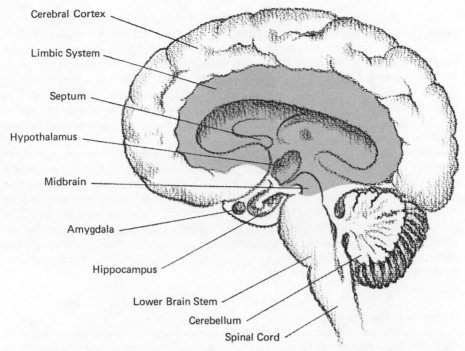

Cerebral Cortex
Limbic System
Septum
Hypothalamus
Midbrain
Amygdala
Hippocampus
Lower Brain Stem
Cerebellum
Spinal Cord

The brain's decisions about violence are made mainly by some of the structures depicted here. The centers that initiate aggressive acts, such as the hypothalamus, lie deep in the primitive part of the brain called the limbic system. Man's more intellectual cortex exercises a restraining influence over the lower brain regions. The brain, scientists speculate, reaches decisions much as a democratic society does. Individual neurons sort out conflicting impulses and decide whether to fire an electrical pulse or not. The sum of such decisions tells a person, for instance, whether to lash out at an enemy or to remain calm.

nections to adjoining cells. When an aggressive act escalates into a violent one, apparently more and more of these neurons are recruited to create bigger pathways for the flow of pulses. Thus violence, as some scientists define it, is aggression gone awry.

The Case of the Enraged Cat

Fortunately for the advance of knowledge about human aggression, the limbic systems of animals have recently been found to bear an amazing functional resemblance to that of man. So laboratory experiments with animals (notably monkeys, cats, and mice) underpin the still limited investigations of aggression systems in the human brain.

Using fine electrodes inserted into animal brains, researchers have induced a fascinating range of aggressive behavior. Cats that normally do not attack rats, for instance, will stalk and kill a rat when stimulated in a certain area of the hypothalamus. On the other hand, a cat stimulated in another nearby region of the hypothalamus may ignore an available rat and attack the experimenter instead. Destruction of the nucleus of the amygdala will turn a friendly cat into a raging beast that claws and bites without provocation, because the signals from the hypothalamus are no longer dampened by the amygdala.

Similarly, a tumor in the hypothalamus or the amygdala can turn a peaceful person into a violent one. Such tumors occur infrequently. Corrective brain surgery remains highly controversial, however, mainly because surgeons lack precise knowledge of the aggression systems and know little about the risk of unwanted side effects from such operations. A surgical lesion—a scar-producing cut, freeze, or burn intended to destroy tissue—can increase or decrease hostile behavior, depending on its location.

Similar gaps in medical information inhibit manipulation of aggressive behavior with drugs that structurally mimic the neurotransmitter chemicals. Recent experiments by Peter Bradley, a British neuropharmacologist, show that a brain cell can be affected in different ways by the same neurotransmitter, depending on the state of the cell, the amount of neurotransmitter, and how often the chemical is administered. It also appears that during an aggressive act a general arousal of the physiological system occurs—the same type of arousal that can be produced by such peaceful activities as jogging or even a concentrated mental effort.

Dynamite in the Genes?

The complex anatomical and biochemical systems of the brain get their "orders" from the genes that determine behavior. Recent studies suggest that males have more brain cells that specialize in aggression than do females. This means that boys are more likely than girls to inherit aggressive tendencies. Very little is yet known, though, about the relationship between specific genetic defects and violence, how many such defects exist, and how frequently they might be inherited. Among the handful of anomalies discovered so far that some scientists have connected with violent behavior is the famous extra Y chromosome, which luckily appears to be inherited by fewer than two men in a thousand. (X and Y are sex chromosomes, with a normal male having an X and a Y, and a normal woman two X's.)

The Y chromosome leaped from the quiet of the laboratory four years ago and landed with a splash in newspaper headlines and courtrooms. The XYY males, usually tall, were said to have a natural propensity for violent crime. Some lawyers tried to gain reduced sentences or acquittal for their clients on the basis of their real or imagined extra Y chromosome. In France, at least, one attorney succeeded.

Some imaginative work now in progress at the University of Connecticut suggests that the Y chromosome story isn't all that simple. Researchers in the department of biobehavioral sciences, led by Benson E. Ginsburg, a noted geneticist, have designed animal breeding techniques that allow them to "tease out," as Ginsburg puts it, the contributions of individual genes and chomosomes to behavior. Their findings strongly hint that an XYY male's tendency to aggressiveness depends on whether he inherited his extra Y chromosome from a peaceful or aggressive father. The Y chromosome may act on the brain through the male sex hormones. Ginsburg and other scientists are trying to find out how this process works.

Elevating genetic probing to a new level of precision, Ginsburg and his colleagues have also shown that a Y chromosome from an aggressive father can combine with another genetic anomaly to make an animal twice as aggressive as it would be with just one genetic defect. They worked with an inbred strain of mice known as DBA 1. These mice are genetically susceptible to epileptic-type seizures that can be initiated by a high-frequency sound from a buzzer, or a bell, or even a jangling set of keys. The sound activates an enzyme system, controlled by a gene as all enzymes are, and located in the hippocampus. In a mouse, the network of neurons involved makes up an area the size of a pinpoint. The enzyme activated by sound, nucleoside triphosphatase, generates epileptic-like brain waves that can be recorded.

Stormy Weather in the Hippocampus

The DBA mice, particularly males, are abnormally aggressive, apparently because of the defect in their hippocampus. In such mice, complex chemical reactions are superimposed on abnormal electrical activity in their hippocampal neurons. "You whip up an electrical storm in that region of the brain," says Ginsburg, describing his work with a touch of poetic license. Chemicals in the brain intensify the storm, he says, "as if you poured gasoline on a fire—and it went whoosh!"

The same type of storm, and in the same spot, rages in the brains of certain humans. They are either pathologically aggressive or have been made aggressive by hippocampal stimulation. This suggests, of course, that Ginsburg and his colleagues have found a genetic anomaly underlying aggression in both mice and men. In recent years, surgeons in some hospitals have been stimulating different parts of the brains of cancer patients in an effort to find an area that might block unbearable pain. In a number of instances, where doctors have stimulated the hippocampus by administering a very mild electrical shock through an electrode, patients showed the type of rage that Ginsburg and his associates found in those DBA mice. One mild-mannered patient in his fifties suddenly brandished his bedpan as a weapon against the nurses and whoever else happened to be around. He later felt quite embarrassed and contrite.

The discovery of the consequences of these anomalies and of other types of brain damage shatters the assumption made by criminologists and sociologists that the vast majority of cases of violent behavior involve people with completely normal brains. Studies of criminals who have repeatedly committed violent offenses show that they have a higher incidence of brain damage than the general population. Moreover, recent research is uncovering subtle forms of brain damage, unrecognized until now. No one knows for sure how many people in the U.S. suffer from brain damage, but some doctors place the number at 10 million to 20 million. Not all of them are violent, of course, but in addition there are many thousands who suffer from delusions or other forms of mental disturbance that make them dangerous. David Hamburg, head of the psychiatry department at Stanford University Medical School, estimates that the nation harbors some 200,000 potential presidential assassins. "Many manage their delusions on the fantasy level," says Hamburg. "Others engage in other forms of violent behavior."

What many people with brain abnormalities may have in common are pathways in the brain that failed to develop properly in infancy because of faulty upbringing, just as visual nerve pathways fail to develop properly in animals deprived of light. The fault, especially during the first two years of life when the brain is growing the fastest, lies in lack of physical affection, which an infant needs as much as nourishment. Earlier researchers had usually blamed emotional, social, or learning deficiencies for behavioral disturbances in infants raised in a foundling home. But James Prescott, a young neuropsychologist at the U.S. National Institute of Child Health and Human Development, suggests that there is a more fundamental biological reason. He maintains that normal pathways in the brain do not fully develop in children deprived of such expressions of affection as touching, cuddling, and being carried about. Instead, he says, this "somatosensory deprivation" leaves them with damaged central nervous systems.

A Chicken-Wire Mother

In a dramatic series of experiments, Harry F. Harlow, a University of Wisconsin psychologist, has demonstrated what happens when baby rhesus monkeys are deprived of their mothers. Harlow placed an infant monkey in a cage with two inanimate mother substitutes. One, covered with terry cloth and equipped with bicycle-reflector eyes, was designed to feel and look somewhat like a real rhesus mother but had no apparatus for feeding the infant. The other "mother," made of unadorned chicken wire, was unattractive to touch but contained a baby's bottle from which the infant could drink milk. Harlow found that the infant rhesus clearly preferred to spend all of its time with the nonfeeding surrogate. Even when feeding from the chicken-wire "mother," the infant would cling to his terry-cloth favorite. Harlow concluded that in infant-mother love, holding and cuddling are even more important than feeding. He also found that female monkeys who grew up with mother surrogates failed to develop maternal affection: they all seemed indifferent to their own children. Like parents who abuse their children, these monkey mothers frequently attacked, and sometimes even killed, their infants. Other researchers have recently traced three generations of human parents who batter and abuse their children. The only common characteristic of such parents, regardless of social or economic class, was that they themselves had suffered from lack of mothering and affection. Harlow wryly concluded a recent paper:

> Hell hath no fury like a woman spurned.
> With love not given, love is not returned.
> The loveless female, human or macaque,
> In place of love will substitute attack.

Can such deprived, aggressive monkeys be restored to normalcy? Experiments in Harlow's laboratory indicate that rehabilitation is possible if it is done early enough. Young monkey mothers reared in isolation sometimes regain most of their normal maternal behavior when locked in a cage with their own babies. The infant clings to the mother so persistently, despite her efforts to put it away, that eventually the baby monkey begins to serve as a therapist. Similarly, some young male monkeys reared in isolation become less aggressive when forced to play with monkeys their own age or younger.

Research into the brains of monkeys raised in isolation is just beginning, but indirect evidence already hints that such treatment induces brain damage.

In humans, brain waves with abnormal, jagged "spikes" are often a telltale sign of damage. Robert G. Heath and Bernard Saltzberg, researchers at Tulane University, have recorded such spikes in the brain waves of monkeys reared by Harlow. The spikes reflect abnormal electrical activity, particularly in the cerebellum.

Why Ding Feared Dong

Further evidence of the cerebellum's role in violence comes from the work of A. J. Berman, a neurosurgeon at Mount Sinai Medical School and the Jewish Hospital in Brooklyn. He has successfully modified autistic and aggressive behavior in isolation-reared monkeys by removing presumably abnormal sections of cerebellum that deal with the reception of sensory signals. In one experiment, Berman performed similar surgery on two monkeys called Ding and Dong, who had fought viciously and continuously. The operation turned Ding into a submissive animal, while Dong remained as aggressive as ever. Berman attributes the difference to the location of the surgery. Some tissue was removed from the midline section of Ding's cerebellum while the excision on Dong was microscopically closer to the side of that brain structure.

Berman suggests that his findings may one day be relevant to treating humans. "Walk into the back wards of any mental institution," he says, "and you'll find children whose behavior is identical with that of Harlow's monkeys."

All these and many other experiments have led a number of scientists to conclude that people who behave overaggressively may have an abnormality in the mechanism by which they perceive pleasure. In animals reared in isolation, as in pathologically violent people, the impulses resulting from the stimulation of movement and skin sensations may not be reaching their normal destinations in the brain. The feeling of pleasure may thus be experienced only partially or not at all.

This may explain, among other things, why both institutionalized children and monkeys brought up in isolation generally rock back and forth for hours on end and respond violently if touched. Adults with damaged pleasure systems similarly may be trying to derive pleasure from the rough physical contact involved in violent acts; they may, in effect, be seeking an additional stimulus. Researchers have also found that electrical stimulation of pleasure centers in the brain eliminates feelings of rage, because the brain seems to contain rival nerve systems that suppress opposing emotions chemically and electrically.

The Scientist Plays Victim

Aggressive behavior doesn't necessarily have to arise as a result of damaged networks of nerve cells; it can be easily learned, too. Albert Bandura, a pioneering psychologist at Stanford University, demonstrated almost a decade ago how effectively aggression can be taught through the power of example. He used as "victims" large, inflated plastic figures known as Bobo dolls. Small children watched both real-life and filmed attacks on the dolls, then were given an opportunity to act aggressively themselves.

In study after study, researchers discovered that boys, especially, easily learn and retain aggressive behavior. They readily act out what they have learned not only on Bobo dolls but on other children and even adults. In one typical and recent experiment, conducted by psychologist Robert M. Liebert and his associates at New York State University at Stony Brook, kindergarten children watched a short film. Later they spontaneously attacked a scientist who had appeared in the film dressed up as a hard-luck clown and had been beaten up by another researcher. Many studies show that televised violence affects children in similar ways.

Violent behavior can be set off by many other environmental conditions. For instance, Leonard Berkowitz, a University of Wisconsin psychologist, showed that the mere presence of firearms can stimulate aggressive action. He tested groups of students who were provoked and insulted by one of his colleagues. Later, the groups had a chance to administer electric shocks to their tormentor. Students in a room where a gun was casually displayed gave the investigator about 25 percent more shocks than those in a room containing no weapons. The findings suggest to Berkowitz and others that easy access to lethal weapons—about 65 percent of homicides in the U.S. are committed with guns—not only facilitates the commission of crimes but creates an atmosphere in which violence is more likely to occur.

As in the laboratory, violence in real life often begets more violence. Marvin E. Wolfgang, a noted criminologist at the University of Pennsylvania, has coined the term "subculture of violence" to describe the cluster of values, attitudes, and life styles prominent among the poor living in the slums. Violence in that setting is so common as a problem-solving mechanism, says Wolfgang, that there is no shortage of real-life models for the young to imitate.

Many other factors—frequent absence of fathers, low income, unstable employment, poor living conditions—also bend the behavior of underprivileged youths toward violence, according to Wolfgang. Under all these pressures, plus in some cases a lack of physical affection at home, adolescent blacks have the highest homicide rate of any group in the U.S.

To complicate matters, they, like other adolescents, undergo a hormonal upheaval. Boys in particular become more aggressive as the amount of sex hormones in their bodies increases. Electron microscopy at Oxford University has recently begun to reveal structural differences between males and females in such control centers of aggression as the hypothalamus, for which hormones have a particular affinity.

Are Men Stronger Than Mice?

The still mysterious workings of hormones on the brain constitute only a small part of the enormous gap between what scientists have discovered and what remains to be learned about the physiology and biochemistry of violence. For example, says Benson Ginsburg, the University of Connecticut geneticist, scientists should find out whether men, through conscious control and training, can override the physiological changes involved in aggression much more effectively than, say, mice can. Another unknown is whether genetic instructions are so strong in some people as to completely mold their behavior. Answers to such questions could open the way to far more specific therapies. More effective anti-violence drugs, for instance, could be developed if we could delineate the particular enzymatic mechanisms in the brain that affect aggression.

Treatment with existing drugs, many scientists feel, is something like using a shotgun where a rifle is needed. Even so, some investigators propose that methadone-type clinics be set up to dispense drugs available now to persons prone to violence. Lithium might be useful because it appears to speed up the release of serotonin, a brain chemical that seems to inhibit aggression. Michael H. Sheard, a Yale neuropharmacologist, has had some success in modifying the behavior of violent prisoners with lithium.

Other novel approaches may emerge from studies that are under way. For example, development of a vastly improved brain-wave recording machine, now in progress at Tulane, would enable doctors to detect signals of trouble from deep in the brain without surgically implanting recording electrodes there. It may also become possible to treat damaged deep-nerve networks ultrasonically, thereby avoiding surgery.

It is clear that much more specific therapies than those in use today are needed for people who have brain damage. Vernon H. Mark and Frank R. Erwin observe in their recent book, *Violence and the Brain:*

> Hoping to rehabilitate such a violent individual through psychotherapy or education, or to improve his character by sending him to jail or by giving him love and understanding—all these methods are irrelevant and will not work. It is the malfunction itself that must be dealt with, and only if this fact is recognized is there any chance of changing his behavior.

No Trouble in Tahiti

To prevent brain damage that may lead to violence, some new tactics could be tried now. "Changing child-rearing practices is probably the most important single thing we can do as a society," says Prescott. "We have to make sure that the children we have are wanted children." Prescott and others also suggest that it might be a good idea to evaluate and treat children as early as age five if they show a tendency to brutalize other children or animals or have episodes of uncontrolled rage. Such youngsters, scientists say, are good candidates for violent behavior later.

Anthropologists have gained some intriguing clues about child rearing by studying peaceful societies. Prescott surveyed data from forty-nine primitive cultures and found in thirty-six of them an amazingly strong correlation between physical affection toward infants and lack of violence. In societies where infants were treated cruelly, violence prevailed. Robert Levy, an anthropologist at the University of California at San Diego who had studied tranquil Tahiti, found that parents on the island seldom punish children by hitting them. Thus the children have no aggressive models to emulate.

Another deterrent to violence may be the habit of arguing it out. Societies that have developed highly elaborate ways of verbalizing violence are quite peaceful. In Tahiti and other Polynesian islands, people engage in "talking out acute anger, rather than taking physical action," says Levy. Similarly, Italians sometimes sound violent, but according to scientists who have studied Italy, there is far less incidence of violent offenses there than in the U.S.

This nation leads the advanced industrialized countries of the world in homicide and other violent crimes. Assaults in the U.S. occur nearly twice as often per capita as in England and Wales, and robberies are ten times as common. In 1971, the latest full year for which figures are available, 17,630 people in the U.S. were murdered. In England and Wales, West Germany, France, and Italy, which have a combined population about 3 percent larger than ours, there were only 1,948 murders—a rate almost ten times lower than that in the U.S.

By contrast with the U.S., these other industrial countries have more homogeneous populations, exert greater control over firearms, and operate with somewhat more rigid social structures. These differences may explain some, though not necessarily all, of the disparities in the rates of violence. In any case, it is clear that our methods of dealing with the problem have not proved particularly effective. Scientific investigation at last is beginning to provide surprising insights into why this is so. In time, the new research may lead to a much broader understanding of violent behavior, and, eventually, to effective means of discouraging it.

"Stress, then, is rampant not in rural or in underdeveloped countries, but in the great urban centers of the industrialized world."

The enormous consequences of stress in our society are expressed in this article, including the fact that many of its byproducts appear to be destructive to human beings. Social demands for achievement, excellence, and competence appear to produce psychological stress effects that are destructive to the human body. Researchers in the area of stress are attempting to understand and to deal with these problems.

It has long been a matter of common intuition that bottled-up anger can crack the bottle, prolonged strain can make people sick. This old folklore now has considerable scientific support. Working independently, several groups of medical researchers—both physicians and psychologists—have collected impressive evidence that emotional factors are primarily responsible for many of the chronic diseases that have been hitting American males hard in middle age, notably the big one, heart disease. Challenging medical dogma, these doctors deny that fatty diet, cigarette smoking, and lack of proper exercise pose the main perils to men in their working prime. Much more important, they say, is stress. Stress might be defined as the body's involuntary reactions to the demanding life that we Americans choose—or that chooses us.

These reactions are rooted deep in the prehistory of the human species. Early man survived in a brutal world because, along with an elaborate brain, he had the mechanisms of instantaneous, unthinking physical response when in danger. Picture a primitive man, many thousands of years ago, lying in the sun in front of his cave after the hunt, digesting. Suddenly he felt the cool shadow of a predatory carnivore, stalking. Without thinking, he reacted with a mighty surge of bodily resources. Into his blood flashed adrenal secretions that mustered strength in the form of both sugar and stored fats to his muscles and brain, instantly mobilizing full energy, and stimulating pulse, respiration, and blood pressure. His digestive processes turned off at once so that no energy

Reprinted from the January 1972 issue of *Fortune* Magazine by special permission; © 1972 Time Inc. Research associate: Varian Ayers Knisely.

was diverted from meeting the threat. His coagulation chemistry immediately prepared to resist wounds with quick clotting. Red cells poured from the spleen into the stepped-up blood circulation to help the respiratory system take in oxygen and cast off carbon dioxide as this ancestral man clubbed at the prowling beast, or scuttled safely back into his cave.

A Cool Memo from a V.P.

Today, say stress researchers, a man in a business suit still reacts, within his skin, in much the same chemical way. He does so although today's threat is more likely to be in the abstract, for example, a cool memo from a vice president of the corporation: "The chairman wants a study of the savings possible in merging your division with warehousing and relocating to South Carolina."

Flash go the hormones into the blood; up goes the pulse beat—but the manager who receives the memo can neither fight physically nor flee. Instead his first tendency is to stall, which only induces guilt, before he plunges into a battle fought with no tangible weapons heavier than paper clips. Under his forced calm builds repressed rage without any adequate target—except himself.

If he is the kind of hard-driving, competitive perfectionist whom many corporations prize, and if this kind of stress pattern is chronic, the stress experts will tell you that he is a prime candidate for an early coronary (an even more likelier candidate than American men in general, whose chances of having a heart attack before age sixty are one in five). If not a coronary, it may be migraine, ulcers, asthma, ulcerative colitis, or even the kind of scalp itch James V. Forrestal developed as he began to give away to interior pressure. Or perhaps a collision on the road—stressed people are more accident-prone.

Chronic strain is so common that there are conventional ways of fighting back. Millions of pills repose in desk drawers, ready to foster calmness or energy. The trouble with them, say the doctors, is that after the calm or the uplift there usually comes a period of depression. Martinis may be better, although they too involve dangers. Some people under stress try to vent their repressed anger in polite violence at a driving range or bowling alley, or by chopping wood or throwing themselves at ocean waves breaking on the beach. But the violent exercisers had better be careful of contracting another common stress symptom, low back pain.

Marriages have to accept a lot of stress, both in hurtful words and yet another symptom, temporary impotence. If a man coming under job stress has been on an anticholesterol diet he had better stay on it, but the competitive strain on him will be upping his serum cholesterol, whatever he eats. In broad terms, man the victorious predator now preys internally on himself.

Lost Consolations

Why has stress become such a problem in today's world of mass-manufactured comforts and conveniences? For most people in industrial nations, after all, life is in many respects a lot easier than it was for their ancestors. Perhaps the answer, or at least part of the answer, is that modern societies have to a great extent lost the supports that helped people in earlier times endure toil, hardship and suffering—religious faith, sustaining frameworks of tradition and custom, a sense of place in the social order, a sense of worth derived from the exercise of craftsmanship, and awareness that toil, hardship, and suffering were likewise endured by the other members of the same community and the same social class. In the twentieth century the great increase in physical abundance has been accompanied by swift and deep erosion of these intangible sources of consolation and support.

Particularly destructive of the individual's sense of security have been the side effects of one of the industrial world's most precious products—social mobility. This bright trophy of our times has its deeply etched dark side. Social mobility has weakened the sense of belonging to a class, the sense of having a place in the social order. More important, social mobility implies that success depends on merit alone, and to the extent that a society believes in such correlation, individual breadwinners are thrust into an endless competition in which losing or lagging can be interpreted as a sign of personal inadequacy.

Stress, then, is rampant not in rural or in underdeveloped countries, but in the great urban centers of the industrialized world. And it is not surprising that external threats to the community tend to decrease individual stress rather than increasing it. In England, for example, two prime indexes of stress, alcoholism and suicide, declined markedly during World War II.

As a recognized factor in disease, stress is very much a product of the twentieth century. When it was still but vaguely recognized forty years ago, the medical historian Henry S. Sigerist foresaw its importance. Every epoch, he observed, has its characteristic ailments. "It seems as though the powers that ordain the style for and stamp their impress upon a certain epoch affect even disease." He pointed out that the Middle Ages were dominated by ills of the common people such as the great plague, leprosy, and the epidemic neuroses, which appeared in the sixth to the fourteenth centuries. The disease that characterized the Renaissance was syphilis, an infection incurred not passively but as a result of an individual act. "In the discordant Baroque era, the foreground is occupied by diseases which might be called deficiency diseases like camp-fever, scurvy and ergotism on the one hand and on the other by diseases which might be called luxury diseases like gout, dropsy and hypochondriasis." Tuberculosis and similar ailments characterized the romantic period, "while the 19th century, with its tremendously increased industrialization, the development of great cities and the accelerated life tempo, brought about industrial diseases, general nervousness and neuroses of many kinds."

The Seeds and the Terrain

Medicine, too, has its epochs. Until late in the nineteenth century, the leading doctors were generalists, devoutly concerned with the "whole man." According to Sir William Osler, the famous Canadian clinician, "It is much more important to know what sort of a patient has a disease than what sort of a disease a patient has." Claude Bernard, the most renowned of nineteenth-century French physicians, maintained that diseases were resisted by a person's central equilibrium, his *milieu intérieur;* the germs were all about, like seeds blown by the wind, but did not take root in his "terrain" unless he had already been weakened.

After the middle of the nineteenth century, however, the medical world's focus of attention began to shift from the patient to the disease. Pasteur and other great scientists achieved glorious successes in identifying harmful micro-organisms, and medicine knocked off one disease after another. Many doctors came to consider the question of the patient's receptivity to illness almost quaint, except in such obvious conditions of weakness as severe malnutrition. By 1943, Dr. Flanders Dunbar of Columbia University-Presbyterian Hospital in New York was able to point out that of the most common dangerous illnesses in America fifty years earlier—infections such as scarlet fever and typhoid—not one was still on the list of the ten most common causes of mortality and morbidity.

Yet the hospitals were still full. It almost seemed that man was inventing new chronic diseases to replace the old infections. The realization sent some medical practioners and researchers back to the whole-man concept. In the vanguard was Dr. Harold G. Wolff of New York Hospital-Cornell Medical Center, who wrote that in infectious disease "the presence of the micro-organism, however indispensable, is not sufficient as the cause of illness ... In a sense, disease is a reaction to rather than an effect of noxious forces."

Through painstaking observation and accumulation of case histories, Dunbar, Wolff, and other investigators were able to demonstrate that many persons who had become vulnerable to certain organisms shared not only physical but also psychological characteristics. This was especially true in chronic conditions such as eczema, gastric ulcer, diabetes, arthritis, migraine, asthma, and ulcerative colitis. The researchers decided that the Victorian novelists had been excellent intuitive diagnosticians in discerning that people who had been through periods of severe emotional upset, such as a broken love affair, or depression caused by the death of a beloved mate, were especially vulnerable to pulmonary tuberculosis. More recently a high incidence of cancer has been found in the same circumstances, but the evidence is less convincing, so far, than with TB. Some studies indicate also that vulnerabilities shift as social patterns change. For example, peptic ulcers used to be primarily a woman's ailment. One retrospective medical study reveals that from 1850 to 1900 close to seven out of every ten patients with perforated peptic ulcers were women. But from 1920 to 1940 nine out of every ten were men. Since mid-century the incidence of ulcers in women has been on the rise again.

A growing accumulation of evidence indicates that a great many bodily ills that afflict human beings are partly psychosomatic in nature. For example, a period of mental depression affects a patient's nasal mucous membranes, making him somewhat more vulnerable to virus infections. As one doctor observed, "You don't have to be depressed to get a cold, but it helps."

Some very different chronic illnesses have been interlinked. The *Journal of Chronic Diseases* several years ago published a paper entitled "Why Do Wives with Rheumatoid Arthritis Have Husbands with Peptic Ulcer?" The answer was a summary of research revealing the existence of a particular type of hostility in such marriages. The wife, conditioned by early childhood, had a yearning for high public esteem, an ambition that her husband could not, or would not, enable her to gratify. Frequently, the husband was of the common ulcer type, in strong need of emotional support, which the wife, because of her resentment, did not provide.

Aggression is likely to be clearer in close business relationships than in marriages, but still not simple. Dr. Sidney Cobb, one of the authors of the paper on arthritic wives and ulcerous husbands, recently noted in conversation that many a quietly aggressive executive unconsciously picks an ulcer-prone assistant, sensing that the assistant can be prodded into anxious action by the boss's failure to say good morning.

Discovering the Ubiquitous

A pioneer investigator into the implications of stress was Dr. Hans Selye, a Canadian who has become the world's acknowledged authority on his subject. Selye, now sixty-four, defines stress as the nonspecific response of the body to any demand made on it. He maintains that stress went unstudied in detail for centuries simply because it had always been so common. "Stress is ubiquitous, and it is hard to *discover* something ubiquitous."

Selye recalls that an intimation of his future specialty came to him in his youth.

I was a second-year medical student in Prague in 1926 when my professor brought in five patients for the students to diagnose—one with cancer, one with gastric ulcer, etc. It struck me that the professor never spoke about what was common to them all, only about what were the specifics of the diagnosis. All these patients had lost weight, lost energy, and lost their appetites.

Ten years later, an assistant professor at McGill in Montreal, Selye observed that various kinds of insults to the bodies and nervous systems of laboratory animals had lasting effects in making them vulnerable to subsequent stress.

I was trying to isolate a hormone in the laboratory. I was working with extracts of cow ovaries and injecting them into rats. All of them, when later subjected to stress, had the same reaction—adrenal overaction, duodenal and gastric ulcers, and shrinking thymus, spleen, and lymph nodes. The worse the stress, the stronger the reaction. Then I tried injecting other materials, even simple dirt. I even tried electric shock, and got the same results.

When he tried inducing fear and rage, results were again similar.

When All the Rats Died

One of Selye's most significant breakthroughs came when he realized he could take two similar groups of rats and predispose one group to heart disease, uncommon in animals, by injecting an excess of sodium and certain types of hormones. Then he would expose both groups of rats to stress. None of the control group suffered. *All* the cats in the predisposed group died of heart disease.

In time, Selye came to the conviction that the endocrine glands, particularly

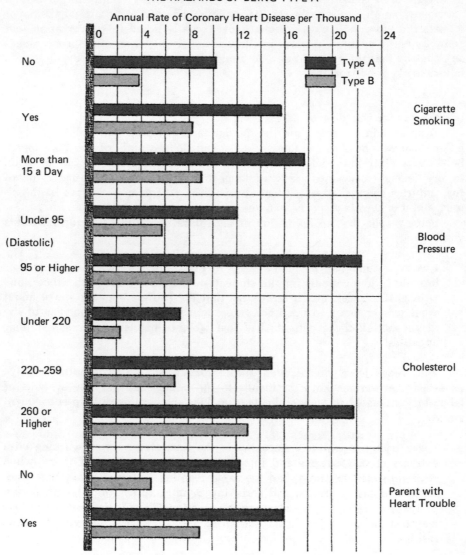

THE HAZARDS OF BEING TYPE A

Annual Rate of Coronary Heart Disease per Thousand

Your temperament is more important in making you a candidate for a coronary than the number of cigarettes you smoke, your blood pressure, the level of cholesterol in your blood, or even your heredity. So say Drs. Friedman and Rosenman. They point to an eight-and-a-half-year study of more than 3,000 American males. First the men were interviewed and classified into the competitive Type A and the more relaxed Type B. Then detailed medical records were maintained. The A's had more coronary heart disease—even, in many cases, when the conventional risk factors predicted more for B's.

the adrenals, were the body's prime reactors to stress. "They are the only organs which do not shrink under stress; they thrive and enlarge. If you remove them, and subject an animal to stress, it can't live. But if you then inject extract of cattle adrenals, stress resistance will vary in direct proportion to the amount of the injection, and can even be put back to normal."

Selye explains that when the brain signals the attack of a stressor—which could be either a predatory beast or a threatening memorandum—the adrenal and pituitary glands produce the hormones ACTH, cortisone, and cortisol, which stimulate protective bodily reactions. If the stress is a fresh wound, the blood rushes irritants to seal it off; if the stress is a broken bone, swelling occurs around the break. The pro-inflammatory hormones are balanced by anti-inflammatory hormones, which prevent the body from reacting so strongly that the reaction causes more harm than the invasion.

Energy That Can't Be Replenished

So the initial reaction to any kind of stress is alarm. It is followed by an instantaneous rallying of the body's defenses. The fight is on—even if the body, in effect, is just fighting the mind. If the threat recedes or is overcome, stability returns. But if the attack is prolonged, deterioration sets in, as the defense system gradually wears down. Selye calls this process the General Adaptation Syndrome, and it is recognized in the field as a brilliant concept.

Stress is not only a killer, Selye teaches, but also a drastic aging force. Different men have different hereditary capacities to withstand stress, but once each man's "adaptation energy" has been expended, there is no way yet known to replenish it. Selye believes that some time in the future it may be possible to produce from the tissues of young animals a substance that could replenish human stress energy. "But that is for the Jules Verne future—soft research, like soft news, that may happen."

Selye likens each man's supply of life energy to deep deposits of oil; once the man has summoned it up and burned it in the form of adaptation energy, it is gone—and so, soon, is he. If he picks a high-stress career, he spends his portion fast and ages fast. "There are two ages," says Selye, "one which is chronological, an absolute, and the other which is biologic and is your effective age. It is astonishing how the two can differ."

At the University of Montreal, Selye conducts research on how to keep the machine, man, oiled in his daily struggle against small and large stressors. His latest news is the work his laboratory has done with certain hormones called catatoxic steroids. "In their protective action, they are almost like a panacea," he claims. "These antistress hormones produce enzymes in the body, most of which destroy toxic substances, or neutralize them. Detoxication is the most effective way to fight disease or stress. Pollutants, nicotine, and carcinogens— all can be detoxified in the body by catatoxic steroids. And, unlike the corticoids, the best of this group, PCN, has no toxicity itself, no hormonal effect."

As an example of the promise of catatoxic steroids, Selye points to cardiac patients, for whom doctors frequently prescribe digitalis. Selye says a doctor is forced to experiment, sometimes almost to overdo the dose, in order to ascertain how much a patient needs. Yet if the patient is given too much digitalis, he will suffer a buildup of toxic effects. The correct catatoxin, says Selye, can neutralize that danger. Many an industrial worker exposed to dangerous fumes, to mercury, or to other poisonous substances will be protected with catatoxic steroids, he predicts, when they are perfected and available. The potential market is so broad that seventeen different chemical manufacturers in the U.S. and abroad are participating in Selye's research.

A Queerly Contemporary Quality

Stress research in the U.S. centers on heart disease, and for good reason. Cardiovascular ailments such as coronary heart disease now take an appalling annual toll in lives of American men in vigorous middle age. Of the 700,000 people who died from coronary heart disease in the U.S. last year, almost 200,000 were under sixty-five.

Yet until this century heart disease was virtually unknown anywhere in the world, and as late as the 1920's it was still fairly rare in the U.S. Dr. Paul Dudley White, the eminent cardiologist, recalls that in the first two years after he set up his practice in 1912 he saw only three or four coronary patients. The queerly contemporary quality of heart disease cannot be attributed to the ignorance of earlier doctors. As far back as the time of Hippocrates, most afflictions were described well enough to be recognizable today from surviving records. A convincing description of heart disease, however, was not entered in medical records until late in the eighteenth century.

Some of the most important research on the effects of occupational stress in the U.S. has been carried out by the University of Michigan's Institute for Social Research, and the experts there are not impressed with the conventional medical wisdom regarding coronaries. Professor John R. P. French Jr., an austere and plainspoken psychologist at the institute, says that the known risk factors do not come close to accounting for the incidence of the disease. He maintains that "if you could perfectly control cholesterol, blood pressure, smoking, glucose level, serum uric acid, and so on, you would have controlled only about one-fourth of the coronary heart disease." There is little solid evidence, he adds, "to show that programs of exercise substantially reduce the incidence of coronary heart disease or substantially reduce some of the risk factors."

To a great extent, argues French, the problem is the job. "The stresses of today's organizations can pose serious threats to the physical and psychological well-being of organization members. When a man dies or becomes disabled by a heart attack, the organization may be as much to blame as is the man and his family." A nationwide survey directed by French's colleague Robert L. Kahn found evidence of widespread occupational stress in the U.S. The results indicated that 35 percent of the employees had complaints about job ambiguity, meaning a lack of clarity about the scope and responsibilities of the work they were supposed to be doing. Nearly half—48 percent—often found themselves trapped in situations of conflict on the job, caught in the middle between people who wanted different things from them. Some 45 percent of the sample complained of overload, either more work than they would possibly finish during an ordinary working day, or more than they could do well enough to preserve their "self-esteem."

Other occupational stresses found by the survey included insecurity associated with having to venture outside normal job boundaries; difficult bosses or

DEATH UNDER SIXTY-FIVE

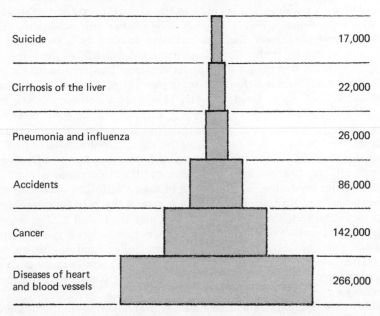

Suicide	17,000
Cirrhosis of the liver	22,000
Pneumonia and influenza	26,000
Accidents	86,000
Cancer	142,000
Diseases of heart and blood vessels	266,000

Cardiovascular disease is leveling off in the U.S., but it is still the principal cause of death—not only among the elderly, but also among people under sixty-five. Middle-aged men are much more vulnerable than middle-aged women. Of the 266,000 young and middle-aged Americans who died from diseases of the heart and blood vessels in 1968 (the most recent year for which accurate figures are available), 183,000—nearly 70 percent—were men.

subordinates; worry over carrying responsibility for other people; the lack of a feeling of participation in decisions governing their jobs—a malaise, adds Dr. French, that distinctly lowers productivity.

Management jobs carry higher risks than most. In a detailed study done for NASA at the Goddard Space Flight Center, the investigators from Ann Arbor found that administrators were much more subject to stress than engineers or scientists. Responsibility for people, French explains, always causes more stress than responsibilities for things—equipment, budgets, etc. The rise in serum cholesterol, blood sugar, and blood pressure among ground managers is much greater during manned space flights than during flights of unmanned satellites. Whatever their assignment, the administrators at Goddard, as a group, had higher pulse rates and blood pressure, and smoked more, than the engineers or scientists. Medical records revealed that administrators also had suffered almost three times as many heart attacks as either the scientists or the engineers.

The Coronary Type
In any occupation, though, people vary a great deal in the amounts of stress they can handle. Some researchers at the institute hope psychologists will be able to work out methods of screening employees for their tolerance of stress. There may even prove to be physiological methods of selection. Dr. French and

his associates have discovered a direct correlation between "achievement orientation" and high readings of uric acid in the blood—regarded in the past principally as a sign of susceptibility to gout. "High serum uric acid persons," French reported, "tend not to see the external environment as a source of pressure. [They] tend to master their external environment, while high cholesterol persons are typified by the perception that the external environment is mastering them."

It is not a new observation that some people are more subject to stress than others. Sir William Osler lived too early to see many coronary cases, but he left a shrewd description of the angina type. "It is not the delicate, neurotic person who is prone to angina," he commented, "but the robust, the vigorous in mind and body, the keen and ambitious man, the indicator of whose engine is always at 'full speed ahead' . . . the well set man of from forty-five to fifty-five years of age, with military bearing, iron gray hair, and florid complexion."

This Osler quotation is a favorite of two California cardiologists, Meyer Friedman and Ray H. Rosenman, who are among the country's leading students of stress. In the past seventeen years they and their staff at the Harold Brunn Institute of Mount Zion Hospital in San Francisco have spent thousands of hours and hundreds of thousands of research dollars building up an impressive case that behavior patterns and stress are principal culprits in the high incidence of coronary heart attacks among middle-aged Americans—and that personality differences are of vital importance.

Until 1955, Friedman and Rosenman were conventional cardiologists, doing research in the standard heart risk factors: serum cholesterol, cigarette smoking, blood pressure, diet, and obesity. They also gave half their time to practice, however, and, says Friedman, "We finally began to look at the individuals. They were signaling us. More than 90 percent showed signs of struggle. An upholsterer came in to redo our waiting room, and pointed out that the only place the chairs were worn was at the front edge."

In studying reactions to stress, Friedman and Rosenman gradually came to the conviction that people can be divided into two major types, which they designate A and B. Type A, the coronary-prone type, is characterized by intense drive, aggressiveness, ambition, competitiveness, pressure for getting things done, and the habit of pitting himself against the clock. He also exhibits visible restlessness. Type B may be equally serious, but is more easygoing in manner, seldom becomes impatient, and takes more time to enjoy leisure. He does not feel driven by the clock. He is not preoccupied with social achivement, is less competitive, and even speaks in a more modulated style. Most people are mixtures of Type A and Type B characteristics, but a trained interviewer can spot one pattern or the other as predominant.

A Rather Grim Chuckle

The extreme Type A is a tremendously hard worker, a perfectionist, filled with brisk self-confidence, decisiveness, resolution. He never evades. He is the man who, while waiting in the office of his cardiologist or dentist, is on the telephone making business calls. His wife is certain he drives himself too hard, and she may be a little in awe of him. The world is a deadly serious game, and he is out to amass points enough to win.

He speaks in staccato, and has a tendency to end his sentences in a rush.

He frequently sighs faintly between words, but never in anxiety, because that state is strange to him. He is seldom out sick. He rarely goes to doctors, almost never to psychiatrists. He is unlikely to get an ulcer. He is rarely interested in money except as a token of the game, but the higher he climbs, the more he considers himself underpaid.

On the debit side, he is often a little hard to get along with. His chuckle is rather grim. He does not drive people who work under him as hard as he drives himself, but he has little time to waste with them. He wants their respect, not their affection. Yet in some ways he is more sensitive than the milder Type B. He hates to fire anyone and will go to great lengths to avoid it. Sometimes the only way he can resolve such a situation is by mounting a crisis. If he himself has ever been fired, it was probably after a personality clash.

Type A, surprisingly, probably goes to bed earlier most nights than Type B, who will get interested in something irrelevant to his career and sit up late, or simply socialize. Type A is precisely on time for appointments and expects the same from other people. He smokes cigarettes, never a pipe. Headwaiters learn not to keep him waiting for a table reservation; if they do, they lose him. They like him because he doesn't linger over his meals, and doesn't complain about quality. He will usually salt the meal before he tastes it. He's never sent a bottle of wine back in his life. Driving a car, Type A is not reckless, but does reveal anger when a slower driver ahead delays him.

Type A's are not much for exercise; they claim they have too little time for it. When they do play golf, it is fast through. They never return late from vacation. Their desk tops are clean when they leave the office at the end of each day.

An Unrecognized Sickness

But in the competition for the top jobs in their companies, says Dr. Friedman, A's often lose out to B's. They lose because they are too competitive. They are so obsessed with the office that they have attention for nothing else, including their families. They make decisions too fast—in minutes, rather than days—and so may make serious business mistakes. They are intoxicated by numerical competition: how many units were sold in Phoenix, how many miles were traveled last month. Also, says Friedman, Type A's frequently have about them an "existential" miasma of hostility, which makes others nervous.

Type B's differ little in background or ability from A's, and may be quietly urgent, but they are more reasonable men. Unlike Type A, Type B is hard to needle into anger. Friedman says, "A's have no respect for B's, but the smart B uses an A. The great salesmen are A's. The corporation presidents are usually B's."

What is most tragic of all in this picture of hopeful, driving, distorting energy is that the Type A's are from two to three times more likely than the Type B's to get coronary heart disease in middle age. In all of Sinclair Lewis' pitiless characterizations of the go-getting American businessman of another era, there is nothing so devastating as these doctors' cool, clinical statistics. Says Rosenman about the Type A condition: "It is a sickness, although it is not yet recognized as such."

The test program that Friedman and Rosenman offer as their strongest body of evidence was undertaken in 1960 with substantial backing from the National

Institutes of Health. A total of 3,500 male subjects aged thirty-nine to fifty-nine, with no known history of heart disease, were interviewed and classified as Type A or Type B. Then came complete physical examinations, which are still being performed on a regular basis as the program continues to accumulate data. So far, 257 of the test group—who are roughly half A's and half B's—have developed coronary heart disease. Seventy percent of the victims have been Type A's.

Even more emphatic is the picture that emerged when A's and B's were evaluated with respect to the generally accepted risk factors for heart trouble. As a group the A's had higher cholesterol levels than the B's. But it was found that even A's whom the conventional wisdom would have rated safer in blood pressure, parental history, or any combination of the usual risk factors were more likely to develop coronary heart disease. Conversely, B's could show adverse ratings in blood pressure and other factors and still be relatively safe. Dr. Rosenman reported that any B whose level of cholesterol and other fatty acids was within normal limits "had complete immunity to coronary heart disease, irrespective of his high-fat, cholesterol diet, family history, or his habits of smoking or his lack of exercising."

What creates a Type B or Type A? These cardiologists do not profess to know the complete answer yet. But to them it is obvious that both heredity and environment are involved. A's are naturally attracted toward careers of aggressiveness and deadline pressure. American life today, Friedman and Rosenman observe, offers plenty of these. What Type A's need but cannot easily achieve is restraint, says Dr. Friedman, who himself suffered a heart attack in 1967.

The medical debate that the Brunn Institute and the other stress researchers have joined is a bitter one, with deeply entrenched positions. The most emphatic opponents of the stress theory are those nutrition experts who, over the past twenty years, have virtually convinced the nation that a diet high in saturated fat and cholesterol is responsible for the epidemic of heart trouble. One pointed criticism that opponents make against the Friedman-Rosenman studies is that their method of classifying individuals into Type A or Type B is subjective, relying heavily on signs of tension as observed by the interviewer. The two cardiologists do not deny this, but point out that a good deal of all medical analysis is subjective. Their independent appraisals of Type A's or Type B's agree, they say, at least as much as doctors' readings of identical x-ray films. Says Rosenman: "Most epidemiologists are incapable of thinking of anything that cannot be quantified. There are no positive links between diet or exercise and heart disease, either. A migraine is subjective, too."

Last Words of a Great Man

Studies of stress and its effects are now under way around the world. In 1950 Hans Selye's pioneering work was the sole technical treatise published on stress; last year there were close to 6,000 separate reports on stress research. At the Brunn Institute, Dr. Rosenman says, "we can't keep up with the requests from all over the world to train people here." During recent years, courts of law in the U.S., in a highly significant switch, have begun to favor plaintiffs seeking compensation for damage related to heart attacks caused by alleged stress on the job.

Now that even cardiologists are beginning to believe heart disease can be traced to unrelenting competitiveness and baffled fury, will a wave of concern over stress sweep over this hypochondriacal country, to match the widespread interest in jogging and polyunsaturated oils? Quite likely. There is nothing more fascinating to the layman than folklore finally validated by reputable scientists. A murmur of assent rises faintly from the past. When the great Pasteur lay in terminal illness, in 1895, he reflected once again on his long scientific disagreement with Claude Bernard. Pasteur's dying words were: "Bernard was right. The microbe is nothing, the terrain is everything."

"Even in their dreams men portray themselves as threatened by imminent body damage more often than do women."

An interesting area of psychological investigation is that of body image. Our feelings about ourselves are partially reflected in the way we perceive our bodies. The correlations between body image and emotional feelings are described by one of the leading researchers in this field, Dr. Seymour Fisher. In this article you will find a wide range of experimental studies on the psychological aspects of body image.

There is no more fascinating sight than your own image looking back at you in a mirror. You are drawn to it in a half-embarrassed way, excited and intensely involved. Do you remember the last time someone showed you a photograph of yourself? Wasn't there a surge of feeling and a deep curiosity about "How do I look?" Perhaps, too, you have noticed the strange entrancement even animals display at the sight of their mirror double.

Your body encompasses a sector of space that is uniquely your own. It represents your base of operations in the world, the outward manifestation of your being and identity. No other object is so persistently with you. Unceasingly, even when you are asleep, you receive enormous quantities of information from your body. Your decisions, fantasies, even your dreams are influenced by the sensations emanating from it. Yet it is only in the last two decades that serious scientific attention has been given to the study of the body as a psychological phenomenon.

For centuries scientists have studied the body as an anatomical structure and a biological system, leaving its psychological aspects to other disciplines. Artists and writers, for example, traditionally have devoted great energy to capturing the "feel" of the body in dramatic contexts. Eastern philosophies such as yoga have enjoyed a considerable measure of Western popularity in recent years, in part because of their supposed power to put the individual closer to his own body. Similarly, the so-called "drug culture" has drawn on body experience; LSD users, for example, report that the chemical frequently produces the feeling that parts of the body have become detached or that the boundary between the body and the outside world has dissipated.

But even the average person must admit to a curiosity about his body and a preoccupation with the psychological experiences it presents to him. He is concerned about the impression his body makes on others; he experiences anxiety about the potential vulnerability of his body to disease and trauma; he uses "gut" cues to help him decide whether or not to get involved with certain people or confront certain situations; he puts out large sums of money to shape and camouflage his appearance so that it will conform to his idealized concept of the "good body." Indeed, a major portion of advertising is devoted to products that claim to improve the individual's relationship with his body—by making it cleaner, more fragrant, stronger, sexier.

The task of making sense of our own bodies is not as simple as we might hope or expect. As each individual matures, he is confronted with the problems of integrating an endless barrage of sensations and assimilating the meanings adults ascribe to various sectors of his frame. He discovers complicated rules prescribing the areas he can touch, talk about, look at, and even think about. He is puzzled by the multiple, and often opposed meanings assigned to the same body area. He learns, for example, that the back of his body is simultaneously a spatial dimension, a place where punishment is applied, and a locus for concern about anal sphincter control; yet the same area also remains obscure because he cannot even get a direct view of it.

The child's attempt to construct a complete psychological map of his body is further hindered by the negative messages he receives from others about such an enterprise. His parents are reluctant to talk about body events and, in fact, become angry or embarrassed when he explicitly mentions certain organs or orifices. He learns that the available vocabulary for describing his own body experiences is sparse and tinged with an illicit flavor. Moreover, the child soon realizes that the culture does not trust body experiences; his education focuses on cultivating intellectual capacities, but his teachers insist that he control body impulses that are likely to "break out" if not closely monitored. Growing up in such an atmosphere, a child finds it almost impossible to examine or codify his body experiences realistically. Hasty glimpses of body terrain and fragments of anatomical information must be pieced together with little or no outside help. For these reasons, the individual is inclined to view his body as having alien qualities and to entertain numerous irrational notions about it.

In fact, although an individual experiences his body more often and in far greater depth than he does any other object in his environment, his perceptions of this, his dearest possession, remain distorted throughout his life. For example, when the average person is called upon to describe or make judgments about his body, he displays considerable inaccuracy. In studies in which persons have been asked to indicate the sizes of various body parts (e.g., head, arms), they often grossly over- or underestimate their true proportions. In one experiment Leo Schneiderman asked subjects to stand in front of a novel full-length mirror consisting of multiple panels that could be moved in such a way as to distort their mirror image in known quantitative terms. When subjects were confronted with the distorted image and asked to reconstruct their true appearance by manipulating the movable mirror panels, they frequently erred. They were indeed surprised to discover how vague their knowledge of their own appearance really was.

Other investigators have found that it is not very difficult to arrange conditions in which the individual fails to recognize pictures of himself. For example, if you take a picture of an individual's shadow profile without his knowledge and subsequently show him a series of shadow profile pictures that include his own as well as those of several other individuals, he will rarely recognize his own. But if you ask him to guess about the personal qualities of each profile pictured, he will say more favorable things about his own silhouette than he will about the others. This repeatedly validated finding suggests that even where there is lack of conscious recognition, one's own image still elicits defensive ego involvement (in the form of self-praise) at the unconscious level. Lack of conscious recognition has also been demonstrated with respect to pictures of one's hands, and even one's face, if presented for only a brief duration.

Freud was one of the first to note, anecdotally, the difficulty we have in identifying our own image when we come across it unexpectedly. The eminent doctor was sitting in a train sleeping car when a sudden jolt opened the door of the washroom and "an aged man, wearing a dressing gown and a cap" entered his compartment. Just as he was about to inform this stranger that he was intruding, Freud discovered that the stranger was actually his own image reflected in the mirror.

One of the problems of maintaining an accurate picture of your own body is that the image needs to be repeatedly revised. There is often a lag between the occurrence of change in your body and the incorporation of this change into your body model. Consider the effects of aging. Many people have been startled to discover on meeting an old friend after a long separation that the friend perceives much greater signs of aging than the individual had recognized in himself. This lag is especially apparent in the blind. For example, a man of middle age who had lost his sight when he was young told me that his image of himself was still that of the child he had last seen in the mirror years ago. Although others responded to him as a middle-aged adult, he could only visualize himself physically in the form of a young boy.

The so-called "phantom limb" provides another striking example of the difficulty in keeping one's body image up to date. When a person loses a projecting body part such as an arm or a nose because of trauma or surgery, he often continues to experience that part as if it were still present. The sensations that seem to emanate from beyond the stump are often so vivid that he may momentarily forget about his loss and try to use the missing part. After a while, however, the phantom limb fades and usually disappears permanently. This phenomenon has been attributed by some to the fact that the sudden loss of a major body sector is too radical a change to "accept." Only gradually does the new pattern of body sensations become assimilated, and the body concept therefore becomes more accurate.

Although the oblique way in which the individual builds up and maintains a model of his body makes it difficult for him to use body cues rationally, there is no doubt that whatever model he *does* evolve strongly influences his behavior. The individual's body concept is an influential intermediary in his transactions with what is "out there." A person who regards his body as weak and fragile will behave less boldly than one who perceives his body as a well-defended place. Similarly, a person who turns away from his body because he experiences it as bad and ugly may turn to intellectual activities as compensation.

Many sophisticated and reliable procedures for evaluating a person's body concept now are available. Reactions to one's mirror image, inkblot interpretations, drawings of the human figure, estimates of body size—such measures of body feelings have proven to be diversely correlated with personality traits, ability to tolerate stress, conduct in intimate group situations, and even psychosomatic symptoms.

Some of the most interesting work being done today by body image researchers is aimed at demonstrating that body experiences can shape an individual's interpretations of the outside world. In a rather ingenious study, Stuart Valins asked men in a laboratory setting to judge the attractiveness of a series of pictures of seminude girls. The men were told that while they were making these judgments their heart rate would be recorded. However, it was added, because of a "defect" in the equipment, they would be able to hear the sound of the heartbeat as it was being picked up. Valins proceeded to manipulate the faked audible heartbeat so that it changed perceptibly while each man was judging certain of the pictures, but remained unchanged for all the others. The final judgments were significant; the men decided that the most attractive pictures were those of the girls they were looking at when they thought their heart rate had changed. The findings of this study, replicated by other investigators, demonstrated that each man's perception of what seemed to be going on within his own body had a definite impact on his opinions of the world around him.

Another experiment found that a person's mood can be influenced by artificially molding his facial muscles. Explaining to his experimental subjects that he was studying the activity of facial muscles, James D. Laird manipulated these muscles so that to an external observer the subjects seemed either to be "smiling" or "frowning." The subjects had no idea what expression the experimenter had "put on" their face by means of his manipulations. Yet when measures of mood were obtained, the "frown" and "smile" conditions were found to produce opposite mood effects. Somehow, the position of the facial muscles was perceived and interpreted, causing a significant shift in how happy or sad the individual felt.

Rorschach inkblots provide another illustration of the influence that one's body sensations have on his perception of the outside world. The Rorschach, of course, is based on a long-standing psychological theory that one's interpretations of ambiguous stimuli will reveal hidden problems that the individual does not consciously recognize or is afraid to talk about freely. But in studies conducted in my own laboratory, Sidney Cleveland and I discovered that feelings about the body alone can influence the way a person interprets the vague patterns presented to him. The way an individual experiences the outer, peripheral regions of his body will be expressed in the peripheral regions of the objects he creates from the inkblots. For example, people differ in how clearly they perceive their body to have a defensive sheath capable of protecting them from intrusion. Some feel open and vulnerable; others feel well-fortified. The more secure an individual feels about his body boundaries, we discovered, the more he produces Rorschach images with protective sheltering qualities: caves with rocky walls, turtles with hard shells, tanks, shields, persons covered with blankets.

An individual's feelings of boundary security are correlated with how clearly he is aware of his boundary sheath—skin and muscle. Heightened awareness of this sheath seems to contribute to a sense of being adequately bounded and thus more secure. Many of us have employed this trick in fearful surroundings. Lying in bed, a home owner becomes anxious about a break-in and pictures the enclosing walls of his house. A driver entering a storm assures himself of his safety by glancing at the walls of his metal cocoon. Perhaps even more common is the preference many people have for small bedrooms or tight-fitting clothing.

With this notion of body security in mind, we conducted several experiments to determine if heightened awareness of the body sheath would have an effect on the interpretation of inkblots. In one experimental condition, subjects were exposed to experiences that caused them to focus on their skin and muscle. They were asked to report the occurrence of sensations in these areas while various stimuli, such as stroking, were applied to the skin. In the second condition, attention was drawn away from the outside of the body and focused upon the interior, with subjects reporting such phenomena as heart sensations or the feel of swallowing a glass of water. The results of these manipulations validated our assumption that awareness of certain body areas will affect one's feeling of security and, in turn, the perceptions of the outside world. When attention was focused on the skin and muscles, the number of protected inkblot images, such as a man in armor, rose; when attention was directed toward the interior, such inkblot fantasies decreased.

A person's body experiences may permeate his outlook in a number of unique ways. Studies have shown that if a subject is asked to compose imaginative stories, his tales will be affected by whether he is lying down or sitting up; his judgment of how far away an object is will depend on whether or not he feels the object has a meaningful relationship to his body; his beliefs about how friendly others are toward him may depend upon his faith in the security of his body boundaries, and so forth.

All of these body experiences will affect the activities of normal, healthy individuals. But what happens to the body model during psychological breakdown? For years psychiatric literature has suggested that schizophrenics suffer gross fragmentation of the body model. Vivid case histories have been published about schizophrenics who fancy that they have lost important chunks of their anatomy or who perceive their bodies as grotesquely altered—"dead," or transformed into the opposite sex, for example. However, more systematic studies have revealed that the body model stands up pretty well to the impact of the schizophrenic process. In fact, investigators have had a difficult time demonstrating truly impressive differences between psychiatric patients and normals in their mode of body experience. When one sifts through the scientific literature about this matter, only a few limited conclusions seem warranted. Schizophrenic patients *do* report a greater number of distorted and unusual body sensations than do normal persons, but the difference is small. And, somewhat surprisingly, schizophrenics do not exceed neurotic patients in this respect. Even in the throes of severe disturbance, the body concept seems to remain relatively well-preserved.

One specific dimension that *has* shown promise in differentiating psychiatric patients from normal persons is perception of body size. Psychiatric patients are concerned about sensations of body shrinkage and smallness. They feel reduced in stature or perceive one or more body parts to be smaller than they should be. When asked to make numerical estimates of the sizes of various body parts, they usually overreact, either underestimating or compensatorily overestimating the true proportions.

I have suggested that these perceptions of shrinkage represent a view of self that is depreciated and devalued. The psychiatric patient is often one who, in his own eyes, has failed or suffered major rejection by the culture. He feels lowly and unwanted, and his Lilliputian sensations reflect his downgraded view of himself.

In the course of probing the nature of abnormal body experiences, we have learned that certain body feelings, once considered as clearly pathognomic, are actually quite normal. A good example is provided by the phenomenon of *depersonalization*. Early psychiatric literature asserted that the patient who reports that his body feels alien, as if it did not belong to him, had a particularly poor prognosis for recovery. Depersonalization was supposed to be a mark of advanced pathology. However, several investigators have recently reported that depersonalization is a common reaction to stress among normal persons. For example, depersonalization has been prominently detected in normal persons who became anxious when swallowing an unknown drug during an experiment. There seems to be adaptive value in responding to stress-induced anxiety by getting "distance" from your own body, thereby decreasing personal involvement with it. Furthermore, normal persons who differ in their use of depersonalization also differ in other aspects of their behavior. For example, they have contrasting ways of responding to certain kinds of sexual stimulation. I have found that women who prefer vaginal stimulation to manual clitoral stimulation in reaching orgasm have an unusually strong depersonalized perspective toward their own body. I have described these findings in detail in *The Female Orgasm: Personality, Physiology, Fantasy*, published by Basic Books.

It would be impossible for anyone to attend simultaneously to all of the things happening in his body. He would be overwhelmed and ultimately confused. Just as one learns to attend to only certain auditory stimuli, each person must learn to attend to the various sectors of his body in some pattern that is meaningful and useful to him. Each individual, we have found, actually is rather consistent in his style of distributing body attention, although such consistency holds true more for men than for women. One man may be unusually aware of his head, another of his legs, and still another of the right as compared with the left side of his body. What is an outstanding body landmark for one may be almost invisible for another. Also, we have learned that each body sector is associated with a fairly distinct conflict or tension theme.

Specific conflict themes turn out to be linked to the following areas: head, back versus front, mouth, eyes, stomach, heart, right versus left. For example, the male with heightened awareness of his back (as compared to the front of his body) is often preoccupied with urges to express hostile soiling feelings toward others that evoke alarm in him because they are experienced as dirty and indicative of loss of self-control (perhaps in a way reminiscent of the child who fails to control his anal sphincter as expected by his parents). The male with heightened awareness of his heart is religiously oriented and especially conflicted about guilt feelings. One of the most intriguing patterns we discovered indicated that the male who is grossly more aware of the right as compared with the left side of his body is in conflict about his sexual relationship with women. He feels inhibited in the presence of women, is less likely to date, and gets anxious when confronted by stimuli with sexual connotations. From such findings we concluded that when an individual habitually concentrates a large amount of attention upon a body sector he is doing so because that sector is linked with a conflictual issue that persistently troubles him. What utility might such an association have? Most likely, the individual's investment of attention in specific body areas has some adaptive or control function. This is somewhat analogous to the piece of string that is tied around a child's finger when he is sent to the store so that he will remember what he is supposed to buy when he gets there. An individual's long-term focus of attention on a body area could serve, therefore, as a kind of "string around the finger" reminding him that certain things should or should not be done.

The persistent concentration of attention upon a body area provides a guiding signal to the individual to restrain the expression of conflictual impulses associated with that area. For example, heightened back awareness would signal that control should be maintained over hostile besmirching urges; or magnified awareness of the right side of the body would warn against heterosexual involvement. Within this framework an individual's style of perceiving his body can be regarded as a part of the elaborate system he evolves to control his behavior. As he develops attitudes toward basic issues in the world, they become coded in terms of differential awareness of specific body parts.

The regulatory function of this concentration of awareness is apparent in the much simpler case of monitoring the muscles of an arm to keep it rigid or the sphincter muscles of a full bladder to inhibit urination. There is also interesting anecdotal information in the psychiatric literature about instances in which patients, having been psychotherapeutically relieved of a preoccupation with sensations or minor symptoms in a body part, suddenly show a dramatic release of affect upon some theme. The investment of concern in the body area apparently served to inhibit awareness of the underlying anxiety that came to the surface when the superficial concern was removed.

We have also completed experiments in which we artificially altered the individual's awareness of a body part to demonstrate the control function of concentration on that region. The greater the amount of attention a man habitually directs to his heart, the greater his religiosity and anxious concern over feelings of guilt. In one experimental procedure a group of men were given exercises designed to heighten their heart awareness; immediately afterward they were briefly exposed to a series of words, half of which referred to guilt themes (e.g., wrong, fault, judge) and half of which did not. They then were asked to recall as many of these words as possible. The purpose of the learning task was to detect defensive emotional attitudes toward the guilt words in terms of the relative proportion of guilt and nonguilt words recalled. Groups of control subjects went through the same procedure, but their degree of heart awareness was not altered. It was found that the group that was made more heart aware had a significantly greater tendency to forget the guilt words. By concentrating a man's attention on his heart, we were able to alter his receptivity to guilt themes.

In view of the obvious differences between male and female bodies, it would be logical to expect that men and women would construct quite different images of their bodies. We do, in fact, find radically different styles of body perception related to sex. At this moment in history the question of body superiority-inferiority most naturally arises. Freud did little for the women's movement by explicitly declaring that the female has a depreciated, inferior concept of her body. A little girl is traumatized, he reasoned, upon discovering that her genital organ is different from the male's, whose phallic attributes are equated with power and strength. Presumably, this trauma leaves indelible scars; she is destined to interpret her lack of a penis as a sign of body inferiority. Thus the idea grew that the average woman is less secure and more disturbed about her body than is the average man.

Body image research, however, indicates that precisely the opposite is true. For example, we put a series of male and female rubber masks on the faces of men and women and requested the subjects to describe each mask as they glimpsed it in a mirror when a light flashed on. To our surprise, the men were made much more anxious than the women by this procedure. They were flustered by the female masks and made significantly more errors when trying to describe the characteristics of their disguised appearance. The solidity of these observations was affirmed by a second study that produced the same results. It was apparent that the men were less able to cope adequately with the change in body concept imposed by the experimental condition.

Other scientific evidence indicates a similar trend. It has been demonstrated that the average woman perceives her body to be better protected and enclosed by a more secure boundary than does the average man. In one study we found that the male was more disturbed by the threat of injecting adrenaline into his body than was the female. Other investigators have observed that men are relatively more preoccupied with themes of body destruction. Even in their dreams men portray themselves as threatened by imminent body damage more often than do women. Several appraisals of males and females hospitalized for surgery reveal greater anxiety in men than in women about the body-threatening implications of the situation. Men may carefully control their open expression of such anxiety, but inwardly they are more disturbed than women.

In addition to the perception of body threat, there is another important difference in the way males and females experience their bodies. Diverse sources have noted that women are more aware of their body feelings than are men and that they are more positive in accepting these experiences. David J. Van Lennep reported that female children not only display greater body awareness than male children, but the magnitude of this difference between the sexes becomes larger after adolescence. In addition, the degree of body awareness in women is known to be correlated with positive attributes such as a clear sense of identity, while in men it is linked with certain categories of conflictual preoccupation. This confirms what we already observe in everyday life. Girls and women invest much more open interest in the body than do their male counterparts. They feel free to study their own appearance and to experiment with techniques for altering it by means of clothing and cosmetics. A male who displays much direct or open interest in his body (except with reference to athletic activities) is regarded as a deviant.

A woman apparently sees a clearer and more meaningful relationship between her body and her life role than a man. Despite the influence of Women's Liberation, the chief goals of most women still revolve about being attractive, entering into marriage, and producing children. Such aims readily permit the female to see her body as a vehicle for her life career. This is not true for the man. Unless he becomes a professional athlete, he can perceive little connection between his body attributes and the requirements for status and success. Male power and accomplishment are increasingly defined in terms of intellect, cleverness, business acumen, and so forth. The low status jobs are the ones that require body strength. As I have reported in *Body Experience in Fantasy and Behavior* (Appleton-Century-Crofts), an important contribution of the research on body experience is that it has cast serious doubt on stereotyped ideas about the inferiority of the feminine body concept.

Our expanding knowledge about the body as a psychological object encourages thought about the potential practical and therapeutic applications of this knowledge. Intriguing possibilities are becoming visible. For example, efforts are under way in both Europe and the United States to evaluate the potentialities of treating psychological disturbance by altering body experience. Austin M. Des Lauriers has suggested that a major problem of the schizophrenic is that he has lost an articulated image of his body; without it he has little individuality or ability to test reality. Des Lauriers has devised therapeutic techniques to make the schizophrenic more aware of his body, particularly its boundary, and claims considerable clinical success with this approach. Others have indirectly affirmed Des Lauriers's concepts by demonstrating that exercise and systematic stimulation that highlight muscle and skin sensations in the schizophrenic individual do, indeed, increase his boundary security.

Alterations of body experience also are being explored with "emotionally disturbed" children and those with serious learning problems. Preliminary findings suggest that certain types of learning difficulties may be improved by giving the child a more realistic image of his body, especially its spatial dimensions.

Research analyses of body feelings may prove to be of value in clarifying puzzling complications that arise when people must adapt to body disabilities and medical procedures. We now know that fantasies of body vulnerability may cause an individual to respond with grossly inappropriate distress to minor body trauma and to fail completely to adjust to more serious chronic disablement. We have leads that suggest that the amount and kind of psychological disturbance evoked by an injury may depend upon subtle differences in its location upon the body. An injury on the right side may pose a different form of threat than one on the left side; trauma to the back may arouse different kinds of anxieties than if it involved the front. Body attitudes also seem to play a role in the perplexing problem of why people delay in seeking medical treatment after they discover a serious symptom in themselves. Often the delay is so great that a disease process will have advanced to a point where it is no longer amenable to treatment. Paradoxically, it appears that the individual who feels secure about his body is most inclined toward such irrational delay. Finally, it should be noted that we are beginning to see body attitudes as potentially powerful predictors of the psychological effects produced by various drugs. This is quite logical if we remember that an important part of the impact of drugs involves alterations of body sensations.

Various individuals and cults currently acknowledge the importance of the experienced body as a basic component of life adjustment. It is interesting that heightened concern with body experience has coincided with the investigation of body image in the psychological laboratories and clinics. Here, however, the similarity ends: Those involved with these cults or movements are unwilling to wait for the facts to come in. Instead, they have embarked on impulsive quests via drugs and meditation, for example, in the hope of hitting upon new principles that will make possible "revolutionary" innovations in the body model and over-all well-being. But the odds are against these haphazard approaches. Only systematic study will provide sound principles and realistic techniques for altering body experience in helpful ways. Indeed, there is little doubt that the body image is one of the most important—and, ironically, most neglected—phenomena in the scientific quest for understanding of our psychological selves.

**Suggested Readings for
Chapter 4**

Delgado, José M. R. *Physical control of the mind: Toward a psychocivilized society.* New York: Harper Colophon Books, Harper & Row, 1969. A brilliant review of Delgado by Delgado written for the intelligent layman.

Pfeiffer, J. *The human brain.* New York: Harper & Row, 1965. A popular presentation of our knowledge about brain functions.

Teitelbaum, P. *Physiological psychology.* Englewood Cliffs, N.J.: Prentice-Hall, 1967. A brief but excellent introduction to physiological psychology for the beginning student.

Wooldridge, D. E. *Machinery of the brain.* New York: McGraw-Hill, 1963. A clear and popular account of the scientific advances in the understanding of brain function.

Discussion Questions

1. How does the brain resemble, and how does it differ from, a computer?

2. Is electrical brain stimulation a technique opening glorious pathways to the future or a first step toward loss of human freedom? How might it move in each of these directions?

3. How does body image differ from a physical representation of the body?

4. What are the relative effects of environmental events and physiological events in determining what you do?

Infancy, Childhood, and Adolescence

From the moment of conception each individual begins a complicated process of biological and social-psychological growth, and as this sequence unfolds, behavior passes through various developmental landmarks that are both peculiar to the individual and typical of the species. The study of human behavior is a search for the patterns of maturation and learning that make a person what he is. How does one acquire a particular set of values, beliefs, ideas, feelings, and all the other distinctly human qualities? For an answer to this question it is necessary to inquire into the history of the organism to learn about the internal and external forces that have shaped his development.

As we grow up, the recollections of our past grow dim. We can focus on bits and pieces of our early experiences but it is impossible for us to completely recapture the joys and pains, the successes and failures, which have so influenced our present life. Yet our identity, who we are and what we are, is part of a long and forgotten evolutionary progression that was set in motion at the time of conception. To many people life seems to begin after birth takes place. However, science is beginning to unravel the extremely critical nature of the intra-uterine environment on the future of a given child. In the uterus the zygote is extremely vulnerable to numerous potential hazards that can arise from disease and hereditary imperfections. These imperfections can produce profound emotional stress in the families of those who are afflicted by mental retardation, birth disease, and physical abnormalities. These are great tragedies of life, yet early diagnosis and treatment of these problems are now possible and hold a promise that someday more complete diagnoses and therapy within the uterine environment can be realized. Furthermore, the rapid advances in genetics might reach the point where undesirable traits could be eliminated through the rearrangement of the molecular structure of the genetic material. In science, all possibilities are open, but it is for the society itself to use the products of science and then judge the consequences.

From the moment a newborn baby leaves the rather pleasant, fluid environment of the womb, he passes into a new and challenging world of people. To the research scientist, the infant is a unique subject for the investigation of a series of controversial problems that have raged in psychology for many years. Stated simply, the issue concerns the relative contributions of biological inheritance and environmental influences to various aspects of human behavior. Those who support the biological side maintain that the genetic attributes of the organism are the major factors in setting the basis for temperament, emotional reactivity, intellectual capacity, and so on. The environmentalists, in contrast, believe that the richness or deprivation of social experience plays a more important part than the basic contributions of biological endowment. Another group stresses the interaction between these variables and considers the interdependence of biological and social conditions to be crucial. Recent evidence in infant behavior suggests that the infant is not a "blank slate" at birth, but that he quite rapidly expresses perceptual preferences that can not be directly related to social training. Also, other data on language and conceptual ability reveal a capacity for very young children to respond in complex and sophisticated ways long before it was assumed that their development would permit. The overall trends in research findings emphasize the crucial nature of heredity in the child's growth towards maturity. However, although the importance of heredity cannot be minimized, each child also grows up in an environment which to a large extent determines his attitudes and directions in life. Recently, due in large part to the energy and dedication of the women's liberation movement, we have become more aware of the biased nature of our "sexist upbringing." The paper by Letty Cottin Pogrebin describes how early training in attitude development tends to orient children toward the acquisition of biased roles in society. For example, boys learn early that being doctors, lawyers, scientists, and so on is mainly men's work, while girls, more likely than not, ought to be trained as nurses, housewives, cooks, and elementary school teachers. Furthermore, the ways in which boys and girls are physically handled is heavily dictated by the culture too. Boys are tossed around and hoisted above the heads of parents, while girls are handled delicately as they "ought" to be. This article vividly describes the stereotyped cultural attitudes toward sex roles and emphasizes how women are socially and vocationally penalized through this early upbringing.

What is it like to be an only child? What does it feel like to have an older brother or to be the middle child with two other siblings? If you're a girl, what is it like to have an older brother who maintains an overprotective attitude when anything goes wrong? A fascinating area of psychological study is the effect of birth order on personality and behavior. For example, to take a reasonably uncomplicated finding, it appears that the only child, often pictured as spoiled and unhappy, does not in reality quite fit this description. Research suggests that the only child frequently bears the brunt of parental pressure, is frequently overprotected but is also quite self-confident and considerably more relaxed than first-born children, who eventually have to contend with other siblings. If you consider all the combinations of birth order, this research area can become extraordinarily complicated. Is the only-born as relaxed and as comfortable as a middle-born, or does an only female grow up in the same manner as an only male? The article by Norman Lobsenz provides some fascinating insights into the personalities and specific difficulties which birth-order sequences may produce.

Discrimination exists in every society. Prejudicial hatreds focus on religious differences, on regional differences, or on nationalistic or tribal conflicts. In the United States prejudice exists on all of these levels. People are rejected because they come from an undesirable region of the country, don't belong to a particular religious group, or are ethnically unacceptable. Prejudice is an insidious companion that overtly and subtly colors our relationships with people outside our primary identity groups. Many ethnic, racial, and religious groups have suffered intensely from discrimination in the U.S. The American Indian, the Puerto Rican, the Chinese- and Japanese-Americans, the Mexican-Americans, Jews, Catholics, hillbillies, and Italian-Americans, to name a few, have experienced painful indignities. Black and Indian persons have always been regarded as inferior by the white community and their position in American society has improved only very slowly. Economically underprivileged, deprived of satisfactory educational opportunities, and socially isolated from the mainstream, they have existed apart and alone. In our recent experience, racial oppression has generated hatred, fear, and unprecedented violence. Yet prejudice continues to be a social psychological reality, and a reality that even the most well-intentioned and broadminded of us have difficulty in resolving. In an article by two black psychiatrists, Drs. Poussaint and Comer, a plan for dealing with prejudicial attitudes in the home is presented. They aptly point out that the seeds of prejudice are often planted by parental attitudes toward other people and that children model and assimilate these preferences. They maintain that white parents have a particularly difficult task in training their children to deal realistically with prejudice. The white child is constantly surrounded by derogatory images of the black person, and unless parents are willing to relate to these influences realistically and directly it is highly probable that their children will easily assimilate cultural attitudes of prejudice and intolerance. The resolution of social and economic injustice, as well as the alteration of deeply entrenched social prejudice, is always a complex matter. Prejudicial beliefs and attitudes are not easily removed, particularly since they are reinforced by such powerful media as books, movies, television, and other powerful sources of biased communication. Fortunately, attitudes are beginning to change. There is a new awareness on the part of the black community that blackness can indeed be respectable and perhaps even desirable. The black movement has ceased to be a passive recipient of oppression and has fought vigorously with varying degrees of success for greater educational and economic opportunities. Given these gains, perhaps in the long run constructive reason will triumph over disruptive passion.

In contemporary times, the label adolescence has taken on added significance through the actions of a youthful generation that has demanded to be heard and recognized. Perhaps at no other point in our history have the voice and energy of youth been so instrumental in augmenting political and social change. It is doubtful also that the "generation gap" between parents and children has ever been so wide. However, the roots of this rebellion are not quite so obscure. Wars in various parts of the world, urban deterioration, racial strife and inequities, and a host of other social realities have created a sense of frustration and anger motivating frantic and often well-organized action. In fashion, music, and art, the influence of this group has challenged the complacency of adults and the shock waves are being felt around the world.

To social scientists, adolescence is a stage of accelerated growth that begins with prepubertal development and ends with the attainment of physical maturity. To the psychologist the course of adolescence is complete when the individual has become socially stabilized as an adult. Within these broad outlines, however, there are many cultural and personal meanings which complicate this age period perhaps more than any other. It is clearly evident in our culture that the most crucial psychological issues confronting the adolescent are his quest for identity, self-awareness, and independence. Toward this goal he is physically able and emotionally geared to experiment with sex, use overt expressions of hostility and rebellion, and relate himself to his peer group with great tenacity; yet this energetic search for meanings relevant to his human condition frequently places him in direct conflict with the adult community, particularly his parents.

In this difficult and conflict-laden stage of life many adolescents have turned to drugs as a source of some combination of relief, insight, and joy. In doing so they model an adult society which has engaged in drug abuse for many years. In an attempt to help students to understand the effects of the variety of drugs which are now available, the University of Michigan prepared a comprehensive guide which is included in this chapter. This article does not advocate any particular position with regard to the use of drugs other than the need for individuals to have accurate information before making critical decisions. Whether or not students use drugs, which ones, how much, and under what circumstances, are all important decisions which may have significant consequences. Decisions such as these are best made with full knowledge of the available information.

Perhaps one of the most difficult, time-consuming, and anxiety-provoking experiences that people encounter is looking for a job. It is difficult enough looking for a job when you have had a little practice and know some of the ropes, but getting into the job market immediately after college can be "a nerve-wracking experience." Application forms, tests to measure your personality and abilities, interviews, and other evaluations are an unpleasant but necessary reality. The article by Nancy Axelrad Comer entitled "Jobhunting Now: The Employee Employers Look for" is a balanced account of the problems of jobhunting and contains bits and pieces of important and useful information that can help you. This article contains a series of brief interviews with personnel directors and other professionals involved in the hiring process who present their opinions on what and what not to do when looking for a job.

18   **Down with Sexist Upbringing!**
Letty Cottin Pogrebin

"Homosexuality is the big worry. The specter of having a son turn out gay haunts nearly every father."

This article deals with how we acquire different attitudes about sex. Why do little girls like to play house and little boys like to be the managers of the house? This article by Pogrebin investigates some of the important social variables which have prepared us for sexist attitudes.

Our twin daughters aren't into Women's Liberation. For all they know, a male chauvinist pig is the fourth little porker on the big bad wolf's menu. They've never suffered job discrimination, never been treated as sex objects and can't be characterized as bra-burners since they're still in undershirts.

But living with Abigail and Robin, age six, is an ongoing consciousness-raising session for my husband and me. In them, and in their three-year-old brother David, we see ourselves. They mirror our attitudes and mimic our relationship. They are constant reminders that lifestyles and sex roles are passed from parents to children as inexorably as blue eyes or small feet.

From empirical evidence our children have concluded that women's work is writing books and articles, having meetings, making dinner, doing puzzles with the kids, and fixing the electrical wiring. (In my husband's presence circuits short and sockets belch fire.) Man's work, on the other hand, is writing legal briefs, arguing cases, having meetings, making breakfast, reading stories with the kids and fixing the plumbing. (I can turn a toilet tank into a geyser with a single glance.)

In our household, whoever can, does. Call it convenience plus ability. I make dinner because I like to and because I cook better. My husband makes breakfast because I simply cannot get up that early in the morning and the children love his pancakes.

In homes where male and female roles are rigidly defined, children would tune in a wholly different picture. If the father restricts himself to the television room, the evening paper and the "masculine" chores in the backyard, his son is not likely to feel that folding laundry is a man's lot in life. If the mother is exclusively engaged in domestic activities, her daughter may question whether women were meant to have other interests.

Reprinted by permission of the author and Ms. Magazine, Spring 1972 (preview issue).

Home environments tend to set the stage for sex role stereotypes. We've all seen little girls' rooms that are so organdied, pink and pippy-poo one would never dream of besmirching them with Play-Doh or cartwheels. We've seen little boys living in nautical decors or in cell-like rooms heavy on athletic equipment but lacking a cozy place to read a book. We've seen boys scolded for parading in their sisters' ballet tutus; girls enjoined from getting soiled; boys forbidden to play with dolls; girls forbidden to wrestle.

Why are parents so alert to sex-typed behavior? Why do they monitor the "masculine" or "feminine" connotations of children's clothes, games, toys, reading material and physical activity?

Homosexuality is the big worry. The specter of having a son turn out gay haunts nearly every father. Mothers seem to join in the obsession—not because they have the same investment in the boys' masculinization, but because they've been made to feel women are responsible for producing Mama's boys who fall prey to homosexual temptation.

The prospect of having a Lesbian daughter doesn't seem quite as threatening. Keeping girls feminine is largely a matter of keeping them attractive, alluring and marriageable. The tomboy is said to be "going through a phase." It can be cured with a lace petticoat and a new hair ribbon. It can even be turned into an advantage: "My daughter throws a ball like a boy," or "I swear, she thinks like a man." While some find it enviable to have a daughter who knows what a gridiron is, a son who likes to iron is another dish of neuroses.

Although male homosexuals are often truck-driver-tough and many heterosexuals are gentle poets, the assumption remains that superficial masculine and feminine identities and activities will prevent sexual confusion.

"There is absolutely no scientific validity to this assumption," says Dr. Robert E. Gould, Director of Adolescent Psychiatry at the Bellevue Hospital Center.

Boys become homosexual because of disturbed family relationships, not because their parents allowed them to do so-called feminine things.

Kids must be allowed all available opportunity to develop and achieve their full potential. They should have free access to *human* toys, books, games and emotions—all of them free from sex-stereotyping.

Dr. Sirgay Sanger, a Harvard-educated child psychiatrist, puts it this way:

In the child's earliest years, masculine or feminine differences are a fake issue. Until three or four years of age children have the same needs. Beyond that age, what they require most is individual differentiation, not gender differentiation. To highlight differences only denies to one sex the advantages and pleasures of the other.

Such differences can be alarming and threatening to children. Unisex clothes and relaxed dating rituals among the young indicate that there's a natural tendency to minimize sex differences and to find comfortable common areas of human communication.

Maybe the next generation of parents will be uncoerced and uncoercive.

Meanwhile, those of us raising children now must face our own prejudices and society's pervasive sexism.

How do you telegraph your prejudices and preconceptions? Blue and pink is the first label. The way you handle and coo to the infant differs. Girls get cuddled and purred over. Boys get swung and hoisted and roughhoused. The choice of toys also tells a child something without words. Mechanical do-it-yourself crib games for boys. Delicate mobiles for girls. And later—he gets baseballs, model ships, Erector sets, chemistry kits. She gets Barbie dolls, tea sets, nurse kits, mini-mops. And still later—he goes skiing, camping, skin-diving and plays football with Dad. She goes to ballet class, piano lessons, art exhibits and bakes brownies with Mom.

And they both get the signal. That they are expected to be very different from one another. That he can experiment, solve problems, compete and take risks. That she is passive, domestic, cultured and cautious. If the profile sounds familiar, your children may need a strong dose of non-sexist upbringing. Open the options. Let your boy know the challenge of tackling a recipe; let your girl know the challenge of tackling another kid. But whatever your best efforts, beware of outside pollutants such as these:

During a visit to their father's office, our three children were introduced to one of his associates. The man told David that when he grew up he could be a lawyer in Daddy's firm. Turning to the twins the man said: "And we can use some new legal secretaries, too."

On a recent plane trip, a stewardess asked my husband how many and "what kind" of children he had. She brought back three gold pins: one Junior Pilot wings and two Junior Stewardess wings. (When my husband gave the pins to the children he told them that all the wings were pilot's.)

When David grazed his knee and started howling I overheard our baby-sitter tell him: "Come on now, boys don't cry." ("Crying is the ultimate human reaction to pain and sadness," says Dr. Gould. "In Egypt men were wailing in the streets when Nasser died. But Americans are trapped in the mystique of the ideal man—someone like John Wayne striding emotionless through a war movie. It's unreal.")

For most of us the problem becomes overwhelming when we examine the educational system and the media. Here's where doctrinaire "experts" legitimize sex roles. And here's where cultural brainwashing techniques are most entrenched and hardest to fight.

In opposition to censorship, Mayor Jimmy Walker once said, "No girl was ever ruined by a book." Well, maybe not by one book. But a cumulative library of negative, stultifying stories, books and poems can go a long way toward ruination of the female spirit.

We didn't really notice them coming at us. The fairy tales that show girls sleeping away their lives until the prince hacks through the underbrush to rescue them. The nursery rhymes in which we are kept in pumpkin shells or crammed into a shoe with a bunch of kids. All of us: Lazy Mary, Contrary Mary, frightened Miss Muffet, empty-headed Bo-Peep—a sorry lot with little relief on the positive side. Even Mother Goose herself was eccentric.

And in school books, the Dick and Jane syndrome reinforced our emerging attitudes. Arithmetic books posed appropriate conundrums: "Ann has three pies . . . Dan has three rockets . . ." We read the nuances between the lines: Ann keeps her eye on the oven; Dan sets his sights on the moon.

Put it all together, it spells conform. Be beautiful, feminine, alluring, passive, supportive. Subvert your energies, dear. Conceal your brains, young lady. Spunky girls finish last on the way to the prom. Tomboys must convert. Boys don't make passes at female smart-asses. We all got the message.

The boy reading the same material is victimized by the reverse effects. If she's all dainty and diaphanous, he has to be strong and assertive. If she faints with love for a fullback then he'd better try out for the team. If Mom and the kiddies are at home all day, then who but Dad must work to keep starvation from the door? The pressure is on.

But suppose he isn't up to jousting with his fellows or scaling palace walls? What if he prefers a flute to a football? Tough luck, and that's why Georgie Porgie runs away. Because there's no place for the tender, sensitive, uncompetitive boy in juvenile books—or in American life.

Children's literature and texts may favor the man-child by investing him with forcefulness, creativity and active virtues. But the concomitant effect is to stunt him emotionally, to teach him that toughness is a prerequisite for manhood, to cheat him of a full and free acquaintance with all forms of culture and to burden him with the identities of soldier and sole support of dependent human beings.

Our children need our help:

To route them to the few realistic books available within each reading category and age level.

To impose an interpretive voice upon their reading experiences.

To seek stories that offer alternate lifestyles and that show men *and* women with cosmic concerns and diverse identities.

To ferret out biographies and history books that give women their rightful place and accord respect to female opinions and perspectives.

Some will rush to buy or borrow recommended books such as those listed below. Some will pass every book under a Geiger counter for sexist overtones. But no one should burn the old stand-bys and the classics in a fit of feminist pique. The simple exercise of adult intelligence and advanced consciousness will do the trick.

As a parent you can become an interpreter of myths. A feminist revisionist. Analyze, discuss, question the given elements. Portions of any fairy tale or children's story can be salvaged during a critique session with your child.

For example, Dr. Sanger suggests a transformation of *Cinderella* from a tale of a hyperlanguishing female to a constructive fantasy. Look at it this way: Cinderella wasn't a victim. She was a strong young woman and a tolerant, understanding human being. She recognized the pettiness of her stepsisters. She endured her stepmother's cruelty. Because she was sympathetic rather than bitter, she gained an ally—the fairy godmother, who epitomizes our ideal of free choice. Cinderella's reward for perseverance and strength of character is entrée into the castle: in other words, a better life.

As for the bit about marriage being a woman's be-all and end-all, you'll have to deal with that inevitable dénouement as you see fit. Most of the time, I figure it's a fair ending. After all, we don't know what the prince did with the rest of his life either.

While the mother who does not work outside the home is in the minority for the first time, you can count on one hand the books that positively reflect the dual-occupation family. No wonder the 22 million children of working mothers feel somewhat deprived. All the printed evidence suggests that the only normal mother is a stay-at-home mother and that a woman should need only a well-frosted cake to feel fulfilled.

Once conscious of this propaganda you can externalize your awareness. Start reading seminars for other parents through the school or community center. Inquire into the contents of your child's reading syllabus.

You'll find, as did a Princeton group called Women on Words and Images, that 72 per cent of the stories about individual children are geared to boys; that the overriding conclusions to be drawn from school readers is that girls are always late, give up easily, don't excel in school (contrary to statistical fact), and need a lot of help solving problems and getting things done.

You'll find more than enough reasons to support activist groups that are closing in on publishers and educators. You may even be outraged enough to join a feminist collective to prepare non-sexist reading lists and to launch honest books of your own making.

You might demand that your bookstore and library stock equalitarian literature. Complain to publishers and editors. And don't spare the Board of Education. Remember that when repressive, slanted books are adopted by an entire school system, their contents are invested with divine authority.

The National Organization for Women's Report on Sex Bias in the Public Schools provides appalling evidence of sexism in the entire system, not just in its books. Girls are barred from 85 per cent of the play areas, from several gym activities, from many field and track sports and from most school teams. They are directed instead to volleyball courts, dancing or cheerleading.

Boys get the special assignments whether on the audio-visual squad, hall patrol or honor guard. While boys may not be welcome in cooking or sewing class (what male would be caught dead electing them anyway?), girls are barred from shop, metalworking, mechanics and printing courses.

How can you raise your kids to be free when they're so systematically shackled within the schools? Emancipation from sex-stereotypes is not possible unless all institutions affecting a child's development are brought into harmonious accord. That's why parents are resorting to legal suits to win their daughters' access to woodworking courses or entry into boys' specialty schools or a deserved place on the varsity tennis team. That's why children's liberation is the next item on our civil rights shopping list.

It will require widespread consciousness-raising courses for teachers. We'll have to stop guidance counselors from programming female students for limited achievement. (Why should gifted girl biology students become science teachers when bright boy students are directed into medical careers?) We want more male teachers at the elementary level and more females in administrative posts. We want our children to know that men can be fine caretakers of the young and that women can be respected authority figures.

If the schools are often a battleground for the sexes, the television screen is an out-and-out disaster area. Situation comedies telecast during children's prime time include such splendid inanities as *I Dream of Jeannie* (a flagrant master-slave relationship between the sexes) or *I Love Lucy* (the scatterbrain embodying the infantilized woman and the henpecking wife).

Even *Sesame Street* is not immune to sexist attitudes. Without impugning its noble educational intentions, we can't fail to note the role rigidity the program teaches along with the letters of the alphabet. Susan is almost always in the kitchen. Puppet families are traditional: Dad works, Mom cooks (an inaccurate portrayal of many black and poor families and of middle class dual-professional families as well). Boy monsters are brave and gruff. Girl monsters are high-pitched and timid. Oscar turns out to be a male chauvinist as well as a grouch. When his garbage-pail home needs a spring cleaning he calls a woman to do it.

And speaking of garbage, the commercials television feeds into our children's minds add up to pure rubbish. Often the indictment of exploitive and insulting commercials has been filed by committed feminists objecting to the assault on women's self-image. However, while most adults have become inured to the high-pressure sales pitch, the crucial point is that children *don't* tune out. They react with interest, not annoyance. We must begin to view sexist commercials as an affront to parents and children, not just to feminist women. The 30- or 60-second commercial has been found so effective a sales tool that it forms the foundation of *Sesame Street*'s format for selling knowledge. Obviously, the technique is potent. According to the Boston group Action for Children's Television, your child will see 350,000 TV commercials by the age of eighteen.

Add it all together and you have a bombardment of cultural conditioning: grown-up men buy rugged cars, drink lots of beer, shave their faces and kiss girls who are pretty enough, thin enough or fragrant enough to warrant it; grown-up women diet for love and approval, serve flavorful coffee or lose their husbands to the morning paper, and use the right soap or lose their husbands to a woman with younger skin.

To defumigate TV programming and set a standard for decent commercial messages is a monumental job. A letter to a network executive has as much chance of making waves as a pebble in the ocean. The F.C.C. should care about sexism but its commissioners have licensing, antitrust and equal time on their collective minds. So the target of our wrath must be the sponsors. They must be taken to task for their pejorative view of women in commercials and their financial support of programs that disparage women's role.

It will be a long time before enough women use their dollars to protect their children from media's warped message. Until then it might be wise to monitor the TV fare for sexism as well as sex and violence. A *Flintstones* program showing how wives play dumb to build their husbands' egos can be more harmful to a small child's developing sense of values than a panel discussion of premarital sex or drug addiction. As with children's books, television shows frequently require parental supervision and sermonizing. Give the commercials a taste of their own medicine: ridicule. Show children the absurdity of three or four commercials and they'll talk back to the television set before you know it.

Clearly, the home influence can go only so far. Parents may renounce role rigidity and set a beautiful example of individuality and gender freedom, only to be defeated when the kid next door calls your free child a dirty name. What is needed then is a radical eradication of sexism, not only in your house but in the house next door and in the culture as a whole.

The stakes are high. If we fail, it's more of the same. And the same is not good enough for our children. Cheating one sex and overburdening the other won't do anymore.

If we win, human liberation is the prize. Our daughters and sons gain the freedom to develop as persons, not roleplayers. Relationships between the sexes can flourish without farce and phoniness. And dignity can be the real birthright of every child.

For the Liberated Child's Library

Not every book listed below is entirely free of sex-role stereotypes. Despite some flaws, each book was chosen because of a redeeming positive theme or constructive moral. Given the dearth of non-sexist children's books, the titles that follow are among the best available at the moment. They are excerpted from a far more extensive bibliography which may be ordered from *Ms.* Magazine, 370 Lexington Avenue, New York 10017.

The complete bibliography is a result of personal choice plus recommendations by Nancy Barron (University of Missouri Center for Research in Social Behavior); Feminists on Children's Media and their bibliography *Little Miss Muffet Fights Back**; Rhonna Goodman (Vocational High School Specialist, New Public Library); Lillian Morrison (Coordinator of Young Adult Services, New York Public Library); Aileen O'Brien Murphy (Children's Literature Specialist, New York Public Library).

Tuning in Early: Pre-school Books

Cecily Brownstone: *All Kinds of Mothers* (McKay). Black and white mothers, working and stay-home mothers all have an important quality in common—their love for their children.

Dan Greenburg. *Jumbo the Boy and Arnold the Elephant* (Bobbs-Merrill). Baby boy and baby elephant are mixed-up in the hospital nursery. A whimsical story showing both fathers and mothers tending the mismatched offspring.

Margrit Eichler. *Martin's Father* (Lollipop Power). Household chores and outdoor adventures are shared by a boy and his father. *(For a brochure and order form from The Lollipop Power Collective, send a stamped, addressed envelope to: P.O. Box 1171, Chapel Hill, North Carolina 27514.)*

Eve Merriam. *Mommies at Work* (Scholastic). Busy moms in various occupations, trades and professions. A must!

Lou Ann Gaeddert. *Noisy Nancy Norris* and *Noisy Nancy and Nick* (Doubleday). Two books about irrepressible Nancy, who is as inventive as she is boisterous.

Sue Felt. *Rosa-Too-Little* (Doubleday). A Puerto Rican girl, who desperately wants a library card, learns to write.

Bill Charmatz. *The Little Duster* (Macmillan). A grown man cleans his messy apartment with the inadvertent aid of a dog.

Phyllis Krasilovsky. *The Man Who Didn't Wash His Dishes* (Scholastic). Cooking for himself is no problem, but cleaning up afterward is.

Edna Mitchell Preston. *The Temper Tantrum Book* (Viking). Animals prove that anger, frustration and humor know no sex.

* To order a copy of "Little Miss Muffet Fights Back," send 50 cents in coin plus a stamped, addressed 4 x 9½" envelope to Feminists on Children's Media, P.O. Box 4315, Grand Central Station, New York, New York 10017.

Humanized Fiction: Girls Who Think
and Act, Boys Who Feel and Care

L. Frank Baum. *The Wizard of Oz* (Reilly & Lee). Dorothy leads the search for brains, heart, courage and honesty. A fantasy for feminists and humanists of all ages.

Betsy Byars. *Go and Hush the Baby* (Viking). Babysitting can be fun for a big brother. (ages 5-8)

Astrid Lindgren. *Pippi Longstocking* (Viking). The escapades of an unreconstructed tomboy. (6-11)

Betty Miles and Joan Blos. *Just Think* (Knopf). Mothers who work, fathers who enjoy their kids, athletic girls, a child-care center . . . just think—reality! (4-8)

Scott O'Dell. *Island of the Blue Dolphins* (Houghton). A strong, self-sufficient Indian girl survives 18 years alone on an island. (9-12)

Ivan Southall. *Walk a Mile and Get Nowhere* (Bradbury). A 13-year-old tests his manhood and finds machismo is meaningless. (10+)

Hila Colman. *Daughter of Discontent* (Morrow). A 17-year-old girl must reexamine her attitude toward her domineering father and men in general. (12+)

Betsy Madden. *The All-American Coeds* (Criterion). How the crackerjack girls' basketball team of a black high school triumphs over the rule against coed competition. (12+)

Maia Wojciechowska. *Don't Play Dead Before You Have To* (Harper). A sympathetic teen-aged boy becomes father and mother to a neglected child (12+)

Let Us Now Praise Famous Women:
Biography and Autobiography

Leah Lurie Heyn. *Challenge to Become a Doctor:* The Story of Elizabeth Blackwell (Feminist Press). Well-illustrated biography of the first woman doctor. (8-12) *(For information about the publications of The Feminist Press, send a stamped, addressed envelope to Box 334, Old Westbury, New York 11568.)*

Susan Brownmiller. *Shirley Chisholm* (Doubleday). The first black woman to be elected to the United States Congress. (9-13)

Bernadette Devlin. *The Price of My Soul* (Knopf). The young Irish revolutionary tells her experiences in Parliament. (12+)

Marianna Norris. *Doña Felisa: Mayor of San Juan* (Dodd, Mead). Twenty-three years at the top. (8-10)

Polly Anne and Stewart Graff. *Helen Keller: Toward the Light* (Garrard). The remarkable handicapped woman and her teacher Anne Sullivan. (6-9)

Terry Morris. *Shalom, Golda* (Hawthorn). Israel's Prime Minister Golda Meir from childhood to world leader. (10-15)

Toby Shafter. *Edna St. Vincent Millay* (Messner). The tomboy who grew up to become a Pulitzer Prize-winning poet. (12+)

Dorothy Sterling. *Lucretia Mott* (Doubleday). The Quaker preacher who crusaded for Abolition and Women's Suffrage for over 50 years. (12+)

Lawrence Lader and Milton Meltzer. *Margaret Sanger: Pioneer of Birth Control* (Crowell). The patron saint of planned parenthood. (12-15)

Jacqueline Bernard. *Journey Toward Freedom: The Story of Sojourner Truth* (Grosset & Dunlap). The former slave turned abolitionist, feminist and spokeswoman for non-violence. (11-15)

The Woman Question
Answered in Fact and Fiction

Karen DeCrow. *The Young Woman's Guide to Liberation* (Bobbs-Merrill). Alternatives to the half-life while the choice is still yours. (14+)

Doris Faber. *Petticoat Politics* (Lothrop). How American women won the right to vote. (12-15)

Elizabeth Hall. *Stand Up, Lucy* (Houghton). A historical novel about a young activist during the period before passage of the 19th Amendment. (8-12)

Lucy Komisar. *The New Feminism* (Watts). The experiences of young women growing up in an age of social and sexual revolution. (12+)

Eve Merriam, Editor. *Growing Up Female in America* (Doubleday). Diaries, journals and letters that reveal the lives of ten American women, famous and unknown. (12+)

Books to Boycott (and Girlcott):
Three Examples of What to Avoid

Whitney Darrow Jr. *I'm Glad I'm a Boy! I'm Glad I'm a Girl!* (Simon & Schuster). Symptom (from the text): "Boys invent things. Girls use what boys invent." Diagnosis: Rampant sexism. For girls it's a quick course in second-class personhood.

The *Sesame Street Book of People and Things* (Preschool Press).   In its "Note to Adults" the writers consistently refer to the child as "he," and they *mean* he. Nearly all the "people in your neighborhood" are men (the one woman in the group is a hairdresser). Where are the role models for 51 per cent of the preschool population?

Frank Jupo. *Just Like Mommy/Just Like Daddy* (Grosset & Dunlap). The all-American division of labor: Mom on the inside with the dishes and dust. Dad on the outside—raking, mowing. Propaganda to perpetuate role stereotypes.

**"If you are the youngest
in the family, researchers say,
you are more likely to feel
dominated by people around you.
But you also have a better chance of
being a creative person."**

For some time psychologists have speculated on the effects of birth order on personality development. In other words, if you are the oldest child you may grow up with a different personality than either a middle or a youngest child. These birth orders can become quite complicated as new children enter the family, and research has yielded some fascinating insights.

• A friend has invited Ellen and her sister to a party where there will be many boys and girls they haven't met before. Ellen thinks it will be fun. But her sister feels ill at ease with people she doesn't know. So she decides not to go.
• Janice has unexpectedly failed an important math test. Her mother comes to her room to try to cheer her up. She always did that when Janice's older sister was unhappy, and it made the girl feel better. But Janice just wishes that her mother would go away. When Janice is depressed, she'd rather be alone.
• You are asked to run for office in the school elections. Two years ago your brother was elected class president, and he urges you to make the race. "It'll be fun whether you win or lose," he says. You're flattered, but the idea of competing for votes turns you off. So you decline the nomination.

Have you ever wondered why brothers and sisters can be so different from one another? Same parents, same home, same kind of upbringing—yet each has a different approach to life.

Part of the reason, some psychologists now believe, lies in the sequence in which you are born—whether you are the oldest, the youngest, or a middle child in your family.

These experts have found that "birth order" might have an important influence in shaping personality, and that it can have a substantial effect on the way you respond to people and to experiences.

For example, if you are an only or an oldest child (they tend to share many of the same characteristics, since an oldest child is also an "only" for a time), you are more likely to be self-disciplined and hardworking. You seek to be the center of attention. Yet you also tend to be more anxious than other people under stress.

If you are the youngest in a family, researchers say you are more likely to feel dominated by people around you. But you also have a better chance of being a creative person.

And if you are a middle child, you probably have a greater-than-average need for affection. At the same time, the chances are you are good at dealing tactfully with friends, classmates and coworkers.

There's a psychologists' joke that goes this way: since there are three diffi-cult positions in the birth order—oldest, middle, youngest—one should try to avoid all three! But there is no "number magic" about the order in which we are born. Neither fairy godmothers nor the science of heredity has earmarked any position in the sequence for overall advantage or handicap.

(Since talking about birth order can get to be cumbersome, both "only" and "oldest" children will be referred to here as O. The last-born in a family will be Y. A "middle" child—one born at any point in the sequence between an O and a Y, whether a second, fifth or even ninth child—will be called M. Brothers and sisters, technically known as siblings, will be "sibs.")

The main reason that birth order makes a difference in how one thinks about himself and reacts to others is that parents usually have a particular "emotional set" toward each child—a pattern of feelings and attitudes—depend-ing on the child's place in the family succession. A second reason is that sibs tend to react with one another in ways directly related to their birth order.

Take, for example, the Jones family. When their first child, Mary, was born, she was her parents' pride and joy. As an O, she was the focus for all their love and attention. Everything Mary did—the first step she took, the first word she spoke, the first day she went to school—was a family landmark. At the same time, the Joneses were always tense when they were raising Mary. They were never sure they were doing the right things for her.

When Helen was born next, the Joneses were pleased but not quite so ex-cited. They took her childhood accomplishments more casually. But they were also a lot more relaxed about her upbringing. Helen wasn't made to toe the mark as much as Mary had been. Of course, Mary didn't have her parents to herself anymore. She felt jealous of Helen, but when she showed it, her parents got angry with her. So Mary decided the best way to keep as much of her par-ents' love as possible was to try to please them, to be a "good" girl.

Several years later the Joneses had another child. Because it was a boy, and because the Joneses had decided it would be their last child, Johnny was "babied" a great deal. A lot less in the way of responsibilities and obedience was demanded of him, even as he grew older. He wasn't disciplined as much as his sisters had been. On the other hand, his childhood accomplishments got little attention or praise because Mr. and Mrs. Jones had been through all that twice before. Johnny's presence didn't affect Mary much. She was still the O. Helen, however, suddenly became an often overlooked M. Both girls lorded it over Johnny—they could do everything better, and they ordered him around. Still, as a Y, Johnny never had to make way, emotionally or physically, for a younger sib.

In short, because the Joneses reacted differently toward each child, all three saw themselves in different family "roles." And in accordance with their roles, each subconsciously developed certain attitudes and behavior patterns that would become the basis for the way they dealt with and felt about life—first within the family and later with the outside world.

What does this mean in terms of the effects of your birth order on your personality? The experts can draw a profile of the typical O, M and Y. But they caution that there are no hard and fast rules because human beings can't be pigeonholed into preset categories. Besides, many of the findings of birth order research are still confusing and even contradictory. Moreover, a good deal depends on how much insight parents have into the way they deal with their children. In general, however, the picture shapes up something like this:

If You Are an O

Not surprisingly, you think of yourself as someone special. Dr. Lucille Forer, a clinical psychologist who has specialized in birth order, points out that since an O has her parents to herself for a year or more—and because the parents make a fuss over everything the child does—an O "develops a feeling of being a rather important person." Thus, you will probably go through life with a strong ego . . . not in the sense of being conceited, but in the sense of feeling loved and sure of yourself.

You probably also grew up under pressure to behave "properly." For one thing, your parents likely saw you as a reflection of their child-raising abilities, so they wanted you to be "good." Too, you were with grown-ups much more than with other children, so you naturally identified closely with the adult world you lived in. You made your parents' values—obedience, conformity, responsibility, hard work, achievement—an integral part of your own conscience.

An O's parents generally have time and energy to concentrate on talking and playing with their child. Therefore, you grasped word and number concepts rapidly, which helped you do well in school. Also, your parents expected a great deal of you; you were the first child on whom they could pin their hopes for the future. As a result, you came to demand a lot of *yourself*. You were eager to succeed.

And O's do succeed. Surveys show they tend to get better grades and score higher on exams; they are more likely to go to college; they are more likely to choose professional careers; they show up in lists of prominent people far more than the law of averages would allow. Indeed, in terms of "achievement of eminence," said psychologist William D. Altus, "the dice are loaded in favor of the first-born."

(*Warning:* On the other hand, some studies show that O's do not perform as well under stress as M's or Y's. Psychologists feel that an O, always under pressure to meet high standards, suffers a lack of self-esteem when she fails to live up to them. This anxiety to shine can sometimes affect her performance. An O may need constant reassurance that she is doing well.)

One major drawback for you as an O is that you were the "practice" child on whom your parents made their mistakes and projected their worries. For example, when an O baby is sick, parents are far more upset than they are with later children, by which time they've learned to take routine childhood illness in stride.

Consequently, you may be overly sensitive to physical problems. You may let minor ailments interfere too easily with your plans. You may even use real or imagined illness as an excuse to avoid an unpleasant situation.

The birth of a second child is the watershed that separates the O's into "onlies" and "oldests." The only child has traditionally been considered spoiled and unhappy. But research shows this is far from true. Onlies do bear the brunt of parental anxiety and pressure and are often overprotected. On the other hand, says Dr. Forer, an only child is more self-confident and relaxed than other first-borns. "He never experiences the disappointment of having others take his place," she writes.

If You Are an "Only"

You have usually had most of the things you need and want since family income doesn't have to be portioned out among other children. With this kind of material status added to your emotional security, you subconsciously feel yourself to be a special sort of person.

As a result, you may go on playing the role of "only child" even when you are grown up. Chances are, you'll virtually take it for granted that people will help you whenever you need help—just as your parents always did. Unlike an "oldest"—who resents taking orders because she has usually struggled to remain the dominant child in her family—an "only" usually feels quite comfortable with people in authority.

As an "only" you probably had a lonely childhood. Yet studies indicate this often gives you greater reserves of independence and self-reliance. (Twenty-one of the first twenty-three astronauts to go into space were O's.) You learned to use your imagination, to fantasize. You may have had a host of imaginary playmates. Yet it is often hard for you to understand how real people of your age think and feel.

If You Are an "Oldest"

You know all about the problems of adjusting to a new baby in the family. You went through the universal spectrum of emotions: bewilderment, hurt, anger, jealousy.

Yet in your parents' eyes, no matter how old you were when your first sib was born, you suddenly became "grown up." You were expected to behave like a "big" girl, because no matter how small you were, the baby was smaller. You were given more chores and responsibilities. In the long run, like most "oldests," you tried to meet these new standards.

Of course, the sex of your sib can make a difference. If you have a younger brother, for example, it may bring out the maternal in you. And because he tends to look up to you, you usually come to have a warm liking for men. If your sib is a girl, there was probably more competition and jealousy between the two of you in early childhood. As the oldest, you usually won—and very likely you still want to triumph in most things you do.

If You Are an M

By tradition, middle children are supposed to be overshadowed by both their older and younger sibs. (Significantly, perhaps, there have been fewer studies made on M's than on either of the other two groups!) But the surveys that have been done show that M's are far better off than anyone supposed.

Studies of M's are complicated by the many possible family combinations that can exist. An M can, for instance, be the middle one of three children, the second or third of four, or the second-to-sixth of seven, etc. An M may have older sisters and younger brothers, or vice versa, or both. And each situation sets up a host of different ways in which you, your parents and your sibs react to one another. In general, experts find that M's enjoy being M's more than O's or Y's enjoy their positions in the birth sequence.

For one thing, as an M you have the advantage, for a while, of being the youngest in the family. And when another child is born you don't suffer as much resentment or jealousy as an O does. After all, you didn't have your parents all to yourself in the first place. You also have the double asset of an older sib to whom you can turn for help and guidance, and a younger sib whom you can to some extent supervise and control.

Because you have learned to be tactful in dealing with sibs, on both sides of you, you are able to get along well in groups. You can deal diplomatically with people above and below you. You make friends easily because you are friendly; M's often feel shortchanged on their share of family attention and affection, so they look for both elsewhere.

You aren't driving or demanding as O's tend to be. But you manage to get your way by subtler means. Dr. Forer points out that an M's ability to be diplomatic, to manipulate people indirectly, can be useful in fields like politics, public relations or salesmanship.

Because M's usually grow up with sibs of the opposite sex, you are likely to get along well with men. Even in women's lib days, a flexible and sharing M—willing and able to mesh her needs with those around her—tends to make an excellent wife. Moreover, because you are less possessive, controlling and impatient than the average O and Y, you will make a good parent.

On the other hand, M's do not necessarily have the best of all possible birth orders. Much depends on the "sex distribution" of your sibs. A genetic psychologist, Dr. M. H. Krout, studying the relationship of behavior patterns and birth order, concluded that the more children of the same sex in a family, the less likely parents were to prefer one of them. Specifically, he found that the middle child of three females will get the least affection and attention.

As a result, it's likely that a girl M will often seek goals or interests very different from those of her sisters. It's her way of trying to single herself out, to achieve some status. An M may tend to emphasize intellectual accomplishments or a business or professional career. Often an M sister remains unmarried —but likes it!

But if a girl M follows a boy O, she's likely to be especially cherished. She's usually close to her mother and identifies with her. If a girl M follows an older sister, chances are the two will compete.

As families grow and the M position gets more complicated, these adjustments may vary. For example, a study of large families by the late sociologist Dr. James H. S. Bossard revealed that though M's enjoyed their positions better than O's, the *first* of a series of M's was seldom as satisfied with her spot as later M's. Indeed, the best adjustment seemed to be made, Bossard found, by fourth and fifth place M's. They had better records for making friendships with groups of other people, rather than singling out one "best" friend as O's tend to do.

In the long run, it seems M's do pretty well. According to child psychologist Dr. Bruno Bettelheim, an M with one or more older sisters "often looks more sparkling . . . and tends to get her way by being charming and capricious." An M with an older brother "feels secure and well-protected," says Dr. Bettelheim, and seldom needs to make demands on other people because "she received so much from the brother who babied her."

If You Are a Y

Less has been expected of you than of your sibs. Because your parents were more experienced at child-raising, they were more relaxed in bringing you up. One result, say the experts, is that having been left more to your own devices than your sibs were, you may be more original and creative in your approach to life.

Since you are the youngest (and, of course, the last) child, you were probably babied too much, too long. You had little chance to be in charge of anything or anyone. No one burdened you with expectations. Since this situation is, after all, a comfortable one, you may still tend to cling to immaturity and dependency. With at least three other people in your family who are older, bigger, stronger—you may have come to feel that you aren't as adequate as others. This attitude may have been reinforced because your parents seldom seemed impressed by your early accomplishments (after all, they'd seen finger-paintings and orange-crate "bookcases" before!)

Some Y's choose to stay babied. They use childish measures—sulking or crying or pleading—to get what they want. Others decide they'll just have to try harder to catch up to their sibs. Thus a girl Y with older brothers sometimes turns into a tomboy for a while.

What is most important for a Y is that she develop her own individual skills and qualities. That is the mature alternative to both remaining childlike and competing with sibs on their own ground. A parent can help by giving a Y more responsibility and by encouraging her to follow her own goals.

Above all, as a Y you are a complex person. You tend to be easy to relax with, but you frequently flare up in sudden resentful angers. At one time you may be more than willing to accept help; at another time you will resent it as "keeping you a baby." You often find it difficult to accept responsibility or to make decisions, and this will frustrate you. On the other hand, all that childhood indulgence may give you a feeling of optimism and well-being . . . nothing can go wrong in your world! You may thus develop an easygoing and even adventurous approach to life.

Obviously, just as with M's, a great deal depends on the age and sex of your sibs. For example, a girl with older sisters is ordinarily a Y, but if she has only older brothers she may—as the family's first daughter—be treated by her parents almost like an O. Similarly, if a girl is born last in a large family, say, ten years after her previous sib, the great age gap could perhaps put her in the category of an "only."

The influence of birth order, psychologists feel, can extend beyond childhood and adolescence into our adult lives. Perhaps more interesting is the fact that birth order can be involved in our choice of the kind of person we marry.

In general, we seem to look for a marriage partner who will let us recapture the childhood environment in which we felt most comfortable. Thus, points out Dr. Forer, O's tend to choose Y's, and vice versa. Because an O is competitive and controlling, marriage to another O would lead to endless arguing.

An M may carry into marriage her childhood desire to be needed and wanted. As a wife and mother, she may cater to her family so much that she neglects herself. But this trait may work in paradoxical ways. One M wife complained that her husband demanded so much of her attention she couldn't go out of the house for fear he might telephone her. Actually, her husband *wanted* her to be more independent. The marriage counselor she went to urged her to develop interests outside the home. When she did the marriage improved because she no longer had to insist on "being needed" at home—she stopped acting toward her husband as she'd acted toward her sibs in childhood.

Y's rarely remain single. Psychologist Walter Toman found that a Y usually selects a husband who is an O, or at least an older M. This choice enables her to continue in the role of the well-loved and cared-for "child." Eventually, however, a Y girl may feel too "dominated" by her O spouse and rebel.

A marriage between two Y's, on the other hand, can turn into an emotional tug of war to see which one can get the "most"—the most love, the most care, the most things. A Y who is used to the affection of all her older sibs needs to sense that she is similarly cherished by her husband. But he may be hard put to cherish her, for being Y's—with fewer responsibilities as children—neither of them may be the most competent or sensitive in meeting a partner's needs and taking on the obligations of home and family.

Throughout this article I've used phrases such as "you *may*," or "O's *tend* to," or "M's are more *likely*." One reason is that many findings by researchers are still ambiguous. Secondly, variations of age and sex in a family sequence can get so complex that it almost takes a computer to sort out the possible combinations and their effects. Thirdly, since people aren't puppets, they don't always react according to classification.

As psychologists continue to study birth order, a clearer picture of its implications may emerge. Even that, however, will not mean that anyone's character or personality is fixed or foreordained by the accident of place in the family.

Yet there are undeniable patterns. Being aware of them can help you to change things about yourself that you may not like, instead of continuing to act out unconsciously the birth order "roles" of your childhood.

Alvin F. Poussaint and James P. Comer

"Children are quick
to adopt the negative attitudes
they've seen their parents display
toward individuals or groups."

In this article two black psychiatrists explain how attitudes about prejudice develop. They stress the importance of being honest and straightforward about prejudicial attitudes rather than hiding behind politeness and false conventionality. This paper describes many of the sensitive issues that parents have to deal with in educating their children to be less prejudiced.

How can we prepare our children for life in a rapidly shrinking and multiracial world? And how can those parents with an ambivalent racial outlook hope to raise children free of prejudice? Can we avoid future conflict between ourselves and our children if their ideas on race turn out to be different from ours? These are just a few of the questions that we, as Black psychiatrists, frequently hear from young white parents.

We are concerned here primarily with those parents who want their children to grow up with healthy attitudes toward people of other racial groups. We do not expect to answer all the questions white parents may have. Nor can we always be very specific. But we can make suggestions and recommendations that may help white parents in their efforts to raise children to be free from bias.

Of course, there are some parents who have no desire to help their children develop free of racial prejudice, and there is little we can say here that will be of value to them. These parents do a disservice to their children and to the country, and they must assume full responsibility for the consequences.

It is commonly agreed that one of the first places children learn prejudice is at home. None of us likes to admit that he—or she—is biased; yet it is almost impossible for most Americans, bred in a society with a history of flagrant racial abuse, to grow up without some prejudiced attitudes. Until recently the white public's attitudes toward Blacks were determined largely at second hand—by books, broadcasts and plays that depicted Blacks as happy-go-lucky and "shiftless," or as criminal, depraved and dangerous.

Reprinted from *Redbook* Magazine, May 1972; copyright © 1972 The McCall Publishing Company.

Although white Americans in recent years have become increasingly aware of these images as insidious stereotypes, many still suffer from the residual hangover of the old attitudes. And many parents, unconscious of this racial bias, pass it on to their children. The first step white parents must take is to face squarely and to control whatever prejudices they may discover in themselves.

When we are not aware of or will not acknowledge our own prejudices, we are likely to be inconsistent and defensive in our attitudes toward race-related matters. And of course, young children are confused when a parent talks one way and acts in another—as, for instance, the mother who says she is not prejudiced but opposes Blacks' moving into her apartment building or neighborhood. If you say "the right thing" in order to sound liberal, and are insincere, one of two things can happen—your children will become hypocritical themselves or they will come to view you as a hypocrite.

Children are quick to adopt the negative attitudes they've seen their parents display toward individuals or groups. Derogatory ethnic "jokes" are but one example. Even when nothing disparaging is said, children may sense that something is unacceptable about Blacks or members of other minorities if parents shun these people at school events or public-affairs meetings.

It is often better for parents who are aware of specific prejudices to acknowledge rather than hide them. In a home where a climate of independent thought is encouraged, open discussions about the reasons for prejudices may help you develop a more mature attitude as well as help your child become a rational thinker. Those parents who force their attitudes on their youngsters deprive them of the opportunity to think for themselves and encourage rebellion. It is important that parents who acknowledge an irrational prejudice allow their children to form more rational attitudes when they are so inclined. Children appreciate honesty and the willingness to permit them to hold different opinions.

Children become aware of racial differences at around three years of age. In particular they are curious about hair and color differences. White parents are often uncomfortable when their children inquire about these differences—particularly in the presence of Blacks—even when the questions are quite innocent. These parents must remember that their discomfort stems from their own feeling that there is something wrong with being Black. Your child's inquiry should be answered without hesitation or anxiety and in terms appropriate to the age of the child.

If a three-year-old child points out that a playmate is brown, an appropriate answer might be: "Yes, some people have brown skin, some white, some black and some yellow." Further elaboration is not needed until the child raises additional questions about color or race.

As they grow and explore their environment, its people and their ways your children will raise more questions—unless your anxiety tells them that they shouldn't. Older children may want to know *why* people have different skin color, eye shape and hair, and they may be curious about the origins of these differences. Honest answers given without anxiety are more effective than lectures on brotherhood and equality.

Of course, the very best way to help your children grow free of racial prejudice is to enable them to have normal relationships with Blacks. Youngsters who come in touch with a wide range of Blacks in school or at home are less likely to develop prejudiced attitudes. A white child who is bounced on the knee of a Black friend of the family won't be uncomfortable with other persons with dark skin. If a white youngster has an opportunity to touch the skin and feel the hair of Black playmates, he won't find these characteristics strange or unfamiliar when he encounters other Afro-Americans.

When contact with people from different racial groups is a new experience, it should be handled in a normal and relaxed manner. Adults should not stand poised to pounce on a child for fear that he or she will display some racial prejudice. We recall an instance where a white youngster excitedly pointed toward a Black man at a swimming pool and said, "Hey, Mom, look at that man ..." The mother, greatly flustered, tried to hush the child, but he continued: "... in the striped bathing suit!" The mother's anxiety clearly had prompted her to anticipate the worst. Innocent or even angry remarks children make often are viewed as racial slurs of significance by parents. You must remember that your youngsters are not as aware of our society's racial problems as you may be.

For example, a situation arose in one nursery school in which a white child and a Black child wanted to play with the same toy. The white youngster told the teacher that she never wanted to play with that "old brown girl" again. She then stalked off to play with another Black child.

A white parent who was present felt that the white child should be warned against the expression of negative racial attitudes. But the teacher responded instead by helping the white child understand that she was angry, and that when she felt better she would want to play with her friend again. She helped both children understand that they could share the toy and did not have to fight over it.

When a child attacks another child, it's often out of frustration or disappointment. A child often sees difference as vulnerability and will strike out at his enemy by singling out what he thinks is a weak spot—"fat Daddy," "mean Mommy" and maybe "old brown girl." In this instance the teacher made it clear to the child that she did not want to play with her friend because she was angry at her, not because her friend was brown. To admonish the child for racial prejudice would have been reading adult anxieties into a situation that did not warrant it.

One of the authors recalls an incident that occurred when he was regularly seeing a five-year-old white boy from a public-housing project. One day the boy walked into the office and announced that he could not see the therapist any longer because he was moving away. He remarked that his mother wanted to get away from the "colored people" because colored people were bad. This five-year-old assured the doctor that he would return to see him as soon as the "colored people" moved from the neighborhood. At no time did he seem to be aware that the psychiatrist was a "colored person."

Unfortunately, this child's mother was planting the seeds of racial prejudice in her son, who was too young to understand her bias. It would have been an unwise approach for a parent, teacher or therapist to reprimand this boy for bigotry. Instead, the therapist explained to the boy that kind people and unkind people come in all colors.

In spite of any efforts you make, your children inevitably will pick up derogatory racial remarks from other children. The name-calling in children's games and ditties is one example. Sayings like "eeny, meeny, miny, moe, catch a nigger by the toe" and calling chocolate or licorice candies "nigger babies" or Brazil nuts "niggertoes" are obvious instances. Some parents become just as alarmed when they hear such terms as they do about the use of "bathroom words" or profanity. There is no need. When you hear your five- or six-year-old using "nigger" or "kike," you might point out that Black children or Jewish children will be angry and will not want to play with him if he uses those words. It is helpful to teach children the proper name for each racial or religious group.

Children do not want to hurt the feelings of others except when they themselves are angry or frustrated. A simple explanation of how others will feel is usually enough to cause them to drop racial slurs.

Just as there is no need to "attack" a child for a remark made in innocence, neither is there a need to accentuate the positive. Some parents feel that because there are many factors in the environment that may lead to prejudice, they must indoctrinate their children with the "right attitude." Because some white parents want to impress upon their children the fact that Black people do indeed have good qualities, they may emphasize clichés. Black people are good dancers, good athletes, good musicians. Unfortunately, this creates more stereotypes.

It is important to permit your children to experience others as individuals and form their own opinions. We should offer them assistance and comfort only when it is clear that they are confused or hurt as a result of a social experience.

If you have the "right attitude" in racial matters, it is likely that your children will develop the "right attitude." When you feel a need to indoctrinate, it often indicates some self-doubt. Honest, straightforward, age-appropriate explanations are far more convincing and effective than lectures. Such explanations convey a message to your child that says: "I trust you, once you are informed, to be fair and just in your relationships with others."

White parents occasionally ask us, "But what can I do when my child is bullied or mistreated by Black children?"

In some cases white children associate aggressive, bullying behavior on the part of a Black child with his race. Usually, however, the assumption at this point is vague, as evidenced by one white seven-year-old who sought the protection of a Black classmate from her block "because the Black kids always fight me on the playground."

In all cases it is important first to be certain that your child is not provoking attack in some way—by a rejecting or condescending attitude or by verbal or physical hostility. When you are sure this is not true, it is important to point out to your child that there are bullies in all races and that all Black youngsters do not behave in this manner. In the case just mentioned, it was a matter of helping the white seven-year-old understand that relating fighting to race was not logical, since her friendly and protective neighbor was also Black.

Too often, white charges of "bullying" arise when Blacks from other communities are introduced through school or play situations to a white neighborhood. In many cases these feelings are prompted by fear of the outsider. It is generally helpful if parents and teachers cooperate to work out arrangements so that the children begin to know one another as individuals rather than unknown "groups" to be attacked or to defend oneself against. Parents might suggest such activities as school parties, trips and other projects open to both children and parents, so that adults and children alike get to know one another. Bullying is often defensive behavior that usually will disappear when a child feels accepted and has no reason to fear or to feel rejected by others.

When bullying behavior is prolonged and the children are older than nine or ten, the problem is more difficult. White parents have told us of situations in which their children developed negative attitudes toward Blacks in spite of home efforts because of difficult school experiences. Today's Black children are not being strapped with attitudes of passivity and low self-esteem, which was the case in the past. In some cases the energy is not appropriately channeled into achievement, and a few children are annoyingly outspoken and angry in their assertion of Black pride. Indeed, in situations where racial discrimination remains, this is justified.

You can help your child understand why some Black children are over-aggressive. You can point out to your nine- or ten-year-old that Blacks have been treated unfairly in the past and do not expect to be treated fairly now.

On the other hand, you should not excuse unjustified confrontation or disruptive behavior by any child. The real issue, of course, is trust. Sometimes to an aggressive, assertive Black child a statement such as "Look, if you're fair with me, I'll be fair with you" can have amazing results. It can be the first step toward mutual respect.

Wholly acquiescent behavior, however, encourages aggressive response. A white eight-year-old child constantly beaten by Black classmates didn't report it because "Blacks have been mistreated too much." Another white youngster went without lunch money because several Black children made daily "collections" for their own pockets. This type of aggression compromises the white child's rights and is damaging to the development of everyone concerned. It is hardly a basis for mutual respect.

White parents must therefore make it clear to their children that no one should permit himself to be victimized—neither white nor Black. If a child is beaten by other children and unable to do anything about it, the parent must intervene, seeking the help of school authorities and of the parents of the children involved.

When children watch news programs about racial conflict or become aware of racial trouble in their city, they often ask questions. It is not helpful to turn off the broadcast or discourage the questions. Children need help in understanding these events or they will feel personally threatened. They will often identify with the "good guys," or keepers of law and order. Developmentally they are very much involved in internalizing the rules and regulations of the world around them.

You can point out that all people who are denied a fair opportunity usually become angry, upset and sometimes violent. With a six- or seven-year-old you might recall what happened when his friend or brother or sister took a toy away from him or did not permit him to play in a game. With a nine- or ten-year-old you can point out that protest and violence occur all over the world in places where people have been treated unjustly; that in the United States workers and soldiers of all colors have protested violently when they felt they were victims of injustice.

You can do this without justifying violence or apologizing for being white. The objective is to help the child understand the importance of fair play, to understand conflict as a matter of disagreement rather than an issue of one race against another. If you want to express disagreement with the method of protest, it should be made clear that you are unhappy with the actions of the protesters, demonstrators or rioters, not with the race involved.

In helping youngsters to understand the events around them, it is important not to convey the impression that a Black child is an emotional cripple who deserves special treatment in a one-to-one contact. Black children, like all children, do not want their playmates to feel sorry for them. Most will be annoyed by solicitous or overprotective behavior.

A white youngster who does not invite a Black friend to her birthday party to spare her possible racial insults or discomfort, for example, creates more problems than she solves. Other solutions are available, all the way from not having the party to not inviting white children likely to insult the Black youngster. The exclusion of the Black child reflects racial prejudice. Besides, Blacks have developed many ways of coping with the everyday reality of racial prejudice.

In much of this discussion we have talked about white families who have some degree of contact with Blacks. The problem is more difficult if you live in an all-white community or in a community where the only Blacks present are engaged in low-income tasks. Your child can develop stereotyped viewpoints about Blacks that can be troublesome later. One white youngster from an all-white suburban community, visiting the city with her mother, exclaimed upon seeing a Black infant, "Look, Mommy, a baby maid!" In another instance a Black professional man moved into a neighborhood previously all white and was greeted by a friendly youngster with, "Hi, Mr. Garbageman!"

Under these circumstances it is especially important that you use other means to expose your children to differences among people in our society.

You might want to see to it that they watch Black or interracial television programs, or that they read some of the books now available for children that skillfully and interestingly discuss racial differences. Storybooks that show children of all races engaged in work or play can be useful. Providing your child with Black and white dolls helps them understand at the very earliest age that ours is a multiethnic society. The *Sesame Street* and *Electric Company* educational television programs, in which children of different races and backgrounds play, sing and learn together, are especially useful in teaching humanitarian values.

There is an increasing appreciation of the richness of the various cultural heritages in America. African and Afro-American art, sculpture and music are featured from time to time at various museums, special exhibits and concerts. In fact, it may be possible to arrange for such exhibits and programs at your church, synagogue, clubs, and so on. Your children will be persuaded of your interest when you take them to Black exhibits and programs. Your involvement in ending exclusionary practices in your community prepares your children to approach Blacks in the larger society without prejudice.

At home and outside the home, the white parent has an awesome task. There is still a great deal of racial prejudice in our society and yet you hope to raise your children free of prejudice. This requires adequately dealing with or discussing your own prejudices. It requires sensitivity to the feelings of frustration and anger in your own children that can lead to racial prejudice and it requires helping them manage these feelings in a healthy way.

This is an important task. Continued racial prejudice can lead to conflict between white parents and their children and even greater conflict between Blacks and whites in the society. If every family does its part, we can begin to reduce the problems created by racial prejudice in our own hearts, in our own homes and in our society.

21   About Drugs Again
Marjorie Schuman, Tom Greenfield, Pat Clayton,
Jane Hassinger, and Jeff Gumbiner

"Pure heroin is not a very toxic substance compared to some other drugs."

People of all ages are being confronted with questions about what drugs to use, in what dosage, how frequently, under what circumstances, and with what presumed effects. Some answers are offered in authoritarian terms based on a system of morality, such as "all drugs are evil" or "drugs are a great turn-on." It makes much more sense to recognize the differences among substances, and to make individual decisions based on one's values and on accurate information about the consequences of the decision. This article provides a great deal of current and relevant information.

Some General Information

In the absence of reliable information about drugs, the risks involved in using them are greatly increased. Excessive dosage, mixing of drugs, ignorance of the dangers, and confused expectations, all contribute to the tragedies we read about, often attributed too simply to drug use per se. However, in giving basic drug information, generalizations are not always easily made. Especially with street drugs, generalizations must always be qualified with the reminder that the actual contents of the drugs are unknown and variable.

People vary a great deal both physically and psychologically in ways which affect their responses to drugs. These differences are by no means trivial. For example, a drug which has stimulant effects for most people may put others to sleep. Set and setting—the circumstances under which a person takes a drug, why he takes it, what he expects from it—also have important influences on the outcome of the experience.

Aside from individual differences in sensitivity to drug effects, dose is another critical variable in determining a person's response to a drug. At the extremes, too little of any drug will have no effect, while too much may be disastrous. The effects of a given dose of a drug will often be modified if other

This article is adapted from a booklet *About Drugs Again*, © 1973, University of Michigan, available from University Publications, The University of Michigan, 409 East Jefferson, Ann Arbor, Michigan, 48104. It was written by staff of the Drug Education Project, Office of Student Services, with assistance of the U.S. Office of Education, federal grant OEG-0-71-1304, under the Drug Abuse Prevention Act of 1970. It does not necessarily reflect the views of the Office of Education.

drugs are simultaneously used. Mixing drugs, or taking drugs when one is drinking without regard to the potent effects of the drug alcohol, often leads to unpredicted effects, sometimes dangerous ones. A special note should also be made of the fact that the use of any drugs during pregnancy, particularly without the advice of a physician, is ill advised since it is impossible to assess the effects on the unborn child.

Repeated use of a drug adds another dimension of complexity. With repeated use of many types of drugs, a person may come to require a higher dose to achieve the same effect; this phenomenon is known as *tolerance*. For some types of drugs, tolerance is closely related to the development of *physical dependence*, which occurs when the body becomes accustomed to the presence of drugs in the system. A person who is physically dependent upon a drug becomes quite sick if the drug is withdrawn (*withdrawal or abstinence syndrome*). *Psychological dependence*, which often develops at the same time, is quite real in its own right and independent of physical dependence. Psychological dependence can, and does, occur with just about every type of drug, in some individuals —caffeine, marijuana, aspirin, or heroin.

The information which follows is arranged according to different classes of drugs. The final section, America, The Drug Culture, gives an overview of some broader issues.

Cannabis

Marijuana and hashish are related forms of the plant *Cannabis Sativa*, a weed which grows freely in many parts of the world including the United States. Marijuana is prepared from the dried flowering tops of the cannabis plant while hash is a more potent form prepared from the resins of the plant. Marijuana has been known since at least the third century B.C., and is in use by upwards of 200 million people all over the world. While no medical use for the drug is recognized at the present time, cannabis has in the past been used for ailments ranging from gout, rheumatism, and malaria to "female-weakness" and absent-mindedness. Marijuana was listed as an official drug in the U.S. Pharmacopoeia until 1937, at which time its use as a medicine declined as a consequence of new anti-marijuana legislation. This followed a campaign against marijuana launched by the Federal Bureau of Narcotics.

A compound called delta-9-THC (tetrahydrocannabinol) is believed to be the major active chemical in cannabis, although other structurally related chemicals present in the plant or occurring in the body after one smokes marijuana may also be active in producing the subjective effects. THC is activated by heating, so that smoked marijuana is more potent than an equivalent dose of the drug ingested by eating. An average joint of marijuana has a THC content of about one percent, while hashish may have as much as 4-5 percent THC. The relationship of marijuana and hashish is, thus, rather analogous to the relationship between wine or beer and whiskey. Lethal doses of cannabis are virtually unknown, although strictly speaking too much of any chemical may be toxic.

There has been some debate as to whether to call marijuana an intoxicant, a hallucinogen or, as is most common at the present time, a sedative-hypnotic. What is most clear is that marijuana is *not* a narcotic; such a classification is misleading where it still exists in law. Marijuana does not create physical dependence, is not a potent painkiller, and shares few properties in common with narcotic drugs.

Marijuana does have hallucinogenic properties, although it is much less potent in this respect than drugs like LSD. From one point of view, it makes little sense to distinguish "mild" from "hard" hallucinogens, since hallucinogenic effects are dose related. Many marijuana users are not aware of this fact, probably because of the weak marijuana that is generally available. A user may feel that he is tripping when he smokes grass, and this is generally not due to adulteration of the marijuana with stronger chemicals (LSD, mescaline, etc.) but rather to the dose of the marijuana. Similarly, there is little likelihood that marijuana will be adulterated with heroin or opium unless one does the adulterating oneself or buys specially prepared opiated hashish.

Marijuana is not physically addicting. It may cause a psychological dependence in susceptible users (as may any drug). The issue of tolerance to marijuana is unresolved. It has not been shown that users need to take more of the drug to get stoned; in fact, there is some evidence that a "reverse tolerance" occurs—in that as a user becomes accustomed to the effects he may need to smoke less. However, many users feel that while they do not need more of the drug to get stoned, when they smoke frequently they may not stay stoned as long.

The performance of some tasks is impaired by smoking grass but, generally, inexperienced users are most susceptible to these impairments while experienced users may be unaffected on the same tasks or may even show a slight improvement of performance.[1] One widely quoted study showed that marijuana impairs driving less than does alcohol,[2] but this study should not be considered conclusive given its methodological flaws. It is likely that given sufficient experience with the drug most of its effects can be overcome for the purposes of driving; but on the other hand, the risks of driving when stoned are certainly greater than normal, partly because of the unknown alteration in judgment and also because of the wide differences found from person to person and from one occasion to another.

The best guess as to how marijuana produces its subjective effects is that the drug somehow alters the way in which the mind processes sequential information; that is, the drug interferes with the serial coordination of memory.[3] Marijuana interferes with short-term memory, causing for example, the feeling of not being able to remember what was just said. It is likely that some of the feelings of depersonalization and unreality that sometimes accompany the marijuana experience are due to this "temporal disintegration" of memory. Other important subjective effects of marijuana include a feeling of euphoria, giddiness, and sometimes a distortion of perceptions (space, time, vision, and hear-

[1] Weil, A. T., Zinberg, N. E. and Nelsen, J. M. (1968) Clinical and psychological effects of marijuana in man. *Science, 162:* 1234–1242.
[2] Crancer, A., Dille, J. M., Delay, J. C., Wallace, J. E., and Haykin, M. D. (1969) Comparison of the effects of marijuana and alcohol on simulated driving performance. *Science, 164:* 851–854.
[3] Melges, F. T., Tinklenberg, J. R., Hollister, L. E., and Gillespie, H. K. (1970) Temporal disintegration and depersonalization during marijuana intoxication. *Arch. Gen. Psychiat., 23:* 204–210.

ing). Some users feel that the drug enhances appreciation of music, art, and other aesthetic experiences; some describe the experience as profound.

In high enough doses (too high), marijuana or hashish may impair judgment, cause confusion, disorientation, or even panic. Adverse reactions to marijuana are most likely to occur in the novice user, although an experienced user may react badly to a dose higher than he is accustomed to. Bad reactions often take the form of panic over the threat of loss of control, fear of dying, paranoia, or the fear that the person won't ever come down. In an unstable person, the panic may precipitate a psychotic reaction.

Although there are conflictiing opinions in the literature, there is no unequivocal evidence that the use of marijuana causes lasting mental changes of any sort.

THC

THC, tetrahydrocannabinol, is the major active chemical in marijuana. Many people feel comfortable with the prospect of tripping on THC because they feel that it will probably be much like smoking marijuana. Unfortunately, purified THC is unstable at normal temperatures and so *there is no real THC around*. What is sold instead is frequently a substance called PCP (see "Miscellaneous Downs," p. 223) and, as a general rule, street THC contains bad quality drugs. Beware.

Alcohol

In the history of man's use of alcohol, nearly every fruit juice, honey, sap, and grain has been fermented to obtain ethyl alcohols (and sometimes undesired by-products). As with many drugs, alcohol was first considered to be a newly discovered "cure-all." Presently it is used medically only as an antiseptic or, if there are no other drugs available, as a mild analgesic or sedative. By far its greatest use is as a social drug. Booze is one of our oldest forms of pharmacological entertainment.

As mentioned in a later section, alcohol is pharmacologically classified as a sedative-hynotic, having many properties in common with short-acting barbiturates. Although it is a central nervous system depressant, in low doses alcohol may have a pseudo-stimulant effect, resulting from the hyperactivity of various primitive parts of the brain being freed suddenly from the inhibitory control of the cortex. This disinhibition may result in an intensification of the person's present mood, or expose underlying impulses—a little sadness may become a depression, suppressed anger may be expressed as aggression.

The response to alcohol is also dependent on expectations, acting as a "pseudo-stimulant" when ingested at a party or inducing sleep if taken before retiring to bed. With increased consumption, greater depression occurs with drowsiness, drunkenness, sleep, and eventually coma (and possibly death). It is seldom realized that the lethal dose of alcohol is not much higher than an amount which causes you to pass out and lose consciousness. Also, a prolonged comatose sleep itself can be dangerous because of the increased susceptibility to infections while in this state.

Alcohol also causes dilation of surface blood vessels, resulting in a flush and warm glow. But beware of drinking to keep warm, e.g., if stranded in a snowstorm—the subjective warmth is coincident with heat leaving your body.

Alcohol also increases stomach acid secretion, and when ingested in concentrated form (straight shots) causes gastric irritation, possibly with prolonged discomfort. Long-term, continuous use is associated with cirrhosis of the liver, low resistance to infectious disease, and a variety of neurological and mental syndromes.

Psychological dependence on alcohol occurs in varying degrees; a minor dependence can develop rapidly and easily and is very common in the U.S., manifesting itself in the drink before dinner, liquor at parties, and socializing in bars. Greater degrees of psychological dependence are defined by the desire to drink beyond the culturally accepted limits. Physical dependence requires fairly continuous consumption over a period of time, but once developed, the withdrawal from alcohol is as severe as the withdrawal from barbiturates and should not be undertaken without medical supervision. Present estimates indicate there are at least ten million American alcoholics.

Physiological tolerance to alcohol develops with physical dependence; however, non-dependent drinkers may exhibit a behavioral tolerance. After sufficient experiences under the influence of alcohol, one may learn to adjust his behavior and compensate for some of the debilitating influences of the drug. This is not to say that practice makes perfect—alcohol has been found to be a significant factor in more than half of all American traffic fatalities. Know your own limits.

Although alcohol is a social drug and often considered separately from prescribed medications, one should realize that alcohol is basically a sedative-hypnotic and combined with prescription downers (tranquilizers and sleeping pills), causes unpredictable and possibly very dangerous depressive effects.

Downers

Sedative-hypnotics are a group of drugs used medically as sleeping pills and sedatives and nonmedically as downers. The most important drugs in this category are the *barbiturates*. There are also many non-barbiturate drugs which are essentially like the barbiturates in their actions, including a sedative-hypnotic called Quaalude® (methaqualone) which recently has enjoyed popularity in many areas of the country. Alcohol is also properly included in this class of drugs, but it is unique by virtue of being a socially acceptable intoxicant and thus has been considered separately.

Sedative-hypnotics are central nervous system depressants. Some important aspects of this depressant effect include calming (sedative) effects, sleep-inducing (hypnotic) effects, muscle relaxation, and an anticonvulsant effect. When first taken, the effects may be feelings of elation, tranquility, well-being, and euphoria. The overall effect varies, according to dose, from a calming action, to sleepiness, to drunkenness (exactly as with alcohol, including slurred speech and lack of motor coordination), to sleep and, ultimately, to coma and death.

An overdose of sedative-hypnotic drugs kills by depressing vital body functions, especially breathing. What sometimes happens is that a person may become confused enough after taking a few pills to lose track of how many he or she has taken and thus take an overdose. Also, combining alcohol and other sedative-hynotics is extremely dangerous, since two depressant drugs taken together (e.g. alcohol and a barbiturate) may have an unpredictable effect greater than the sum of their individual actions. Many accidental suicides (notably Jimi Hendrix's death) may be attributed to drug combinations of this sort.

Barbiturates and related drugs can be extremely habit forming and, in fact, produce a physical dependence that can be far more dangerous and life-threatening than addiction to narcotics. This dependence will not ordinarily occur at the usually prescribed dose but rather follows a course of developing tolerance, increasing dosage, and greater and greater dependence. It is important to note that one does not develop tolerance as far as the effects of a lethal dose are concerned. (One might develop tolerance and feel little effect from four or five capsules of a depressant but still OD or go into a comatose state on the sixth).

Despite these dangers, it is claimed that there is sufficient medical use of barbiturates to necessitate the manufacture of enough for 25 doses for every man, woman, and child in the U.S. each year. Perhaps this accounts for the fact that, unlike most street drugs, downers are likely to come from a commercially manufactured source. In any case, barbiturates account for 15 percent of all poisonings in this country.

Barbiturates are combined with stimulants in two fairly common drugs: Dexamyl® (d-amphetamine + amobarbital) and Desbutal® (methedrine + pento-barbital). These combination drugs are effective stimulants but they are also "double jeopardy" in this it is possible to become dependent simultaneously on the stimulant and the down.

Miscellaneous Downs

Quaalude® (Methaqualone)   Quaalude shares many of the same effects as the other drugs discussed in this section: it depresses the central nervous system to produce a drunken-like, sleepy, tingly, downed-out feeling. However, Quaalude has less effect on respiration and pulse than the other sedative-hynotics. That is, a person can OD on Quaalude without showing the typical signs of depressed respiration and pulse. While on the one hand this means that Quaalude has a somewhat better margin of safety than other sedative-hynotics, an overdose is still not to be taken lightly. If this should happen, medical attention or knowledgeable assistance is advisable. Note should be made of the fact that Quaalude can produce physical dependence just as barbiturates do, and withdrawal should be medically supervised.

Tranquilizers   There are two different kinds of tranquilizers, categorized as "minor" and "major." The "major" tranquilizers are generally used for the treatment of psychotic patients in psychiatric hospitals (e.g. Thorazine®). The "minor" tranquilizers—Librium®, Valium®, Serax®, Miltown®, and others—calm anxiety, relax muscles, and are essentially like barbiturates except that they have milder actions in the usual prescribed dose. The same caution as for barbiturates should be observed when mixing these drugs with alcohol, although they are somewhat less dangerous. Extended use of tranquilizers may result in a mild physical dependence, but this will not generally be a problem in usually prescribed doses.

PCP   Phencyclidine or Sernyl®, which may be sold as THC, is a tranquilizer-anesthetic that is used in veterinary medicine. (Its use is not approved for human consumption.) The drug, commonly known as PCP, is rather unique in its effects, considered by some to be a "psychedelic down." A person on PCP will commonly seem somewhat dazed, downed-out, and yet also seem to be tripping.

Many bizarre reactions occur with this drug. The person may be confused and out of contact and may have marked sensory disturbances, including numbness in the face and extremities; speech may be impaired and thinking may be delusional. This is frequently not a pleasant experience for the user, although if the dose is moderate, some people find this to be an enjoyable experience. PCP is probably as dangerous an adulterant in street drugs as any around, because of unpredictable effects such as respiratory depression (breathing becomes irregular or sometimes stops, especially when the drug is mixed with alcohol).

Drugs as Downers for Psychedelic Trips   Downers frequently do not bring someone "down" from a trip. They may help to calm and relax the tripper but they do not reliably terminate the trip. In view of the unknown content of street hallucinogens, it is unwise to use downers for this purpose, especially without medical advice. Generally, it is much more helpful to talk someone down. (For further information, see Lampe's *Drugs: Information for Crisis Treatment.*)

SEDATIVE-HYPNOTICS

Generic Name	Brand Name
BARBITURATES	
pentobarbital	Nembutal®
secobarbital	Seconal®
secobarbital + amobarbital	Tuinal®
amobarbital	Amytal®
phenobarbital	Luminal®
OTHER	
methaqualone	Sopor®, Quaalude®
alcohol	Johnny Walker®, Gallo®, Millers®, etc.
marijuana(?)	
TRANQUILIZERS	
minor:	
meprobamate	Miltown®, Equanil®
chlordiazepoxide	Librium®
diazepam	Valium®
oxazepam	Serax®
major:	
chlorpromazine	Thorazine®
prochlorperazine	Compazine®
thioridazine	Mellaril®
trifluoperazine	Stelazine®

Stimulants

Stimulants, including the amphetamines (Dexedrine®, Benzedrine®, methedrine, etc.) have come to be known as speed or ups because of the strong psychological and physical stimulation derived from using them. These drugs stimulate those parts of the central nervous system which are responsible for maintaining wakefulness and alertness. This effect may make sleep virtually impossible.

Along with the stimulation generally goes an extreme feeling of well-being, or even euphoria. There is often a feeling of tremendous energy and motivation and a sense of heightened mental ability and clarity. One may get a feeling of boundless power, as though one could do anything in the world; while this may be reflected in heightened performance, judgment may also sometimes be impaired. Another major effect of amphetamine-like drugs is the depression of appetite; hunger is absent and food becomes unappealing.

Amphetamines and other stimulant drugs have had few legitimate medical uses although until recently they have been widely used (and misused) in medical practice. For example, these drugs have been prescribed to people who are mildly depressed, because they elevate mood and give a sense of well-being. This is of dubious value to the person, first, because ultimately he or she can't rely on these habit-forming drugs to feel good, and second, because as the stimulant effects wear off, it is common to crash and to become even more depressed than before.

Another common use of the amphetamines has been as diet pills, based on the decreasing of appetite for food by the drugs. Again, this use is not now recommended because it does not help the obese person learn new food intake habits. Moreover, the appetite-decreasing effects wear off in about ten days. One use of amphetamine-type drugs which has generally been approved in the field of medicine (although vigorously opposed by some) is the use of stimulants to calm (paradoxically) the behavior of hyperkinetic children whose hyperactivity may indicate minimal brain damage.

Another recognized use of amphetamines in medicine is for the treatment of narcolepsy, a rare neurological disorder. Despite the few legitimate uses, amphetamines have been so widely produced as to necessitate new governmental controls on their manufacture and prescription.

In February, 1973, the Food and Drug Administration issued a national recall on all combination amphetamine prescriptive substances (e.g., Dexamyl-d-amphetamine + amobarbital). In addition, drug companies have been ordered to include on labels of single amphetamine preparations the warning that amphetamines are not effective as anoretic aids and should only be used prescriptively in cases of extreme obesity as a short-term (no more than two weeks) adjunct to dieting.

Apart from once legitimate prescriptive uses, amphetamines are sought after by those who want the benefits of a stimulant substance either to aid in staying awake (studying all night is a common example), to lose weight, or just because they enjoy the feeling of speeding. In high enough doses or when used intravenously, speed may cause an intense rush of thoughts, feelings, and sensations, an amphetamine trip. When used in this way, amphetamines have a seductive appeal which makes their use liable to becoming habitual. First, as tolerance to the effects develops, a person gradually takes more and more to get the same effect. Further, as the effects of a dose wear off, the after-effect may be a devastating depression, lethargy, and loss of energy for living (often complicated by lack of sleep and food)—a perfect reason for needing more speed. Until very recently most pharmacologists considered the intense craving for the drug upon withdrawal to be the result of psychological rather than physiological dependence. The clinical state upon withdrawal mentioned above is very different from—in a sense the inverse of—the abstinence syndrome associated with opiate withdrawal which had been taken as the model. The exhaustion or crash after discontinuing amphetamine use is now known to have physiological roots and some consider these drugs' addictive potential greater than that of heroin. Those interested in reading more about amphetamine dependence might consult Grinspoon's excellent recent article "Amphetamines Reconsidered."

Amphetamines are quite toxic and stressing to the body, particularly to the heart and circulatory system. Drowsiness and fatigue ordinarily protect the body from undue depletion of energy, a mechanism which is short-circuited by amphetamines. Thus, while amphetamines increase alertness and efficiency for a short time, the after-effects may include fatigue, dizziness, headache, and an inability to concentrate. The physical signs of toxicity include a very rapid heart rate, high blood pressure, headache, and fever; convulsions may occur. In high enough doses amphetamine also has a toxic effect on behavior: the user becomes more and more agitated, more and more paranoid, until eventually, he or she becomes psychotic and fails to realize that the delusions and hallucinations are drug effects. While this is not extremely common, it can happen to anyone given a high enough dose.

Cocaine

Cocaine, like amphetamine, is a strong stimulant to the central nervous system, with many of the same effects. The user may take this drug, a white powder, by snorting it or by dissolving it in water for intravenous use. Unlike amphetamine, it is not effective orally. Also, cocaine has local anesthetic properties, so that it will numb the nasal membranes and throat when snorted. Since cocaine is expensive, the drug may be cut with novocaine as a cheap substitute. With chronic use of cocaine, there is a decrease in blood flow to the nasal membranes which causes tissue damage to the nasal walls.

The effects of cocaine are rapid in onset and are subtle to the novice user. The drug will produce a euphoric excitement, an excitement of orgastic proportions when taken intravenously. Cocaine's effects are short-lived, the peak effect occurring in 15-30 minutes. As with amphetamine, signs of excessive stimulation and toxicity include a rapid heart rate, high blood pressure, agitation, and paranoia. Psychological dependence on cocaine does occur. Although there is no tolerance to repeated use of the drug, the potential for mild physical dependence does exist.

Caffeine

A discussion of stimulants is not complete without some mention of the most common one, caffeine. We consume 100-150 mg. of caffeine for every cup of coffee or tea and 35-55 mg. for every cola beverage that we drink. Caffeine is a milder stimulant than amphetamine but has the same ability to produce a more rapid and clearer flow of thought and to allay drowsiness and fatigue. Few people think of their morning cup of coffee as a drug habit, but that's what it is, even though the practice may not be particularly harmful. Potential for mild physical dependence exists with regular use of caffeine, along with a fairly predictable abstinence syndrome (headache, fatigue, irritation, agitation, cramps, etc.).

Nicotine

Another socially accepted drug, nicotine, also has stimulant properties, although some people feel that smoking calms them down. Since these common stimulant substances are frequently used in combination with other drugs, such as speed or hallucinogens, it should be remembered that they can add to the overall stimulation.

Recent studies concerning the addiction potential of nicotine indicate that heavy smokers (a pack a day or more) smoke to obtain a needed dose of nicotine. Experiments done at The University of Michigan reveal that if the amount of nicotine per cigarette is varied, the individual adjusts his consumption to meet the dose requirements. The new low-tar, low-nicotine cigarettes therefore encourage an increase in smoking among those addicted. A relatively mild abstinence syndrome is also involved (agitation, fatigue, headaches, dizziness, and a slight weight gain).

The potential for habituation to nicotine is enormous. The odds seem to be that if a young person smokes a cigarette three or four times and accustoms himself to the initial adverse reaction (dizziness and nausea), he will likely become a regular smoker in the future. For many people this possibility is further increased by the social reinforcements involved in cigarette smoking.

Given the possibility of an individual rapidly developing both physiological and psychological dependence on tobacco, it is clear why the anti-smoking campaigns of recent years have failed. They have relied on the threat to physical health demonstrated by research connecting smoking with serious respiratory and heart disorders and all but ignored the addictive qualities of the drug nicotine. The consumption of tobacco and the number of smokers in this country is still increasing. This discussion is based on information contained in the excellent chapter on nicotine in the new book from Consumers Union, *Licit and Illicit Drugs.*

STIMULANTS

Generic Name	Brand Name
d-amphetamine	Dexedrine®
methamphetamine (methedrine)	Desoxyn®
d-l-amphetamine	Benzedrine®
amphetamine + d-amphetamine	Biphetamine®
phenmetrazine	Preludin®
methylphenidate	Ritalin®
ephedrine	
COMBINATIONS	
methamphetamine + pentobarbital	Desbutal®
d-amphetamine + amobarbital	Dexamyl®
OTHERS	
cocaine	
caffeine	Liptons®, Coca Cola®, Maxwell House®, NoDoz®, etc.
nicotine	Marlboro®, Camel®, Kool®, etc.

Narcotics

Like alcohol, narcotics have been known and used since antiquity for their depressant effects. In addition to producing drowsiness and relaxation, these drugs have a potent pain-killing action which has been exploited by man from 3000 B.C. to the present time. Narcotics include opium and its derivatives (hence the synonym "opiates"): heroin, morphine, codeine, and synthetic substitutes for morphine, including meperidine (Demerol®) and methadone.

Medically, the most important effect of narcotic drugs is analgesia, deadening of pain. The subjective effects include a feeling of floating relaxation, peaceful lethargy, and drowsiness. Dreams or vivid dreamlike imagery may occur. (Morphine was named after Morpheus, the Greek god of dreams.) The physical actions include constriction of the pupils to pinpoint size, slowing of breathing, tightening of the bowels, nausea, and itching; the extremities feel heavy and the body warm. All in all, this experience may be extremely unpleasant to one who has never before used a narcotic. However, those who use narcotics repeatedly soon come to experience these effects as desirable.

Despite what we have all heard about heroin—"death drug" . . . "killer" . . . "the worst substance on the path of pharmacologic degradation"—pure heroin is not a very toxic substance compared to some other drugs. The damage to health that one associates with use of heroin is related less to any harmful effects of heroin per se than to the life style of addicts whose drug hunger compels them to use impure, often contaminated drugs under unsterile conditions.

The realistic fear about heroin is that of becoming addicted. As tolerance to the effects of narcotics occurs, the user is prompted to take more and more, and a dependence on, and liking for, the drug begins to grow. The dependence on narcotics is both physical and psychological. Physical dependence occurs when the body becomes accustomed to the depressant effects of narcotics in the system; after a while, the user will become quite sick if the drug is withdrawn (withdrawal or abstinence syndrome). Psychological dependence may be associated with this physical dependence, particularly because the user may look to the physical symptoms as signs of being hooked. However, psychological dependence is quite real in its own right, and independent of physical dependence. In fact, many users feel quite hooked on doses of heroin too low to produce much physical dependence. Physical dependence takes some time to develop depending on how much drug is used, how often, and whether one shoots up the drug or snorts it. It is impossible to say exactly how long, since the process varies from case to case, but it may take as long as several weeks or more. Psychological dependence also depends on the individual's susceptibility. Some people can use heroin on a limited basis, on weekends for example, for a long time and keep the dependence under control, while others will escalate their drug use and become addicts. It's a good idea to keep a healthy respect for the addictiveness of narcotics, despite the more commonplace casual use of heroin than before. Probably few addicts ever expected to become addicted.

Aside from dependency, the major hazards involved in the use of narcotics seem to stem directly or indirectly from their illegality. Street heroin can consist of from one percent to perhaps 15 percent heroin; the rest is usually quinine, milk sugar, and other white powdery substances—and often, lots of bacteria. Because of the lack of control of quantity and quality of illicit drugs, heroin users sometimes die of overdoses, allergic reactions, and bacterial infections, including hepatitis. Intravenous use of heroin, especially, entails serious risks of infection, particularly if needles are not sterilized. As far as social consequences are concerned, it is important to realize that heroin itself does not incite a person to crime. Crime is directly related to drug addiction only by virtue of the junkie's drug hunger and the high cost of an illegal drug habit. An addict with access to plenty of drug—for instance a doctor, or nurse—can live a long time with a narcotics habit and lead a normal life without anyone suspecting. Addicts are not necessarily depraved!

No "cure" for heroin addiction is known. At the present time, large amounts of money have been committed to the support of programs which dispense methadone (also a narcotic) to addicts as a substitute for heroin. The rationale behind this treatment raises certain political as well as medical issues. The use of methadone as a "treatment" for heroin addiction is reminiscent of the claim made long ago that heroin would be the "cure" for morphine addiction.

Treating a drug problem with another drug can never really resolve all of the problems involved in drug dependence, for the individual or the society at large.

NARCOTIC ANALGESICS

Generic Name	Brand Name
OPIUM AND DERIVATIVES	
morphine	
heroin	
codeine	
paregoric	
SYNTHETICS	
hydromorphone	Dilaudid®
methadone	Dolophine®
meperidine	Demerol®

Hallucinogens

The years of the late 1960s were hailed as the dawn of the psychedelic age. We tend to forget that, despite the fairly recent discovry of LSD, a wide variety of hallucinogens—the legendary soma, ololiuqui, peyote, amanita muscaria, and others—have been used to alter, explore, and control the workings of man's mind since ancient times.

Hallucinogens, i.e. drugs of the LSD type (mescaline, psilocybin, and others), have been the focus of so much controversy nationwide that it is particularly difficult to provide pertinent "objective" information. Information comes from disparate sources, ranging from the experiential, drug-taking counterculture on the one hand to the conservative medical establishment on the other hand. The media have been used in a campaign against the use of hallucinogenic drugs, with medical science claiming terrible adverse consequences of such use, including chromosome damage, brain damage, and deterioration of personality. At the other extreme, there are those who deny all risks and see hallucinogens as a panacea. In a sense, these issues cannot be decided fully on a factual basis at this time; there is so much contradictory information available that anyone can find factual support for almost any point of view. So, in the final analysis, each individual must evaluate the risk for himself or herself. Hallucinogens are powerful, mind-bending chemicals with somewhat unpredictable effects, both potentially beneficial and potentially harmful.

While there are many different hallucinogens—LSD, mescaline, psilocybin, MDA, DMT, DET, STP, etc.—and, in street lore, many "kinds" of each—white lightning, purple haze, chocolate mescaline, etc.—there are probably few people even among the most experienced drug users who really "know" the differences in terms of the subjective effects of each drug. It is not even certain whether, in equivalent doses, one hallucinogen is distinguishable from another. A particular batch of a particular drug often gets a reputation as good dope, smooth dope, or whatever, although such differences should probably be regarded more as myth than anything else. What is a smooth trip for one person may be so only because the dose of the drug is just right for that person. In any case, when two people take exactly the same drug, it can often happen that one will have a good trip while one will have a bummer. To give another common example, chemical analysis has shown that there has been no genuine mescaline in the Ann Arbor area for quite some time, despite persistent rumors of "good mescaline," "organic mescaline," etc. being available. Most of the chemicals sold as psychedelics are LSD or decomposition products of LSD, sometimes other substances such as speed, belladonna, or PCP (see Adulterants, p. 233).

Hallucinogens have been variously called psychedelic or psychotomimetic depending on how one views the experience. "Psychedelic" means "mind-manifesting," implying that the nervous system ("mind") becomes evident to itself. The "trip" is the exploration of previously unnoticed domains of mind— the journey to new places inside your head.

As a result of his hallucinogenic experiences, Aldous Huxley theorized that the function of the brain and nervous system is primarily selective, screening out a mass of sensations which would be largely irrelevant for survival. According to this view, that which manages to pass through the "reducing valve of the brain" is merely a trickle of our potential consciousness. Psychedelic drugs appear to create temporary bypasses of the "reducing valve," allowing one to become aware of sensations and mental processes previously unnoticed.[4] For example, while tripping, one may become profoundly conscious of the fact that his whole field of vision with its vast multiplicity of colors and shapes is a state of affairs inside his head.[5]

In contrast to a psychedelic or consciousness-expanding view of hallucinogenic drug experience, some have interpreted these experiences as a confusion of consciousness, or even as a psychotic experience—hence the term "psychotomimetic" that is sometimes used for hallucinogenic drugs. Indeed, there are some remarkable similarities between the drug-induced hallucinogenic experience and the experiences of those undergoing psychotic changes in their personalities. Similarities may include alterations in the sense of self and reality, changed experience of the boundaries between oneself and "external reality," perceptual distortions and hallucinations. However, it is also generally recognized that psychotic experiences differ in important ways from the kinds of experiences people generally have on hallucinogens. For one thing, the psychotic person does not have the reassurance that he will come down after a certain number of hours. Thus, the psychotic is in a distinctly different position than the tripper. Perhaps psychosis can best be compared with the experience of

[4] Huxley, A. (1963) *Doors of Perception*. New York: Harper & Row.
[5] Watts, A. (1962) *Joyous Cosmology*. New York: Pantheon Press.

someone who is panicked or freaked out on drugs and no longer recognizes his experience as drug-induced nor the fact that he will eventually return to normal.

Drugs, particularly hallucinogens, affect the coping mechanisms we use to structure and relate to external reality. This may result in profound insight and an immediate reorientation of values, or may be so threatening that one becomes totally disoriented and panicked—a bad trip. Much of what the drug experience *is* depends on what the tripper and those around him *expect it to be*. The person's frame of mind before hand and his environment during the experience have a great deal to do with whether or not the trip is enjoyable. For example, tripping among frightened people would emphasize feelings of fear and anxiety, so that being in a comfortable situation is important. Vibes are a very real and important part of the environment.

If a tripper does happen to become disoriented or panicked, a friend or helper can possibly assist by reassuring the tripper that he is safe and will not be left alone, by creating a more secure environment (fewer people, less noise, etc.) or by encouraging him to try to relax into the experience. While generally someone who is tripping can be "talked down," some skill is necessary in recognizing and dealing with the various situations that can arise, and it may be advisable to call for assistance.

Despite a voluminous medical literature on hallucinogenic drugs, there is little certainty about how these drugs act in the brain to produce their effects. This is really not surprising in view of the limited understanding of how the brain works without drugs. Several neurochemicals found in the brain, particularly one called serotonin, have been implicated in a possible mechanism of action. Those familiar with chemical structures will recognize that hallucinogenic chemicals such as LSD and mescaline resemble these naturally occurring chemicals quite closely. It is likely that the presence of hallucinogenic chemicals in the nervous system alters the functioning of the natural chemicals in the brain's sensory systems, particularly the visual system, and in that part of the nervous system concerned with focusing attention.

The long-term effects of hallucinogens have never really been adequately investigated. Both negative and positive life-changes have been ascribed to the use of hallucinogens; some people do not feel that the drug experience has made much of a difference either way. These outcomes are difficult to evaluate because the drugs have such different effects on everyone. How often one trips, what happens during the experience, how one integrates the experience afterward, are all extremely important.

For example, flashbacks—recurrent experiences of drug effects long after the drug is gone from the system—occur in some people but not in others. A flashback may be a vague feeling described as being "like tripping" or may be a very specific memory of part of the drug experience. People react to flashbacks in very different ways, ranging from curiosity or enjoyment to anxiety. Often, a flashback may call to the surface fears a person may have that drugs have endangered his sanity or injured his brain. The most likely explanation is that a flashback is a recurrent memory, relived until the drug experience can be integrated, be mastered.[6] Flashback-like experiences are not unique to acid.

[6] Freedman, D. X. (1968) On the use and abuse of LSD, *Arch. Gen. Psychiat.*, **18:** 330-347.

In fact, for most people there have been times when some present event triggers an unusually vivid reexperience, or a strong feeling associated with a previous intense experience. Many professionals believe there is an essential similarity between such normal "flashbacks" and those following drug experiences.

In the literature on LSD, it has frequently been asserted that flashbacks are due to persistent changes in the nervous system, part of the alleged brain damaged wrought by hallucinogens. These hypotheses are little substantiated by sound medical evidence, although it would be equally hard to demonstrate the complete absence of physiological changes. Some people who have done a lot of hallucinogens respond atypically on certain kinds of psychological tests and do seem to change, to think and act somewhat differently. While this might suggest minimal organic brain damage, other explanations have also been advanced.[7] For example, different patterns of perception and thinking may be learned during repeated experiences in a drug-induced altered state of consciousness. It is not clear to what extent the drugs are responsible in these instances. The outcome is always an interaction between the drug and the mind of the person taking the drug. For example, some people have an interest in tripping to explore the "crazy" parts of themselves and "get into" these experiences more completely and increasingly often. Some have been known to take acid with accelerating frequency as they became more and more fascinated with the bizarre, without apparent awareness that others are seeing them as falling apart, or feeling that they are becoming impossible to "get through to." In brief, hallucinogens can be used to go down as well as up, to integrate or to fragment.

The possible adverse effects of hallucinogens on genetic tissue have received much publicity. Quite a few scientific reports have claimed to show that LSD causes chromosome damage, and a few reports found evidence of fetal abnormalities in cases where pregnant women had ingested the drug. However, an equal number of contradictory reports also appeared in the scientific literature. All of the evidence bearing on the truth of these rather alarming claims has been reviewed recently by N. I. Dishotsky, et al. in the journal Science.[8] These authors concluded that chromosome damage, when found (and such damage is not universal among users of hallucinogens), is related to the effects of drug abuse in general and not, as initially reported, to LSD alone. Further, Dishotsky and his associates concluded that evidence of birth defects, in rats and mice, much less in man, could not be confirmed. The design of proper experiments for testing for these kinds of consequences of drug use is complicated by many difficulties—uncertainty as to what substance a person taking "LSD" has actually taken, what other drugs this person uses, his or her state of health, and many others—so that conclusive evidence is hard to obtain. It would seem that, along with claims of brain damage, the threat of chromosome damage has been exploited in an attempt to discourage the use of hallucinogens. One seldom sees reference made to the chromosome damage caused by other drugs, such as aspirin, caffeine, and others. However, this is not to minimize the risks involved, especially given the uncertainty of what substances are contained in street hal-

---

[7] Dusen, W. V. and Metzner, R. (1968) The long-term effects of psychedelics. *Clin. Toxicology, 1(2)*: 227–234.

[8] Dishotsky, N. I., Loughman, W. D., Mogar, R. E., and Lipscomb, W. R. (1971) LSD and genetic damage. *Science, 172*: 431–440.

lucinogens. It is possible that impurities in street drugs and/or other factors may cause chromosome damage in susceptible individuals; it is not clear what the consequences of such damage are to the health of the individual.

HALLUCINOGENS
lysergic acid diethylamide (LSD)
lysergic acid monoethylamide
mescaline
peyote
psilocybin
dimethytryptamine (DMT)
diethyltryptamine (DET)
2, 5-dimethoxy-4-methylamphetamine (DOM, STP)
methylenedioxyamphetamine (MDA)

Adulterants
Street drugs today are rarely, if ever, pure. Most drugs are cut with other substances to dilute the strength of the pure drug or, as in the case of psyche-delics, in the belief that they will enhance the trip. And in many instances there is a monetary advantage to selling impure drugs since additives reduce the amount of the pure drug used and thus increase the margin of profit.

Although it is impossible to tell what adulterants are found in a particular drug unless the drug is chemically analyzed, certain adulterants are traditionally found in common street drugs. Heroin is never found in pure form in the United States, although purer forms are found overseas. Usually heroin is cut with milk sugar or quinine, the latter being responsible for the bitter taste of the drug, though many other adulterants may also be used. Cocaine is also cut with adulterants similar to those found in impure heroin. These adulterants may be harmless, but there are cases where death has resulted from dangerous impurities in heroin or cocaine; it can never be taken for granted that all adul-terants are safe.

The supply and demand for drugs may also affect the amount or type of impurities found in drugs. Mescaline is a case in point. Mescaline, especially pure mescaline, is rarely available on the streets. In fact, it has been found that almost all chemicals sold as mescaline have no mescaline in them and are instead combinations of different drugs such as LSD, speed, and PCP. Mescaline, however, is a marketable commodity and dealers often sell "mescaline" (regard-less of its true ingredients) because people want it.

Psychedelic drugs are a rather unstable breed of chemicals which often break down simply with the passing of time. Since these chemicals are some-times ineffective by the sime they are used, adulterants may sometimes account for the effects, if any, that do occur.

Often LSD and other less common psychedelic drugs such as STP and MDA are cut with speed to enhance their effects. These drugs, however, are closely related chemically to other stimulants and have a stimulant effect of their own. Thus, people may fear they have taken LSD "laced with speed" when they are actually responding to the stimulant effects of LSD itself. (This is not to say that speed is never found in "LSD.")

Another additive less frequently found in psychedelic drugs is atropine, an alkaloid of Belladonna. Atropine can produce delusions, delirium, or may disturb memory functions. Its specific physiological effects are raising of body temperature, dry flushed skin, and increased pulse rate. When atropine poisoning is acute these symptoms are very visible and it is quite possible that delirium may cause extreme agitation, even violence. Although many of the symptoms of atropine poisoning, such as flushed skin, very high pulse rate, and delusions, may occur to some degree with other hallucinogenic drugs, symptoms stemming from a dangerous dose of atropine will usually be dramatic.

An even less common adulterant found in psychedelics is strychnine, a strong stimulant. Strychnine is added for the same reason as other stimulants, to enhance hallucinogenic effects. With high doses, the first effects—tightening of face and neck muscles and stomach cramps—can progress to convulsions and, in extreme cases, to death. While the dangers of strychnine should not be overlooked, the effects of LSD may include minor stomach cramps. Often people suspect strychnine poisoning when in fact there is none. Despite their rarity, if severe cramps or convulsions should occur, medical attention is needed immediately.

PCP (phencyclidine or sernyl) is often found as an adulterant in street LSD, mescaline, or THC. PCP is a tranquilizer, used for animals, which has both depressant and hallucinogenic qualities (see Miscellaneous Downs, p. 223, for more information).

Solvents

Certain volatile solvents are sniffed to achieve some kind of high. Among these are glue (toluene is the active ingredient), ether, gasoline, lighter fluid, freon, and paint thinner. The effects may include inebriation, exhilaration, hallucinations, and stupor. The effects usually last only a short time. They may, however, last one to two hours.

In general these substances are extremely dangerous and on occasion are lethal. Most are irritating to the mucous membranes and eyes and can cause damage to internal organs including the brain. If freon or other solvents used for refrigeration are inhaled, freezing of the throat and lungs is possible. Death may occur by suffocation if solvents are inhaled from a paper bag or similar device.

While dangers of drugs often are blown out of proportion, this is not true with solvents. They are dangerous, and if used, extreme caution should be exercised.

Laughing Gas

Nitrous oxide is a short-acting anesthetic gas ("laughing gas"), still used by some obliging dentists and also for surgical anesthesia. The gas enjoyed considerable nonmedical use at the turn of the century and, recently, there appears again to be a trend toward experimentation with the drug. It is for the experience that precedes anesthesia that most nonmedical users inhale the gas. Subjective accounts paint the picture of an extremely elusive, ineffable, and rapid high. Many people inhaling a small amount of the gas, perhaps an average balloonful, will feel giddy with a light-headed sense of relaxation. It may be that, as William James described at the end of the last century, others may experience, "the tremendously exciting sense of an intense metaphysical illumination. ... As sobriety returns, the feeling of insight fades, and one is left staring vacantly at a few disjointed words and phrases. ..."[9] The effects are therefore intense but very short-lived, and coming down will often leave a sense of cosmic irony. ... Some class nitrous oxide as a minor psychedelic alongside marijuana.[10]

With small doses of nitrous oxide, the user usually will not lose all sense of volitional control. Even in larger amounts, its use presents little hazard if professionally administered. (It is a prescription drug.) However, a word of caution is in order for those who may use the substance illicitly. If the gas is breathed exclusively for even a relatively short period, more than a minute or so, a person may progressively lose consciousness, become unable to initiate movements, and succumb to a fatal oxygen starvation. Provided adequate oxygen is inhaled, however, there is relatively little danger either from licit or illicit use.

America, the Drug Culture

There is a question about the extent to which any one of us can be free of a prejudiced view in the area of drug use. From infancy we have been bombarded with cultural education about drugs. As John Corry says,[11]

> There is no end to the ways in which Americans can be manipulated and made to feel that there is something wrong, and that whatever it is, it can be solved by something or someone.

In other words, for every uncomfortable or socially undesirable feeling state there is a "fix." The billion dollar drug industry spends over $500 million annually in advertising or $4,000 per physician in what the Food and Drug Administration calls a promotional overkill.[12] Bent on expanding its market, the pharmaceutical industry has frequently resorted to distorted advertising. This has been a principle factor in creating an increased need for psychoactive drugs—stimulants, sedatives, tranquilizers, and antidepressants: in 1970, 202 million legal prescriptions for these drugs were filled in pharmacies, a figure which does not include institutional prescriptions.[13]

As Lennard points out,[14] the pharmaceutical industry has been ingenious in inventing illnesses and cures for questionable complaints. One drug company, for instance, possibly with tongue in cheek, even invented and advertised a malady they called "The Blahs" and sold its own product as the specific cure. We

[9] James, W. (1888) Subjective effects of nitrous oxide. In Tart, C. T. (ed.), *Altered States of Consciousness.* New York: Anchor Books, Doubleday & Co., 1972.
[10] Tart, C. T. (1972) *Altered States of Consciousness.* New York: Anchor Books, Doubleday & Co.
[11] "The Politics of Style," *Harper's* (1970) 241: 1146.
[12] *Ann Arbor News,* May 10, 1972.
[13] Lennard, H. L., Bernstein, A., Epstein, L., and Ranson, D. (1971) *Mystification and Drug Misuse.* San Francisco: Jossey-Bass.
[14] *Ibid.,* p. 17.

are all familiar with quasifactual commercials in which people's heads turn to sink drains to bring home the efficacy of decongestants, or in which a woman finds that she no longer feels the impulse to yell at her nosy kid because she has taken _____. The mass media are thus used to provide reinforcement of the erroneous redefinition of human problems as medical ones. Thus the pharmaceutical industry mystifies both physician and the public about the effect of drugs.

Lennard says, ". . . only to the extent that interpersonal and other problems can be construed as medical-psychiatric problems can they be considered appropriate targets for drug treatment."[15] The medical profession and especially the drug companies have an interest in defining diverse human situations in just these terms. Lennard sees drug promotions as deliberate attempts to mystify both physicians and the public. (When one person creates a false impression by giving another person distorted information, often with direct benefits to the former and cost to the latter, the process may be called mystification.) He cites, for example, a 1969 advertisement in the *Journal of the American College Health Association*[16] which states:

"A whole new world . . . of anxiety . . . To help free her of excessive anxiety . . . adjunctive Librium." Accompanying the bold print is a full-page picture of an attractive, worried woman, standing with an armful of books. In captions surrounding her, the potential problems of a new college student are foretold: "Exposure to new friends and other influences may force her to reevaluate herself and her goals . . . her newly stimulated intellectual curiosity may make her more sensitive to and apprehensive about unstable national and world conditions." The text suggests that Librium (chlordiazepoxide HCL), together with counseling and reassurance "can help the anxious student to handle the primary problem and to get her back on her feet."

It is likely that if a student, beset by such matter-of-course life problems, were to take drugs such as marijuana, seeking relief through self prescription, this action would be labeled escapist by many of his or her elders and contemporaries. A growing group of doctors is becoming concerned about the too-ready prescription of drugs such as amphetamines and tranquilizers without a weighing of the possible costs, not the least of which is reinforcement of the view that taking a drug represents part of a solution for personal and interpersonal problems. Particularly in the past, though holdovers of this attitude survive, physicians have considered information about possible side effects and alternative therapeutic strategies as their professional province. Some drug companies disclose such information only to doctors. The patient's right to be given unmystifying information so that he can form his own judgment on such matters is increasingly recognized.

Nowhere is it more true than in the realm of behavioral and emotional difficulties that the professional you choose to consult may have more to do with the kind of treatment you receive, including or not including the prescription of medication, than the condition you present as patient or client. Professionals

[15] *Ibid.*, p. 18.
[16] *Ibid.*, p. 19.

differ as regards the appropriateness of drug treatment, above and beyond the fact that doctors can prescribe while the other professions cannot. If this issue concerns you, it may be worthwhile for you to consult your psychiatrist, social worker or psychologist about any psychoactive drugs which may be prescribed for you.

Mystification exists also in the use of "social drugs" like alcohol and marijuana, and others. It is ironic that the counterculture has incorporated many of the mystifying distortions promoted by the Establishment. For example, in the *Making of a Counterculture*, Roszak notes that some hippies wore buttons quoting the duPont company, "Better Things for Better Living Through Chemistry":[17]

The gadget-happy American has always been a figure of fun because of his facile assumption that there exists a technological solution to every human problem. It took only the great psychedelic crusade to perfect the absurdity by proclaiming that personal salvation and the social revolution can be packed in a capsule.

What emerges in part from this mystification phenomenon is the message that drugs are magic—that they can do what we cannot do for ourselves. The espoused view of many drug educators these days is often that such a message is not only false but also dangerous in that it encourages us to rely on chemicals rather than on ourselves. They are fast to point out that drugs are not magic and that their action can be explained in clear, scientific terms. But things are defined as "magic" when people cannot explain what things are, how they work, or why they work. And in fact, drugs do work in mysterious ways. Nobody really knows how it is that aspirin relieves headaches; however, most of us know it does and we take it for that reason.

When we take a drug, the way we interpret our experience has to do with many factors other than the physiological effects of the drug. Often this involves a mystique surrounding the experience, for example, the interpretation of physical numbness as pleasurable or transcendent. Since we frequently enjoy being mystified, we are prone to attributing quite specific effects to the drug that we have ingested, whereas even in large doses, the effects of psychoactive drugs may be nonspecific—about as general as to be conveyed by such labels as "uppers," "downers," or "psychedelics." For the rest, we ourselves, including those alien and unexplored parts of us, are each the singer and the song.

Given that drugs do what people want them to do, what is it that people seek in drug-taking? It is almost impossible to describe motivations without being evaluative. Take "fun" for example. Many people use drugs like alcohol and marijuana in social settings because they find it fun and pleasurable to do so. To attempt to analyze the infinite subjective varieties of fun reveals a prejudice that fun is something more than fun—for example, a screen for undesirable escapist behavior. Unless we become convinced otherwise, we can accept fun as a legitimate reason for taking drugs. And it is well to give some thought to the value judgment that escapist behavior is always undesirable.

Some people, as mentioned earlier. like the experience of being "mystified," or feeling something magic or undefinable occur within and around them. Other

17 Roszak, T. (1969) *The Making of a Counterculture*. New York: Doubleday & Co.

people report that drugs, notably hallucinogens but other drugs as well, facilitate self-discovery, disinhibition, and expansion of awareness—experiences which they find entertaining and exciting, and possibly growth-inducing. Kenneth Keniston calls such people "seekers"—individuals who are looking for expanded meaning and energy in their lives.[18]

Another reason for using drugs is the specific intention of making oneself "feel better." Feeling better may encompass a large spectrum of different meanings for different people. For some, it means the elimination of physical pain, and/or the alleviation of emotional pain. For others, feeling better may mean not feeling at all, becoming numb to oneself and one's surroundings. For still others, it may mean becoming more receptive to oneself, one's energies, and outside stimulation. Students who use drugs sometimes claim that using drugs, hallucinogens for example, helps to alleviate the boredom they experience in school. Boredom is one form of human suffering that is little attended to in our society.

Since such drug-taking in our society is illegal, using drugs can become a convenient vehicle for expressing rebellion. However, group standards may also have the opposite effect. In groups where drug-taking is accepted, it can be an alienating experience not to participate. Certainly, many of us took our first alcoholic beverage or smoked our first cigarette so as not to feel excluded. Drugs are potentially dangerous substances, sometimes lethal in certain quantities and combinations. This destructive potential allows drugs to be used by some people as dramatic communications of a wish to hurt themselves, or of the fact that they are already hurting. People may or may not be aware of what this behavior communicates to others, or may not want to know. Taking drugs about which one knows nothing or mixing drugs may have overtones of self-destructive feelings, though not as dramatic as a deliberate suicide attempt.

So it seems that people take drugs to entertain themselves, to explore themselves, to soothe their pain, both physical and emotional; sometimes to hurt themselves or communicate hurt, and probably for many other reasons. The fact is that many people make the decision to experiment with drugs, and if they discover that the drugs they take work in whatever ways they were supposed to work, many of these people will keep taking drugs. Those who find alternatives that also work may stop or modify their drug-taking. However, until alternatives are readily available to most people which satisfy needs for entertainment, pain-killing, awareness expansion, and self-discovery, "drug magic" may be hard to beat.

[18] Keniston, K. (1970) Drug use and student values. In Horman, R. E. and Fox, A. M. *Drug Awareness*. New York: Avon Press.

22   Jobhunting Now: The Employee Employers Look for
Nancy Axelrad Comer

"Rule number one:
know where to look.
Some cities have higher unemployment
rates than others."

Finding the right job is one of the most important decisions anybody
makes. This article by Nancy Comer describes some of the issues, pit-
falls, and valuable hints people can use in finding a job. Getting yourself the job you like is not always easy. Some of the information in this
article might go a long way in helping you find the situation you want.

The mahogany curtain. Or oak, teak or steel. That huge, immaculate or paper-
littered expanse of desk whose air space you, the prospective employee, must
penetrate in order to engage and conquer the Enemy, that most benevolent of
despots, the prospective employer.

It's superfluous to repeat those horrible statistics about the number of jobs
available today versus the number of applicants. Any idiot worth her resume
already knows them. But what she may not know, or has despaired of ever
discovering, is that there *are* needles in the haystack; she just needs a good
magnet to find them.

Jobhunting, even if you're independently wealthy, is not fun. Even in the
best of times it's a nerve-wracking experience, humiliating to the modest, hum-
bling to the proud, and just plain terrifying to the uninitiated, recent college
graduate. The most seasoned jobhunters still quail at the sight of an application
form or x-ray visioned interviewer who can take one look at you and discover
that you swiped three erasers from your last employer and haven't made your
bed that morning. Some applicants take the cloak of power from an interviewer
by imagining him naked; others stare at a point two inches beyond his left ear
and pretend they're talking to Mother. But nothing really helps when you're the
supplicant in the employer's market. Nothing except perhaps the knowledge that
he's (she's) human, too, with all the foibles and frustrations, fears and fantasies
that you have—only different. Maybe he didn't make his bed that morning
either.

We asked a variety of (human) employers what sort of applicant they'd
most likely hire and we discovered that jobhunting today, minus the white

gloves, is not much different from 20 years ago. There are still the same unwritten rules which vary slightly according to the company, its location, management's conservatism, the interviewer's prejudices and the length of his sideburns (most interviewers for professional positions seem to be male).

Rule number one: know where to look. Some cities have higher unemployment rates than others. In San Francisco, for instance, any beginner job is scarce. Laverne Coleman, Employment Counselor at the State Department of Human Resources, admits that "most graduates who come to our office want to work in social service agencies, but the jobs just aren't there, at least not in San Francisco, not even for people with M.A.s. And a lot of employers are saying they don't want liberal arts graduates for low-level positions because 'they're overqualified and will get bored.'" By checking state employment offices, applicants can get a good idea of where jobs aren't in their field. They could find out that even to get an interview with some public school systems, they might have to wait a month.

There are job listings other than newspaper want ads. The personnel office at the University of Texas does no campus recruiting for non-teaching jobs, but does post openings on campus bulletin boards, and spreads the word to the Texas Employment Commission and private agencies. Companies with a large percentage of union employees like newspapers, auto manufacturers and television studios are often required by their unions to post available jobs on company bulletin boards. This does give the advantage to present employees and their relatives and friends, but does not preclude an outsider's coming in to peruse the boards from time to time (as long as she doesn't resemble a mad bomber casing available sites, but has permission to wander aimlessly about the premises). Some companies use their own professional association's placement services; The Connecticut Public Television Corp. (CPTV) in Hartford, Conn., relies on the National Association of Educational Broadcasters as much as write-ins and walk-ins. Some lean heavily on the College Placement Annual (available in most libraries), particularly for finding engineers and sales trainees. A few still do on-campus recruiting at nearby schools, but more and more are going off-campus to student conventions, minority gatherings, military centers, etc.

The Wichita (Kansas) Eagle and Beacon Publishing Co., Inc. replenishes its reporter staff almost exclusively through its intern program, carried on through journalism departments of nearby universities, as do many other papers who have volunteers if not interns. Department stores and banks have management training programs as entrees to top-level positions.

Once you've decided on the company to tackle, what then? Employers vary on whether they'll see any old pavement-pounder off the street, or require written or telephone contact first. Woody Sudhoff, managing editor of the Cincinnati *Post and Times-Star*, doesn't like applicants to come through employment agencies.

> I like them to come straight to me. If they need an agency to talk for them, they don't have the qualities I'm looking for. I think it's rude for a person to come in without an appointment; it shows a lack of understanding and sensitivity of what kind of business I'm in. It saves me time, too, if they make an appointment. I can often do some homework on them. Coming in unannounced is sort of a sneaky approach.

However, William Ludders, former personnel manager of Jantzen, Inc., in Portland, Oregon, feels it would be "unrealistic" if they treated people without appointments indifferently. "Eastern companies may be more formal about appointments; we have to be more open and receptive." But he does recommend that jobhunters looking for jobs on the professional level write a letter requesting an appointment and enclosing a resume. One West Coast public relations firm insists that the resume be mailed in first; if the applicant fits their needs, they'll invite him in for an interview. One method to follow: the bigger the company, the more likely they are to have an extensive personnel department able to see anybody, anytime. The smaller the firm, the better it is to write or phone ahead.

While a few companies prefer their own carefully completed application forms to resumes (the Civil Service, for one), most depend on resumes as an indication of character and efficiency. Any good book on employment can supply the standard form to beginning resumeers. It should be carefully done though. "It's discouraging," complains John Lennhoff, Vice-President of CPTV, "to get a Mimeographed resume addressed to 'General Manager' at an incomplete address. You know that these are probably being sent to every educational TV station in the United States, and that the applicant hasn't even bothered to get an up-to-date name and address." (A simple matter of checking annual reports, listings in *Literary Marketplace* or *Madison Avenue*, or even a quick call to the company switchboard operator.) "But when we get a personal letter with a resume, we do everything we can to grant an interview. We'll see people even if there's no opening—you never know when something may come up and we keep applications on file."

Graphic and film design consultants Kramer, Miller, Lomden & Glassman of Philadelphia prefers portfolios to resumes. But they must be well-organized, give a clear picture of the type of work the applicant has been doing, and should be packaged well—not oversized with a stuck zipper and pieces falling out—since much of their work deals with packaging.

Once an applicant is granted an appointment, he should find out all he can about the company, if necessary by unobtrusively standing outside and watching the type of employee going in and out. A more practical way is to send for the company's literature—employment brochures, annual reports for the big ones—or try to get a look at their product. For a public relations firm or ad agency, find out whose accounts they handle; if you want to work for a magazine, read past issues. Most jobhunters, according to Theodore Miller, a partner of Kramer, Miller, Lomden, et al., who sees about three applicants a week despite his firm's small size, are poorly informed not only about the job market, but about the firms they apply to.

They seem to open a telephone book and first comb the large print, then seek out the smaller. And I would say that many of our applicants lack a sense of history in relation to the advertising field. It's a big handicap because they've lost a tremendous hunk of nomenclature and background information that we find is necessary. If we tell an employee to design a piece using an effect employed by a particular sculptor, for instance, and they haven't heard of him, we're wasting an awful lot of time.

The chief recruiting personnel supervisor of a major Houston, Texas, oil company is concerned about many jobhunters' inability to understand the difference between a liberal arts background and jobs available in his industry. "Too many of our female applicants come from women's colleges. A B.A. degree in geology won't find oil. Those schools simply don't offer enough calculus, computer sciences, etc. Too often women and minorities go into political science, history and English literature rather than the hard sciences; when they graduate, their job markets in these areas are severely limited. It's to their advantage to think of their vocational choice *before* they pick a college"—and to have enough sense not to try for a technical job with a technically oriented company without the background. A little research into the jobs available would save a lot of time. Managing Editor Sudhoff complains that

> sometimes I have to explain our setup and this vexes me. They should have done some homework about our editorial policy, people and practices. I question them about both our editorial policies and our copy. If they *admit* they haven't checked it out, that's a point in their favor, though. I like for them to be candid; I admire that.

The way you look when you first walk through the door may make all the difference between a job and "don't call us, we'll call you." Unfortunately, every interviewer has his own idiosyncrasies as far as appearance is concerned, and there's really no way to ferret them out ahead of time (unless you know someone he's interviewed). The first thing most interviewers notice is neatness. "I don't mind long hair or a mini-skirt," explains Woody Sudhoff, "but the general look must be well-groomed. If an applicant is careless about his person, he's going to be careless about his work."

Robert F. Darrow, Executive Director of Teacher Personnel for the Columbus Public School System is concerned with the way an applicant looks, walks, talks, shakes hands, and looks at the interviewer. "Above all, we don't want a mask."

The applicant who makes the most favorable impression on a college personnel representative is the one with

> medium-length dress, the more conservative hairstyle—not long, straight hair, which is a sign of immaturity, really. Many of our applicants are surprised that we're not interested in hiring student types who aren't going to stay very long. But we're looking for the permanent employee, just like IRS, IBM or anybody else.

Jobhunters who chew gum don't bother an interviewer at a New York City ad agency,

> as long as they don't crack it. It's really irritating, and, besides, I've never been able to learn how. The ones who really get me are the people who bite their nails. I always wonder what sort of psychological hangups this 25-year-old has that he has to bite his nails, and I can't stand people who walk in with a lit cigarette.

One hospital administrator is maniacal about smoking (he doesn't). His advice: "Don't, unless you're offered one." And a lot of interviewers are turned off by fishy handshakes.

Grades are extremely important to interviewer Jerry E. Johnson of the Chemical Abstracts Service, in Columbus, Ohio, since technical expertise is a prerequisite, and they have 3000 applicants a year to fill 50 positions. Many of their employees have doctorates and a grade point average of 3.5, although someone who's supported herself (or a family) through school might be considered with a lower average than someone who's had no such responsibility. One ex-teacher complains that most public school systems won't hire A graduates—they're too likely to be controversial. "The System prefers the C students."

Many of the companies who do look at grades look at them in terms of performance patterns rather than averages. At Pillsbury Company in Minneapolis, Henry A. Brown, Manager of Manpower Planning, "is interested in the pattern, is it consistent, does it show improvement? Subject matter or subjects taken aren't weighed too heavily, except for electives. We'd want to know which ones were chosen and why."

Extracurricular activities in high school and college are also important to Mr. Brown, if they show the applicant demonstrated leadership or the ability to bring about change. "We would be more interested in a person who was able to put the sorority or fraternity house on a good cost control basis than one who was a cheerleader just to be a cheerleader."

The Cincinnati *Post and Times-Star* is impressed by extracurricular experience too—

> if it's in a field relative to the one they want to write about, i.e., someone with a sports background would have the knowledge to cover sports. The person who had worked on his high school or college publication would be assumed to have more than a passing interest in journalism. It's especially helpful for an applicant to have worked on his college *daily* paper. These kids do desk work, mark wire copy, do makeup, heads. The more expert they are at all these chores—like typing, and even a good telephone voice helps—the better chance they have with us, even without fulltime experience.

And there's the rub: experience. Every employer interviewed placed experience as the top priority. It didn't have to be fulltime—they could have done volunteer work in hospital administration or worked at a day camp. At the Wichita Eagle and Beacon, Eldon Case, the personnel manager, says that "if someone walks in who says he's worked for three years as a reporter, we're *very* interested even if he's a high school dropout." Jantzen's Mr. Ludders even "likes to hire the gal who picked beans during the summers, because she knows what work is." Every employer checked the business references, and woe to the applicant who falsified his application or resume—this was usually considered rejection grounds even after the employee was already hired. (Few companies bother to check personal references unless there is a question or an applicant they are undecided about; some do check professors, though, and the advisor for a Master's thesis or the applicant's immediate superior at his volunteer job.)

So much for the tangibles. But what if you've got reasonably short hair, long nails (unless you're applying for a secretarial position), decent grades and a little experience? What makes you more special than all the other applicants with the same qualifications to a particular employer?

The ability to communicate is of prime importance to Ted Miller. An employee must be able to understand his client's problem when it's explained and discuss it clearly with her superior. So Mr. Miller likes a completely filled out application form,

> or one that indicates the applicant has seen the question and checked it if it's not applicable. It's one more example of ability to communicate. The people who come in here are moved around in a labor-pool situation; it's not a team setup. So it's important that they communicate well with several different personalities. If the employee can only communicate with one designer, after a while she becomes staffed to that one designer, and this creates a problem.

Norbert J. Nickel, vice president of the Merchants & Savings Bank of Janesville, Wisconsin, rates the ability to get along with people high. "We have no product to sell except service."

Public relations firms hunt for common sense, intelligence, taste, the ability to publicize a client well without indulging in ego massage, tact, grace under pressure, the ability to get along with people.

Jerry Johnson at Chemical Abstracts looks for the opposite. "Abstracting is not for someone who wants to deal with people. I look for someone who's happy reading books, and being alone, with a good vocabulary and literary ability."

Several companies expressed interest in the applicant with innovative—but practical—ideas. At some "the individual with innovative ideas is sought for merchandising and design jobs, but how much imagination do you want your accountant to have?"

Mr. John Douglas, Manager of Recruitment, Placement and Employee Benefits at Rich's, in Atlanta, one of the Southeast's largest department stores, looks for applicants with proven leadership ability—such as presidents of the student government or campus store managers.

Managing editor of the Cincinnati *Post and Times-Star*, Woody Sudhoff looks for the applicant with "writing skills, integrity, poise, grooming, an attitude of self-respect. Perhaps that's most important. These are people who have to go out and represent us, interview for us. They must command respect, and they can't get it if they don't have self-respect."

The Pillsbury Company is attracted to jobhunters

> with a high level of adaptability, a capacity to deal with a variety of problems or projects. Sometimes a particular academic background can't be used straight across, but those who can sense how their training might be adapted to business needs are the ones we'd hire.

The U.S. State Department's Employment Division, also feels that flexibility is the single most important quality a person should have; next, maturity and the potential to assimilate new things easily. Production assistants at CPTV must meet Vice-President John Lennhoff's requirements: "an understanding of television, manual dexterity and the ability to make quick decisions. Versatility is necessary since personnel doubles up in assorted roles according to the needs of the moment. Our people aren't limited to the title."

"Nothing destroys an intelligent person quicker than a stupid question," asserts Jerry Johnson, and it's true that thoughtful questions can bring a dead interview to life. Employers expect applicants to ask about the company, the job, salary, but the order of questions and how they're asked is important. "There's nothing they *can't* ask," according to Woody Sudhoff.

Though it turns me off if the first question is about parking arrangements or days off. I want 'em nosy as hell. That's what makes a good reporter. I spell out the details of the job, hours, salary and welcome questions after that. I *want* them to ask about their future, about serving with one of our bureaus, possibilities for transfer and promotion. I like for them to have thought about it and want advancement. I want them to have goals.

Ludders of Jantzen—and most of the employers interviewed—doesn't mind if a woman applicant asks about maternity benefits as a matter of course. "But if it's the first thing she asks, a little red light flashes and we're suspicious."

Many companies, with the Equal Employment Opportunity Commission breathing hard down their necks and fearful that government contracts might be revoked, bend over backward to be fair—or at least appear so—to women and minority applicants. But women should ask where the job will take them and what happened to their predecessor, particularly if she was a woman. The employer's answer or the way he answers can give the applicant a good indication of the company's attitude toward promoting women, and whether they'd want to work there.

Not so tangible, but equally important is the attitude the jobhunter brings to the interview. To Henry Brown of Pillsbury "the only real offense is a poor attitude toward employment, the way they feel about the working world and their lack of eagerness."

Gary Waren at the University of Texas feels that

if a person comes in to an interview with us and expresses a feeling of frustration because he's been turned down on other jobs, I have the feeling, "well, you're not going to get hired here, either." You're got to have that confidence, you've got to keep going. Before you start looking for a job (other than secretarial) you must be financially and emotionally prepared for two or three months without one, if you're bound and determined to get a job that requires your specific training. During the interview you should be attentive, *very* attentive, to everything that is said by the interviewer. Even if it's just small talk. Most interviewers use it to find out a little more about the individual.

The employers we interviewed would probably all agree with Stanford Levy, Production Manager of CPTV. "Hiring is the hardest thing I do. It's like marriage. You never know how it will work out until afterward."

Suggested Readings for
Chapter 5

Blaine, G. B., Jr., McArthur, C. C., and others. *Emotional problems of the student.* New York: Anchor, 1966. Discussions of personality problems as seen in a university clinic. Actual cases are used as illustrations.

Erikson, E. H. *Childhood and society.* (2d ed.) New York: Norton, 1963. A classic presentation by an eminent psychoanalyst of early stages of development with many interesting case studies and cross-cultural material.

Grinder, Robert E. *Studies in adolescence.* New York: Macmillan, 1969. A group of interesting research papers and clinical reports of adolescent behavior.

Nowlis, Helen H. *Drugs on the college campus.* New York: Doubleday, 1969. A comprehensive summary of current information about the properties of various drugs and the nature and extent of their use on college campuses.

Spock, B. *Baby and child care.* New York: Pocket Books, Inc., 1957. An authoritative handbook for parents which provides a wealth of information about practical problems in the physical and psychological care of children.

Stone, L. J. & Church, J. *Childhood and adolescence.* (2d ed.) New York: Random House, 1968. A well-written textbook presenting the developmental sequence according to age stages and covering recent theory and research.

Discussion Questions

1. How do you plan to raise your child: what goals do you have in mind?

2. Should boys and girls be treated identically from birth onward?

3. How can a classroom contribute more than education to the growth of a child?

4. Why are you the way you are?

MERRILL LYNCH, PIERCE, FENNER & SMITH INC

**Chapter 6
The Adult
Personality**

The study of the human adult personality is one of the fascinating topics of contemporary psychology. It is an area of research useful to the psychologist who wants both to understand and to treat their emotional difficulties. The term "personality" is also an intriguing mystery to anyone who wants to satisfy his curiosity about what makes people tick. Unfortunately, to define exactly what is meant by the term "personality," whether it be child personality or adult personality, can be extremely subjective. However, to most theorists the term "personality" refers to the sum of all the learning experiences, perceptions, habits, and distinctive behavior which produce what we might best characterize as a unique individual. Along with "uniqueness," a particularly important aspect of personality is "consistency." While the term "uniqueness" suggests how different I am from other people in some significant ways, the term "consistency" refers to how similar I am to myself over time. In other words, if you saw me today and then tomorrow, you would be able to identify me as the same person each time. Generally, the terms "uniqueness" and "consistency" are so naturally taken for granted in the study of personality, that we hardly bother to ask the crucial questions such as, unique in what way, or how consistent, and under what conditions are we most consistent. Interestingly enough, most contemporary research seems to indicate that people are unique, but not necessarily that unique. Furthermore, while there is obviously consistency in much of our behavior, the environment may influence our basic emotional responses more than will our internal personality traits. Thus we may not always be consistent, depending upon the situation which affects our behavior. This chapter examines a variety of aspects of personality functioning, and explores some of the influences on adult behavior.

Personality requires an interaction between internal and external forces. As people grow older there are circumstances of life such as changes in the family, children growing up, boredom in vocational activities, and so on which appear to create what might be termed a "personality crisis." The article, "Husbands in Crisis," is a description of some interesting and important research on males between the ages of 35 and 45. What these researchers discovered was that this period in life was an extremely unsettling one and tended to induce stress reactions in many men. The research team found that men during this particular age level seemed to undergo a profound psychological reorientation which altered their perception of life and raised serious questions about how they wanted to spend their remaining years. Interestingly, not only does stress produce anxiety, frustration, and feelings of unfulfillment, it may also generate instructive changes in relationships with other people, and produce a more mature sense of one's own identity. This article describes both aspects of this complicated period of life.

Consciousness-raising groups have become a useful vehicle for sharing intense, honest, and difficult emotional feelings. The women's liberation movement has discovered the usefulness of these groups for developing healthier attitudes in women toward childrearing, sexuality, and relationships with men. The next paper in this chapter, "A Report on a Consciousness Raising Group," is a transcript of one woman's experience. The group's task was to discuss attitudes toward sex, more specifically, female sexuality. It is an unusually open account of the sexual attitudes and experiences of some adult women in our society.

Some years ago a brilliant black novelist by the name of Ralph Ellison wrote a now classic novel called *The Invisible Man,* which was a description of the black experience in America. The hero of Ellison's novel was a black intellectual who struggled vainly to define his identity and, in the process, to escape the invisibility of being a black man in a white man's society. The article by Sylvester Monroe, "Guest in a Strange House: A Black at Harvard," is not far removed from Ellison's theme. Monroe describes his experiences and that of his fellow blacks at Harvard University, perhaps the most elite university in the United States. Monroe's account is particularly interesting because it traces the development of black and white consciousness during the 1960s up to the present. Harvard was a totally unique experience for black students because of its image as the most prestigious white establishment university. Monroe describes his four years at Harvard as an extremely frustrating experience because the attitude toward blacks was so often negative and demeaning. It is difficult to say whether or not Monroe's experience at Harvard was typical of all the blacks attending that institution, but it is brutally clear that the black intellectual feels alienated and forcibly excluded from the rest of society.

The psychoanalytic theory of Sigmund Freud was an early effort to develop a systematic and comprehensive approach to understanding personality. Freud observed in his patients both rational behavior having easily understood motives, and irrational behavior such as dreams, distortions of reality, and fears which were not easily explained. In attempting to understand such disparate behavior within a given individual, Freud highlighted the differences between conscious and unconscious mental processes, and pointed out the great influence unconscious factors can have on our behavior. He also developed a theoretical picture of three basic areas of mental functioning. Personality was then seen as evolving from the interplay of these three areas. The id was seen as a storehouse of impulses which constantly sought gratification for the individual. The superego was likened to the conscience and was thought to govern the standards of right and wrong. The ego's responsibility was to mediate the demands of the id and superego, to coordinate these with the realistic considerations of the individual's environment, and to regulate the behavior which ultimately developed. While there is still a small nucleus of psychologists who adhere to orthodox psychoanalytic theory, a number of new approaches to the understanding of adult personalities have been developed. It is a tribute to Freud that many of the current theories either represent slight modifications of his initial thinking or, where very different, grew in reaction to his original, provocative theory.

The existential school of psychology was a major development in reaction to strictly psychoanalytic thinking. The theorists of this school emphasize the importance of immediate experience and are much less concerned with understanding the historical roots of behavior. Erich Fromm has written a paper, "Do We Still Love Life?" which is very much in tune with the thinking of many contemporary existential theorists. He emphasizes that continuous growth and change must be seen as an essential part of life, and that the use of force and control to influence or inhibit this growth is detrimental to the achievement of a mature life style. Love is contrasted with force, and is seen as a process which allows life to develop in a free, ever-changing, and ever-growing manner. This is true for both love of one's self, which would encourage personal growth and development, and for love of others, which would be marked by an understanding and tolerance that would allow the other to develop in his own way without trying to influence him to do as we would want. Dr. Fromm also indicates the importance of our culture in influencing our ability to grow and to change in positive ways. By taking into full account the environment as a source of influence in the development of personality, he reflects an important modification of psychoanalytic theory. He finds our culture to be excessively mechanical and overly bureaucratic, and to emphasize results and objects. This type of culture encourages control and prevents love from developing fully.

"The clearest and most obvious difficulties a man goes through at this time have to do with the simple fact that he has lost the sense of growing up; he has begun growing old."

This article examines a critical phase in human development, middle age. What happens when a man reaches middle age? What are the effects of self-examination, of self-appraisal, and of prospects for the future? Maggie Scarf puts these problems in sharp focus and comes up with some very interesting observations.

Why does a rising corporation executive suddenly, in his early forties, quit his job and go off with his family to a new kind of life on a farm? What makes a seemingly happy husband leave his wife for a girl not much older than his daughter? Why do so many men, at about this time in their lives, begin to drink too much, become discontented and depressed for no clear reason, undergo what appears to be a distinct personality change?

Wives usually know, or sense, that something mysterious comes over a man as he approaches his middle years—not a physical change, such as they themselves experience in menopause, but a psychological one. But what, exactly, brings this change about? Why does it so often erupt in crisis? And how are women to understand and deal with it?

According to a group of six researchers at Yale University, now involved in the third year of a four-year study of males between the ages of thirty-five and forty-five, this ten-year period is often the strategic turning point in a man's life. Led by Dr. Daniel J. Levinson, a psychologist of fifty-one, the research team has been conducting intensive interviews with a carefully selected group of forty men in this critical time of their lives. Ten of the men are executives, half recruited from a large, settled firm, half from a smaller, more experimental company; ten are blue- and white-collar workers from the same two companies; ten are writers, some well known, some not; ten are biologists at different stages of their academic careers.

"Husbands in Crisis," by Maggie Scarf, in *McCall's,* June 1972. Reprinted by permission of the author and The McCall Publishing Company.

Acknowledging that what will emerge from these interviews is not going to be *universally* true for men in their middle years, the Yale team nevertheless started out with a few general questions. Were all the men in the study group heading toward, or going through, or just recovering from, some experience of crisis? If so, did this crisis tend to vary in intensity for men in different occupations? Or—despite differences in type of work, degree of success, and so on—were their problems basically similar, and linked (like those of early adolescence) to their age?

Now, with all of their major interviewing completed, and the follow-up interviews (two years later) well under way, the researchers have come to several tentative conclusions.

"We're always asked whether or not we've found that there is such a thing as a 'male menopause,' " Dr. Levinson says.

But as far as I'm concerned, this phrase is misleading. The period we're studying is some ten years earlier than the female change of life. Still, as to whether a male "crisis" exists, I would say that if one means this in the sense of "turning point," then such a thing does take place.

It generally begins somewhere in the late thirties, and the most fundamental thing about it is that it's a part of normal development: a man at this stage *can't* go on unchanged. He's at the end of something, his early adulthood, and moving toward another period—middle age. There's a discontinuity at this point in his life. He's coping with a variety of new circumstances, like the first indisputable signs of aging; and at the same time, he's assessing old things—fantasies and illusions about himself which he's sustained up until this point.

How men respond to mid-life stress varies, according to Levinson, as widely as does the degree of stress itself. At one extreme would be someone like Gauguin—who, in his mid-thirties, shed his wife, family, and career as a bank clerk to become a painter and go off to live in the South Seas. At the other extreme would be the man who feels depressed and upset as he moves toward forty, but does nothing, makes no change in his occupation, marriage, or way of living. In between is the man who perhaps takes flight in a series of extramarital affairs, does poorly in his work for awhile; then the flurry dies down, he stays put and doesn't change anything in his life at all.

Yet, regardless of what a man does or doesn't do during this decade, he emerges from it "different"—restabilized, in his mid- or late forties, on another personality level. "Even if nothing whatsoever in his external life is different," Dr. Levinson observes, "*he* is, and it's all going to have a different meaning for him."

If men do undergo some profound psychological reorientation between thirty-five and forty-five, the Yale team reasoned, there ought to be earlier, clearly identifiable stages in their adult development that led them to that point.

In analyzing their interviews, the researchers found that there appear to be three such stages. The first, which they call "Getting into the Adult World," starts around the time a man is in his early twenties. At this point, the men interviewed had all been exploring sexual and marital opportunities, different work possibilities, varying kinds of adult group memberships—but had not made firm internal commitments. Quite often, during this exploratory phase, they pursued contradictory goals—one man was working toward success as a businessman and as a writer at the same time. Later, as he integrated his life into a meaningful pattern—and firmly committed himself to it—he let go of those half-formed goals and dreams that did not fit in.

"Getting into the Adult World" might, for one man, last throughout the entire period of his twenties, while for another the phase could be extremely brief. But the common experience was that by the age of thirty to thirty-two, a man had moved into the next stage of adult life, which the research group called "Settling Down." During this period, he became absorbed in the major tasks of his early adult life: proving himself in an occupation, establishing a family, working out a set of values and beliefs that would cement and give meaning to the "life" he was creating. During this phase, he was obviously far less free to explore alternate occupational or sexual options. Those aspects of his personality that had no place in the life he had built for himself tended to be pushed aside or left dormant.

During this "Settling Down" phase, he was deeply influenced by the values and judgments of those around him: He wanted to "make it" in terms of beliefs he shared with his group at large. Spurred on by some vaguely perceived goal (for many of the biologists in the study, it was related to dreams of someday winning the Nobel Prize), he struggled forward toward a satisfaction that always lay ahead, just over the horizon.

"But by age forty," points out Mrs. Charlotte Darrow, the one sociologist in Dr. Levinson's group, "a man has reached his horizon. Whatever illusions he might have had before, this is, inevitably, a time of assessment. He knows fairly clearly just where he has placed in life's battles—and just about how much farther he can go."

If he has failed, either in his own eyes, or in others', or in both, there is the pain of making peace with that knowledge. But even when he has not failed—when he has won the very professorship or high executive position he set out to achieve—he often must come to terms with feelings of futility and meaninglessness. In reality, the dream he has achieved turns out to be far more limited than was his original vision.

"At this point," Mrs. Darrow explains,

many beliefs and values—all of those obvious "truths" that support a man while he is Settling Down—may suddenly come into question. For he's been engaged in a huge effort, working toward the thing that was supposed to make him happy in some glorious distant future. And now here he is, and and things suddenly don't seem so clear. And he starts asking himself: Is this what I really wanted? Was it worth all I had to give up? Do I want to go on doing these same things for the years I have left?

At the same time, those inner voices that he silenced or ignored earlier now make themselves heard again, and with a new urgency. "After all," Mrs. Darrow notes,

in order to do this masculine thing—I mean, to move out and to achieve in the external world—he simply has had to sacrifice, to neglect or suppress certain parts of his self. For example, some of the research biologists felt they had had to emphasize the more rational, consciously intelligent, tough-minded aspects of their personality. This often meant defending against another whole area having to do with more emotional, softer, less masculine wishes and feelings.

The restlessness and discontent that a man may begin to experience more and more intensively toward the close of his thirties is, in the view of the Levinson team, a forerunner of normal personality growth and change. At this stage, a man begins to feel a new kind of freedom from external pressures: the long work of making an identity and place in the world is almost completed. But at the same time, an often painful process of reevaluation and reappraisal is getting under way. Now he wants to find out who *he* really is, what *he* really wants—and, perhaps, what doors are still left open to him.

This process of self-questioning, affecting not only his view of himself but of those about him, brings with it profound inner changes. These changes may take place quietly, almost unnoticed. The biologists mentioned earlier might, on nearing forty, feel a new desire to be related to *people* rather than ideas or things—and shift undramatically into more administrative jobs. Or, such inner changes might be reflected in a man's profound modification of his own ideas about himself. As one thirty-nine-year-old writer taking part in the study put it:

. . . Phrasing it melodramatically, I feel a weakening of the need to be a great man. And an increasing feeling of: "Let's just get through this the best way we can. Never mind hitting any home runs: let's just get through the ball game without being beaned." He noted that his whole early adult career had been guided by a dream of success and fame, which had never been realized, but now, ". . . when I think of giving these things up it doesn't pain me any more . . ."

The changes may be more fundamental, as they appeared to be for one forty-four-year-old businessman, whose marriage was flowering after twenty years of what he called "dormancy." As he said,

From an emotional standpoint, ours has probably been a very one-way relationship, with my wife doing most of the giving. I suspect . . . it hasn't gone very far in terms of enrichment. I know I'm the one who's contributed most of the control, kept us on this lousy monotonous plateau. But I'm going through some kind of change, becoming less 'intellectual' about feelings and so on. Like, the other night my wife had her menstrual period, and we got into bed, and well, she was just very nervous. You know, rolling and tossing. I don't know why, but I just started rubbing her back, and soothing her. And then I just held her face to face. I put my arms around her, and we just stayed that way. And this seemed to comfort her quite a bit, and she quieted down and had a good night. . . . You see, I felt this might do her good, and I tried it. Which I'm not sure I would have thought of six months or a year ago. In fact, I suspect a year ago I might have lain there for a while and then said, "Well, I'm going to have a cigarette." And then I'd have gotten a blanket and gone to sleep on the couch . . .

The mid-life decade, like adolescence, appears to be a crossroads—a time when new personality growth is possible, and some degree of personality change inevitable. A man may now move toward a new kind of intimacy in marriage, toward a greater self-fulfillment in his work life, toward deeper, more realistic relationships with his children. Or, he may be stopped at this point, suffer a developmental defeat. For this period of a man's life holds its threats also: in this decade the incidence of alcoholism, hypochondria, and obesity—all connected to depression—show a marked rise. Sexual difficulties, if they existed before, are exacerbated. The divorce rate leaps. As long ago as 1965, statistics indicated that nearly one-fourth of all persons filing for divorce in this country had been married for longer than fifteen years. And the incidence of marital breakup, in what experts have dubbed the "twenty-year slump," appears to be increasing every year.

What, then, are the specific problems a man is dealing with in this transitional period between early adulthood and middle age? And if he can be expected to emerge from the decade "different," to some degree, in what way is he likely to change?

The clearest and most obvious difficulties a man goes through at this time have to do with the simple fact that he has lost the sense of growing up; he has begun growing old. He is no longer in the stage of "apprenticeship," of being the young man with promise. As he approaches forty, he moves into a new position. And beyond, as he perceives with a fresh and painful clarity, lies old age—and his own death.

The knowledge that one will someday die is difficult to deal with psychologically. As Freud observed: "No one believes in his own death . . . in the unconscious, everyone is convinced of his own immortality." But death's reality presses on a man now in a host of new ways: through the aging or dying of parents, through the deaths of friends, through obvious signs of his own aging. He must inevitably confront the growing evidence that his control over his own body is limited.

As one forty-four-year-old taking part in the study recalled:

. . . I understood (suddenly, waking up after a party one morning) that I could not, that I did not have an absolute capacity for sleeplessness and alcohol. . . . It was a very dramatic and distinct change, because up until then I could stay up until dawn or 7 or 8 a.m. . . . But in the summer of my thirty-seventh year I realized I could no longer do that. I felt terrible. I got the message very radically. I suddenly realized I was no longer twenty-four years old. I was getting on toward forty.

As the same man related in a subsequent interview:

I tend to notice it in the newspapers nowadays when people my own age die. Which is something you don't seem to remark on much when you're in your thirties. But then, people at that age die in accidents; in their forties they start to keel over from heart attacks. . . . Hardly a day goes by when I don't say—I don't mean it preoccupies me, by any means—but I play the awful game. I'm sure many people do. Where you say: "God, in six years I'll be fifty. . . ."

Here is the way another man, a black industrial worker in his early forties, expressed it:

I'm working in the business, hard. And I'm getting older, and the energy I started with is running out. Sooner or later I'm not going to be able to work as hard, and I really haven't gotten any place. As you get older, you begin to think of yourself as a man in a hurry. The years are going by, and you want to know your life meant something . . .

Another man, who had thrown over a successful business career a few years earlier in order to go into full-time writing, described himself this way: "I don't make love as much, I play doubles instead of singles. I try to substitute technique for that earlier, animal energy." He often suffers from bouts of insomnia, and "when I'm awake, alone in the night that way, I think about my own death."

The paradox of these years, the time of a man's "prime" and his "fulfillment," is that they bring with them an ineluctable realization of how fleeting are those years, and that prime. It is this new and vivid encounter with Death, taking place at mid-life, that lends the period its painful tone and precipitates its often critical nature.

Another central set of problems has to do with a man's changing experience of fatherhood. During this decade of his life there are generally new, sometimes overwhelming cries and criticisms and demands coming from his own near-adult children. Here, for example, is what four men, chosen at random from the study sample, faced.

An executive: His oldest daughter had just had what he termed a "tantrum" and dropped out of college. His "Number One Son" was not working up to the level of his ability.

An industrial worker: His oldest child, a stepson, "cannot seem to learn . . . He's not as smart as he might be." His own son could get all A's, but "doesn't cooperate . . . seems emotionally unstable, never hears what you say, can't keep his mouth shut."

A novelist: His oldest son, age thirteen, was in a "terror of a rebellion." He was a "dropout," had "run away," was "into drugs," and was doing no work at school.

Another writer: His oldest child, an eighteen-year-old-boy, was "tall, handsome, swinging away. . . ." But he was a political revolutionary, had been picked up by the police three times. He was attending a private boarding school: "That is, *when* he is there. . . ."

According to Dr. Edward Klein, one of the three psychologists on the research team, "As father to a baby, you can entertain all kinds of illusions about your own power and omnipotence: there is that child whose very fate depends upon you, whom you're going to mold and shape into some ideal being." But during his children's adolescence, a man must inevitably compare that fantasy with what is now becoming reality—and accept the limited nature of his own influence.

Almost simultaneously, his relationship to his own father is changing. The fathers of the four men quoted earlier, for example, were either dead, frail and helpless, or—in one case—slowly dying. (" 'Painful' is the way I would describe my own feelings. . . . This isn't the man of my childhood.") The man at mid-life thus seems to be caught in a generational cross fire: as well as being father to his own children, he often must be, in effect, father to his aging or dying parents as well.

"The essence of what is happening," observes Dr. Klein, "is that as a man is having to let go of his own dependency, he's getting a lot of new problems and flak from his sons. And by that I don't mean only from his real sons, but his 'symbolic sons' also. Because his paternity, at this point, doesn't extend only to his own children, and perhaps to his parents. It comes to be expected of him by other, younger adults."

That this is so can in itself come as a shock: Many men in their late thirties retain the illusion that they are still young, or, as Klein says with a smile, "simply ageless." A chance word, however, a remark made by a younger colleague, may bring to them the sudden realization that people in their late teens and early twenties see them as vaguely parental—as middle-aged or even old.

A man between thirty-five and forty-five is moving (perhaps feeling shoved) into a variety of new relationships that involve, in the widest sense of the word, "bringing up" the succeeding generation. This is what the psychoanalyst Erik Erikson calls the stage of generativity. Erikson views this development of a newer, more altruistic, more "fathering" stance toward younger adults, as a normal stage of emotional growth. "Individuals who do not develop generativity," he has written, "often begin to indulge themselves as if they were their one and only child."

The difficulty is, however, that assuming fatherhood in its fullest sense involves letting go of certain fantasies about the self. As Dr. Klein puts it,

> In a way, this final taking-on of responsibility is like the last bite of the Biblical apple. You're no longer the "son," the one who can't do certain forbidden things without full awareness of the consequences: you're the guy who's in charge of the whole show, the one who's entrusted to *take care* of others. The trouble [he adds with a rueful laugh] is—who wants to let go of the apple?

Concerns about sexuality—fears about the possibility of waning virility, allusions to worries about declining sexual attractiveness—were another of the major problem areas emerging from the Yale interviews. Less than one third of the men taking part in the study were actually involved in extramarital relationships; but there was much fantasy about possible affairs, and a good deal of psychological conflict around the issue. A number of the men were, for the first time, consciously and seriously considering a relationship with some other woman. Said one man who had recently made a small beginning toward a liaison of this kind: "I haven't had the nerve (to begin a physical sexual affair with her). I set these things up, and then I don't go through with it . . . (but) I cannot pass her house, I cannot think of her without the most excitement and an energy change coming over me."

Another man described the way in which his thought processes were diverted by fantasies of women. Even at home, while telling a story to his children, he found that a woman often appeared on the horizon of the tale, interjecting herself between the "King" and the "Queen," and laying claim to the male. "I'm rarely at peace inside," he remarked. "What I'm torn about is whether my commitment to my wife is the thing I really want . . ."

According to Dr. Ray Walker, psychiatric resident working on the Yale team, the commonness of sexual fantasy among men in this decade is related to a heightened sense of loneliness. For most men this doesn't have to do simply with a search for sexual variety or adventure. The whole question of one's marriage and family are part and parcel of the far more general question of one's life. And in the mid-life period, when a man is searching for goals which are more true to his inner self, then he may come face to face with something fairly disquieting: an awareness of what is missing in his relationship with his wife."

(These remarks were virtually paraphrased by a biologist taking part in the study: "I feel much more lonely now than I did in the earlier years of marriage. There is this feeling I have, yes, that maybe out there there is someone who might share a more intellectual kind of life with me.")

Dr. Walker notes that during the first half of a man's life his dominant feminine image is related to the ideal of the Mother: "the Nurturer, the one who feeds him, builds up his ego, makes his life easier." At the time when a young man chooses a wife, this feminine ideal prevails strongly in his unconscious thought: He projects onto the woman he marries many of the wishes and illusions and feelings that relate to the archetype of the Mother.

But, as he approaches middle age, his overriding feminine image begins to change: He now wants to relate to a woman much less as Mother and far more as Lover and Companion. As this change occurs, Dr. Walker explains, a man becomes ready to stop projecting his own more childish wishes and feelings upon his wife. At this point, the entire relaitonship will either go through a phase of restructuring and change, or the husband will feel "stuck." He will begin to experience his wife in a new way: "She'll remain the Mother, but now it will be the Dark Mother—the negative feminine, the one who is holding him back from realizing himself. At this juncture, she starts becoming in his mind, at least—the personification of the Entrapper."

In an interview with a forty-one-year-old executive who described his marriage as "solid, one that would go on forever," the coexistence of conscious loyalty and an unconscious movement in a totally different direction, were demonstrated in a striking way:

> My wife isn't an oversexed individual [he began comfortably]. I think we've got a good match there. If it wasn't, either one way or another, my attentions would have turned a long time ago. Still . . . you know, sometimes I see a movie or read a book and I think, Gee, she's frigid compared to what I'm seeing, or this thing I'm reading. . . . But in my evaluation, she's not a frigid person. She has deep feelings, she's warm, she's a devoted mother. . . . [But] you never know what will happen as you get older. They say once the kids grow up, then divorces occur. I can't predict that something won't happen once the kids are gone . . .

Perhaps the most fascinating and suggestive phenomenon to emerge from the study thus far has been the appearance, in the case histories of most of the men interviewed, of a kind of relationship that the Yale group has come to call the "mentor relationship." Almost every man who had achieved a degree of success in the world had had, during the period of his early adult life, one or more "mentor" figures.

A mentor, explains Dr. Braxton McKee, who is the only practicing psychiatrist in the study group,

> is a person who is at least a bit older, usually eight to ten years, and who has some expert knowledge or wisdom, or personal qualities or skills, which he offers to share with the younger man. A mentor could be someone like a professor, a more established executive, an older relative—but he is usually someone connected with a guy's occupation.

For the younger man, the mentor represents a point of development that is higher than his own, and to which he himself aspires. The mentor is in this sense a parental figure, and yet he is also a friend. He is someone who, by his attitude, more or less says to the younger man: "Here is the world, of which I am a part; and into which I invite you—to become my peer and colleague." He offers, as the actual parent never can, the possibility of a real equality with him.

"Generally speaking," observes McKee,

> it is assumed that once a person separates from his father, and leaves home, he is independent. But that's simply not true. What seems to be consistently overlooked is the parental function of the organization the man becomes involved with—and also the fact that, despite his newfound 'independence,' he starts almost immediately to seek out these semiparental mentor figures. And develops much further, by the way, if he succeeds in finding them.

Mentor relationships, the Levinson group believes, may be a crucial part of early adult development—possibly *the* crucial part. A break with the mentor is very often the signal that a man has come to the third stage of early adult life, which the researchers call "Becoming One's Own Man."

In this phase, a man does just that—he assumes more responsibility for himself in the world, insists on speaking with his own voice, becomes more autonomous, less dependent, more authoritative in his work and family life. This new state of being is brought about in part by external happenings: He may have just reached the top of the ladder in his job, received his professorship, won a prize. On the other hand, the new feeling he has about himself can also be self-generated. Explains Dr. McKee:

> For a sizable number of individuals, there just seems to be this sense that one ought to be making a step toward something a little better, more responsible, or creative. Something that comes out of a man's own inner goals—perhaps a new kind of job he goes after now. There is this sudden reaching toward something that is in some way different—independent of the tasks he's been working on, and independent of the mentor.

After "Getting into the Adult World"—the period of exploration—and "Settling Down"—the phase of intense commitment to building an identity and a life for himself—"Becoming One's Own Man" marks the conclusion of a man's struggle to adapt to and conquer his external environment. It sets the stage for the more internal battles and self-questionings that follow—for the period of crisis and change that characterize the mid-life transition.

A flurry of letters always reaches the Yale group's research offices shortly after any public mention of their project. Says Maria Levinson, one of the team's psychologists and wife of its director, "Most of the mail we receive is fairly typical. Wives who write in—from 'the two of us'—on behalf of a husband who seems to have caught some kind of virus, something which attacks men at mid-life. The wife's initial response is often a kind of frenzy of mothering: Her husband is sick with this thing and her question is how can she cure him?"

What if a woman has lived happily with a man for some fifteen or twenty years and he suddenly begins changing. What can she make of it?

"She should view it as a stage in the developmental process," Mrs. Levinson says,

> not as a kind of flu. As a period during which a man is going to go through some painful changing of gears. When he's starting to experience himself as "older," and having come to terms with that, and with the task of making way for the upcoming generation. In brief, as a time when a serious transition is being made—which involves feelings of unsettlement, and sometimes turmoil.

But what advice might one offer to a woman whose husband is going through this period of turmoil?

"In some of our cases," Mrs. Levinson remarks thoughtfully,

> it was the wife, not the husband, who upset the equilibrium, who made demands for him to get out of his rut and start changing. In general, however, what she does depends very much on the stage she herself is at—and on her capacity to tolerate her husband's depression. And, of course, it depends on the amount of understanding and intimacy that has existed between them.
>
> You know [she observes], in the love of young adults there is a great deal of projection and fantasy: A young wife projects onto her husband many of her feelings about her father, and a young husband projects onto her feelings and fantasies about his mother. But now, in the mid-life period, when one is being freed of many of these earlier illusions, the question is: Can that younger love become something more adult? If there is a good communication between the two people, then they are probably developing in parallel ways. In that case, there will be change on both parts: they'll reintegrate at a higher, more honest level.

But suppose a man becomes disturbed and won't talk about it to his wife? Suppose he can't show his weaknesses to her? Or that his dissatisfaction with himself has something to do with a dissatisfaction with her—and he finds some other woman to talk to?

"You are not talking about something so simple as mere dissatisfaction," Mrs. Levinson says firmly.

You are talking about an existential condition. A man comes to feel disappointed, humiliated, violated by what he has done with his life and the part he feels his wife has played in this process. What can *she* do, if she doesn't happen to feel the same way—if she feels, instead, that their life is tolerable if not ideal, and if she feels that he, in seeking an illusory change, is betraying her and abandoning their children?

To the extent that the wife is in the grip of feelings of moral outrage and victimization by him [she continues], there is probably nothing she can do to keep the marriage together. And perhaps, if they have been moving apart over a period of years, the marriage isn't worth saving: it might be liberating for both, and a relief for the children, if they simply went their separate ways. A real reconciliation would have to involve important changes in the relationship; the choice would be between renewal or stagnation.

If a man can leave his marriage with little or no pain [she adds], then obviously it has become empty, without real meaning for either partner. But in our experience, where a man seriously considered breaking up his family, he went through enormous suffering.

In such a case [Mrs. Levinson says], it would not be enough for his wife to be sympathetic, or to try to make herself more "alluring." She would have to be prepared to grasp the magnitude of his despair, to share in it in whatever ways she could, to come to terms more fully with her own suffering, and to see their joint plight as containing also the possibility for their further development.

The crisis that confronts a man at mid-life is, by its very nature, a turning point for his wife as well. It almost goes without saying that the more fully they both understand the changes, the better they will be able to weather them. This decade by no means represents the beginning of the end: It often signals a movement into something newer, stronger, and more profound for both partners.

"Then I felt so guilty that, by the end of the marriage, I had allowed him to completely dominate me."

The women's liberation movement has helped women achieve greater understanding of their position in society and has encouraged them to adopt different attitudes about their femininity. One of the important vehicles for sharing personal insights is the consciousness-raising group. In this group experience, people try to unravel some of the complicated features of their lives and then develop a greater awareness of their identity. This article describes one such group and gives an intimate portrayal of the personalities involved.

Editor's Note

One of the components of Women's Liberation is the phenomenon called "consciousness-raising" which involves a group of say six to ten women meeting regularly to talk to one another about being women. Some have called them gripe sessions, other have dismissed them as amateur group-therapy. They are neither. The group is leaderless, the attitude, supportive (which accounts for the lack of close, pounce-on questioning in the transcript that follows—no one's allowed to play pseudopsychiatrist), and the procedure, in this group at least, is to have each member speak in turn.

The women in this group, meeting for nearly a year, are:

Sally, 26, a rather plump, married mother of two, housebound, but very eager to write and publish.

Nancy, 30, a very pretty and, despite her current distaste for clothes, unavoidably chic photographer. She is separated from her husband and has one child.

Jean, 39, an art director separated from her husband, by whom she has two children. Small, direct, she looks at least ten years younger than she is.

Jane, 34, divorced, a teacher in a very famous school. Clear-eyed, clear-skinned, handsome, she would be recognized anywhere in the world as an American.

Ann, 29, probably the most intellectual in the group, certainly the one with the most degrees. Sad-eyed, soft-voiced, she is a film director and critic.

Susan, 26, a speech therapist. In face, figure, clothes she is very contempo-

rary; her voice is slightly hoarse, which makes it curiously engaging.
Margaret, 23, small, with large eyes. She is a TV production assistant.

The meeting was held in Jane's apartment. The topic was female sexuality.
In the transcript, which was edited, the sections in italics are the interjections of
group members or of the *MLLE* editor who taped the evening.

Sally: I get a much more positive feeling when I think about my emotional
responses toward my children and my husband—my sense of love and sentiment
and responsibility—then when I think of a biological, sexual response. And I
have to say that my husband is the only man with whom I've ever had sexual
relations. I married him relatively young, because I was pregnant. Before I
married, I was, in terms of sex, a babe in the woods. For as long as I can remember, I was bright but terribly unattractive—and, really, as a little girl, I was
horrible, much worse than I am now—but I never worried about it. I concentrated on being top of the class, and when my young, pretty friends were going
to their early dances and I wasn't—well, if it did bother me, I didn't admit it.
This ended when I got to college, because I was in a school where brains were
easy to come by. I tried a few mixers and when I wasn't the first one looked at,
I suddenly realized that I wasn't making it as a woman, the feminine image. I
found my answer by getting involved in the college newspaper, but I had a very
minor social life. So when I graduated, I chose to take a job where I would
realize some great career or intellectual potential. And it happened exactly as I
wanted it to. I came to New York and had a very good time, and made up in a
couple of years a lot that I had missed. By this time I was aware of what I was
doing, and of the emptiness of my life in terms of my personal ambitions. I was
very ambitious and very aggressive and still am, but I got entangled with the
pregnancy and marriage and the sudden realization that it was too late, that it
was all over. I had gone too far with trying to realize what these girls had had in
college that I hadn't. I had made a deliberate choice as to what I wanted, but had
stopped thinking along the way. But I don't regret it. It's worked out well.
Because what I've discovered is based on the basic dichotomy of the female
going one of two routes in her life. Either through men, by relying on her female-
ness to achieve success, or by relying on her innate human potential, maybe her
intellect. Now that I'm married, I've been able to combine the two. The thing
about concentrating on intelligence is that it's a very lonely kind of life, and so
is being single. Now I'm in constant communication with people I enjoy—my
children and my husband. One thing I still wonder about is being asexual. I have
a lot of hangups about how close I can be to my husband in some ways, particularly in terms of sex. But I think that's improving too as I'm feeling more secure
within myself. This afternoon, I was standing in the window of my new apartment painting the windowsill and suddenly I had a sense of looking at myself,
of seeing myself framed. And I said, "Who am I right now?" I am a wife. I am
a mother. I am a person with projects important to me. And I am a happy
person.

Nancy: I have always been one of those people who have been, supposedly,
very strong and independent but, really, it was all forced to hide my vulnerability. I was domineering in relationships in order not to be swallowed up in
them. When I was single, I was OK until Sunday afternoon which was just

excruciating because it was the only time during the week that I didn't have someone telling me where to be. I'd cry and say nobody loves me, and what I wanted was to be loved because a woman without a man is a ship without a sail and I needed to be completed. That was always number one—to be loved. The idea of loving didn't even occur. I married a man who was very uptight about his sexuality and I was very uptight about mine; and I repeated my parents' pattern and started to dominate him. Then I felt so guilty that by the end of the marriage, I had allowed him to completely dominate me. I joined Women's Liberation May 3rd of last year and by May 16th I had separated. I guess it was about July that our group could handle talking about sex. And it's funny, I have said things in the meetings that I had not yet previously admitted to myself. We were talking about sex and I said "Well, frankly I can take it or leave it." That's a very heavy thing for someone who is uptight about her sexuality, or lack thereof, to say. The following Monday I discovered sex. Now I know I'm a woman and how to communicate physically, beautifully, in bed. That one thing, really loving sex, is the most important thing that has made me feel secure as a woman, more than any of my achievements. It's communication that makes me feel like a woman. All communication—communication with my child, communication with my sisters, communication with men. To me, communication is everything.

When you say you like sex, is it for the communication or the physical pleasure?

Nancy: It's the sum total. I have had sex with about ten men since I'd discovered sex in July and I've had only one bad experience. My lovemaking now is sometimes like a ballet. For 30 years I felt that every bit of my sexuality was something I could put on top—my false eyelashes, my straightened hair, my chic clothes. I did the disguise fantastically; nobody would have guessed that I had this interior problem. But I was just one big need. I fell in love in a very deep way about two and a half months ago, but it ended, and since then I haven't slept with anybody. I have felt myself getting frantic and panicky and like a little girl, and at one point I got very sick and thought I was going to die and what's worse, I didn't give a damn if I did. It had been such an emotional and complete thing for me that not only have I not slept with anybody since, but I've had trouble masturbating. But I read this article about Wilhelm Reich who says that orgasm gets rid of all neuroses, and so I decided that I'm going to give myself a really big fabulous—at least one every day—orgasm. In a way, it's made me feel even more like a real woman because what I'm aiming for is to be an autonomous woman.

Jean: My whole life has been a quest for what my sexuality is, and it's far from ended. As a child, I had much more than the usual sexual curiosity. I spent my whole childhood under bushes and in closets with all the neighborhood children, male and female. And I was continually caught and punished. There was something there I just couldn't find out about. When I was a young adolescent, I went to a girl's school and had lots of crazy lesbian experiences. When I was at the dating age, I was very unsuccessful with boys which made me terribly unhappy, but by the time I got to college I was tremendously successful. But I was fairly sexually inhibited in the sense that I refused to go all the way. I did everything else of an experimental nature, still continued to experiment with girls, and had affairs going with boys and girls simultaneously. But through it all,

I knew I was going to get married, and when I was almost 25 I picked a man of whom I was very fond, who seemed to be not too threatening, and we had a good marriage for about five years.

Was he the first man you slept with?

Jean: No, I had slept with a couple of people ... but I can't remember it. I mean there was no orgasm involved or anything exciting. My sexual life with my husband was not terrific. He was fairly inadequate and I was inexperienced. But it all seemed right because I really didn't know anything else. I had a feeling of ... not inadequacy—unfulfillment, like if I suddenly died what would I say to St. Peter ... you know, like what have I done with my life? In our sixth year of marriage we had our first child and I was quite surprised because I really hadn't wanted children. But I felt that I'd done my bit and could rest on my laurels. And we had a second and I continued to feel the same way, but the marriage began to fall apart. After about three years, I finally fell into bed with a house-guest and don't remember much about that. But that became the continuing pattern for the next year, and I went to bed with quite a few different people, and it got to be better and better and more and more interesting.

All men?

Jean: All men. And then about that time my husband said he wanted a divorce and it came out that he'd been unfaithful to me for six years. Suddenly I was all by myself and realizing how dependent I'd been on him. I'd always felt I was very independent because he went to work and I did everything else. But I was really very high and dry. Since then I haven't found myself. I haven't found anything except I know what I want to do now, which is to be an autonomous person. I would like to be able to love somebody, and I think I will be able to. But I will never consider getting married again.

Do you think all the experimentation was an attempt to feel something?

Jean: Well, when I was a child I sort of got cut off from all kinds of feeling. And it's been very hard for me to express feelings or accept them from other people.

Can you go to bed with somebody and leave your head out of it?

Jean: That's the thing I was doing with all those experimental extramarital relationships and the ones I'm still carrying on. And it's a very masculine thing to do. I mean it's just going out and getting laid. Just purely sexual. I mostly go to bed with people I know. And it's purely satisfying.

And you can walk away from it and if you never see that person again never feel any sort of hurt or rejection or anything?

Jean: It's a set-up situation where everybody knows in advance that it's going to be casual. Because these people have other commitments or I do.

Sally: At this point in my life there is nothing I would rather do than experience sexual relationships with other men, although I love my husband very much. And I tried to explain this to him. All I said was ... "I'd just like to know about it." He said ... "You're ridiculous." I said I would like a relationship where you'd go out, you know, and have your thing and I would do mine, and we wouldn't exactly come home and exchange all the details. But this, I think, would add a dimension to our relationship.

Why? How?

Sally: Just maybe from the sake of . . . experience. . . .

Like going to a movie . . . or theatre . . . ?

Sally: I admit I don't go around looking but I feel there's a great danger for my family—that my feelings may get involved. You can't say that they won't, but still I feel there's a wonderful positive thing of experiencing other people. . . .

If you did do this—let's say you picked out a man, found him physically attractive, and said, "OK I'm going to sleep with him" and found it more enjoyable than you did with your husband. . . .

Sally: That would be a problem [laughter]. But I haven't done it and I've listened to these other women saying that they feel very much in touch with their sexuality because they give when they want to give. . . . I feel that I'm deliberately holding on to a tradition in which I've been raised—that I'm married, and should be devoted to this one man. And I . . . it's all mixed up.

I think it's wonderful that you're becoming an open woman instead of a whole lot of rules.

Jane: The trick is to move with that and not destroy something. You have to separate what you want to do in your head from some of the realities in your life, and you have to be very careful.

Nancy: You can have an on-going relationship with someone that lasts for years, but that doesn't mean that you shouldn't have moments. As long as the moment is real. Your feelings are there, but they're there for then, and when the moment's over, it's something in your scrapbook.

Jane: The whole topic of sexuality is one that interests me enormously because I am full of sexual hang-ups and have been in analysis for ten years and am not rid of them yet. I went into analysis ostensibly because I wasn't orgastic. Ten years later I'm still there. I don't know how much of it has to do with not giving—to the man, and to myself. At the same time, I'm wrecking it for me, and for him, too.

Do you feel you owe the man you sleep with an orgasm?

Jane: Not consciously. But you get into a whole thing—is there something wrong with them? Because, by and large, the men who are most concerned about orgasm and whose performance it affects are the ones who seem to be the most insecure about their own masculinity.

Nancy: When I say that I discovered sex suddenly—I didn't have an orgasm that night. This whole emphasis on the orgasm and if it's a clitoral or a vaginal or whatever . . . it's, like, not sex. I don't need a man for an orgasm, I need a man for the contact. Too much is made of the orgasm . . . because any way you get it, it's nice.

Jane: That's what my analyst keeps saying to me—you know—"like forget about that orgasm for a while and enjoy yourself."

But you do have climax?

Jane: Yes, but it seems to me that an orgasm from intercourse must be the best.

Why?

Jane: Well, it's because you're sharing—that's the ultimate in communication with the man if you're in there together.

Can you have relationships with men—either long or brief—without committing yourself?

Jane: Yes, to a certain extent. For example, recently I've been seeing a man who, for whatever reason, has trouble making it. So I have since gone to bed with another man for the release of the sexual tensions from the other one I really care more about. Is that sort of what you mean? But I can't do that for very long. At all. Because I have to at least have the fantasy that the relationship is going somewhere, or that I care about the person, that I want to be with him, and if I project that fantasy far enough it always gets to marriage.

How old were you when you had your first complete sexual experience?

Jane: Twenty-one, when I was married. I was one of those people who did everything in every kind of way but you don't have intercourse until you are married. I was scared and felt very guilty about those other things and it was very important to me to talk with my college roommates. These talks made an enormous difference in how much I could enjoy my sexual activity. In a sense, that's partly what I want to use this group for. I think it's sort of pathetic, 16 years later, to be still in the same place. But I am still there. And it doesn't work like it worked when I was 18. When I was married I felt much more a woman. Much more female—and that somehow is involved in female sexuality—than I do now. A man, A MAN is very important to me in terms of how I feel about being female and sexual.

And you can't feel it by yourself?

Jane: No. I have been going out with somebody very exciting, and he was saying that a friendly relationship was most important between us, and I didn't like that. Because a sexual relationship is really the heart of a male-female relationship. Another man I'm seeing said, "Do you like sex?" and I said, "Oh yes, I like it a lot ... like every day." Well, it turned out that that frightened the hell out of him. I said, "... what is going on in this world with these guys?" There are lots of men around who have sexual problems too, and it adds to our confusion. Particularly for me, who has always been accustomed to taking what a man says as gospel.

Ann: I've never been able to separate my head/heart or whatever it is from the sexual thing. In fact, there are several times when I've met men who've looked enormously attractive and have thought, "Wouldn't it be great to have this one-night stand?" But I've never been able to. I like to form deep friendships that can't be kept up by seeing someone just once a year. With girls as well as men. Sexually, I'm very much the same way. All the relationships that I've had have come from good friendships first and so the sexual thing was a communication, just another step along the way. When I was younger, I was enormously affected by what might be called the sociology or the mores of the times. There were things that good girls did and things that bad girls did. And I always resented the fact that men had to prove their masculinity at your expense. So I would play games. I remember when I was in high school going with a boy who was one of the fastest guys in town. I went out with him something like 14 times and never kissed him. And I enjoyed it because I was paying him back for all the humiliation that I felt. I remember another time when I decided virginity was a terrible thing and I was going to get it over with. I went to bed with this guy and we both took our clothes off and just as he was coming at me I noticed that he had his socks on. I also knew that he didn't care about me. Suddenly I grabbed the bed sheet and said, "I can't. You're going to hate me, but I can't." And he really did hate me, because I'd one-upped him. Not because he cared about me. Still, I always think that my being a woman, in spite of my allegiance to Women's Liberation, is very much defined by men, by how men respond to me.

Men in general . . . or a specific man?

Ann: A specific man that I care about. I don't think I would ever enjoy going it alone, although there are times when I have. I can't imagine long periods of my life in which there wasn't a man involved.

Do you feel like a woman without a man?

Ann: My life constantly involves interacting with men, either professionally or not. Do you mean, do I feel like a woman when I'm with other women?

I don't think that you can be an autonomous, self-determining person unless you see yourself as a woman, and then if you're with a man, groovy. But part of the way you know you are a woman is because of the thing that's set up with a man. So it seems to me that if you're living in a vacuum, you're not a woman. You're just a person.

Nancy: I don't need a man to define me.

From what you said in other meetings, it seems your work is a major part of your life. Does sexuality enter your career? Or are you basically neuter when you work?

Ann: I'm not a neuter person. I am definitely female. But it's not a voluptuous kind of sexuality and I tone it down.

Are you able to raise the heat, once you get off work?

Ann: Oh, once I get out of work I just take off my masks. But not with people I work with. I felt that when the sexual thing came into my work, people would stop taking me seriously. There are certain rules that you do have to follow or you will have problems.

Susan: When I was around 10, I was a tremendous tomboy. And I said to my father, "Why wasn't I born a boy instead of a girl?" He said, "God made you a girl and you should start being one." That's when I realized that I could still do all the things I had been doing—racing, and being with guys and fighting —but I had this new awareness of myself. When I think of sexuality, I think of it sexually. I'm aware of it in everything I do—in my work, in the way I relate to my friends, men, my family. Until recently though, I always thought of myself as a girl who went out with boys. And I've begun to see that's no good anymore. That's not expressing my sexuality, or the way I feel. And I'm trying very hard to think of myself as a woman. Because I'm not making it as a girl anymore. I'm getting more womanly feelings, maternal, sexual feelings. I want a child badly and, of course, I'm not in a situation to have one. But that's another thing that's taken me from this girl image. And it's hard to deal with, because sometimes I have difficulty handling myself as a woman, and fall back on the girl. Sex is something that I look for and crave with a man, and most of the time if I'm without it I feel . . . I can feel that I'm wanting it, desirous of it, and to me that's a very feminine, womanly feeling. But I don't have an orgasm as from the books. I've redefined it for myself so I can deal with it. And it's not exact, physical release, pinpointed to a specific part of my body. It's this total, wonderful . . . a total release for my mind, my heart and everything. I've only felt this way twice. But to me that's an orgasm. I don't care if I never have the other kind. It might feel great, physically—a clitoral orgasm you have from masturbating— but it doesn't matter if I ever have that. The two times I have had the other, I burst out crying. Not out of sadness, and not out of happiness . . . just this outpouring of every emotion I can have. And it's definitely a head trip more than a body trip. It's not that I want the sex, I want the man.

Can you sleep with somebody and have a great time if your feelings aren't involved?

Susan: My feelings become involved. If they weren't before, while I'm having sex, all of a sudden they are. Technique-wise, I know more than most guys and it's hard for me to deal with someone who might be very sweet and wonderful but inexperienced. They turn me off. One thing my mother taught me to believe, which is really weird for an uptight Jewish mother, was that sex is a great, great part of marriage and of a relationship and it will hold you together when a lot of things are going wrong. I'm in love with a friend of mine, and he's everything I could ever want in a husband. But I couldn't even kiss him, no less sleep with him. And I wish I didn't have this strong sexual feeling, because he probably could make me happier than anyone I know.

Not without sex he couldn't. I guarantee that.

Susan: It's hard for me to find my sexuality because I think I live it a lot. And it's hard for me to say exactly what it is for me, because I feel it all the time. It's not really great because I've been hurt a lot lately. Someone just said to me, "Do you think our relationship is mostly sex?" and I said, "uh huh," without thinking. And he said, "Wow, you really told the truth, good for you." As soon as he said that I thought, "God, that really wasn't the truth." Because I would never have had sex with him if I didn't care about him. It's hard for me to understand how a man, how anyone, can separate his head from his body. How a man can just sleep with you, if he doesn't care about you. Yet I know girls who can go out and make a guy as easily as a guy can make a girl.

I talked with a female psychiatrist and she says that any woman who says she can is kidding herself.

    Susan: If women can't do it, why can men?

    Nancy: Because they are so out of touch with their feelings. They're out earning a living and getting on top and competing and pushing away. They just don't know where they're at. I couldn't think of sleeping with someone I didn't care about. I'm very into the present tense so, like, I don't have to have the promise of life, 'til death do us part, to be able to care. But when I'm in bed, boy, I'm caring, really caring. That person is like *it*.

    Susan: Once, I thought, "Wow, I've got to marry this guy because I'll never find anyone like this in bed." He lived, breathed and everythinged sex. Then I found—he was only the second person I'd ever slept with—it's not really if they're good, it's how you feel about them. Because, then, it becomes super between you.

    Margaret: Female sexuality is something I've never really thought about defining before tonight. When I heard we were going to be discussing it, I suddenly said to myself, "What am I gonna' talk about?" First of all, I have not had that much sexual experience. I didn't start dating until college. I went to a school where all the girls are gorgeous and tan and blonde and rich. I happened to be a poor, kind of homely girl from Boston who never set her hair or wore any makeup, and didn't know how to. The first thing that happened was that three of my girlfriends grabbed me, plucked my eyebrows, curled and dyed my hair and I was a platinum blonde when I came home in the spring. I was unaware of sexuality, because my mother wasn't aware of it. So all I knew was that I could be kind of pretty, and maybe could get a date here and there, and even then it still took me four years before I had a boyfriend. Just recently I've discovered why. Whenever I've liked a guy, I've always felt, how could this guy like me? Finally, I had a very good experience. I went to a party and met a married man. He was older, 37, and I was 22. It was like all the things I had dreamed about. We went out for about six or seven weeks, maybe just once a week, and I knew it could never be anything. I didn't have to be committed to him, and I knew that I could never call him, because I felt very guilty about the fact that he was married. But he thought that I was so fantastic! He spent every minute of every hour telling me how great and fantastic and delightful and charming I was, and how much he adored me, and how much he couldn't wait to go to bed with me. I wouldn't go to bed with him because I was not ready to handle a married man—I couldn't even handle a single one—and thank God I knew it. Even though this is what terminated our relationship, it terminated only because of that, and not because we didn't respect each other. That was beautiful. It was beautiful that such a really wonderful person could love me. I have since had one other relationship, in which I had sex for the first time, and that was lousy. It's funny. Even though I've never had much sexual experience I know when it's good or not. Maybe it's intuition, or maybe I feel that I'm not insecure about having good sex. Once I do, it'll be great.

Do you think someone 23 has a freer head about sex than someone ten years older?

    Margaret: I really don't think so. I think I am representative of my generation, or maybe a certain part of it. There are a lot of young people today who, because of the Pill or whatever being thrust at them at a high-school age are very much into sex. Still, I have friends who are very sexually aggressive and who feel very free and relaxed about making it. I have one friend who'll make a guy and walk away from him, and has probably slept with more men than most men have slept with women in their lives. But I think it catches up with her once in a while. She'll get into a superdepression and say, "What do I have for this 75 guys I slept with? Nothing." The most exciting thing is this—sitting here and becoming aware of yourself. The fact that the Pill is there, or that the freedom is there, doesn't necessarily make it that easy. This is what we need, to become self-respecting persons.

Nancy: I think the whole truth is consciousness. Because of Calley there is a new consciousness about Vietnam, because of Women's Liberation there is a new consciousness about women. People are developing a new consciousness about themselves. And I don't think it has that much to do with age.

Susan: It's the time, and whatever age you are, you are still in this time. The girl who's 21, and all of a sudden becoming liberated and understanding a lot more about herself, was in the same place everyone else was three years ago. There isn't any generation gap; it's a communication problem. When women talk with women there is no gap. So, we're raising our consciousness and getting it together, but if men stay where they were at, then we will still have loneliness.

Nancy: I was thinking it would be marvelous if everyone could join a consciousness-raising group—men *and* women—because the kind of communication we've achieved here among, not just women, but among people, is making it a much more valuable world to live in. It's not things, it's not clothes, it's just this exchange, and that's the mark of Utopia. It is so beautiful when you have this kind of reality.

"The main topics of discussion always centered on our daily experiences on a white campus or on the similarities of our past lives in inner-city ghettos."

This article by Sylvester Monroe is a sensitive portrait of a black student finding his way through what many consider to be the most prestigious university in America. But more than that, "A Black at Harvard" describes the dilemma of the black intellectual and his difficulty in coming to terms with a white society.

I am part of a new and growing group of black students for whom Harvard is a new experience. In fact, until I was a sophomore in high school, I had never even heard of Harvard College. When I graduate from Harvard this June, I will be the first member of my family to receive a college degree. But, even after three-and-one-half years at Harvard, I still find it extremely difficult—even impossible—to think of myself as a "Harvard man." Instead, I feel more like a guest in a strange house where my welcome has all but run out. I am nearing the end of a four-year visit during which I have never felt at home.

The problem is that the traditional Harvard just isn't my Harvard. The Harvard of my experience has been three years of a totally black experience—black roommates, black friends, black dining-hall tables, black dances, black student organizations, black building takeovers, black studies, and black ideology, all isolated within the confines of an otherwise white university.

A recent black graduate of Harvard told me that although black students have studied here for more than a century, their experience really represented only a passing through in which they were always careful never to upset the status quo. "For more than one hundred years," he said, "black students have found themselves, in effect, in a revolving door that has momentarily offered access to Harvard and then quickly spun them out into the cold world again."

After almost a century without change the 1960s created a new kind of black student, full of the awareness that black is beautiful and proud and powerful and often violently antiwhite. Responding to the militant stance of urban black people during the Sixties, Harvard and other prestigious white colleges started to recruit those students. The big push came in 1968, when for the first time there were almost 100 black students in Harvard's freshman class. (As late as 1965 there were less than two dozen black students in the entire college.) Each year since 1969, when I arrived, Harvard has admitted about 130 black freshmen, bringing the current black enrollment to more than 520 in a total undergraduate population of about 6,000 students.

Wherever they could be found—in the graduating classes of inner-city high schools or on ghetto street corners—young black kids who had never even heard of the Ivy League were brought to Harvard "to make it" in the white world. Unquestionably, it was a bold and—in one sense—even admirable venture; yet it also was blind. For, in essence, Harvard was bringing black students to a swimming hole and telling them to swim.

Consequently, a lot of black students were able to stay afloat only with the aid of summer enrichment programs like ABC (A Better Chance), Upward Bound, and others designed to help bridge the enormous gap between black inner-city schools and prestigious white ones. In my own case the jump from the 100 per cent black Wendell Phillips High School on Chicago's South Side was bridged by a year at the Duke University ABC program in 1966, and then three years at St. George's prep school in Newport, Rhode Island.

But there were countless others who, without the benefits of such transition, were simply left to drown. Harvard did not recognize any responsibility to black students beyond the initial step of bringing them here.

Beginning in the mid-Sixties, Harvard and a steadily growing group of black students began feeling their way through a totally new experience—a kind of "great experiment" in which a handful of confused and frightened black youths found themselves charged with the mammoth task of developing better racial relations with a scared and uncertain white college community.

Even as late as 1969 black students were coming to Harvard *expecting* to be accepted and absorbed into the mainstream of university life. Although filled with anxiety about a variety of concerns, including the fear of failing academically, very few came with any intention or desire to separate themselves from white people.

In fact, in those years between 1965 and 1969 most blacks still had white roommates, and many of them even participated in white social activities. (They did so partly because the number of blacks hadn't grown sufficiently to form black organizations and partly because blacks were genuinely seeking to get along with the white community.)

When I first came here, I had two white roommates—by choice. Although I got along well with them during my freshman year, relations with other whites often were not as pleasant, for it seemed at times that there was just too much that white Harvard students did not know.

I remember vividly the questions they would ask: Someone would want to know whether my parents grew up on a plantation or whether my grandmother was a slave. Or someone else might ask whether my family's diet consisted mainly of soul food or whether anyone in my family had ever won a dance contest because of natural rhythm. I recall a friend's telling me once that a white girl even wanted to touch her (Afro-styled) hair.

Although I had experienced much the same kind of ignorance and naïveté in prep school, somehow it all seemed a lot worse at Harvard. It was with increasing difficulty that I tried to ignore feelings that I was being used as a guinea pig, a black showpiece for the Harvard administration—which, in fact, was what most of us were.

As it turned out, rather than suffer the tongue-in-cheek naïvéte so evident in many of those questions, many of us began desperately seeking other black students while consciously avoiding any unnecessary contact with anyone white —student or faculty.

It didn't take long to find a small group of blacks who felt pretty much as I did, and we began meeting for late evening bull sessions anywhere we could be assured of being alone. The main topic of discussion always centered on our daily experiences on a white campus or on the similarities of our past lives in inner-city ghettos. But, better than anything else about those meetings, I remember the deep sense of closeness and solidarity we felt. It was like a breath of fresh air after we had put up all day with the patronizing attitudes of white students and professors. After several of these bull sessions I decided about midway through my freshman year that I would have black roommates for the rest of my stay at Harvard. For the past three years that is exactly how it has been.

It was early in that first year also that I became influenced by the black ideology of the Association of Afro-American Students (Harvard Afro)—at that time a highly active and political black student organization that was partly responsible, during the student strike in the spring of 1969, for bringing about the establishment of an Afro-American Studies Department.

Because everybody around me had been black on the South Side of Chicago, I wasn't confronted with my blackness until I had arrived at St. George's School. But even there I never really had to put it into any particular perspective. Instead, I always told myself that although I am black, I am first of all a human being, and that ultimately the latter fact would prove more important than the former in whatever I might do. But as a result of my associations with Harvard Afro, the emphasis gradually shifted, despite the many attempts I made to prevent it. For the first time in my life I realized that the facts of race and color do not change simply because one goes to a white prep school or college. Everything I have done since then has been guided by a conscious black perspective.

To understand the profound effect this change of attitude had upon me is to understand how I suddenly felt about the classes I was taking, indeed, about almost every facet of my life at Harvard. For example, in the spring term of my freshman year, during a humanities lecture, I suddenly found myself wondering what possible connection there could be between *Beowulf* (the subject of the lecture) and any solution to the problems of black people in America. Quickly I decided there was none, walked out of the lecture hall, and stopped attending the course.

In the same way I canceled my participation in many other black-white activities that seemed to me of no particular value in preparing to help better the plight of all the black people I'd left back home in Chicago. I stopped eating at mixed dining-hall tables in order to avoid going through the empty motions of talking to white students. I stopped taking courses that weren't taught entirely in lectures, because I didn't want to talk with white teaching fellows. Our desire to avoid any kind of exchange with whites was so intense that during the annual sophomore dinner in the Leverett House dining hall, after finishing a specially prepared dinner of steak and wine and apple pie, about ten of us—all sitting at the same table—walked out just as the house master began his welcoming address!

In other words, for the past three years my stance—and that of the great majority of my contemporaries—has been that I simply have no time for those parts of the Harvard College curriculum and social life that seem to have nothing positive or relevant to offer to my experiences and goals.

What has been most frustrating in my four years here is that I have found so very little in any aspect of the school that has not reflected a negative attitude toward black people and their worth as contributing members of the human race. It is that way in history courses. It is that way in English. It is that way in house activities. It is that way in sports (according to one of my roommates who is a leading member of the varsity basketball team).

Intellectually, I still believe there is a great deal to be gained by staying here. Thus, I have remained, but not without suffering the painful experience of fulfilling academic requirements that adopted a negative posture toward black people. In my major, social studies—a combination of American history and economics—I was required to take one-and-a-half courses in history. One of these was an intellectual-history course covering the span of American history from the beginning to the present in sixty-seven lectures. Black peoples' contributions were mentioned in only two of those during the entire year: once with respect to the issue of slavery and once to explain black intellectuals' involvement with socialism and communism in the early twentieth century.

Similarly, my other roommate, an economics major whose interest is economic development, had to take a course in which the professor would ask such questions as: "Why hasn't black Africa developed economically?"

As the years have brought more black students to Harvard, more of them have found it easier to live and interact among themselves, developing cultural and educational programs that meet their own needs. Harvard is today confronted not only with more black students than ever before but with increasingly louder and more militant demands for "relevancy" in the college experience. The black challenge has become a demand for Harvard's acceptance of the full responsibility for bringing black students here, in the same way that the students have had to wrestle with the keen sense of guilt they feel being here while their families still struggle in black ghettos.

I remember well the guilt my roommate and I felt as sophomores living in a plush, apartmentlike dormitory suite equipped with such luxuries as a refrigerator, private bath, private bedrooms, and a living room with a large plate-glass picture window looking out over the banks of the Charles River. To this day it still seems terribly inconsistent that we are actually living better as students in a college dormitory than we have ever lived in our own homes in two of the many overcrowded, dirty housing projects of Chicago and New York City.

The one sure way of easing such guilt was to demand "relevance" from Harvard, which means, in effect, instruction that can be directed toward improving the quality of life for blacks as a whole in this country. I recall my participation in the 1969 black student takeover of a Harvard administration building. The issue we demonstrated against was alleged hiring discrimination by the university against black painting contractors and construction workers.

But when a university dean shouted through a bullhorn that unless we left the building immediately we'd all be suspended from school, I suddenly couldn't think of any good reason for being there in the first place, except that I felt if I hadn't gone in, I'd have been a traitor to the black cause. Much later in the summer I realized that I had occupied University Hall not so much for the sake of the painters but instead to convince myself and my peers that being at Harvard had not made me forget where I came from.

By seeking to relieve their guilt via building takeovers, strikes, and other kinds of demonstrations and by exercising their desire for "privacy," black students have baffled and embittered the white Harvard community.

To them black isolation is an ambivalent stance. As one white educator reflected, "It is like an incredible paradox in which black students who once objected to separatism in all-black colleges now shun the mainstream of college life at Harvard and develop isolated programs of their own."

In 1969, when blacks demanded that the university make some changes in its curriculum, many white faculty were frightened by the students' implied threats of violence if their demands were not met. Consequently, motivated by fear more than reason, the faculty voted to support the students' demands for a separate black-studies program, which is today essentially a social science and humanities-oriented program of readings in the history of black culture.

I think the faculty vote reflected also a conscious desire to "give the niggers anything they want so long as it will keep them quiet." It was also, I think, an easy way of washing their hands of the whole matter, leaving to the students themselves the responsibility of educating black students.

The situation is similar with respect to the other aspects of black isolation. Even though whites at all levels of the university have complained about such things as being denied seats at all-black dining-hall tables, none of them, it seems, has been particularly disturbed enough really to do anything about it. Neither does there seem to be much concern at all that more frequently black students are missing classes and subsequently not receiving the instruction they desperately need. Instead, under the pretense of "respecting their wishes" whites are simply ignoring black students altogether, leaving them to sink or swim on their own.

But the blame does not belong only to the whites. Blacks have been equally complacent about their own responsibilities as students. More and more young blacks who come here are becoming much too comfortable behind a superficial shield of black solidarity. Somehow they are blinded, it seems, by the small amount of effort it takes to isolate oneself from almost everything that isn't particularly appealing.

In essence, too many blacks simply misuse the ideological strength of black solidarity as a kind of cover to dupe the white community into believing that behind their united front of blackness they are mature, self-confident, and functioning black individuals, who know exactly what they want and how they will get it. But what I see and hear instead are insecure and frightened young black men and women, who—in the words of a James Brown song—are constantly "talking loud and saying nothing" in an attempt to persuade themselves, more than anybody else, that they have the right answers.

Eating lunch with a group of black freshmen and sophomores last spring, I overheard one of them say to another: "You know, I'm really glad I'm at

Harvard and not Howard. I've heard they [the Howard faculty and administration] don't take no stuff down there." I realized that he was glad to be at Harvard because here, being black, he can get through without ever really applying himself. Yet maybe he should have preferred being at Howard, where the instructors would make certain he got the basic remedial skills that so many of us never mastered before coming to Harvard. Black students often do not get adequate remedial preparation before entering Harvard through no fault of their own. What is in part their fault is that in four years of college many never even attempt to acquire these skills.

On the other hand, it is quite difficult to get that kind of extra help at Harvard without asking for it, which only compounds the problems of black students who are isolated from the white college community. "There are a number of black students now doing B work who could be doing A work," says Archie C. Epps, Harvard's black dean of students. "The reason they are not is that they have isolated themselves from the intellectual strength of the Harvard community."

Martin A. Kilson, a professor of government who is one of the most powerfully influential black individuals at Harvard, adds, "The problem with black students at Harvard is that they are too caught up in ideology. Most people who deal in ideologies believe only ten per cent of it, at most. But blacks at Harvard want to believe ninety per cent of their own ideological bullshit."

Meanwhile it is 1972, and increasingly I hear of blacks—just three or four or five years out of school, holding degrees from Harvard or Yale—who discovered that they could not handle the everyday demands of their jobs. The world, it seems, has suddenly caught up with many of them and pulled the covers from an empty four years in the Ivy League. One by one, they've thrown up their hands to the realization that there is no great demand for "showcase niggers" today.

The first fifteen black students with degrees in Afro-American studies have already graduated from Harvard. While a couple of them have gone to law school or divinity school, the overwhelming majority are now teaching black history. I cannot help thinking that if the future holds nothing more for the graduates of black-studies departments than teaching jobs in the black community, then who will be the black doctors, the technicians, and the architects of the future black community? I cannot help thinking also that it might have been better for many of us to have gone to Tougaloo College in Mississippi or Fisk or Howard or anywhere other than a place like Harvard, where if one is black, he must necessarily shut himself off from the strength of the institution in order to affirm his self-identity.

As for me personally, I am on the brink of being thrust out into that same complex and demanding white world, and, quite frankly, I feel very inadequate about my past three years at Harvard, which were lived in an almost totally isolated black vacuum. To be sure, I am thoroughly confused.

"Life is not a means to an end, it is an end in itself."

Erich Fromm is one of the great men of contemporary psychological thought. Besides his creative contribution to personality theory, he has written a number of popular books. One of them, *The Art of Loving,* is similar in theme to this article. Think of what you mean by "love," and then compare it to the definition used by Dr. Fromm.

To some of you this question may be puzzling, or it may even sound senseless. Do we not *all* love life? Isn't this love of life the ground from which all our activities spring? How could we even stay alive unless we loved life and made continuing efforts to sustain and improve it?

Of course it is true that without some love for life, neither an individual nor a culture *could* exist. We see examples of this all the time. Individuals who have lost all love for life become insane, commit suicide, become hopeless alcoholics or drug addicts; we also know that whole societies have been so emptied of love of life and filled with destructiveness that they crumbled and perished, or almost perished. Think of the Aztecs, whose power vanished like dust before a small group of Spaniards; or think of Nazi Germany, which would have committed mass suicide if Hitler's will had prevailed. Thus far we in the Western world are not crumbling, but there are indications that this could happen.

Before we speak any more about the love of life, however, I think we should try to understand what we mean by the word "life." To some people this seems very simple. Life is the opposite of death. The person or animal that is alive can move by himself and react to stimuli; the dead organism can do nothing of the kind, and in addition, it decays and cannot preserve itself, as a stone or a piece of wood can. True enough, that is an elementary way to define life; but I should like to carry the definition a little farther. Life always tends to unite and integrate; in other words, life by necessity is a process of constant growth and change. Indeed, when growth and change cease, there is death. Life does not grow wild and unstructured; every living being has its own form and structure implanted in its chromosomes. It can grow more fully, more perfectly, but it cannot grow into what it was not born to become.

An apple tree can never become a cherry tree; but each can become a more or less beautiful tree, depending on its constitutional endowment and on the

From *McCall's Magazine,* August 1967. Reprinted by permission.

environment in which it lives. The degree of moisture and sun that may be a blessing to one plant will be a curse for another. It is not different with man; but unfortunately most parents and teachers know less about humans than a good gardener knows about plants.

To say that life grows according to a structural pattern, and not wildly and unpredictably, does not mean. however—except in a broad sense—that the very individual aspects of a living being are predictable. This is one of the great paradoxes of all life. It is predictable—yet it is not. We know more or less, in a broad outline, what any living being is to become; yet life is full of surprises—it is disorderly compared with the order that nonliving matter presents.

If one is so filled with expectations of "order"—which is, after all, a category of his own mind—that he expects order in a living being, he will be disappointed. If his desire for order is very strong, he may try to force life into orderly patterns to control it, and in his frustration and fury when he finds out that it cannot be controlled, he may eventually try to strangle and kill it. He has become a hater of life because he could not free himself from the compulsion to control. He has failed in his love for life because, as a French song puts it, "love is the child of liberty."

It should be added that this holds true not only in our attitude toward the life of others, but also toward the life within ourselves. We all know the person who can never be spontaneous, who can never feel free, because he insists on controlling his feelings, thoughts and actions; he can never act unless he knows precisely what the result will be; he cannot stand any doubt; he frantically seeks certainty, often to be tormented by more doubt when this certainty cannot be found. Such people who are obsessed with the need to control may be kind or cruel, but one condition must be fulfilled: the subject of their interest must be controllable. When this need for control reaches a certain point, the psychiatrist says that such a person suffers from an obsessive-compulsive neurosis and a good deal of sadism. This is a good way of expressing it if one is dealing with the classifications of mental illnesses. From a slightly different viewpoint, however, one might say that this person is suffering from his inability to love life, that he is afraid of life, just as he is afraid of everything that he cannot control.

And this brings us to a principle inherent in love, whether it is love for life or love for a person, an animal, a flower. I can love only when my love is adequate and corresponds to the needs and the nature of that which is loved. If a plant needs little moisture, my love is expressed by letting it have the moisture it needs. If I have preconceived ideas of "what is good for the plant"—for instance, the idea that lots of water is good for everything—I will cripple or kill the plant, because I was not capable of loving it in the way it needed to be loved. It is simply not enough "to love"; it is not enough "to want the best" for another living being; unless I know the need of the plant, the animal, the child, the man or woman, and unless I can let go of my wish to control. my love becomes destructive, a kiss of death.

Many people cannot understand why, in spite of loving another person deeply or even passionately. they fail to keep his or her love or even drive him away. They complain about the cruelty of their fate, and they cannot understand why their love fails to evoke love in the other person. If they can stop feeling sorry for themselves and blaming life, it would help them. and it might even change the tragic course of events if they would ask themselves whether their love corresponds to the needs of the loved person or whether it is a result of their own fixed ideas about "what is best."

There is only a small step from controlling to using force. What holds true of the former is equally true of the latter; love and force are irreconcilable contradictions, and perhaps there is no more fundamental polarity in human behavior than that between love and force. Both are deeply rooted in our nature; they are the basic possibilities of approaching the world and coping with it. To most people the principle of force appears so natural and self-evident that they do not even recognize that it is a principle and not just part of "human nature." The principle of force often appears to be the most adequate and simple solution of a problem.

Think of a mother whose child refuses to do what is necessary. What gets better and quicker results than to force him? You have the power; he must give in—why not use it? Of course, there are many ways of making use of your force, some friendlier and some nastier ones. You can begin by persuading him and not even mentioning the threat of force, which you keep only as your last resource; or you can threaten immediately. You can use force moderately and only to the extent to which the purpose requires it; or you can, if you are sadistically inclined, use force immediately and far beyond the needs of a situation. Force is not necessarily a physical threat; it can be psychological, using the child's suggestibility or ignorance to deceive him, lie to him, brainwash him.

In adult life, force is applied even more ruthlessly, since the feelings of tenderness most of us have for children are less likely to soften our attitude toward people our own age, especially strangers. In most social situations, it is the law that mitigates the use of force. There are many instances in which the law inhibits my use of force as a means of getting another person to act according to my will. But the law represents only the very minimum of protection against force. In most personal relationships, the law is not effective. The father who prevents his adolescent son from choosing the career he wants by stopping his allowance, the mother who uses tears and appeals to the son's generosity to dissuade him from marrying the girl of his choice are using force, the employer who threatens to fire a man, the teacher who insists that his students accept his views and gives them poor marks if they fail to do so—all are using force, aware of it or not.

When it comes to the relations between nations, we seem to have even less trouble persuading ourselves that our use of force is justified, whatever the damage to other human beings. We have become so desensitized, in fact, that most of us can enjoy our breakfast while reading newspaper accounts of men, women and children being killed or maimed.

History, however, shows, better than individuals, that efforts to secure permanent superiority through the use of force invariably fail. What in the flush of victory seems to be the foundation for centuries of unchanged stability based on superior force, invariably crumbles after a few decades before the assault of new force or inner devitalization. Hitler's Thousand-Year Reich that lasted only fifteen years is not untypical of triumphs based mainly on force.

Indeed, even when force seemingly brings about the desired results, it has what we would call in a drug dangerous "side effects." On a national scale, it leaves a passionate desire in the injured to retaliate, and at the same time it gives them the moral justification for their own use of force when circumstances permit.

Equally dangerous is the side effect that force has on the people who use it. The user soon begins to confuse the strength of his means of force (wealth, position, prestige, tanks and bombs) with the strength of his own person. In fact, he does not try to make *himself* stronger, his mind, his love, his aliveness; but he puts all his energies into the attempt to make his *means* stronger. He becomes impoverished while his force capacity increases; after he arrives at a point of no return, he can do nothing but continue to deal with the world by force and stake everything on his success with his method. He has become less alive, less interested and interesting, more feared and by many, of course, more admired.

The approach of love is the opposite of the approach by force. Love tries to understand, to convince, to stimulate. In doing so, the loving person constantly transforms himself. He becomes more sensitive, more observing, more productive, more himself. Love is not sentimentality or weakness. It is the method of influencing and changing that does not have the dangerous side effects of forcing. Unlike force, it requires patience, inner effort and, most of all, courage. To choose to solve a problem by love requires the courage to stand frustration, to remain patient in spite of setbacks. It requires real potency, rather than its perverted facsimile: force.

Love is always an active concern for the growth and aliveness of the one we love. It cannot be otherwise, since life itself is a process of becoming, of unification and integration, and the love of life, as I have already tried to show, is the kernel of all love; it is the love for the life in a person, in an animal, in a flower. Anyone who believes he loves a person and who does not also love life may desire, want, cling to a person—but he does not love him.

That this is so is known to us, although we are often not consciously aware of this knowledge. When someone says about a person that "he really loves life," most people understand precisely what is meant. We refer to a person who loves all phenomena of growth and aliveness, one who is attracted to a growing child, the growth in an adult, a growing idea, a growing organization. To him, even that which is not alive, like a stone or water, becomes alive and that which is alive attracts him not because it is big and powerful, but because it is alive. Often you can even recognize the lover of life by his facial expression. There is a radiance in his eye and also in his skin, something glowing in and around him. When people "fall in love," they have life, and that is the reason they attract each other. But if this love of life is too weak to last, they fall out of love again and do not understand why their faces are the same and yet not the same any longer.

Is the love of life something in which people differ only in degree? How good if this were so; but, infortunately, there are people who do *not* love life, who "love" death, destruction, illness, decay, disintegration. They are not attracted by growth and aliveness, except that they dislike and want to strangle them. They hate life because they cannot enjoy it or control it. They suffer from the only true perversion that exists—i.e., to be attracted to death rather than to life. In my book *The Heart of Man*, I have called these people *necrophiles*, "lovers of death," and indicated that the necrophilous orientation, in its extreme forms, is, from a psychiatric point of view, indicative of severe mental illness.

If you observe and watch, you will discover that you have known lovers of death as well as lovers of life; but perhaps you did not dare to think in these terms, because on the surface everyone is "nice" and "loving," and when it happens that a man is gripped by the desire to kill people, we tend to shrug off his condition by calling him "sick." He may be sick, but how can we be sure that we, too, do not suffer from this same sickness? What makes us so certain we are lovers of life rather than lovers of death?

Actually, there are grave symptoms in our culture today that suggest we are already infected by an insidious attraction to that which is not alive. We see manifestations of this attraction all around us: destructive violence and sadism on the international level, crime and cruelty on the national level; the degree of tension and anxiety, which can almost be measured quantitatively by the amount of tranquilizing pills sold in our country; drug addiction, which is an effort to substitute thrills and excitement for a genuine love of life. We do not need statistics to be convinced. Most of us show the symptoms in one degree or another. Consider the need so many of us have to take a drink before we can be comfortable in company; our synthetic expressions of gaiety and sorrow when the occasion seems to demand them; our tendency to *think* rather than to *feel* what is appropriate to the situation (a wedding, a funeral, the painting of a celebrated artist); the increasing use of sex to achieve intimacy and excitement without any feeling toward the other person except desire.

To some extent, of course, these symptoms are individual problems; but to a larger extent they are the result of our way of living in the industrial age. First of all, we are more concerned with *results* than with the *process* that leads to them. These results, in the sphere of industrial production, are brought about by machines and gadgets, and it has reached a point where we consider ourselves as machines, too, expect quick results and look for gadgets that produce the desired effect.

But we are not machines! Life is not a means to an end; it is an end in itself; the process of living, that is, of changing, growing, developing, being more aware and more awake, is more important than any mechanical achievement or result—if, and this is a very important qualification, we love life. If you were asked why you love another person and answered, "Because he is successful, famous, rich," you would probably feel a little uneasy because you know all this has nothing to do with love. But if you would say, "Because he is very alive," that you love his smile, his voice, his hands, his eyes because they radiate life— then, indeed, you would have given a reason. It is not different with yourself. You are interesting because you are interested. You are loved because you can love and because in yourself and in the other person you love life.

This attitude, however, is difficult to experience in a culture that emphasizes results instead of processes, things instead of life, that makes means into ends and that teaches us to use the brain when the heart should be involved. Love for another person and love for life are not something that can be achieved in a hurry. Sex, yes, but not love. Love requires a pleasure in stillness, an ability to enjoy *being* instead of *doing, having* or *using*.

Another factor that makes it difficult to love life is our increasing, never satisfied appetite for things. True enough, things can, and should, serve man; but if they become ends rather than remain means, they tend to sap man's interest in and love for life and to make him an appendix of the machine, a thing. Things can produce many results, but they cannot love, either a person or life. We have been so indoctrinated as consumers that we have come to believe that almost no pleasure is complete unless it includes something you can buy. We have lost the knowledge that a few generations ago was quite widespread—i.e., that the most exquisite pleasures of life do not require gadgets. But they do require the capacity for stillness, for "letting go," for concentration.

Travel to the moon, which excites the fantasy of millions of people, is more fascinating to most than giving oneself fully to looking at a person, a flower, a river or into oneself. Certainly, in the travel-to-the-moon orientation there are intelligence, perseverance, courage, daring, but there is no love. Travel to the moon is only a symbol of living with mechanical gadgets, admiring them and using them. This world of man-made things and their use is our pride and our danger. The more the "thing" aspect of the world becomes prominent, the more we are interested in the manipulation of these things, the less we experience the quality of life and the less can we love life. Indeed, there is reason to suspect that we are more fond of the technical miracles that can destroy life than we are of life itself. Could it be that the people of the industrialized world do not succeed in achieving effective nuclear disarmament because life has lost much of its attraction and things have become the object of our admiration?

Still another obstacle to loving life is the ever-increasing bureaucratization of our activities. You can choose nicer names for it; "teamwork," "group spirit" or whatever you like. The essential fact, however, is that, for the sake of maximal economic efficiency, we tend to cut each individual down to the proper size that makes it possible for him to become one of the group—efficient, disciplined, but not himself, not fully alive and hence paralyzed in his capacity to love life.

But what can we do to change all this, you may well ask at this point. Is it necessary to give up our system of mass production, our technical achievements, in order to love life again? I do not think so. But what *is* necessary is to be aware of the danger, to put material things in their place, to cease transforming ourselves into things and manipulators of things. If instead of manipulating, we love all that is alive, then even a thing—a glass, for instance—can become alive through our life-giving approach to it, such as the artist has. Then we shall learn that if you look at someone or something long enough, he or it will talk to you. But you must truly look, forget about getting something out of it and be able to be really still. If you find it necessary to describe your feelings with enraptured statements like "Isn't it divine" or "I am dying to see it again," then your sentiments are not likely to be worth much; if you can look at a tree in such a way that it seems to be looking back at you, you probably will not feel like saying anything.

There are no prescriptions for loving life, but much can be learned. If you can shed illusions, seeing others and yourself as they are and you are, if you can learn how to be still rather than always "going places," if you can grasp the distinction between life and things, between happiness and thrill, between means and ends, and—most of all—between love and force, you will have made the first steps toward loving life. After you have made these first steps, ask again. You will find meaningful answers in a number of books—and most of all within yourself.

One question should not be ignored: You might be afraid that the more one loves life the more one suffers from the hourly assault on truth, beauty, integrity and life. Indeed this is so and especially today. But to save oneself from pain by becoming indifferent to life produces only greater pain. Any severely depressed person can tell you that to feel sad would be a relief from the torture of feeling *nothing*. Happiness is not the most important thing in life—aliveness is. Suffering is not the worst thing in life—indifference is.

One more remark: If we suffer, we might try to stop the causes of suffering. If we feel nothing, we are paralyzed. Thus far in human history, suffering has been the midwife of change. Should, for the first time, indifference destroy man's capacity to change his fate?

Suggested Readings for Chapter 6

Bardwick, Judith M. *Psychology of women: A study of biocultural conflicts.* New York: Harper & Row, 1972. This book throws the many aspects of the psychology of women into bold relief.

Birren, J. E. *The psychology of aging.* Englewood Cliffs, N.J.: Prentice-Hall, 1964. A presentation of the characteristics and problems of the aging individual.

Fromm, E. *The art of loving.* New York: Harper, 1956. A bestseller which examines many of the different meanings and expressions of love. Some of Dr. Fromm's ideas are presented in his article in this chapter.

Southwell, E. & Merbaum, M. *Personality: Readings in theory and research.* (2d ed.) Belmont, Calif.: Wadsworth, 1971. A presentation of significant theories of personality with related research and articles of criticism.

White, R. W. *Lives in progress.* New York: Holt, Rinehart and Winston, 1966. A complete presentation of three case studies of essentially normal people, illustrating the manifold factors that contribute to personal growth.

Discussion Questions

1. What are the problems created for men by women's liberation, and what are some possible benefits?

2. What are the benefits of women's liberation for women, and what are some possible drawbacks?

3. What is love? Why do some people experience it constructively, while others cannot promote growth through it?

4. What is it like to be a minority-group member in a majority-group society? Have you ever experienced that feeling, and how did you cope with it?

Chapter 7
Marriage
and the Family

The family is the major social unit in our society. A person's development occurs within the structure of the family and is strongly influenced by it. In fact, one of the most important personal decisions that faces any individual is the choice of a spouse. Since a great deal of the time, energy, and gratification of the adult occurs within the family unit, an understanding of the family is of critical importance to psychology. For some reason, however, the amount of research effort expended in this area does not seem to be consistent with the importance of the topic. There has been a good deal of speculative anecdotal material along with some clinical case histories, but little in the way of sound research. Sociologists have been much less at fault in this area, and many of the articles presented in this chapter are the product of sociologists rather than psychologists.

The first paper, by Lael Scott, entitled "What You Should Know before You Marry," is a description of the pros and cons of premarital counselling. With the divorce rate reaching epic proportions in the United States and many other parts of the Western world, it is obvious that the institution of marriage is undergoing some drastic revisions. In particular, census data indicate that girls who marry in their teens and boys who marry before the age of twenty-two are twice as likely to get divorced. In order to help young adults approach marriage with a more mature attitude, premarital counselling can be a valuable experience. What does a premarital counselor do, and what are the kinds of problems which can be handled within a counselling situation? Premarital counselling, like any other therapeutic encounter which examines feelings and attitudes, is not easy to define. However, any good premarital counselor would probably examine attitudes about sex and about the handling of finances, and also try to stimulate open discussion about issues that might be hidden or partially disguised. The importance of direct communication, realistic appraisal of competition and conflict, and the mutual understanding of the nature of love and sex would undoubtedly be a primary focus. This article presents a balanced description of the premarital counselling experience and offers practical details as to who is trained to do marital counselling, what agencies provide this service and other useful information.

One of the proposed solutions to the "marriage in crisis" in our society is to change the institution by providing new alternatives for traditional marital life styles. The article "Brave New Marriage" by Melvin Maddocks examines some of the more recent ideas and proposals for marital change by various liberal activists and women's liberation advocates.

In the past few years psychological research on the topic of sexual behavior has increased substantially. One recent study, conducted by Dr. Seymour Fisher, focuses on the psychology and physiology of the female orgasm. The women in Fisher's study took many psychological tests and were interviewed in depth about their early life experiences, their adulthood, and how they felt about their bodies. The interviews took place during pregnancy, during menstruation, and were repeated over a significant length of time to establish the consistency and change in sexual feelings. One of the most important findings was that a woman's orgasm appears related to the amount of self-confidence she has in feeling that the people she loves and feels comfortable with will not leave or abandon her. Some aspects of this study are discussed in the article by Norman Lobsenz.

The final article in this chapter, by Hugh Carter, examines some of the important facts about divorce. He does not, however, attempt to build a theory about marriage and the family out of an examination of these facts. Two points are made striking by this approach. First, the facts about divorce are a good deal different from many common beliefs, indicating the necessity for research and its advantage over speculation as the source of information. Second, the call for increased information about divorce through better public records is similar to the call for increased research about sexual behavior. This reflects a general recognition that research is appropriate in areas which previously have been considered private, and is in fact necessary for any meaningful understanding of these areas.

"Penny and Jim: this pregnancy thing was just an accident."

Marriage counselling is a professional therapeutic activity which can often be extremely helpful. Entering into marriage can be a difficult decision with current as well as future problems to contend with. This article describes some of the important aspects of marriage counselling and some of the things to look for if and when one decides counselling might be helpful.

At a time when teen-age marital discord has reached almost epidemic proportions, more young people than ever before are turning to premarital counseling.

A technique that has come into its own in the last decade, premarital counseling can be a significant step toward divorce prevention. As a method of working with couples *before* marriage, it is the natural child of both marital and family therapy.

Certainly, recent statistics from the United States Census Bureau point out the urgent need for such counseling. These figures show that girls who marry while in their teens and boys who marry before they're twenty-two are twice as likely to divorce than those who wait. As Dr. Mary Calderone, executive director of SIECUS (Sex Information and Education Council of the U.S.), quipped: "If teen-age marriage were a ship of state, Lloyd's of London would probably refuse to insure it."

Success in marriage isn't something you learn from books; it's not just a golden promise that will be magically fulfilled for you. Real success comes from knowing, in every sense, the one you love, and he you. This state of complete knowing doesn't just happen; it requires work. That's where the premarital counselor plays such a vital role. "As marriage approaches," explains counseling expert Dr. Aaron Rutledge of the Grosse Pointe (Michigan) Psychological Center, "all the forces of nature—sex, love, self-fulfillment, relating—are available to be guided into renewed personality growth. There's still time to effect adult personality changes, which is at the same time an investment in soon-to-be-born children: a chance to influence both the chicken and the egg."

Now tune into some of the ominous warning signals that have been uttered by young people, all in their teens, prior to their own Big Day. You may find that you are in a similar situation.

Mary: We're so much in love. John's just the kind of boy I always wanted. He's tall and handsome, and my parents are kind of impressed by his family. He's what I'd call the strong, silent type. We never seem to disagree. I'm beginning to wonder if that's because we never really discuss anything—anything important, I mean. Maybe it's because each of us is afraid we'll rock the boat if we do—after all, the wedding is in three weeks . . .

George: I want to marry Gail because she's so mature, even though she's only eighteen. She seems to be able to handle everything so cool-like. She's a lot like my mother, but not so bossy. And Gail doesn't treat me like a kid. But between you and me, I'm still seeing some of my old girl friends. Guess I'm kind of kicking up my heels for the last time; Gail would die if she found out. I'd actually like to postpone the date till I get it all out of my system, but the invitations have been printed—everyone knows we've set a day—and my mother would kill me if I didn't go through with it now . . .

Janice: I'd like to work, but Joe believes a wife should stay home. I'm sure I'll be able to change his mind *after* we're married . . .

Bob: Sure, she has a small sexual problem now, but I know I'll be able to change all that . . .

Sheila: My parents say I have to marry Steve because I'm pregnant. But I don't love him. I feel pretty panicky . . .

Penny and Jim: This pregnancy thing was just an accident. We really do want to marry each other but think maybe we ought to put the baby up for adoption so that later on we won't feel it's got us trapped. Then we can plan for other babies, later on . . .

Joyce: I didn't think we ought to have sex, but when Josh proposed marriage, well, then we started having a sexual relationship too. We've even planned what we're going to call our first child. I'm so happy. We are really in love, aren't we? It all seems like a fairy tale . . .

If you listen closely, you can detect undertones that are, perhaps, just beginning to trouble these couples, areas that could be explored with a counselor who is qualified to help them discover, together and separately, the depth of what's worrying them.

Who, then, should consult a premarital counselor? The professionals in the field are rather evenly split on the answer to this question. "I think *everyone* intending to marry should see one," says Dr. Laura Singer-Magdoff, the new president of the American Association of Marriage and Family Counselors (AAMFC), a standard-setting organization with some 1,500 members. Those professionals who don't agree that everyone should seek premarital counseling do, however, concur on the following: Any couple (often it's only one of the partners) who feels there are real questions about the proposed marriage, or even some nagging doubts—whether they be about sex, money, in-laws or who's going to run the home—should definitely see a counselor. Many times these doubts will turn out to have no real substance; they may be simply normal symptoms of bride or bridegroom jitters. You owe it to yourself, however, to check them out with a trained professional.

Qualified premarital counselors come from many fields: they may be ministers, psychologists, psychiatrists, gynecologists or social workers. What they have in common is substantial supervised clinical training in family and couples therapy, which they may have received from medical schools or reputable family-centered institutions like the Marriage Council of Philadelphia, the American Foundation of Religion and Psychiatry, or the Family Institute, Inc.

A premarital counselor wants to find out about your own and your fiancé's hidden selves and to help you understand each other's needs. The counselor will also try to nudge some of your more inflexible attitudes, the ones which could eventually get in the way of a growing marriage. He or she will remind you, too, of the humorous side of marriage; after all, not every problem need be the death knell of your relationship. Premarital counseling is, in a way, like a polio shot; it is preventive medicine. Except that by the time such counseling is required, the paralysis has probably already started to set in.

Here is the typical procedure followed during the four sessions usually suggested.

At the first meeting the counselor evaluates how well the boy and girl open up to each other. Often the couple presents small problems: differences over whom to invite to the wedding; should both of them work; the girl's fear that the boy depends more on his mother's opinion than on hers. Very important during this initial session, according to noted psychologist Dr. Wardell Pomeroy, is how the two go about solving problems. Frequently they don't, says Dr. Pomeroy. Rather, they may look to him as a judge—someone who will tell them that the boy is right and the girl wrong, or determine whether they're "really in love." This is clearly not the counselor's role, which is explained at the outset.

The second and third visits are devoted to each partner separately. Problems mentioned quite casually in the opening session are gone into more deeply. For instance, a boy and girl from Long Island, New York—she seventeen and he nineteen—went to a Jewish Family Service agency to talk about their upcoming marriage. John said he really didn't want Judith to work. When John went alone for the second visit, he confided that what actually bugged him was that Judith would have to work in order to put him through college. He felt terribly guilty— "I'll be living off her!"—yet he hadn't been able to tell his fiancée about these feelings. The other side of the coin was revealed during Judith's single session, when she disclosed that she had every intention of going to college herself after John finished. Not only that, but she was eagerly looking forward to working in the interim. In no sense did she feel used, as John was seeing the situation. Trouble was, she had never told John what she wanted for herself. She had always put his needs first, figuring everything could be worked out after they were married. The confusion engendered by their mutual silence—all based on their fear that anything said out loud might break them up—was quite suddenly and easily lifted.

By the fourth session, the pair had learned new, more constructive techniques for communicating with each other.

The experience of Carl and Ingrid, a young couple from the West Coast, clearly illustrates how important counseling can be in helping build a future together. "We were very different when we first met," says Carl, a twenty-two-year-old college student. "I was a street person from L.A. I had hung around with a block gang. And Ingrid? She was so clean, and so quiet. I was the loud-mouth." The two saw a lot of each other over the next six months; they decided they would probably marry, so they went about finding an apartment together. The bliss of planning a marriage, of "playing house," as Ingrid puts it, outshone the bitter moments. Like the time Carl said he had to move back with his mother because she was sick. Ingrid didn't think he had to do it. Carl now admits he wanted to get away.

When he returned he found Ingrid growing more and more sullen. "I didn't know why," she told me. "I just felt there was less joy in our lives." Carl added, "It was going downhill and I knew it too. I told Ingrid that we owed it to ourselves and our future to see someone before we got married."

They consulted a therapist at Carl's college who frequently worked with engaged couples. They saw him separately and together once a week for several months—longer than the more usual four to six weeks. Ingrid, it turned out, needed time to gain inner strength and self-confidence. She had been brought up to keep her feelings to herself; it was rare that she expressed any anger toward Carl. When she felt stronger, however, she announced to the therapist and a shocked Carl that she was going to go into analysis and that she also wanted to live by herself—at least for a time. The presence of the counselor allowed the two to break up more easily than might have been the case otherwise. "We separated as rational human beings, not fighting animals," Ingrid recalls. "I was very angry with the counselor at first," Carl admits. "I thought it was his job to help us make it. But it was true what he had been indicating to me. I had no understanding of Ingrid's feelings."

The pair stopped seeing each other for a while, then started up again. "Now she stands up to me," Carl says with obvious relief. "There's no more Miss Goody-Goody Two Shoes about her. And friends notice that we're really talking to each other for the first time."

Carl and Ingrid returned to the counselor, seeing him a total of about six months—and then at their wedding. They saw him once again a year later for what they called "a thousand-mile checkup." They're still checking out okay.

I asked Dr. Pomeroy—himself married thirty-three years—what he looks for in the relationship of a young, about-to-be-married couple.

I want to see how well they communicate with each other, first (he said). Second, how freed are they from their parents? The process of becoming an adult is the process of losing parents as parents. You can retain them as friends or peers or enemies, but you must lose them as Mommy and Daddy. Third, I look for what their concept of marriage is—their expectations. More and more—perhaps because of the impact of women's lib, I look for an egalitarian approach to solving problems. What if they think that marriage per se will resolve all their difficulties? Then they're in trouble and have to be brought back to reality. Marriage isn't a magic wand.

Young people today, on the whole, are much more open about sex and intimacy. Yet, says Dr. Pomeroy, young people have many of the same sexual inhibitions they've always had. Dr. David Reed, assistant director of the Marriage Council of Philadelphia, says that 90 percent of the premarital couples who come to the Council are engaging in sex—and having problems with it. Much of this, he feels, is caused by what he calls a magical obedience to romantic love. "If either the boy or the girl says, 'You're the only one I'll ever love,' then there's got to be an implication of immaturity. As a counselor, I get very uneasy when I hear that. It often means the impending marriage is a set-up by one or the other's family."

The prestigious Marriage Council of Philadelphia and Jewish Family Services agencies agree that often the easiest, most effective way of working with engaged couples is in small groups of four or more pairs. The reasons are apparent. If, for instance, you and your fiancé come from different religious backgrounds, you may also have different ideas about the use or nonuse of birth control. This might be an area the two of you haven't yet recognized as a potential problem. But if you are in a couples group, and another girl starts discussing the advantages of, say, oral contraceptives, you might find yourself agreeing with her while your fiance takes a strong stand against her views. Signals go off in your head: you and he had better face this issue—right now! And what could be a better place than here, in front of a trained counselor, with the added support of other couples concerned about similar problems?

In the last few years, according to Dr. Reed of the Marriage Council of Philadelphia, his organization has emphasized what he calls pre-premarital counseling. This is more of an educational process than the specific premarital counseling which is often employed during crisis situations. In addition to sending counselors out to schools to lecture on problems concerning interpersonal relations, the Council also holds group sessions for couples who are living together or intending to marry. Male and female team leaders get groups of from four to twenty-five couples to interact with each other through the use of role-playing games. For example, one of the engaged couples will volunteer to thrash out—by play-acting—a typical teenage problem. Take "Should we live together before marriage?"

Boy: A marriage ceremony is not that necessary if we love each other.

Girl: But I'm afraid of what my parents and friends will think. And besides, there's always a possibility I might get pregnant.

Boy: I think we should live together so we can really enjoy each other right away. And it'll save money.

Girl: Then the romance will fade and the boredom of marriage will probably set in *before we're even married.*

As the couple role-plays the particular situation, other members of the group throw in suggestions which often turn out to be extensions of their own personal anxieties about the subject.

Pre-premarital or "un-marital" counseling should be available in every high school, says AAMFC's president Dr. Singer-Magdoff. She feels that such inter-relationship training should be included in family living and sex education programs, since "we're not taught how to relate to one another; we're just never given that opportunity as we grow up."

"Barbers, bartenders and ministers all think they can do marriage counseling," says the Rev. C. Clifford McLaughlan, a teacher and counselor with the American Foundation of Religion and Psychiatry. Dr. McLaughlan, along with other professionals, suggests the following methods for finding a premarital counselor:

1. Write the American Association of Marriage and Family Counselors for the names of qualified premarital counselors in your area and general guidelines for seeking their help. Address: AAMFC, 6211 West Northwest Highway, Suite 2900, Dallas, Texas 75225. If you and engaged friends of yours are interested in starting your own couples group, write to Dr.

Laura Singer-Magdoff, in care of the AAMFC, for the name of a group leader to work with you.
2. The Family Services Association in your area can refer you to well-trained professionals.
3. The Jewish Family Services and Catholic Charities agencies also make referrals from most of their offices.
4. Ministers, doctors and teachers can usually refer you to a qualified person if they themselves are not trained in this area. Watch out for those who aren't trained, but who, because of the nature of their work, may feel a need to help you themselves. Don't be timid. If you think you need more help than they can offer, ask for a referral.

Expect to pay around $35 for private session per couple with a competent professional. In groups the cost is less—something from $10 to $20 a session for each couple, down to zero—depending on your income.

Charlatans can still be found in the field of marriage counseling, mainly because very few states have license requirements. Even recent licensing laws set standards so low that few of the incompetents have been weeded out. The number one rule for avoiding a charlatan is: don't turn to your telephone book yellow pages. Anyone can advertise there.

When you have received a proper referral from any of the above groups, ask the counselor what kind of theoretical—and especially, clinical—training he or she has had in marriage and family therapy. A psychiatrist, for example, is not necessarily qualified to help you, unless he has had that type of additional training.

Divorce is bad news, no matter how you look at it, and no one can guarantee that there won't be one in your future. California's divorce rate is so astronomical that not long ago it passed a law *requiring* premarital counseling for couples if one partner or both are under eighteen. The couple must still obtain parental permission to marry, plus the permission of a judge of the Superior Court, who bases his decision heavily on a confidential report coming out of the counseling sessions.

California is the only state thus far with such a law. But the majority of premarital counselors there, according to one official, is already looking forward to the day when counseling will be a nationwide requirement for every couple intending to marry. Whether or not other states follow suit, the idea does excite the imagination, in much the same way that an experimental vaccine does. There is great hope that it will, if not totally eradicate the disease, at least help to control the epidemic of teenage divorce.

"Romeo and Juliet are alive and well in a Westchester suburb— $60,000 English Tudor house with real crushed seashells in the driveway."

Recently there have been a series of books questioning the conventional institution of marriage and suggesting possible alternatives. This article by Maddocks evaluates some of the proposals suggested in these books, and critically evaluates the conclusions and future prospects for different forms of marital relationships.

Who can help knowing by heart the myth of the American marriage? For those with a taste for metamorphosis, the standard scenario goes like this:

Romeo and Juliet are alive and well in a Westchester suburb—$60,000 English Tudor house with real crushed sea shells in the driveway. Despite early marriage and two children (a boy for him, a girl for her), R. has managed to acquire a college degree and a $27,000-a-year job with a New York life insurance company as an actuary, an absolute genius at double indemnity. He is in his late thirties and slightly gone to paunch: waistline expanding, hairline receding. After three drinks tiny red veins appear on his cheeks. The boy who used to climb balconies now commutes on what is left of the New Haven Railroad, solving the crossword puzzle in the New York *Times*.

Juliet is still slim but severe, almost knife-edge, wearing the slightly vengeful look of a woman to whom all-night lovemaking is an event of the past— about fifteen years past. She is forever frantically smoothing things down: her hair, her furniture, her husband and children. If R. is going soft, J. is going hard; and both are turning sour. They have Made It, and so what? The passionate lovers have become sick-and-tired dialecticians. What they do now until the lark sings is argue.

At this point in the familiar scenario two endings become available to scriptwriters:

Option A: One perfectly tip-top spring afternoon while strolling through Rockefeller Center, Romeo meets Rosaline again (or Juliet meets Mercutio—that boy always had a certain something), and the trusty old heart cries: "I married the wrong woman!" or "I married the wrong man!" as the case may be.

Option B: One dark night Romeo Jr., thirteen, almost dies during an appendectomy. The next morning R. and J., haggard but hyper-alive with relief, take a second cup of coffee under the rose arbor. The Westchester sky is memorably blue. Juliet Jr., ten, followed by her beagle, Friar Laurence, comes running to Mummy with a single flawless tulip in her hands, and Mummy thinks: "This is all there is, and it's enough."

In either option, the moral stays the same: marriage is Right, but people can be Wrong. When people "grow up," when they find out who they really are and what they really want, they learn this.

How suddenly quaint the premise sounds today! When R. and J. '72 glare across their pillows at three o'clock in the morning, her punch line is no longer, "I married the wrong man," but, "I married." Period. And there's no nonsense about "This-is-all-there-is-and-it's-enough." The line now reads: "This is all there *is*? It's *not* enough."

The same Americans who all these years blamed their bad marriages on themselves, now, if they seem less than happy or good, blame themselves on marriage. *Is marriage really necessary?* At one time only Bohemians and socialists—people like that—asked the question. Now it has become the property of the middle class: the people who twenty years ago talked about togetherness; the people who ten years ago thought once you had *her* orgasm straightened out, that was that; the people who faithfully kept saying that marriage has its ups and downs and, you know it's a compromise and you have to work at it but, taken all in all, it's still the best shot at happiness. These are the people who are now saying, "Marriage is hell"—and maybe the hell with it. It is "as obsolete as the piston-engine plane." It is "the triumph of hypocrisy." It is "a ghetto of lunacy." Suddenly priests seem to be the only people left who really want to get married. In effect, a new myth of American marriage is being written with a credo that goes more or less like this:

Brave Old Monogamy was serviceable in its day: on the frontier certainly and probably for as long as America was "agrarian." But the "nuclear" family loses its social and economic advantages in an "urban-industrial" culture.

Furthermore, marriage suits Americans less and less as a psychological arrangement. Monogamous expectations are badly out of line with man's (and woman's) sexual nature. The marriage contract—the very word is repulsive—has become a false and punitive convention. "Holy matrimony" is no longer a sacrament but a "piece of paper," a contradiction in terms: legalized love.

Marriage has become one of those antiquated institutions—another dirty word—that bricks people in. They are forced to play out obsolescent "roles," neglecting their own self-interest. Indeed they are not allowed to "be themselves." Condemned, before they start, to boredom and resentment, they are also doomed in a reprehensible number of instances to divorce.

A whole new genre—a kind of Brave New Marriage Lit.—has been invented to confirm the disenchantment with traditional monogamy and to codify the new "alternatives." As with most movements of piquant discontent today, the generous impulse of Brave New Marriage Lit. is to "liberate" men and women not only from their actual traps but from their "hang-ups" too. Brave New Marriage Lit. is the seventies equivalent of Norman Vincent Peale or Dale Carnegie: it is here to *help*. How? Consider *Open Marriage: A New Life Style for Couples* (Evans, $6.95) by Nena and George O'Neill. In the political spectrum of Brave New Marriage, the O'Neills are liberals rather than radicals. They are for small mercies: extending the permissible boundaries of proper conduct, raising the ratio of pleasure to sacrifice without disturbing the conscience. They want to ease the general strain by semantics, by redefinition.

Noting the increased life-span of today's couples—to say nothing of their accelerated capacity for using up experience—Brave New Marriage moderates like Margaret Mead have protested that "till death do us part" is getting to be an awfully long time. As a first small mercy the moderates proposed "serial monogamy." Liberals like the O'Neills have moved one step beyond this "plural-ism"-in-sequence. Protesting that Brave Old Monogamy or "closed" marriage means "rigid role behavior," "excessive togetherness," and "possessiveness," they advise pluralism with marriage—"a little additional sharing," as they put it.

Does "open" marriage include adultery? The O'Neills are anxious to play down the question. With anthropologists' detachment they indicate that adultery is "another option that you may or may not choose to explore." In redefining fidelity with kindly vagueness as "commitment to your own growth, equal com-mitment to your partner's growth," they are, to all intents, granting the sort of under-the-counter permission to extramarital sex that "situation ethics" moral-ists granted to premarital sex a decade ago.

The O'Neills see the need of their constituency as gratification with honor. Reconcilers of the new and old moralities, they do their best to demonstrate that ecstasy and self-improvement are often the same thing. Their thesis can be read as a compassionate resolution of Freud's dilemma: that civilization has been "built up upon a renunciation of instinct."

The O'Neill school of Brave New Marriage Lit. belongs to what is loosely referred to as the sexual revolution. Another school of compassion takes its direction from another revolution: Women's Liberation. If the assumption of the O'Neills is that marriage forces couples to do an injustice to nature, the assump-tion of Jessie Bernard is that marriage forces partners to do an injustice to each other—particularly the husband to the wife. "Being married," she states in *The Future of Marriage* (World, $9.95), "is only half as good for wives as for hus-bands." As a frankly partisan sociologist she sees her mission to "reorient the public's thinking."

All the options get chalked on the blackboard: traditional nuclear family; serial monogamy; communes and cooperative households; short-term contracts; ménage à trois; group marriage; swinging; even celibate marriage. At the bottom, Dr. Bernard prints in block letters—underlined until the chalk breaks—her own opinion: "Needed: new social spectacles." Then she asks her pointed question: what will these "alternatives" do for women? She is not at all sure; the book ends under the caption: "No final conclusion."

The New Woman, she does suppose, will avoid "sensory overload"—that is, sex is not the solution. Rather, the answer is "personhood," and "temporarily permanent" relationships may best lead to "personhood." At any rate, the New Woman will not describe herself as "married." Perhaps "pair-bound" will do. "Once we have words for the new statuses," Dr. Bernard writes, with at least as much goodwill as naïveté, "we can clarify their nature."

All these are reasonable and humane objectives as stated; one is tempted to say that the chief motive of the Brave New Marriage author is to relieve suffering. So far, the new "alternatives" under scrutiny are just that: practical solutions designed for specific problems. If this were all there was to Brave New Marriage, it would be just another case of American pragmatism: a few inspirational mottoes and a lot of intuitive tinkering. But beneath the conspicuous common sense there is concealed an astonishing ideology—at times, virtually a secular vision of salvation—which threatens to set up an equally romantic myth to replace the one it has rejected. Its metaphysics may be paraphrased as follows:

Man is innocent—or at least lovers are. All they need is their freedom. The restrictions that frustrate them also corrupt them, making them feel anxious, guilty, and causing them to behave vengefully toward one another.

Sexual love is a benign act. "Make love, not war"—meaning, as long as you're making love, you will never make war. The lover is man at his purest-in-heart; allow him his pleasure, and his "hang-ups" and "hostility" will disappear. (Freud may be parenthetically recalled here to voice his dissent. Though he stipulated that civilization was built upon "renunciation of instinct," he went on to say that if we were to allow "complete freedom of sexual life, thus abolishing the family, the germ-cell of civilization, we cannot, it is true, easily foresee what new paths the development of civilization could take; but one thing we can expect, and that is that this indestructible feature of human nature [aggressiveness] will follow it there.")

With graphic little arrows the O'Neills diagram the promises of Brave New Marriage:

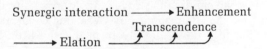

These promises may be as extravagant, as perfectionist as any promises in the history of marriage, and that, as the O'Neills would be the first to point out, is saying a lot. What does the pie in the sky cost? Little more than the courage to throw off your chains, to "be yourself." Or so the manifestos read in bold type.

Alas, nothing exposes more mercilessly the romanticism of Brave New Marriage than a comparison of its bargain price tag with its hidden costs. In exchange for releasing poor harassed humans from the harsh injunctions of monogamy, Brave New Marriage—without apparently noticing the fact—imposes even more exacting imperatives. Examine the fine print in this casually worded rule for "pluralism" drafted by the O'Neills: "If partners in an open marriage do have outside sexual relationships, it is on the basis of their own internal relationship—that is, because they have experienced mature love, have real trust, and are able to expand themselves, to love and enjoy others and to bring that love and pleasure back into their marriage, without jealousy."

In other words: thou shalt not be possessive; thou shalt not be jealous; thou shalt not object to thy planned obsolescence; and so on—commandments that by contrast make "thou shalt not commit adultery" look like rolling off a log.

Brave Old Monogamy called for rather ordinary virtues—principally patience. Brave New Marriage, under the advertisement of reducing expectation, calls for a sort of Renaissance man of the heart, with apparently unlimited time and energy, the balance of a tightrope walker, and the tact of a diplomat.

If taken seriously, the ideology of Brave New Marriage could produce anxieties at least as onerous as sexual guilt. They already have, if one believes the advance frontiersmen (or more often frontierswomen) in places like the *Village Voice* who are turning their dissatisfaction with the new "alternative" into a confessional art form. "Sex, yes. Lots of sex, more than ever," reports one self-styled "casualty of the sex war." But, Karen Durbin gloomily continues, it all "seems bleak and a little dead. A year or so ago, so much seemed possible, and even if it didn't seem possible, the try itself was worth making. New worlds were going to be forged. New men, new women, free of sex roles and competition, free of all the sexual levers that a sick, aggressive society had manipulated us with. Now here we are.... Society doesn't have to manipulate us, we can manipulate ourselves."

Then there is Kathrin Perutz, another agonized New Woman, writing practically in blood. As her title indicates—*Marriage Is Hell* (Morrow, $5.95)—she is as down on Brave Old Monogamy as anybody else, and more vehemently, more personally so. Yet a reader could imagine her composing a sequel: *Brave New Marriage Is Hell Too*. For she is half in rebellion against her own rebellion.

She points out what is cruel in the New Freedom: this leaving everything up to "each individual." Speaking of herself as lost in "a sea of alternatives," she complains: "We are given choice and conflict, but not the means to resolve either." Nor does she like the fact that "it's become unusual for an ambitious woman to admit great joy in her child. Why should a 'liberated' woman feel that deep love for her child is somehow ignominious?" She is discontented with the plans for accommodating children to Brave New Marriage by theorists reporting on the good word from the kibbutzim, or by Germaine Greer, recommending that one have one's child, then quite literally farm out the little him or her to an Italian peasant family.

What makes "emancipated" people like Karen Durbin and Kathrin Perutz look Brave New Marriage's gift horses (freedom, pleasure, a serene conscience) so querulously in the face? Perhaps a self-preserving sense that each individual, each generation can afford just so many investments in hope. But perhaps, too, a hunch that Brave New Marriage prophets have less control over their prophecy than they imagine.

Futurologists, for all their lip service to naturalness and spontaneity, tend to be bureaucrats at heart. They are looking for what T. S. Eliot once called a system so perfect that no one will have to be good. And so, in the end, Jessie Bernard wonders if a "national family policy" might not make things easier all around. "Policy in the future," she writes, "is going to make it possible for more and more people to achieve good marriages. ... The shape of the distribution of happiness in marriage will change; the mode will shift to the right. It will be possible for people to be as unhappy as in the past; but fewer will be." In short, the marriage of the guaranteed minimum: freedom and innocence gently nudged along by the "social engineer," supervised no doubt by a U.S. Department of Pair-Bound Relations.

Robert Francoeur, in *Eve's New Rib: Twenty Faces of Sex, Marriage, and Family* (Harcourt Brace Jovanovich, $6.50), goes so far as to suggest that the options he is enumerating will produce "a new world for mankind"—if not indeed a new mankind.

Every ideology earns its embodiment. Medieval Christianity has the Gothic cathedral. American business has the skyscraper. If the reader trusts Dr. Francoeur, Brave New Marriage has the Sandstone Foundation for Community Systems Research north of Los Angeles.

"It is impossible," Dr. Francoeur cries, "to verbalize the realities of the diffused, low-keyed, 'McLuhanesque cool" sensuality-sexuality which permeates the Sandstone community." But he tries.

The physical design of the SFCSR is late-period Hugh Hefner. The main building features a hundred-foot plush-carpeted living room with a mammoth womb of a fireplace; an enormous buffet dining room; and a paneled lounge with strobes and colored lights that illuminate a pool table, a bar, and water beds. Off the lounge is a "cozy" room with wall-to-wall mattresses. Nearby there awaits an indoor swimming pool, warmed to body temperature.

What is happening at that bar, in that ninety-nine-degree swimming pool, on those water beds? "Feedback and constant re-evaluation within a basic but flexible process philosophy."

Here at last we may have arrived in a blaze of jargon at what the signals are all about: philosophy—though not necessarily "flexible process" philosophy. The quarrel over Brave New Marriage is a quarrel over Brave New World. Sexual ethics—the comic debates of reluctant prudes versus determined lechers —are the least of it. What is happiness? What even is pleasure? What—dare one say it—is *real*? These are the ridiculous portentous questions that keep worrying their way into a reader's mind. Along with that other question: *Do these people know?*

It makes a mad scene, begging for satire—but melancholy satire. Two armed camps of sentimentalists—the future people and the past people—dispute whether they are talking about a dream or a nightmare. On the one hand, mod prophets are running to keep up with their own Zeitgeist; on the other hand, Cassandra's warning (about two hundred years too late) against the "deauthorization" of Western civilization. And in the middle: just plain sad, complicated people with people's sad, complicated needs.

A final prediction:

The future people demanding change, more change, are getting to be like those back-seat fanatics in Keystone Kops chase scenes whose lips shape screams of "Faster! Faster!" as the steering wheel comes loose and the tires fall off. Even without their help marriage in America is moving at superspeed.

The will to condemn has gone out of society in the matter of divorce and abortion, and these changes in attitude are slowly being legalized. ("No-fault" divorce laws will come close to sanctioning "serial monogamy.")

People don't lose their jobs or even their "reputations" because of adultery, though they may lose their reputations now by indulging in too much chastity. Sexual varietism, including homosexuality, is "understood" to death.

In practice, moderate Brave New Marriage is here, and the ideologues shouting "Repression!" are fighting a battle largely won. The real danger is that, out of their excesses of utopian zeal, they may change a quite tolerable equilibrium into something worse. To paraphrase Santayana, those who don't know their puritanism are condemned to repeat it. If the Brave New Marriage-makers were dealing with tennis instead of marriage, they would listen to the curses of the players, then sympathetically solve the problem by lowering the net and stipulating "limited and temporary" base lines. They leave their players relieved of all special demands but also near that intolerable point where total freedom becomes total responsibility. You *must* do whatever you think you want to— this last imperative of American puritanism is likely to prove the harshest as well as the most impossible ideal of all.

A final scenario:

Don't look now, but who is that trim and tanned couple in the Sandstone corner, he nicely slimmed down, she nicely rounded out? Paddling in the pool, feeding back and re-evaluating like mad, are R. and J. in their latest metamorphosis. In *Brave New World,* Huxley visualized another Shakespearean character —Edmund in *King Lear*—"sitting in a pneumatic chair, with his arm around a girl's waist, sucking away at his sex-hormone chewing-gum and looking at the feelies."

Let us imagine one last three-o'clock-in-the-morning dialogue, R. and J., as part of their "flexible process philosophy" program, have been reading *Romeo and Juliet* aloud. Now it is "personhood"-assessment time for Shakespeare and, of course, for them. R. rolls over on their water bed with a squish and begins:

"God, all that morbidity. Love and self-sacrifice and *death*. I mean, Shakespeare's perverse."

"It's as if suffering *meant* something, as if unhappiness were a civil right," J. agrees. "But sometimes a sort of—you know—bell rings, and I almost think I get what he's saying . . ."

"Time to swim," R. interrupts brusquely, waking Rosaline on the next mattress. With J. holding one hand and Rosaline the other, he takes the plunge. The ninety-nine-degree blandness dissolves the odd tweak of distress their conversation had given him. He has a sudden, grateful impulse to explain how right, how honest, how—well—moral it is to arrange life as pleasantly as possible. But he can't find the words, so he only says:

"This beats climbing balconies."

And, of course, when you look at it one way, it really does.

"The women took dozens of psychological tests. They were interviewed in depth about their childhood, their marriage, their sexual experiences."

In an earlier paper in this volume Seymour Fisher wrote an article about experiencing your body. Now Norman Lobsenz describes some other important research from the laboratories of Dr. Fisher on the female orgasm. This work by Dr. Fisher is one of the most intensive and well-researched studies that has been carried out on various psychological aspects of the female orgasm.

Despite all the talk these days about female sexuality, little is actually known about its essential nature. The two major studies of the subject—the Kinsey Report's statistical survey, and Masters and Johnson's laboratory research on how a woman's body reacts during sexual arousal and climax—concerned themselves primarily with external, objective facts. But so far, there has been virtually no investigation of how a woman's personality affects her ability to experience sexual satisfaction.

Now, in a survey destined to be a controversial landmark in the field, a clinical psychologist named Seymour Fisher has explored the emotional background of female sexuality. He has tried to discover exactly what a woman *feels* before, during and after intercourse; *why* she feels the way she does; and how those feelings influence her sexual attitudes and capacities. Dr. Fisher's findings, published in a 250,000-word book, *The Female Orgasm: Psychology, Physiology, Fantasy* (Basic Books, Inc.), yield important and surprising insights into a woman's sexual life. Some of these insights help to unravel the complex psychological elements involved in sexual arousal. Others bluntly challenge traditional theories and widely held beliefs that have been the basis both for disparaging the so-called frigid woman and also, paradoxically, for treating her "problem."

Still other of Dr. Fisher's insights raise questions about what up to now have been considered established facts. Indeed, says the psychologist, "There seems to be good reason for questioning practically every accepted idea" about female sexuality. These negative findings may eventually help to allay many fears, prejudices and old wives' tales. More significantly still, Dr. Fisher's research may ultimately lead to new knowledge that will help women better understand their sexuality and improve their ability to enjoy it.

Dr. Fisher, a professor of psychology at the Upstate Medical Center of the State University of New York, in Syracuse, built his monumental study on what he calls the "trust and verve" of 300 middle-class wives who volunteered to take part in it. The women ranged in age from 21 to 45, though most were in their 20s and early 30s. They had been married two to three years on the average, and all had at least a high-school education. But though they came out of a similar social and economic background, the women represented a diversity of emotional personalities. Writes Dr. Fisher: "There were the tense, the relaxed, the loud, the quiet, the shy, the exhibitionistic, the dull, the creative, the warm, the cold. . . ."

For five years he and his research team—laboratory technicians, psychological-testing experts, statisticians and other professionals working under a grant from the National Institute of Mental Health—studied the sexual behavior and personality characteristics of this group. The women took dozens of psychological tests. They were interviewed in depth about their childhood, their marriage, their sexual experiences. They talked about how they felt toward their own bodies, about the ways they preferred to make love. They described the intimate physical aspects of their lovemaking, as well as their feelings and fantasies during intercourse. Many of the tests and interviews were repeated at various times, such as during and after pregnancy and during and after menstruation. Meantime, Dr. Fisher analyzed virtually every scientific survey ever made in the field of female sexuality in the hope that correlating this mass of information for the first time would produce new insights.

With professional caution, Dr. Fisher urges that the conclusions he has drawn from this vast wealth of data be considered only tentative and exploratory. For one thing, the women he studied are a highly limited sampling. For another, he believes it is risky under any circumstances to generalize about the nature of sexual responsiveness in women. Nevertheless, he flatly declares that "I privately believe that the findings will prove to be validly applicable to middle-class women in the United States."

Here are the highlights of his findings:

• A woman's ability to achieve orgasm consistently is linked to how much (or how little) confidence she feels in knowing that persons who are close and important to her will always "be there." The "low-orgasm woman," to use Dr. Fisher's language, is likely to be subconsciously concerned about the dependability of those she loves, and to worry about losing them. (Research over the years has repeatedly indicated that about 30 percent of all wives never, or only occasionally, reach a climax. Despite today's greater sexual knowledge and more open sexual attitudes, the women in the Fisher panel were not much different from the women Dr. Kinsey studied 20 years ago; there were close to 40 percent of Dr. Fisher's group whose capacity for orgasm was inconsistent.) Dr. Fisher's first clue was that the low-orgasm women in his panel were far more preoccupied than other women with hidden fears of loss and separation. In Rorschach tests, where they interpreted inkblots, in making up stories based on pictures they were shown; and in answering questions about the kinds of thing they worried about, low-orgasm women repeatedly mentioned themes of death, estrangement and loneliness. "It is as if these women assumed that union with someone else could not be counted on to persist, but rather to be terminated unexpectedly," he writes.

To Dr. Fisher, this tendency ties in with another key finding. When the women in his study were asked to describe the mental processes involved in achieving climax, most of them emphasized the importance of detaching their conscious attention from their surroundings, and of focusing intently on themselves and their feelings. "In that sense, attaining orgasm means, at least for a short period, giving up some measure of one's attachment to objects 'out there,' " he says.

As sexual excitement builds, everything else becomes vague, distant, fades out. Thus, says Dr. Fisher, a woman's reaching orgasm means giving up her hold on the world around her and letting herself be carried away. And in a woman who subconsciously feels that people and things are undependable or transitory, this fading process can be so alarming that it can prevent her sexual excitement from building up.

There is still another important skein in this pattern: a woman's childhood feelings about her father. Dr. Fisher found a tendency among the high-orgasm women to recall their fathers as having high moral values, being demanding and holding high expectations for them.

"My father was warm," said one such woman, "but he looked down on people who were pals to their children. He said children needed a father." Said another: "I had to live up to strict standards of behavior."

Conversely, low-orgasm women for the most part remembered their fathers as being casual, permissive and short on definite values.

A demanding father, Dr. Fisher speculates, gives his daughter the feeling that he is interested enough in her to devote much of his time and energy to trying to guide her, to help her succeed in life. Even if she resented this discipline, he believes, she would still feel that her father was dependably concerned about her, and that he would go on being that way.

On the other hand, the permissive father may give his daughter the feeling that he is not terribly committed to her, that he does not care too much what happens to her. Just as a child may translate a lack of discipline as a lack of love, she may subconsciously take her father's permissiveness as a lack of real concern about her.

How does this link up with her capacity to achieve orgasm when she is grown? Dr. Fisher points out that when a woman is "carried away" by sexual feelings—when the world around her begins to fade—these sensations are being caused by a man. To reach orgasm, she must trust him. "So it would be logical," Dr. Fisher writes, "that her feelings about the dependability of the prime male figure in her early life . . . should carry over to her later sexual relationship with men. All we can say is that to some significant but unknown degree, the nature of a woman's transactions with her father as she is growing up will probably affect her orgasm capacity. . . . They could even be *the prime determinant* of orgasmic potential."

• Indeed, Dr. Fisher says in one of his more startling conclusions, it's possible that the mere presence of a man during the sexual act creates a psychological barrier. He begins with the fact that research suggests that far more women can reach orgasm through masturbation than by intercourse.

How, then, explain this paradox? It is not that a man is necessarily less skillful in stimulating a woman than she herself can be, says Dr. Fisher. Rather, he sees the answer as a corollary to his main finding—that orgasm is inhibited by a woman's fear of "loss," tied into feelings about her father. Thus a man's presence during sex increases her anxiety to a critical level. "One could say," the psychologist observes, "that she finds herself a more dependable object to which to relate than she does a man."

• Even women who have trouble reaching orgasm find sexual arousal important and rewarding. This rebuts the traditional view that wives who seldom or never achieve climax must be uninterested in lovemaking.

Many low-orgasm women Dr. Fisher interviewed mentioned such emotional rewards as feelings of tenderness and intimacy toward their husbands. Some wives take pleasure in the sensations of their own bodies. "My thoughts are on my movements, my skin," one woman said. "I concentrate on the way our skin feels against each other . . . I make every nerve in my body come alive and think." Other women remarked that the buildup of sexual tension, even without release, was an "intriguing" and "exciting" experience.

For the most part, the Syracuse women were extremely interested in sex. They had frequent sexual fantasies and wanted to make love often. Perhaps because of this attitude, they were willing and able to describe in detail their actions and feelings during sexual arousal.

Almost all enjoyed foreplay, frequently referring to "growing feelings of warmth" around the pelvis and thighs. Others mentioned tickling and tingling sensations. Nevertheless, many of them struggled with unpleasant tensions during arousal. Some were concerned that they would not reach orgasm, or that it would take them so long that their husbands would lose interest.

Orgasm itself was described as everything from "exploding" to "something breaking," "a rigid knot bursting." One out of every five women observed that at the peak of intercourse she felt a sense of merging with her husband, a loss of self. Sometimes this made for heightened intimacy and sometimes for a sense of being "unbelievably alone."

• Dr. Fisher's study goes a long way toward ending a lot of cherished but apparently baseless beliefs about the connections between a woman's ability to achieve climax and various aspects of her personality. For example, there seems to be absolutely no relationship between a woman's potential for orgasm and such things as her age, religious feelings, her parents' attitude toward sex, her sex education, premarital sex experience, traumatic events such as rape or abortion, her physical development, her husband's personality, or even her physiological reaction to erotic material.

Only two items seem to be accurate predictors of a woman's sexual capacity: The more education she has, and the higher her social class, the more orgasmic she is likely to be. To Dr. Fisher, this is further confirmation of his theory about a woman's need to feel certain that those around her are dependable. A lower-class, less-educated woman, he reasons, is more likely to have grown up in a family whose financial situation was uncertain and insecure, where at any moment the father might lose his job, become seriously ill or even desert his family.

Moreover, Dr. Fisher finds no strong correlation between orgasm, or the lack of it, and a number of emotional difficulties: aggressiveness, passivity, guilt, narcissism, a lack of femininity. He tartly observes that "one can no longer glibly speak of orgasm as more likely to occur in women with certain personality traits."

By the same token, one can no longer glibly label some women frigid because of certain personality traits. There is no relationship between a woman's ability to respond sexually and either her emotional maturity or her mental health. Since sex is only one aspect of life, says Dr. Fisher, "there is no persuasive reason for viewing low-orgasm consistency as just another example of a woman's general inability to cope adequately with the world. . . ."

This finding clashes with some major psychiatric theories, and with some of the therapies used to counsel women with sexual problems. "However," Dr. Fisher declares, "it is clearly necessary to challenge those who use limited sexual responsiveness in a woman as a sign of poor mental health."

• The old idea that the "feminine" woman is able to have a more satisfying sex life than the "nonfeminine" is also denied by the Fisher report. "It's unlikely that the housewife or the model is more orgasmic than the woman engineer or taxi driver," he says. Indeed, a woman's sexual response, or lack of it, seems to bear no relation to whether she conforms to the cultural stereotype of the female image. The woman who fits the feminine mold may seriously lack the ability to be sexually aroused. Conversely, women who deliberately reject conventional femininity may be highly responsive.

"It is too easy," Dr. Fisher writes, "to slip into simplistic notions that women are neatly ordered into 'sexy' and 'nonsexy' categories. . . . For example, the extremely sexy woman who always achieves intense orgasms may not get as much satisfaction out of intercourse as the apparently less sexy woman whose orgasms are inconsistent and of less strength."

Furthermore, it's almost impossible to predict, from one aspect of a woman's sexual behavior, how she will react in another aspect. Thus, a woman who likes to make love frequently may have a low rate of orgasm; a woman who has a climax easily may still feel unhappy during or after orgasm. There are also women who reach orgasm easily *and* enjoy it a great deal—yet who still prefer to have sex infrequently.

• Along the same lines, Dr. Fisher's study puts to rest the popular theory that a sexually adequate woman will also have a well-functioning reproductive system. It's a plausible theory, he admits, based on the fact that sex and reproduction involve the same organs, and that both are considered aspects of femininity. But he finds no sustaining evidence that women who have menstrual difficulties, or who have difficulty becoming pregnant, are any less able to enjoy sex than other women.

Another bit of folklore is that a woman cannot achieve maximum sexual satisfaction until she has had a child. This notion has led many women with orgasm problems to become pregnant in the hope of solving them. Dr. Mary Jane Sherfey, a researcher cited these days by many ardent feminists, believes that pregnancy helps "orgasmic competency" by increasing the blood supply in the pelvic area. Yet the women in the Syracuse panel who had babies were no more orgasmic than those who were childless.

Given the complexity of female sexuality, "it is extremely unlikely that any one psychological or physiological event will drastically alter a woman's sexual responsiveness," says Dr. Fisher. He flatly states that to advise a woman with an orgasm problem to get pregnant, or to quit work to be a housewife, or to find a new sex partner is totally unrealistic.

• If any further evidence were needed to set aside the Freudian idea that a clitoral orgasm is somehow less mature or healthy than a vaginal one, the Fisher study provides it. Yet it also offers several startling findings about the two kinds of climaxes:

1. The women Dr. Fisher interviewed insist that—contrary to what Masters and Johnson, among others, have observed—there *is* such a thing as a separate and specific vaginal orgasm. And the women say that they can distinguish patterns of sensation from it that are quite different from those of the clitoral orgasm. "It's the difference between someone violently tickling you and someone caressingly stroking your bare back," said one wife. Observed another: "Vaginal stimulation is like a warm bath of pleasure; my whole body responds to it. In clitoral stimulation my whole body is rigid with the expectation of continuing pleasure. From clitoral, my body demands to be satisfied; from vaginal, my body is content if it's not."
2. Despite the widespread belief that a vaginal orgasm is somehow bound to be more fulfilling, some of the women said that clitoral orgasms produced far higher "charge" and "ecstasy."
3. In their ability to reach orgasm consistently, Dr. Fisher found no difference between the vaginally and clitorally oriented women. And though his panel ranged from those who wanted only penile-vaginal contact and found clitoral manipulation unpleasant, to those who preferred only the latter, most women used—and needed—both kinds to reach a climax. *But when all the women were asked which they'd prefer if they had to choose permanently between clitoral and vaginal stimulation, two thirds of them opted for clitoral.*
4. Since elements of both kinds of stimulation are generally present in intercourse—vaginal stimulation exerts pressure and tugging on the clitoris, and clitoral manipulation sets up vaginal pulsations—what is the emotional basis for a woman's preferring one over the other? Dr. Fisher's study seems to provide the answer.

For one thing, tests of the Syracuse group showed that the vaginally oriented woman tends to feel "depersonalized" during intercourse—distant and estranged from her own body. She tends to see it as lacking vitality and sensitivity. At the same time, she is inclined to hold down her sense of excitement, to dampen emotional arousal. In other words, she tends to be a more anxious personality type than the clitorally oriented woman.

For such a woman, Dr. Fisher theorizes, vaginal stimulation—which produces less intense excitement—may be less emotionally threatening. She may also need the extra "commitment" from a man, symbolized by penetration, before she can let herself respond to him fully.

Dr. Fisher also points out that in vaginal stimulation, the act is a *mutual* one, in which the woman is both giver and taker, whereas in clitoral stimulation the woman is primarily a taker, the object of her husband's attention.

To the woman who prefers vaginal orgasm, all this may represent a subconscious feeling that "she has no right to feel that her body belongs to herself, or to enjoy body experiences that only gratify her personally. . . . Sexual arousal should only occur when a male sex partner . . . is sharing in the responsibility" and in the pleasure. Conversely, the woman who prefers clitoral stimulation needs to feel that her body and its exciting feelings belong to her alone.

Dr. Fisher stresses that one reaction is neither better nor worse than the other. Each simply represents a different sexual orientation.

He speculates that these attitudes develop in childhood. The "vaginal woman," he writes, can be pictured as having had parents who strictly controlled her physical activities, from eating and toilet training to sex: "They would in essence be telling her that she dare not have a really important body experience unless it was approved by, or shared with, some other significant figure." The "clitoral woman," rather than giving in to these demands, may have rejected them and psychologically decided that she would not allow anyone to intrude on the autonomy of her body.

• In sex, practice does not make perfect—despite some claims that regular intercourse increases a woman's ability to reach orgasm. In an analysis of available figures, Dr. Fisher points out that between the first and fifth year of marriage there is only a 1 percent increase in the number of wives who "almost always" climax. After ten years of marriage the increase is 3 percent. Even among women who climax with less regularity to begin with, ten years of marital sex produces only a 5 percent improvement in orgasm consistency. And even those small increases, Dr. Fisher thinks, may be due less to sexual experience than to a woman's growing confidence that her marriage will endure, her husband remain loyal.

Similarly, elaborate sexual techniques have little effect on female responsiveness. Despite the gaudy claims of some marriage manuals, neither length of foreplay and varied intercourse positions, nor the use of exotic procedures produces more or better orgasms.

"Women with orgasm difficulties," Dr. Fisher writes, "probably try to convince themselves that if only they could master some new sexual technique, all would be well. Or they may irrationally criticize their sex partners for not being sufficiently expert to stimulate them properly. In other words, the attainment of orgasm is often perceived as a motor act which can be mastered in the same way as any muscular maneuver. . . . But it is doubtful that a woman's sexual responsiveness can be looked upon as an athletic skill."

• Does a high-orgasm woman, or one who seeks intercourse frequently, show the same gusto toward other forms of physical gratification? Dr. Fisher found only a few isolated links between sexual and other appetites. The sexy woman is no more likely to enjoy food or alcohol or tobacco than is the less sexy one. Similarly, a woman who feels sexually unsatisfied does not seem to compensate by indulging her other physical desires.

By extension, this last point is extremely important. For one traditional view compares female sexuality to a hydraulic system: If tension isn't released in one outlet, the pressure on others will grow. But the Fisher survey shows that low-orgasm women are no more tense, irritable or anxious than high-orgasm women. "This suggests," the psychologist says, "that a married woman is able to adapt to the level of sexual satisfaction that's available to her."

How much sexual release does a woman ordinarily need? The women in the Syracuse study averaged three and a half sex acts a week, with enormous individual variations in that rate. But women who are narcissistic—greatly concerned with their own bodies, clothes, grooming, cosmetics—make love more often. Dr. Fisher believes that one of the reasons a woman may desire frequent intercourse is her wish to be the center of attention. In lovemaking, she finds not only sexual excitement but also the excitement of having a man lavish interest and admiration on her. One wife put her feelings this way: "I like to feel my husband is paying strict attention to my pleasure—treating me in regal fashion. This is a selfish attitude . . . but it is important to me."

Dr. Fisher's study was not made, or his book written, with the prime intent of finding ways to help women with sexual problems. Before real progress can be made on that score, the psychologist feels, science must learn far more about the orgasmic process.

He points out that—because even the best of words are still poor conveyors of emotion—we don't *really* know how a woman feels during arousal, during orgasm, or when arousal fails to lead to orgasm. We know far too little about the psychological factors that differentiate clitorally oriented from vaginally oriented wives. Do women, for example, subconsciously choose different kinds of men when they marry—an aloof spectator type, as against one who expects rights over her body? Does her preference change with the length of her marriage or with different partners?

If Dr. Fisher's theories prove true, it may be that a woman's orgasmic potential is determined *before* she becomes sexually active—during childhood, when her anxiety about the loss of loved ones may be intensified by a distant or permissive father. A young girl's father, aware of such potential problems, might take steps to compensate for them.

As far as the grown woman is concerned, Dr. Fisher makes these suggestions:

First, a husband can make an effort to be more emotionally dependable, to give his wife the feeling that she can count on his loyalty, interest and love. He can cut down on work that keeps him away from home or that takes too much of his energy. He can communicate more openly and intimately—talking out his resentment or anger, for example, rather than going off and sulking, thus leaving his wife feeling alone.

Second, counselors and therapists could focus on a woman's feelings about separation and loss and on her memories of her father. With more insight, Dr. Fisher feels, a woman might be better able to compensate for her anxieties or to understand that she is irrationally transferring to her husband those qualities she felt her father lacked.

However much is yet to be learned, Dr. Fisher's research thus far offers some encouraging new conclusions for women with sexual difficulties.

Perhaps most important is his reassurance that "There are many pathways open to a woman in the process of becoming a sexually adequate person. She need not grow up with any special set of traits in order to be sexually responsive. She need not conform to any fixed stereotype of what is feminine."

30   Eight Myths about Divorce—and the Facts
Hugh Carter

"Frequently, because of marital discord, a couple separates, but without serious thought of divorce."

Is divorce increasing? What is the most difficult year of marriage? Can children hold a family together? What are the prospects for the future of divorced people? Much of our information in this area is based on rumor and misconception. Carter helps to clear up a number of such questions by reference to factual data.

This year, close to 400,000 couples will be divorced in the United States. The figure is one that many people find alarming, but much of the talk about the divorce problem in America seems to be based on misunderstandings or fallacies. Here are some of the most frequently encounterd myths about divorce:

1. *The divorce rate is going up rapidly.*

The figures do not support this. For more than 20 years nothing drastic has happened to the divorce rate except for a brief, sharp increase caused by the war, followed by a decline. In 1946—when many war marriages ended—the rate was 4.3 per 1,000 of the population, an all-time high. In that year, more than 600,000 couples were divorced. For the next five years the rate fell, reaching 2.5 in 1951. In 1960 the rate was 2.2 per 1,000 of the population, identical with the 1941 rate. Provisional figures point to no drastic change in the rate through 1963. It is true that the rate is higher now than it was 40 years ago; it stood at 1.5 in 1923.

2. *The divorce rate is about the same in all parts of the United States.*

Actually, the rate in the Western states is 3.4 per 1,000 of population—almost four times as high as the rate in the Northeastern states of 0.9. The remainder of the country is in an intermediate position, the rate being 2.1 in the North Central states and 2.8 in the south.

It is true that the rates are affected to some extent by migratory divorce—establishing residence in a state in order to obtain a divorce. Then, too, since most divorcing persons are young adults, the divorce rate depends, in part, on the age distribution of the population. Where there is a heavy concentration of young adults, the divorce rate tends to increase. There are also marked differences in divorce laws and in the strictness with which judicial authorities interpret the laws. However, the differences among the four regions are greater than could be explained by these factors.

There is a good deal of speculation that because the West is a new region its people have a relaxed attitude toward divorce. On the other hand, the South, which has the second highest rate, cannot be considered a new region. The truth is that we really do not know the reason for the regional differences in divorce rates.

3. *Most divorces are granted in Reno and similar places.*

The evidence indicates that migratory divorces are only a small fraction of the total. *All* Nevada divorces equal less than 3 per cent of the national total. The figures probably seem high because of the great amount of publicity attending them. The majority of divorcing persons cannot afford to establish residence in another state to obtain a divorce. This seems to be true also of divorces for American citizens in Mexico and other foreign countries. From time to time there is a great deal of publicity about divorce mills, but the number of cases involved is small compared with the national total.

4. *The third year of marriage is the hardest.*

A first glance at divorce statistics may seem to support this myth. In some divorce tables the largest number of divorces is shown after three years of marriage. (In other tables the peak comes after two years, or after one year.)

However, the facts are more complicated than appears at first glance. Frequently, because of marital discord, a couple separates, but without serious thought of divorce. Months, or even years, may pass before the beginning of legal action.

After a decision is made for divorce, the plaintiff, usually the wife, consults a lawyer. He, in turn, must inquire into the pertinent facts. If the grounds appear adequate, he prepares the case and has it entered on the appropriate court docket. In due time, the case is heard and the decree granted. All these steps require time—from several months to several years.

An analysis of the statistics and related facts leads one to conclude that the first year of marriage is the hardest, even though the peak in divorces may come after three (or two) years. It also appears from the statistics that each year of marriage is less likely to end in divorce than the immediately preceding year.

5. *Having children will prevent divorce.*

Latest published statistics show that more than one-half of divorcing couples have children.

Two opposing views are sometimes presented on marital stability and children. On the one hand, children are said to provide a common interest and a focus for family life. On the other hand, children may serve to intensify an existing conflict. In any event, in recent years the proportion of divorcing couples with children has been rising. Whether the number of divorces would have been larger or smaller if there had been more or fewer couples with children is unknown.

6. *The wealthy and the highly educated have a higher divorce rate than the poor and those of limited education.*

Although comprehensive national statistics are not available on this point, a number of excellent research publications indicate that the higher professional and business groups have the lowest divorce rates, while the highest divorce rate is found among working-class families. The great publicity attending divorce actions of wealthy and prominent persons may account for the popular myth that these groups have the highest divorce rate.

7. *Because of the high divorce rate, there are enormous numbers of divorced persons in the population.*

Census figures do not support this view. A 1962 sample survey indicated about 3 million divorced persons—that is, about one divorced person in the population to every 29 married persons.

Remarriage, of course, is the main reason for the relatively small number of divorced persons. In the same survey, the Census Bureau reported more than 14 million persons who had been married more than once. Some had been widowed, but the majority had been divorced.

8. *Divorced persons are less likely to remarry than are the widowed.*

Just the opposite is true: About three out of four marriages involve a divorced person. The reason is the early age of most couples at the time of divorce. Age at widowhood has been advancing in recent years and the likelihood of marriage declines with age. Most remarriages of persons past 55 years of age are of the widowed: however, the majority of remarriages occur at younger ages and involve divorced persons.

While it is easy to point out some of the obvious misinformation about divorce—the myths—it is not easy to obtain the comprehensive facts the importance of the subject warrants. An insurance actuary estimates the risk of death from a study of death statistics. Excellent divorce statistics would make it possible to calculate the risk of divorce from such facts as age at marriage, differences between ages of husband and wife, number of previous marriages and whether they were dissolved by divorce or death.

Unfortunately, persons interested in the stability of family life cannot get the needed facts from official sources. With considerable chagrin, after years of working to improve them, I must make it clear that the United States is far behind most countries of Western Europe in the accuracy of its divorce statistics.

Why is this true? For one thing, the vital statistics (including divorce statistics) of the United States are different from the national censuses of population. The latter are provided for in the Constitution as a responsibility of the Federal Government. Vital statistics are a responsibility of the states.

Early in this century births and deaths were not fully reported. That they are now is the result of a campaign led by public-health specialists and leading physicians. Similarly, the American Bar Association has urged its members to support the central registration of divorces. Leading social scientists in the 28 states not now participating in the Divorce Registration Area program are actively urging their states to join. It can be hoped that it will not be long until all 50 states are cooperating. Then there will be fewer myths and more solid facts about divorce.

**Suggested Readings for
Chapter 7**

Framo, James L. *Family interaction: A dialogue between family researchers and family therapists.* New York: Springer, 1971. An unusual conference with many well-known scholars interested in family development and process.

Katchadourian, H. A. & Lunde, D. T. *Fundamentals of human sexuality.* New York: Holt, Rinehart and Winston, 1972. An excellent introductory work which reviews the biological and cultural aspects of sexuality and sexual behavior.

Mead, Margaret. Culture and commitment. New York: Doubleday, 1970. The famous anthropologist's book discussing her views about the generation gap. The distinction between postfigurative, cofigurative, and prefigurative cultures—respectively, where children learn from adults, both learn from peers, and adults learn from their children—is elaborated.

Murstein, Bernard I. *Theories of attraction and love.* New York: Springer, 1971. A series of papers on theory and research in interpersonal behavior.

Patterson, Gerald R. *Families.* Champaign, Ill.: Research Press, 1971. A coverage of family intervention techniques inspired by behavior modification theory and practice.

Discussion Questions

1. What would constitute an ideal date for you? How do your recent dates compare to this ideal? Why the discrepancy?
2. Is marriage an outmoded institution?
3. Is the divorce rate increasing? Why? Can anything be done about it? Should anything be done about it?
4. What are the social implications of abortion?

Abnormal Behavior

The most common method of diagnosing abnormal behavior is based on a manual published by the American Psychiatric Association. This manual divides the spectrum of abnormal behavior into a variety of subcategories, many of which are illustrated by some of the material appearing in this chapter. This traditional psychiatric classification describes various types of neurotic conditions as well as more serious disorders that are labeled psychotic. An amusing distinction between neurotic and psychotic disorders is captured by the saying that the neurotic builds castles in the sky, the psychotic lives in them, and the psychiatrist collects the rent.

The article in this chapter by Don A. Schanche, "Can a Psychiatrist Help Normal People," describes some of the common problems which might be helped through psychological assistance, and some expert comments about the importance of psychological counselling with "normal people." During our life there are special conditions and situations which arise that produce stressful side effects. Unless checked these difficulties could expand to produce more serious disturbances. Often these problems do not require intensive or long-term treatment but rather swift and direct therapeutic intervention.

Emotional disturbances can take on many forms. For example, one form, more or less psychological, is characterized by obsessional, anxiety-provoking thoughts and ideas which persistently preoccupy a person throughout the day. Another typical style of responding to emotional distress is by experiencing various bodily symptoms such as fainting, pounding in the chest, nausea, and other physiological reactions. It is not so surprising that emotional distress can be powerfully reflected in physiological reactions. We have all experienced profuse sweating under tension or unpleasant feelings in the pit of the stomach when confronted with a potentially fearful challenge. The name given to physiological disturbances which seem to have an emotional cause are psychosomatic disorders. Psychosomatic medicine has for many years been an intriguing yet puzzling area of study. There have been many different theories about why some people tend to develop psychosomatic reactions, but unfortunately the research evidence has not sufficiently clarified the exclusively "emotional nature" of these disturbances. The article by Michael Halberstam, "Can You Make Yourself Sick?" deals with some perplexing questions in psychosomatic medicine. He examines the psychological as well as the organic medical evidence for different types of "psychosomatic" illnesses and attempts to present a balanced picture of this syndrome. Halberstam suggests that both the mind and the body are involved in psychosomatic problems. Therefore, treatment should investigate the emotional factors which might create a tendency to use physical complaints as a substitute for psychological symptoms. However, comprehensive diagnosis must also consider genetic and physiological variables which could also contribute to the psychosomatic behavior. The treatment of psychosomatic disorders is at present variably successful. There are no easy solutions, although recent advances in behavior modification, especially the voluntary self-control of various internal processes, are promising. Similarly, the use of drugs such as tranquilizers and antidepressants are producing useful results.

Some people who are troubled do not restrict their symptoms to ones which trouble themselves, but instead develop behavioral problems which can be destructive to others as well. Alcoholism is a condition which causes enormous personal distress and also a great deal of suffering in people who must live with the alcoholic or come into social contact with him. It is the most prevalent form of drug abuse in our society, and the most costly to society in both personal and economic terms. The article by Knox explores this problem in a manner that may shed light on it for the reader.

Depression in its most extreme form is a thoroughly miserable condition. Despair, intense feelings of helplessness, feelings of physical weakness, and a desire to simply fade away from most human contacts is a typical depressive profile. Hundreds of thousands of people suffer from extreme forms of depression. In some instances mental and physical suicide may be a direct consequence of depressive preoccupation. To a milder degree, most people experience some sort of depression intermittently throughout their lives. Feeling blue, feeling low, just feeling sad and unhappy is a reality with which we all have to cope from time to time. Most of us are able to break out of these depressive traps but a good many people aren't. In chronic depression some individuals even have difficulty in distinguishing when they are and are not depressed. Theoretically, depression is an intriguing puzzle. One theory suggests that depression is a consequence of some real or imagined loss that has created an intolerable grief reaction. It is easy to see depression mainly as a consequence of observable loss, such as that of a loved one, but it is more difficult to understand depression when there is no apparent identifiable cause. The article "The Anatomy of Melancholy" by David Elkind and J. Herbert Hamsher delves into this complicated problem. The process of depression is described, and some of the most recent treatment methods highlighted.

The most common type of psychotic disorder is schizophrenia. The individual given the label of schizophrenic is characterized by personality disintegration which prevents effective functioning. His perception of reality is severely impaired, and unconventional behavior such as hallucinations—seeing or hearing things that nobody else can see or hear—are frequent. In addition, the acceptance of false beliefs called delusions may also be present. Aside from hallucinations and delusions, which are principally thinking disorders, there are affective symptoms of schizophrenia such as depression, marked elation, emotional overreaction, or flatness of affect which characterize the schizophrenic's emotional state. The final article in this chapter, "Schizophrenia: Is There an Answer?" is a general summary of what is known and unknown about the causes and general characteristics of schizophrenia. The article discusses questions about schizophrenics such as "Are schizophrenics likely to be violent?" "Is schizophrenia inherited" "Are the parents of schizophrenics at fault?" and so on. There is a great deal of inaccurate information about schizophrenia being circulated without corrective feedback. This article is an excellent antidote for these unscientific ideas. Schizophrenia is a complex riddle, and it is only through the support of extensive research that additional truths about schizophrenia will be uncovered.

"So many people think you have to be crazy to go to a psychiatrist, or you have to be helpless to go."

Little by little seeking help from a professional who specializes in psychology is becoming less of a stigma. Many people need and find helpful some form of psychological help during periods of emotional crisis. This article describes the usefulness of psychological intervention with people who are *not "insane."*

Here are four healthy people who feared they were mentally ill and thought they had evidence to prove it. All of them discovered that with a little preventive foresight, mental health was only a therapist's office—and a few hours of counseling—away.

• An elderly woman whose husband has been clinging to life in a near-vegetative state in a nursing home for five years suddenly becomes deeply depressed and convinced that death has overtaken her. "It's as if my own body no longer belongs to me."

• A suburban mother of three small children, whose ambitious husband not only travels often but frequently works nights and weekends, feels herself isolated, friendless and imprisoned in thankless domestic routine. She lies sleepless at night, weeps uncontrollably and is convinced that her "entrapment" has made her a "nervous wreck."

• A 62-year-old executive who has helped to build one of the top 500 companies in the U.S. suddenly loses the confidence and decisiveness that made him a success and is convinced that he is becoming senile. Certain that he is near life's end, he permits business and personal affairs to fall into chaos.

• A former child prodigy, now a brilliant and successful 27-year-old bachelor scientist, feels such a deep emotional malaise that he has trouble concentrating on his work and decides that mental illness has cut him down in the prime of life.

No matter how convinced each of these unhappy people is that his mind is failing, all four are neither mentally ill, nor even abnormal. They are simply suffering from common emotional discomforts that can be easily pinned down

From *Today's Health*, January 1973. Reproduced by permission of the author and *Today's Health*, published by the American Medical Association.

and remedied. The cases are real, and they are typical of hundreds of thousands of Americans who "let their troubles get them down." Each was helped to regain a satisfying, socially constructive life by psychological counseling that took no more time out of their lives than a visit to the movies.

• The elderly woman realized the cause of her grief-like depression and conquered it in two hours of conversation with a skilled psychiatrist. Sensibly admitting that her vegetating husband would soon die, she had made arrangements to will his body for medical research, and at the same time she had willed her own body for the same purpose. Her depression literally was grief, not only for her husband but for herself, because from the moment that she signed the will, she felt separated from her own body, as if she had already died.

• A psychiatrist chatted with the young suburban mother for a little over an hour, during which he got her to list the important aspects of housework and motherhood vs. the relatively unimportant ones. By organizing her work and her time, she was able to get out of the house more often, expand her circle of friends, and guiltlessly hire a babysitter so she could travel occasionally with her husband.

• The aging executive who thought he was senile discovered in two therapeutic sessions that he was only worried about his approaching retirement, for which he was utterly unprepared. The worry had so preoccupied him that the attendant forgetfulness falsely convinced him that he was becoming senile when, in fact, he was in perfect mental and physical health.

• The malaise that the brilliant young bachelor thought was connected with his work actually was caused by a common social problem. After a few hours of therapy he recognized that while he longed for feminine companionship, he had never learned how to meet young women. As a child prodigy he moved so quickly through school that he missed the normal boy-girl dating games. Now, as a 27-year-old, all he had to do to solve his problem was reach out for feminine companions and fill that important gap in his education.

We asked Jack Weinberg, M.D., a psychiatrist and clinical director of the Illinois Psychiatric Institute and professor of psychiatry at the University of Illinois Medical School, this question: "Can psychiatry help healthy people stay that way?" His answer is unequivocal. He points out that you don't have to be mentally ill, or even neurotic, to benefit from psychiatric advice, any more than you have to be at death's door to benefit from an annual physical checkup. In fact, the healthier you are, the easier it is for a professional to help you work your way free of troublesome hangups.

Dr. Weinberg tells two true stories to illustrate his belief in the importance of preventive psychiatry—seeking psychiatric, psychological or even pastoral counseling *before* there is serious trouble. Both involve Air Force enlisted technicians whose behavior around nuclear weapons literally threatened national catastrophe.

The first of the two men, according to Dr. Weinberg, forgot to ground a nuclear warhead that he was working on. A charge of static electricity, such as you get when you walk across a thickly piled carpet on a dry day, detonated the conventional triggering explosives in the warhead. Fortunately for the state of New Mexico, where the accident took place, the blast did not touch off a full-scale nuclear explosion, but only scattered radioactive debris around a limited area.

The second Air Force man flipped after brooding for weeks over a withheld promotion. He climbed to the warhead level of a missile silo with a cocked pistol and called to his superiors, "If I'm not promoted, I'll set it off." He was lured down and hospitalized with severe mental illness.

According to Dr. Weinberg, the almost catastrophic actions of the two men —one of them forgetful, the other irrational—probably could have been averted if the Air Force at that time had been more attuned to viewing psychiatry as a preventive resource rather than as a last resort for very sick minds. The "forgetful" technician, for example, was actually seething with anger and disappointment over his wife's infidelity when he forgot to ground the warhead. If the Air Force at the time had encouraged its men to take their problems to the base psychiatrist or chaplain without automatically branding them as "psychos" or "sissies," he might have relieved his anger, and his "forgetfulness," by talking out his problem, and the lapse of memory that almost turned part of New Mexico into a cinder probably would not have occurred.

Similarly, if the Air Force then had used thorough psychiatric screening methods, as it does today, the irrational technician would have been weeded out of the nuclear weapons work force long before he ever got the chance to blow up an ICBM. With understanding therapy earlier in the course of his illness, the emotional crises that built up to such a horrifying climax could quite possibly have been so relieved that he may have been able to lead a stable, happy life in another job.

"So many people think you have to be crazy to go to a psychiatrist, or you have to be helpless to go," says Jarl Dyrud, M.D., professor of psychiatry at the University of Chicago's Pritzker School of Medicine.

The two views commonly held are that you go four or five times a week for four or five years and it's all terribly expensive and impractical or that you go helplessly in and get medicated or have electric shocks and come out somehow or other changed. As a matter of fact, if you go when you are only moderately uncomfortable, it may be much easier. Very often it is with this less intense problem-solving that we do our best work.

As an example of the kind of non-critical psychiatric help he is talking about, Dr. Dyrud cites the case of a physician with whom he once worked. The doctor was an amiable, well-adjusted man with no obvious emotional problems. But he was worried, as any man would be, by transient chest pains. As a doctor, he naturally had his heart and lungs checked out very carefully, but the doctors could find nothing wrong. Finally, he sat down to talk to Dr. Dyrud. In the course of only two relatively brief sessions, the source of the chest pains emerged. The physician was undergoing a great deal of anxiety over his middle-aged wife's pregnancy. Naturally, he was anxious about her health and the possibility that she might give birth to a defective child, since such births occur more frequently in middle-aged mothers. But he was also angry, a feeling that he had unconsciously repressed, because his wife had insisted on having the child, and would henceforth have someone other than him to care for. "He put this all together in the course of a couple hours, and sort of chuckled about it," recalls Dr. Dyrud. "And he stopped having the pain."

The important thing to recognize about the doctor's case is that he was not mentally ill or paralyzed by his anxiety. There was no need for him to spend months or years on a psychiatrist's couch rummaging through his childhood in search of Oedipal hangups or primal screams. He was simply having trouble with one situation in an otherwise comfortable life. If he had hidden it and let it fester, the problem might have led to marital conflicts and serious emotional troubles. Instead, he prevented it by seeking treatment early, like knocking out an infection with antibiotics before it gets out of hand.

"Sometimes an aspect of life gets jammed up," the psychiatrist explains.

> We can help a person release it so it starts running again. He may encounter another obstacle, but chances are that once the jammed aspect gets running again, enough good things happen so that it tends to keep going.
>
> I think the main thing we treat is demoralization. If we simply start the sorting process and begin to lay things out so that the individual can look at them one at a time, we've begun to treat the demoralization.

Sometimes, according to Dr. Weinberg, all the process requires is an ear "loaned" to the patient for a very brief time. He recalls one man who came to his university clinic for help. Routinely, Dr. Weinberg sat down with the man for an hour to elicit his history before referring him to another psychiatrist for treatment. "He talked and I grunted and nodded at the proper times to show that I was interested, then explained to him that he would be assigned to another doctor." As it turned out, the patient did not follow up on the treatment. Five-and-a-half years later he called on Dr. Weinberg to say, "You helped me so much when you saw me that one time that I'd like to see you again. I have a question to ask."

"What did I do" asks Weinberg. "I did nothing but listen to him. I didn't give him one piece of advice. It was just the understanding that somebody was willing to listen, spend some time with him. That was sufficient for this man to go on for five-and-a-half years. With so many persons, all one needs is a listening ear. There is no doubt in my mind that it would do tremendous good if people would come in before there is a crisis; if they felt the freedom to do it and if society sanctioned the idea that there are places that you can go for help. Even if you are told when you get there that you shouldn't have any therapy, it is a help."

While there are many psychiatrists and psychologists who believe as deeply as these men in the efficacy of preventive psychiatry, few of them are doing as much about it as Gilbert Kliman, M.D., and his associates in White Plains, New York. Dr. Kliman, a child psychiatrist, his psychologist wife, Ann, teacher Doris Ronald and Myron Stein, M.D., established the nonprofit Center for Preventive Psychiatry there seven years ago. They have since drawn together a staff that includes psychiatrists, physicians, psychologists, psychiatric social workers, teachers and volunteer laymen in an organized attempt "to keep healthy people healthy while they are experiencing a difficult emotional crisis in their lives."

Such crises may be as minor as a child's fear of starting school for the first time or as major as a natural disaster that throws an entire community into emotional turmoil, and the Center has handled both. For example, when last June's flood waters receded from the city of Corning, New York, they left mental as well as material chaos in their wake.

The town's main employer, Corning Glass Works, inspired local officials to call on the Center for help. Ann Kliman rushed to Corning to begin a unique program of psychiatric "first-aid," which was still continuing half a year after the flood. Among other things, she helped establish centers where the flood victims could talk about their problems, and trained 60 local professionals in the techniques of crisis intervention so they could actually give preventive psychiatric aid to those who needed it. As a result, the incidence of mental illness and suicide in Corning remained stable after the flood whereas, by comparison, both doubled after the same extensive flood damage in other storm-struck cities such as Wilkes-Barre, Pennsylvania.

However beneficial it might be, preventive psychiatry has not yet reached the stage where everyone can run down to the corner psychiatrist for a quick shot of help whenever he feels emotionally uncomfortable. For example, Saul Kapel, M.D., a busy child psychiatrist who is an ardent believer in short-term preventive psychiatry, complains that he simply does not have enough time to practice much of it. Almost all of his patients are seriously troubled families and individuals who need long-term therapy, the kind that requires many visits and sometimes years to accomplish. He knows that many of these who seek his help would benefit from shortterm, problem-solving assistance—perhaps only a "listening ear"—but he has to turn them away because there are others waiting who need help more. Actually, preventive psychiatry often is practiced by family doctors, clergy and other family counselors.

"Parents and teachers can actually do preventive psychiatry," says Dr. Kliman.

Think about the role of parents in health generally. They are in a way, the children's first doctors. They understand that a child has to have clean skin in order to prevent abscesses, and that he has to have good food in order to prevent malnutrition; these are preventive medical functions. The same is true with mental health. Even such things as neuroses, psychoses or psychologically-based retardation are things that parents can to some extent prevent, although less easily than they can prevent an abscess on a baby's skin.

It's a lot easier to keep a baby bathed and changed than it is to practice the kind of prevention I'm talking about. Perhaps it will help to give it some labels. For example, in preventive medicine we talk about skin hygiene; in preventive psychiatry, let's talk about the hygiene of honest communication and the truthful sharing of reality that is a very simple first step in any mental health procedure.

As an instance of poor mental hygiene, Dr. Kliman's associate, Dr. Myron Stein cites an all-too-common case of an insensitive teacher. In this true story, a youngster entered his third-grade classroom one recent morning and told his teacher, "My grandfather is dead." The teacher hesitated, then said, "Well, sit down and open your book to page 32."

"It's highly unlikely that the child got much out of that day's work," notes Dr. Stein with quiet understatement. "Perhaps if the teacher had said, "Oh, I'm sorry, when did it happen?' the child would have felt that she was concerned, and he could have relieved himself by talking about it for a few minutes, then turned to page 32 and read the whole page."

"In a way, the teacher was lying to the child," says Dr. Kliman. "Not deliberately, perhaps, but she was concealing an honest shocked reaction. She failed to communicate honestly."

Like the teacher, most of us become so inured to the major and minor crises of life that we forget how common, and how upsetting, they are. Actually, potentially damaging emotional situations arise frequently, particularly in the lives of small children. Dr. Kliman and two associates once tabulated the crises of a 16-member nursery school class during an ordinary two-week period. This is what they found: A tonsillectomy, the injury of a relative in a car crash, sudden hospitalization of a sister in the middle of the night, a brother's operation, a grandmother's death, the departure of parents for a two-month trip abroad, the deaths of a turtle and a cat, and the revelation to a child that his uncle had died. All that among 16 children in only two weeks.

Deaths, divorce, separation, the trauma of going to the hospital, moving, entering school, going away to camp and many other troubling but ordinary events in a young child's life often lead to emotional crises. These crises, in turn, can be the source of severe psychological problems that in many cases become debilitating many years later, when the child reaches adolescence or adulthood. Therefore, Dr. Kliman and his colleagues believe that it is the first task of preventive psychiatry to cope with the crises when they arise, not wait for them to mature into full-blown mental illness.

The Center concentrates on children under six and has handled severe psychological stresses as the result of bereavement, divorce, parental drug addiction and numerous less grave situations. Many of the youngsters need only brief, crisis-oriented therapy to help them deal positively with the situation. Usually their parents benefit from the same short-term help. Children who require more intensive treatment enter the Center's Cornerstone School, a day-care center/nursery school that combines preschool education with psychotherapy. Others are helped on an individual basis by the psychiatrists and other mental health professionals on the Center's staff.

As word of the Center's interest in preventive psychiatry has spread in the local community, more and more people have begun to anticipate crises in their children's lives before they occur. "Ten years ago I would never have believed the preventive cases that are coming in to us now," says Dr. Kliman. "It's almost staggering."

Kliman and his colleagues view much of their work as a sort of immunization program. Such psychological immunization works wherever there are psychological hazards, according to Kliman. Basically, the immunization process involves little more than being honest with a child without overwhelming him, and sharing anxieties and concerns with him rather than attempting to shield him from them, but the task must be undertaken with warmth and affectionate understanding. It is axiomatic among professionals who work with children that you cannot hide from them the realities of such unhappy events as divorce and death, and it is not only fruitless but damaging to try.

"There are strategies emerging, ways of working with young children that are preventive in and of themselves, and you really don't have to master the entire body of psychoanalytic literature or the psychoanalytic development of young children to practice them," says Mrs. Phyllis Schwartz, a Center staff member.

For adults, the practice of preventive psychiatry isn't always so direct, but there are many equally forthright strategies for dealing with situations that put healthy men and women under psychological stress. Depending upon the person and the problem, the process may be as simple as the time-honored practice of talking things over with an understanding minister, family. doctor, close friend or relative. Or it may involve, on a shorter basis, the skilled techniques of a trained psychotherapist.

Almost any psychiatrist could cite numerous cases in which basically healthy people—individuals who have long managed to live stable lives without cracking up or giving in to crises—have actually gained strength and improved their lives by brief therapeutic help when troublesome situations arose. As one of the most common examples, Dr. Dyrud describes the almost universal feeling among young housewives that they are trapped by children and home care. While they remain emotionally healthy, many of them feel extremely uncomfortable. "They devalue what they are doing," says Dr. Dyrud, "and at the same time they work even harder, trying to get more satisfaction out of it. The result is that they dig themselves in deeper and see fewer adult friends."

Paradoxically, the husband often devalues the young mother's role even more than she does and makes her feel worse by constantly feeling sorry for her, stuck in a dull, unrewarding job. Dr. Dyrud has found that by simply sorting out the most meaningful elements of the young mother's role and the husband's contribution to it, about 70 percent of the couples who have come to him have benefited by drastically revising their opinions of themselves. After only a few visits, they go away feeling both relieved of a burden and proud of what they are doing. Thus, if a truly damaging emotional crisis comes along, such as a death or separation they are stronger and better able to cope with it.

While the professional movement toward preventive psychiatry is relatively new, the practice of it—without the label of "mental hygiene"—is probably as old as mankind. In tribal societies, for instance, the cooperation and support that each tribesman gave the other was preventive because it forestalled isolation, created a feeling of belonging and provided needed succor in times of stress. The large families of generations past performed the same preventive role. Although death and other critical situations were at least as frequent as they are today, there were grandmothers, aunts, cousins, uncles and numerous brothers and sisters to comfort the grieving and the hurt. "I suspect that's one of the reasons why divorce is having such a bad mental health effect in this day and age," says Dr. Kliman. "Without large families, they are isolated victims. They don't have a network of community support that was once common."

The fact that mental health improves when people are not so isolated is one of the reasons why Dr. Kliman and others are anxious to see preventive psychiatry viewed not as a narrow professional specialty, but as a general concern, like good nutrition, that can and should be practiced by everyone.

While it is true that most of us know we should eat a well-balanced diet, still many of us over-indulge in favorite, but not soundly nutritious, foods or drinks. Still, we try to lose weight, to guard ourselves against the temptations of gluttony. We don't realize, though. that one should also have a well-balanced emotional regimen, as well. Too much of a feast of guilt, of self-deprecation, of anxiety, shows up just as inevitably on the scales of unhappiness and impaired functioning. We need to weigh ourselves in the emotional balance from time-to-time to check on whether we are *mentally* overweight—and, if so, see a professional to help us go on a mental health diet.

Just how widely a balanced emotional program's effects might be felt is perhaps best illustrated by Dr. Weinberg's story of the Air Force nuclear technician. After the near-catastrophe, the Air Force came to the Group for the Advancement of Psychiatry, of which Dr. Weinberg is treasurer, to ask for help in devising tests and screening methods that would cull the mental health risks out of the 300,000-man force which handled the dangerous weapons. The GAP carefully studied the problem and prepared a booklet which the Air Force used as a guide in removing some 3,000 psychological "risks" from work on, or near, atomic warheads.

"The colonel in charge of personnel came to a GAP meeting to thank us for what we had done, and provided Air Force copies of our booklet for all of us," recalls Dr. Weinberg. "I was horrified, because on top of the booklet it said, 'CLASSIFIED.'

" 'Do the Russians know about this?' I asked.

" 'Of course not, it's classified material,' the colonel said.

" 'Well, what good does it do us to cull out *our* emotionally-bothered individuals? If *they* have an emotionally bothered individual, he could start something that could be detrimental to mankind.

" 'Will you do us all a favor, colonel? Pass by the Russian embassy tonight and drop one of these booklets over the wall.' "

That's preventive psychiatry.

"What is a psychosomatic illness? Is it a cause, an effect, or both? Is it a real, or an imaginary condition?"

Psychosomatic illnesses are a puzzling phenomenon. Frequently people complain of various physical disabilities without any apparent organic cause. This article by Dr. Halberstam examines some of the theories and empirical work being carried on in the area of psychosomatic illness. It makes for fascinating reading.

Bill Steinmetz felt a twinge in his stomach, just as Barnes the division manager started the monthly sales meeting on the stroke of 10:00 o'clock. With the economy the way it was, nobody in the division was picking up contracts, but he had a feeling he might have fallen behind the others. Each of the salesmen reported on his month, and as Bill suspected Aiello was doing particularly well with franchised services while Bill had always concentrated on individual companies. Soon it would be his turn to speak. Bill's attention wandered—Aiello's voice drifted off as Bill could only think of the recurrent pain waves that knotted his stomach into a ball. He began to feel sweaty and cold; then the chills alternated with hot flashes so that his face felt momentarily as though it were burning up. Then the pain settled in the lower part of his abdomen. He began to think that if he went to the bathroom maybe he'd feel better. But how would it look if he suddenly walked out of the meeting?

Bill's secret fear as he excused himself was that he was experiencing the first symptoms of cancer. Actually, though his discomfort was real enough, he was among the uncounted millions, whose organic ailments are caused by anxiety, fear, tension and emotional stress. Now, research has opened up new avenues of therapy which promise that people like Bill soon will be able to control and offset the destructive physical effects of their emotions by a process of "thinking them away."

Inside the toilet Bill already felt safer. After a few minutes he expelled some gas and then a small bowel movement, smaller than usual. He was frightened, but not too surprised, when he noticed some white mucus-like material in the bowl. Maybe cancer, just as he had dreaded. This time he would make an

From Today's Health, December 1972, published by the American Medical Association.

appointment with Dr. Glaser, the way his wife had been nagging him to do.

Back in the conference room he settled himself quickly at his place. When his time came to present, he didn't flub anything, but he could tell he wasn't as sharp as usual. As the meeting ended, Barnes came over to him with a look of concern. "Anything the matter, Bill?" he asked.

The cramp came back again, ever so slightly.

"So you see, Bill," Dr. Glaser went on, "there's no sign of cancer at all. Both the barium enema X-rays and my visual examination of your colon with the sigmoidoscope showed no abnormality. But that doesn't mean that you're not sick or that you're imagining anything. What you have is what we call a spastic colon or mild colitis. It means that your lower intestine—your colon—isn't functioning smoothly as a unit the way it should be, gradually propelling material toward evacuation. Instead, some parts are contracting when they should be relaxing—one contraction is forced upon another and pain results."

"Now I know it's not cancer I'm not so interested in what causes it. I just want to know how to make it go away and not come back."

"Sure, but in order to help on that I'm going to have to go over some of the questions I asked you when you first came in. You said then that there was no particular pattern to when these cramps occur. What about when you're anxious or upset?"

"Well, I don't know . . . maybe they could be a little worse then."

"You told me everything was OK in your personal life. Let me get more specific—what about at work?"

"Work's been sort of tough, come to think of it. Lot of worry there. Business hasn't been too good."

"Has it ever been this bad before?"

"To tell the truth—no. And I've never been so uptight about it before, either. Do you think that has anything to do with these pains?"

"It sure could. We'll have to ask a lot more questions, but it certainly could."

"Like, could you call what I have, you know, 'psychosomatic'?"

Dr. Glaser smiled. "You certainly could."

Bill's question is typical of the curious fact about psychosomatic ailments— just about everybody knows the word and uses it, but relatively few of us know what it means. People like to say of a persistent backache or a headache that just wouldn't go away—or an attack of the "virus"—"Don't worry about it, it's probably only psychosomatic."

What is a psychosomatic illness? Is it a cause, an effect, or both? Is it a real, or an imaginary, condition? When a person, such as Bill with his spastic colon, develops such a disease, what kind of therapy is indicated? The quest for answers to these and other questions has led an ever larger number of physicians into a new specialty, a combination of physiological and psychological therapy: psychosomatic medicine.

The most startling advance in psychosomatic medicine in the past five years has come out of the basic animal psychology labs of such men as Neal Miller, Ph.D., and B. F. Skinner, Ph.D. Briefly stated, Miller's thesis is that all bodily activity—human and non-human—is learned, and that this includes the functioning of the autonomic nervous system. If dogs can be conditioned to produce saliva by the ringing of a bell, then by systematic rewards humans can be taught to regulate their pulse rates, blood pressures, stomach emptyings, and a host of other "involuntary" functions. The method used to teach people how to control their autonomic functioning is called "operant conditioning," and it takes advantage of modern electronic devices to give the patient a constant impression (the rewards) of how he is doing.

For example, the patient whose heart is subject to premature beats ("skipped beats") does not get a shock every time he "allows" his heart to beat abnormally, as in the traditional aversive conditioning. Instead, he receives a constant visual signal in the form of a yellow light when his heart is beating regularly. When a premature beat disrupts this sequence, a red and then a green light goes on. Attached to this apparatus, the patient is told merely to keep the yellow light on as much as possible. In experiments reported by Theodore Weiss, M.D., and Bernard Engel, Ph.D., five of eight patients showed a statistically significant ability to reduce the number of skipped beats while on the machine, and in four this ability persisted long after the experimental period ended.

No one knows what mechanism is involved in "thinking away" actual disturbances of bodily function. Hormone studies are being done in patients receiving operant conditioning, as they have been done for some years now on certain famous Indian yogas and as they may be done in the future on Western practitioners of "transcendental meditation." What seems clear is that by consciously shutting out certain outside stimulae and, perhaps, by activating areas of the brain (especially the hypothalamus), we can achieve psychosomatic health as well as psychosomatic illness.

Any illness a human develops, in fact, can be called "psychosomatic" because the word implies an interaction between the mind ("psyche") and the body ("soma"). Even the most classically "organic" diseases, such as tuberculosis, where the actual infecting bacillus is well identified, bring along with them profound conflicts in the patient's mind—Will I die? Will I be able to go back to work? Will I get too far in debt? The emotional impact of a so-called "organic" disease can often be more devastating than the physical illness. Many research studies have shown, for example, that heart attack victims return to work at a rate determined not so much by the actual heart damage as by their attitudes toward their work, illness, and life is general.

After recognizing that every physical illness has its accompanying—and truly inseparable—emotional component, physicians in the 1930's and '40's began to talk about an extension of this concept. Led by the famed psychiatrist Franz Alexander, and aided by a series of brilliant experiments, they helped formulate the concept of "psychosomatic illness"—demonstrable physical illness actually caused by underlying mental conflicts. (Note the definitional difference between psychosomatic illness and hypochondria, in which concern about bodily function usually wanders from one part of the body to another, and in which no physical organ changes occur. See Today's Health, November 1971.)

Among the key experiments which structured this idea were a series of observations on a patient known as "Tom," who, after a childhood accident, had part of his stomach looped outside his skin, easily accessible to researchers. Stewart Wolf, M.D., and Harold Wolff, M.D., studied Tom for a period of years and found a close relationship between the way Tom felt emotionally and the way his stomach functioned. The interactions between mind and the digestive tract had, of course, been known for many years, but the experiments of Wolf and Wolff showed conclusively that strong emotions could produce marked changes in the muscular tone, secretions, and blood supply of the gut.

It should come as a surprise to no one that emotions can directly cause profound changes in the physical functioning of the body. The blush we experience when embarrassed is just as red as one from heavy exercise, the pounding of the pulse just before first making love to a beloved is as fast as that after a race, the nausea we feel when we see something disgusting is just as real as that from motion sickness—yet in none of the examples above has one's body actually been touched.

Fainting, blushing, pounding in the chest, nausea—all these are commonly produced by emotion alone. What was new in the concept of psychosomatic medicine was that *long-term* emotional stress could cause chronic illness. Believers in the psychosomatic theory pointed to the same bodily mechanism that underlies the acute psychosomatic examples mentioned above—the autonomic nervous system, divided into two components (sympathetic and parasympathetic), which through unconscious signals sent out from the brain and the endocrine glands regulate the involuntary functions of the body. "Involuntary" and "autonomic" because no one is able to decide to slow up his pulse or relax his stomach entrance or move food along faster in the intestinal tract—at least, no one had been until recently!

Because the ultimate transmitter of signals from emotional centers in the brain to the autonomic nervous system to the end-organs they controlled (intestine, bronchial tubes, heart, etc.) was known to be a pair of compounds called acetylcholine and adrenalin (epinephrine), research attention focussed on these. Generations of experimentation from the late 19th century to the present by such men and women as Claude Bernard, Walter Cannon, and Flanders Dunbar culminated in the work of the Canadian Hans Selye, who demonstrated that emotional stress and tensions directed increased hormonal outpouring of the adrenal glands. The adrenals produce not only cortisone and its derivatives, but adrenalin.

The stage was thus set for the great psychosomatic stampede of the 1950's, a time when practically every disease of unknown origin (and some of known origin) was attributed to a primary psychologic problem. The equation in its simplified form went like this:

Emotional stress (conflict, loss, anger)—continual overactivity of the adrenal glands—continued over-stimulation of the autonomic nervous system—blood vessel spasm and other end-organ change—actual physical findings in the diseased organ. In one classic form of the theory specific emotions were believed to cause specific diseases: Frustration predisposed to ulcer, for example.

Instant candidates for "psychosomatic illness" were such diseases as neurodermatitis, hyperthyroidism, high blood pressure, rheumatoid arthritis, asthma, peptic ulcer, and ulcerative colitis—the so-called "holy seven" of psychosomatic research. I happened to go to medical school at a time (1953-57) and a place (Boston University Medical School) when great advances were taking place in psychosomatic illness, and many of my classmates felt that the secret of such illnesses would be found just as definitely as Koch found that a tiny bacillus caused tuberculosis.

These hopes have faded. Today's textbooks of medicine list no illnesses under the general heading of "Psychosomatic," and researchers continue to argue whether patients with ulcerative colitis get the disease because they have a distinctive personality or develop a distinctive personality because they have the disease. The same debate, supported by research work on both sides, goes on about duodenal ulcers, coronary heart disease, high blood pressure, and many other conditions.

But despite the failure to pin down certain diseases as "caused" by the emotions, the field of psychosomatic medicine has advanced enormously since I left medical school. The emphasis is no longer on proving emotional causes for certain illnesses, but on exploring the indivisible, barely detectable interplay between mind and body. It has been conclusively shown that, if worry and tension by themselves can't make everyone sick, they and other emotions play a vital part in how our bodies feel, how illness develops, and how the individual copes with and recovers from sickness.

The new research in the field takes advantage of the same space-age technology which has advanced all other fields of medicine. Rather than relying on a subject's own testimony that he felt pleasure during a certain experiment, researchers can now measure his pupil size from instant to instant, correlating dilated pupils with pleasurable emotions. This couldn't have been done ten years ago with the cameras then available. Similarly, miniaturized, unobtrusive testing devices can be worn all day to measure pulse and blood pressure, giving the researcher a chance to relate changes in those measurements to periods of strong emotion during the patient's day.

A whole host of new chemical determinations has been opened up. The day when it was sufficient to measure the amount of adrenal hormones or adrenalin a subject put out in a day as an indication of "stress" are almost over. Today a variety of neuro-humoral transmitting substances can be measured, and some can be measured minute-to-minute, giving a more precise correlation with rapidly-changing emotions. Scientists are coming to the view that no single chemical mediates "stress," but rather that a complex interrelationship of many chemicals is involved.

Psychological testing has become infinitely more refined than it used to be. Instead of administering a standard "personality index test," doctors can devise specific questionnaires for certain experiments, and have the results correlated by computers in one day, a task it used to take six graduate students six weeks to do. More questions can be asked, more subtle and unexpected relationships uncovered. Experimenters are also freer to ask volunteer subjects directly about sex and to measure their emotional response to sexually laden material.

Another major effort in the field, led by George Engel, M.D., and his colleagues in Rochester, New York, has been to focus on the mental and social events in a patient's life just before he develops a clear-cut "organic" illness, such as stroke or heart attack. Engel has found that a higher percentage of patients than could be expected from chance alone have suffered a major setback in their personal lives just before the onset of these "organic" diseases. Overwhelmed by such conflicts as a loved child in trouble with the police or the financial need to stay with a distasteful job in which every day is torture, some patients enter what Engel calls "the giving up, given up" state. They feel they can no longer control their own lives, and are at the mercy of powerful, unstoppable forces. In this state, probably because of the altered hormone balance which it induces, they are more prone to serious organic disease.

Engel, as well as Thomas Hackett, M.D., of the Massachusetts General Hospital, has also studied the recovery phase from illness in psychosomatic terms. Working in a coronary care unit, Dr. Hackett has found a high degree of anxiety, then depression, then "coping," in patients who have just had heart attacks. It is in those patients who fail to cope adequately, who either deny they had any illness at all or who become paralyzed with fear that another attack may occur, that recovery is most prolonged. This coping ability may relate to the patient's childhood, when initial experience with illness or hospitalization induced a lifelong fear of sickness, or, instead, a continuing need for dependency, for handing his body—and his problems—over to other people to take care of.

The biochemistry of the emotions is also coming into view, like a statue gradually taking form as the sculptor laboriously chips away at a block of material. We cannot yet say—"Depression—not enough noradrenalin—just add a little more to his soup," or "Anger—too much adrenalin—just take a couple blocking pills," but we are on the verge. The work of Joseph Schildkraut, M.D., and Seymour Kety, M.D., formerly of the National Institutes of Health has shown significant differences in adrenalin-related compounds in such disorders of mood as depression and mania. From their work has come not only an understanding of the kind of profound depression that seems inexplicably to strike such successful people as Senator Thomas Eagleton, but also insight into the day-to-day emotional variations we all experience. Working on a fundamental level with enzymes which block certain steps in the formation of noradrenalin and related compounds, Kety and others have also pointed the way to future medicines which will be even more effective in treating depression and mania than the ones now available.

The psychosomatic literature is bursting with developing research. The scientific study of sleep, now possible for the first time, is being correlated with mood changes. Studies on infants are being done which indicate—just as parents have always suspected—that some children from their very birth are more prone to anxiety (this inborn or "constitutional" factor may be the reason that, while we are all subject to loss, anger, and conflict, and while our body chemistries all react to such emotions, we do not all develop illness or even nervousness).

Recent experiments have shown that the blood cholesterol level increases during periods of tension, that the adrenal hormone levels shoot up to extremely high percentiles in the Navy radar operators in two-man planes landing on aircraft carriers (interestingly, the pilots show a smaller increase, suggesting that the fact they have control over the landing and are not merely passive participants is a less anxiety-inducing situation). Several experimenters have correlated mood changes during the menstrual cycle with varying hormone levels, an old subject for research, and then gone on to study the effect of the birth control pill on these feelings. Besides the entries on the "holy seven" diseases, the pages of the journal *Psychosomatic Medicine* are filled with references to diseases and emotions encountered in daily living and the experimental laboratory. The number of biochemical substances being measured has increased enormously and sophisticated analyses of such substances as serotonin and 3-methoxy-4-hydroxyphenylglycol have replaced—or supplemented—the questionnaires that psychosomatic researchers depended heavily on 20 years ago.

There is nothing really mysterious about psychosomatic health and disease. Its basic principles have been known from the time of the Bible and Shakespeare. Its scientific principles have been steadily clarified for the past 100 years. But it is only recently that those principles have begun to be systematically applied by physicians like Dr. Glaser to help patients such as Bill Steinmetz.

Bill was sitting in the doctor's office waiting for the discussion to end. He was starting to feel uneasy again. He never told anyone about the problems at work, not even his wife. It was easier to avoid questions. Now the doctor was asking questions. Maybe he could avoid them too. Why can't Dr. Glaser just give me something to get rid of the cramps? he wondered.

But the doctor wanted to know when the last attack came on. He asked questions about the people Bill worked with. What about this young guy, Aiello? Did Bill get along with him at all, could he be jealous? What about Barnes? Maybe he was in a bad temper because things weren't going so well for him either.

Bill squirmed in his seat. If all this was at the bottom of the problem, what could he do about it? He couldn't stop going to work.

The doctor agreed. But there were things Bill could do to help alleviate the tension he built up at work.

"You're in good physical condition, Bill," said the doctor. "Some vigorous exercise outdoors will do you a lot more good than an afternoon of sitting in front of the television. Go out and take a walk in the evenings, clean up the yard on Saturday, borrow a bike from one of your kids and go for a ride. Take a train to work instead of driving your car. Be more receptive to new ideas at work. Get off the defensive—and try being a little more cheerful. You'll be more relaxed and you'll probably be able to work better."

The doctor gave Bill a prescription for a mild tranquilizer. "It will help keep the brain from overstimulating the nervous system when you feel a tense situation coming on," he explained. "You'll be able to function a little more confidently and, hopefully, as things start getting better, the pressure will lessen and you'll be back to your normal capacity without the medication."

"We'll have to treat the cramps, too, physiologically. The other prescription I'm giving you is a muscle relaxer. It acts directly on the colon and will help prevent the contractions and the pain."

Bill was amazed at how much better he felt already. It hadn't really been so difficult to talk to someone about his problems and worries. They loomed large before, all bottled up inside of his head. But he found that when he put them outside himself, they didn't look so big or menacing. Wait 'til his wife heard about this.

Though Bill already feels better, and will probably show gradual improvement, he has only begun his course of therapy with Dr. Glaser.

As we have seen, Dr. Glaser started by attempting to give his patient insight into some of the fears or angers which help cause symptoms. Bill will need to cooperate in the months ahead by learning to avoid situations in which emotions trigger symptoms. Dr. Glaser, as he told Bill, will prescribe tranquilizers, which tend to act on that area of the brain—the hypothalamus—which sends out signals to the nervous system when strong emotions are evoked. With tranquilizers the emotions may still be perceived properly by the patient—"I'm nervous because I have to fly to Cleveland tomorrow"—but the unconscious overstimulation of the sympathetic nervous system is blocked. In addition to tranquilizers, other medications are used which act at the sensitized end organ itself.

Thus another patient whose asthma follows periods of stress may not only get a tranquilizer, but another medicine which works directly on the bronchial tubes to keep them out of spasm. In cases where severe symptoms and emotional tension are problems, psychiatric consultation and treatment will often proceed simultaneously with physical and pharmacologic therapy.

This combined approach recognizes that the physician is not treating a diseased *part*, but a whole human being.

"What actually does cause alcoholism is still a mystery."

A great many stereotypes exist about the effects of alcohol and the characteristics of the alcoholic. Research has enabled us to study these stereotypes and, in many cases, to dispel them. In this article Knox presents a series of popular misconceptions and then the most recent relevant scientific information. Unfortunately, in some cases the certainty of the myth can only be replaced by uncertainty rather than a definitive solution.

In the past, an alcoholic usually got censure instead of help; today he is viewed as the victim of a disease. The change came about through renewed efforts to understand his complex problem. And with greater understanding has come the opportunity to clear away the cloud of misconception that obscured the true nature of alcoholism—and condemned him in the first place.

Each of the following statements in italics is a common misconception about alcoholism. After each statement, we supply the medical facts.

Most alcoholics are on skid row

No. Though the word "alcoholic" sometimes brings to mind a reeling, rheumy-eyed derelict, few alcoholics actually fit the description. According to recent calculation, 95 to 97 percent of our alcoholic population are *not* found staggering down dingy streets or huddled in dark doorways, but leading responsible lives in respectable communities. As a group, they're indistinguishable, representing both sexes, a variety of ages, and every race, creed, and calling. As individuals, most of them meet the criteria of middleclass America; they're married, have nice homes, raise a couple of kids or more, live with their families, and go to work or keep house. In numbers, they add up to an estimated nine million.

Alcoholics can stop drinking if they really want to

The alcoholic has gained an undeserved reputation for being a weak-willed person who drinks because he likes to. In the light of what is known about alcoholism, the strength of his resolve has little to do with the compulsion to drink, and he would crave alcohol even if he disliked the taste of liquor.

According to leading authorities on the subject, alcoholism is a form of drug addiction and, like other forms, involves changes in the chemistry of the body that lead to physical dependence. On withdrawal, the alcoholic becomes subject to real, not imagined, pain. Depending on how advanced his case is, he can be subjected to a nightmarish range of discomfort such as: extreme nervousness, night "sweats," leg and arm cramps, stomach pains, nausea, dizziness, uncontrollable trembling, hallucinations, convulsive seizures similar to epileptic attacks, and delirium tremens which can be fatal if untreated. Considering that relief comes with alcohol, one can readily understand why an alcoholic would be unable to simply "stop drinking" without help.

An equally difficult problem is the alcoholic's psychological dependence. He feels an overwhelming need to drink in order to cope with his problems, even though he knows that his drinking may have destructive consequences on his health, job, arrest record, marriage, and family.

Alcoholics don't want to be helped

While authorities concede that the alcoholic seems to be singularly help-resistant, they do not interpret this as a sign that he doesn't want help. They attribute it instead to an underlying tendency to deny his condition by failing, or refusing, to recognize alcoholism in himself. Many more alcoholics, they say, would seek help if the stigma attached to the disease were removed, and the alcoholic could openly admit to his problem without risking scorn and reproof.

Authorities also agree that at some level of understanding all alcoholics are aware of the destruction in their lives. In many cases, alcoholics become help resistant because they've been subtly (or not so subtly) rejected by people who should have helped them in the past, or because efforts to help them have not been particularly well tailored to their needs.

Women rarely become alcoholics

Current statistics indicate that nearly two million women are alcoholics, dispelling the notion that an alcoholic woman is a rarity. And while these statistics show that four or five times as many men as women are alcoholics, not all authorities are convinced the reading is dependable. Some, in fact, maintain that the incidence of alcoholism may well be just as high among women as it is among men, but that intensified efforts to protect female problem drinkers against exposure lowers the probability of detection. Also, men usually feel less need, and have less opportunity, to drink unobserved, making it more difficult for them to keep alcohol addiction a secret.

Alcoholics drink to escape reality

It isn't so. Saying that an alcoholic drinks to escape reality implies that he sets out to drink himself into a state of oblivion, where his problems can't reach him. Actually, what he's looking for is a way to cope with, not to escape from, reality. If he looks for it in drinking, it's because alcohol has an anesthetic effect and dulls the sensibilities. By depressing the brain's nerve centers it not only takes the edge off physical pain, fatigue, and emotional stress, but seems to cancel out inhibiting personal characteristics—self-consciousness and timidity, for example—that might otherwise act as a barrier in dealing with everyday tensions and situations. His motive in drinking, in other words, is not basically different from that of the estimated 86 million Americans who drink and don't have any problem with it.

Heavy drinkers are alcoholics

Not necessarily. Many authorities feel two main distinctions can be made between heavy drinking and alcoholic drinking. First, the alcoholic builds up a tolerance to alcohol, which means that his capacity for alcohol increases and it constantly takes more alcohol to have an effect on him. In the heavy drinker, the same amount of alcohol generally produces the same effect: if he drinks more than he usually does, he is affected more. Second, someone who is a heavy drinker and not alcoholic can choose where, when, how much, and with whom he drinks; he can drink or not, as he likes. In short, he has control over his drinking. With the alcoholic, it's the other way around.

Some experts, however, feel such definitions may be too narrow. Dr. Morris E. Chafetz, director of the new National Institute on Alcohol Abuse and Alcoholism, says "Alcohol abuse, in one sense, is present any time a person becomes drunk. And repeated episodes of intoxication or heavy drinking which impairs health—or the consistent use of alcohol as a coping mechanism in dealing with the problems of life to a degree of serious interference with an individual's effectiveness on the job, at home, in the community, or behind the wheel of a car—is alcohol abuse, and may raise the strong suggestion of alcoholism."

Alcoholism strikes without warning

Not really. Experts consider the prodromal, or early, stage of alcoholism a time of warning before the actual onset of the disease. It is a period when a person continues to function, at least outwardly, as he always has, but displays signs of psychological dependence on alcohol, such as the following:

■ He tends to drink on "signal": before starting the day's work, with lunch, after dinner, at bedtime; when he's bored, when he's keyed up, when he's tired, when he's upset, when he's elated.

■ He always drinks more than his companions, often more than he intended, and a great deal more than he used to.

■ He can't have a good time without drinking; it's a "must" for picnics on the beach, golf, fishing, card-playing, attending football games, and the like.

■ He doesn't sip his drinks, but gulps them down.

■ He indulges in some solitary drinking, often on the sly.

There is, in addition, one important warning sign that is significant in itself. It's called a "blackout."

A blackout is not the same as "passing out"; the person doesn't lose consciousness, and he behaves in what appears to be a normal manner while he's drinking. He may not even have had more than two or three drinks, although "blackouts" are usually produced by heavy drinking. Afterward, the drinker has no recollection of episodes following his drinking, or even that they took place.

It takes years of heavy drinking to become an alcoholic

Not always. Once a person's drinking has gone out of control and is creating problems in the different areas of his life, he is said to have become addicted to alcohol and in the acute stage of alcoholism. Generally, it takes an average of ten years of heavy drinking to reach that point. But there's no rule about it. For some individuals, the disease begins with the very first drink. With others, it takes three to five years of what experts consider moderate drinking. And there are people who drank heavily for 20 and 30 years before they showed signs of addiction, while others have been drinking as much and as long with no apparent ill effects.

Only a certain type of person can become an alcoholic

Researchers used to think so, too, and tried to paint a personality picture of addiction-prone individuals by studying the behavior and characteristics of chronic alcoholics. In doing so, they noted many striking similarities. The subjects were, for example, typically sensitive, easily frustrated, unable to cope with anxiety or tension, and tended toward feelings of depression and inferiority; many showed signs of emotional immaturity; hostility, guilt, and sexual problems.

But the theory simply could not stand up to scientific scrutiny, mainly because no set of characteristics could be assembled that would apply to them all. Furthermore, it could not be determined if the traits they exhibited were an inherent part of their personality, or had developed as a result of their addiction. Most authorities, in fact, are inclined to say there is no such thing as an "alcoholic personality," and any type of person is a candidate.

Alcohol is the sole cause of alcoholism

Obviously, no one can become an alcoholic without the use of alcohol. But authorities regard it as an *agent*, and not the cause of alcoholism. If it were the cause, they say, everyone who drinks would become addicted to it. Which isn't, of course, the case.

What actually does cause alcoholism is still a mystery, although several unproven theories recently have been advanced. It has been suggested, for example, that there is a basic physical difference in the way alcohol is disposed of in the body of an alcoholic. Another theory is that alcoholism is caused by a glandular malfunction, and nutritional deficiency is also suspect. Some say the disease is due to an abnormal emotional background, while others attribute it to serious psychiatric illness.

The informed consensus is that psychological, physical, social, and cultural conditions all contribute to alcohol addiction. However, most authorities do not discount the possibility that a single underlying cause, sometimes referred to as the X-factor, may be at the root of the problem.

A person can't inherit alcoholism

No evidence has been unearthed to specifically relate alcoholism to heredity, but there is a substantial amount of research that indicates alcoholism does run in families. Children of alcoholic parents, for example, are considered by authorities to be extremely high-risk individuals. And while their greater susceptibility might be accounted for by an unfavorable home atmosphere, learned attitudes regarding drinking, and imitation of adult behavior, some experts feel that the discovery of a direct genetic connection—either as a predisposition to alcoholism or an immunity to it—is not as remote as most people think.

Alcohol doesn't cause cirrhosis of the liver

It's long been known that only a small percentage of alcoholics—an estimated ten percent—develop cirrhosis of the liver. If alcohol were the cause of cirrhosis, the reasoning once went, a much greater percentage of alcoholics would get this disease. Most medical authorities assumed that the true cause of the prevalence of cirrhosis of the liver in alcoholics (eight times more frequent) was malnutrition, caused by the inclination to drink rather than eat. But now they're not sure.

Cirrhosis of the liver means scarring of the liver, and recent studies have shown that even small doses of alcohol unquestionably cause scar tissue in the liver. Other studies confirm that when people with advanced cirrhosis of the liver stop drinking, their condition shows striking improvement. As for the theory that malnutrition is the cause of this disease in alcoholics, studies say that it's simply not so.

"For the first time," says Dr. Frank A. Seixas, medical director of the National Council on Alcoholism, "we're getting medical evidence which confirms the observations doctors have made—and dodged—for years: alcoholism and cirrhosis are very closely linked."

Alcoholism is an allergy

Former alcoholics sometimes refer to their addiction as an "allergy," but do not use the word in its scientific sense. What they mean is that they react to alcohol differently.

It is possible, of course, for an individual to be allergic to any of the ingredients used in the distilling process, as well as to the alcohol itself. But if he were, his allergy wouldn't manifest itself as alcoholism. In such cases, the sensitivity would more likely produce symptoms similar to those that occur in other allergies, such as sneezing in hay fever or hives in food allergy. Also, allergies do not ordinarily lead to a craving for the substance that causes them *after* the reaction.

Alcoholism can't be cured

To be technical about it, an alcoholic can't be "cured." It would mean restoring him to a condition that enables him to drink in a controlled manner, and the majority of experts agree that, because alcoholism is a lifelong addiction, this usually can't be done. But the illness can be interrupted, and he can recover through abstinence and treatment.

Modern methods of treating alcoholism include: *medication*, which is used to ease the discomforts of withdrawal, to treat any medical complications that may be present, and sometimes to induce an aversion to alcohol; *counseling* or *therapy*, which consists of treating the psychological or emotional aspects of the problem; and *Alcoholics Anonymous*, a worldwide fellowship of nearly half a million people who succumbed to alcoholism and now share their own experiences in the hope of drawing strength and inspiration to solve their common problems.

Reports of success from various sources range from 15 to 80 percent, but the method employed seems to be less of a determining factor in recovery than early treatment, the patient's earnest desire to get well, and the support of those close to him.

"In children, however, psychiatrists seldom see the prolonged and deep seated depression they observe in adolescents and adults."

Depression is probably the most unpleasant emotional experience felt by man. Sometimes depression can be a minor annoyance or can develop into an intensely painful reaction. This article by Elkind and Hamsher describes various theories of depression, some treatment methods to overcome depression, and clinical material describing the various forms of depression.

It is an anguish of the mind that has as its companions fear and sadness—Freud might have described depression this way. Hippocrates, calling it melancholia, knew it in these terms. But that common voice in all of us, speaking in low and pained syllables, has taught us the sorrowful dialogue of feeling down and out.

If it is an unwelcome intruder—and who can say otherwise?—depression probably has never been a stranger. It would be correct to attribute as much of history and literature to it as to any other single emotional dominant. Both the commonest of men and the greatest of leaders have been victims of deep depression. Abraham Lincoln was well known for his despondent moods, which affected both his staff and his family. Winston Churchill referred to the "black dog" of depression that often overwhelmed him with a sense of futility and hopelessness. More recently Sen. Thomas Eagleton was forced to withdraw from the campaign because of the public debate over his past depression and its treatment.

Depression is a very human condition. In its least intense form it is not much more than an unpleasant symptom of everyday stress and strain, and as such it is experienced, at one time or another, by everyone. Yet each year a surprisingly large number of Americans—as many as eight million, the National Institute of Mental Health estimates—suffer depression severe enough to be treated by a physician, and another 250,000 people require hospitalization, often because of suicidal intentions. Suicide is the eleventh most common cause of death in this country and the fifth most common among children and adolescents.

Despite the prevalence of depression, its inner workings—what it is that causes feelings of despair—have eluded the doctor's grasp almost to the point that the medieval explanation of an imbalance among the bodily juices, however archaic, does not seem too far removed from the realm of possibility. Until the early part of this century melancholy feelings were popularly thought to arise from indifference of the mind, neglect of the spirit, or as a consequence of physical imprudence.

The modern breakthrough in our understanding of depression was made by Freud in a paper written in 1917 titled *Morning and Melancholia*. Building upon the writings of one of his students, Carl Abraham, Freud drew an analogy between grief reactions and depression. Although noting differences between these reactions, he also pointed out that both had their roots in attachment and subsequent loss.

Depression is still regarded as involving loss (real or imagined) of a particular person, object, belief, or value to which one is normally or inordinately attached. This attachment and loss phenomenon can be seen in many different forms of depression.

After the recent floods caused by Hurricane Agnes many people whose homes or businesses were destroyed showed depressive symptoms: They were dejected, had lost interest in the external world, were lacking in motivation, and were virtually unable to perform any useful activity. At the same time they did not have the characteristic self-reproach and self-abasement found in other, more serious, forms of depression.

Notably, a person who had lost a rowboat was sometimes more depressed than one whose home had been destroyed by the storm. The extent of depression did not directly coincide with the extent of material loss. This phenomenon, observed in countless other situations involving loss, is considered one of the foremost characteristics of depression. It can be applied with equal justification to the stockmarket trader who takes a large market swing in stride while the small investor may get upset by the slightest down-slide. It is the degree of attachment one has to things, and not their material worth, that determines the extent of depressive reaction to their loss.

If the attachment is minimal or the setback temporary, then the reaction may be normal feelings of low mood that disappear in a short while. At the other extreme are the abnormal feelings of intense hopelessness—a sense of losing all that makes life worth living.

This variation in intensity of the response to losing something—or someone—helps to explain why in fiction, as in reality, lovers will kill themselves upon the death of their partner. Romeo and Cho Cho San (in *Madame Butterfly*) committed suicide at the loss (again, real or imagined) of their lovers. In such instances the emotional attachment is so strong that loss of a lover or mate makes the world empty and devoid of meaning.

Other attachment and loss relationships exist besides those between lovers. A study of twelve manic-depressive patients at the Washington School of Psychiatry, for example, revealed that such patients tended to be the most talented members of the family and were pushed into achievement by their parents. Love and acceptance came to be associated with achievement and compliments from their peers and superiors. When these individuals failed or did not achieve their highest goals, they often became depressed.

Although other studies have not entirely confirmed these findings, they do suggest that depression can result from an excessive attachment to a career or public image. Depression occurs when the treasured career or image is tarnished, in fact or in prospect.

Loss is not always this straightforward or obvious. What is known as "success depression" is a frequently diagnosed condition for which there is no readily apparent cause. A man receives a promotion or reaches a long-sought goal, such as getting a house of his own. Then, inexplicably—to family, friends, and to the individual himself—he experiences depression. Most psychiatrists believe that the depression is caused by two factors. First, the intense pressure necessary for attaining the goal becomes a needed impetus to activity. Without this pressure bewilderment replaces decisiveness, and the patient feels hopeless and at sea. The second factor involved in success depression is the person's reaction to the possibility that he will somehow ruin his accomplishment.

Although this and all other types of depression—from the normal feelings of unhappiness to a pathological sense of despair—are common phenomena in adults, they are less frequently encountered in infants and children. It is probably more exact to say that depression in infants and children is not the same as in adults. Among infants who have been abandoned and unloved, psychiatrists sometimes find a type of withdrawal called anaclitic depression, which involves apathy, listlessness, loss of appetite, and retardation of growth. Infants who have not been mothered (hugged, held, cooed to, rocked, kissed, etc.) may even die despite the fact that they have received physical care.

In children, however, psychiatrists seldom see the prolonged and deep-seated depression that they observe in adolescents and adults. The reasons for this provide additional insights into the anatomy of depression. Basically, children lack the intellectual ability to see themselves from another person's point of view. Thus, they cannot really evaluate themselves objectively, and they believe that whatever they want they can achieve. Of course, children are unhappy at times when they fail in what they undertake or lose something they cherish, but the perennial mood of childhood is one of optimism—just the opposite of the depressed mood.

A case in point is the child with a visible physical defect, such as a deformed arm or a harelip. Such youngsters often appear to be outgoing, gutsy kids who are cheery, optimistic, and happy. Upon reaching adolescence, these individuals often become depressed. For the first time the young person during adolescence begins to see himself as others do and comes to recognize that his own view of himself as being the same as everyone else may not be shared by others. It is at this age that prolonged depression, as occurs in adults, may arise.

Aging is but one of the processes necessary to the more severe forms of depression. Not surprisingly, another factor related to depression in adults is loss of a parent during childhood or early adolescence. To be sure, this is not always the case. Nonetheless, such loss, particularly of the father, probably should be considered a predisposing factor toward adult depression. It also is common to other psychiatric disorders as well.

Nothing as dramatic as the loss of a parent is a necessary or inviolable precursor of depression. Something as ready-made as gender alone may bring on a low mood. Despite the controversy that exists among professionals over the diagnosis of depression, they all agree that depression is more frequent in women than it is in men. This is true both for cases seen in private practice and in hospital admissions. The reasons are not entirely clear. It could be woman's place in society (being a housewife can be a depressing role) or hormonal or psychological factors that make her susceptible to depressive feelings.

It also may be that men, socialized to be more oriented toward achievement and activities outside the family, are not as sensitive to the family's ups and downs. Women historically have been required to center their entire emotional lives on the family, and any loss is felt intensely since it represents a major portion of a woman's life. Psychiatrists are frequently confronted by a depressed woman whose children have married or left for college or a career. The woman's loss in such situations is the loss of her own utility and purpose in life. On the other hand, the frequency of depression in women could be related at least in part to the fact that men are more reluctant to confess their depressive episodes than are women. Because men usually conceal their intentions, they are more often successful in committing suicide.

Depression can be triggered by something as innocuous as weather or seasonal variations. Although one might expect that Christmas would be a peak period because it symbolizes home, family, interpersonal relationships, this is not the case. Most depressive illness among students, including suicides, appear in the spring and fall and are least frequent in the summer. The anticipation of failing an exam, psychologists believe, is a more potent factor in causing depression during these two seasons than the actual fact of failure.

A problem in uncovering some of the factors related to depression is diagnosis. Psychiatrists are far from agreement as to the classification of these emotional disorders. Some regard all depressive reactions as falling on a continuum, while others tend toward the theory that depressive reactions in a normal individual are qualitatively different from those in the neurotically or psychotically ill individual. Some of the most generally accepted classifications of the affective disorders are as follows:

Involutional psychotic reaction (also known as involutional melancholia) is seen in middle-aged people who are confronted with growing old. In the majority of instances there has been no previous history of depression. These people tend to have been compulsive individuals and to have led orderly lives. Their depressive illness often involves guilt, anxiety, difficulties in sleeping and eating, and hypochondria. Such reactions are typically long-lasting and often require hospitalization.

Manic-depressive reaction, manic type, is characterized by people who are excitable and elated most of the time. They talk a great deal about grandiose plans and projects and seem to be bundles of energy and activity. They often seem to be carried away by their ideas, which become diffused and disorganized. Occasional depressive moods may appear momentarily, but the dominant mood is one of optimism and activity.

Manic-depressive reaction, depressed type, individuals generally are unhappy, mentally dull, and physically slow. Sometimes the individual will be frightened and apprehensive to the point of cowering against the wall or in a corner. At other times he will appear to be perplexed or in a stupor and will be unresponsive to questions and requests.

Manic-depressive reaction, mixed type, individuals show signs of both the manic and depressive features described above.

Psychotic-depressive reaction, in addition to the classic signs of depression, low mood, and lack of interest, produces the classic features of delusions (false beliefs) and hallucinations (false sensations). In such patients there is often a specific precipitating factor. For example, soldiers who accidentally kill a buddy or an officer often show this type of reaction.

Psychoneurotic-depressive reaction is characteristic of people who tend to be anxious and to rely on rationalization to defend their positions. When such persons experience the loss of a loved one, or the loss of self-confidence or esteem, they suffer depression and self-deprecation. At the same time, however, the anxiety is somewhat allayed. This patient often feels guilt for past failures and deeds but shows none of the severe fantasies of the patients in the psychotic category. Analogous to this type of reaction is the student who imagines that one of his parents has died and that this will provide him with an excuse from exams. The depression associated with the loss of a parent relieves the anxiety associated with taking exams. Many psychiatrists equate neurotic-depressive reactions with an actual loss whereas psychotic depressive reactions are not related to any external event.

With suicide at one end and the blue feelings on a down day on the other, depression basically has three degrees of severity. Mild depression involves low mood and pessimism about the future. At this level of depression the individual is lethargic and feels unable to deal with simple, everyday affairs. Moderate depression is characterized by markedly slowed thinking and action. It is during this stage that the individual blames himself for everything, and minor setbacks become catastrophes in his mind. This is perhaps the most dangerous of depressions because it generates suicide. In the most extreme form—severe depression —the patient is completely withdrawn and unresponsive.

Although mild depressions almost always disappear without treatment, the two more serious degrees of depression, in most cases, do not respond merely to primarily verbal therapy. They are responsive to certain drugs and to electroconvulsive (ECT), or shock, therapy; however, the reason for success of these two treatments is not understood.

Although many psychiatrists dislike them, chemical and convulsive therapies usually do alleviate depression. The first use of convulsions for the treatment of mental disorders began in 1934 when L. V. Meduna, a Hungarian physician, injected a syringefull of camphor oil into one of his patients. As had many physicians before him, Meduna observed that patients who experienced naturally occurring convulsions—as in epilepsy—appeared to be free of psychotic symptoms after an attack. To Meduna this observation suggested the use of artificially induced convulsions as a therapy.

Although he tried several other substances after the camphor oil proved too unreliable, it took three years before a team of Italian physicians discovered the technique of producing convulsions electrically. This method is still the most widely used; however, though not as troublesome as when it was first employed, it is not without its problems.

As short a time ago as the early 1960s, ECT required assistants to control the patient. Typically, a different aide would be stationed at each of the patient's arms and legs. When the current was turned on, the patient became rigid and his limbs flailed out unless held down. Unlike epileptic convulsions, however, artificially produced ones sometimes resulted in fractured bones and joint dislocations. Such undesirable experiences with ECT caused many people to rail against it as barbaric, medieval, and inhumane. Such reactions persist today though these undesirable effects have been virtually eliminated by the use of anesthesia and muscle relaxants.

Today ECT is a relatively harmless treatment, not significantly more distasteful than having a tooth filled under Novocain, though it is usually done in a hospital. In preparation for the shock most physicians anesthetize the patient. The electrodes, through which the current travels, are two metal disks held in place on the temples by a band around the head. The only visible effect of the 100 or so volts at 200 to 1600 milliamps passing through the brain for about one second is a slight twitching of the toes.

The recovery from an ECT treatment normally begins within a half hour when the patient wakes up somewhat groggy and slightly disoriented. Particularly after several treatments, patients tend to become temporarily forgetful and confused. While frustrating, this condition is transitory, and many studies have shown that, except for the rare patient who has undergone more than fifty treatments, there are no lingering harmful effects of ECT.

The results of ECT are not only dramatically successful but immediate. Many patients show improvement after only one or two treatments, and it has been estimated that 80 per cent of all depressives fully recover after six to eight treatments.

The reason for the effectiveness of ECT is largely unknown. Some psychiatrists claim that the shock leads to a reorganization of the thoughts that produced the disorder. A more widely held, but equally speculative, view is that ECT is an unpleasant experience that is likened by the patient, on a subconscious level, to a punishment. After the treatment the patient feels that he has atoned for whatever in his past caused the depression. Since it is based on the belief that depressed people feel guilty about real or imagined shortcomings and only subconciously experience the shock as punitive, this theory remains an untestable hypothesis.

Until the late 1950s ECT unquestionably was the best treatment for depressive disorders. In 1957 the first of the antidepressant drugs became available. Originally designed for schizophrenic disturbances, these drugs were found to be more effective in alleviating the low mood of depressed patients.

The earliest drugs used to reduce depression were the amphetamines. The various side effects, including habituation, made the continued use of these a questionable price to pay for relief of depression, and by 1958 researchers produced other depression-combating drugs with fewer side effects. Not as rapidly effective as the amphetamines, these newer drugs, called by such names as Elavil and Parnate, are widely taken by persons suffering mild-to-moderate depression.

Research on all of the antidepressants has produced findings that are as confusing and contradictory as they are extensive and specific. Differences in research approaches, in dosages used, in types of patients treated, and in a host of other factors produce controversial results. An additional problem is the different purposes of research projects. Some investigators have attempted to assess the degree of effectiveness of one or more drugs, while others have focused on the comparative merits of specific drugs as compared with alternative therapeutic approaches, such as ECT and hypnotherapy. Most psychiatrists say that more work is needed before drug therapy can be considered superior to ECT.

Evaluation of drug treatment is complicated by value judgments such as "ECT is barbaric" or "drugs are crutches that help the patient avoid dealing with the real problem," and also by the fact that drugs have one distinct advantage and one equally significant drawback. The advantage is that patients who are only mildly affected by depression can be treated with a less extreme method than ECT, hospitalization, or long-term psychotherapy. This permits many patients to be treated by their personal physicians without being identified as having a mental-health problem. The striking disadvantage of drugs lies in their unwanted but undeniable side effects.

No drug has been developed that does not have negative secondary results in addition to its positive primary ones. It is common in drug therapy to prescribe one chemical for a wanted effect and one or more additional ones to offset the concomitants of the first. This may lead to a cycle of chemical complications.

The alternative to ECT or drugs is psychotherapy, in which the psychiatrist works with the depressed patient to uncover the emotional roots of the disorder and to help alter the patient's personality so as to effectively reduce the chance of recurrence of the depression.

Depressed people may recover spontaneously, without any treatment, just as most people are able to come out of normal low moods in a day or so. The tendency of depressed patients to recover spontaneously is a problem in evaluating the results of any treatment. This is particularly true of psychiatric treatment since therapy of this nature usually involves many sessions over months or even years. A large number of patients may lose their motivation when they begin to feel better and may drop out of therapy before it can be judged whether the sessions have been effective.

It seems clear that depressive disturbances, even if they involve a physiological or biochemical component, are primarily emotional phenomena. Thus, supportive or searching psychotherapy is undoubtedly a potentially valuable aid to the depressed patient. There is, however, considerable disagreement as to when in the course of the depression psychotherapy is most helpful.

Until more, much more, is learned about the subtle intricacies of the human mind, depression can be only partially understood. For the more serious forms of depression there are treatments that provide relief. Most of us who know what it is to feel the blues need only reassurance to snap the mood. Often a sunny day or a pleasant exchange is enough.

"His distortions confuse him; his confusion frightens him; his fear becomes so overwhelming that he withdraws from people and his withdrawal from human contact leaves him painfully alone."

What is schizophrenia? What are some of the behaviors that characterize schizophrenia? How true are some of the myths about it? All of these questions and many more are taken up in this article. Here you will find a review of some of the most current information about schizophrenia.

What Is It?

At first it was as if parts of my brain "awoke" which had been dormant, and I became interested in a wide assortment of people, events, places, and ideas which normally would make no impression on me.... The walk of a stranger on the street could be a "sign" to me which I must interpret. Every face in the windows of a passing streetcar would be engraved on my mind, all of them concentrating on me and trying to pass me some sort of message.[1]

Schizophrenia is a word used to describe a complex mental disorder. It describes a set of conditions which are not constant, but ever changing, a way of behaving that is not general among all sufferers, but highly personal.

In contrast to many illnesses, it is not localized in one part of the body. Rather, it affects all aspects of an individual's personality—the way he thinks. acts, and feels. No generalizations hold true for all schizophrenics. In fact, it is possible for two people to be labeled "schizophrenic" and to show entirely different symptoms.

Reprinted by permission of the Center for Studies of Schizophrenia, Clinical Research Branch, Division of Extramural Research Programs, National Institute of Mental Health.

[1] (Quotations are used with permission of the publishers). MacDonald, Norma. Living with schizophrenia. *Canadian Medical Association Journal, 82*:678–681, January 23, 1960. In: Kaplan, Bert, *The Inner World of Mental Illness: A Series of First-Person Accounts of What It Was Like.* New York: Harper & Row, 1964, p. 175.

The World of the Schizophrenic

Unusual Realities Each person looks at the world from his own point of view. If four people go to see a trapeze show, they might talk about it afterwards very differently. One person might talk about the danger and risks involved in doing somersaults in the air. Another might talk about the beauty and grace of the act and compare it with a ballet. Another might talk about the sturdiness of the ropes and pulleys. And yet another might be impressed most with the attractiveness of the performers.

A person diagnosed schizophrenic might see any one of these four images just as a "normal" person sees them. Or he might see laughing hyenas, instead of people, swinging on the ropes. Just as each "normal" individual views the world from his own perspective, the schizophrenic, too, has his own perceptions of "reality." However, his view of the world very often is strikingly different from the usual "reality" seen and shared by those who are well.

Illusions The world of a schizophrenic may be timeless, flat, without depth, without dimension. It may appear dull, simply black and white, without color. Faces may seem to alter. The kind, loving face of a wife may suddenly appear harsh and cruel. The schizophrenic knows that in actuality his wife's face has not changed; but for him, it has. He may blink his eyes once or twice to try to see again his wife's loving expression. These are "illusions" which can come to plague his everyday life.

Very often he knows that what he is perceiving is not accurate, but he is unable to alter his view. As a schizophrenic girl described the experience:

> I went to my teacher and said to her, "I am afraid...." She smiled gently at me. But her smile, instead of reassuring me, only increased the anxiety and confusion for I saw her teeth, white and even in the gleam of the light. Remaining all the while like themselves, soon they monopolized my entire vision as if the whole room were nothing but teeth under a remorseless light. Ghastly fear gripped me.[2]

Hallucinations The world of a schizophrenic also may be filled with hallucinations; a person actually may sense things which in reality do not exist. For example, he may see his dead mother walking through his bedroom, or he may feel fingers touching his body, or he may hear voices telling him what to do. These visual, tactile, and auditory hallucinations are very frightening to him.

Fear and Loneliness Living in a world that is distorted, changeable, and lacking the reliable landmarks we all use to anchor ourselves to reality, the schizophrenic feels confused, and unbearably frightened. Because he has lost his sense of the "usual" reality, he feels at a distance from others, and very much alone. To him, life seems a vicious cycle. His distortions confuse him; his confusion frightens him; his fear becomes so overwhelming that he withdraws from people and his withdrawal from human contact leaves him painfully alone. Being alone is what frightens him most; being alone prevents him from easing the confusion; being alone perpetuates his madness.

The overwhelming fear the schizophrenic experiences has a powerful im-

---

[2] Sechehaye, Marguerite. *Autobiography of a Schizophrenic Girl.* New York: Grune & Stratton, Inc., 1951, p. 2.

pact on the way he behaves. He may feel so frightened that he will sit rigid as a stone, not moving for hours, not uttering a sound. Or he may move about constantly, always occupied, wide awake, vigilant, alert. These are two very different modes of behavior that two individuals may exhibit; or one schizophrenic individual may exhibit this different behavior at different times.

Disordered Thinking   Very often the schizophrenic's thinking is affected by his disorder. He may endure many hours of not being able to "think straight." Thoughts may come rapidly, so that he cannot "catch them." He may not be able to stay with one thought for very long and he becomes easily distracted, unable to pay attention. As one patient reported:

My concentration is very poor. I jump from one thing to another. If I am talking to someone, they only need to cross their legs or scratch their heads and I am distracted and forget what I was saying.[3]

He may not be able to sort out what is relevant and what is not relevant to a situation. As a result, he may dwell on a single thought for hours, such as thinking about how many times he has brushed his teeth that day. Or he may be unable to connect his thoughts into logical sequences; his thoughts may be disorganized and fragmented.

Half the time I am talking about one thing and thinking about half a dozen other things at the same time. It must look queer to people when I laugh about something that has got nothing to do with what I am talking about, but they don't know what's going on inside and how much of it is running around in my head. You see I might be talking about something quite serious to you and other things come into my head at the same time that are funny and this makes me laugh. If I could only concentrate on one thing at the one time I wouldn't look half so silly.[4]

Such jumping from topic to topic may be totally confusing to another person.

My thoughts get all jumbled up. . . . People listening to me get more lost than I do.[5]

The lack of logical connectedness in thoughts, or "thought disorder" as it is termed, makes conversation very difficult. If people cannot seem to make sense of what an individual is saying, they tend to be driven away, and to leave him alone.

Dispelling Some Myths

At times, "normal" individuals may feel, think, or act somewhat in a way that is characteristic of schizophrenia. Often "normal" people are unable to "think straight." They can be made so anxious by speaking in front of groups, for example, that they will feel confused, unable to pull their thoughts together,

[3,4,5] McGhie, Andrew, and Chapman, James. Disorder of attention and perception in early schizophrenia. *British Journal of Medical Psychology,* 34:103–16, 1961.

and "forget" what they had intended to say. This does not mean that they are schizophrenic.

Often schizophrenics exhibit what is called "inappropriate affect." This means showing emotion which does not seem to be consistent with the situation. For example, a schizophrenic may say that his mother has died and then laugh instead of cry. But this can sometimes be seen in the behavior of "normal" individuals, when for instance, they giggle nervously after a minor accident.

Just as "normal" people might occasionally do "crazy" things, a schizophrenic very often thinks, feels, and acts in a "normal" fashion. Unless he is in the midst of an acutely disorganized state, a schizophrenic knows that most people eat three times a day, sleep at night, and use the toilet. He does have a sense of the common reality. Being "out of touch with reality" (which is perhaps one way to describe schizophrenia) does not mean that an individual is living totally in another world. Rather, there are certain aspects of his world which are not shared by anyone else and which seem to have no real basis. Hearing a voice of warning talk to you every morning is not an experience shared by most people and is clearly a distortion of reality; but it is only a distortion of one part of the reality; everything else may be in place. A schizophrenic therefore may appear quite "normal" much of the time.

There is a very prevalent notion that schizophrenia is a split personality or a Dr. Jekyll-Mr. Hyde switch in character. This is not an accurate description of the disorder. A woman who is mean and cruel to her children and then kind and thoughtful to her neighbors is not necessarily schizophrenic. She is acting in a different fashion in different situations and does have some control over her behavior.

A schizophrenic is not a dope addict or an alcoholic. He may use alcohol or drugs to help him deal with his problems, but schizophrenics do not use this means of escape any more than does the average person.

A schizophrenic is not simply a happy-go-lucky person delighting in his madness. For the most part he feels plagued and tortured. One need not try to convince a man that he is mad. Despite how he acts, he knows it; he is very much aware of his difference and his agony. He is tormented and frightened by his voices and distorted perceptions. He is confused and made lonely by his inability to order and control his thoughts and to carry on a "normal" conversation. He knows his disorder all too well.

I felt all this tumult of madness—all this stark, lonely living which is worse than death—and the pain, futility and hopelessness of it all—and the endlessness, the eternity.[6]

Schizophrenia, then, is a complex disorder. It affects *all* aspects of an individual's personality. It is expressed differently in different people, and within a single individual its characteristics may vary and change.

As a woman diagnosed schizophrenic said:

[6] Jefferson, Lara. I am crazy wild this minute. How can I learn to think straight? In: Kaplan, Bert, *The Inner World of Mental Illness: A Series of First-Person Accounts of What It Was Like.* New York: Harper & Row, 1964, p. 12.

Since it is a law of nature that no two snowflakes are alike, and that no two human beings are alike, it is practical to realize that no two minds are very similar at all, even in the more understandable part. Since the schizophrenic wanders about in a bottomless unconscious, and I suspect on by-paths leading into a far-reaching collective consciousness, it is not likely that I will ever know what goes on in the mind of a fellow-sufferer.[7]

A person does not *have* schizophrenia as he might have an ulcer in his stomach or a cold in his head. He *is* schizophrenic; he *is* the disorder. It pervades his entire being.

Is Schizophrenia a New Disease?

While the term "schizophrenia" was not used until the early 20th Century, the disorder has existed throughout history. In times past, and even now in some places, man has looked at peculiar behavior and considered it a sign of magical powers (as in medicine men), or possession by the devil (as in the witches of Salem). Only relatively recently has it been thought of as an incurable hereditary disease, and, most recently, as a treatable medical illness.

In Western society, "madness" or "insanity" was not regarded as a responsibility of medicine until the early 19th Century. At that time, a movement to offer more humane treatment to the mentally ill made it possible for them to receive more scientific medical treatment. The insane were unchained, released from prison, and accorded decent care. Several categories of mental disease were identified. By the early 20th Century dementia praecox (schizophrenia) had been distinguished from manic-depressive illness, and subcategories of the disorder had been described. In 1911, the Swiss psychiatrist Dr. Eugen Bleuler first used the term "the group of schizophrenias." Despite disagreement among scientists as to precisely what conditions should or should not be included in this group, the term has been used commonly since 1911.

Can Children Be Schizophrenic?

Children have been known to exhibit schizophrenic-like behavior, although its relationship to the adult disorder, if any, remains poorly understood. Two major categories are generally recognized: severe disorder in children under 5 who usually have no speech and are very withdrawn; and serious difficulties in children under 5 who do have some language, but are withdrawn and relatively uncommunicative. The first is most often termed infantile autism, the latter, childhood schizophrenia.

These conditions are much less common than the schizophrenias of adolescence and adulthood. This booklet applies principally to adults. If you are concerned about a child, have him seen by your family doctor or pediatrician, who can refer him, if necessary, to a child psychiatrist or child guidance clinic.

Are Schizophrenics Likely To Be Violent?

It is true that some acutely disturbed patients may become physically vio-

---

[7] MacDonald, Norma. Living with schizophrenia. *Canadian Medical Association Journal*, 82:678–681, January 23, 1960. In: Kaplan, Bert, *The Inner World of Mental Illness: A Series of First-Person Accounts of What It Was Like.* New York: Harper & Row, 1964, p. 179.

lent. However, since the introduction of tranquilizing drugs, such outbursts are relatively infrequent. There is no evidence that, after having been released from a hospital, people diagnosed as schizophrenic are more prone to violence than the average person.

What about Suicide?

Suicide is a potential danger in any disturbed individual, including schizophrenics. If an individual tries to commit suicide or expresses plans to do so, he should be given immediate professional help.

What Causes Schizophrenia?

There is no known single cause of schizophrenia, just as a man's personality is the result of an interplay of cultural, psychological, biological, and genetic factors, a disorganization of personality (in other words, schizophrenia) may result from an interplay of the same factors. Scientists do not agree on a specific formula which is necessary to produce the disorder. No "bad" gene has been found; no abnormal chemical has been detected; no one stressful event (such as a death in the family) seems sufficient, by itself, to produce such a shattering disorder as schizophrenia. But scientists do agree that it is most likely that *combinations* of these factors produce schizophrenia.

Is Schizophrenia Inherited?

A decade ago, it was believed that schizophrenia had a very strong hereditary basis. Over the last 10 years, however, increasingly sophisticated twin and adoptive research has led to a reassessment of the role of genetics in schizophrenia. There is probably a hereditary aspect of the disorder, but the exact extent of its influence needs further explanation. Most scientists agree that schizophrenia *itself* is not inherited. Rather, what may be inherited is a predisposition to the disorder, an inherited potential.

It is not known whether this predisposition is specific to schizophrenia or to a broader category of mental illness; nor is the magnitude and mode of genetic influence on the development of schizophrenia known. As there is no genetic marker for schizophrenia, it is very difficult to determine the genetic influence. Undoubtedly, inheritance is not the sole factor.

Are the Parents at Fault?

There is wide agreement that a child's experience in his family plays a major role in the development of his personality. The child's patterns of emotional expression, thought, and action are shaped by his parents.

Most parents have noted traits in their children which resemble their own characteristics, such as a child's sense of humor or temperament. This resemblance has been shown to depend on more than heredity. Imitation, modeling, and identification with certain aspects of one or both parents have a powerful influence on personality development.

Just as parents have an impact on the development of healthy aspects of their child's personality, they can also contribute—unwittingly—to the development of unhealthy aspects. Parents do not intentionally, maliciously influence a child to become deviant. However, it is generally agreed that environment, family, peers, and school—all can contribute to the development of the illness.

Some studies have shown that in families with schizophrenic offspring, communication among family members is unclear and the parents themselves often exhibit illogical thought processes. Other studies have found that contradictory communication seems to be important in the development of the disorder. For example, a parent may push a child away and at the same time express great affection for the child. The confusion which might be engendered in the child as to which part of the message is "really" meant seems to have a parallel in the difficulty experienced in trying to sort out what is "really" meant by an individual schizophrenic. However, it is not yet known whether these difficulties are a *cause* or a *result* of schizophenia. In other words, the unclear thinking in families with schizophrenic offspring may come as a result of its schizophrenic member.

Is Schizophrenia Caused by Poverty?

Poverty itself is not a direct cause of schizophrenia. Conditions associated with poverty, however, may be implicated in the development of the disorder. Indeed schizophrenia appears to occur more frequently among the lower socioeconomic class than any other.

Low-income mothers often receive inadequate care during the prenatal period and at the time of delivery. They are also more apt to receive poor care both for themselves and their baby immediately following the child's birth. Poor nutrition and inadequate care before, during, and after delivery are associated with increased risk for the children; one of those risks is the development of schizophrenia.

Poverty is frequently accompanied by a disordered family life. For a growing child, this presents serious difficulties in adjustment which could lead to an emotional disorder. While broken or otherwise disturbed homes are not in any way the sole cause of schizophrenia, they can contribute—in combination with other factors—to its development.

Is Schizophrenia Caused by a Chemical Defect?

At the present time, no biochemical cause has been found for schizophrenia. A number of biochemical abnormalities, however, have been reported in schizophrenics over the years. For example, many acutely ill patients excrete in their urine a compound which, when analyzed by a particular chemical method, produces a pink spot. The substance which produces the pink spot is of special interest because of its possible hallucinogenic qualities. Scientists have related the production of such compounds by the body to the occurrence of schizophrenia because people under the influence of chemicals such as mescaline and LSD experience hallucinations. Unfortunately, whether the pink spot can be found *only* in schizophrenic patients (and not in normal persons), and whether it is a cause or a result of schizophrenia is still unknown.

How Is It Treated?

Since schizophrenia is not a single condition, and is expressed differently in different individuals, with symptoms constantly changing, there is no one best treatment. Instead, a number of treatments have been found to be helpful, and more are being developed.

What about Tranquilizers?

The major tranquilizers (such as chlorpromazine or thorazine) available since the mid-1950's, have proved valuable to most schizophrenics and are a standard treatment for the disorder. They greatly improve—directly and indirectly—the outlook for individual patients. They decrease the patient's fear and lessen acute symptoms; they enable him to think more clearly and function more appropriately. The choice of drug can be made only by a qualified physician.

The introduction of psychoactive drugs has had a powerful effect on the attitudes of professionals and laymen toward the possibility of successful treatment for schizophrenia. Hospital nurses, attendants, and doctors feel more comfortable when a patient is calm and is behaving in a sociably acceptable fashion. They feel more hopeful that the individual will soon be able to function "normally." This feeling in turn enables the patient to feel more hopeful about himself and to begin to form meaningful contacts with other people. These contacts and this hope are of tremendous importance in helping the patient recover.

What about Other Forms of Treatment?

Almost every authority agrees that tranquilizing drugs should be supplemented by other forms of treatment. While the drugs have proved crucial to the positive outlook for schizophrenia they are not in themselves curative. Combining several forms of treatment, especially those which add human contact, seems to hasten and make more complete the recovery of the schizophrenic. It has been demonstrated repeatedly that continued involvement with people is essential to prevent a state of "chronic" illness.

Are Electroshock and Insulin Coma Treatment Still Used?

In particular situations, electroshock treatment may be useful. It can be of help, for example, if a severe depression occurs in the course of a schizophrenic episode. Insulin coma treatment is used less often now because electroshock treatment seems to be equally effective and has fewer side reactions.

Is Lobotomy Still Recommended?

This brain operation, formerly used in some patients with severe chronic schizophrenia, is now rarely used. Its discontinuation is due both to the serious, irreversible personality changes which the surgery may introduce and to the fact that better results can be attained from less hazardous procedures.

Are Large Doses of Vitamins Useful in Schizophrenia?

Good physical hygiene, including a nourishing diet and proper exercise, is always important. Whether or not large doses of vitamins are specifically therapeutic for schizophrenia remains unresolved. Since vitamins have few serious side effects, adding them to other forms of treatment is considered relatively harmless. Their specific value for the treatment of schizophrenia, however, is still in question. In no case should vitamins be the sole form of treatment.

What about Psychotherapy?

Individual psychotherapy or psychoanalysis is a form of treatment in which an individual talks for a specific period of time (usually 50 minutes) on a regular basis (ranging from once a month to 5 days a week) to a psychiatrist or other mental health professional. By sharing his experiences with a trained, empathetic person and by talking about his world with someone outside it, the schizophrenic may gradually come to understand more about himself and become able to sort out the real from the unreal and distorted. This process can prevent his being driven further into a world of fear, confusion, and isolation. Experience with such a helping relationship can enable him to trust others and to come out from his shell of withdrawal, into contact with the world at large.

Group Therapy

Group therapy sessions usually involve about 10 patients and one or two trained therapists. Here, the focus is on learning from the experiences of others, testing out one person's perceptions against those of others, and correcting distortions and maladaptive interpersonal behavior by means of feedback from other members of the group.

Family Therapy

Family therapy is a technique which has only recently come into wide use. As usually practiced it involves the patient and his parents or spouse and a therapist. Brothers and sisters, children and other relatives may also be included. The purposes vary. Meeting in a family group can enable various family members and the therapist to understand better the points of view of others, can help with treatment planning (such as hospital discharge), and can modify a family's attitudes and behaviors which seem to be related to the development or maintenance of "illness" in the patient.

Hospitalization

Prolonged hospitalization, especially in large, distant, and impersonal institutions with few doctors, nurses, and other staff members is now believed to be antitherapeutic. What seems to prolong schizophrenia is the absence of social contacts, the lapse of ties with family, acquaintances, and the community. Often a schizophrenic is isolated in his own world of fantasy; to be brought out of that world, he must make meaningful contact with people, which is virtually impossible in poorly staffed facilities.

Well-staffed facilities and removal from stressful situations, however, can provide a protective atmosphere for the troubled patient and relief for the family.

Many schizophrenics can benefit from partial hospitalization (day care or night care), from outpatient treatment (going to a clinic or office regularly for individual, group, or occupational therapy), or from living in a halfway house (designed to aid patients in bridging the gap between 24-hour hospitalization and independent existence in the community). The treatment of schizophrenia is becoming increasingly community-centered. Attempts are being made to minimize the actual time a person must spend in a hospital. The treatment of schizophrenia is taking into account the adverse effects of prolonged hospitalization and the positive effects of continued contacts with family and friends.

What Lies Ahead?

Given its complexity, the riddle of schizophrenia—its characteristics, causes, and treatment—is unlikely to be solved in the near future.

The major changes in the next decade probably will come in changes of treatment philosophy and facilities. Hopefully, institutions for the treatment of schizophrenia will be small and well-staffed with flexible, accepting, and sensitive individuals who can facilitate changes rather than reinforcing their patients' mistrust and rigidity.

The development of a variety of treatment facilities is of crucial importance because schizophrenics vary so greatly in their needs for treatment.

Alternatives must be found between the relatively nonintensive treatment offered in outpatient clinics and the highly regulated treatment of 24-hour supervision. With a wide variety of facilities available, doctors will be better able to tailor treatment to the widely different needs of individual patients rather than, as is all too often the case, tailoring the patient to the treatment. Some patients need constant care and attention, while others need a place to be responsible, without constant supervision. Only by having several types of services available can we maximize the effectiveness of our treatment of this complex disorder.

Can Schizophrenia Be Cured?

Schizophrenia is no longer viewed as a chronic, progressive, hopeless disease. Many schizophrenic patients improve to such an extent that they lead independent, satisfying lives. Indeed, they may even grow from the experience to become fuller human beings. To do so, they integrate the experience into their lives—make it a part of themselves—instead of trying to isolate or ignore it. The schizophrenic experience is so powerful that it is almost certain to have a crucial impact on an individual's life. Trying to "forget it" seems to be not only difficult, but detrimental; trying to accept it and learn from it is also exceedingly difficult, but potentially growth enhancing. In this sense, a schizophrenic episode can be a creative experience.

As one schizophrenic individual said:

> Living with schizophrenia can be living in hell, because it sets one so far apart from the trend of life followed by the majority of persons today, but seen from another angle it can be really living, for it seems to thrive on art and education, it seems to lead to a deeper understanding of people and liking for people, and it's an exacting life, like being an explorer in a territory where no one else has ever been. I am often glad that illness caused my mind to "awaken" eleven years ago, but there are other times when I almost wish that it would go back to sleep.[8]

However, there is no single cure for schizophrenia. No simple operation, no single drug, no instant magic has been found. The public should beware of purveyors of "the cure" for (or "the cause" of) schizophrenia. Such claims lead to

[8] MacDonald, Norma. Living With Schizophrenia. *Canadian Medical Association Journal*, 82:678–681, January 23, 1960. In: Kaplan, Bert. *The Inner World of Mental Illness: A Series of First-Person Accounts of What It Was Like.* New York: Harper & Row, p. 184.

disappointment, resentment, and withdrawal. It is this process of unrealistic expectations followed by equally great disappoinments which has so frequently led to despair and the consequent neglect of schizophrenics.

Indeed, it is probably unrealistic to expect cure in the sense of complete restoration to former functioning. That is rarely expected of any branch of medicine. X-rays reveal that even a completely healed broken leg, for example, shows bone changes associated with healing. Thus, in the absolute sense, the broken leg is not "cured" but "repaired." Applying this analogy to the recovered schizophrenic, one would expect "scars" or changes from previous characteristics. When a man comes out of the hospital or other treatment center, one should not expect that he will be the same as he was before the disorder. Much as a survivor of a fire, he has lived through a powerful experience, and one should not expect him to remain untouched by it. As one woman said, even when she was in the midst of an acute schizophrenic episode:

I cannot escape from the Madness by the door I came in, that is certain— nor do I want to. They are dead—past—the struggles of yesterday. Let them lay in the past where they have fallen—forgotten. I cannot go back— I shall have to go onward.[9]

Perhaps the greatest roadblock to recovery a schizophrenic faces is a lack of attention from others because they are afraid of him. They may fear, for example, that a small patch of irrationality within him may someday expand until, unchecked, it dominates his personality. Given the almost universal fear of "losing one's mind," it is small wonder that society too often neglects the schizophrenic and keeps him at a distance. Unfortunately, this distance only reinforces the schizophrenic's difficulty with relationships, and will, therefore, tend to reinforce his illness.

How To Help

It is generally best to seek advice first from a family doctor, or from a local medical society that can recommend a physician, clinic, or psychiatrist. Don't hesitate to seek help for fear that a friend or relative will have to be hospitalized for the rest of his life. *Schizophrenia is treatable* and in most instances the treatment can allow return to a relatively normal life within a fairly short period of time.

The best advice is not to be concerned about "schizophrenia" itself. Rather, concern is due any person who appears seriously troubled, in whatever ways the difficulty is shown, whether depression, excessive drinking, prolonged personality change, withdrawal from friends and relatives or serious interpersonal difficulties. Any or all of these characteristics may be indicative of schizophrenia. Good professional advice should be sought for anyone who seems seriously troubled—not because he may be schizophrenic—but because he needs help.

[9] Jefferson, Lara. I am crazy wild this minute. How can I learn to think straight? In: Kaplan, Bert, *The Inner World of Mental Illness: A Series of First-Person Accounts of What It Was Like.* New York: Harper & Row, 1964, p. 7.

Suggested Readings for
Chapter 8

Beck, A. T. *Depression: Causes and treatment.* Philadelphia: University of Pennsylvania Press. An excellent work from both a research and a clinical perspective. It is an outstanding review of a very complex clinical syndrome.

Landis, C. *Varieties of psychopathological experience.* F. A. Mettler (Ed.). New York: Holt, Rinehart and Winston, 1964. A series of autobiographical statements by individuals who have undergone a period of abnormal behavior.

Rabkin, L. Y. *Psychopathology and literature.* San Francisco: Chandler, 1966. Abnormal behavior as it is illustrated in famous literary works.

Zax, Melvin & Cowen, Emory. *Abnormal psychology: Changing conceptions.* New York: Holt, Rinehart and Winston, 1972. An excellent new textbook that reviews the entire field of abnormal psychology with particular emphasis on the new developments such as community psychology.

Zax, Melvin & Stricker, George. *The study of abnormal behavior.* (3d ed.) New York: Macmillan, 1974. A collection of papers concerning issues in abnormal psychology, types of abnormal behavior, the treatment of abnormal behavior, and community psychology.

Discussion Questions

1. How would you decide whether or not you were in need of help for a mental health problem, and how would you go about getting it?

2. What is abnormal behavior?

3. How does your physical health and wellbeing relate to your emotional condition?

4. Is a mental illness like any other illness? How is it different?

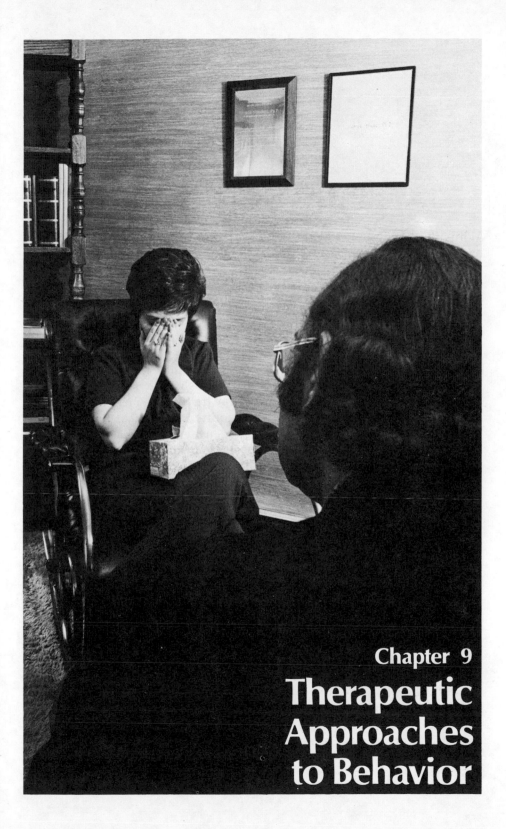

Chapter 9

Therapeutic Approaches to Behavior

While the study of abnormal behavior is of great interest in its own right, serious research would be an empty academic exercise if it did not result in the development of procedures useful in the modification of such behavior. A long-time concern of psychologists, the treatment of abnormal behavior has followed a fairly stable and uniform pattern for many years. Such treatment has traditionally consisted of either individual psychotherapy sessions based primarily on the theoretical formulations of Sigmund Freud or else hospitalization in an institution which was essentially custodial in nature. In recent years, however, there has been a revolutionary change in the approach to abnormal behavior. For the outpatient, there have been several variations in the traditional procedure. Modifications of basic Freudian theory have proliferated, so that the individual psychotherapeutic sessions are now guided by many theoretical frameworks other than Freud's. More important, a development such as the behavior modification school has discarded the psychoanalytic framework altogether, preferring to approach patients from a theoretical viewpoint heavily influenced by learning theory. Even more revolutionary are the many attempts to go beyond the one-to-one relationship and invoke various resources of the community in order to treat the patient within his own environmental setting. For the inpatient, many hospitals have now become treatment agencies rather than custodial institutions. The use of drugs has also revolutionized inpatient care and has led to a much greater turnover in hospital admissions. For the field as a whole, there has also been a growing tendency to use nonprofessionals for psychotherapeutic purposes and to discard traditional models whenever they have proven to be inadequate. The articles included in this chapter discuss many of these developments.

The forerunner of all attempts to modify disturbed behavior was the theoretical system developed by Sigmund Freud. Kaplan describes some of Freud's early cases, showing how he first approached these problems. His method emphasizes the basic rationality of conduct and the need to search the early history of an individual in order to uncover the roots of behavior. While unconscious processes can make behavior seem irrational, such behavior should be rationally explicable once we understand all of the antecedent conditions.

The heart of Freud's approach to the patient is in his conviction that with understanding comes improvement. Kaplan's article is an intimate description of Freud as a therapist. He stresses the fact that we often forget that not only was Freud an ingenious and provocative theoretician, but he was also a decent, involved, and superbly helpful clinician.

The behavior modification approach assumes that much of psychopathology is acquired through experience and learning. Unlike psychodynamic approaches, which tend to blame certain unspecified internal processes as the causes of disturbed behavior, the behavior modification approach regards the disturbed behavior as the psychopathological target. Thus an appeal to mysterious causes such as "the unconscious" or other motivational states is abandoned in favor of an assessment of the environmental reinforcement conditions which control and/or influence behavior. This approach does not in any way ignore the idiosyncratic nature of the individual behaving organism, but in fact tends to emphasize the extraordinarily unique properties of a person's interaction with his special social environment. Interestingly enough, many of the behavior modification research studies use a relatively small number of subjects. These subjects are studied intensively under as controlled therapeutic conditions as possible. The case study by Merbaum, describing the use of a punishment technique to extinguish self-destructive behavior in an autistic child, is one example of a behavior modification treatment program. Parenthetically, most behavior modification procedures do not rely upon punishment or aversive stimulation, but use positive reinforcement incentives as the core of the therapeutic program. This case happens to be one in which other alternatives failed, and more extreme measures were necessary to extinguish this very distressing behavior. Two points are worth noting in this case study. The first has to do with the programming of the aversive stimulation. The original program required that the child be administered an electric shock following each incident or response of hitting himself. This was very rarely accomplished because most of the people who administered the shock were very reluctant to administer punishment on a continuous reinforcement schedule. The second point describes the inclusion of the child's mother as a behavior modifier for her own child. This paper shows one type of behavior modification program at work.

If you were "sane" and acted "sane" in an "insane" place, there is no assurance whatsoever that you would be regarded as "sane." The research paper by Dr. David Rosenhan presents a unique social psychological experiment. In this study Rosenhan placed perfectly "sane" people in mental institutions and evaluated the reactions of professionals working in these institutions to these "sane" patients. What Rosenhan discovered was that even if people act sane within insane places, they are still usually labeled as insane. In other words, the label insanity is so powerful, especially in places designed to house the insane, that sane behavior is ignored, minimized, or regarded with disbelief. Of course,

Rosenhan's paper raised a furor within the professional community. A number of professionals have argued that the deceptive practices used in this research were unfair to the diagnosticians in these institutions who operate from within a different set of observational vantage points. In any event, this paper seriously calls into question the utility and general validity of psychiatric diagnoses and the often disastrous side effects of applying psychiatric labels to institutionalized people. Rosenhan's paper is a classic and should be read carefully.

Some of the more recent innovations in psychological treatment have occurred within the group-therapy field. Group techniques have been employed for patients from a wide variety of social backgrounds by therapists with an enormous diversity of training, ranging from professionals skilled in group process to laymen with little experience beyond a single participation as a group member in a prior session. Group members range from middle-class, well-functioning individuals to severely disturbed psychiatric inpatients. Some of the techniques used include sensitivity training, T-groups, laboratory sessions, encounter groups, and confrontation groups. The unsophisticated layman seeking a group experience can easily be befuddled by the choice open to him, and he would be well advised to exercise some caution before entering a potentially powerful experience under unskilled and possibly destructive leadership. An example of a group setting that is becoming increasingly popular is marathon therapy, where a number of group experiences are used in an extended session capable of lasting well over twenty-four hours. Lamott describes his experience in a marathon session under the leadership of George Bach.

Often when people discuss psychotherapy they assume that psychoanalysis is the only type of treatment available. The paper by Ernest Havemann, describing the various alternatives to analysis, should definitely clarify this misconception. Havemann estimates that there are perhaps two hundred different schools of therapeutic thought and thousands of therapeutic techniques devised to change, alter, influence, and help people who are emotionally troubled. The problem is, with this proliferation of therapeutic gimmicks, to find out which ones are really useful, and for what specific problems. In this paper several popular treatment approaches are described and briefly evaluated. Included are the behavior therapy technique of systematic desensitization of Dr. Joseph Wolpe, the reality therapy approach of Dr. William Glasser, Carl Roger's client-centered interviewing, and a description of some group techniques. In contrast to strict psychoanalytic method, these approaches involve active participation on the part of the therapist. Rather than confining himself to the role of observer and reflector of what the patient presents, here the therapist directly and actively works to elicit new and more constructive behaviors from his client.

The large number of new ideas and methods of treatment indicates that the field of psychology has entered a creative and experimental phase.

One problem that has arisen in this context is that members of differing schools of thought have sometimes tried to present their particular views as the key to the solution of all problems. This phenomenon has been called "the overgeneralization of insight," and occurs in all fields of study. When a technique has been found useful for a particular problem, or an idea has been very useful in explaining a particular observed event, this is what should be stated as precisely as possible. This is the way accurate scientific information is accumulated. There is no need to take one's good insight and generalize it in a global and unrealistic way to all situations. In this context, in thinking about different therapies it is sometimes helpful to ask oneself, "What kind of problem would this therapy probably be useful for?" "In what way can I imagine this therapy being useful for me?" and "What part of me would it touch, what real situations I encounter would it influence?" This kind of filtering of ideas through one's personal experience is helpful in keeping oneself open to new approaches, and is a means of generating good research questions as well. Clearly many questions need to be researched so that we can come progressively closer to knowing what will be most effective in helping a given individual with his particular pain, disorganization, and difficulty in achieving his goals. Hopefully, some of the students reading this book will be intrigued and eager to participate in the search for this knowledge.

"....His almost naïve earnestness— found expression in his daily clinical practice...."

Sigmund Freud was one of the great minds of the twentieth century. His fame is traced to the impact of his theories concerning personality and psychopathology. But what kind of a therapist was this brilliant thinker? Did his skills extend from the abstract to the real? Kaplan examines these questions in this article.

When Sigmund Freud was in his middle thirties, his medical career began to take an alarming turn. This was in the early 1890s, years before his thinking attained that conceptual shape we call psychoanalysis. A gifted neuropsychiatrist of increasing reputation, Freud was becoming alienated from the professional community of Vienna. The personal advantages his brilliance had already achieved were beginning to slip away, at first into indifference, then derision. For a man approaching middle age and shouldering responsibility not only for his wife and children, but for his parents and sisters as well, the financial jeopardy was nerve-racking. That his professional plight was not the result of something suddenly bizarre or iconoclastic in his assertions about mental illness compounded his frustrations. Iconoclastic opinions were to damage his career much later, and when they did, he readily accepted it. At this point, his was a case of exasperating an establishment not yet prepared for reformation.

For example, Freud's early proposals about the sexual factor in the psychoneuroses were not sensational novelties. They were quite consistent with prevalent opinion. A relationship between the sexual life of patients and their nervous disorders was a suspicion widespread among medical practitioners of the time. Freud credited Charcot, one of his most esteemed teachers, with the remark referring to mental patients, *"Mais, dans des cas pareils c'est toujours la chose génitale, toujours, toujours, toujours"*—with such patients, it is always a matter of sex, always, always, always. It was Josef Breuer, physician to many luminaries of Viennese society, who said to Freud about a neurotic patient, "These things are always secrets *d'alcôve*—questions involving the marriage bed. Another indelible reference to sex came from Professor Rudolf Chrobak, the most eminent gynecologist of Vienna. In connection with a woman he sent to Freud for treatment, he recommended with cynical despair: "Rx. *Penis normalis dosim repetatur"*—the best medicine would be an ordinary penis, repeatedly.

Thus when Freud initially codified these ideas into a scientific position, it was not his originality that scandalized his colleagues. What was disturbing was something about Freud's character. As he commented years later, those notions that his colleagues casually flirted with, he married—and took the consequences. Indeed, genius without character is hopeless; for it is character that dares to carry ideas beyond the judgment of a given time and place, into the more risky tribunals of Destiny.

Naturally Freud's character—his almost naïve earnestness—found expression in his daily clinical practice, in his actual conduct with patients. In his therapeutic activities, which flash with character, there are awesome glimpses of his great purpose that have remained comparatively neglected in the dissemination of his thought.

Vienna abounded in so-called classically hysterical women, patients free of physical lesions but nevertheless given to fainting spells, shortness of breath, ill-temper, depression, amnesia, nausea, delusions, migraines, paralyses—the list could be extended to a full page. The male neurotics tended toward elaborate and incapacitating obsessions and compulsions. Theories about the psychoneuroses were far in advance of therapeutic techniques, not unlike the situation today with, say, cancer. To the Vienna medical society (which was one of the best in the world), hobbled as it was by an ignorance as to how to treat the psychoneuroses, neurotic patients were regarded as annoyances, malingerers, pests. Treatment consisted of talking, suggesting, and commanding the neurotic out of his symptoms. This failing, mild electric shock, rest cures, warm baths, and other techniques were called in, largely to emphasize the doctor's determination that the patient get well. The doctor-patient relationship could be described as one of mutual harassment.

I have mentioned that Freud took quite seriously the business of sexuality. Another idea—somewhat less common, because it was more complex, was that neuroses had something to do with the lengths a patient had to go to avoid unsavory thoughts and memories of painful events. This Freud also took seriously, and he pronounced the idea in an italicized maxim in one of his earliest papers: *"Hysterical patients suffer principally from reminiscences."* For the psychotherapy of neurosis, the consequences of this idea were extraordinary. It meant that the doctor should listen to his patient's verbal reports and try to locate the morbid feeling and ideas his neurotic symptoms replace. With typical plausibility, this is precisely what Freud did, for hours on end, day after day. But he not only listened to the nonsense of his patients; he began to demand that they amplify details that were obscure and incomplete. Inevitably, Freud was becoming, as David Riesman once called him, a "rate buster." Where all around him superficial dispatch prevailed, Freud found it necessary to prolong therapy to unheard-of-lengths.

Like Philoctetes, Freud now possessed a wound and a bow, for which he was both shunned and sought. In practicing psychiatry, this means that you become one of the list of "extreme measures," and you are referred the most intractable cases. These days you would have to ransack your directory for a colleague who would take on the kind of case that routinely filled Freud's practice at the height of his physical powers. Yet in all his published accounts of treatment, there is not a breath of self-pity or self-aggrandizement.

Reason versus Obsession

What was it like to be a patient of such a doctor? It has been said that Freud was a severe rationalist who reduced human vitalities to barren mechanics. But this is true only if pettiness is proof of passion. When a patient consulted Freud, he was in the presence of a man deeply involved in an enterprise larger than the patient and larger than Freud. It was the absence of personal pettiness in the situation he created that liberated the patient's secrets. There was nothing a patient could tell this man that he couldn't find a proper niche for in the human design. He could walk through nightmares and humanize all demons. He was the passionate enemy of every fear that made freedom of thought less than an absolute principle. Though he staked everything on the power of reason, the scheme that reason served could have occurred only to a man of transcendental sensibilities.

All of this springs to life in the case histories that appear now and again in the long shelf of Freud's writings. The Rat Man case—we shall learn momentarily the reason for this grisly appellation—comes to mind first, because I can't imagine another psychiatrist in practice at that time who, upon hearing the complaints of the Rat Man, would not have come forth promptly with the well-meaning voice of conventional reassurance and thereby blown the case.

The Rat Man (this is his nickname among analysts: "Notes Upon a Case of Obsessional Neurosis" is his original name) was a young law student who had recently done military training, and consulted Freud in connection with proliferating obsessions. Their grip upon him could be regulated only by the patient's performing nonsensical acts, which were consuming years of his life. Typical was an irresistable urge to interrupt his studying at a given hour in the evening and retire to a downstairs vestibule where he had to expose his genitals in a mirror while thinking about his deceased father. Many of his compulsions were not so easily carried out, and some demanded exhausting restraint, as when, for example, it occurred to the patient that to remove a jinx from a particular person he was fond of, he would have to slit his own throat with a razor.

Other compulsions existed as far back as the patient could remember, and previous therapy had failed to ameliorate his suffering. What drove the Rat Man into further treatment at the moment was an especially maddening incident involving a fellow army officer. He sought Freud in particular, having chanced upon Freud's just-published *The Psychopathology of Everyday Life.* In the pages of that book he thought he recognized himself. This was shortly after the turn of the century, when Freud was wholly in disrepute, so that a patient's coming to Freud was a good indication of desperation.

A large part of the notes of the case is given over to the multitudinous details of the army incident that brought the patient to treatment. What was immediately helpful was Freud's unreserved interest in these details. Roughly, the patient had gotten it into his head that he owed a particular army officer a trifling sum of money for the delivery to the patient of a small package. However, the fact was that the patient owed the money to the postal clerk who had received the package and had advanced the COD charges. Though the patient was fully aware of this fact, he could not shake himself free of the compulsion to pay the money to the army officer instead. The package, incidentally, contained eyeglasses, a replacement for a pair the patient had lost on maneuvers. Knowing that the officer would think him crazy for insisting upon paying a debt that was not actually owed, the patient concocted devious plots to get the money into the officer's hands. As if this were not bad enough, these plots had to accommodate all sorts of ridiculous compulsive conditions. One, for example, was that the money had to be paid through a go-between, another officer. I shall forego a recounting of the patient's final turmoil, which reached its climax on a train speeding back to town. The prospect of even suggesting the patient's agitated ruminations about switching train connections so that he could finally execute his compulsion sets my teeth on edge. Freud marked every detail without contention.

But very soon the patient's recital to Freud struck an obstacle. Before the patient could proceed with the further details of his obsessional debt, he had to bring into his story still another officer. This was the person who had wrongly told the patient which officer had laid out the money for the package. The patient knew the money was really owed to the postal clerk. Why, then, was this person's misinformation so compelling? The patient's attempt to dodge this matter evoked a great instance of Freud's singularity of purpose (but notice the gentility with which Freud exorcised a malignant thought).

On maneuvers, just before losing his eyeglasses, the patient had gotten into conversation with the officer now in question. This officer, the patient told Freud, began to describe a horrible torture used in the East . . . Here the patient broke off. He got up from the analytic sofa, unable to continue, and implored the doctor to spare him the report of the details. Freud assured him that the treatment was not designed to torment the patient. The patient roamed about the room, pleading. But the doctor could not grant something which was beyond his power. (The power was now in the idea and no longer in the man who had invented the idea.) "He might just as well ask me to give him the moon," Freud wrote. "I went on to say that I would do all I could, nevertheless, to guess the full meaning of any hints he gave me. Was he perhaps thinking of impalement?" "No, not that—" the patient hesitated—"the criminal was tied up—a pot was turned upsidedown on his buttocks—some rats were put into it—and they— bored their way in—" Into his anus, Freud completed the sentence. Whereupon a dam of reserve cracked, and a flood of rat fantasies poured forth, so upsetting that by the end of the session, the patient was calling Freud "Captain."

For months thereafter they sifted the patient's thoughts to try to find out how the idea of rats had acquired its overwhelming effect. They discovered, for example, a forgotten story of the patient's father who had been, during his own army service, a *spielratte*—a gambler—and had lost at cards small sums of money entrusted to him in his duties as a kind of quartermaster. The story mortified the patient, who held his father in impeccable esteem. And they happened upon a memory so vague the patient had to act it out with Freud to gain conviction about it. This memory had to do with his father's physical violence after the patient had (like a rat) bitten someone as a very young child. The patient couldn't reconcile the idea of this beating with the image of his father's gentility, until a point in treatment when the patient found himself moved to rebuke Freud bitterly but unaccountably, for he had grown immensely fond of Freud. What enforced the conviction about the memory was the fact that these verbal attacks on Freud could not be made from the analytic couch. The patient had to leap up and shout his abuse from across the room, thus avoiding the retaliatory thrashing he expected from Freud. Where else but from the example of his otherwise benevolent father could the patient have learned to defend himself against the absurd idea of Freud's punching him in the face? Piece by piece, the rat symbol was dismantled, and what conspired in its symptoms, conspired in other symptoms, which fell away under these auspices.

There is a final footnote, which Freud was moved to furnish for a 1923 printing of the case: "The patient's mental health was restored to him by the analysis which I have reported upon in these pages. Like so many other young men of value and promise, he perished in the Great War."

The Lady in the Alps

When he treated the Rat Man, Freud was already a mature and seasoned psychoanalytic therapist—the only one in the world. The case of Katharina affords a glimpse of Freud when his intellectual and clinical enthusiasm estranged him professionally from his colleagues. The events took place around 1892.

We know about Katharina from an afternoon's consultation with Freud in a rather surprising setting. It was summer. Freud was on vacation in the Eastern Alps and one day happened into a mountaintop hotel to rest after a strenuous climb. Katharina was the young daughter of the landlady. When she learned from the visitor's book that Freud was a doctor, she approached him and asked for his help. She had "bad nerves." Freud noted that she was a robust, sulky-looking young lady, culturally rural, and that she spoke in a regional dialect. Her politeness and despondency overcame his reluctance to have his holiday intruded upon.

Her complaint, as she described it, was of a sort common in Freud's clinical experience. During the past two years, Katharina had suffered periodically from a syndrome of pressure on the chest with suffocating shortness of breath, nausea, and terror at the apparition of an anguished, unrecognizable face, a man's face. She would faint and have to be put to bed for several days. Anxiety hysteria, Freud mentally remarked, was obviously not limited to cosmopolitan society.

Two theories informed Freud's questioning of Katharina as she sat across from him at a secluded restaurant table. One theory involved the sexual factor, the other, the traumatic event itself. His technique at this time was—to be charitable—naïve: He told her he knew how her attacks had come on two years ago. She had seen something embarrassing that she would have preferred not to have seen. Katharina was stunned. It was a perfect hit.

Immediately, Katharina recalled that her first attack occurred two years ago, shortly after she happened to see her father in bed with one of the maidservants. She caught the scene through the window of a ground-floor bedroom, but it was too dark to make out exactly what they were doing or whether they were clothed or not. Katharina lost her breath, reeled against the wall and several days later went to bed with her first full-blown hysterical attack.

A mind less ardent than Freud's might have stopped here, with this gratifying confirmation of his sense of things. But Katharina's reaction really confirmed very little. Why exactly the pressure on her chest? Why not some other symptom? And whose face appeared in the apparitions? Her father's? But, then, why was it anguished, when the scene involved the father in an act of pleasure? Not least, why did the scene have the effect it did? Such reactions as Katharina's are not inevitable.

Direct questioning about these matters got them nowhere, though Katharina was getting caught up in the spirit of the inquiry. At the height of their frustrations, Freud made a grand appeal to a fresh agency—the mind's own lawfulness. "I told her to go on and tell me whatever occurred to her, in the confident expectation that she would think of precisely what I needed to explain the case."

At first Katharina rambled on about her present circumstances but soon gravitated toward several earlier incidents. They were not very remote in time, and they had to do with her father's unsuccessful sexual advances toward her. The first proved very much to the point. It contains every element of her syndrome:

Katharina was fourteen when she went on a particular overnight trip with her father. They shared the same room but slept, of course, in different beds. In the middle of the night, Katharina awoke suddenly shocked to find her father in bed with her, his body pressing against her. She rushed to the doorway, nauseous and breathless. "What are you up to!" she remonstrated. "Go on, you silly girl, keep still. You don't know how nice it is." Katharina threatened to take refuge in the hallway, at which her father soured his face and returned to bed. Katharina also returned to bed and slept the night through unmolested.

As for the sight of her father in bed with the maidservant, Freud was able to show her that her reaction was not so much to that but to the memories that the sight stirred up in her. The more recent scene, in short, was charged with her memories.

"She was like someone transformed," Freud observed. "The sulky, unhappy face had grown lively, her eyes were bright, she was enlightened and exalted."

Freud left his card in the event that she needed more help. Evidently she never felt the need, for he never saw her again.

I might add that this incident of a single consultation was not an isolated one. Throughout much of his life Freud kept open his noon hour for single consultations. Quite often he gave very significant help in a single hour, without recommending a long course of formal psychoanalysis, which spells the lie to the myth that Freud believed everyone ought to undergo analysis. Indeed, from various accounts we know that Freud treated the conductor Bruno Walter in a single consultation, when Walter became panicky about not being able to conduct with an almost paralyzed arm. Walter recounts in his autobiography how Freud examined his arm and concluded hysteria.

"But I can't move my arm," Walter objected.

"Try it at any rate," Freud urged.

"And what if I should have to stop conducting?"

"You won't have to stop."

"Can I take upon myself the responsibility of possibly upsetting a performance?"

Freud puffed his cigar. "I'll take the responsibility."

Walter conducted beautifully.

Of course, Freud never suggested that such encounters substituted for psychoanalysis. Theodor Reik has a letter from Freud concerning Reik's inquiry about Freud's four-hour consultation with Gustav Mahler in 1910. Mahler apparently benefited immensely, but, as Freud put it in the letter: "It was as if you would dig a single shaft through a mysterious building."

A Failure with Dora

Did Freud ever mishandle the clinical situation? He was sufficiently secure in the knowledge of his powers to confess his limitations, but even these are full of instruction.

The case of Dora has been a subject of lively dispute. Anticipating future criticism, Freud did attempt to acquit himself in regard to the outcome of the case. But he had obvious doubts. The story is this:

Dora was a mature eighteen-year-old young lady, bright and vivacious. An hysteric with migraines, nervous coughing, fainting spells, irritability, she had run through a succession of doctors in a short span of years. Finally she planted a histrionic suicide note on her family that drove them to their wits' end, and they dragged her off to Freud "to talk some sense into her." Her emotional blackmailing and tyranny were evident to Freud almost at once. (She got increasingly better at these things in the course of her long life. She nagged her husband literally to death. Her attending physician at her own deathbed in New York some dozen years ago referred to her as one of the most repulsive individuals he had ever come across.)

However, the story she related to Freud was very poignant. For years, she told Freud, her father had been carrying on an affair with a close friend of the family. Dora's mother, incidentally, was a hausfrau whose days were spent covering and uncovering the furniture in a constant battle against dirt. Her father made no bones about his infidelity. But much worse, when Dora developed into a lovely adolescent of fourteen, her father began to encourage an affair between Dora and his mistress's husband in the hope of buying off the husband's interference. The husband—I have always thought him a rather decent, though pathetic, fellow—read the father's encouragements gladly and began to ply Dora with gifts and attention. As this charade went on, the husband could contain himself no longer; how much Dora must have provoked this was beyond her awareness. He trapped Dora in a hallway and mauled her passionately. She threw him aside and fled. Shortly thereafter, she had her first hysterical attack. And so began her series of high-strung bouts with Viennese psychiatry.

Dora told Freud these things with outraged righteousness and demanded Freud's cooperation in her wish for vengeance. Freud believed the facts of Dora's story. But many hold that he made his first mistake in attempting to analyze her straight off, a doomed undertaking with a patient thoroughly consumed by the merits of her immediate crisis, as Dora was. While she wanted Freud to agree that her symptoms were the appropriate reactions to her father's infamous conduct, Freud wanted her to see how she participated, unwittingly but nevertheless actively, in her own victimization. It was as though Freud took his vehicle for a bulldozer. With Dora, he was driving it right into a mountain.

The "analysis" lasted three months. During this time Freud exercised his finest ingenuity in proving to Dora how her symptoms were her self-punitive moral judgments on her own unconscious envy of her father's mistress and on her actual erotic desires for the man who finally forced himself upon her in the hallway. As with her would-be lover, Dora's cooperation with Freud was a setup. She produced astonishing confirmations in her dreams and mental associations, which aroused Freud's therapeutic hopes and theoretical interests. At the peak of his involvement, and at what he deemed the brink of her cure, Dora cut him down. This was the cunning moment her vindictiveness chose for the cool opening remark of what was to be her last session. "Do you know that I am here for the last time today?" Freud recovered in a wink. When had she come to this resolve, was all he asked. She had made up her mind two weeks ago—which drew her thoughts, with Freud's continued collaboration, to a particular incident involving the dismissal of a governess. Like an unwanted servant, Freud had been put on two weeks' notice.

I have suggested one possibility of error, that Dora was simply in no condition to be analyzed. She may have needed perhaps years of weaning from her narcissism in preparation for analysis.

Another possibility of error was Freud's neglect of the "transference." Dora had succeeded in repeating in the analytic situation what she had done with her aroused pursuer in the hallway. Freud should have known that she was bound to do this and should have taken interpretive steps to prevent it before it got out of hand. Was he too involved at the time in his personal scientific curiosities? Or was he just no good with petulant women?

Erik H. Erikson, among others, has argued that Dora, who was merely eighteen at the time of treatment, was entitled to Freud's support and commiseration, that a sense of fidelity is as much an unconditional right of the adolescent as food is of the infant. Was Freud's analytic neutrality too harsh? Freud's own conclusion leaves this question moot: "Might I perhaps have kept the girl under my treatment if I myself had acted a part? If I had exaggerated the importance to me of her staying on, and had shown a warm personal interest in her . . . ? I do not know. . . . . In spite of every theoretical interest and every endeavor to be of assistance as a physician, I keep the fact in mind that there must be some limits set to the extent to which psychological influence may be used, and I respect as one of these limits the patient's own will and understanding."

What a discrepancy between this ethic and the hucksterism of some activities of today's psychiatric movement, where the public can find just about anything it wants, so long as the fee can be met. Dora did return to Freud fifteen months later, "to finish her story and ask for help once more." Goodness knows, Freud needed the fee. "But one glance at her face was enough to tell me that she was not in earnest over her request." They talked. She spoke of her gains and setbacks. At the end of her hour Freud sent her on her way. Should he have taken her back? It has been reported that in Dora's subsequent life, first in Paris, then in America, she never missed a chance to aver, with bashful pride, that she was the Dora of Freud's famous "Fragment of an Analysis of a Case of Hysteria." Her three months with Freud may have been the only experience with unimpeachable integrity in her long, unhappy life.

Money

The prosperous psychoanalyst is a nepotist. But Freud constantly found it hard to make ends meet. At first there was his falling out of favor, his "splendid isolation," as he called it. Afterwards he was still too busy with the theory and practice of psychoanalysis to make any real money out of his international reputation. In 1924 McCormick's Chicago *Tribune* offered Freud an open price— any amount—to cover the Leopold-Loeb trial in Chicago. Freud turned this down, as he had turned down a similar offer from the Hearst empire, which included a chartered ocean liner all to himself. When Freud's nephew Edward L. Bernays eagerly wrote to him from New York about the possibility of a $5,000 advance and vast sales for a brief autobiography, Freud was appalled, though not without good humor, at the very idea of getting "a hitherto decent man to commit such an outrageous act for $5,000." He added: "Temptation would begin for me at a sum a hundred times as great and even then the offer would be rejected after half an hour."

In renouncing such opportunities, Freud often cited his health, which was very bad during the latter span of his life. But this was never the crucial reason because, despite his physical discomfort—he had cancer—and the wear and tear of advancing years, his output was unflagging. The truth was that he didn't have forever to insure the future of psychoanalysis, and he knew that this would be best accomplished by his technical writing and teaching, activities that kept him respectably poor. For example, he did write a brief autobiography not long after his nephew's overture, but he wrote it for a technical rather than commercial publisher, and received a pittance for it. His own Psychoanalytic Press, whose original editions are now treasures, continued to take every spare dollar. He was once upset for months over a consultation with a renowned oral surgeon who was passing through Vienna, because the fee he paid the man had been earmarked for the Press.

Thus Freud lived mainly from his daily labor with patients. He averaged between seven and ten cases a day, each patient attending six sessions a week. Later the number of sessions was established at five a week to make time for an extra student Freud had inadvertently permitted to come to Vienna, when his schedule was actually full. At the height of his fame in the 1920's, Freud's fees were $20 per session for regular patients and $10 for students undergoing training analyses; in New York, his former students were already getting $25 a session. Royalty and celebrities paid him more, but there were always too many students in his practice for this to make much difference financially. He was forever mortgaging his present for the future. By and large, these students went on to redeem his great sacrifice. A handful survive. In their sixties and seventies, their contributions are worthy of an army of workers.

The mystique that shrouds the analytic fee is not Freud's legacy. Nowhere did he claim that the analytic cure depended upon a painful financial sacrifice by the patient. Freud counseled a straightforward attitude about money, as he did about sex. The fee is the analyst's livelihood. It benefits the analyst, not the patient. So long as the analyst receives his wages from some source, there is no evidence that free treatment is less effective than costly treatment. Karl Menninger has underscored this simplicity. He has written that the best source of money for analysis is a dormant savings account.

What would Freud do with those who came with little means, with those whose "dormant savings accounts" and gainful employment were wiped out by Europe's periodic depressions and political upheavals? His students tell how he was always pestering them to find time for indigent patients. They would have turned down the request of a do-gooder, a sentimental charity-monger. But Freud's character instilled in the merest project a sense of great enterprise.

Indeed, at this writing there is an aged man in Vienna, the only direct representative of Freud in the city that was the birthplace and one-time capital of psychoanalysis, for psychoanalysis perished there with the Nazi occupation. A former patient of Freud's, this man is called the Wolfman because his treatment centered on the analysis of a dream of a tree full of white wolves. The treatment became Freud's masterpiece in clinical exposition, and the Wolfman sometimes grants appointments to analytic students who continue to research his case. The Wolfman earns his bare living as a writer of sorts.

The point is that he was Russian nobility when he came to Freud. Incapacitated, he settled with his entourage in Vienna to undergo what he now refers to as his "cure with the Professor." After several years, the Bolshevik revolution destroyed his holdings. Overnight he became a destitute refugee. Freud carried him for years thereafter with no hopes of financial repayment. When the Wolfman later required further treatment, Freud thought it better for his case to continue with a woman analyst. He prevailed upon and secured a gifted British analyst for his patient, who was still living from hand to mouth. Until he no longer needed it, the Wolfman continued to receive the very best treatment.

It is no insult either to myself or to my colleagues to observe that our attempts at such gestures, which to Freud had all the grace of life-long manners, invariably come to grief in anxiety and resentment. The gap between Freud's practices and ours is not cited in order to humiliate, but to reveal the challenges we have still to meet, challenges generated not by his genius so much as by his vision and character.

That we have gone beyond Freud is a figment, unless the windy evangelism of our latter-day psychiatry is an advance on his eagerness to surpass easy solutions to tragic problems. Nor is the adventurism prevalent today what he really meant by versatility in psychotherapy. Beyond Freud? On the contrary. Benjamin Nelson has put it exactly: "Too few years are left in the present century to exhaust the dimensions of his message or to approximate the substance of his hopes."

And that tiresome cliché: "Freud was a brilliant theoretician, but not a very good doctor." Not a very good doctor? Compared to whom?

37 The Modification of Self-Destructive Behavior by a Mother-Therapist Using Aversive Stimulation
Michael Merbaum

"With both hands he would beat his face furiously and, as a result, his face was terribly bruised and his cheeks grotesquely swollen."

Behavior therapy is a form of treatment which focuses on disturbed behavior and tries to eliminate it. To the behavior therapist, psychopathological behavior is the target for treatment, rather than assuming, as in other therapies, that there is something within the mind that causes the disturbed behavior. This paper is an example of the use of punishment in extinguishing self-destructive behavior that had been quite unmanageable for many years. While you read this paper it is important to consider the ethical pros and cons about the use of punishment.

Aversive stimulation, particularly shock, is now an important therapeutic tool in the treatment of various forms of behavior pathology. One promising application is in the systematic use of a shock punishment paradigm in suppressing self-destructive behavior in seriously disturbed children (Tate & Baroff, 1966; Tate, 1972; Lovaas & Simmons, 1969; Corte, Wolf, & Locke, 1971). However, a practical problem complicating the effective use of aversive methods is a restriction of the punishment effect to the specific situation in which the punishment was originally presented. Thus, a common finding is that punishment contingencies programmed in one situation do not automatically generalize to other social contexts unless similar stimulus elements are present in both (Bucher & King, 1971; Corte, Wolf, & Locke, 1971; Risley, 1968; Birnbrauer, 1968; Lovaas & Simmons, 1969).

The present case study deals with the generalization of punishment in the control of extensive self-destructive behavior in an autistic child. The crucial aspect of the treatment program was the involvement of the child's mother as an active treatment collaborator. The training of parents, especially mothers, in the therapy of their own children, has been the subject of a number of research reports (e.g., Salzinger, 1967; Patterson & Brodsky, 1966). The behavioral ration-

From *Behavior Therapy*, 1973, 4, 442–447. Reprinted by permission of the publisher.

ale for the training of parents in this role assumes that the attempted elimination of deviant behavior in the school or clinic will not necessarily extend to the home environment as long as parents continue to arrange reinforcement contingencies as before. The home environment should be part of the total therapeutic package for optional progress to be initiated and maintained.

Methods
Subject

Andy was a 12-yr-old boy, the first of two children. His sibling, a girl of 7, was reported by the parents as normal. Andy, however, had been variously diagnosed as autistic, schizophrenic, retarded, brain damaged or combinations of these. His behavior was extremely primitive. He was virtually non-verbal, but had learned to communicate his basic needs through gestures and crude sounds. There was almost no evidence of peer contact and his social interaction with teachers at a day school for the seriously emotionally disturbed consisted of awkward and inconsistent demands for attention and affection. He seemed easily frustrated and often lapsed into temper tantrums at the slightest provocation.

Treatment Problem

Andy's self-abusive behavior had been a constant problem at home and in school for at least five years. With both hands he would beat his face furiously and, as a result, his face was terribly bruised and his cheeks grotesquely swollen. The fleshy part of his hands were calloused, discolored and also swollen. During the past five years intensive therapeutic programs all failed completely (including chemotherapy, mega vitamins, patterning, physical restraints and conventional psychotherapy). Prior to the onset of the aversive treatment program, parents and teachers reported that the problem was becoming more severe and that they were fearful that more serious damage might occur to his head.

Treatment Procedure and Results

A time sampling procedure consisting of a series of 10-min intervals was arranged to determine the frequency of blows to the face. Andy was observed for 5 days at lunch, play and during motor-training periods at school. Ten behavior samples were obtained with a digital hand counter. The number of beatings ranged from a high of 419 to a low of 55 during the 10-min segments. His average number of blows was 221 per 10-min period. Observational data suggested that his constant attacks to his face were habitual and that even while laughing and playing the beatings persisted. Nonetheless, when agitation was present the frequency of blows increased and their intensity appeared more vigorous.

The punishment contingency was administered by a Hot Shock stock prod. The prod, 18 in. in length with two end terminals about 0.5 in. apart is battery operated and gives off 150–300 mA peak amperage, with output from 200–500 V.

The treatment program was arranged as follows. The therapist (the author at the beginning of the project) waited until Andy hit himself and then presented the shock. Andy's initial reaction to this experience was surprise, a cry of pain and immediate fear of the device. Paradoxically, his reaction to the therapist was one of approach and desire for closeness. Tenderness and affection were freely expressed by the therapist and Andy responded warmly to this attention. For the next 2 hr, with the shock prod visible to him, there was not one instance of self-abusive behavior.

Andy's teachers, carefully instructed in the use of the shock device, played an essential role in the treatment program. The shocker, carried around constantly, was immediately available when Andy began to beat his face. On those rare occasions on which he would hit himself a shock was immediately forthcoming along with a resounding NO from the teacher. It was estimated that Andy received no more than 17 shocks at school before the behavior appeared to be under tight stimulus control. Throughout subsequent weeks the teachers continued to carry the shock prod wherever they went and Andy was constantly exposed to the threat of shock.

During the school program continual communication with his parents indicated that not only was the amount of self-destructive behavior at home the same, there even seemed to be a slight increase in their frequency. At this juncture a second program was established. Andy's mother was trained to use the shock apparatus. In addition, the practical value of positive reinforcement was explained and the behavior contingencies for the presentation of punishment and positive reinforcement worked out. The mother was instructed to use the shock on a response contingent basis, and to take a frequency count of the target behavior a day prior to the introduction of the shock. In addition, she was to keep a running diary of her reactions to the use of the shocker and the changes observed in Andy's behavior.

The first day the mother took two 15-min time samples, during which periods Andy hit himself 253 and 358 times respectively. Following these time samples she introduced the shock with a simultaneous NO as the shock was presented. The following are some excerpts from her diary:

> May 7th. 5:00 P.M.—He started to hit himself. I gave him one shock and a loud NO. He screamed and ran away but did not hit himself again. He turned the water on in the bathroom for the first time and was very pleased with himself.
>
> May 8th. A.M.—He has not hit himself for 1 hr. When he wanted more toast he became upset when I told him he would have to wait. Instead of hitting his face he went into his room.
>
> May 8th. P.M.—Hit himself only about four times between 5:00 and 7:30 P.M. when he went to bed.
>
> May 9th. A.M.—Hit himself only three times. Stopped when I said No.
>
> May 9th. P.M.—Hit himself four times total. He seemed to be in a very relaxed mood right from school.
>
> May 10th. A.M.—Did not hit his face even when he made a fuss about having to brush his teeth.
>
> May 10th. P.M.—Was in a happy mood. He is eating much more and has gained three pounds.
>
> May 11th. A.M.—We went to my in-laws for the day. They could not get over the way he was behaving. He did what he was told and we had a very relaxed day. He was also very happy.
>
> May 13th. A.M.—There was no hitting.

May 13th. P.M.—Was upset at dinner and was banging his elbow on the table. When I told him to stop he went to his room. After he came out and had finished his dinner he was very relaxed. He went to bed at 9:00 P.M. and was up all night. He did not have any of his vitamins this day.

May 25th. A.M.—Not too happy this morning. He was hitting his face. We had to take him for a ride to the beach. He was good and did not bang his face. We went for hamburgers and he really enjoyed this. I would say this is the first time he waited in the car and was not hitting himself.

May 28th.—Andy has been in a good mood most every day. I use the shock stick to make him stop hitting his arm, it worked. This has been the first long weekend for him to be so good. He was happy and was not hitting his face. He went to bed a little later than usual but then he went right to sleep.

June 17th.—Andy is behaving about the same. He will still hit his face every now and then. Saturday, Andy took his bath sitting down in the tub. This is the first time he has done this in about five years. He was playing with a new hand hose I just bought and when I said to him to sit he did. The next thing I did was to put in the stopper and let the tub fill up from the hose. He really enjoyed himself. I don't know how long this will last but we were very pleased.

The following is the mother's summary of July and August:

Andy responds very quickly to the shock stick. I have used it about eight times. I used the stick when he woke up in the middle of the night and would not go back to sleep. He was hitting his face and stamping his feet. I have used the stick in this manner only twice and it worked immediately. He laid down and went to sleep. When he came home from camp he was upset and crying. When I asked him what was wrong he said "I am hungry." He has said this before. Other words he has said are "cookie," "dog," "apple," "go car." He can turn on the water in the tub and sink. He will now climb up on a stool and not be afraid to come down. I now carry the stick whenever we go and just the sight of it makes him behave.

September 8th.—I took a count in the morning last week from 7:00 A.M. to 8:45. He hit his face 28 times. The hitting was not hard and at times, he was laughing. I cannot find the counter. I think Andy has hid it some place. He is very good at doing this. Andy seems to be more verbal. He greets people with a hug and a "hi." He goes twice a week for his vitamin shots. Our Doctor can't get over how quiet he has become. Not once has he hit himself even though he doesn't like what happens to him. Yesterday, he was yelling to the doctor "I am a good guy" over and over as he was getting his shots. He is starting to eat with a spoon.

Finally, a year later, I contacted her and the following report was given:

I haven't used the shock stick since some time back in the winter, but I can't really remember when. They used it at the school only once this summer. The frequency of hitting is almost nil. He is quieter, happier, and wonderful around the house. We now go on trips with him and the family all appear to enjoy each other more." The mother estimates that she has used the shock stick about 25 times throughout the entire treatment program. When he does start to hit, and this is very infrequent now, a strong "NO" is sufficient to stop the behavior. The mother was terribly pleased about his progress and recalled that during the long period of time he was abusing himself the family couldn't eat, travel or spend any pleasant times together. Now this has changed dramatically.

Discussion

Behavioral training for parents has usually focused on the virtues of positive reinforcement in creating the most optimal conditions for behavioral change. Partially out of ethical and humane considerations, most behavioral programs have discouraged aversive methods which produce excessive physical discomfort. However, since punishment is often the most convenient and perhaps, momentarily, the most successful way parents have of suppressing annoying or deviant behavior, the tendency to punish is extremely powerful. Thus, to counter this pattern, parents are urged to exercise restraint or to present mild punishment only if more positive reinforcement approaches fail. In contrast, the ethical acceptability and therapeutic utility of administering intensive physical punishment by professional personnel is relatively well documented. Interestingly enough, the training of parents in these methods has not been reported in the literature.

It almost goes without saying that, when a punishment program is arranged, it is important to use care in selecting the parent to dispense the aversive contingency. If, for example, a parent has had a history of using punishment in a sadistic or tyrannical way it makes little sense to encourage these methods even with close therapeutic supervision. In the current case Andy's mother had rarely used punishment as a device to obtain compliance. Part of her abhorrence of punishment seemed to grow out of a sense of guilt for her own responsibility in producing the kind of child she had. Thus, the use of punishment involved a hard decision that required extensive support from the experimenter and many follow-up conversations during the program. Interestingly enough, it became clear that if she could limit Andy's self-abusive behavior with an emphatic "No" or, a visual display of the shock prod, she would avoid the shock contingency, a path she was often relieved to take. Despite her reluctance to use shock, on some occasions she did independently experiment with the shock method to influence her son's behavior. In the diary it is noted that shock was presented when Andy hit himself on the arm, a behavior which was not originally selected as a target for shock. This event presented an interesting problem. Observing that punishment appeared to suppress the appropriate maladaptive target behavior, Andy's mother was tempted to use the procedure in situations other than the one for which it was directly assigned. While this phenomenon was not excessive, there were indications that his mother was also tempted to use the threat of shock whenever she considered his behavior deviant in other than self-abuse situations. Thus, if an aversive program is developed it is crucial that there be ample supervision to keep the program within its defined limits.

References

Birnbrauer, J. S. Generalization of punishment effects—a case study. *Journal of Applied Behavior Analysis*, 1968, *1*, 201–212.

Bucher, B., & King, L. W. Generalization of punishment effects in the deviant behavior of a psychotic child. *Behavior Therapy*, 1971, *2*, 68–77.

Corte, H. E., Wolf, M. M. & Locke, B. J. A comparison of procedures for eliminating self-injurious behavior of retarded adolescents. *Journal of Applied Behavior Analysis*, 1971, *4*, 201–215.

Lovaas, O. I., & Simmons, J. Q. Manipulation of self-destruction in three retarded children. *Journal of Applied Behavior Analysis*, 1969, *2*, 143–157.

O'Leary, K. D., O'Leary, S., & Becker, W. C. Modification of a deviant sibling interaction in the home. *Behaviour Research and Therapy*, 1967, *5*, 113–120.

Patterson, G. R., & Brodsky, G. A behavior modification programme for a child with multiple problem behaviors. *Journal of Child Psychology and Psychiatry*, 1966, *7*, 277–295.

Risley, T. R. The effects and side effects of punishing the autistic behaviors of a deviant child. *Journal of Applied Behavior Analysis*, 1968, *1*, 21–34.

Salzinger, K., Feldman, R. S., & Pornoy, S. Training Parents of brain injured children in the use of operant conditioning procedures. *Behavior Therapy*, 1970, *1*, 4–32.

Tate, B. G. Case study: control of chronic self-injurious behavior by conditioning procedures. *Behavior Therapy*, 1972, *3*, 72–83.

Tate, B. G., & Baroff, G. S. Aversive control of self-injurious behavior in a psychotic boy. *Behaviour Research and Therapy*, 1966, *4*, 281–287.

"Eight sane people gained secret admission to twelve different hospitals."

Dr. Rosenhan's controversial research project startled many people. His work directly challenged some of our most cherished notions about insanity by suggesting that the terms "sane" and "insane" are not as clear as most professionals present them to be.

If sanity and insanity exist, how shall we know them?

The question is neither capricious nor itself insane. However much we may be personally convinced that we can tell the normal from the abnormal, the evidence is simply not compelling. It is commonplace, for example, to read about murder trials wherein eminent psychiatrists for the defense are contradicted by equally eminent psychiatrists for the prosecution on the matter of the defendant's sanity. More generally, there are a great deal of conflicting data on the reliability, utility, and meaning of such terms as "sanity," "insanity," "mental illness," and "schizophrenia."[1] Finally, as early as 1934, Benedict suggested that normality and abnormality are not universal.[2] What is viewed as normal in one culture may be seen as quite aberrant in another. Thus, notions of normality and abnormality may not be quite as accurate as people believe they are.

To raise questions regarding normality and abnormality is in no way to question the fact that some behaviors are deviant or odd. Murder is deviant. So, too, are hallucinations. Nor does raising such questions deny the existence of the personal anguish that is often associated with "mental illness." Anxiety and depression exist. Psychological suffering exists. But normality and abnormality, sanity and insanity, and the diagnoses that flow from them may be less substantive than many believe them to be.

From Science, January 19, 1973, 179, 250–258. Copyright 1973 by the American Association for the Advancement of Science.
* The author is professor of psychology and law at Stanford University, Stanford, California 94305. Portions of these data were presented to colloquiums of the psychology departments at the University of California at Berkeley and at Santa Barbara; University of Arizona, Tucson; and Harvard University, Cambridge, Massachusetts.

[1] P. Ash, J. Abnorm. Soc. Psychol., 44, 272 (1949); A. T. Beck, Amer. J. Psychiat. 119, 210 (1962); A. T. Boisen, Psychiatry, 2, 233 (1938); N. Kreitman, J. Ment. Sci., 107, 876 (1961); N. Kreitman, P. Sainsbury, J. Morrisey, J. Towers, J. Scrivener, ibid., p. 887; H. O. Schmitt and C. P. Fonda, J. Abnorm. Soc. Psychol., 52, 262 (1956); W. Seeman, J. Nerv. Ment. Dis., 118, 541 (1953) For an analysis of these artifacts and summaries of the disputes, see J. Zubin, Annu. Rev. Psychol. 18, 373 (1967); L. Phillips and J. G. Draguns, ibid., 22, 447 (1971).
[2] R. Benedict, J. Gen. Psychol., 10, 59 (1934).

At its heart, the question of whether the sane can be distinguished from the insane (and whether degrees of insanity can be distinguished from each other) is a simple matter: do the salient characteristics that lead to diagnoses reside in the patients themselves or in the environments and contexts in which observers find them? From Bleuler, through Kretchmer, through the formulators of the recently revised *Diagnostic and Statistical Manual* of the American Psychiatric Association, the belief has been strong that patients present symptoms, that those symptoms can be categorized, and, implicitly, that the sane are distinguishable from the insane. More recently, however, this belief has been questioned. Based in part on theoretical and anthropological considerations, but also on philosophical, legal, and therapeutic ones, the view has grown that psychological categorization of mental illness is useless at best and downright harmful, misleading, and pejorative at worst. Psychiatric diagnoses, in this view, are in the minds of the observers and are not valid summaries of characteristics displayed by the observed.[3-5]

Gains can be made in deciding which of these is more nearly accurate by getting normal people (that is, people who do not have, and have never suffered, symptoms of serious psychiatric disorders) admitted to psychiatric hospitals and then determining whether they were discovered to be sane and, if so, how. If the sanity of such pseudopatients were always detected, there would be prima facie evidence that a sane individual can be distinguished from the insane context in which he is found. Normality (and presumably abnormality) is distinct enough that it can be recognized wherever it occurs, for it is carried within the person. If, on the other hand, the sanity of the pseudopatients were never discovered, serious difficulties would arise for those who support traditional modes of psychiatric diagnosis. Given that the hospital staff was not incompetent, that the pseudopatient had been behaving as sanely as he had been outside of the hospital, and that it had never been previously suggested that he belonged in a psychiatric hospital, such an unlikely outcome would support the view that psychiatric diagnosis betrays little about the patient but much about the environment in which an observer finds him.

This article describes such an experiment. Eight sane people gained secret admission to 12 different hospitals.[6] Their diagnostic experiences constitute the data of the first part of this article; the remainder is devoted to a description of

---

[3] See in this regard H. Becker, *Outsiders: Studies in the Sociology of Deviance* (Free Press, New York, 1963); B. M. Braginsky, D. D. Braginsky, K. Ring, *Methods of Madness: The Mental Hospital as a Last Resort* (Holt, Rinehart & Winston, New York, 1969); G. M. Crocetti and P. V. Lemkau, *Amer. Sociol. Rev.*, 30, 577 (1965); E. Goffman, *Behavior in Public Places* (Free Press, New York, 1964); R. D. Laing, *The Divided 'Self: A Study of Sanity and Madness* (Quadrangle, Chicago, 1960); D. L. Phillips, *Amer. Sociol. Rev.*, 28, 963 (1963); T. R. Sarbin, *Psychol. Today*, 6, 18 (1972); E. Schur, *Amer. J. Sociol.*, 75, 309 (1969); T. Szasz, *Law, Liberty and Psychiatry* (Macmillan, New York, 1963); *The Myth of Mental Illness: Foundations of a Theory of Mental Illness* (Hoeber-Harper, New York, 1963). For a critique of some of these views, see W. R. Gove, *Amer. Sociol. Rev.*, 35, 873 (1970).
[4] E. Goffman, *Asylums* (Doubleday, Garden City, N. Y., 1961).
[5] T. J. Scheff, *Being Mentally Ill: A Sociological Theory* (Aldine, Chicago, 1966).
[6] Data from a ninth pseudopatient are not incorporated in this report because, although his sanity went undetected, he falsified aspects of his personal history, including his marital status and parental relationships. His experimental behaviors therefore were not identical to those of the other pseudopatients.

their experiences in psychiatric institutions. Too few psychiatrists and psychologists, even those who have worked in such hospitals, know what the experience is like. They rarely talk about it with former patients, perhaps because they distrust information coming from the previously insane. Those who have worked in psychiatric hospitals are likely to have adapted so thoroughly to the settings that they are insensitive to the impact of that experience. And while there have been occasional reports of researchers who submitted themselves to psychiatric hospitalization,[7] these researchers have commonly remained in the hospitals for short periods of time, often with the knowledge of the hospital staff. It is difficult to know the extent to which they were treated like patients or like research colleagues. Nevertheless, their reports about the inside of the psychiatric hospital have been valuable. This article extends those efforts.

Pseudopatients and Their Settings

The eight pseudopatients were a varied group. One was a psychology graduate student in his 20's. The remaining seven were older and "established." Among them were three psychologists, a pediatrician, a psychiatrist, a painter, and a housewife. Three pseudopatients were women, five were men. All of them employed pseudonyms, lest their alleged diagnoses embarrass them later. Those who were in mental health professions alleged another occupation in order to avoid the special attentions that might be accorded by staff, as a matter of courtesy or caution, to ailing colleagues.[8] With the exception of myself (I was the first pseudopatient and my presence was known to the hospital administrator and chief psychologist and, so far as I can tell, to them alone), the presence of pseudopatients and the nature of the research program was not known to the hospital staffs.[9]

The settings were similarly varied. In order to generalize the findings, admission into a variety of hospitals was sought. The 12 hospitals in the sample were located in five different states on the East and West coasts. Some were old and shabby, some were quite new. Some were research-oriented, others not. Some

---

[7] A. Barry, *Bellevue Is a State of Mind* (Harcourt Brace Jovanovich, New York, 1971); I. Belknap, *Human Problems of a State Mental Hospital* (McGraw-Hill, New York, 1956); W. Caudill, F. C. Redlich, H. R. Gilmore, E. B. Brody, *Amer. J. Orthopsychiat.*, 22, 314 (1952); A. R. Goldman, R. H. Bohr, T. A. Steinberg, *Prof. Psychol.*, 1, 427 (1970); unauthored, *Roche Report*, 1 (No. 13), 8,1971).

[8] Beyond the personal difficulties that the pseudopatient is likely to experience in the hospital, there are legal and social ones that, combined, require considerable attention before entry. For example, once admitted to a psychiatric institution, it is difficult, if not impossible, to be discharged on short notice, state law to the contrary notwithstanding. I was not sensitive to these difficulties at the outset of the project, nor to the personal and situational emergencies that can arise, but later a writ of habeas corpus was prepared for each of the entering pseudopatients and an attorney was kept "on call" during every hospitalization. I am grateful to John Kaplan and Robert Bartels for legal advice and assistance in these matters.

[9] However distasteful such concealment is, it was a necessary first step to examining these questions. Without concealment, there would have been no way to know how valid these experiences were; nor was there any way of knowing whether whatever detections occurred were a tribute to the diagnostic acumen of the staff or to the hospital's rumor network. Obviously, since my concerns are general ones that cut across individual hospitals and staffs, I have respected their anonymity and have eliminated clues that might lead to their identification.

had good staff-patient ratios, others were quite understaffed. Only one was a strictly private hospital. All of the others were supported by state or federal funds or, in one instance, by university funds.

After calling the hospital for an appointment, the pseudopatient arrived at the admissions office complaining that he had been hearing voices. Asked what the voices said, he replied that they were often unclear, but as far as he could tell they said "empty," "hollow," and "thud." The voices were unfamiliar and were of the same sex as the pseudopatient. The choice of these symptoms was occasioned by their apparent similarity to existential symptoms. Such symptoms are alleged to arise from painful concerns about the perceived meaninglessness of one's life. It is as if the hallucinating person were saying, "My life is empty and hollow." The choice of these symptoms was also determined by the *absence* of a single report of existential psychoses in the literature.

Beyond alleging the symptoms and falsifying name, vocation, and employment, no further alterations of person, history, or circumstances were made. The significant events of the pseudopatient's life history were presented as they had actually occurred. Relationships with parents and siblings, with spouse and children, with people at work and in school, consistent with the aforementioned exceptions, were described as they were or had been. Frustrations and upsets were described along with jobs and satisfactions. These facts are important to remember. If anything, they strongly biased the subsequent results in favor of detecting sanity, since none of their histories or current behaviors were seriously pathological in any way.

Immediately upon admission to the psychiatric ward, the pseudopatient ceased simulating *any* symptoms of abnormality. In some cases, there was a brief period of mild nervousness and anxiety, since none of the pseudopatients really believed that they would be admitted so easily. Indeed, their shared fear was that they would be immediately exposed as frauds and greatly embarrassed. Moreover, many of them had never visited a psychiatric ward; even those who had, nevertheless had some genuine fears about what might happen to them. Their nervousness, then, was quite appropriate to the novelty of the hospital setting, and it abated rapidly.

Apart from that short-lived nervousness, the pseudopatient behaved on the ward as he "normally" behaved. The pseudopatient spoke to patients and staff as he might ordinarily. Because there is uncommonly little to do on a psychiatric ward, he attempted to engage others in conversation. When asked by staff how he was feeling, he indicated that he was fine, that he no longer experienced symptoms. He responded to instructions from attendants, to calls for medication (which was not swallowed), and to dining-hall instructions. Beyond such activities as were available to him on the admissions ward, he spent his time writing down his observations about the ward, its patients, and the staff. Initially these notes were written "secretly," but as it soon became clear that no one much cared, they were subsequently written on standard tablets of paper in such public places as the dayroom. No secret was made of these activities.

The pseudopatient, very much as a true psychiatric patient, entered a hospital with no foreknowledge of when he would be discharged. Each was told that he would have to get out by his own devices, essentially by convincing the staff that he was sane. The psychological stresses associated with hospitalization were considerable, and all but one of the pseudopatients desired to be discharged almost immediately after being admitted. They were, therefore, motivated not only to behave sanely, but to be paragons of cooperation. That their behavior was in no way disruptive is confirmed by nursing reports, which have been obtained on most of the patients. These reports uniformly indicate that the patients were "friendly," "cooperative," and "exhibited no abnormal indications."

The Normal Are Not Detectably Sane

Despite their public "show" of sanity, the pseudopatients were never detected. Admitted, except in one case, with a diagnosis of schizophrenia,[10] each was discharged with a diagnosis of schizophrenia "in remission." The label "in remission" should in no way be dismissed as a formality, for at no time during any hospitalization had any question been raised about any pseudopatient's simulation. Nor are there any indications in the hospital records that the pseudopatient's status was suspect. Rather, the evidence is strong that, once labeled schizophrenic, the pseudopatient was stuck with that label. If the pseudopatient was to be discharged, he must naturally be "in remission"; but he was not sane, nor, in the institution's view, had he ever been sane.

The uniform failure to recognize sanity cannot be attributed to the quality of the hospitals, for, although there were considerable variations among them, several are considered excellent. Nor can it be alleged that there was simply not enough time to observe the pseudopatients. Length of hospitalization ranged from 7 to 52 days, with an average of 19 days. The pseudopatients were not, in fact, carefully observed, but this failure clearly speaks more to traditions within psychiatric hospitals than to lack of opportunity.

Finally, it cannot be said that the failure to recognize the pseudopatients' sanity was due to the fact that they were not behaving sanely. While there was clearly some tension present in all of them, their daily visitors could detect no serious behavioral consequences—nor, indeed, could other patients. It was quite common for the patients to "detect" the pseudopatients' sanity. During the first three hospitalizations, when accurate counts were kept, 35 of a total of 118 patients on the admissions ward voiced their suspicions, some vigorously. "You're not crazy. You're a journalist, or a professor [referring to the continual note-taking]. You're checking up on the hospital." While most of the patients were reassured by the pseudopatient's insistence that he had been sick before he came in but was fine now, some continued to believe that the pseudopatient was sane throughout his hospitalization.[11] The fact that the patients often recognized normality when staff did not raises important questions.

Failure to detect sanity during the course of hospitalization may be due to

[10] Interestingly, of the 12 admissions, 11 were diagnosed as schizophrenic and one, with the identical symptomatology, as manic-depressive psychosis. This diagnosis has a more favorable prognosis, and it was given by the only private hospital in our sample. On the relations between social class and psychiatric diagnosis, see A. deB. Hollingshead and F. C. Redlich, *Social Class and Mental Illness: A Community Study* (Wiley, New York, 1958).

[11] It is possible, of course, that patients have quite broad latitudes in diagnosis and therefore are inclined to call many sane, even those whose behavior is patently aberrant. However, although we have no hard data on this matter, it was our distinct impression that this was not the case. In many instances, patients not only singled us out for attention, but came to imitate our behaviors and styles.

the fact that physicians operate with a strong bias toward what statisticians call the type 2 error. This is to say that physicians are more inclined to call a healthy person sick (a false positive, type 2) than a sick person healthy (a false negative, type 1). The reasons for this are not hard to find: it is clearly more dangerous to misdiagnose illness than health. Better to err on the side of caution, to suspect illness even among the healthy.

But what holds for medicine does not hold equally well for psychiatry. Medical illnesses, while unfortunate, are not commonly pejorative. Psychiatric diagnoses, on the contrary, carry with them personal, legal, and social stigmas.[12] It was therefore important to see whether the tendency toward diagnosing the sane insane could be reversed. The following experiment was arranged at a research and teaching hospital whose staff had heard these findings but doubted that such an error could occur in their hospital. The staff was informed that at some time during the following 3 months, one or more pseudopatients would attempt to be admitted into the psychiatric hospital. Each staff member was asked to rate each patient who presented himself at admissions or on the ward according to the likelihood that the patient was a pseudopatient. A 10-point scale was used, with a 1 and 2 reflecting high confidence that the patient was a pseudopatient.

Judgments were obtained on 193 patients who were admitted for psychiatric treatment. All staff who had had sustained contact with or primary responsibility for the patient—attendants, nurses, psychiatrists, physicians, and psychologists—were asked to make judgments. Forty-one patients were alleged, with high confidence, to be pseudopatients by at least one member of the staff. Twenty-three were considered suspect by at least one psychiatrist. Nineteen were suspected by one psychiatrist *and* one other staff member. Actually, no genuine pseudopatient (at least from my group) presented himself during this period.

The experiment is instructive. It indicates that the tendency to designate sane people as insane can be reversed when the stakes (in this case, prestige and diagnostic acumen) are high. But what can be said of the 19 people who were suspected of being "sane" by one psychiatrist and another staff member? Were these people truly "sane," or was it rather the case that in the course of avoiding the type 2 error the staff tended to make more errors of the first sort—calling the crazy "sane"? There is no way of knowing. But one thing is certain: any diagnostic process that lends itself so readily to massive errors of this sort cannot be a very reliable one.

The Stickiness of Psychodiagnostic Labels

Beyond the tendency to call the healthy sick—a tendency that accounts better for diagnostic behavior on admission than it does for such behavior after a lengthy period of exposure—the data speak to the massive role of labeling in psychiatric assessment. Having once been labeled schizophrenic, there is nothing the pseudopatient can do to overcome the tag. The tag profoundly colors

[12] J. Cumming and E. Cumming, *Community Ment. Health, 1*, 135 (1965); A. Farina and K. Ring, *J. Abnorm. Psychol., 70*, 47 (1965); H. E. Freeman and O. G. Simmons, *The Mental Patient Comes Home* (Wiley, New York, 1963); W. J. Johannsen, *Ment. Hygiene, 53*, 218 (1969); A. S. Linsky, *Soc. Psychiat., 5*, 166 (1970).

others' perceptions of him and his behavior.

From one viewpoint, these data are hardly surprising, for it has long been known that elements are given meaning by the context in which they occur. Gestalt psychology made this point vigorously, and Asch[13] demonstrated that there are "central" personality traits (such as "warm" versus "cold") which are so powerful that they markedly color the meaning of other information in forming an impression of a given personality.[14] "Insane," "schizophrenic," "manic-depressive," and "crazy" are probably among the most powerful of such central traits. Once a person is designated abnormal, all of his other behaviors and characteristics are colored by that label. Indeed, that label is so powerful that many of the pseudopatients' normal behaviors were overlooked entirely or profoundly misinterpreted. Some examples may clarify this issue.

Earlier I indicated that there were no changes in the pseudopatient's personal history and current status beyond those of name, employment, and, where necessary, vocation. Otherwise, a veridical description of personal history and circumstances was offered. Those circumstances were not psychotic. How were they made consonant with the diagnosis of psychosis? Or were those diagnoses modified in such a way as to bring them into accord with the circumstances of the pseudopatient's life, as described by him?

As far as I can determine, diagnoses were in no way affected by the relative health of the circumstances of a pseudopatient's life. Rather, the reverse occurred: the perception of his circumstances was shaped entirely by the diagnosis. A clear example of such translation is found in the case of a pseudopatient who had had a close relationship with his mother but was rather remote from his father during his early childhood. During adolescence and beyond, however, his father became a close friend, while his relationship with his mother cooled. His present relationship with his wife was characteristically close and warm. Apart from occasional angry exchanges, friction was minimal. The children had rarely been spanked. Surely there is nothing especially pathological about such a history. Indeed, many readers may see a similar pattern in their own experiences, with no markedly deleterious consequences. Observe, however, how such a history was translated in the psychopathological context, this from the case summary prepared after the patient was discharged.

This white 39-year-old male . . . manifests a long history of considerable ambivalence in close relationships, which begins in early childhood. A warm relationship with his mother cools during his adolescence. A distant relationship to his father is described as becoming very intense. Affective stability is absent. His attempts to control emotionality with his wife and children are punctuated by angry outbursts and, in the case of the children, spankings. And while he says that he has several good friends, one senses considerable ambivalence embedded in those relationships also. . . .

---

[13] S. E. Asch, *J. Abnorm. Soc. Psychol.* 41, 258 (1946); *Social Psychology* (Prentice-Hall, New York, 1952).
[14] See also I. N. Mensh and J. Wishner, *J. Personality*, 16, 188 (1947); J. Wishner, *Psychol. Rev.*, 67, 96 (1960); J. S. Bruner and R. Tagiuri, in *Handbook of Social Psychology*, G. Lindzey, Ed. (Addison-Wesley, Cambridge, Mass., 1954), vol. 2, pp. 634–654; J. S. Bruner, D. Shapiro, R. Tagiuri, in *Person Perception and Interpersonal Behavior*, R. Tagiuri and L. Petrullo, Eds. (Stanford Univ. Press, Stanford, Calif., 1958), pp. 277–288.

The facts of the case were unintentionally distorted by the staff to achieve consistency with a popular theory of the dynamics of a schizophrenic reaction.[15] Nothing of an ambivalent nature had been described in relations with parents, spouse, or friends. To the extent that ambivalence could be inferred, it was probably not greater than is found in all human relationships. It is true the pseudopatient's relationships with his parents changed over time, but in the ordinary context that would hardly be remarkable—indeed, it might very well be expected. Clearly, the meaning ascribed to his verbalizations (that is, ambivalence, affective instability) was determined by the diagnosis: schizophrenia. An entirely different meaning would have been ascribed if it were known that the man was "normal."

All pseudopatients took extensive notes publicly. Under ordinary circumstances, such behavior would have raised questions in the minds of observers, as, in fact, it did among patients. Indeed, it seemed so certain that the notes would elicit suspicion that elaborate precautions were taken to remove them from the ward each day. But the precautions proved needless. The closest any staff member came to questioning these notes occurred when one pseudopatient asked his physician what kind of medication he was receiving and began to write down the response. "You needn't write it," he was told gently. "If you have trouble remembering, just ask me again."

If no questions were asked of the pseudopatients, how was their writing interpreted? Nursing records for three patients indicate that the writing was seen as an aspect of their pathological behavior. "Patient engages in writing behavior" was the daily nursing comment on one of the pseudopatients who was never questioned about his writing. Given that the patient is in the hospital, he must be psychologically disturbed. And given that he is disturbed, continuous writing must be a behavioral manifestation of that disturbance, perhaps a subset of the compulsive behaviors that are sometimes correlated with schizophrenia.

One tacit characteristic of psychiatric diagnosis is that it locates the sources of aberration within the individual and only rarely within the complex of stimuli that surrounds him. Consequently, behaviors that are stimulated by the environment are commonly misattributed to the patient's disorder. For example, one kindly nurse found a pseudopatient pacing the long hospital corridors. "Nervous, Mr. X?" she asked. "No, bored," he said.

The notes kept by pseudopatients are full of patient behaviors that were misinterpreted by well-intentioned staff. Often enough, a patient would go "berserk" because he had, wittingly or unwittingly, been mistreated by, say, an attendant. A nurse coming upon the scene would rarely inquire even cursorily into the environmental stimuli of the patient's behavior. Rather, she assumed that his upset derived from his pathology, not from his present interactions with other staff members. Occasionally, the staff might assume that the patient's family (especially when they had recently visited) or other patients had stimulated the outburst. But never were the staff found to assume that one of themselves or the structure of the hospital had anything to do with a patient's behavior. One psychiatrist pointed to a group of patients who were sitting outside the cafeteria entrance half an hour before lunchtime. To a group of young

15 For an example of a similar self-fulfilling prophecy, in this instance dealing with the "central" trait of intelligence, see R. Rosenthal and L. Jacobson, *Pygmalion in the Classroom* (Holt, Rinehart & Winston, New York, 1968).

residents he indicated that such behavior was characteristic of the oral-acquisi-
tive nature of the syndrome. It seemed not to occur to him that there were very
few things to anticipate in a psychiatric hospital besides eating.

A psychiatric label has a life and an influence of its own. Once the impression has been formed that the patient is schizophrenic, the expectation is that
he will continue to be schizophrenic. When a sufficient amount of time has
passed, during which the patient has done nothing bizarre, he is considered to
be in remission and available for discharge. But the label endures beyond discharge, with the unconfirmed expectation that he will behave as a schizophrenic
again. Such labels, conferred by mental health professionals, are as influential
on the patient as they are on his relatives and friends, and it should not surprise
anyone that the diagnosis acts on all of them as a self-fulfilling prophecy. Eventually, the patient himself accepts the diagnosis, with all of its surplus meanings
and expectations, and behaves accordingly.[16]

The inferences to be made from these matters are quite simple. Much as
Zigler and Phillips have demonstrated that there is enormous overlap in the
symptoms presented by patients who have been variously diagnosed,[17] so there
is enormous overlap in the behaviors of the same and the insane. The sane are
not "sane" all of the time. We lose our tempers "for no good reason." We are
occasionally depressed or anxious, again for no good reason. And we may find
it difficult to get along with one or another person—again for no reason that we
can specify. Similarly, the insane are not always insane. Indeed, it was the
impression of the pseudopatients while living with them that they were sane for
long periods of time—that the bizarre behaviors upon which their diagnoses
were allegedly predicated constituted only a small fraction of their total behavior. If it makes no sense to label ourselves permanently depressed on the basis
of an occasional depression, then it takes better evidence than is presently available to label all patients insane or schizophrenic on the basis of bizarre behaviors or cognitions. It seems more useful, as Mischel[18] has pointed out, to limit
our discussions to *behaviors*, the stimuli that provoke them, and their correlates.

It is not known why powerful impressions of personality traits, such as
"crazy" or "insane," arise. Conceivably, when the origins of and stimuli that
give rise to a behavior are remote or unknown, or when the behavior strikes us
as immutable, trait labels regarding the *behaver* arise. When, on the other hand,
the origins and stimuli are known and available, discourse is limited to the
behavior itself. Thus, I may hallucinate because I am sleeping, or I may hallucinate because I have ingested a peculiar drug. These are termed sleep-induced
hallucinations, or dreams, and drug-induced hallucinations, respectively. But
when the stimuli to my hallucinations are unknown, that is called craziness, or
schizophrenia—as if that inference were somehow as illuminating as the others.

The Experience of Psychiatric Hospitalization

The term "mental illness" is of recent origin. It was coined by people who
were humane in their inclinations and who wanted very much to raise the sta-

---

[16] Scheff, 1966.
[17] E. Zigler and L. Phillips, *J. Abnorm. Soc. Psychol.*, *63*, 69 (1961). See also R. K.
Freudenberg and J. P. Robertson, *AM.A. Arch. Neurol. Psychiatr.*, *76*, 14 (1956).
[18] W. Mischel, *Personality and Assessment* (Wiley, New York, 1968).

tion of (and the public's sympathies toward) the psychologically disturbed from that of witches and "crazies" to one that was akin to the physically ill. And they were at least partially successful, for the treatment of the mentally ill *has* improved considerably over the years. But while treatment has improved, it is doubtful that people really regard the mentally ill in the same way that they view the physically ill. A broken leg is something one recovers from, but mental illness allegedly endures forever.[19] A broken leg does not threaten the observer, but a crazy schizophrenic? There is by now a host of evidence that attitudes toward the mentally ill are characterized by fear, hostility, aloofness, suspicion, and dread.[20] The mentally ill are society's lepers.

That such attitudes infect the general population is perhaps not surprising, only upsetting. But that they affect the professionals—attendants, nurses, physicians, psychologists, and social workers—who treat and deal with the mentally ill is more disconcerting, both because such attitudes are self-evidently pernicious and because they are unwitting. Most mental health professionals would insist that they are sympathetic toward the mentally ill, that they are neither avoidant nor hostile. But it is more likely that an exquisite ambivalence characterizes their relations with psychiatric patients, such that their avowed impulses are only part of their entire attitude. Negative attiudes are there too and can easily be detected. Such attitudes should not surprise us. They are the natural offspring of the labels patients wear and the places in which they are found.

Consider the structure of the typical psychiatric hospital. Staff and patients are strictly segregated. Staff have their own living space, including their dining facilities, bathrooms, and assembly places. The glassed quarters that contain the professional staff, which the pseudopatients came to call "the cage," sit out on every dayroom. The staff emerge primarily for caretaking purposes—to give medication, to conduct a therapy or group meeting, to instruct or reprimand a patient. Otherwise, staff keep to themselves, almost as if the disorder that afflicts their charges is somehow catching.

So much is patient-staff segregation the rule that, for four public hospitals in which an attempt was made to measure the degree to which staff and patients mingle, it was necessary to use "time out of the staff cage" as the operational measure. While it was not the case that all time spent out of the cage was spent mingling with patients (attendants, for example, would occasionally emerge to watch television in the dayroom), it was the only way in which one could gather reliable data on time for measuring.

The average amount of time spent by attendants outside of the cage was 11.3 percent (range, 3 to 52 percent). This figure does not represent only time spent mingling with patients, but also includes time spent on such chores as folding laundry, supervising patients while they shave, directing ward cleanup, and sending patients to off-ward activities. It was the relatively rare attendant who spent time talking with patients or playing games with them. It proved impossible to obtain a "percent mingling time" for nurses, since the amount of time they spent out of the cage was too brief. Rather, we counted instances of

---

[19] The most recent and unfortunate instance of this tenet is that of Senator Thomas Eagleton.
[20] T. R. Sarbin and J. C. Mancuso, *J. Clin. Consult. Psychol.*, 35, 159 (1970); T. R. Sarbin, *ibid*. 31, 447 (1967); J. C. Nunnally, Jr., *Popular Conceptions of Mental Health* (Holt, Rinehart & Winston, New York, 1961).

emergence from the cage. On the average, daytime nurses emerged from the cage 11.5 times per shift, including instances when they left the ward entirely (range, 4 to 39 times). Late afternoon and night nurses were even less available, emerging on the average 9.4 times per shift (range, 4 to 41 times). Data on early morning nurses, who arrived usually after midnight and departed at 8 a.m., are not available because patients were asleep during most of this period.

Physicians, especially psychiatrists, were even less available. They were rarely seen on the wards. Quite commonly, they would be seen only when they arrived and departed, with the remaining time being spent in their offices or in the cage. On the average, physicians emerged on the ward 6.7 times per day (range, 1 to 17 times). It proved difficult to make an accurate estimate in this regard, since physicians often maintained hours that allowed them to come and go at different times.

The hierarchical organization of the psychiatric hospital has been commented on before,[21] but the latent meaning of that kind of organization is worth noting again. Those with the most power have least to do with patients, and those with the least power are most involved with them. Recall, however, that the acquisition of role-appropriate behaviors occurs mainly through the observation of others, with the most powerful having the most influence. Consequently, it is understandable that attendants not only spend more time with patients than do any other members of the staff—that is required by their station in the hierarchy—but also, insofar as they learn from their superiors' behavior, spend as little time with patients as they can. Attendants are seen mainly in the cage, which is where the models, the action, and the power are.

I turn now to a different set of studies, these dealing with staff response to patient-initiated contact. It has long been known that the amount of time a person spends with you can be an index of your significance to him. If he initiates and maintains eye contact, there is reason to believe that he is considering your requests and needs. If he pauses to chat or actually stops and talks, there is added reason to infer that he is individuating you. In four hospitals, the pseudo-patient approached the staff member with a request which took the following form: "Pardon me, Mr. [or Dr. or Mrs.] X, could you tell me when I will be eligible for grounds privileges?" (or ". . . when I will be presented at the staff meeting?" or ". . . when I am likely to be discharged?"). While the content of the question varied according to the appropriateness of the target and the pseudopatient's (apparent) current needs the form was always a courteous and relevant request for information. Care was taken never to approach a particular member of the staff more than once a day, lest the staff member become suspicious or irritated. In examining these data, remember that the behavior of the pseudopatients was neither bizarre nor disruptive. One could indeed engage in good conversation with them.

The data for these experiments are shown in Table 1, separately for physicians (column 1) and for nurses and attendants (column 2). Minor differences between these four institutions were overwhelmed by the degree to which staff avoided continuing contacts that patients had initiated. By far, their most com-

[21] A. H. Stanton and M. S. Schwartz, *The Mental Hospital: A Study of Institutional Participation in Psychiatric Illness and Treatment* (Basic, New York, 1954).

mon response consisted of either a brief response to the question, offered while they were "on the move" and with head averted, or no response at all.

The encounter frequently took the following bizarre form: (pseudopatient) "Pardon me, Dr. X. Could you tell me when I am eligible for grounds privileges?" (physician) "Good morning, Dave. How are you today?" (Moves off without waiting for a response.)

It is instructive to compare these data with data recently obtained at Stanford University. It has been alleged that large and eminent universities are characterized by faculty who are so busy that they have no time for students. For this comparison, a young lady approached individual faculty members who seemed to be walking purposefully to some meeting or teaching engagement and asked them the following six questions.

1. "Pardon me, could you direct me to Encina Hall?" (at the medical school: ". . . to the Clinical Research Center?").
2. "Do you know where Fish Annex is?" (there is no Fish Annex at Stanford).
3. "Do you teach here?"
4. "How does one apply for admission to the college?" (at the medical school: ". . . to the medical school?").
5. "Is it difficult to get in?"
6. "Is there financial aid?"

Without exception, as can be seen in Table 1 (column 3), all of the questions were answered. No matter how rushed they were, all respondents not only maintained eye contact, but stopped to talk. Indeed, many of the respondents went out of their way to direct or take the questioner to the office she was seeking, to try to locate "Fish Annex," or to discuss with her the possibilities of being admitted to the university.

Similar data, also shown in Table 1 (columns 4, 5, and 6), were obtained in the hospital. Here too, the young lady came prepared with six questions. After the first question, however, she remarked to 18 of her respondents (column 4), "I'm looking for a psychiatrist," and to 15 others (column 5), "I'm looking for an internist." Ten other respondents received no inserted comment (column 6). The general degree of cooperative responses is considerably higher for these university groups than it was for pseudopatients in psychiatric hospitals. Even so, differences are apparent within the medical school setting. Once having indicated that she was looking for a psychiatrist, the degree of cooperation elicited was less than when she sought an internist.

Powerlessness and Depersonalization

Eye contact and verbal contact reflect concern and individuation; their absence, avoidance and depersonalization. The data I have presented do not do justice to the rich daily encounters that grew up around matters of depersonalization and avoidance. I have records of patients who were beaten by staff for the sin of having initiated verbal contact. During my own experience, for example, one patient was beaten in the presence of other patients for having approached an attendant and told him, "I like you." Occasionally, punishment

Table 1. Self-initiated contact by pseudopatients with psychiatrists and nurses and attendants, compared to contact with other groups.

Contact	Psychiatric Hospitals		University Campus (Nonmedical)	University Medical Center Physicians		
	(1) Psychiatrists	(2) Nurses and Attendants	(3) Faculty	(4) "Looking for a Psychiatrist"	(5) "Looking for an Internist"	(6) No Additional Comment
Responses						
Moves on, head averted (%)	71	88	0	0	0	0
Makes eye contact (%)	23	10	0	11	0	0
Pauses and chats (%)	2	2	0	11	0	10
Stops and talks (%)	4	0.5	100	78	100	90
Mean number of questions answered (out of 6)	*	*	6	3.8	4.8	4.5
Respondents (No.)	13	47	14	18	15	10
Attempts (No.)	185	1283	14	18	15	10

*Not applicable.

meted out to patients for misdemeanors seemed so excessive that it could not be justified by the most radical interpretations of psychiatric canon. Nevertheless, they appeared to go unquestioned. Tempers were often short. A patient who had not heard a call for medication would be roundly excoriated, and the morning attendants would often wake patients with " Come on, you m——f——s, out of bed!"

Neither anecdotal nor "hard" data can convey the overwhelming sense of powerlessness which invades the individual as he is continually exposed to the depersonalization of the psychiatric hospital. It hardly matters *which* psychiatric hospital—the excellent public ones and the very plush private hospital were better than the rural and shabby ones in this regard, but, again, the features that psychiatric hospitals had in common overwhelmed by far their apparent differences.

Powerlessness was evident everywhere. The patient is deprived of many of his legal rights by dint of his psychiatric commitment.[22] He is shorn of credibility by virtue of his psychiatric label. His freedom of movement is restricted. He cannot initiate contact with the staff, but may only respond to such overtures as they make. Personal privacy is minimal. Patient quarters and possessions can be entered and examined by any staff member, for whatever reason. His personal history and anguish is available to any staff member (often including the "grey lady" and "candy striper" volunteer) who chooses to read his folder, regardless of their therapeutic relationship to him. His personal hygiene and waste evacuation are often monitored. The water closets may have no doors.

At times, depersonalization reached such proportions that pseudopatients had the sense that they were invisible, or at least unworthy of account. Upon being admitted, I and other pseudopatients took the initial physical examinations in a semipublic room, where staff members went about their own business as if we were not there.

On the ward, attendants delivered verbal and occasionally serious physical abuse to patients in the presence of other observing patients, some of whom (the pseudopatients) were writing it all down. Abusive behavior, on the other hand, terminated quite abruptly when other staff members were known to be coming. Staff are credible witnesses. Patients are not.

A nurse unbuttoned her uniform to adjust her brassiere in the presence of an entire ward of viewing men. One did not have the sense that she was being seductive. Rather, she didn't notice us. A group of staff persons might point to a patient in the dayroom and discuss him animatedly, as if he were not there.

One illuminating instance of depersonalization and invisibility occurred with regard to medications. All told, the pseudopatients were administered nearly 2100 pills, including Elavil, Stelazine, Compazine, and Thorazine, to name but a few. (That such a variety of medications should have been administered to patients presenting identical symptoms is itself worthy of note.) Only two were swallowed. The rest were either pocketed or deposited in the toilet. The pseudopatients were not alone in this. Although I have no precise records on how many patients rejected their medications, the pseudopatients frequently found the medications of other patients in the toilet before they deposited their own. As long as they were cooperative, their behavior and the pseudopatients'

[22] D. B. Wexler and S. E. Scoville, *Ariz. Law Rev., 13*, 1 (1971).

own in this matter, as in other important matters, went unnoticed throughout.

Reactions to such depersonalization among pseudopatients were intense. Although they had come to the hospital as participant observers and were fully aware that they did not "belong," they nevertheless found themselves caught up in and fighting the process of depersonalization. Some examples: a graduate student in psychology asked his wife to bring his textbooks to the hospital so he could "catch up on his homework"—this despite the elaborate precautions taken to conceal his professional association. The same student, who had trained for quite some time to get into the hospital, and who had looked forward to the experience, "remembered" some drag races that he had wanted to see on the weekend and insisted that he be discharged by that time. Another pseudopatient attempted a romance with a nurse. Subsequently, he informed the staff that he was applying for admission to graduate school in psychology and was very likely to be admitted, since a graduate professor was one of his regular hospital visitors. The same person began to engage in psychotherapy with other patients —all of this as a way of becoming a person in an impersonal environment.

The Sources of Depersonalization

What are the origins of depersonalization? I have already mentioned two. First are attitudes held by all of us toward the mentally ill—including those who treat them—attitudes characterized by fear, distrust, and horrible expectations on the one hand, and benevolent intentions on the other. Our ambivalence leads, in this instance as in others, to avoidance.

Second, and not entirely separate, the hierarchical structure of the psychiatric hospital facilitates depersonalization. Those who are at the top have least to do with patients, and their behavior inspires the rest of the staff. Average daily contact with psychiatrists, psychologists, residents, and physicians combined ranged from 3.9 to 25.1 minutes, with an overall mean of 6.8 (six pseudopatients over a total of 129 days of hospitalization). Included in this average are time spent in the admissions interview, ward meetings in the presence of a senior staff member, group and individual psychotherapy contacts, case presentation conferences, and discharge meetings. Clearly, patients do not spend much time in interpersonal contact with doctoral staff. And doctoral staff serve as models for nurses and attendants.

There are probably other sources. Psychiatric installations are presently in serious financial straits. Staff shortages are pervasive, staff time at a premium. Something has to give, and that something is patient contact. Yet, while financial stresses are realities, too much can be made of them. I have the impression that the psychological forces that result in depersonalization are much stronger than the fiscal ones and that the addition of more staff would not correspondingly improve patient care in this regard. The incidence of staff meetings and the enormous amount of record-keeping on patients, for example, have not been as substantially reduced as has patient contact. Priorities exist, even during hard times. Patient contact is not a significant priority in the traditional psychiatric hospital, and fiscal pressures do not account for this. Avoidance and depersonalization may.

Heavy reliance upon psychotropic medication tacitly contributes to depersonalization by convincing staff that treatment is indeed being conducted and that further patient contact may not be necessary. Even here, however, caution needs to be exercised in understanding the role of psychotropic drugs. If patients were powerful rather than powerless, if they were viewed as interesting individuals rather than diagnostic entities, if they were socially significant rather than social lepers, if their anguish truly and wholly compelled our sympathies and concerns, would we not *seek* contact with them, despite the availability of medications? Perhaps for the pleasure of it all?

The Consequences of Labeling and Depersonalization

Whenever the ratio of what is known to what needs to be known approaches zero, we tend to invent "knowledge" and assume that we understand more than we actually do. We seem unable to acknowledge that we simply don't know. The needs for diagnosis and remediation of behavioral and emotional problems are enormous. But rather than acknowledge that we are just embarking on understanding, we continue to label patients "schizophrenic," "manic-depressive," and "insane," as if in those words we had captured the essence of understanding. The facts of the matter are that we have known for a long time that diagnoses are often not useful or reliable, but we have nevertheless continued to use them. We now know that we cannot distinguish insanity from sanity. It is depressing to consider how that information will be used.

Not merely depressing, but frightening. How many people, one wonders, are sane but not recognized as such in our psychiatric institutions? How many have been needlessly stripped of their privileges of citizenship, from the right to vote and drive to that of handling their own accounts? How many have feigned insanity in order to avoid the criminal consequences of their behavior, and, conversely, how many would rather stand trial than live interminably in a psychiatric hospital—but are wrongly thought to be mentally ill? How many have been stigmatized by well-intentioned, but nevertheless erroneous, diagnoses? On the last point, recall again that a "type 2 error" in psychiatric diagnosis does not have the same consequences it does in medical diagnosis. A diagnosis of cancer that has been found to be in error is cause for celebration. But psychiatric diagnoses are rarely found to be in error. The label sticks, a mark of inadequacy forever.

Finally, how many patients might be "sane" outside the psychiatric hospital but seem insane in it—not because craziness resides in them, as it were, but because they are responding to a bizarre setting, one that may be unique to institutions which harbor nether people? Goffman[23] calls the process of socialization to such institutions "mortification"—an apt metaphor that includes the processes of depersonalization that have been described here. And while it is impossible to know whether the pseudopatients' responses to these processes are characteristic of all inmates—they were, after all, not real patients—it is difficult to believe that these processes of socialization to a psychiatric hospital provide useful attitudes or habits of response for living in the "real world."

[23] Goffman, 1961.

Summary and Conclusions[24]

It is clear that we cannot distinguish the sane from the insane in psychiatric hospitals. The hospital itself imposes a special environment in which the meanings of behavior can easily be misunderstood. The consequences to patients hospitalized in such an environment—the powerlessness, depersonalization, segregation, mortification, and self-labeling—seem undoubtedly counter-therapeutic.

I do not, even now, understand this problem well enough to perceive solutions. But two matters seem to have some promise. The first concerns the proliferation of community mental health facilities, of crisis intervention centers, of the human potential movement, and of behavior therapies that, for all of their own problems, tend to avoid psychiatric labels, to focus on specific problems and behaviors, and to retain the individual in a relatively nonpejorative environment. Clearly, to the extent that we refrain from sending the distressed to insane places, our impressions of them are less likely to be distorted. (The risk of distorted perceptions, it seems to me, is always present, since we are much more sensitive to an individual's behaviors and verbalizations than we are to the subtle contextual stimuli that often promote them. At issue here is a matter of magnitude. And, as I have shown, the magnitude of distortion is exceedingly high in the extreme context that is a psychiatric hospital.)

The second matter that might prove promising speaks to the need to increase the sensitivity of mental health workers and researchers to the *Catch* 22 position of psychiatric patients. Simply reading materials in this area will be of help to some such workers and researchers. For others, directly experiencing the impact of psychiatric hospitalization will be of enormous use. Clearly, further research into the social psychology of such total institutions will both facilitate treatment and deepen understanding.

I and the other pseudopatients in the psychiatric setting had distinctly negative reactions. We do not pretend to describe the subjective experiences of true patients. Theirs may be different from ours, particularly with the passage of time and the necessary process of adaptation to one's environment. But we can and do speak to the relatively more objective indices of treatment within the hospital. It could be a mistake, and a very unfortunate one, to consider that what happened to us derived from malice or stupidity on the part of the staff. Quite the contrary, our overwhelming impression of them was of people who really cared, who were committed and who were uncommonly intelligent. Where they failed, as they sometimes did painfully, it would be more accurate to attribute those failures to the environment in which they, too, found themselves than to personal callousness. Their perceptions and behavior were controlled by the situation, rather than being motivated by a malicious disposition. In a more benign environment, one that was less attached to global diagnosis, their behaviors and judgments might have been more benign and effective.

[24] I thank W. Mischel, E. Orne, and M. S. Rosenhan for comments on an earlier draft of this manuscript.

"...Genuine emotions are forced to break out of their protective shells of status and image and social convention."

Therapy sessions are ordinarily scheduled for one hour, which often turns out to be a 45-minute hour. Group sessions are longer, usually taking between one and a half and two hours. In contrast, marathon groups last an uninterrupted twenty-four hours or longer. Presumably the gathering fatigue makes resistance more difficult and treatment more intense. Lamott attended one such group and describes his experience.

Last summer I became involved for a time with a psychotherapy group of a classic and traditional sort, a group whose common denominator was that its members were intelligent and well-educated neurotics who were managing with the help of tranquilizers and sleeping pills, as well as with the help of the group itself, barely to cope with the everyday problems presented by their jobs and their domestic situations. It was a long-standing group, some of its members having attended the twice-weekly meetings for more than a year. During the six weeks or so that I spent with them, several members showed some improvement, if by improvement we mean an adjustment to the often-preposterous demands of our personal worlds.

Recently, I had the opportunity to contrast this conservatively organized group with its diametric opposite, a 24-hour marathon group which was offering the hope of virtually instant improvement. Unlike the members of the traditional group, who in extreme cases were like people hanging onto the edge of a cliff by their fingernails, the marathon groupers were either trying to respond to immediate problems, such as the shock of separation and divorce, or trying to break through their personal limitations in order to expand their participation in the banquet of life.

It struck me as I took part in the marathon, which was in Hollywood, that it was an intensely California phenomenon, for, like Synanon, the Esalen Institute, nude therapy and feeling therapy, the marathon is a California invention, and I think it would be hard to consider the marathon outside the context of the civilization which produced it. In California, the promises are more golden and—as demonstrated by the statistics for suicide, alcoholism and divorce—the confrontation with reality is often more tragic. Furthermore, Californians have often shown a touching faith in the power of absolute sincerity to solve their personal problems.

The night before I joined a marathon that was to take place under his direction, I had dinner in a Chinese restaurant in Beverly Hills with Dr. George R. Bach, a clinical psychologist who believes that he and Dr. Frederick Stoller ran the first marathon in 1963. A native of Riga, Latvia, and a Ph.D. from the University of Iowa, Dr. Bach is short, plump, extroverted, tanned, white-haired, uninhibited, warm, charismatic and immensely voluble. He is an enthusiast, a missionary whose gospel is that of the overriding necessity for human beings to achieve openness and transparency in their dealings with each other. (One of Dr. Bach's current interests besides the marathon is his "fight clinic," in which married couples are trained to combat each other constructively.)

Over a couple of Scotches and plates of shrimp and vegetables, Dr. Bach explained that the point of the marathon was to bring about permanent changes in the behavior of the participants by breaking down their usual defenses through simple fatigue and the workings of group pressure.

"Five years ago, when Fred Stoller and I invented the marathon, our wives thought we were crazy," Dr. Bach told me. "We'd been carrying out weekend retreats at Palm Springs, but we found that in a group session of ordinary length, it was too easy for some of the people to put off really leveling with the rest of the group. The pressure never really built up to the point where they dropped their defenses and stopped playing games or going off into great safaris into their pasts.

"Well, we decided to try running a group without any breaks except for food. We didn't have the least idea how it would turn out. Maybe half the people there would have bad trips and come out of it depressed and even suicidal. Thank God, that wasn't what happened. The marathon worked."

Dr. Bach went on to say that the marathon, which is usually scheduled for 24 hours but sometimes for longer, was a psychological pressure cooker in which genuine emotions are forced to break out of their protective shells of status and image and social convention. When I reminded him that, at a meeting of the American Group Psychotherapy Association last February, Dr. S. R. Slavson, one of the founders of that organization, warned against the potential dangers of marathon and some other newer forms of group therapy, Dr. Bach waved his arms and raised his voice. (Among other things, Dr. Slavson had said: "Obviously, latent or borderline psychotics with tenuous ego controls and defenses may, under the stress of such groups and the complete giving up of defense, jump the barrier between sanity and insanity.")

"Slavson doesn't have any idea what he's talking about," Dr. Bach declared heatedly. "We've devoted a lot of energy to research, and we know what we're talking about. When we started, we were getting maybe 10 percent bad trips. Now it's 1 or 2 per cent."

(Later, I talked to Dr. Donald A. Shaskan of San Francisco, a pioneer in group therapy and a past president of the group psychotherapy association, who told me: "Marathon therapy is in the experimental stage, and its safety is still being debated in the professional organizations. Certainly, it requires a therapist who takes the responsibility of following up his patients after the marathon is over.")

The next day, as the marathon approached, I found myself feeling thoroughly depressed for no good reason that I could explain. It was a sort of free-floating depression that attached itself to whatever was handy, and as I looked down from the balcony of my dreadful room on the 12th floor of a dreadful Los Angeles-style hotel, I was reminded of Dr. Bach's comment that some people, even though a comparative few, came out of a marathon in a deep depression. I didn't feel at all comfortable about taking this chance and would have been happy for an excuse to pack up and go back home.

A little before 10 in the evening I presented myself at Dr. Bach's Mediterranean villa on a hillside street in Hollywood. I was welcomed by his wife, Peggy, a painter and art historian who acts as her husband's co-therapist. A slender, handsome woman who was bearing a black outfit of blouse and slacks, she introduced me to the other participants by their first names as we gathered in her vaulted living room. (The anonymity of first names is a condition of a marathon; it not only encourages candor but also acts as a social equilizer between the movie star and the saleswoman.) With one exception, the women were wearing slacks with sweaters or blouses. The men, too, tended toward slacks and sweaters.

As we drank coffee and waited for Dr. Bach, who had been detained at a speaking engagement at a church, I exchanged notes with my neighbor, an attractive but rather brittle-looking woman in her 40's named Paula. It was, I confessed, my first marathon. Paula told me she had completed three or four marathons. She and her husband, who was also present, were leaving town the next week and they thought it was important to take part in another marathon while they had the chance. I said that I was a little concerned at the prospect of staying awake for 24 more hours. "Oh, you won't have any trouble," she told me. "Once it starts, the time goes by so fast that you'll be surprised how soon it ends." Paula knew some of the other people there—there were eight women and seven men—having met them at previous marathons. Others, I gathered, took part in Dr. Bach's regular group-therapy sessions.

Dr. Bach arrived, bouncing into the room as he greeted people he knew and introduced himself to the one or two he didn't. It was clear that, unlike my earlier experience in group therapy, in which the therapist had been a quiet, benevolent supportive presence, this was to be Dr. Bach's show; he would be the impresario, the stage manager, the gadfly, the *agent provocateur*.

After changing his suit for slacks and a persimmon-colored sweater, Dr. Bach reminded us of the 10 commandments of the marathon, which we had been asked to study before coming. Boiled down somewhat, these are that everybody would stay until the end, that only Dr. Bach and his wife would be allowed to take naps, that physical assault was forbidden but brutal frankness was encouraged, that no booze or drugs were allowed, that openness, transparency and intimacy were the watchwords, and that our behavior in the group itself and not our standing in the outside world was the only matter of importance. In addition, there were housekeeping details such as the presence of a buffet in the dining room, an interdiction against dawdling in the bathroom and the rule that whenever anybody left his seat somebody else would take it in order to keep the group constantly changing.

The marathon began with each person taking the "hot seat," which happened to be in front of the fireplace, for two minutes to describe what he expected to gain from taking part. Our aspirations were clearly a large order to be coped with in only 24 hours. Doris, a woman of about 40, and Sherry, a strikingly constructed girl in her 20's, were each recovering from the shock and dislocation of recent separations that they expected to lead to divorce. Deborah, also young and attractive, was in much the same situation. Paula, the woman with whom I'd been talking, and her husband, Max, were trying to salvage their 20-year-old marriage. Clint was having trouble with his third wife. Gene was depressed by the loss of his mistress. Cathy, who felt overshadowed by her successful husband, was trying to find her own identity. Karl and Amy were concerned about whether they should marry each other. Margot, the least attractive woman present, had never had a satisfying relationship with a man. Of those with other problems, Molly, who looked barely old enough to be out of high school, turned out to be a 24-year-old who was trying to find out who she was. Sig, an experienced marathoner, was following the road of self-realization. Otis, too, said he wanted to learn more about himself.

When it came my turn, I told the group about my generally depressed condition and went on to say that, in the context of the marathon's goal of open communication, I had sometimes regretted using a too-easy glibness and a cocktail-party variety of charm to fend off intimacy when it was offered. (As I write this I am reminded that I must have become thoroughly Californian in the 18 years I've lived in the state. We Californians are surely more vulnerable than anybody else when we are accused of not being honestly and genuinely and truly sincere and open and receptive.)

Like private confession, public confession has its forms and rituals. Some, such as psychodrama and the dialogue, are common currency in the group-therapy movement. Others, such as the haircut, have their roots in the games played in Synanon groups. (A haircut is a direct attack by one person on another. The victim is not allowed to defend himself.) There is also a specialized language: to *level* is to speak with absolute sincerity; *feedback* is criticism; to *gunnysack* is to pack away grievances; to *museum* is to wander back through the debris of one's psychological history; to *redcross* is to give aid and comfort to somebody under attack, and is not encouraged.

About midnight, after some preliminary skirmishing, Paula and her husband became involved in a dialogue. (In reporting this, as well as in what follows, I have changed identities and circumstances sufficiently to avoid easy identification.) Dr. Bach directed Paula and Max to sit facing each other, their knees a couple of feet apart, in two straight-backed chairs in the center of the room. Tall, slender and dark, Max was the only person in the group who gave signs of being there under compulsion. The reason for his presence under duress became apparent as soon as Paula began to talk. She was angry to the point of threatening divorce.

"I don't think you're ever going to change," she told him. Dr. Bach stood behind her as she talked, his hand on her shoulder, a sort of psychic prompter, urging her to go on whenever she hesitated. "I've about given up hope, I really have," Paula said. "I simply can't stand any more of your damn smugness. There you are, the Great Big Important Colonel who never makes a mistake. It's always somebody else who makes the mistakes, never you. When you come home, it's the same thing. You never listen to me. Aren't you ever going to try to listen to what I say to you?"

Max said, "I'm listening right now." Dr. Bach moved behind his chair. "I do try to listen to you, Paula. I listen very hard, but I can't respond the way you want me to because your demands don't have anything to do with reality."

"Oh, God!" Paula cried, holding her head in her hands. She lifted her head and said, "They don't have anything to do with your reality. But what about *my* reality? Don't you ever let yourself consider that my reality is just as important to me as your reality is to you? Just because I don't command a bomber with a hydrogen bomb in it doesn't mean that I'm not real. Whenever I talk to you I get the feeling your mind is 50,000 feet in the air."

"I don't know what I can do that I'm not already doing," Max said. "I do try to listen to you. But I don't think I'm at fault if I don't understand what you really mean."

"You don't ever try to understand me," Paula said. Her hands were in her lap now, fingers intertwined, knuckles tight. "I'll bet you can't remember anything I've ever said to you."

Max said, "But I can. I remember a great deal you've said. I remember that last week you told me that if I didn't come to this marathon you were going to see a lawyer. So I came with you, even though I couldn't believe that talking for another 24 hours would do us any good."

"I'll bet you can't remember anything else."

"I remember your telling me that you had to have a life of your own that didn't have anything to do with the Air Force. I told you that was fine, that I understood, that I thought it would be a good thing if you got a job in town, off the base. And you said that was fine, but the trouble was that nobody wanted to hire a middle-aged woman who'd forgotten all the typing and shorthand she'd ever known. You said the only job you could get would be behind the counter at the five-and-ten. I told you that a colonel's wife couldn't work at Woolworth's. And you blew up and locked yourself in the bedroom for the rest of the night."

"That's exactly what I mean," Paula cried triumphantly. "You never try to understand. If you'd tried to understand you'd know that I didn't really mean I was going to get a job at the five-and-ten."

"But that's what you said," Max objected. "How can I understand you if you don't say what you mean? If you didn't mean you wanted to work at Woolworth's, what *did* you mean?"

Paula said, "If you'd listened to me instead of playing Great Big Colonel, you would have found out what I meant. What I was going to tell you was that I want to go to State College and get teaching credentials. I want a career of my own. I want to be a schoolteacher."

Max looked puzzled. "Why didn't you say so?"

"You didn't give me a chance," Paula said, breaking into tears.

Somebody gave her a box of tissues and Dr. Bach let her cry for a while. Then he said, "All right, it's time to negotiate." He took Paula's hand. "Tell us what you want Max to agree to."

"I want Max to try to understand why I have to go to college and become a teacher. I want him to listen to me when I come home from school. I want him to help me and support me, and when he's with me I want him to stop thinking about the Air Force."

"Can you agree to that?" Dr. Bach asked Max.

Max nodded. "Sure," he said.

"Paula wants to hear you say it," Dr. Bach said.

With some prompting, Max repeated the terms of the negotiation. "I will try to understand why Paula has to go to college and become a teacher. . . ."

"Now kiss her," Dr. Bach said when Max was through.

Max stood up, bent down to Paula's face and kissed her lightly and rather formally. She looked appeased. They got up and sat down together on a couch. Self-consciously, Max put his arm around Paula's shoulder. She smiled, but a little thinly.

After a moment's silence, Cathy, a pleasant-looking young woman, said to Max, "I think you're a dreadful person. I don't think you mean a word of what you've said. You've done it just to keep Paula quiet. You're not leveling. I hate liars."

"I'm not a liar," Max said stiffly.

"Oh, yes, you are," Cathy said. "You're trying to tell me that colonels don't lie, but I'm telling you that colonels lie just like anybody else."

"I don't have anything to say to you," Max said.

Cathy looked angry.

Clint, tall, rangy and bushy-haired, said: "Now, just a minute. Let's not assume that Paula's all right and Max is all wrong. I went through something like this with my second wife. It's easy to say that Max is a heel because he won't let Paula do what she wants to do, but what I want to know is this: Does Paula really want to become a teacher, or is this just a game to put Max on the defensive?"

"I really want to be a teacher," Paula said.

"I'm afraid I don't believe you," Clint said.

"Why don't you believe her?" Cathy asked.

"Just because I don't," Clint said. "Furthermore, I think you're a stupid, castrating bitch."

"Maybe that's your problem," Cathy said.

"Maybe it is," Clint said.

A little later, I found myself involved in a psychodrama as a result of having brought up a recent argument about money with my wife. Dr. Bach urged me to pick as my partner in the drama the woman present who most resembled my spouse. I picked Cathy because, like my wife, she is dark-haired and plump and because I admired her fighting style.

We took off from the financial quarrel and had a spirited interchange about the rights and duties of husbands and wives. Alas, if my goal really was to achieve openness, I committed a mortal sin by letting myself be carried away to the point of inventing a couple of monster children who had no resemblance to my own three and, picking up a cue that Cathy tossed me, played the part of a ferociously Victorian husband and father, a sort of Theobald Pontifex translated into 20th-century California. After Cathy and I had run out of steam, Paula and Doris told me what an obnoxious person I was, and from what the others contributed it became clear that among the women I had nominated myself as the least popular candidate for any sort of intimacy.

Yet, in spite of my guilt at having lied to the group, I found that I was feeling a good deal better. Whether it was simply the benevolent effect of adrenalin being released or of some more subtle psychic process, my depression was lifting. Something, at any rate, was going on, for a little later I found myself talking at length about matters that have caused me real pain and that I wouldn't have conceived a few hours earlier of bringing up to anybody except the closest of my friends.

At 3 A.M., Dr. Bach told us that he and Peggy were going to bed for four hours so they would be as alert as possible during the coming day. We were to be on our own until 7.

There was a general air of irritation and dissatisfaction after the Bachs left. I was beginning to feel tired and not particularly happy at having exposed myself. Judging from the quarrelsomeness of the group, some of the others were feeling the same way. We jockeyed around, psychically speaking, for a while without getting much of anywhere until suddenly Margot screeched: "Damn it, I'm part of this group, too, and I want somebody to listen to me. All I've been hearing is about married people, married people, married people. Well, I don't give a damn about you married people. I want to talk about me."

"Nobody's been hogging the floor," Otis told her. He was a strong-featured man with close-cropped yellow hair. "If you want to talk about yourself, why don't you just speak up? You don't have to get all up-tight and make a speech about it."

"If I talk to you, will you listen to me?" Margot asked.

"I don't know," Otis said. "Every time you've opened your mouth tonight you've been a real bitch. I don't know if I want to hear any more from you."

"God, I hate you!" Margot said.

"It's mutual," Otis told her. Sig spoke up. "Now that you've got that out of the way, why don't you give Margot a chance to talk?"

Margot looked at Sig fiercely, as if, in spite of his help, she knew that he really belonged to the enemy.

"Go on," Sig urged her. "Nobody's going to interrupt you."

A tall, big-boned woman with heavy legs, the only woman there who was wearing a dress, Margot was not in fact a particularly prepossessing female. She was at her worst when her face was ugly with anger. She told us that her main trouble was that, although she liked men, she'd never had a close friendship with a man. She knew she wasn't attractive but she felt she had a lot of love to give.

"The love certainly isn't showing tonight," Sig said.

"How can it?" Margot cried. "Every time I try to make friends with a man, he runs away as if I had leprosy."

"Judging from what I've seen of you, I don't blame them," Sig said.

"You can say that again," Otis said. "One brush with you and I'd run for the hills."

Margot began to cry noisily. She went all in a heap in her chair. Doris brought her the box of Kleenex; she sobbed into the tissues for a while. When she was through, she was red of eye and puffy around the cheeks, but she spoke in a much better-controlled voice.

"I want you all to level with me," she said. "I want every man in the room to tell me if he finds me at all sexually attractive." She turned toward the nearest man, who happened to be Max, the Air Force colonel.

Max looked uncomfortable. He pursed his lips and looked steadily at

Margot for a while. Then he said, "I don't find you at all attractive right now. If you took better care of yourself and had somebody help you pick your clothes, you wouldn't be unattractive. But I don't think it's just a matter of looks. You'll never get a man to feel warmly toward you so long as you come at us as if we were the enemy."

"Thank you," Margot said. As she went around the circle, we other men answered much as Max had. She accepted our comments quietly, and as her face lost its flush she did in fact begin to look more attractive.

Otis was the last of the men, and as Margot reached him, she said, "I'm curious what you're going to say."

Otis shook his head. "I can't tell you if you're sexually attractive or not. You see, I only like boys."

Nobody noticed the dawn. While the sun came up we talked about Molly and Deborah and why, though they were almost exactly the same age, Deborah seemed several years older. Karl had stretched out on the floor and closed his eyes. When Amy noticed that he was asleep, she leaned down and pinched the lobe of an ear. He sighed, opened his eyes and drew himself up. "Oh God," he said, "I feel like the whole Sahara Desert has got under my eyelids." He got up heavily and went into the dining room to get some coffee.

It turned out that breakfast was just then being set out by the Bachs' house-man. There were fruit juice and scrambled eggs and bacon, coffee and toast. Dr. Bach and Peggy came downstairs, looking somewhat refreshed.

Dr. Bach, who was wearing a jogging outfit, announced that anybody who wanted to come along with him on his morning jog was welcome. Molly and Karl joined him, and they went out into the hillside streets while the rest of the group drank more coffee. Then Sig, who had been studying yoga, gathered the rest of us outside by the swimming pool, where he put us through some deep-breathing exercises.

When we had come together again in the living room, Dr. Bach, who had changed from his jogging outfit back into sweater and slacks, raised the issue of what the group ought to do next. Before we had got very far in this discussion, Karl said to Dr. Bach, "Let me level with you. I don't like to see you pawing young girls."

It turned out that Dr. Bach and Molly had engaged in some horseplay, mauling each other as they jogged along.

"Well," Dr. Bach said cheerfully, "that's just the way I am. I like touching people. I like girls."

"I still don't like it," Karl said. "There's something about the spectacle of a middle-aged man like you laying hands on a young woman that makes me uncomfortable."

"What I don't like," Sig said, "is the idea that you're taking advantage of your position of authority and maybe the girl is putting up with it because you're the great Dr. Bach."

Dr. Bach whooped joyfully. "A palace revolution!" he cried. "Always we have a palace revolution. Now, let us ask Molly. Tell us, Molly, was I taking advantage of you?"

"We were just hitting each other," Molly said. "We were just having fun. Honest."

"You see?" Dr. Bach asked triumphantly.

Karl shook his head. "I'm not just talking about Molly. I'm talking about all the other people you're always laying your hands on."

"Perhaps the trouble isn't me," Dr. Bach suggested. "Perhaps the trouble is you. You're holding yourself in, you think there's something evil about establishing physical contact with another human being."

"Perhaps that's true," Karl said. "I still don't like it. What does Peggy think about it?"

"Let us ask Peggy," Dr. Bach said. "Let us ask the beautiful and intelligent and understanding Peggy." He turned grandly to his wife of 28 years, with whom he boasts of having carried on several thousand constructive domestic fights. "What do you have to say about this grave accusation, Peggy?"

"I don't mind seeing you kiss other women, but when you put your hands on their breasts or their bottoms, I think it's disgusting," Peggy said crisply.

Dr. Bach gave signs of extreme combative pleasure. "A real palace revolution! Everybody is against me! Even my beautiful and loving wife! Hah!" He sat down, smiling, and threw his arms wide in the air. "What are we to do about this situation?" He folded his arms and looked penitent. "I am sorry. I am not sorry for myself, I can't help that. But I am sorry if I distress you. I will try to control my evil nature. I will try not to be a dirty old man. Is that all right with everybody?" He looked around and, satisfied, said, "Now that we have settled this extremely important matter, what are we going to do next?"

What happened next was that Deborah gave Sherry a haircut. They were both good-looking girls in their early 20's, both separated from their husbands. They had been together in previous groups, and until then they had seemed to be on extraordinarily good terms with each other.

Deborah was slender, dark and intense. Sherry, who had one of those lush Southern California figures and a soft, pretty, self-indulgent face, had been sitting cross-legged on a couch, her shoulders thrown back, clearly inviting the men's admiration. The two girls sat in the straight chairs in front of the fireplace.

"I've been getting sick to my stomach with the show you've been putting on for the men," Deborah said. "You keep coiling and uncoiling yourself on the couch as if you were the sultan's favorite slave girl or something. What did you come here for, anyway, to look for a quick pickup? Well, any man who went home with you would be out of his mind. All you are is a squashy, bosomy body and there's nothing inside at all. You make me puke."

When she paused, Dr. Bach rose from where he had been squatting by the hearth and, taking Deborah's right hand in his, held it so that her index finger pointed accusingly at Sherry.

"Furthermore. . . ." Dr. Bach urged.

"Furthermore," Deborah said, "whenever you say anything it's always about yourself and how attractive you are to men and what a tragedy it is that your husband wasn't satisfied with this precious thing you gave him and instead got involved with another woman. Well, I don't blame him at all. What he couldn't stand was never hearing you say anything but me—me—me—me—me—me. Me—me—me—me—me. *Me—me—me—me—me.*"

"Furthermore. . . ." Dr. Bach said.

"Furthermore," Deborah began, and then stopped. "I guess I've said what I wanted to say."

Sherry cried.

At 10 in the morning the group threatened to bog down. About half—men who had brought razors and clean shirts, women who had changed their outfits and freshened their faces—looked comparatively spruce. The real feeling of the group, however, was carried by the rest of us, who were beginning to look seedy and rumpled. Otis, the man who had sexual feelings only for boys, complained twice that he'd paid his $90 fee like everybody else but was getting nothing from the group. Margot had reverted to bitchiness and managed to throw verbal obstructions into every promising beginning. Paula called Max up again for another dialogue that didn't seem to get much of anywhere except to demonstrate her conviction that her husband wasn't leveling and that he had no honest intention of changing his high-handed ways.

At that time, with the marathon halfway through its course, the prospect that any of us might come anywhere near the goals we had set didn't seem at all good. I was feeling tired and cranky and thoroughly skeptical of Dr. Bach's theory on the benevolent effects of fatigue. Remembering his comparison of the marathon to a psychic pressure cooker, I was prepared to argue that, as sometimes happens with pressure cookers, the outcome would be a soggy mess. We had, clearly, achieved a level of intimacy that doesn't come out of the usual dinner party or even the day-after-day-contact between people working in the same office, but it didn't seem, then at least, to be an intimacy that would lead anywhere worth going to.

On looking around the group, I found myself reacting strongly to each of the people. I rather resented Dr. Bach, with his obvious pleasure in his virtuoso performances, but increasingly liked his wife, who displayed a nice gift for abrasiveness ("I thought what you just said was pretty slimy"). Margot, I decided, thoroughly deserved her lonely state. Paula was a 24-carat specimen of tyrannous virtue. Clint thought he was too damn clever by far. Gene, a bearded, pipe-smoking man who had something to do with television, was the most distasteful of all. Fast with his footwork, he had managed to avoid giving away anything about himself except that he was a pretty important fellow and that he felt an inordinate amount of nobility in bringing a recent love affair to an end. I felt rather sympathetic toward Max; I liked Deborah, who had a nice straightforward style, and Cathy remained attractive although she bounced alarmingly from niceness to brutality and back again. Of all of them, I felt most warmly toward Doris, and, on looking back, I think it wasn't only because she was a good-looking woman who was troubled and who was appealing for help, but because her behavior actually had been changing for the better. There was, perhaps, hope for the rest of us.

Sometime during the long reaches of the night, Doris had asked if she could tell us about her troubles. Just a couple of weeks earlier, she said, she had found out that her husband had been carrying on with another woman. She had ordered him out of the house. Since then she had been torn between a conviction of her own rightness and acute feelings of loneliness and fear for the future. When she began to cry, her face seemed actually to dissolve into an appalling mess of self-pity.

We had been stern and critical with Doris for her self-pity but had told her that a new world was opening up and that what she made of this world was the only thing that should concern her now. (Even in therapy groups we fall back on clichés when faced by the real crises of living.)

After a good cry, Doris looked much more cheerful. Now, eight hours later, she showed no signs of reverting to weepiness. Instead, when one of the other separated women spoke bitterly of her husband's running after another woman.

Doris said briskly: "Oh, come on now. When I first found out about my husband, I was sure he'd been chasing some sexy young chick who probably looked like Marilyn Monroe. Well, when I finally saw her she turned out to be a quiet woman of about my own age. She wasn't even as good-looking as I am." Doris laughed. "Maybe that was what hurt most of all."

Paula had been right when she told me how fast the 24 hours would go by. Dr. Bach, sensing the general grogginess of the group and warning us that we didn't really have much time left, took the men out to the poolside patio, where we drank beer and talked man-talk. The women stayed indoors with Peggy Bach.

The surprise of the pool-side session was Otis, who for the first time began to talk about himself and his troubles in a world dominated by heterosexuals. The police generally left you alone, he told us, if you did your thing in the gay bars and other institutionalized meeting places of the homosexual community, but if you liked young boys you were fair game. He went on for quite a while; as he talked his manner became less brittle and hostile, and even Max, who had shown a good deal of antipathy toward Otis, drew himself into the conversation. After we went back to the living room, it became clear that something had changed in Otis's relations with the group. Where, before, he had been tight and defensive with the women, he now seemed relaxed and—well, open and transparent. Cathy and Doris told him what an attractive person he really was.

After lunch—fried chicken, ham and salad—we started down the home stretch with more dialogues, more haircuts and a drama or two. There were a couple of casualties. Gene simply disappeared after he had been told by virtually everybody present what a generally disagreeable person he was. When he protested that in the real world he didn't have any trouble communicating with people, particularly with women, there had been a burst of unbelieving laughter from the women.

As the afternoon went on, Margot became increasingly shrill, unreasonable and stubborn. Several people suggested firmly that if she didn't have anything more useful to say it would be much better if she kept her mouth shut. Finally Clint said, "Damn it, Margot, if you went out and cut your throat, I don't think anybody here would waste a tear on you."

Margot got up and went into the music room for her coat and purse. We watched her go to the front door and leave.

Doris, looking alarmed, said to Clint, "That was cruel."

Clint shrugged. "If we let her go on, she'd turn this into a bad trip for all of us."

"I think we ought to find out if she's going home or what," Doris said. "She may really be doing something serious."

"Like suicide?" Peggy Bach asked.

"Oh, God," Clint said with disgust.

"You didn't have to suggest it to her," Doris said.

"Margot is not going to kill herself," Dr. Bach said. "You must not worry about her."

"I'm not convinced," Doris said, but we went on to something else.

Margot came back in about half an hour. She left her coat and purse in the music room and sat down in a corner. She was very quiet.

At the end, each of us was judged by a jury of four other people whom we had chosen ourselves. How open and honest had we been in the course of the marathon? Had our behavior actually changed? Did the change seem to be a real one that might be permanent?

As the judging went on, it became apparent that there weren't going to be many surprises. We *had* come to know each other pretty well, having penetrated at least the first layer of social defenses. Otis was congratulated on overcoming his initial uptightness. Cathy told Max that she still didn't like him and didn't see much hope for him in the future. Doris was told to go forth and blossom in her new life. I was urged to keep working at becoming more open and transparent, but the consensus was that I had a long way to go.

The last person to be judged was Dr. Bach himself. Finding myself on his jury, I took the occasion to tell him that in spite of the skill with which he had led us through the marathon, I thought he was at least half charlatan, with a vast talent for exhibitionism and showmanship. The other half, I conceded, probably contained some genius.

Dr. Bach responded with good humor and irony, declaring with a flourish that a bent for showmanship was part of himself and that he couldn't act otherwise. He went on to say that it had been a good marathon, in spite of our tendency to intellectualize our problems instead of responding to them directly with our feelings. He asked us to join Peggy and himself in a "love feast" to celebrate the end of the marathon and to bridge our return to the world outside.

The buffet dinner centered on roast beef and several bottles of a good Burgundy. Somebody turned on music and Clint and Deborah danced. Sig and Sherry became involved in an intense private conversation. Max and Paula ate together in apparent domestic contentment. Most of the rest sat on the floor around a coffee table. Margot sat by herself.

On looking around the room I found that, now that the marathon was about to break up, I felt an extraordinary sense of concern about all my 24-hour companions. I cared, and cared strongly, that Doris and Deborah and Sherry should find their ways out of the debris of their marriages, and that Otis should make a better accommodation with the non-homosexual world, and that Karl and Amy should make the right decision about whether to get married. For myself, I felt, a grateful sense of release from the depression that had blackened my mood at the beginning. To this extent, at least, the marathon had been a success for me. (Looking back on it now, however, I am obliged to add that I can detect no evidence that there has been any change in my behavior. I am still as quick as ever to throw up a defensive verbal screen whenever my privacy seems threatened.)

Taking my plate and my glass of wine, I sat down next to Margot in her corner. She told me she thought the marathon had been a waste of time and money. Nobody had cared about her and her problems. I told her that, on the contrary, when she'd walked out the group had been upset and worried about her. She looked surprised, but then went on: "I still don't think this was a good marathon. I wonder why nothing ever seems to work for me. Nothing ever seems to work."

The love feast broke up between 9 and 10. Dr. Bach put on a jacket and Nehru cap and prepared to take his dog for a walk. He paused at the door, where I was saying good-by to Peggy, and commented: "Three or four more marathons and you won't recognize yourself." Then, Nehru cap on head and dog on leash, he trotted briskly down the road, leaving each of us to find his own way back into the greater world outside.

"Even the new one-to-one therapy is much less expensive than psychoanalysis, if only because it is faster."

Encounter groups, behavior therapy, reality therapy, T-groups, and a wide range of therapeutic procedures are currently being practiced. Frequently it is assumed that psychoanalysis is the only therapeutic procedure used by psychotherapists. This is obviously a myth as you will discover after reading this article by Havemann. In it he presents an overview of some of the most interesting and potentially useful therapeutic approaches currently being applied to a wide range of emotional problems. In some cases there are more assumptions than facts supporting the use of one therapeutic procedure over another, but, hopefully, this will change as research progress.

John Blank, at the age of 33, was in many respects a model husband and father. He was also, as it happened, a confirmed, habitual, compulsive transvestite. He had started before he was 12 to dress up in his mother's or his sister's clothes whenever they were away from the house. By the age of puberty, he was hooked.

Service in the Army forced him to give up the habit for a while—a barracks being hardly the place to practice transvestitism. It was a miserable period for John Blank. By the time he got out of the Army and back to a secret wardrobe of women's clothing, he had developed a full-fledged ulcer.

Civilian life and marriage, though they calmed his ulcer, did nothing else to change him. He found, indeed, that he could not have sexual relations with his wife unless he dressed up first. Every now and then, he had an irresistible urge to spend an evening in public in a dress, nylon stockings, high-heeled shoes and a woman's wig.

As he neared his mid-30s, John Blank was almost as unhappy as he had been in the Army. He worried about being arrested some night and losing his job. He wondered how long his wife would put up with him. Above all, he worried about the fact that his son was getting to the age where the boy would surely discover his secret. In addition to being addicted to the strange wardrobe, he was now also addicted to sedatives, which he gulped constantly to soothe his jangling nerves.

In desperation, John Blank sought help from a new kind of treatment, totally different from psychoanalysis in theory and practice: behavior therapy. The treatment prescribed for him was extremely simple. He did not lie on a couch and try to produce free associations about the childhood origins of his compulsion; indeed, he hardly talked to the therapist at all except to explain his problem. On each visit to the therapist's office, he merely undressed, put on a dressing gown and went behind a screen, where his favorite outfit of women's clothing was laid out on a chair. On signal from the therapist, he took off the gown and began dressing in this clothing. At some point, at times soon after he had started, at other times when he was nearly finished, he was rudely interrupted by a jolt of electricity delivered through a grid on the floor. He then, as instructed by the therapist, began to remove the clothes. The shock—or sometimes just the sound of a buzzer—was repeated at intervals, until he had them all off.

At each session in the therapist's office, this process was repeated five times. John Blank never knew when the electric shock would hit him, whether to expect the shock or just the buzzer nor how many times shock or buzzer would be repeated while he pulled off the clothes. After 80 visits to the office, he had had his fill of this kind of nerve-racking waiting for the blow to strike—and the therapist figured he had also lost his taste for women's clothing.

The treatment proved to be a striking success. When the therapist looked him up six months later, John Blank reported that he had not once gone back to his secret wardrobe. He felt better than he had felt in years; his worries were vanishing and he was tapering off his use of sedatives.

Behavior therapy, which produced such remarkable results for John Blank, is one of many forms of patching, refurbishing and expanding the human psyche that have begun to flourish as the influence of psychoanalysis has waned. By the careful count of one observer of the psychotherapeutic scene, there are now no fewer than 200 different schools of thought, most of them very new, on how to make Americans less neurotic, more normal, more "fulfilled" than they have been in the past.

The new schools of thought cover a broad and baffling range, from the commonsensical to the exotic. At one extreme is the growing number of psychiatrists who believe that mental disturbances are caused by faulty brain chemistry and can best be treated with the new personality-control drugs. Near this end of the scale is behavior therapy, a product of the psychology laboratory. At the opposite end are numerous methods that have no scientific basis at all, such as the mystical tenets of yoga and Zen Buddhism.

Some methods are still based, like psychoanalysis, on a one-to-one meeting of therapist and patient. But the great move today is toward groups—all kinds of groups made up of young and old, men and women, single and married, rich and poor, black and white, sometimes led by professional therapists and sometimes meeting on their own, seeking in various ways to help one another get over their hang-ups. The most publicized branch of the group movement is Esalen Institute, high on a cliff above the Pacific Ocean, where, on almost any day of the year, 20 or 30 people at once can be found running across the magnificent California landscape, singing, shouting, dancing, looking into one another's eyes and otherwise engaging in a mass effort to help their inner feelings bubble to the surface.

There are not only 200 different approaches but roughly 10,000 specific techniques, most of them developed for use in groups. At any given moment of the day, most or all of these techniques are being practiced somewhere. Groups of ordinarily staid businessmen work as if their lives depended on it to build playhouses of index cards; a college professor and an unemployed chorus girl sit back to back on the floor and try to "communicate" with their shoulder muscles; a plump California housewife and an ascetic clergyman stand barefoot on a bed sheet, trying to tune their senses to the feel of the grass beneath; a man who earns $100,000 per year breaks down and weeps in front of a dozen strangers because nobody likes him; another group of strangers, men and women, shed their clothes and plunge naked into a swimming pool with a therapist who belives that nudity frees the emotions. All this varied activity goes on not only by day but often through the night; one of the most popular new approaches is the "group marathon," which continues for 24 hours without interruption or sleep, leaving its members weary and groggy but somehow exhilarated.

The new brands of therapy and the new group encounters have been sampled by hundreds of thousands more Americans than ever have had any personal experience with psychoanalysis. For one thing, they are far more available. There are more psychiatrists and clinical psychologists using various new methods and techniques of therapy than there ever were analysts in the U.S. As for the groups, these are springing up everywhere; they have even been conducted by television, with everybody within the station's broadcasting range welcome to tune in and take part. For another thing, the new methods are far cheaper. Even the new one-to-one therapy is much less expensive than psychoanalysis, if only because it is faster; the 80-session treatment of John Blank, though far above average for behavior therapy, was still much shorter than the three to five or more years usually required in psychoanalysis. Groups are cheaper yet. It costs nothing at all to organize your own group and as little as $50 to attend a group or marathon led by a professional. You can spend a weekend at Esalen, the holy of holies of the group movement, for as little as $65, including room and board.

Psychoanalysis has never promised its patients very much—only that if they were willing to work long enough and hard enough on the couch, and then the rest of their lives on their own, they might be able to conquer their most crippling conflicts. Most of the new schools of thought, by contrast, have a kind of evangelical optimism and fervor. One of the Esalen psychologists, William C. Schutz, has written a book on Esalen's methods and goals; he calls it *Joy* and his subtitle is "Expanding Human Awareness." Other terms popular among spokesmen for the new schools are mind expansion, self-realization, self-fulfillment, bodily awareness, personal growth and ecstasy. Spurred on by these slogans and, evidently, by pleasurable experiences in group encounters, quite a few Americans have turned into a new kind of fanatic; they are not alcohol addicts, not heroin addicts but group addicts, eagerly tracking down every new group encounter and rushing to every one that they can possibly attend.

Americans, of course, have had many previous infatuations—in recent years, bowling, astrology, the hula hoop, isometric exercises, jogging, health foods and the drinking man's diet. Are the new alternatives to psychoanalysis also fads, or are they the way of the future? Since the new methods vary so widely, from the fact-conscious products of the psychology laboratory to the hashish-inspired visions of Oriental mystics, from the commonplace to the far-out, there is probably no single answer. An examination of some of the most prominent of the new methods, however, will offer some clues.

Behavior therapy, the newest treatment method with a truly scientific basis, is in large part the creation of Joseph Wolpe, a psychiatrist who teaches at Philadelphia's Temple University School of Medicine. Dr. Wolpe was originally a follower of Freud, but changed his mind after studying the learning theories that have been developed by psychologists; he was particularly influenced by the evidence that behavior that is in some way rewarded tends to be repeated, while behavior that is not rewarded or is punished tends to be abandoned. To Dr. Wolpe, a neurotic symptom such as John Blank's transvestitism, far from representing an unconscious conflict, as maintained by Freud, is, in fact, "just a bad habit." It was acquired through some unfortunate quirk of learning and is in some way rewarding to the patient—but it can be eliminated or modified by taking away its reward value.

Dr. Wolpe spends no time at all discussing a patient's childhood or trying to probe into the patient's unconscious mind. Instead, he and his followers make a direct frontal attack on the current problem. John Blank, for example, was treated by associating the wearing of women's clothing with the punishment of electric shock, rather than the reward of whatever kind of pleasurable feelings it previously produced. Similarly, Dr. Wolpe has successfully treated a homosexual by strapping an electrode on the man's calf and showing him pictures of naked men and women. When a man appeared, the electrode produced a shock; when a woman appeared, the electricity went off.

Most people who visit a psychotherapist, however, do not have a simple "bad habit" such as transvestitism or homosexuality. They are more likely to be troubled by anxiety—for example, by a fear of entering an elevator, going to social events, meeting the opposite sex or talking to the boss. For such patients, Dr. Wolpe has developed a method that he calls "desensitization." One of his patients was a 52-year-old housewife terrified by thoughts of death. She had feelings of anxiety every time she saw an ambulance or a hospital, much stronger feelings when she drove past a cemetery and intense fear when she thought of her first husband dead in his coffin. Dr. Wolpe treated her by having her relax completely, then asking her to think about the sight of an ambulance but to stop thinking about it if she began to feel at all anxious. Step by step, he led her to remain relaxed while thinking about all the things that had previously frightened her. By the end of the treatment, she had been fully "desensitized"—the sights and thoughts once associated with anxiety were now associated, instead, with feelings of relaxation.

Recently, the school of behavior therapy has been given a new dimension through an experiment conducted by Albert Bandura, a psychologist noted for his studies of the learning process. Dr. Bandura, who teaches at Stanford University, advertised in the local paper for people who were disturbed by a fear of snakes. To his surprise, since Stanford is in the San Francisco metropolitan area and hardly infested with snakes, nearly 100 people responded. To his further surprise, about a third of the volunteers turned out to have diagnosed themselves incorrectly; when actually confronted with a snake, they were not afraid at all (a fact that has led Dr. Bandura to suspect that perhaps many people only *think* they are neurotic).

From the volunteers, Dr. Bandura finally selected 48 people, both men and women, young and old, who were genuinely terrified of snakes. Among them: a plumber who was afraid to work outdoors, a real-estate salesman who could never bring himself to show a house in which there was a pet snake and two members of the Peace Corps who were frightened by the very thought of being assigned to jungle country. From the Freudian viewpoint, all of them would have been considered victims of deep-seated sexual conflicts, for a snake is the most obvious kind of phallic symbol. Dr. Bandura, however, chose to regard them as the victims of something quite different—namely, a pure-and-simple fear of snakes.

To one third of the volunteers, Dr. Bandura applied the Wolpe desensitization technique. Another third were turned into their own therapists; they were shown how to relax completely (by first tensing and then slackening all the muscles of the body) and asked to watch a moving picture of children and adults approaching and finally playing with snakes, as shown by a projector that the patient himself could stop and turn back if the pictures became disturbing. The remaining third watched through a window while one of Dr. Bandura's colleagues, in the next room, approached a snake, touched it and, after a time, let it crawl around his neck. Once these patients had got up their courage, they were invited in to imitate this procedure.

All the volunteers lost some of their fear of snakes—the third group most quickly and completely of all. Within an average of two hours, indeed, many members of the third group were playing with snakes the way they might play with a puppy. The two other groups, switched to the method of watching through the window, quickly reached the same level of almost complete fearlessness.

The significance of Dr. Bandura's experiment is its indication that at least one kind of neurotic fear can be conquered through the simple process of imitating another person. To psychologists, imitation is one of the most effective forms of learning; babies learn to speak in large part by imitating the sounds their parents make; older children learn to write by imitating the strokes the teacher makes on the blackboard; all of us learn to dial a telephone, play baseball and drive an automobile through imitation. Dr. Bandura's new experiment seems to indicate that people can learn how to be normal instead of neurotic in the same fashion—a finding that may open up an entirely new frontier in psychotherapy.

Another new kind of treatment, called reality therapy, developed by Los Angeles psychiatrist William Glasser, is of special interest, because it appears to produce good results even though it is the exact opposite of psychoanalysis in every respect. The psychoanalyst speaks of mental illness; Dr. Glasser believes that there is no such thing. The psychoanalyst searches for the origins of the patient's problems; Dr. Glasser believes that there is no point in dealing with past events, because these events are over and done with and cannot be changed. The psychoanalyst tries to remain as neutral and anonymous toward the patient as possible; Dr. Glasser tries to establish a strong, intimate personal relationship.

The psychoanalyst looks for the patient's unconscious conflicts and motivations; Dr. Glasser holds that these matters, though perhaps interesting, have nothing to do with helping the patient. The psychoanalyst avoids making any moral judgments of the patient; Dr. Glasser makes the patient face up to the question of whether his behavior is right or wrong, not necessarily in the ultimate moral sense but in terms of social realities and his own desires. ("If a patient says he's a thief and is willing to accept the consequences of being a thief, that's all right," says Dr. Glasser. "I don't judge it, but it's basic to reality therapy for him to judge it.") Finally, the psychoanalyst avoids giving advice, on the theory that the patient should find his own way of living; Dr. Glasser tries to help the patient plan better ways of fulfilling his needs.

The basic problem of all people who require therapy, in Dr. Glasser's view, is that they are "irresponsible." They have never learned, or have forgotten, how to accept the world as it is, take responsibility for their own lives, get along in society and meet their needs while respecting the needs of others. Dr. Glasser worked for many years with the inmates of a California school for delinquent girls; possibly as a result, there is a very down-to-earth and even hard-boiled quality in his thinking. He rejects as "psychiatric garbage" the long, sad stories of unhappy childhoods with which patients often attempt to justify their present inadequacies. "A lot of people," he states, "are looking for excuses. Reality therapy says the hell with the excuses; let's get on with the business of improving our lives."

As a therapist, however, Dr. Glasser radiates a good deal of warmth, and he is regarded with much affection by his former patients, including some of the once toughest of the delinquent girls. His therapy proceeds in three steps. First, he attempts to establish what he calls "involvement" with the patient—so that the patient, who in all probability has been feeling friendless, realizes that he is genuinely eager to help. Next, while preserving this close relationship, he begins to ask the patient to examine his behavior for signs that it might be irresponsible and unrealistic. Finally, he tries to help the patient find more responsible and realistic ways of behaving. Throughout this process, he talks almost entirely about behavior, seldom about the patient's motives or feelings. Once the patient can be taught to behave more responsibly even in one small area of his life, Dr. Glasser maintains, this often sets up a chain reaction in which better behavior leads to better attitudes, which lead, in turn, to more forms of better behavior.

Compared with psychoanalytical theory, reality therapy is the height of simplicity; indeed, Dr. Glasser says he could teach any bright young trainee all he needs to know about the theory in a day. Applying it to patients, however, is another matter. As Dr. Glasser puts it, "Psychoanalysis is difficult to learn but easy to practice; reality therapy is easy to learn but difficult to practice." The psychoanalyst mostly listens. The reality therapist engages in an active, close and often exhausting dialog. He must establish a genuine friendship with patients who may resist it, feel a genuine sympathy with their sufferings, yet be tough enough never to let his sympathy divert him from getting along with the hard task of improvement.

Of all the new schools of thought that constitute today's alternatives to psychoanalysis, reality therapy is at the farthest extreme of the plain-spoken, the nonmystical—and the modest. Far from promising joy or ecstasy, Dr. Glasser warns his patients that reality therapy is not even primarily directed toward making them happy. In his opinion, people can find happiness only for themselves; therapy can only give them a reasonable chance at finding it. In his book *Reality Therapy*, he describes a woman patient, a divorcee, who was given to promiscuous and unhappy love affairs, emotional outbursts and fits of depression; since treatment, she has abandoned her frantic "scrambling for love" and has learned to control her emotions and is depressed less often. She also has found a better job and moved from a shabby furnished room to an apartment. However, she is still a divorcee with few friends, living in a strange city and without much income. Dr. Glasser says bluntly, "No one would describe her as happy, because she hasn't that much to be happy about, but she is no longer painfully unhappy."

Dr. Glasser is by no means the only member of the new breed of psychotherapists to conclude that the key to successful treatment is a warm, close human relationship between therapist and patient. The same idea has been adopted by many other therapists, including some whose theories are otherwise quite different. It is, indeed, a sort of common denominator that runs through most of today's nonanalytical office therapy. It is also the basic principle behind the various kinds of group activities that have sprung up outside the office setting.

The man responsible for popularizing the idea of the intimate therapist-patient relationship is Carl Rogers, a psychologist who founded what is known as client-centered therapy. This is not one of the newest methods; in fact, it goes back to the early 1940s. But it has been one of the most widely used and influential; and Dr. Rogers, who has now turned his attention from individual treatment to groups, continues to be among the most respected of today's innovators.

Client-centered therapy is based on Dr. Rogers' view of the human personality, which is quite different from the psychoanalytical or any other theory of personality that preceded it. Dr. Rogers believes that each person has a self-image—that is, a picture of himself as having many polarized characteristics, such as brave-cowardly, friendly-unfriendly, aggressive-submissive, ambitious-lazy, and so on. Ideally, the self-image is built up out of clear and honest observation of one's experiences, behavior, thoughts and feelings. In the maladjusted person, however, there are many disturbing conflicts between the self-image and the actual facts; it is these conflicts that explain why he is neurotic.

A simple example of conflict would be this: A man who has an image of himself as completely honest cashes a check at his bank one day, is overpaid ten dollars by the teller and knowingly walks off with the money. He is now caught up in a psychological crisis. One way of meeting it is to face the facts, see clearly that he has committed a dishonest act and admit to himself that, although he is generally a very honest person, he is not above an occasional slip. This is the healthy course; it keeps his image of himself in line with reality. On the other hand, the man may be so afraid of condemnation by society or by his own conscience that he cannot bear to own up to the truth. He may try to deny that he stole the ten dollars by telling himself that he kept the money to avoid embarrassing the teller. Or he may try to justify his action by telling himself that the teller had tried to cheat him in the past. In this case, he tries to maintain a self-image of total and unbending honesty that is simply not in accord with reality.

The well-adjusted person, says Dr. Rogers, is one whose self-image is realistic and flexible, changing constantly to take honest account of new experiences. The maladjusted person has a self-image so rigid that he cannot bear to accept any unpleasant truths; he must set up more and more defenses against reality, resulting in more and more tension and anxiety.

The basic technique of client-centered therapy is to provide an atmosphere of great warmth and empathetic understanding in which the patient feels free to begin exploring his true thoughts and feelings and to discover and remedy the conflicts. In Dr. Rogers' many years of treating individual patients, he attempted at all times to be a sensitive and understanding friend to the patient, displaying complete acceptance of all aspects of the patient's personality. As the patient began to feel freer to discuss what he considered to be his faults, Dr. Rogers never acted surprised and never criticized; he was totally permissive toward even the cruelest expressions of hostility or the strangest sexual fantasies. As he has said, his aim was to offer constant assurance that he regarded the patient "as a person of unconditional self-worth; of value, no matter what his condition, his behavior or his feelings." Given this kind of unqualified support, the patient gradually came to acknowledge his true thoughts and feelings, learned for the first time what he was really like and began to revise his self-image in line with reality. As with the rest of the treatment, its conclusion was also permissive; Dr. Rogers let the patient himself decide when it was successful and could end.

To many people who hear about client-centered therapy for the first time, it sounds downright dangerous. If everybody were encouraged to be completely himself, it seems only natural to ask, how could society survive the sudden appearance of hordes of self-seeking, brawling, murderous, lustful, rapacious brutes? A psychoanalyst would certainly worry, for, according to Freud, the human psyche has a dark and evil side; one of man's basic instinctual drives, constantly struggling for expression, is the blind urge to annihilate anyone who dares try to keep him from getting his own way in all matters, large and small. Dr. Rogers' therapy, however, is based on the optimistic assumption that all human beings, if only they have the chance, will grow in the direction of social cooperation. "The individual has a very strong drive toward wholesome self-actualization," he says, "What we have to do is give him a climate in which this can thrive."

Providing a climate in which the human psyche can thrive is also the general purpose of the various kinds of encounter groups that have come to dominate, in sheer numbers, at least, the American psychotherapeutic scene. The group movement has expanded rapidly in the past few years; new Esalen-type centers have opened in all parts of the nation; the professionals who are experienced at conducting groups receive more invitations, from all kinds of people in all kinds of cities and towns, than they can possibly accept. Yet, though it seems to have sprung up almost overnight, the movement actually began more than 20 years ago and struggled along inconspicuously for a long time before achieving sudden popularity.

The strange thing about the group is that nobody invented it; its birth was strictly an accident. The event took place at a conference, held in Connecticut in 1946, on the training of community leaders. Among the professors and Government officials present was the late, highly regarded social psychologist Kurt Lewin, a tireless student of group dynamics (the processes through which groups are formed, go about their business and succeed or fail). With him, Dr. Lewin had brought four members of his research staff—not to participate in the conference but to study it by recording their observations of how individual delegates and their committees behaved and reacted to one another. Somebody suggested that the findings of the four researchers, if presented in the evening when there was no other conference activity, might be a valuable form of feedback that would help the people at the conference judge their own effectiveness and work together more smoothly and efficiently. The first evening, only a few people showed up; these few were so excited by the feedback that the word quickly spread and next evening, everybody was there. After that, the original purpose of the conference was almost forgotten, as the delegates became absorbed in such questions as how each of them looked to the others, how they succeeded or failed at communicating their ideas and how committee decisions were influenced by the interplay of personalities (what a psychologist might call the "interpersonal relationships") among committee members.

The unexpected turn taken by the Connecticut conference seemed to prove that people are fascinated by their behavior in groups—also that, if they are helped to understand their behavior, they tend to become more open, more honest, more aware of their own feelings and more spontaneous. Hot on the trail of something new in human experience, some of the conference leaders quickly set up a non-profit institute called the National Training Laboratories, to refine the techniques of group self-studies and promote their widespread use.

N. T. L. describes itself as being in the business of encouraging social change through sensitivity training—that is, the attempt to teach people to become more aware of their own feelings and motives and the feelings and motives of others, and thus to become more perceptive, open-minded, understanding and creative members of the organizations to which they belong. (N. T. L.'s first groups were for psychologists and other educators; it since has expanded into group training for corporation executives, administrators and teachers in public school systems and universities and community leaders.) Its method is the T group, the T standing for training.

In a typical T group, 12 to 14 business executives meet with a professional leader from N. T. L. The leader announces that the group will gather at certain specified times—say, for six hours a day over a five-day period—to try to learn about the forces that influence the behavior of individuals and groups; the learning will come from the members' own behavior, reactions and feelings; there are no rules of procedure and the group is free to go about the task in any way it sees fit; the leader will try to help the members learn from their experiences in the group but will make no attempt to direct or influence their activities.

To most businessmen, used to attending meetings with a formal agenda and conventions with a formal program, the T-group leader's announcement is a surprising and even frightening introduction to a whole new world in which the ordinary rules of conduct are suspended; there are no lines of authority and

each individual must make his own way without benefit of guidelines or cor-
porate title. What usually results, after an initial confusion and hesitation, is a
remarkably frank group discussion in which individual members feel perfectly
free to reveal their own deepest problems and their opinions of one another,
whether affectionate or hostile. Given the candid atmosphere of the group and
the honest feedback on how their behavior appears to others, the members often
become aware of feelings, fears, guilts, desires and frustrations they had previously concealed even from themselves. Abraham Maslow, a past president of the
American Psychological Association who has conducted T groups, says, "It's
very hard to believe in sober minutes that a dozen utter strangers will suddenly
let all their defenses clatter to the floor like old shoes—but I've seen it happen."

Out of the T group have risen the other kinds of shoulder rubbing and
psyche baring, usually called encounter groups, that take place at Esalen and
other centers and under the direction of individual leaders throughout the country. Whereas the members of T groups usually have a good deal in common in
their working-day lives, the members of encounter groups usually do not; they
get together haphazardly from all walks of life. What takes place, however, is
quite similar to the activity of the T group. Members of encounter groups tend
to let down their defenses, reveal their self-doubts and tell each other frankly
what they like and do not like about one another. There are occasional flare-ups
of hostility and moments of deep affection. There is a good deal of laughter—
also, to a greater extent than in T groups, a good deal of weeping.

Why are people so willing—even eager—to bare their souls to strangers?
Dr. Rogers says it is a sign of the times, something that could never have happened at an earlier stage of history. "When a man is scrambling very hard to get
his three meals a day," says Dr. Rogers, "he doesn't have time to feel alienated
from his fellow human beings. Now that we have the affluent society, we do
have the time and we realize that we are alone and lonely, lacking deep contacts
with others. We begin to say, 'I wish there were someone I could talk to honestly; I wish someone cared about me.' " Charles Seashore, a psychologist with
N. T. L., says, "There's a kind of immaturity and thwarted growth in all of us.
As human beings, we have all kinds of potentialities—to be warm or stand-
offish, loving or hostile, open or suspicious, enthusiastic or constrained, adven-
turesome or cautious, emotional or reserved. But our society rewards some of
these traits and discourages others, and most of us wind up as adults with just
one or two stereotyped responses that we display automatically to all the hundreds of different situations in which we find ourselves. The popularity of
groups rests on the fact that most of us feel deprived; probably 85 to 95 percent
of us feel that we're not as close to people as we'd like to be, or that we're not
as open and honest about our feelings, or that we have an anxiety over sub-
mitting to or exercising authority, or that our lives are too boxed in and nar-
rowly predictable from day to day. Since the group encourages intimacy, honesty and adventure, it's a great experience even if its effects are only temporary."

Is the group a form of therapy? Dr. Maslow says no: "Although I'm very
impressed with groups, I don't think they can help with serious problems—only
minor hang-ups. A neurosis just won't fade away at a T group or a weekend
marathon." The N. T. L. staff is careful to call its aim not therapy but "personal
learning and personal growth." Dr. Seashore points out that he himself once

experienced what he considered a therapeutic breakthrough in a T group—but that it occurred in the 139th group he attended or conducted, a figure hardly likely to be reached by nonprofessionals.

Dr. Rogers, on the other hand, has no doubt that the group is a form of therapy and a highly effective form, at that; he has come to believe that 20 hours in a group are more effective than 20 hours of one-to-one treatment. The secret of the group, he thinks, is that "it gives people permission to be helpful to one another"—a privilege that is not generally available in society and that is grasped eagerly and often with great skill, resulting in very much the same kind of support offered in client-centered therapy. In one way, says Dr. Rogers, the group is superior to client-centered therapy as he practiced it in the past; this is the fact that members of the group freely express their negative as well as their positive feelings toward one another. Thus, each person in the group is at times deeply liked and supported for his good qualities and, at other times, confronted with harsh criticism of the bad, a push-pull process that seems to speed awareness of the true self. If Dr. Rogers returned to one-to-one practice, he says, he would be very free to give his patients constant feedback on his inner reactions to them, pro or con.

Whether the encounter group should properly be called therapy or just a form of education, it certainly does *something* for people. At the Western Behavioral Sciences Institute, psychologists gathered interviews from 1000 people who had taken part in groups; these people agreed almost unanimously that they had greatly enjoyed the experience and had been profoundly influenced; typical comments were, "It was the most important thing that ever happened to me" and "It changed my whole life." What, exactly, about the group had produced this effect? As the psychologists had expected, the one thing mentioned most frequently was some particularly dramatic example of deep exchange of understanding and emotion between two or more members of the group—sometimes an incident in which they themselves had taken part, sometimes an incident that they had merely observed (another example, perhaps, of Dr. Bandura's learning through imitation). To the psychologists' surprise, however, these outstanding incidents did not necessarily involve the therapist who led the group; in fact, the therapist was responsible for no more of them than anybody else. To psychologist Richard Farson this suggested a strange possibility: To the extent that the encounter group is therapeutic, is it a form of therapy that requires no therapist? In other words, can a group succeed without a professional leader?

Dr. Farson's idea of experimenting with leaderless groups was opposed by every therapist he knew. Without professional guidance, he was warned, members of the group would quickly be at one another's throats. Nonetheless, he went ahead, though with extreme caution. The first leaderless group was watched anxiously by two profesisonal therapists behind a one-way see-through mirror, ready to intervene quickly if the group got stalled or out of hand. As it turned out, the two observers were unneeded. In fact, every time the group seemed on the verge of serious trouble, the two therapists were amazed to see some completely untrained member step in and do exactly what they themselves would have done. With this reassurance, Dr. Farson then set up a full-scale experiment comparing leaderless groups with groups led by professional therapists. It developed that the leaderless groups, even when composed of people who had never

Some Other Alternatives to Psychoanalysis

In addition to the types of psychotherapy discussed in the text, there is a wide variety of other methods available. (Note: Some forms of psychotherapy use the Freudian technique of having the patient free associate while in a relaxed position, usually on a couch, but reject Freud's theories of the structure of the mind and the causes of personality disorders. Others retain the Freudian theory but use different methods of therapy; still others have abandoned both the theory and the practice of psychoanalysis. These brief and necessarily simplified descriptions emphasize the ways, theoretical or practical, in which various psychotherapies most sharply depart from classical psychoanalysis.)

Chemotherapy concentrates on chemical imbalances in the nervous system that may be the causes or the results of mental disorders and attempts to treat these disorders with drugs such as tranquilizers and psychedelics. Chemotherapy may be used as an aid to other kinds of psychotherapy, and is often effective in dealing with severe psychoses.

Directive psychotherapy assumes that the patient is not in a condition to work through his own problems or to establish therapeutic goals, and the therapist undertakes these responsibilities. The therapist uses any technique that seems indicated and tries to base his plan of action on all available scientific knowledge.

Existential therapy is based on the existentialist philosophical belief that each individual has to choose his values and decide the meaning of his life. The therapist attempts to achieve an authentic, spontaneous relationship with the patient to help him discover his free will and make his choices.

Experiential therapy is a system in which therapist and patient jointly enter the patient's fantasy world, often acting out fantasies together. The resulting emotional experiences aim at re-educating the patient on the deepest level of his psyche.

General semantics postulates that neurotic behavior results from unrealistic use of words, especially the error of identifying the word with the object for which it stands. The therapist tries to teach the patient to use language more accurately and realistically in thinking and communicating, thereby achieving a more effective orientation.

Gestalt therapy focuses on the patient's difficulty in forming meaningful, organized "wholes" (referred to by the German word *Gestalt*) out of experiences that have left him with unresolved problems. Through encounters between therapist and patient, usually in the presence of a group, the therapy seeks to restore the individual's fragmented integrity of thinking, feeling and acting so that he can regain contact with reality and resume personality growth.

Horneyan psychology was developed by Karen Horney, who believed that neurosis springs from basic anxiety acquired in childhood. Horneyan therapy aims to overthrow the idealized self-image the patient is trying to live up to, making him face his actual self and release his potential for healthy personality development.

Hypnotherapy uses hynosis to increase the patient's suggestibility and to lift repressions, to remove neurotic symptoms when they prevent progress in therapy or to persuade the patient to adopt more constructive general attitudes.

Interpersonal psychology locates the causes of personality disorders in the relations between the individual and society rather than in purely internal psychological developments and aims at improving interpersonal attitudes and relations.

Learning-theory therapy treats mental disorders as self-defeating behavior patterns that the individual has learned to rely on when he feels anxiety. The therapist applies all available scientifically discovered principles of learning to make the patient unlearn these patterns and to countercondition him against the attitudes that produced them.

Orgonomy is based on the theory of Wilhelm Reich that there is a specific energy—called orgone—that accounts for life. Reichian therapy combines psychoanalysis with manipulation of the patient's body in order to remove muscular armor—muscular attitudes an individual develops to block emotions and organ sensations.

Psychodrama is a form of improvised play-acting of certain roles and dramatic incidents resembling those situations that produce problems for the patient in his daily life. The purpose is to provide the patient with both theoretical insight and corrective emotional experience. This acting out is often conducted before an audience.

Rational-emotive therapy, developed by Albert Ellis, asserts that emotional disturbance arises when individuals mentally reiterate unrealistic, illogical, self-defeating thoughts. The therapist identifies these thoughts, argues against them and persuades the patient to undertake actions that will disprove the undesirable beliefs and, hence, strip them of their power.

Transactional analysis postulates that all interpersonal communications spring from specific ego states called Parent, Adult and Child. The therapist attempts to identify the ego state producing each communication from the patient with the aim of discovering the plan the individual has unconsciously chosen for his life and of replacing it, if necessary, with a more realistic and constructive one. Transactional analysts prefer to work with groups.

before taken part in an encounter, behaved very much like the led groups; their members got right down to business, avoided excess hostility and did a good job of helping one another. To Dr. Farson, the experiment suggests a startling answer to the problem of how the nation can possibly train enough therapists for all the people who need help. "It may turn out," he says, "that our greatest resource for solving human problems is the very people who have the problems."

One immediate result of Dr. Farson's experiment has been a do-it-yourself kit for nonprofessionals eager to organize their own groups. The kit was created largely by a young psychologist named Betty Berzon, a former associate of Dr. Farson at the Western Behavioral Sciences Institute; it is a set of tape recordings, each running about an hour and a half, designed to be played by a group that will hold eight meetings. For each session, the voice on the tape suggests various activities that have been found helpful in groups. For example, all members but one are asked to form a tight circle, into which the missing member then tries to break. Or the members are asked to write down, anonymously, some secret of which they are ashamed; the slips are shuffled and handed out; each member, in turn, then reads the paper he has drawn and discusses how it might feel to have such a secret. Following each suggestion, the tape goes silent, to give the group time to carry out the instructions; then the voice returns with something new. The recordings are called Encountertapes and are manufactured by the Human Development Institute of Atlanta, a subsidiary of Bell & Howell (an indication that the group movement has grown big enough to interest the multimillion-dollar corporation world).

"What we've done," says Miss Berzon, "is package the group experience and make it available to schools, churches and industries. This takes it out of the esoteric centers like Esalen and right into the mainstream of everyday life." Miss Berzon was one of the several thousand people marooned for three days at New York's Kennedy Airport by an unexpected snowstorm last winter. Listening to the incessant bulletins over the airport loudspeakers, and watching her frustrated fellow travelers grow increasingly bored and glassy-eyed, she kept grieving at the lost opportunity for playing her Encountertapes over the speakers and turning an ordeal into a delightful mass initiation into the marvels of the encounter group. She can never pass a tall office building without thinking of it as a place where a public-address system and a single set of Encountertapes could bring the group experience to many thousands of people at a time.

Even enthusiasts such as Miss Berzon, however, concede that the group has one serious defect for which no remedy is as yet apparent. It is one thing to confess your secrets, pour out your angers and break into tears among a few people gathered expressly in behalf of this kind of free and frank communication; it is quite another thing to do so at home or in the office. Says Miss Berzon, "Once you've had this taste of honey—once you've had the opportunity to really relate in depth to other people—it's hard to go back to the cocktail-party kind of superficiality. But everyday life isn't like the group. And your family, your boss and your friends probably have a vested interest in keeping you just as you've always been. So the effect tends to get dissipated when you go home." Says Dr. Farson, "People *feel* they're changed by the group, but no matter how you observe them, test them or question their families and friends, you don't find any significant changes in their actual behavior. The reason is that what happens in the group is something that a person can't make happen anywhere else."

Trying to transfer the atmosphere of the group into real life can, in fact, be downright dangerous. One businessman who attended a T group reports, "I learned that I had been making myself miserable by bottling up my hostilities and being overpolite to everybody, so I decided to change all that. Three days later, I realized that I was losing my customers, my employees and my wife—and I changed back in a hurry." Dr. Glasser, who is skeptical of encounter groups, says, "They're based on a false premise. Until all people are open and honest at all times, it's unrealistic to think that you can be—without getting hurt."

In one way or another, most leaders of the group movement are now grappling with this problem. Many of them believe that the solution is to expand the movement, through Encountertapes and the establishment of hundreds of new Esalens, until millions of Americans have had group training of one kind or another; these millions will then reshape society into a sort of single big, happy, uninhibited, affectionate, turned-on encounter group. But as one skeptical psychologist has said, "There are a lot of religious overtones to the movement; these people are like the early Christians, who thought that all of society's problems would vanish as soon as everybody became a Christian."

Others are making a more direct attempt to bring the group and everyday life closer together. The National Training Laboratories, for example, has made some significant changes in the way it organizes its T groups. One N. T. L. psychologist says, "We used to be willing to take just one person from a business organization; we'd get him all revved up and then send him back to office colleagues and a job that hadn't changed a bit. Now we try to get at least two men from the firm, so that they can support each other after they go back. And what we really like is to have many people from the same company and work with the management to open up the lines of communication and creativity; we're trying to change the climate of the big organizations, such as corporations and universities, in which people are embedded." Dr. Farson has been thinking about what he calls "social architecture," a possible new science of the future. "If you want to help people transcend themselves," he says, "you've got to rearrange the social situations in which they constantly find themselves—the job, family, school and church." Thus, the attempt to heal and bolster the human psyche, having already expanded from couch to group, seems likely to expand further into all kinds of social situations. What started as Freud's first modest efforts to help a few hysterical patients has indeed come a long way.

Suggested Readings for Chapter 9

Brenner, Charles. *Elementary textbook of psychoanalysis*. New York: Doubleday, 1957. A very readable paperback that outlines the essentials of psychoanalytic theory in an accurate but not overly technical manner.

Cowen, E. L., Gardner, E. A., & Zax, M. *Emergent approaches to mental health problems*. New York: Appleton-Century-Crofts, 1967. An account of a conference at which many noted authorities presented details of new approaches to problems of mental health, emphasizing the creative use of community facilities and resources.

Frank, J. D. *Persuasion and healing*. New York: Schocken, 1963. A very stimulating review of many approaches to psychotherapy, and their relationship to other forms of behavior modification like primitive healing and brain washing.

Kesey, K. *One flew over the cuckoo's nest*. New York: Viking Press, 1962. A humorous, though frightening novel about a mental hospital and the patients and staff who occupy it.

Lazarus, Arnold A. *Behavior therapy and beyond*. New York: McGraw-Hill, 1971. A recent statement about the orientation and methods of behavior therapy by one of its founders. This is particularly instructive because of its relatively eclectic approach.

Discussion Questions

1. What do the various approaches have to offer to the patient, and how could you choose among them?

2. If you were a pseudopatient, how would you get out?

3. Is therapy of potential help to everyone? To anyone?

4. How can information from the science of psychology be of value to the therapist?